"Television is the world's first truly democratic culture, the first culture available to everyone, and entirely governed by what people want. The most terrifying thing is what people <u>do</u> want."

Clive Barnes

"In the end, of course, the issue is not whether Merv Griffin's secret would be buried with him. In the age of Wikipedia, it's a given that anyone interested enough to Google Merv would quickly get the gist of the story, if not the gory details, or even the less savory details, such as those recounted by Michelangelo Signorile in his 1993 book *Queer in America,* in which an unnamed Hollywood "mogul" is described as firing men from his company for being openly gay. The real point of the episode is the enduring power of the Hollywood closet that held even a billionaire locked in its embrace, paying homage to the presumed prejudices of the public."

Larry Post, author of
***Truthdig--Merv Griffin's Bodyguard of Lies* (2007)**

"This is an unauthorized biography"

Blood Moon Productions

MERV GRIFFIN

A Life in the Closet

OTHER BOOKS BY DARWIN PORTER

Biographies
The Secret Life of Humphrey Bogart
Katharine the Great: Hepburn, Secrets of a Life Revealed
Howard Hughes: Hell's Angel
Brando Unzipped
Jacko, His Rise and Fall
Paul Newman, the Man Behind the Baby Blues

And Coming Soon:
Steve McQueen, King of Cool (Tales of a Lurid Life)

Film Criticism
Blood Moon's Guide to Gay & Lesbian Film (Volumes One & Two)

Non-Fiction
Hollywood Babylon-It's Back!

Novels
Butterflies in Heat
Marika
Venus
Razzle-Dazzle
Midnight in Savannah
Rhinestone Country
Blood Moon
Hollywood's Silent Closet

Travel Guides
Many editions of the Frommer Guides to Europe and the Caribbean

MERV GRIFFIN

A Life in the Closet

by Darwin Porter

BLOOD
MOON
Productions, Ltd.

MERV GRIFFIN
A Life in the Closet

by Darwin Porter

BLOOD MOON PRODUCTIONS, LTD.
WWW.BLOODMOONPRODUCTIONS.COM

ISBN 978-0-9786465-0-9
Copyright 2009 Blood Moon Productions, Ltd.
First Edition, Second Printing, July 2009

Blood Moon's products are distributed in the U.S., Canada, and Australia
by the National Book Network (www.NBNbooks.com)

The author dedicates this book to Danforth Prince

Merv

Prologue

All heads turned as Merv Griffin made his way across the floor of L'Escoffier—"the most exclusive restaurant in the world"—on the eighth floor of the Beverly Hilton. And well they should. He not only owned the hotel but was the chief honcho of a multi-billion empire. The maître d' rushed toward him to usher him to the best table in the house. In fact, legend had it that Merv had bought the hotel to make sure he always had his favorite table.

Leading the march across the elegant room, with its panoramic views, was the Hungarian beauty, Eva Gabor, who'd become his permanent "arm candy." He'd never seen her look more stunning in her taupe gown and what she called "my Cinderella slippers." Around her swan-like neck was a diamond-and-ruby necklace he'd presented to her only that afternoon. He told her that it had once belonged to Marie Antoinette, knowing that she didn't really believe that but would loudly advertise it as fact.

She loved the necklace but had really wanted an engagement ring to solidify their relationship. He knew, however, that wasn't going to happen. There would be no other Mrs. Merv Griffin. It'd taken him three years to untangle himself from his one and only marriage. He had no interest—certainly no sexual interest—in entering into another permanent bond with a woman.

Earlier in the evening he and Eva had stopped off at the hotel bar, making the rounds and encountering Steven Spielberg, Harrison Ford, and Nancy Sinatra. She told him that she'd come just to sample the egg rolls at Trader Vic's that night.

He also ran into a deeply suntanned George Hamilton, who said, "Look around you. There are at least five or six big-time movie stars here with their off-the-record girlfriends. But it's so God damn dark you can't make out anybody. Thank God there are two entrances. If a wife walks in one, the waiter can hustle the mistress out the other door."

In spite of the sad news he'd learned earlier in the day, Merv had a light step as he made his way through the restaurant greeting guests. He'd long ago learned to disguise his true feelings. He was still "every mother's favorite son-in-law," although getting a bit long in the tooth for that appellation.

He always felt more of a man when he had a beautiful woman like Eva on his arm, even though she was an expensive adornment. Hollywood was nothing if not public images. It was a city where truth didn't matter. Only the

1

method you chose to deceive the public. All his life he'd believed in playing by the rules, not changing the game.

Still eager to accomplish bigger and better deals in the future, he could rest secure that he'd become The King of Television. He'd failed to make it as the replacement for singing star Gordon MacRae in the movies, but he ruled the tube.

After all, for nearly a quarter of a century he'd been a household word as host of the Emmy Award-winning *The Merv Griffin Show* where he'd interviewed everybody from John Wayne to Joan Crawford. He'd created and launched TV's two most successful syndicated game shows—*Jeopardy!* and *Wheel of Fortune*. The Beverly Hilton was just one property in his empire.

He estimated he had another ten to fifteen years to live, and he wanted to maintain his image until his dying day—and even after death if that were at all possible.

He didn't want to die like his best male friend, Liberace, did in disgrace, succumbing to AIDS and having his reputation destroyed. If Merv could control events, there would be no notoriety to surround his death the way it had in the case of Rock Hudson, his former lover in the 1950s.

Unlike Rock and Liberace, Merv knew how to protect himself. No virus would get to him. As he candidly told Eva, his most trusted confidante, who knew all his secrets, "I plan to die of natural causes. Not some disease I picked up from an overnight trick."

He had spent a lifetime creating the character of Merv Griffin. If his true character was never revealed, and his self-created image could prevail, even beyond the grave, then he felt his life would have been a success. To most of his fans, he symbolized the good life, a man who had it all. One day he was

Eva Gabor with **Merv**

2

going to write a book about being on top of the world, the way he felt tonight as he looked out over the sparkling lights of Los Angeles.

The title was already spinning in his head—*Merv: Making the Good Life Last.*

As he'd once told Liberace, "You and I have tasted the best that life has to offer, even if we had to spend our lives in the closet. For us, that closet was a jewel box, luxurious and spacious. Not a bad place to be. We've lived in worst dives. And what we did in private was our own fucking business."

"Didn't Rosalind Russell say it all in *Auntie Mame?*" Liberace asked. "Something about life's a banquet—and most poor fools are starving to death, something like that."

"Not us, pal," Merv chimed in.

Seated at table in L'Escoffier, and looking like a Hungarian princess, Eva didn't have to request her drink of the evening. Her champagne was already chilling. "Could you imagine a Gabor drinking anything else?" she had once asked him. Indeed he couldn't.

But there was one big change on her menu for the night. She'd abandoned her usual caviar for a treat the chef had secured for her. The best salami from Budapest had been flown in.

Eva would give up anything for salami. "It is a delicacy created by the Gods," she told him.

To take the "curse" off such a lowly cold cut, Merv had ordered the most beautiful orchids placed on their table. Eva said that when she consumed salami, she always wanted to be wearing diamonds and surrounded by orchids. In fact, she'd called her tell-nothing memoir, *Orchids & Salami.*

Tonight in familiar, swanky surroundings, Eva was in what she called "my gay mood"—she still used the word in its old-fashioned sense. Skilled as a courtesan and arguably trained at the role since birth, she knew her job was to entertain Merv.

She told him that at three o'clock in the morning she'd been caught swimming nude in his pool by two businessmen from Arizona.

When the men spotted her, they plopped down in a chair waiting for her to emerge from the water. "Hi, Eva," the taller of the men called to her. "No, *dahlink,*" she shouted back at them, "it's Zsa Zsa."

After that pronouncement, she emerged completely nude from the pool and grabbed her robe, before disappearing into the elevator to her suite upstairs.

Merv might have laughed at a story like that. But tonight he didn't even smile.

"What is it, *dahlink?*" she asked, sympathetically taking his hand. "You look so sad, so blue." Usually he was jolly and fun, filled with amusing anecdotes. After all, he'd interviewed or else had known practically every celebrity in the world from Marilyn Monroe to Marlon Brando. "It's Nancy," he said, looking depressed and dejected.

Eva knew that Nancy Davis Reagan was his best friend. He'd canceled many an engagement with Eva to escort Nancy to some function. Once when Eva had an argument with him, she accused him of plotting to marry Nancy after her husband, Ronald Reagan, died. "That would be the ultimate triumph for you," she charged. "Marrying the woman who presides over the Free World. You could get a lot of publicity marrying the First Lady. Aristotle Onassis did. Did you know he proposed marriage to me before he asked for the hand of Ms. Jacqueline Kennedy?"

"In your dreams," he said.

Eva had stormed out of his living room, but the next morning they made up at breakfast. It seemed that every night they had some silly argument, yet in most ways, she, not Nancy, was his best friend. He privately told his confidants that "Nancy is best friend, Eva first mistress." He always laughed at his own joke, and so did his staff, although no one seriously believed that he'd ever gone to bed with Eva.

"You still haven't told me why you're so sad," she said.

"You've got to keep this a secret," he said. "Nancy will break it to the world when the time comes. No one must know."

"What is it?" she asked, genuinely interested.

"Nancy called me this afternoon from Washington with the bad news. She's just found out: even Ronnie doesn't know yet. But the President has been diagnosed as having Alzheimer's disease."

"Oh, my God!" she gasped. "No one must find this out. The Stock Market would crash. There could be calls for his impeachment."

"That's why you're going to keep this news under that pretty blonde wig of yours."

After fifteen minutes of trying to console Merv, she said, "You need some serious distraction. You need some fun and games, and I know you've got something planned later in the evening to take your mind off the Reagans. Your mother knows about such things."

The Reagans

4

"You're so understanding," he said.

"But you're such a cad. You could have planned some fun and games for little ol' Eva. Perhaps that handsome lifeguard you hired two weeks ago. Don't tell me you've not had him already."

"You know too much," he said. "Fortunately, you're not in a habit of calling the *National Enquirer*." After dinner, Merv ostentatiously escorted Eva to her suite. Passers-by in the hall saw him as he disappeared inside with her, an indiscretion he wanted them to publicize. But he was going only for a nightcap.

She poured him a drink and gave him a feather-light kiss on the mouth before heading into her boudoir and dressing room to begin her nightly beauty treatments designed to keep her, in her own words, "forever young."

He called down to Hadley Morrell, his most trusted employee whose name would never appear on his payroll. He was paid only in cash. The Minnesota-born Hadley had been Merv's lover in the 1950s. When passion dissipated, he'd stayed on as Merv's private assistant. For the sake of anonymity, Hadley was almost never seen in public with Merv. He wanted both Hadley's identity and their personal relationship kept secret. Merv once told Eva, "Hadley is the most trusted man in the world. What a guy! If you ever murder someone, call Hadley. He'll quietly dispose of the body—no questions asked."

When Hadley picked up the phone, Merv anxiously asked, "Is the kid here?"

"He's in bed buck naked and waiting for you," Hadley told him. "All bubble bathed and raring to go. He's very excited to meet *the* Merv Griffin. He claimed he'd rather meet you than any movie star, even Tom Cruise."

"That's the way I like to hear them talk," Merv said. "It looks like I'm in for a very special evening."

"The best. The agency said the kid does everything. And I mean *everything*. You deserve the very best."

"And so I do," Merv agreed. "This is one Depression Baby that didn't always get the best. Far from it!"

"But you're making up for it now," Hadley assured him.

"Hell, yes!" Merv said. "I didn't begin life in style. But I'm sure ending it with the most succulent prime rib. Let my enemies gossip. I don't care."

"They're just jealous of you, jealous of what you can get."

"You mean what I can pay for?" Merv said.

"That, too," Hadley said.

"My good man, just remember my motto: Living well is the best revenge."

"A Master of Talk TV"

Chapter One

"Please don't take my toys. Please, mister. I've been good." It was almost a scene out of Charles Dickens. The year was 1930, and the place was San Mateo, California, a small community about 21 miles south of San Francisco.

A five-year-old Merv Griffin was in tears when a burly, moving man carted off his rocking horse, his favorite toy. "Not Smiley. That's my horse. He belongs to me. He's mine!" He rushed to retrieve the toy from the man but his mother restrained him.

Even at his age, Merv knew that the men sent by the bank were taking over their home, and even all of their possessions. At the height of the Depression, his father wasn't selling enough football and baseball equipment in the sporting goods store where he worked. It was hard enough to keep food on the table, much less pay the mortgage.

Like so many other families in the nation, the Griffins were six months behind in mortgage payments. The bank, within its legal rights, moved in to evict them and seize their possessions. The bankers had ordered the movers to "take everything," hoping to find something of value. It seemed that bankers all over the country were doing that, humiliating their former clients by taking not only the roof over their heads but their meager goods as well.

The moving men left only some clothing, which seemed to have little value even to the Salvation Army. Merv hugged Barbara, his sister, who was two years older. She was crying. The two children joined their parents in gathering up their remaining belongings. They had until twelve o'clock to evacuate their former home.

Standing in the front yard, Merv in tears looked back at the only home he'd ever known. It was where he'd been brought on July 6, 1925 when he'd been named Mervyn Edward Griffin Jr.

He'd been born to Irish Catholic parents, Rita Robinson, the daughter of a newspaperman, and Mervyn Edward Griffin Sr., a tennis pro who'd won both the California State and Pacific Coast singles title. Rita had fallen in love with the athlete watching him play on the courts.

Behind the wheel of the family jalopy, which somehow still belonged to them, Merv Sr. called to his son to hurry up. Holding his mother's hand, Merv looked once more at their former home. "One day I'll be rich," he vowed to his mother. "Richer than all those bankers. I'll build a palace for you, mama."

"I'm sure you will," she said. "Now c'mon, Buddy. We're going to my mother's. Bless her, she's agreed to take us in."

The Griffins left behind only a toilet seat. In the late 1970s, Merv learned that the seat had sold for $2,000 at a charity auction in San Mateo. "To think some idiot would pay good money for a toilet seat," he said. "Maybe I should sell the fool other souvenirs. Instead of flushing toilet paper I wipe my ass on, maybe I should save it. Put it up for auction. I could make a whole new fortune. The pizza crust I didn't eat. A pair of shoes I'm throwing out. My soiled underwear."

Merv would remember the morning of the family's eviction in San Mateo for the rest of his life. That gray day left a deep scar on him. Decades later he would tell Eva Gabor, "That eviction changed my entire life, the way I looked at things. In the years ahead, I would become obsessed with material things. Far more than a desire to perform, it was

Rita Robinson Griffin in 1927 with **Merv**, age 2

the hope of getting rich that drove me into show business. I listened to Bing Crosby on the radio. I heard he was getting rich singing. My family and friends told me I could sing. Even though I was a chubby little brat, I decided that I was going to go to Hollywood and replace Bing Crosby. Get rich by using my singing voice. There were times in my future when that dream of mine became a nightmare. But I never gave up hope. Never! Even on the darkest of nights."

Eva would always listen patiently to him. Like a good courtesan, she would be reassuring. "You succeeded beyond your wildest fantasies, I am sure. You became not only rich, but the wealthiest man on the planet."

"I wouldn't go that far," he cautioned her.

"Rich and also adorable, an irresistible combination," she said. "Zsa Zsa and I have found that rich men are all bastards. You're a marvelous exception to that rule. Who on Earth doesn't adore Merv Griffin?"

***

"From the age of five, I became a showman," Merv later recalled. "I've spent my entire life putting on a show." At his grandmother's house on South Eldorado Street in San Mateo, he took down the curtains from her living room and used them as a stage curtain. "I started putting on shows for our neighborhood on her back porch. By the time I turned seven, I was known as the P.T. Barnum of San Mateo. No one could believe a kid as young as me could have such talent."

A neighbor, Sally Paule, told him, "If you were a girl, I bet you could go to Hollywood and replace Shirley Temple."

"That was music to my ears," he said. "For a while I actually believed her, almost up until the time I began to face the disappointments and realities of show business."

Merv was the producer and emcee of all the shows, recruiting any kid in the neighborhood who had even a modicum of talent. All the shows began at three o'clock on Saturday afternoon, and tickets sold for a dime. Merv preferred musicals. He ripped off plots and scenes from almost any Shirley Temple movie, especially *Stand Up and Cheer*, *Little Miss Marker*, and *Wee Willie Winkie*.

He was also fascinated by "The Three Stooges" reserving the character of Moe Howard for himself. "I liked Moe the best. He was cranky and sour-faced, and I could do that. But what I liked most was his tendency to inflict violence on the other Stooges. I perfected the two-fingered eye-poke, and nobody slapped faces better than I did—or pulled hair. Yes, I even yanked noses with pliers. Once I got carried away and broke this fat kid's nose. He screamed bloody murder. My parents vetoed all further Stooges shows."

Mervyn Edward Griffin Jr.
aged 5

Once when asked why he was so attracted to The Three Stooges, Merv said, "In show business you can't go wrong being gloriously lowbrow. But I soon got back to my singing. Slapstick comedy was just a detour for me."

When not staging shows, Merv published a local gossip rag, *The Whispering Winds*. He was only eight years old when he launched that sheet printed on an old Ditto machine. Nearly all the neighbors bought copies since it was filled with local gossip. *Whispering Winds* also

9

contained rave reviews for any show Merv produced.

Mr. and Mrs. George Faber lived three doors down from the Griffins. When Mrs. Faber went to Oregon to visit her relatives, Merv noticed a beautiful blonde woman, perhaps from San Francisco, slipping into the Faber household. In the next edition of *The Whispering Winds*, he reported this tidbit of gossip. The issue became a best-seller, and screams could be heard coming from the Faber household when Mrs. Faber returned home.

Publication was suspended when Merv printed a dirty joke he didn't understand. Neighbors complained to the Griffins that their eight-year-old son was a pornographer. *The Whispering Winds* whispered for the last time.

From that early mimeographed paper, Merv developed a life-long love of gossip that would never leave him and which would become in time one of the underpinnings of his empire.

Rita Griffin, Merv's mother, had been born into a family of musicians, and she encouraged her son not only to sing but to take piano lessons. To earn extra money during the Depression, Claudia Robinson, Merv's aunt, gave piano lessons to some of the teenagers in the neighborhood. She also began giving Merv piano lessons when he wasn't even tall enough to sit on a piano stool and reach the keyboard. He had to stand.

Both Rita and Claudia knew that the lessons had to be kept secret from Merv Sr. He disapproved of a boy taking piano lessons, viewing most musicians as "long-haired sissies. Boys should be taught sports. Leave the piano playing to the fat lady at the church."

After weeks of constant practice, Merv learned to play better than Claudia herself. "He's learned every one of my tricks," she said. "The little devil plays better than I ever did. It's time he received more advanced lessons."

Rita agreed and began to cut back on the grocery money, saving quarter by quarter to secure a more professional instructor for her son. She even baked cakes—a pineapple and coconut custard was her specialty—and sold them to her neighbors for fifty cents each.

Shortly before his thirteenth birthday, Merv Sr. learned that his son was a talented piano player. About thirty-five people, including relatives, had been invited to Merv Sr.'s birthday party. A neighbor, Betty Paulson, told him that she'd wanted to spend money on piano lessons for her own son. "But after hearing your Buddy play, I decided that I should encourage my boy to become a fireman or a policeman or something. I've never heard talent like Buddy's. He's a budding Mozart."

Merv Sr. disguised his shock until he could corner his son alone. "Do you know how to play the piano?" he demanded.

"Yes, dad."

"Then God damn it, sit down and play something. Play and sing *Danny*

Boy." After *Danny Boy*, Merv played *Tea for Two*, one of his father's all-time favorites.

From around two-thirty that afternoon until shortly after five, Merv never left the piano. He was occasionally joined by others at the party for a sing-a-long.

"Merv Sr. was stunned at the talent of his son," Claudia later said. "And also angered that Buddy's piano lessons had been kept a secret from him."

"From that day on," Merv said, "my dad encouraged me to sing and play the piano as much as mom and Aunt Claudia did. When all the neighbors complimented him on my recitals, dad decided that having a talented musician as a son was something to be proud of—not ashamed of."

In time Merv was taught by a mysterious woman named "Madame Siemmens," who incorporated green and purple eye shadings in her makeup, giving her a vampiric look.

Merv dreamed of being a classical musician—Edvard Grieg was his favorite composer—and he temporarily abandoned his plan to go to Hollywood and replace Bing Crosby. When not playing Grieg's music at the piano, he became adept at mastering the works of Chopin and Beethoven.

One day he came across some sheet music resting on the piano. A big hit in its day, the song was called "In a Little Gypsy Tearoom." He played the song and loved it so much that he didn't get up from the piano until he'd mastered it.

That night he couldn't sleep, as he kept hearing the sound of the song over and over in his head. The next morning he went to see his Aunt Claudia, informing her that he was going to devote his life—"from this moment on"—to pop music.

She was shocked at his sudden conversion, later telling the family, "It was like the most rigid Christian converting to Buddhism overnight. But I went along with it, because I knew he was sincere. I told him to follow his instincts. It was good-bye Grieg, hello Rudy Vallee."

She was referring to Rudy Vallee, the very square, wavy-haired crooner with the quivery vocals who had all the women screaming, just like Frank Sinatra, Elvis Presley, and The Beatles would do years later. "I got pretty tired of hearing Merv sing 'I'm Just a Vagabond Lover,' and was happy to see the day come when he dropped Vallee as his idol. I kept telling him to develop his own style. I even urged him to take acting lessons, pointing out that singing in night clubs was limited. 'A singer who can act *and* sing can make it big in the movies,' I told him. Of course, I also pointed out to him that he'd have to lose a few pounds if he wanted to become a romantic singing star in films like Nelson Eddy."

"If Dad continued to be worried about me becoming a sissy, he never confronted me with it," Merv later told his close confidant, Hadley Morrell. "I was a bit of a sissy when I was growing up. I don't mean effeminate or limp-wristed, nothing like that. But I just wasn't interested in football—maybe football players—and certainly not in gals. Instead of being on a baseball field or a basketball court, I'd rather sit in my room listening to Ethel Merman sing hits from Broadway shows. I also loved Billie Holiday."

Merv hated St. Matthews grade school, rebelling at its strict code of discipline and rigidly enforced draconian rules. He was constantly sent to the principal's office for disrupting class.

When he was enrolled in San Mateo High School, he found the atmosphere more relaxed. Perhaps as a defense mechanism to protect himself from being too fat, he became the class clown. As he told Rita, "If they're laughing with me, they aren't laughing at me." He became known as "that funny little fat boy," a roly poly bundle of charm and humor. He was especially popular among girls, although not in any romantic sense.

He was terribly bright, one of the brightest boys in his high school. Yet because of an attention deficit syndrome, he made only Ds or even Fs, getting an occasional C.

As he grew older, he became interested in boys, developing one crush after another, usually on one of the handsome school athletes, especially football players. But the objects of his affection always seemed to have a girlfriend waiting for them at the end of the game. "Saturday's Hero always had a Saturday night date with a beautiful girl," Merv later told Hadley.

"No one wanted to make it with a 240-pound boy," Merv later recalled to Hadley. "Of course, in those days I didn't know what 'make-it' really meant. First things came first. My goal was to get a kiss on the lips. I'd seen girls getting them from handsome boys, and I wanted to know what it was like. Instead of lovers, I settled for male friends, both gay and straight."

One such friend was Bob Murphy, whose parents had bought him a mother-of-pearl drum set for Christmas. When he grew up, Murphy would pursue a career in real estate, although he maintained a taste for show business. In the early 1960s, Merv, remembering his long ago friend, hired him to work behind the scenes on

Merv as a plump teenager

his game show, *Wheel of Fortune*. In time Murphy became producer—later executive producer—of *The Merv Griffin Show* on TV.

Merv also became close friends with Cal Tjader, who would become one of the foremost popularizers of Latin music in 1950s America. He primarily played the vibraphone, but was also accomplished on the bongos, congas, timpani, drums, and, like Merv, on the piano.

At the age of seven, Tjader was brought by his parents to San Mateo where he became friends with Merv. His father had danced and his mother had played the piano on the vaudeville circuit. His father taught Cal to tap dance, and he became billed in the Bay area as "Tjader Junior," a tap-dancing *wünderkind*.

Merv would call Cal in 1980 to congratulate him on his Grammy win for his album, *La Onda Va Bien*, capping off a career that spanned more than forty years.

But decades before that, Cal invited Merv to join him every afternoon at his parents' dance studio. Merv would later credit Cal and the Tjader family for "pushing and shoving me into show business."

Although Merv hardly had the physique of a ballet dancer, he began to hang out at the dance studio after school let out. He watched the boys and girls go through their routines, and often accompanied dancers on the rickety piano during rehearsals. At no point did he ever attempt to learn dance steps himself. He didn't want the other students making fun of him and his weight.

It was at the Tjader Dance Studio that Merv met three of his future best friends, who would remain early confidants of his until time and distance eventually separated them. Paul Schone, Bill Robbins, and Johnny Riley.

Unlike Merv, each had a lithe, agile body, and each aspired to pursue dancing as a career. None of them had an interest in football either. Of the three, Johnny danced to a different drummer. He was bold in stating his wish "to become the greatest ballet dancer in the world." Bill and Paul had more modest goals and would happily settle for the role of chorus boys on Broadway. Merv quickly bonded with these young men, especially the handsomest one, blond-haired, blue-eyed Johnny, who was the most charismatic of the lot.

Soon all three dancers became star performers in Merv's Saturday afternoon shows. "We were a precursor to those Mickey Rooney and Judy Garland movies where they were always putting on a show," Merv said. Later he would talk about these shows of his to the real Judy Garland herself.

Merv Sr. had grown comfortable with the

An adult view of Merv's childhood friend **Cal Tjader**,

13

idea of his son becoming a singer or a piano player. But young Merv always thought his father disapproved of his dancer friends and really didn't want them in his house. He found Bill Robbins "too girlish" and once asked Merv not to hang out with him any more.

"He's my friend," Merv protested. Since his father never brought up the subject again, Merv continued to see all three dancers. "My father was a kind man," Merv later recalled. "I think he saw how I was developing and wasn't too happy about it. But Aunt Claudia was in my corner. For a woman born in her age and time, and with her strong religious beliefs, she was hip for her age. She assured my father it was just a stage I was going through."

"He'll grow out of it," Claudia told Merv Sr. "One day he'll settle down with a beautiful gal—that is, if he takes off some weight—and raise a house filled with happy kids. You'll be the proudest grandfather on the block."

"I'm not so sure that's how it'll work out," Merv Sr. told her. "Not if he goes into show business. We know the kind of men who inhabit the world of show business. Bad influences, every one of them." But in spite of his reservations, Merv Sr. never again interfered in his son's present or future friendships.

Merv later told Johnny, "I think dad was disappointed in me, in the way I was growing up, but he never said anything. I sensed a growing separation between us, though we were very limited in what we could talk about. Many subjects were taboo, and we never went there."

Of the three dancers, Merv grew closer to Johnny than all the others. Even though he was only fourteen, he seemed more experienced than Bill or Paul. Johnny sensed Merv's growing physical attraction to him and quickly deflected it. "Let's be sisters," Johnny said. Merv had never heard a man refer to himself as a "sister." "You're just not my type. It's better that we remain friends. I like sports heroes, men like that."

To soften the blow, he invited Merv to "be my date" at a Saturday afternoon football game. "But you hate football," Merv said.

"I may hate football, but not the boys who throw the balls. Especially one named Terry Fletcher."

Merv knew the name. He was the stud of the school. All the girls were after him. A rumor had spread that the school bad boy had gotten one of the girls pregnant, and she'd had to drop out.

Merv attended the game with Johnny, who seemed mesmerized not by the game but by any play Terry made. It was a custom in those days that fathers of the players, perhaps their younger brothers as well, join the players in the locker room to congratulate them after the game or beef up their sagging spirits if they lost.

Although Merv was reluctant to come along, he was urged on by Johnny.

14

In the locker room visitors were dressed in suits, the players in jock straps, uniforms, or nothing at all. Terry had been instrumental in winning the game, and he received most of the congratulations.

As the crowds thinned out, Johnny urged Merv to stick around. Both boys were there to watch Terry undress and head for the shower, where he lathered his body with soap. The athlete seemed to be aware that he had an audience. If anything, he didn't attempt to shoo them away or conceal himself. Merv noted that he paid special attention to soaping his penis, which was beginning to grow hard.

When a coach came over, he threw a wet towel at Merv. "Get the hell out of here!"

But for some reason the coach shook Johnny's hand. "Welcome," the coach said.

Merv waited outside for Johnny, only to learn later that he'd been given the job of water boy. "Oh, the fun I'll have. That Terry baby can be had."

"Do you think?"

"Do I think? *I know.*"

As they were heading across the field, Merv had a question for Johnny. "Until today I didn't know that boys grew *that* big."

"You mean Terry? Girl, you ain't seen nothing yet."

***

Johnny turned out to be a prophet. In later years, a type of young man like Terry would be referred to as "gay for pay." Long before that, he would have been called "rough trade." Soon Johnny was spending all his money on private sessions with the school athlete.

One day he wanted to show off Terry's prowess to all his friends, including not only Merv, but Bill Robbins and Paul Schone. When Johnny's parents were gone one afternoon, he invited his friends to his basement where they sat around Terry, watching him masturbate. The athlete was paid five dollars for his performance, money the boys earned by staging Merv's Saturday afternoon shows.

Before putting back on his blue jeans that day, Terry told the boys that he was available for private sessions with each of them, granting the three the same privileges he gave Johnny. "But it'll cost you," he said as a final warning.

As far as is known, Merv had his first sexual experience with Terry. Merv later told Johnny that Terry "didn't find me much of a cocksucker compared to you, but he took my five dollars anyway." There were many repeat performances, not just between Merv and Terry, but between the football player and

15

both Bill and Paul—that is, when Terry wasn't engaged by Johnny, who always got first choice. Before the end of the school year, Terry had saved up enough to buy a car. Sometimes Merv and Johnny saw him riding around town with the campus beauty queen in the front seat with him. "I bet we get more of Terry than that stuck-up bitch does," Johnny told Merv.

***

The greatest mystery of Merv's early years revolves around "America's Bishop," Fulton J. Sheen, the leading American Catholic of the 20th Century.

In time Merv would meet and in many cases get to know the most famous people on the planet, from Richard Nixon to Jacqueline Kennedy, from Elizabeth Taylor to Pablo Casals. Merv began meeting famous people when he was still in grade school, and Fulton J. Sheen, an American archbishop of the Roman Catholic Church, arrived on the Griffin doorstep to play tennis with Merv Sr. The two men had become great friends and both were avid tennis players.

Whenever Sheen was in California, he always called on Merv Sr. "Tennis is my only form of relaxation," he once said. "You can't do God's work twenty-four hours a day, only twenty-three."

The few times Sheen had visited the Griffin household had been during the day when Merv was in school. Usually Merv Sr. drove to San Francisco to give tennis lessons to Sheen, whose visits to San Mateo were extremely rare.

But one day, quite unannounced, Sheen had arrived at the Griffin household to be greeted by Merv, the only family member at home that day. Merv later told Johnny that he was awed by the presence of such an august person and was tongue-tied for a minute.

Sheen at the time was one of the most distinguished-looking men in America, with a slender build, wavy hair, and a rather thin face which made him look ascetic.

What Merv would forever remember was Sheen's deep-set, penetrating eyes. "It would be impossible to lie to a man like His Worship," Merv later told Johnny. "He seemed to see right through me. It was like he was reading all those dark secrets I kept hidden from my family. I knew at once I wasn't fooling him for a minute. It was like going to confession without confessing anything. He just knew!"

It is not known what transpired during the approximate three hours that Sheen spent talking to Merv that day. "Merv didn't share all the dirt with me," Johnny said. Whatever happened, a bond seemed to have formed between Sheen and the young boy. The relationship would last a lifetime.

Apparently, Sheen had been intrigued by Merv's ambition, particularly

16

when the kid told the older churchman, "Some day I'm gonna become more famous than you." The bishop was far more amused than insulted by this brassy young boy.

"Merv trusted Sheen completely, the way he had Father Lyon when he was fourteen years old back in San Mateo," Bill Robbins later said. Like Merv, Bill was a member of the church choir.

At his young age, and in a surprise move by Father Lyon, Merv was made director of the church choir at the local Catholic church, a post usually held by an older man. Father Lyon also turned over complete creative control to the teenager. "What Father Lyon liked about me was my sense of drama," Merv later said. "He liked it when I hit chords on the organ that made his entrance into the church seem like the Second Coming of Jesus Christ."

Merv's unorthodox handling of the music at the church in San Mateo upset many members of the congregation. A visiting priest from San Francisco wrote a letter to Father Lyon suggesting that Merv be "excommunicated." That same priest, knowing of Griffin's relationship with Sheen, also wrote the bishop a letter citing Griffin's outrageous direction of the church choir. "His music is more Glenn Miller or Tommy Dorsey than church music," the priest charged.

When he was next in San Francisco, Sheen asked for a private meeting with Merv to discuss his music and why it was causing some concern among parishioners. The details of that meeting aren't known, but Merv spent the night in Sheen's private quarters and drove to Los Angeles with him the following day where he spent another five days with the bishop.

In the days and years to come, whenever Sheen was in California, he met privately with Merv, and they often spent weekends together. In those days, when a Catholic priest took an interest in a young boy, it was assumed that it was for spiritual guidance instead of a sexual adventure.

All three of Merv's friends, Johnny, Paul, and Bill, later claimed that Merv had told them that the relationship had become sexual. "Merv didn't sound like a whining child bitching about getting molested," Johnny recalled. "If anything, he seemed to enjoy his time with Sheen, and was excited that of all the boys in America, Sheen had singled him out. That made Merv special, and he loved it. I didn't see anything wrong with it, because at the time I was having sexual relationships with older men myself."

Merv grew so intimate with Sheen that he began to call him "Uncle Fultie." "After all, this guy chose me," Merv told Bill Robbins. "He's dined with

Bishop and TV Evangelist
Fulton J. Sheen

17

popes and princes and is on friendly terms with the President of the United States. And yet he chooses to be with me."

When he was growing up in the 1930s, Merv gathered with his family to listen to Sheen's Sunday night radio broadcast, *The Catholic Hour*. By 1950 the radio show had a devoted following of four million people. But by this time Sheen was growing increasingly fascinated by the new medium of television.

He became the country's first TV preacher to achieve nationwide fame. His TV show faced serious competition, especially from Milton Berle, "Mr. Television" himself. At the peak of his popularity, Sheen drew more TV viewers than Milton. Newspapers called the rating battle "Uncle Miltie faces Uncle Fultie." For his Catholic TV broadcasts, Sheen in 1952 won an Emmy as "The Most Outstanding Television Personality." In accepting the award, he thanked "my writers—Matthew, Mark, Luke, and John." It was Sheen's great success on television that encouraged Merv himself to try to conquer the medium in years to come.

As host of *Life Is Worth Living*, Bishop Sheen became a household word in the 1950s, beginning with the DuMont Television Network. Later he appeared on ABC from 1951 to 1957. At the end of his run, he was attracting an audience of thirty million TV viewers. In time he would also write 70 books—many of them ghost written—including his first, *God and Intelligence* (1925), and his last, *Treasure in Clay*, published in 1980 after he died on December 9, 1979.

Sheen appeared on TV in his full bishop's drag, the envy of his bitter rival in New York, Cardinal Francis J. Spellman, whom Vatican insiders had nicknamed "Nellie" Spellman because of his secret homosexual lifestyle. He was fond of hiring only the most expensive hustlers in New York. Homosexual rumors also plagued Bishop Sheen throughout his life.

Sheen appeared on TV wearing bright green alligator shoes, which were covered by his gown, and hand-sewn red silk underwear. He also became known for constantly checking his regal appearance in the mirror or in reflective glass. He did that at every opportunity. "I'm not vain," he once said in answer to his critics. "I think a servant of God should look his best at all times, even if summoned on a mission of mercy in the middle of the night."

Merv later told his friends that Sheen

Legal at Last: **Bishop Sheen** on TV with a grown up **Merv**

spent at least two hours every morning bathing, doing his hair, and getting dressed. He also was an artist at applying makeup skillfully. "You never know," he told Merv, "when a photographer might be lurking in the bush."

Merv later said that it was Sheen's formidable powers of articulation that helped him become glib on TV instead of tongue-tied. "I could listen to him talk for hours. God, did he have a way with words." Merv cited such statements made by Sheen as "Christ without The Cross is effeminacy, degeneration, LSD, and mysticism which settles for pharmaceuticals instead of sacrifice."

Sheen, whose TV programs are still broadcast, came back into the news as late as 2006. Two packages, containing documentation of two alleged miracles attributed to him, were sent to the Vatican where a panel of priests, doctors of divinity, and theologians have been examining them. After what may be years of study, the panel will "verify if indeed the alleged miracles are authentic." Some of Sheen's most avid supporters want the Vatican to bestow sainthood on their hero.

***

Like his father, two of Merv's uncles, Elmer and Peck, were also champion tennis players. The smallest brother, Peck, was actually the national doubles champion. But it was Elmer who made "Ripley's Believe It or Not" by winning three state titles in Oregon, all in one afternoon. Soon tennis-obsessed movie stars in Los Angeles were seeking the Griffin brothers out, wanting to hire them for tennis lessons.

Elmer became so popular as a tennis pro to the stars that in 1936 he launched the West Side Tennis Club in Los Angeles. Within months it became a rendezvous and social center for movie stars and film executives.

In time Douglas Fairbanks, Jr. showed up, as did a drunken John Barrymore, Clark Gable, Rod La Rocque, Johnny Mack Brown, and Louis B. Mayer himself.

As a very young teenager, Merv was allowed to journey to Los Angeles on occasions to stay with his Uncle Elmer and to hang out all day at the tennis club, watching the stars. On those occasions, Merv rarely left the locker room. Whether his uncle noticed that or not is not known.

It was at this club that Merv met his first movie stars. It was to become his life-long obsession. But instead of a locker room, he would meet many of the stars for the first time on television in front of millions of people.

One day at the club he spotted a hot, sweaty Humphrey Bogart stripping down to take a cold shower. Merv had seen Bogart and Bette Davis in *The Petrified Forest*. Back home in San Mateo, Johnny Riley pressed Merv to divulge all the details. "Bogart has a long thing, but it's a bit on the skinny side."

Elmer wasn't too fond of another member, Cesar Romero, who appeared frequently at the club. During one of Merv's many visits, he saw Romero with the actor, Tyrone Power. The two stars later played tennis together.

That afternoon Merv heard Elmer telling another tennis pro, "That Romero guy has fallen in love with Tyrone Power. I've already warned that Latin sleazeball, 'No funny business in the locker room.' Have you noticed that the other guys cover their privates with a towel every time Romero comes into the room? Word has gotten out about him."

Back home, Merv told Johnny that "Ty Power is the second handsomest man in the world. No one, but no one, is as beautiful as Errol Flynn. He's the most beautiful man on the planet." Although Flynn was a regular member of the club, he never appeared there when Merv was present.

In addition to Flynn, Merv had another idol, the Olympic athlete and movie star, Johnny Weissmuller. Merv had seen all his Tarzan movies. Begging his parents to let him go to Los Angeles, Merv made a special trip there just to meet Weissmuller. He wasn't disappointed.

Back home, he supplied another Johnny, his friend, with all the juicy details. "Tarzan needs a big loincloth to cover all that. I couldn't believe it. He put all the other guys in the locker room to shame. And he likes to show off what he's got. He parades around naked in front of all the others to make them jealous. But I never got to see the head of it even in the shower. He never

Johnny Weissmuller
as Tarzan, King of the Jungle

skinned it back even though I was standing nearby waiting for the unveiling. Oh, well. Maybe some other time. I hear some of the guys get big erections when they're massaged. Maybe I'll get lucky and see Tarzan put on a show."

Merv got lucky, but with another actor, his all-time favorite, Errol Flynn, "Satan's Angel" himself. At the tennis club, the reputation of the handsome star had already preceded him.

Merv was all ears as he listened to stories in the locker room about his swashbuckler super hero. He'd seen *Captain Blood* nine times, and planned to see it nine more times if he had a chance. When Merv sat through the first showing of *The Adventures of Robin Hood*, watching Flynn in green tights at his most charming and daring-do best, in Technicolor no less, he later admitted to Johnny: "I've fallen in love with Errol Flynn. He's the man of my dreams."

Merv shared all the gossip he'd learned about Flynn with Johnny. Was it really true that he had been a slave trader in New Guinea? Was he also a drunkard, lecher, pervert? Merv had heard that he had an amazing appetite for handsome young boys and underage girls. With his astonishing good looks, stunning physique, and legendary endowment, it was said that all he had to do was look at his conquest for the night, and any beautiful girl or boy would rush to the bed of this incorrigible hedonist to be deflowered.

Merv had heard Elmer telling of a visit to the tennis club by Jack L. Warner, head of Warner Brothers, Flynn's studio. "You know Errol. He's either got to be fighting or fucking." The studio mogul also said, "The guy's so well hung that he often unzips on the set in front of everybody, whips it out for all to see. Just to set the record straight about who's the best and the biggest. It's hard to get him to appear on the set. He's often in his dressing room having sex with four different starlets a day."

Years later in Las Vegas, Merv rewatched *Captain Blood* with his best friend, Liberace. One of Liberace's boyfriends heard Merv say: "For a fat little boy growing up in San Mateo, this film was a feast of homoeroticism. I never grew out of the letch I had for Errol. He was my dream man. When I saw him without his shirt in *The Perfect Specimen*, I sat in a dark corner of the theater and masturbated. The film had the most accurate title of any movie Hollywood ever turned out."

In a memoir, Merv recalled his first solo trip at the age of sixteen to visit his Uncle Elmer in Los Angeles. Memory did not serve him well. Actually he'd made nearly a dozen trips to visit his uncle before. When Elmer told him that Flynn was his house guest, Merv was "trembling with excitement" when he walked into Elmer's house to confront his idol.

"What I didn't expect was that my film idol, fresh from the shower, would be sitting *starkers* in Elmer's living room. Now, how shall I put this? I think it's fair to say that Errol Flynn brandished a sword both on and *off* the screen."

"Hi, kid," Flynn said. "Come on in."

Merv later recalled that he was so mes-

Swashbuckler and debauched heartthrob, **Errol Flynn**

21

merized by the sight of his nude hero that he couldn't speak. He knew that Johnny back in San Mateo would be eager to hear all the details. When Flynn saw that Merv's eyes were fixated on his private parts, he said, "Enjoy the free show. To see me on the screen will cost you twelve cents."

Merv was even more surprised when three beautiful girls arrived an hour later. He discovered that the swashbuckler had a date with all of them. To Merv's surprise, Flynn did not put on any clothes but sat drinking, talking, and fondling the girls on Elmer's big sofa. The star seemed oblivious to the little fat boy staring intently at them. Finally, Flynn got up with a big erection and proceeded to get dressed, stuffing his hard-on into his pants. Merv stood at the window watching the four of them disappear into the late afternoon in a white convertible.

He shared a bedroom with Flynn, who always slept nude and uncovered on the sheets. Merv would wake up early in the morning just to stare for an hour or so at Flynn's large penis, which was often erect.

One drunken night, Flynn came into the room and pulled off his clothes, flopping down on the bed. "For the first time in weeks, kid, I didn't get lucky. Those girls must have been lesbians." After about fifteen minutes, Flynn whispered to Merv. "Come on over here and play with it, kid. You know you want to. You can't take your eyes off it. If you play with it enough, I'll make *leche* for you."

Back in San Mateo, Johnny insisted that Merv tell him that story of masturbating Flynn over and over again.

Before leaving Los Angeles, Elmer had taken Merv to his favorite restaurant, Romanoff's, where all the stars gathered. They stopped briefly at Humphrey Bogart's table. Even though it was only one o'clock in the afternoon, the star appeared drunk.

When Merv spotted his favorite character actor, Monty Woolley, at the bar, he excused himself from Elmer's table and walked over. Merv thought Woolley could spit out insults with his razor-sharp tongue better than anybody on the screen.

He also knew that the bearded actor was the best friend of Cole Porter, and Merv knew all the composer's songs. Getting up the courage to approach Woolley at the bar, Merv said, "May I have your autograph, Mr. Woolley?" Forgetting Errol Flynn for the moment, he added, "You're my favorite actor."

"Kid, if you were a Botticelli angel, I'd give you my autograph—and a lot more. But you're nothing but a roly-poly fatso. Fuck off!"

Back at table, Merv told his uncle about the rude rejection. "Stay away from him. He's the biggest pervert in Los Angeles. I mean, how sick can you get? He and that Ty Power sicko have private parties where all the guests eat shit for a sexual thrill."

22

Merv was astonished, thinking at first Elmer might be joking. It was years later that he learned about coprophagia (feces eating).

***

Merv got his driving license at the age of sixteen, just months before the Japanese attack on Pearl Harbor, and he often drove Johnny Riley into San Francisco for the weekend. Johnny was having an affair with a 45-year-old stockbroker, who often gave both boys twenty-dollar bills for fun and games. Merv slept on the sofa in the living room of the stockbroker, where he heard noises coming from the bedroom at night.

During the day Johnny and Merv cruised the streets of San Francisco on the search for good-looking sailors. "Johnny got lucky . . . always," Merv later told his gay pal, Liberace. "I rarely did unless Johnny fixed me up with one of his rejects. When I got to give a sailor a blow-job, he was too drunk to care if some little fat boy was doing the job or a beautiful blonde."

Merv was drafted in 1942 after he'd graduated from San Mateo High School. He stood 5'9" at the time and still weighed slightly more than 240 pounds. "As remarkable as it seems, I had to show up at the induction hall in San Francisco ten different times for physical examinations," Merv said. "I sort of got used to doctors playing with my balls and urging me to cough. On the final exam, the doctor discovered a heart murmur. He considered it serious enough to send me to the hospital. When I was released from the ward and went back to San Mateo, I learned that at long last I'd been classified 4F."

His buddies, Paul Schone and Bill Robbins, had joined the U.S. Navy and were serving on battleships in the Pacific. Bill Robbins might have been "too girlish" for Merv Sr.'s tastes, but apparently he found no objections from the Navy. He later wrote Merv: "I'm making my way through the entire ship's crew. Only the captain has eluded me so far."

Johnny Riley was more masculine-looking than Bill and would not have been rejected by the draft board as an obvious homosexual. However, he bluntly told the Army doctor examining him that, "I'm a cocksucker." There were thousands upon thousands of homosexuals who fought in World War II, but Johnny and Merv were not among them.

Johnny agreed to help Merv sell War Bonds by staging entertainment on the streets of their hometown San Mateo and later in San Francisco.

"I became an early Bob Hope," Merv later said, "staging shows for soldiers on the nearby bases in San Francisco. These guys were about to be shipped out to the Pacific Theater, and we knew—*and they knew*—that many of them would never see San Francisco again."

Years later, when Merv met playwright Tennessee Williams, both of them

23

privately agreed that for a gay male, being in San Francisco was the place to be in the early 1940s. "If a homosexual man couldn't get laid back then, he couldn't get laid anywhere," Tennessee said. "The young sailors virtually lined up to get one final blow-job before sailing away. Perhaps no city in America has ever been so hedonistic. When you're facing death, conventional sexual morality no longer matters. Although Merv and I didn't know each other, we were taking advantage of these fresh-faced young men, some of whom came from the Middle West and had never confronted a gay man below. Many had never received a blow-job before, certainly not from their uptight girlfriends back home."

"Merv and I agreed that it was a heady time for both of us, but it was also sad to realize that the young men we were servicing might be blown to bits by soldiers of the Japanese Empire," Tennessee said. "What a waste! Wars always sacrifice the best of us, and leave rejects like Merv and me at home."

When he wasn't singing on street corners, heckling residents to buy War Bonds, Merv and a civilian watch team scanned the skies of the Bay area looking for unauthorized aircraft. A sneak air attack from Japan was greatly feared. He and various friends used the tower of the San Mateo High School for their lookout post.

"The nights were long and cold," Merv remembered. "Even if we spotted aircraft, I don't know if we would have known the Jap planes from our own Air Force fighters."

One night one of his fellow skywatchers, a handsome, seventeen-year-old boy who was still a senior in high school, brought along a bottle of gin. He and Merv got drunk. Merv later told Johnny, "We fooled around some that night. I think he felt guilty about the experience. The next day he didn't speak to me, even though he'd shot off the night before. I was assigned a different guy the following night. We never saw any planes with the Rising Sun on them."

His friend, Johnny, continued to prostitute himself with older men, but Merv never did that. "There was no demand for me," he jokingly told his pals. Instead he made his money for gas (which was rationed) by playing the organ at weddings. He charged fifteen dollars for a wedding, commanding an extra five for funerals.

The worst year for the U.S. military both in Europe and the Pacific was 1942, and despite some success selling War Bonds, 4F

Tennessee Williams in the '40s, camping it up in Provincetown

Merv wanted to do more. He took a temporary job in the provisions section at Hunter's Point Naval Station outside San Francisco. From here, provisions were trucked to transport ships in the San Francisco harbor. These life-saving supplies were then loaded aboard cargo ships for soldiers and sailors fighting the Japanese in the Pacific.

Merv lost his job at the naval depot supply station when a sailor reported that Merv had propositioned him in the men's toilet. Although Merv adamantly denied this, he was still dismissed from his job. This would be the beginning of several sexual harassment charges that would be made against Merv by men during the years to come.

Through an acquaintance of Merv's father, his son was given a job as a bank teller at the Crocker National Bank. "You can't make a living as a piano player," his father told him. "You need a steady job."

"I lasted one day on the job," Merv recalled. "I talked to a late middle-aged bank teller next to me. He'd worked there for twelve years until his salary was raised to thirty-five dollars a week. The next day I barged into the bank manager's office and quit. I was still determined to make it in show business . . . or else."

At the time, Merv was also enrolled in San Mateo Junior College where he majored in music.

While enrolled in Junior College, Merv developed a crush on his handsome male music teacher, who was about twenty-eight at the time and very popular with his students. Conveniently for Merv, the teacher turned out to be gay.

His name and the details of their brief romance are lost. Merv later confided to Johnny, "He was the first man to break my heart, the first of many I might add. It lasted about three weeks, and I was in Heaven which soon became Hell for me. Suddenly, my teacher didn't have any more time for me. I later learned that he was dating a very cute—*and much slimmer*—blond-haired boy. I was history. I moped around the house for weeks. My revenge came after two or three months when Blondie dumped the teacher for one of the football coaches."

After junior college, Merv enrolled in the University of San Francisco but dropped out before earning a degree. "I just couldn't concentrate on what the professors were saying," he later said. "I spent all my time in class day dreaming about breaking into show business."

"I educated myself by reading a lot," Merv later said. "In the years to come, I interviewed every prominent person in the world, except the Pope. Not only that, I hung out with many of these people. Like a sponge, I listened to them and learned things I would never have learned in college."

"Boy, did I learn," he said. "Stars were discreet on camera, but once backstage or in their dressing room they seemed to want to share all their secrets with me. I guess I looked like a Father Confessor. If I would ever write a book about the secrets of the stars, it'd be a best-seller for sure. But then I'd lose the money in libel suits."

***

Johnny kept urging Merv to lose weight, assuring him he'd be attractive if he got rid of the pudge. Merv tried dieting, but for his whole family weight remained a problem. "We kept eating and eating. I wanted to diet but had no willpower."

In spite of his weight, Merv still wanted to break into show business. While still in college he met Barbara McNutt, "a fat gal with pudgy hands," who, like Merv, had a beautiful singing voice. They teamed up and appeared on *Budda's Amateur Hour* for the local radio station KFRC.

Merv sat at the piano and sang patriotic songs, including "God Bless, America," "The Star-Spangled Banner," and George M. Cohen's "Yankee Doodle Boy." The two-fatsos, as Merv called Barbara and himself, were clearly the best act but lost to a country fiddler from Kentucky who was also in the U.S. Army. Two show business pros, Gertrude Niesen and Billy ("Sneezy") Gilbert, decided to vote for a man in uniform even though Merv and Barbara should have won.

Merv got really mad at Niesen, a big band singer. He vowed to turn off the radio if she came on again, although he loved her brief 1943 film appearance in *This Is the Army*.

Billy Gilbert realized he'd greatly undermined the boy's self-confidence and tried to befriend Merv after he lost. Since 1934 Gilbert had become one of the screen's most familiar faces, and Merv was enthralled when the star was cast as the voice of Sneezy in the 1937 *Snow White and the Seven Dwarfs*. He'd even thrilled Merv when he'd danced with Alice Faye and Betty Grable in *Tin Pan Alley* (1940).

"I'm sorry, kid," Gilbert told Merv. "You deserved to win, but there's a war on. We had to vote the way we did. It'll give a boost to our troops. When the war's over, I predict you'll become a big-time star. Even bigger than Frank Sinatra and Bing Crosby."

"Do you really believe that?" Merv asked.

"Not really. But I can't resist a good line when it comes to my head."

Merv would later claim, "Barbara and I looked like Tweedledum and Tweedledee." Even though they came in second, the host of the show, Dean Maddox, liked their music and secured bookings for Barbara and Merv all over San Francisco. Once they journeyed to Los Angeles for an engagement.

26

At some point, he deserted "fat Barb" and teamed up with a slimmer Janet Folsom, who was also the social director of the swank Pebble Beach Lodge on the Monterey Peninsula. At the time, it was a secret hideaway for movie stars, many of whom were there as part of an off-the-record weekend, with spouses back in Hollywood, or else partners in Palm Springs indulging in their own infidelities.

Janet told Merv that there was an opening at the hotel for the job of pianist, so he journeyed to Monterey for an audition.

Mrs. Lent Hooker liked the audition of Merv and Janet, and hired him as a party pianist to entertain the guests. Her father, Sam Morris, was the owner of the lodge.

With his jovial personality and perpetual smile, and his good—not great—singing voice, Merv became an instant hit with guests at the lodge. One morning at breakfast, Janet introduced him to her friend, Dinah Shore. Merv was in awe of the singer, one of his favorites.

Sitting next to Dinah, and looking rather stoic but devastatingly handsome, was the actor George Montgomery, Dinah's recently acquired hunk of a husband. Other than Tyrone Power and Errol Flynn, Merv thought Montgomery was one of the sexiest men on the screen.

Montgomery was in his soldier's uniform, and his much publicized marriage to Dinah had earned him fame. Merv and Johnny had thrilled to him when he appeared as the leading man opposite Ginger Rogers in *Roxie Hart* (1942) and opposite Betty Grable in *Coney Island* (1943).

Back in San Mateo, Merv later confided to Johnny, "One night I got to stand next to Montgomery at the urinal. Lucky Dinah, I'd say. He talks like he's speaking through clenched teeth. But what a man. He was a heavyweight boxer before becoming a movie star."

Three views of **George Montgomery:**
Above, with then-wife, **Dinah Shore**

"I read in a fan magazine that he studied to be an interior decorator," Johnny chimed in.

"I don't believe that," Merv said, trying to defend this macho star. "Those fan magazines make up a lot of shit."

That night as Merv sat in the

27

lounge of the Pebble Beach Lodge at the piano, he was shocked when Dinah herself got up to sing a duet with him. She asked him if he knew the words and music to her hit, "You'd Be So Nice to Come Home To."

"Do I ever!" he told her. "Let's go for it."

The applause was so deafening that Merv and Dinah did an encore, "I'll Walk Alone." The guests applauded even more wildly the second time around. "Kid, you and I should form an act and take it on the road," Dinah said before kissing him on the cheek and returning to her table. Later, on his resumé, Merv claimed that he'd sung professionally with Dinah Shore. While technically true, the credit was misleading.

Relaxing by the pool the following day, Merv was surprised when Ann Sothern came over and joined him on a chaise longue. "Miss Sothern," Merv said. "What an honor! My God, there are more stars at this lodge than there are in heaven."

"I like your music, big boy," she said, "but you've got to take off a few pounds. I fear that both you and I are going to spend the rest of our lives fighting the battle of the bulge."

With such an unlikely beginning, a friendship was formed that would last for years. No one in movies, at least in Merv's view, could deliver wisecracks better than Ann. "The Queen of the Bs" at Columbia Pictures had come up in show business "one hard knock at a time."

At the time she met Merv, Ann had been cast as the irrepressible namesake of the *Maisie* movies, films that evolved into at least seven sequels based on the original *Maisie* (1939) in which she had been cast as a brash vaudevillian stranded in a small town. Most of the Maisie films were released during the dark years of World War II, frothy comedies with names that included *Congo Maisie (1940), Gold Rush Maisie (1940), Maisie was a Lady (1941); Ringside Maisie (1941), Maisie Gets Her Man (1942),* and last in the series, *Undercover Maisie* (1947).

Addressing his future, she became one of the first show business personalities to urge him to abandon movies and break into television. When her own film career virtually collapsed in the 1950s, Ann turned to the tube, playing the role of Susie in *Private Secretary* (1953), which ran until 1957. The following year she starred in *The Ann Sothern Show*, which ran until 1961. Over the years, Merv faithfully watched most of her appearances on

Lesser Diva: **Ann Sothern**

28

TV and often talked over career moves with her.

He always admired her brutal honesty about herself. "Frankly, she said, "Jean Harlow was slated to play Maisie before she died. I won the role by default." Merv was saddened when he talked to Ann in the 1970s and 80s. She called those decades "drought ridden. The buzzards are circling over me."

In a mood of nostalgia, as he was getting old and blubbery, Merv visited Ann "for old time's sake." He'd obtained a copy of his favorite film of hers, *A Letter to Three Wives* (1949), in which she played a writer married to a younger man, Kirk Douglas.

At the end of the movie, which Merv adored, she turned to him and said. "You know something? I'm always amazed at what a lousy actress I was. I guess in the old days we just got by on glamour. Today's actresses and actors have real talent. Good looks are no longer an essential part of this rotten business."

He was gladdened when she was nominated for an Academy Award playing Tisha Doughty in the 1987 *The Whales of August*. "It's my Last Hurrah," she told Merv in a phone call. "But I truly believe that working with Bette Davis has shortened my life span, and at my age I ain't got that many years to spare."

***

One high-profile regular guest at the Pebble Beach Lodge was even more famous than either Ann Sothern or Dinah Shore. She was Joan Crawford, who happened to be a friend of the socially connected Janet Folsom. To Merv's astonishment, Janet told him that she had checked into the lodge with her longtime flame, Johnny Weissmuller. Janet said that "Tarzan and Joan are sometime lovers . . . sometimes, on occasion. But they can't be seen together in the public rooms."

Merv was hoping for another glimpse of one of his idols, which he'd seen in the nude at his Uncle Elmer's club. But Johnny made no public appearances that weekend, but stayed in Joan's suite.

Joan came down to dinner by herself and made a stunning entrance into the dining room, wearing all white, including those famous high heels that later became known as Joan Crawford "fuck-me shoes." Even though Merv knew that Joan's days as the Queen of MGM were over, and she

Major Diva: **Joan Crawford**

29

was struggling to reinvent herself, she was the epitome of self-confidence and graciousness when Janet introduced him to her.

When not entertaining guests, Janet and Merv wrote music and lyrics together. The following night, they composed one for Joan herself when she came down, again alone, to the dining room. She sat at a front table and had to suffer through:

Someone's out to kill me
'cause
I'm honestly acting like a dilly
I'm silly
'cause I'm in love,
I'm horribly, borably
So in love.

Joan's reaction? "I think you kids have come up with something *terribly*, even *horribly*, cute. Maybe a bit too cute. Try harder next time."

Mrs. Lent Hooker not only got Merv his gig at Pebble Beach, but she also arranged for him to play the piano at private parties for twenty dollars. "I'd play in a treehouse for twenty bucks," Merv said at the time. At a Halloween costume party at Mrs. Hooker's estate, everyone except Merv showed up in masks.

After midnight Merv was joined by a rather dashing figure dressed all in black, with a black mask concealing his features. In his autobiography, Merv remembered the guest disguised as a ghost, but other guests claimed he was actually in disguise as The Cisco Kid.

For about an hour "The Kid" joined Merv in a round of songs, Merv finding his voice "acceptable—not great." But they were having fun, and by that time the other guests were too drunk to care.

At one point, the mystery man handed Merv some sheet music from the film, *Springtime in the Rockies*, one of Merv's favorite movies, starring Carmen Miranda, Betty Grable, and Cesar Romero. He asked Merv if he would play a few

Cesar Romero in his most famous role

numbers from this film.

"Do you know the lyrics?" Merv asked.

"I most certainly do," said the guest, removing his mask to expose the face of Cesar Romero himself.

The Latin star sat with Merv until around three in the morning, playing requests from the other guests. The two men got along famously, laughing and joking, with Cesar telling the more innocent Merv dirty jokes. Romero had been drinking heavily all evening, and Merv was given four cocktails, although liquor went to his head.

When Cesar invited him to join him in the back seat of his imported car, Merv went along with it. "I usually like them a little thinner, but all cats are gray at night," Cesar said. In the rear of the car, Merv received a blow-job from one of the most talented and experienced mouths in Hollywood.

After that night, Merv and *The Gay Caballero* (the name of Cesar's 1940 film) never became lovers again, but their friendship would last for several years to come. One night when Merv was singing for the Freddy Martin band in San Diego, he was surprised to see Cesar seated at a front table with Desi Arnaz. Desi was also appearing in the San Diego area but had the night off.

After the show, both Cesar and Desi came backstage to congratulate Merv on his show and to invite him for a nightcap in their suite.

After an hour, Desi disappeared into the bedroom while Cesar and Merv kept talking. About thirty minutes later, Merv was startled to look up at the doorway to the bedroom. Desi stood completely nude with an erection.

"Griffin, it's time to say good night," Desi called out. "I need that cock-sucker to give me a blow-job so I can get some sleep."

***

Merv fell in love with the Pebble Beach area, and years later when he became rich and famous, he often took handsome young men here for his own off-the-record weekends.

Three decades would go by before Merv purchased his own vacation home in the area. He invited Janet to meet several of his famous friends, but one hour before the housewarming party was to begin, he received a call that she'd suffered a heart attack and had died in an ambulance rushing her to the hospital.

There was another ironic twist to those Pebble Beach days. Years later when the gay talent agent, Henry Willson, showed up at Merv's door, he spotted a fellow house guest, George Montgomery, sprawled nude out by the pool.

Merv explained George's presence to Willson, claiming that he had commissioned the actor to make some elegant cabinets for him.

31

While appearing in action movies, George, an excellent craftsman, ran a cabinet shop for four decades, making furnishings for the stars. He also designed and constructed a dozen beautiful homes for friends and family.

Henry and the handsome actor bonded, and Merv noted that they left Pebble Beach together that weekend. The agent had promised the hunk that he could revitalize his career, which he never did. At that point in their lives, both Montgomery's and Willson's sun had already sunk in the West.

But the question remains: Years after his gig as the entertainment maestro at the Pebble Beach Lodge, did Merv ever manage to seduce George Montgomery, the then-newlywed who had previously accompanied Dinah Shore to her suite?

***

Even though he didn't win first place in the singing contest, Merv did not give up on the radio station, KFRC. One afternoon when he was in San Francisco with Cal Tjader, Merv was urged to apply for a job as a staff musician. Tjader had heard that there was an opening.

Affiliated with the Mutual Network, KFRC would "birth" such famous TV personalities as Art Linkletter and Mark Goodson, the game show producer. Both Goodson and Linkletter would become powerful role models for Merv.

Alan Lisser, the program director, agreed to see Merv and Tjader. "Your friend here has told you wrong," Lisser said. "We don't need a piano player. What we need is a singer. You sing?"

At first Merv started to say no because, in spite of all his public appearances, he still did not think of himself as a singer. "Merv's the best singer in San Francisco," Tjader told Lisser. Urged on by his pal, Merv sang for the director in a voice that was no longer the school soprano but had developed into a melodious baritone.

That morning he'd been listening to the smooth sounds of Dick Haymes singing "I Was Taken for a Sleighride in July." He chose that song for his audition. Lisser was so impressed he brought out Bill Pabst, the station owner.

Merv went through the number again and was hired on the spot to appear every Thursday on *The San Francisco Sketchbook,* a fifteen-minute morning program. His salary would be one hundred dollars per show.

After signing the deal, Merv was told that he'd be backed up by a twenty-two man orchestra. That flabbergasted him. He felt he was on his way up the long ladder of show business.

At this point in his career, Merv had not found his own distinctive voice and was heavily influenced by other popular singers of his day. When he was hired for his first professional show, he'd focused on Dick Haymes as a role model.

Later, Merv attended many of Dick's nightclub shows and got to know him more or less well. Merv told bandleader Freddy Martin, "Never meet your singing idols. Regardless of how smooth they appear on stage, they will always disappoint you in private."

Argentine-born Dick burst into prominence during the Big Band Era of the 1940s, appearing with such bandleaders as Tommy Dorsey and Harry James (who was married to Betty Grable).

"I admired his singing voice," Merv later said. "When I got to know him personally, I thought he was a bastard. He was a hopeless alcoholic but that was only part of his problems. He was also reckless with money. I heard he squandered four-million dollars in just a few years."

As his career headed to the graveyard, Dick met Rita Hayworth in 1953 when she was filming the W. Somerset Maugham story, *Miss Sadie Thompson*, at Columbia. "He didn't love her," Merv later said. "At the time I knew Rita only casually but warned her not to marry the bastard. But she was too much in love to listen to me. The results were a disaster. To beef up his audience, Haymes insisted that Rita sit at the front table for all his nightclub appearances. The spotlight would often be turned on her. Even if the crowd didn't want to hear Haymes sing, *everybody* wanted to get a look at Rita. She was a goddess. Eddie Fisher pulled the same stunt when he married Elizabeth Taylor and hauled her out for public viewing at his nightclub appearances. It's amazing what fading crooners will do to hold onto their popularity—not me, boy. When fans no longer wanted to hear me sing, I switched professions. And how!"

After just one appearance on *The San Francisco Sketchbook,* Merv was offered a bigger and better deal by Bill Pabst. Beginning that Monday, he was to be the star of his own *The Merv Griffin Show*, at a beginning salary of $1,100 per week, which was soon raised to $1,500 per week. The station billed him as "America's New Romantic Singing Star."

In just three weeks, Merv got his show picked up by the Mutual Network, of which KFRC was a member. He learned that his singing was being broadcast across wartime

Rita Hayworth with husband #4, Argentinian crooner (and Merv's role model) **Dick Haymes**

33

America, earning new fans for him in places like Los Angeles, Denver, Chicago, and New York.

"I became filthy rich," Merv said, perhaps unknowingly predicting his own future. "I went out and bought two new cars, one a white convertible just like the one I'd seen Errol Flynn drive away in with those broads. I joined three country clubs, and I didn't even play golf. One membership would have been more than enough. My underpaid dad thought I'd opened a string of bordellos in San Francisco."

Even though his newly emerging fans liked his singing, Merv was smart enough to realize that he was no Frank Sinatra or Bing Crosby. He arranged to study voice with Bill Stoker, a Mormon who once sang with the orchestra of Kay Kyser. It was while attending one of Bill Stoker's voice lessons that he met another aspirant star, Al Cernick.

As Guy Mitchell, Al would become what Merv never became, a singing sensation across America.

***

The same age as Merv, good-looking Guy Mitchell entered the world as Albert Cernick in 1925 in Detroit, the son of Croatian immigrant parents. After meeting his fellow pupil at Bill Stoker's vocal classes, Merv was immediately captivated by the young man's looks, charm, and personality. The first day they met, Guy was wearing his sailor's uniform, having been honorably discharged from the U.S. Navy.

"There was something about his smile that made me tingle all over," Merv later told Johnny Riley. "He also has the kind of hair you want to run your fingers through." After their vocal lessons, Guy and Merv spent hours together talking about their dreams for stardom.

In the 1930s Guy (or Al Cernick) had been signed by Warner Brothers to be groomed as a child star. He later became known as a singer on San Francisco radio, like Merv himself. Surprisingly, Merv did not feel threatened by Guy and didn't view him as a competitor. Instead they developed an unusual rapport with each other. Merv seemed thrilled when Guy, still billed as Al Cernick, got his big break when Carmen Cavallero signed him as the lead singer for his Big Band sounds in 1946.

Before that break came, Guy had supplemented his income working as a saddlemaker, a trade he'd learned from his father. Rather athletic, he also rode horses, and invited Merv to accompany him on trips into the wilds of northern California. Merv wasn't that much into horseback riding but gladly went along to be with the object of his desire.

Somewhere along these trails, Merv fell hopelessly in love with Guy. It was hopeless because Guy was basically straight, although he admitted to "having fooled around a bit in the Navy." At some point on these long horse-back-riding weekends, the relationship between Guy and Merv turned sexual.

One of Guy's closest friends at the time, Ralph Laven, later claimed that Guy told him that the relationship, in spite of his wishes, had become sexual. "I love Merv, but I don't *love* him," Guy reportedly told Laven.

Merv confided the details of his relationship with Guy to his gay friends, including, as always, Johnny Riley. "Al [meaning Guy] wasn't really into it from what I gathered," Johnny said. "He let Merv blow him—and that was it. He did not reciprocate. Merv told me that Al wouldn't even let him kiss him except on the cheek. Poor Merv. He wanted deep French kissing and all the works, but Al just couldn't go that far."

Thus Merv shared something in common with gay boys all over America who fall for straight men. It was a pattern he would continue throughout the rest of his life.

Even after learning how Merv felt about him, Guy did not break off with his close friend, but continued in a relationship. Merv could not have been ful-filled by it, but he wanted to remain at Guy's side regardless of the price.

Putting any jealousy aside, Merv felt pride when Mitch Miller, in charge of talent at Columbia Records, discovered "Al Cernick." "The name's got to go," Miller said. "How about Guy Mitchell?"

Merv did a skip and jump of joy when Frank Sinatra turned down "My Heart Cries for You." Mitch Miller then offered it to Guy, who scored his first million seller for Columbia. Even the B side of the record, "The Roving Kind," was also a big hit. Guy quickly became a household name in the 1950s, with other hits to follow, including a 1956 biggie, "Singin' the Blues." His decade of the 1950s came to an end with yet another mil-lion seller, "Heartaches by the Number."

Like Merv, Guy also wanted to break into the movies, and he did in 1953 when he starred with Rhonda Fleming in *Those Redheads from Seattle* and a year later with Rosemary Clooney in *Red Garters*. Merv was even around in 1957 to toast Guy when he starred on television in *The Guy Mitchell Show*.

Merv had dinner with Guy to console him

Merv's boyfriend, teen idol and singing sensation **Guy Mitchell**

35

when he was booted out of Columbia Records in 1961. "We talked about old times like two geezers, even though both of us had decades yet left to live." Merv confessed to having a tear in his eye in 1965 when he heard the news over the phone that Guy was retiring from show business.

Upon learning of Guy's death at the age of 72 on July 1, 1999, Merv fondly recalled his friend and long-time companion, a man he'd never stopped loving. "Like me, Guy in his music evoked the last years of America's innocence in the 1950s. The world of music, even life itself, would never be the same when that decade came to an end. The horrible Sixties were upon us. Watching Guy's decline only reminded me what would have happened had I not reinvented myself after my decline as a pop singer and a so-called movie star in the Fifties."

***

Even though he continued to sing in San Francisco during the mid-Forties, Merv as a romantic singer was also developing a fan base in Los Angeles. The beautiful Joan Fontaine, star of one of Merv's all-time favorite movies, *Rebecca* (1940), listened to him along with her husband, the producer William Dozier. The "son of Nebraska" had only recently married Fontaine and would go on to wed actress Ann Rutherford after his divorce from Fontaine in 1951.

Joan and Bill became so enamored of Merv's singing that they called him and agreed to drive to San Francisco to meet with him at their suite at the Fairmont Hotel. Bill had hopes of turning Merv "into the next Dennis Morgan," a singing star and fixture at Warner's during the 1940s.

Based on Merv's singing voice, and in advance of their first meeting, Bill judged him to be handsome and romantic with a big future in movie musicals.

It was Joan who answered the door of their suite. Merv recalled that she looked astonished. "*You* are Merv Griffin?" Quickly concealing her embarrassment, she invited him into her suite. "Bill, darling," she called to her husband. "You've got to come out and meet Merv Griffin, the singing sensation."

Merv later recalled that Bill's face "just dropped when he saw me. I could tell how disappointed he was. He knew at once that I wasn't going to be Hollywood's next romantic leading singer in films. But Bill and Joan were terribly polite and recovered brilliantly like the pros they are and invited me in for a drink."

The only humor associated with that afternoon drink came when Joan said, "I really should introduce you to Olivia in case she ever does a musical. You'd be perfect as her leading man." Joan, of course, was jokingly referring to her estranged sister, Olivia de Havilland.

Since Bill and Joan obviously couldn't talk about promoting Merv as a romantic singing film star, the conversation quickly turned to Bill's early days in Hollywood.

In 1935 he came to California as an agent for writers F. Scott Fitzgerald and Sinclair Lewis, and he had many stories to tell about his misadventures trying to get serious writers launched. It made Merv sad to hear Bill tell about Fitzgerald's declining years.

At the door telling Merv good-bye, Bill finally got to the point. "Take off eighty pounds, kid, and then we'll talk."

During the years that followed, Bill and Merv encountered each other on occasions and laughed about their first meeting. "If I knew you were going to become the richest man on the planet, I would have signed you at once," Bill told him. "Fat or not. I could have become Col. Tom Parker to your Elvis. A fifty-fifty split, of course."

Merv also followed Bill's career in television. He was amused as Bill demanded the insertion of phrases like *"Pow!," "Wham!,"* and *"Zowee!"* as a means of infusing camp into the *Batman* TV series in the late 60s. Encountering Bill at Restaurant "21" in New York, Merv came up to him and extended his hand. "The King of Camp himself!"

Later Merv recalled, "Believe it or not, Bill thought camp was a place you sent your kids every summer. I guess he hadn't read Susan Sontag's article defining a new kind of camp."

"As the Batman craze swept the country," Bill said, "I learned what camp was. There are those who say I invented it." Later Bill was accused of ushering in trash TV. But he told Merv, "I'm not ashamed. Were F.W. Woolworth and J.C. Penny ashamed because they weren't Tiffany and Cartier?"

In time Bill became a TV reformer, teaching college courses on Network Television, in which he urged his students to "reshape the tube." He admitted to having produced, in addition to Batman, the *Green Hornet* and *The Tammy Grimes Show*—"the most conspicuous failure ever on television."

But to his classes, whose members included U.C.L.A. undergraduates as well as Hollywood directors, producers, and press agents, he expressed admiration of Merv for bringing serious talk to television, citing interviews with everybody from the Kennedys to Martin Luther King Jr. "Of course," Bill added, "he also had to bring on Burt Reynolds and Sophia Loren to keep the ratings high."

***

In San Francisco, with his new-found money from his successful singing career—"I was making the kind of money my old man could only dream about"—Merv established Panda Records in 1946 with Janet Folsom. With her help and professional advice, he recorded his first album of easy-to-listen-to melodies, including "Falling in Love with Love," which remained his favorite on the road for many years to come. Even though the album, *Songs by Merv Griffin*, didn't sell well, it had its moment in music history.

Fresh from the battlefields of Europe, the album's recording engineer had made great strides in experimental technology. Merv's album was recorded on magnetic tape, the first U.S. label to be recorded in such a way. As such, it is displayed today in museums devoted to music history.

It was not the experience with Bill Dozier and Joan Fontaine, but an encounter with another star named Joan—Joan Edwards—that finally convinced Merv he had to take off the pounds if he ever wanted to be a star in the movies or even in the newly emerging industry of television.

Without ever knowing what he looked like, Joan Edwards had become a faithful fan of Merv's, listening to his romantic singing voice every chance she got. She was one of the most popular radio singers in America, and was regularly featured on the highly rated *Your Hit Parade* between 1941 and 1946.

She'd also been a featured singer with the Paul Whiteman Orchestra between 1938 and 1940, at which time Merv had become an ardent fan.

From her hotel room in San Francisco, Joan called Merv to tell him, "You sing like an angel." Flattered at her attention, he invited her to appear the next morning on his show. "I'll be there with bells on," she promised.

Merv later claimed she was shocked when she encountered him for the first time. Unlike the socially graceful Joan Fontaine, Joan Edwards was a very blunt woman. "You sing a romantic ballad better than Sinatra, although I'm sure you don't fuck as well. I'm speaking from personal experience. But that blubber has to go. There aren't too many Moby Dick scripts being written for whales these days."

Merv later claimed that, "I almost cried when I heard her say that. But it was the truth. I just hadn't faced up to it. I knew my career could really get moving, but only when I shit and pissed away all that God damn fat."

No more visits to Blum's Soda Fountain for his beloved hot fudge sundaes—"with extra fudge, please." No more big bowls of puffed rice in which he dripped honey and added two bananas for breakfast. No more spaghetti dinners with three desserts.

On a rigid diet for the first time in his life, Merv ate nothing but rare steak and salads without oil, only vinegar. Amazingly he managed to take off twenty pounds a month. Standing nude in front of a mirror, he admired his body for the first time in his life, at a fighting weight of 160 pounds.

"I suddenly saw that I was a handsome man, not a Guy Madison, but not a bad-looking guy either. I was just as pretty as Gordon MacRae, who had been signed by Warners and cast in *The Big Punch*. I could sing better than

MacRae too."

Although Merv had not been jealous of Guy Mitchell, he would become locked into a bitter rivalry with MacRae, even at the very beginning of that star's rise to fame.

Merv would become particularly agitated sitting through any movie in the future, such as *Tea for Two* (1950), that co-starred Doris Day and MacRae. "I tried to blot out MacRae's image and sub my own. I felt that I, not MacRae, belonged up there on the screen in Doris's arms."

Merv's weight loss gave him a self-confidence he'd never had before. He even began to feel that he could compete with other gay men for some of the handsome hunks walking around San Francisco. "I would no longer be ashamed to take off my clothes. In fact, I had hopes to find someone who would love me back so my life wouldn't be entirely about servicing rough trade," he told his friend, Bill Robbins.

With his new self-assurance, Merv even gave in to Johnny Riley's request to take off all his clothes to show off his new physique. Johnny later recalled, "I was so impressed with Merv's new look that I tossed in a mercy fuck that night just for old time's sake. After all, he'd been lusting after me ever since grade school, and I felt he deserved some kind of reward."

Heady days remained ahead for Merv as he spent his last months in San Francisco, with continued success for "The Merv Griffin Show," which was presented until that day in 1948 when he resigned. Another offer came in that was far more tempting than the radio show, which had begun to bore him.

At night he hit the gay bars of San Francisco. "With my newly acquired physique, and with certain good looks that had emerged from behind the blubber, I became a whore on the make," he told Johnny. "I was like a kid just released in the candy store and told to pick up anything I liked. I was enjoying a sex life for the first time in my life. I was far too young to settle down, and I wanted to have experiences that had been denied me up to now. I broke a few hearts back then. How different that was for me. Up to now, I'd had my heart broken lusting after 'The Guy.' Get that? Guy Mitchell and a few others."

Merv's life was about to change, although he had no clue as to what was about to happen.

At the St. Francis Hotel in San Francisco, Freddy Martin stepped out of the shower. The radio was on. On the air he heard the romantic, melodious voice of Merv Griffin singing "Let There Be Love."

The popular bandleader was looking for a "boy singer" for his orchestra, and he was captivated by Merv's voice, feeling that the singer would blend in with his music. Before appearing that night in the hotel's club, he ordered his secretary, Jean Barry, to "get me Merv Griffin."

Jean contacted Merv that day and agreed to have lunch that Saturday afternoon. The Merv Griffin she encountered was a newly created man— young, handsome, and *slender*. In Jean's view he possessed one of the most romantic singing voices in America.

"I knew after lunching with Merv that Freddy had found his man," Jean later recalled. "Before I'd left the hotel that day, Freddy said to me, 'I just pray the fucking kid is a looker. The horny women who dance to our music like romantic ballads sung by a guy they'd want to go to bed with.'"

Back at the hotel that night, Jean gave Freddy the good news. "He's a handsome—not pretty—boy, and you already know how he sings. There's a possible problem that I don't think will be any trouble at all. I suspect he might be a homosexual. But if he's got the looks and the voice, what does that matter?"

"Half the boys in my band are homosexual, at least when they're on the road," Freddy said. "This Merv Griffin will fit in just fine with my boys."

Merv's breakthrough as a "boy singer"
in the waning days of ballroom dancing
was with big band legend **Freddy Martin**

Chapter Two

Merv stayed awake all that night, pondering Jean Barry's offer to make him the lead singer with Freddy Martin's band. As dawn came up over San Francisco, he decided to go for it. The way he figured it, being the lead singer of Freddy's band would take him across the country, where he hoped to make millions of new fans. Reflecting on that career-changing choice years later, he said, "I was too much of a fool to realize that I was hooking up with one of the Big Bands just as that musical form was entering its death throes. It had peaked in the 1930s and during the war years. But I never regretted my decision to join Freddy and his boys."

Appearing at the St. Francis Hotel's Mural Room that night, Merv met his mentor, Freddy himself. "He was such a nice guy I couldn't believe he was for real," Merv said. "I thought his politeness might be a cover-up for the monster that lurked beneath." Merv not only met Freddy but was asked to sing—unrehearsed—with his orchestra. Freddy asked him if he knew "Where or When."

"Does a bear shit in the woods?"

"You're on, kid," Freddy said.

"I don't know how I got through the number, but my voice held out," Merv later recalled. "My legs were shaking more than those of Elvis in the years to come. But the audience clapped wildly, and I knew I'd made the right decision."

The next day he began to feel he'd made a very rash decision when he was told that Freddy would pay him only $150 a week. Previously, he'd thought that it would be $150 a night. He was already pulling in $1,500 a week, very good pay for a singer in 1948.

Later Merv claimed that the actual money was not that important to him. That was hardly true. To this Depression era kid, money was vital.

Even so, he shrewdly interpreted this new job as a career advancement in spite of the low pay. "I decided it could lead to fame and fortune eventually. I'd be singing at the Starlight Roof in New York, the Cocoanut Grove in Los Angeles. Meeting all the big stars."

The next day he barged into Bill Pabst's office at the radio station and resigned. It was easy to do since he didn't have a contract with the station manager. Pabst warned him he was making a big mistake and was shocked at the enormous cut in pay he'd be taking. What Merv didn't tell Pabst was that he planned to use his exposure with Freddy Martin's orchestra to launch a screen career. "Just think," Merv said to Pabst, "with Freddy Martin's band, I'll be singing to Elizabeth Taylor, Frank Sinatra, Clark Gable, Lana Turner, and even Judy Garland." As his own fortune teller, he was right on target.

"I see," a skeptical Pabst said. "But think about this. What if Sinatra shows up one night at the Cocoanut Grove? He's highly critical of other singers, you know. You may be too sappy for him. What if he's drunk, a likely scenario. He might let out a catcall to disrupt your act. Embarrass you in front of everybody in Hollywood. And by the way, your act rips off Bing Crosby even more than it does Sinatra, and what if *Der Bingle* shows up to comment upon that personally?"

"I'll shit my pants and keep on singing."

When joining Freddy Martin's band, Merv knew his new boss didn't rule the music scene in the 40s the way that Benny Goodman, Guy Lombardo, Glenn Miller, and Jimmy and Tommy Dorsey did. Even so, Merv daydreamed that he could pull off what Sinatra did when appearing with Tommy Dorsey, recording such hits as "Hear My Song" and "I'll Never Smile Again."

Post-war dollars earmarked for entertainment were meager compared to what they'd been during the war years when men spent heavily, not worrying about saving for tomorrow when they didn't know if they'd have a tomorrow.

Now those same men who'd survived the war were moving to the suburbs where they built homes and began to raise families. The king of the Big Bands, Glenn Miller, was presumed to have died when his plane disappeared in December of 1944, and back home many ballrooms and nightclubs were either closing or doing poor business. Not only that, but many musicians returning from the battlefields, including Ray Anthony and Buddy Rich, were once again competing within the overcrowded field. "The competition was keen," Merv said. "With more and more musicians on the scene, that pie was being sliced into thinner and thinner slices. Even admission prices to ballrooms dropped. Some of the lesser known bands 'disbanded.'"

Frankly, Freddy Martin—nicknamed "Mr. Silvertone"—did not lead Merv's favorite band. He much preferred the sounds of Glenn Miller's band or even the Dorsey Brothers. The kindest word Merv had for Freddy's boys was that they played "likable music."

As a kid, he'd listened to their music, which went back to 1932 when they'd recorded for Columbia Records. His favorite among their repertoire was "Tonight We Love," with Clyde Rogers performing the vocal. Freddy had based the arrangement on the first movement of Tchaikovsky's B-flat piano concerto.

When Merv joined Freddy's orchestra, it employed six violins, four brasses, and an equal number of sax. Freddy was a mean saxophone player himself—in fact, he was hailed as the best tenor saxophonist of the Big Band era.

By the time Merv joined the band, the orchestra had already been the focal point of a film, *Melody Time* (1948), which is interpreted today as a camp classic. In it, Freddy Martin appeared as himself, as did the Andrews Sisters and the homophobic Roy Rogers with his horse, Trigger. Regrettably, the scenes of "Pecos Bill" which appeared within the original were edited out of its re-release years later as a DVD.

Merv also watched as Freddy Martin and his Orchestra appeared as themselves in *Seven Days' Leave* (1942) in which Victor Mature starred opposite Lucille Ball. Merv told Johnny Riley, "I'd even give up Errol Flynn, I think, for Victor Mature. He's too hot to handle."

Merv had seen *Stage Door Canteen* (1943) six times, little knowing that one of its cast members, Tallulah Bankhead, would become his lifelong friend. It starred some of the great ladies of the theater, including Helen Hayes and Katherine Cornell. Even Katharine Hepburn made an appearance. Merv thrilled to the appearance of "Tarzan," Johnny Weissmuller, but was more intrigued by the orchestra conductors cast in the film. They included not only Freddy Martin, but Guy Lombardo, Kay Kyser, Benny Goodman, and Xavier Cugat. He later claimed that watching this movie made him a lifelong fan of Count Basie.

Merv told Freddy that he hoped more movie roles would lie in the orchestra's future now that he'd joined as lead vocalist.

"I'm not sure movies in the years to come will feature 1940s orchestras with boy or girl singers," Freddy said. "Even The Andrews Sisters are fading. What went over during World War II is dying out. The 1950s demand a new kind of sound."

The following night, waiting backstage at the Mural Room, Merv watched as Stuart Wade, the singer Merv was slated to replace, sang his last songs for Freddy's band. At the end of Stuart's act, Merv shook his hand as he came off stage. "Great show!" Merv said with all the enthusiasm he could muster. In the background, he could hear Freddy Martin introducing him as the band's new singer.

To be polite, Stuart also waited backstage for Merv to finish his act. "You were fabu-

Young **Merv**

43

lous," he told Merv. "You'll go over bigger and better than I ever did."

It would take months before Merv learned that compliments one performer makes to another are usually insincere.

"What's next for you?" Merv asked.

"Tomorrow, I head for Hollywood where I'm going to become the hottest actor in show business. The Robert Taylors, Tyrone Powers, and Errol Flynns are getting long in the tooth. They're going to have to move over and make way for me."

As Merv watched Stuart depart, he knew enough at the time to realize that most dreams of show business success end when you wake up. But not in his case. He was determined. The Stuart Wades of the world would come and go, perhaps into oblivion. But he was determined to make it . . . and big.

At the end of Merv's first week of performing with Freddy, the orchestra leader raised his salary to $175 a week because he also wanted Merv to be his second piano player. He promised more $25 raises every thirteen weeks. "But you've got to knock off some more pounds, kid."

"I'm a skeleton compared to the balloon I used to be," Merv said. "But I'll keep eating those rare steaks and salads."

"Merv was not a natural in front of a live audience, but I took a chance on him anyway," Freddy later recalled. "He was very stiff and rigid. Very unsure of himself. It took weeks before he became natural."

"The boys in the band kidded him because every week he sounded like somebody else," Freddy said. "The first week we thought we'd hired Perry Como. The next week Merv sounded more like Bing Crosby. My God, one night I thought he'd been listening to Doris Day sing. I put a stop to him listening to her voice. We didn't want to signal to the ladies in the audience that Merv was a homo."

"Another thing," Freddy continued, "in the beginning Merv waddled on stage like a duck. When he came out with that walk, some people in the audience laughed at him. I think that waddle came from his fat period. I got around his awkward entrance by eliminating his walk-on. I had the boys kill the house lights. Merv could slip out onto the stage and stand before the microphone. The house lights would go on and the audience would see Merv standing in the spotlight instead of waddling on."

It was a sad day in San Francisco and San Mateo when Merv told his family and friends good-bye. It was the beginning of a nationwide tour of seventy-four one-night stands in towns he'd never heard of.

His introduction to life on the road as a "boy singer" began in the hardest, most grueling way. "Almost from the first, my daydreams about making it big in show business came crashing in on me," Merv said. "I was introduced to the realities of show business in Eureka, California. Reality instead of dreams was setting in."

He was heartsick after a long bus ride to Eureka, and he became even more so when he saw the patrons file in. They were loud and raucous, and many had already consumed far too many beers.

In the big cities such as New York, Freddy's band was known for attracting what was left of "café society." But the Eureka audience looked like farmers.

The club was dreary, but Merv did all his big numbers such as "Never Been Kissed" and "Wilhelmina." He tried his best and the audience clapped but with no enthusiasm. He felt the patrons would much rather be hearing Roy Rogers singing about how the stars were big and bright, deep in the heart of Texas.

It was clearly understood that after each of the one-night stands, Merv had to be packed and ready, following his performance, for a late-night supper at one o'clock in the morning. Immediately after that, sometime before 3am, Freddy and his boys would climb onto the bus for transit to the next performance. Often they pulled into town just before the beginning of the next evening's show. They slept on the bumpy bus.

"My god," he complained to Freddy. "I don't even have time to wash the piss stains out of my underwear."

Long used to life on the road, the band leader just smiled. "Then don't wear underwear."

Merv recalled celebrating his twenty-third birthday in Prairie du Chien, Wyoming, where the band threw him a surprise party. Even that wasn't spontaneous. Merv later learned that before leaving San Francisco, Jean Barry had been given a one-hundred dollar bill from Merv's mother, Rita, to honor him on the occasion. "At that point I felt so homesick I cried," he said. "Except for visits to Los Angeles, I'd never really been anywhere but the Bay area."

"Those tears finally came, and when they did, they rained like buckets," Merv said. It was early one morning as he walked the bleak streets of Fargo, North Dakota, with not a soul in sight. "It was my first time away from home, and I missed all my family and my friends like Johnny Riley. I kept in touch by phone on occasions, but calls were expensive and my new salary didn't allow for a lot of luxuries. My support group was gone. But I did make a friend in Jean."

Freddy's secretary traveled on the road with what she called "my boys." She bonded so well with Merv and spent so much time with him that some members of the band suspected a romance. "Far from it," Jean said. "We were good buddies—and that was that. I became the first of what Merv called his gal pals."

Beginning with Jean Barry, and ending with the glamorous Eva Gabor,

Merv over the years formed relationships with a number of women. "From what he told me, no sex was involved, only good times," Johnny Riley later recalled. "He was like many gay men in the late Forties and Fifties who formed superficial relationships with women and 'dated' them."

"But after a kiss on the cheek at the doorstep, it was good night, sweetheart," Johnny claimed. "These romances of Merv's in New York and Los Angeles were about as serious as Tab Hunter dating Debbie Reynolds in the 1950s."

Bill Robbins, the other close friend of Merv's, said, "Of course, Merv had male friends. Take Paul Schone, Johnny, and me for an example. Even Cal Tjader. But he also sought out women to pal around with him. He genuinely liked women, and he liked to be in their company. He enjoyed taking them out. In the years to come, it was fun for him to be seen with Elizabeth Taylor on his arm. But I doubt if he ever fucked Elizabeth Taylor. For fucking, she had to turn to Richard Burton, Frank Sinatra, whomever."

On that first road tour with Freddy and his boys, Merv sat up front in the bus with Jean beside him. "As we crossed the American Plains, some trips lasting twelve hours, I grew bored. Freddy always had his nose buried in a book, and some of the boys played cards. I didn't play poker, and I didn't like to read. To pass the time, I invented word games, including one called 'Twenty Questions.'"

"I was just trying to kill the time, little knowing that I would one day make millions of dollars in television off word games," he said. "I guess I had to start someplace, and I got my start in word games on those long, long rides to Rinky-Dink, U.S. of A. Almost every night in some hell-hole, some drunk would call out for me to sing 'Melancholy Baby.' I got so tired of that I began to close my act with that song, anticipating a drunken request."

The members of Freddy's band were of two minds, the more naïve musicians thinking Merv was having an affair with Jean, the other players suspecting that he might be a homosexual. "A few of us were birds of a feather," one of Freddy's band members later said. "We suspected that Merv might be one of us. After all, musicians are the hippest people in America. We smoked pot decades before it caught on, and we were using the word *gay* when the rest of the world thought it meant *happily excited*."

"One night, three of us were in a hotel room playing poker when one of the guys asked, 'Don't you think Merv is gay?' I

Studio Spin: **Debbie Reynolds** "fake dating" with **Tab Hunter**

46

thought for a minute and said, 'By God, I think you're right.' In those days, we got our rocks off wherever we could going from town to town."

"We agreed that night that one of us should test the waters, and I was selected because the guys said I was the best looking. After I showered the following night, I knocked on Merv's door wearing only a towel. I made up some excuse that I wanted to borrow something. I brought along a couple of cold beers. One thing led to another, and in a couple of hours Merv was bobbing up and down between my legs. He was pretty good at it, too, and I knew he'd done this before. Perhaps many times before."

"When I left the room that morning, I told the guys, 'He's up for grabs, but remember I saw him first.' Throughout the rest of the tour, Merv kept me happy, and he also kept some of the boys walking around with smiles on their faces. I don't think Freddy ever found out what was going on. Maybe he did. Knowing Freddy, I don't think he would have given a damn."

In what Merv would later refer to as "one of the most memorable moments of my life," he was able to see what was keeping the audiences away from ballrooms and nightclubs. That momentous event took place backstage at the Riverside Theater in Milwaukee.

An RCA television dealer brought in "a funny little box" (Merv's words) to demonstrate to Freddy Martin's band what their competition was. "I remember Milton Berle was appearing in drag of all things," Merv said. "The picture was fuzzy. For a person who grew up watching Judy Garland in Technicolor on the big screen, I was very disdainful of this new invention. I thought TV was a novelty. How could I have known back then that it would dominate most of my life—and also be the key to my fortune?"

After what seemed like endless weeks on the road, Freddy Martin's bus approached the skyline of New York City as dawn was coming up. Merv was in awe. "Even though I was from San Francisco, I'd never seen anything like it. It was like a mirage to me. The tall buildings. I spent my first day just wandering around with my mouth open. I must have looked really dumb."

"San Francisco has beauty but in those days it didn't have the hustle-bustle of New York," he recalled. "Every person I encountered looked fired up and in a hurry to get somewhere like they had some important mission to perform. After that first day of rubber-necking, I knew I'd found my city. I also knew that someday I'd live in New York and establish my roots here. Yes, I knew it was in New York that I'd become famous . . . and rich."

After all those one-nighters, Merv was happy to be booked for ten nights at the swanky Waldorf-Astoria. "I'd seen *Week-end at the Waldorf* with Lana Turner, and I was impressed. I even got to stay at the hotel, although I was assigned the maid's room. It must have been the maid's closet. Lana fared better in the movie."

After closing at the Waldorf, Freddy told Merv that their next booking was the Strand Theater where the orchestra would entertain between showings of *Johnny Belinda*, a film that would bring its star, Jane Wyman (Mrs. Ronald Reagan), an Oscar.

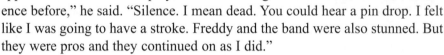

Merv remembered "shaking all over" as he made his first big appearance at a New York theater. The Waldorf debut had been in a relatively intimate night-club, like the Mural Room in San Francisco, and he felt comfortable there. "I feared I'd forget the words to even my familiar songs. But when I led off with 'Because,' I knew I'd hit my stride."

"At the end of the number, I expected deafening applause since I'd never played to such a big audience before," he said. "Silence. I mean dead. You could hear a pin drop. I felt like I was going to have a stroke. Freddy and the band were also stunned. But they were pros and they continued on as I did."

"I did all my hits," he said. "Again nothing but silence. Even my novelty song, 'Pecos Bill,' didn't go over, and all the audiences went for it. I bombed with my popular 'Miserlou,' as well. Nothing but silence. I wanted to die. I'd bombed in a New York theater. I figured then and there that New Yorkers were the toughest audiences in the world."

It was only when the curtain went down that both Freddy and Merv understood the deafening silence. The theater manager, as a publicity gimmick, had invited members of an organization of the deaf to see Wyman as a deaf mute. On screen they read the lips of Wyman and her co-star, Lew Ayres, but could not hear Merv's singing voice.

Benny Stillman, a music critic, covered the performance, writing the next day: "Merv Griffin has a compelling baritone voice. But I feel he is destined to enter the ranks as a second-rate Dennis Morgan since he doesn't have the range to take on Bing Crosby or Frank Sinatra. Yet Griffin sings as well as Fred Astaire if that is a compliment. There was something about him that made me think he would have done better singing with a Big Band in the 1930s. I think it highly unlikely that he will carve out much of a career as a crooner in post-war America."

A few weeks later in Los Angeles when he would actually meet the star of *Johnny Belinda*, Jane Wyman herself, he'd relate the story of singing to a deaf audience. She did not seem amused, but her companion and her co-star in the picture, Lew Ayres, laughed.

As a kid growing up in San Mateo, Merv had read in all the fan magazines that Jane and her husband, Ronald Reagan, were the ideal American couple—

he in uniform serving the country and she waiting at home for him with freshly baked cookies.

After meeting her, Merv understood a different reality. Jane appeared
obviously in love with Lew Ayres. "The way she was holding onto Lew told
me that the gal had gone bonkers over this handsome fella," Merv said. "I was
shocked to see her carrying on this way in public, as I hadn't read about her
separation from Reagan. I was nervous and blurted out something stupid.
'Where's Ronald Reagan? You should be with him—not this guy.' Needless to
say, I wasn't asked to join them at the table."

"In time Jane forgave me for my insensitivity," Merv recalled. "Over the
years we never became friends but acquaintances who nodded politely at parties. I think she resented my close bond with Reagan's new wife, Nancy. But
Jane and I did have one great moment together in Los Angeles. One night
when I was singing, she got up from her table and joined me in a duet. After
hearing 'In the Cool Cool Cool of the Evening,' the audience applauded wildly."

***

While still appearing at the Strand in New York, Merv used to go out into
the alleyway beside the theater for a breath of fresh air between performances. The alley opened onto the stage door of the Ethel Barrymore Theater,
which had a hit play, *A Streetcar Named Desire* by Tennessee Williams, starring Marlon Brando as Stanley Kowalski and Jessica Tandy as Blanche Du
Bois.

Every night Merv would encounter a young actor in the play, who was
always polishing and checking out his motorcycle, which he'd parked in the
alley. Even when he introduced himself to Merv as Marlon Brando, Merv did-
n't realize that the actor was the star of the play. "I thought he was an extra,"
Merv said. "I'd never heard of Tennessee Williams either, and I just assumed
that *Streetcar* was a musical, no doubt set in my native San Francisco, which
is known for its streetcars, of course."

At one point Merv asked Marlon if he sang any solos in the show. The
actor burst into laughter and offered Merv one of his house seats for the
Saturday matinee.

Marlon seemed less inclined to talk about *Streetcar* and pumped Merv for
all the information he could about Freddy's band. "I'm a jazz musician
myself. Just wait until you hear me play my bongo drums."

Marlon was perhaps the most natural and uninhibited man Merv had ever
met. "When he wanted to take a piss in the alleyway, he pulled it out in front
of me and let it rain," Merv recalled. "He made no attempt to conceal himself.

For some reason, he liked me. I don't know why. He was so hip and I was so square."

Years later, Merv recalled that he was shocked by Marlon's brutal but brilliant portrayal on stage. "The first shock came when I realized that he was the star of the show—not an extra. The second shock came when I saw that *Streetcar* wasn't a musical. In my naïve mind, I thought Broadway was nothing but musicals. At any moment, I expected to see Ethel Merman emerge to belt out a song, or at least Mary Martin. I was mesmerized and glued to my seat watching Marlon tangle with Jessica Tandy. In my future I'd see dozens of plays, but *Streetcar*, the first play I ever saw on Broadway, has remained my greatest moment in the theater. How could I have known that I'd become friends with not only its star but with Tennessee Williams, its author?"

Meeting Marlon that night in the alleyway between the theaters, Merv had nothing but effusive compliments for Marlon's performance. The actor seemed immune to praise and brushed off Merv's comments. "You seem to have a schoolgirl crush on me," Marlon said. "Maybe we'd better do something about that. After we both get off tonight, meet me here in the alleyway, and we'll go for a ride on my motorcycle."

Midnight found Merv holding onto the muscled chest of the wild, sexy rebel, Marlon Brando, as they sped through the nearly deserted streets of New York City. At 2am, they ended up at Marlon's apartment on 57th Street.

Marlon woke up his roommate, the comedian Wally Cox. The men had been childhood friends when growing up in Nebraska. Naïve though he may have been, Merv soon realized that Wally and Marlon were lovers. The clue came when Marlon, in front of Merv, gave Wally a long, sloppy wet kiss with tongue.

Wally brought out a bottle of cheap red wine, and the men shared its contents in dirty, chipped glasses. The apartment smelled of feces and urine and was littered with garbage. Wally explained that Marlon kept a pet raccoon but that it had escaped that day. "It'll come back," Marlon predicted. "It always does."

To Merv's surprise, Marlon stripped completely nude and began to play his bongo drums, even though Wally warned him that the neighbors had been complaining about the noise.

"God damn it, Wally, don't be such a fussy old lady," Marlon chastised him. "I want to show Merv here what a great jazz musician I am. If this acting thing doesn't work out, maybe Freddy Martin will hire me for his band."

At 4am, Marlon finally abandoned the drums and

Marvelous **Marlon**

rose to his feet. Merv could hardly miss the actor's erection. "Come on, Merv," he said to his new friend. "I want you to join Wally and me in bed. He looks like just a little guy, but he's got a big surprise waiting for you."

Although the details are missing, Merv later confided in Johnny Riley that he'd had a three-way that morning with Marlon and Wally. "They were lovers," Merv said, "but hardly faithful to each other. Apparently, I wasn't the only guy they'd invited into their love nest. There had been many others."

According to Johnny, Merv never had sex with either man again, although he became friends with both of them. "Marlon Brando loomed in my future," Merv said. "When I left that dingy apartment about nine that morning, I didn't know I'd be taking over that rat-hole from them on a sublet. What an adventure that would be for me."

Further New York adventures for Merv were put on hold when he reported to the Strand that night. In Merv's dressing room, Freddy informed him that the boys would soon be back on the bus heading for Los Angeles after a string of one-nighters in hick towns across America. He'd just booked the boys in his band into the legendary Cocoanut Grove at the Ambassador Hotel in Los Angeles.

After the engagement came to an end at the Strand, Merv had only one free night, during which he attended a performance of Damon Runyon's *Guys and Dolls*. Unlike *Streetcar*, *Guys and Dolls* was what Broadway symbolized for him. It was a musical, even though he didn't understand most of the street talk delivered by the actors with their New York accents.

Years later, Marlon would star in the movie version of the musical. After seeing the film, he called Marlon. "And you laughed at me when I asked if you had any numbers in *Streetcar*," Merv said. "Well, I've seen you in a musical after all, and you can sing. Sort of . . . not as good as me, of course."

"I may not have sounded as good as you," Marlon countered, "but I sure beat out that rat fink, Frank Sinatra. What an asshole! Okay, so I've done a musical. Now it's your turn. Let me see you play Stanley Kowalski."

***

Heading west on Freddy Martin's tour bus, Merv became bored with the series of one-night stands. After the excitement of New York, the American Heartland held little promise for him. "If you're an American, it makes sense to live only in New York or California," he said.

Looming before him was a four-month engagement at the Cocoanut Grove. All the movie stars went there every night, and Merv was determined to meet all of them.

"Merv was a star-struck kid," Freddy later recalled. "When we weren't

51

playing, I retired to my dressing room, but Merv worked the room. He was a charming fellow, and nearly all the stars invited him to join their table. He got to know everybody who was anybody, and he had his radar out as to which table was the most important. He also formed friendships with some of the younger stars—Jane Powell, Elizabeth Taylor, Roddy McDowall, and especially Peter Lawford. Roddy in particular took to Merv right away and introduced him to an insider Hollywood that I had only heard about. I knew stars casually, but not intimately the way Roddy did, the way Merv would come to know them."

One night Merv was invited to join Clark Gable's table. "The King" introduced Merv to a young brunette starlet, Nancy Davis. Merv found her charming, and as the future Mrs. Ronald Reagan she would in time become his best female friend. When Nancy got up to "go powder my nose," Clark whispered to Merv, "You can have her if you want her. I'm dumping her. Go for it! She gives the best blow-job in Hollywood." Merv turned down the offer.

Still seated at Clark's table, Merv stood up to welcome Nancy back from the powder room. He couldn't believe that Clark had made such a disgusting remark about her. Nancy looked so prim and proper. He finally concluded that Clark was drunk and just making a vulgar joke.

He was stunned when Spencer Tracy and a companion walked up to Clark's table and was invited to sit down. Spencer and Clark had been friends since the 1930s, although it was clear to Merv that there was a sharp rivalry between them. At first Merv thought Spencer was dating a boy that night. After all, he'd heard all those homosexual rumors. It turned out to be Katharine Hepburn wearing pants, a hat pulled down over her face, and sunglasses. When she shook his hand and spoke to him, he immediately recognized her distinctive voice.

Katharine and Nancy had nothing to say to each other. At this point, Merv's new friend, Roddy, kept him abreast of all the Hollywood gossip. He already knew that Nancy had been a former lover of Spencer's, so the two women were not overly fond of each other.

"Clark, you made a big mistake when you turned down *The Philadelphia Story*," Katharine said. "You would have been great in it."

On the Town: **Clark** ("The King") **Gable** with starlet **Nancy Davis (Reagan)**

52

"Correction," Clark said. "That was your picture. With you on the screen with me, I would have been no more than a prop."

"Spencer here was supposed to play the other male lead," Katharine said, turning to him. "Too bad, old man. You, too, missed out on doing a classic with me. "Could you imagine? Starring Katharine Hepburn, Clark Gable, and Spencer Tracy."

"Watch it, kiddo!" Spencer cautioned. "I don't like the billing."

Since Merv was left out of the banter, he drifted off to the next table of celebrities where he was welcomed by Joan Crawford, who remembered him from Pebble Beach. She, too, had been the lover of both Clark and Spencer. She introduced him to the handsomest man Merv had ever met in Hollywood. Rock Hudson, a young actor fresh out of the Navy. He was appearing in a small role as a pilot in *Fighter Squadron* at Warners. "He's new in town," Joan said. "I'm showing him the ropes."

"I like your singing," Rock said. "Very romantic, and I'm a romantic kind of guy."

Did Merv detect a wink? Even though Rock was dating a woman, Merv suspected that he was a homosexual. He became certain of it when Rock slipped him his phone number when Joan got up to greet Henry Fonda, who had costarred with her in *Daisy Kenyon*. During the filming, and again according to Roddy, Joan and Henry had had a brief, unsuccessful affair.

Hours before he actually appeared at the club that night, rumors spread that Frank Sinatra had booked the best table in the house. Merv knew that as a singer he wasn't in the same league as Frank and was "already shaking all over with nervousness at the prospect of singing before 'The Voice.'"

"Sinatra can take a song and wrap his soul around it before one word comes out of his lips," Merv said to Freddy. "His crooning makes girls swoon. But look at me. Chopped liver."

"You'll do just fine," Freddy assured him. "In fact, I want you to sing 'I'll Never Smile Again' and dedicate it to Frank."

"I'd rather die!" Merv said.

"You're not going to get out of life that easy," Freddy said.

Two hours later, at Freddy's command, Merv was indeed singing "I'll Never Smile Again."

"I thought I heard my knees knocking," he later said to Freddy. He feared that Frank would be rude during his number and perhaps talk loudly to a companion while Merv sang. He'd been known to do that when faced with performers he didn't like.

But on this night he did just the opposite. He paid attention. Too much attention as far as Merv was concerned. Although his face was enigmatic, Frank seemed to be studying him intently, as he smoked a cigarette and occasionally belted down some Scotch from a glass.

To make Merv even more nervous, Frank's companion that night was Lana Turner, who'd made a spectacular entrance into the club, wearing ermine and a white satin gown cut low. Roddy had told him that Lana had turned to Frank to help her get over a broken heart after Tyrone Power had jilted her.

After his number, Merv went backstage. He didn't dare approach Frank's table in the way he'd done with so many other stars. At Merv's request, a waiter brought him a glass of Scotch and soda. Merv felt he needed a bolt of liquor before attempting to go on again. Freddy's band was playing dance music as Merv looked out surveying the club audience. Frank was dancing with Lana.

"What's a gal like Lana doing with a skinny little wop like Sinatra?" Merv asked the waiter. "She could have any handsome hunk in Hollywood she wants. I bet his dick is no more than four inches long at full mast."

"Don't kid yourself," the waiter said. "The showgals here at the club claim he's got the biggest dick in Hollywood."

"Oh, shit! A great voice and a big dick to go with it. I can't stand the competition."

To his surprise, Freddy's next music was the song, "I'll Never Smile Again." At the mike, Freddy announced, "Ladies and gentlemen, I give you a special surprise performance tonight. The one, the only Frank Sinatra." The singer's appearance was met with thunderous applause.

Taking the microphone, Frank said, "Ladies and gentlemen, here's how 'I'll Never Smile Again' should be sung."

Merv burst into tears. He later told Freddy, "It was the most humiliating moment I've ever had in show business. I don't think I can face an audience again. I think I hate that bastard for what he did to me."

"You'll recover," Freddy said. "Get ready for your next number."

"I can't go on in front of Sinatra again," Merv protested.

"Don't worry! He and Lana have already left the room. But you're not off the hook yet."

"What do you mean?"

"I just got word. Judy Garland has entered the room. She's sitting up front with Peter Lawford and another guy waiting for you to go on."

"Oh, my God. Will my humiliations never end?"

Unlike Frank, Judy Garland was one of the most gracious stars he'd ever met. After his performance she invited Merv to join Peter Lawford and her at her pri-

Merv

vate table. There Merv met a handsome young actor from Brooklyn, Tom Drake, who he immediately recognized as Judy's screen boyfriend in *Meet Me in St. Louis* (1944), one of Merv's all-time favorite films.

More than any other actor in Hollywood, Tom fit the description of "the boy next door." Indeed, his lasting claim to fame was those very words sung to him by Judy in the St. Louis film.

The sweet, soft-spoken Tom was in direct contrast to the charismatic Peter Lawford, whom Merv considered one of the handsomest actors in films. Tonight he was drunk, as was Judy. Only Tom seemed sober. At one point in the evening, he whispered to Merv. "Someone has to drive these two home tonight."

Merv knew that Peter and Judy had had an affair in the early 1940s, which didn't last long. From it, a friendship had emerged. The night he met her, Merv sensed that Judy's emotional state was fragile. He appreciated Peter's sensitivity to the star. "To say that Peter was handling her with kid gloves is an understatement," Merv later told Freddy. Even though Peter was drunk, he sensed how emotionally troubled Judy was and tried to soothe her, as if expecting an emotional disturbance at any minute.

Filled with too much booze, Judy was one of the most direct women Merv had ever known. Sometimes her honesty could be brutal. She didn't seem to mind whether she shocked people or not.

After he'd been at her table for less than 30 minutes, the talk became embarrassingly personal for him. "Do you know why I took up with Peter?" she bluntly asked Merv while glaring at Peter almost defiantly. "My fucking husband at the time, David Rose, was repulsed by cunnilingus, which is one of my favorite things. Peter here prefers that form of sex and is the world's expert on it. He won me over at once by giving me what David didn't. But, frankly, I think Peter likes to suck cock more than eat pussy. Don't you Peter?"

"From what I hear, Merv sucks cock too. We can be frank with each other.

Judy Garland with **Peter Lawford**

After all, we're family. Let's invite Merv to join our little group."

"I'd think that after this introduction, Merv might run in the other direction," Peter said.

"Not at all," Merv chimed in. "You people are the most fascinating I've met so far in Hollywood. I want to be a part of your group."

"Okay, kid," Peter said, "But you don't know what you're getting in for. Before the night ends, we'll give you our phone numbers."

That night didn't end until dawn. By four o'clock Merv was holding a sobbing Tom Drake in his arms, trying to comfort him. The actor had confessed that he was madly in love with Peter, who betrayed him at every turn. "He's never faithful to me," Tom said. "I wait by the phone for him to call. I never know where he is from night to night. One night he's in the bed of Robert Walker, the next night with Lana Turner. Imagine being in love with a man who can't decide on his sexual preference."

"Been there, done that," Merv said.

For the past hour and a half, Peter had been upstairs in Judy's bedroom. He finally emerged, and Merv saw him walking down the steps clad only in his underwear. Pouring himself another drink, he told Merv and Tom that Judy was threatening suicide, and he had to spend the rest of the night with her. He'd promised to drive her to her psychiatric session that morning. "She's upstairs unleashing all those pent-up emotions. Right now she's launched into an attack on Vincente Minnelli, not that that rotten bastard doesn't deserve it."

"Can I be of help?" Merv asked.

"You sure can," Peter said. "Go upstairs and look after Judy until daylight comes." He walked over to the sofa where Tom sat. "Right now I've got to look after Tom."

As Merv left the room and headed up the stairs, he looked back at Peter and Tom. Tom was unfastening Peter's underwear.

In Judy's bedroom, he found her sobbing and demanding more booze. When she became aware of him for the first time, she reached out her arms. "Peter, hold me," she said. "I'm afraid. Really afraid. I fear everything's about to come crashing in on me."

He joined her in bed, holding her as she pressed her body up against his. He realized that she didn't want sex but love and comfort.

Before she drifted off into a coma-like sleep, she said, "Dear Peter, you've always been there for me. Hold me tight. Never let me go."

He was still in her arms when a maid knocked on the door and entered. It was ten o'clock. "Please wake up Miss Garland," the maid said to a sleepy Merv. "Mr. Lawford is waiting downstairs to drive her to her psychiatrist. Mr. Drake is with him."

"Okay, we're getting up," Merv said. "I'll wake up Judy."

"That's easier said than done," the maid said before leaving the room.

That night and early morning marked the beginning of Merv's tortured involvement with Judy Garland. For reasons known only to himself, he would leave his thick chapter on Judy out of his memoirs, and would even mislead his fans about when he'd actually met her. Perhaps he wanted to keep the Judy part of his life private from his public.

Before that troubled night had ended, Judy had finally figured out that it was Merv, not Peter, holding her. It was the beginning of a friendship, even a love affair, that would last until the day she died.

He later told Peter Lawford, "It was like a wild race around a mulberry bush, a race that had no ending and one that went on day and night, especially in the wee, wee hours of the morning, a time of terror for Judy."

***

Merv wanted to call Rock Hudson for a date but was afraid of rejection. "Yet he gave me his phone number," he told Johnny Riley in a phone call. "Why would he do that if he didn't want me to call?"

"Call him," Johnny urged. "It'll probably be the thrill of your life."

The problem was solved when Rock showed up stag at the Cocoanut Grove one Friday night, sending a note backstage to Merv to join him after the show.

When Merv went on that night, he was more nervous than ever, knowing that Rock was out front, watching him, judging him. He wished that he'd taken his diet a little more seriously for the past month.

When he joined Rock later at table, Merv was put at ease at once. Rock seemed the most easy-going person he'd ever met. He was without airs and pretensions, and he spoke honestly and with candor about his life when he invited Merv to go for a midnight drive in the Hollywood Hills.

To test the waters, Merv said, "I was surprised when you asked me out. I feared my competition was that effervescent blonde, Vera-Ellen."

"Oh, please," Rock said. "Let's get serious. My agent, Henry Willson, is deliberately trying to create a scandal. He knows that Vera is five years older than me, and Henry is hoping the scandal mags will pick up on my having an affair with an older woman. Actually, I'm not having an affair at all."

Rock Hudson

"Why would he want to provoke a scandal anyway?" Merv innocently asked.

"Better an exposé of me with an 'older' woman than the fact I'm living with a hot young guy at the moment."

"If he's so hot, why are you out with me?"

"It's my love of the chase," Rock said. "It's good to have prime beef at home, but even more exciting to capture something outside on the hoof."

"Thank God you chose me," Merv said. "I think

you're the biggest stud ever to land in Hollywood."

"You flatter me." He looked into his rear-view mirror. "I do look pretty good. Henry thinks I should be more discreet. He's always trying to fix me up with guys from his stable. I don't want that. I think the chase is more thrilling sometimes than the actual sex." He paused. "Of course, both are great!"

Before the night ended, Rock had driven Merv to a lonely motel where they spent a total of three hours.

By the time Merv had kissed Rock good-bye and was delivered back to his hotel room, he placed an immediate call to Johnny Riley to tell him the news. "I got my man," he practically shouted into the phone.

"You are one lucky queer fellow," Johnny said.

Merv hesitated. "Well, half the night was great, but I don't know about the other part."

"Exactly what does that mean?" Johnny asked.

"I loved the sucking part, although the guy is a bull," Merv said. "But I'd never been penetrated before."

"I bet you loved every inch of it," Johnny said.

"Not at all," Merv said. "It was very painful. I even bled. The more I urged him to stop, the more excited he became. I don't know why guys like to get fucked. All pain, no pleasure."

"Does that mean you won't see Rock again?" Johnny asked.

"I've got a date with him tonight. He's a pain in the ass but the most exciting man I've ever been with in my life. Just to be with him, I'd go through torture."

"Merv Griffin, you may be the only homo in America who doesn't like getting fucked by Rock Hudson. If only it could have been me."

Details about the above-noted encounter between Merv and Rock were widely publicized in the late 1970s when Johnny Riley, after his breakup with Merv tried to shop a book proposal about his former friend to publishers in New York City. Merv had become a powerful figure in show business by that time, and each publisher who saw the material turned it down as too hot, and too potentially libelous, to handle.

Merv himself confirmed the details of his sexual and emotional encounter with Rock to show-biz agent Henry Willson when he and Merv became friends as a result of their mutual contact, Guy Madison, whom Merv had met during their appearance together in the 1953 film, *The Charge at Feather River.*

***

Merv had met Roddy McDowall at least six times at the Cocoanut Grove before their friendship turned into something more intimate. Roddy always showed up at the club with a female star on his arm, even though it was no secret that the British-born actor and former child star was "one of Hollywood's leading homos," as gossip maven Hedda Hopper always claimed in private—never in print.

Merv had watched Roddy grow up on the screen, and had been captivated by him in such pictures as the 1943 *Lassie Come Home* and the 1944 *The White Cliffs of Dover*, in both of which he'd co-starred with Elizabeth Taylor, a child star Merv found mesmerizing.

Of all the male stars he'd met so far, Merv found Rock Hudson the handsomest and the sexiest. But for his tastes, Roddy was the most charming and charismatic. When Roddy talked, he brought you into his world and seemed to suck you into his orbit.

Even at that early stage in his career, Roddy seemed to know virtually everyone in Hollywood and was called "a friend to the stars." At table at the Cocoanut Grove, Merv always admired Roddy's perfect diction and the way he spoke in clever lines. "I was a child thesp," he once told Merv. "That's thespian with a T, my dear." For the rest of his life, he would refer to Merv as "my dear."

Roddy knew more about the secrets of Hollywood than any other star Merv had met—the covered-up scandals, the abortions, the furtive affairs, especially among married stars, the closeted homosexuals, the back alley deals, even the penis size of every popular male star, gay or straight. He worshipped the stars of the Golden Age—for example, tracking down Jean Arthur when she went into seclusion. He even kept in touch with the faded stars of the silent screen, including Louise Brooks and Alice Terry.

Roddy also told the most amusing stories, but never at the expense or embarrassment of anyone else.

"When I was appearing in *How Green Was My Valley*," he said to Merv, "a studio publicist came to my dressing room. He'd been assigned to publicize me in the fan magazines. 'What, little boy, would you like?' he asked me. 'A chocolate sundae with extra fudge?'"

"'No,' I almost shouted at him. 'I want to meet Bette Davis!'"

The publicist set up such a meeting, taking Roddy to the star's dressing room at Warner Brothers where she reigned as Queen. Ushered inside, Roddy met the great screen diva in person. Being worked over by a male hairdresser, Bette

Roddy McDowall

sat at her dressing room mirror, surveying her face. She looked Roddy up and down. "What do you want with me, young man?" she asked in that unmistakable voice of hers.

"When I grow up, I want to marry you," he blurted out.

She burst into hysterical laughter before leaning over and giving him a big, sloppy, wet kiss on the mouth. "That, kid, is just a preview of the pleasures awaiting you. Now, go home and grow up! In the meantime, I've got to make up this tired old face of mine."

Backstage at the Cocoanut Grove, Merv received a note delivered by a waiter. "Join us at table," it said. "Love, Roddy." Merv had finished his appearance for the night and eagerly entered the main floor of the club, wanting to know which star Roddy had brought to see him tonight. At table, Roddy introduced him to the bubbly, effervescent Jane Powell, whom Merv thought was "the cheeriest of the cinematic sopranos" on the screen.

It was the beginning of a long-lasting friendship between Merv and the star. Years later in recalling the beginning of their relationship, Merv said, "Dear, sweet Jane Powell belonged to a time when the world appreciated nice girls who lived next door with their rosy cheeks and birdlike voices. Those days are gone forever."

Merv had seen Jane playing Walter Pidgeon's daughter in *Holiday in Mexico*, in which the character she played developed a crush on pianist José Iturbi, much to the chagrin of a young Roddy, playing her lovesick beau in the picture.

Roddy and Jane had bonded during the making of that film, and the singing star had become a regular fixture at the famous Sunday afternoon gatherings at his house. Many of the young stars of Hollywood gathered at Roddy's Sunday afternoon bashes. These gatherings were considered one of the most coveted invitations in Hollywood.

The night Merv met Jane was the same night Roddy invited Merv to his bash the following afternoon. Although it was only Saturday night, Merv could hardly wait. He felt that his invitation to Roddy's house meant he'd been accepted into the inner circle of young Hollywood stars, even though he lacked the film credits of the other guests.

Roddy was popping up and down, constantly excusing himself to get up and greet other stars at table. This allowed Merv a chance to get to know Jane. Like all young stars of that time, she had only one thing on her mind—her career. "My great fear," she confided, "is that Hollywood will grow tired of wholesome gals and will only cast *femmes fatales* in future roles, stars like Hedy Lamarr and Lana Turner. Elizabeth [Taylor] is a great friend of mine, but I think she's growing up too fast. She's appearing in her first adult film role with Robert Taylor. I predict she's going to turn sultry on the screen and dethrone Hedy herself."

"Just keep on doing what you do best," he told her. "The world will always love you for that. You and Judy Garland. I can't imagine Judy ever being a *femme fatale*."

"Thanks, Merv," Jane said, kissing him on the cheek. "Do you think Roddy is getting jealous having me sit here all alone talking to you?"

"Yeah, right," Merv said. "Roddy is only jealous of you *in* the movies."

She smiled that knowing smile of hers, and Merv sensed she wasn't as innocent about the dark alleys of Hollywood as she appeared.

That night at Freddy Martin's request, Jane agreed to perform what became one of her most famous musical numbers, "It's an Unusual Day," from her latest film release, *A Date With Judy*. Merv was impressed with her delivery, a style she'd begun perfecting when she was only two years old. In spite of the sunny disposition she presented to the world, he suspected a lonely person lurking inside her. She seemed a bit lost in the confusing maze of Hollywood, and he knew of the enormous sacrifices she'd made to get as far in the business as she had.

Back at table, she received his congratulations on her number. "All my life I've wanted to be a singer. How about you?"

"All I wanted was to be a piano player," he told her. "But other people had other ideas."

Later, when Jane excused herself to go to the women's room, Roddy whispered in Merv's ear that he'd like to get together with him for a drink in Merv's hotel room. Merv eagerly invited him, suspecting how the night might go. Rumors of Roddy's fabulous endowment had already reached his ears.

He found Roddy handsome and sexually appealing but feared he wouldn't live up to Roddy's standards as a lover. After all, Roddy had seduced some of the biggest male stars in Hollywood. Only two years or so ago, as the rumor mill had it, Roddy had shared Peter Lawford with both Lana Turner and Elizabeth Taylor.

After Roddy had put Jane in a taxi to take her home, he accompanied Merv up to his hotel room at the Ambassador. Merv would remember that early morning as one of the most memorable experiences of his life.

He was eager to tell someone about it, but had no confidant he could trust until his friend from San Francisco, Johnny Riley, arrived in town the following week. Merv supplied Johnny with all the juicy details.

"Roddy was all over me the moment we got into my room," Merv claimed. "As you well know, I'm pretty basic when it comes to sex. Roddy, on the other hand, is the world's greatest oral artist. He knows erotic zones on the human body I'd never even contemplated. Only problem is, he wants you to reciprocate. It was a bit much for me. I call him the jawbreaker. That damn thing of his looks halfway normal when it's soft, but it just grows and grows and grows."

"We carried on so much Saturday night that it was all we could do to make it to Roddy's Sunday afternoon house party," Merv claimed. "The host was almost late for his own party."

Merv was so foolish and naïve in those days that he virtually confessed to Roddy that he'd fallen for him, all in one night. Roddy quickly realized he had a lovesick puppy on his hands. With great kindness, Roddy had to inform Merv that sex could only be a sometime thing between them.

"I was heartbroken and terribly disappointed," Merv told Johnny. "I thought I'd found the man of my dreams, only to learn that Roddy had a constant string of boyfriends coming and going."

"I wanted the relationship to be permanent," Merv told Johnny. "But Roddy had other ideas. He was always after the next cute boy, and I wanted to settle down. Alas, my life. He would have been a great lover—and most amusing—to come home to."

Roddy had such a great capacity for friendship that he managed to lower Merv down to earth gradually without tramping on his feelings too harshly. He was known in Hollywood for sustaining relationships, even with lovers he'd more or less discarded. Merv would be among them.

They became friends for life, standing by each other as their careers went on roller-coaster rides. Their relationship would continue even more deeply into the 1950s when Roddy left Hollywood, a town that had more or less abandoned him, to try his luck on the Broadway stage and in stock. Roddy's film career had more or less collapsed, and he stood by Merv when the same thing happened to him.

"Roddy was not only a supportive friend," Merv later recalled to Johnny, "but he kept me supplied over the years with more boyfriends than I could handle. I once called him in New York and said, 'Hey, pal, cool it with all those handsome hunks. Who do you take me for? The Whore of Babylon? On second thought, keep sending 'em!'"

***

Merv arrived with Roddy at his house just as Ann Blyth was emerging from her car. After Roddy introduced them, he disappeared to get ready for the remaining guests. Merv agreed to serve as bartender, which wasn't difficult since all Roddy served were soft drinks.

At that point in her life, Ann had long grown tired of hearing compliments and comments about her role as Joan Crawford's bitch daughter, Veda, in the classic, Oscar-winning wallow, *Mildred Pierce* (1945). He had heard of how she'd suffered a broken back in a sledding accident at Lake Arrowhead and had to spend a long convalescence, more than a year and a half, in a back brace.

After inquiring about how she felt, Merv and Ann talked about what a wonderful woman Joan Crawford was, and about Ann's ambitions as a singer. By the time the next guest arrived, Merv and Ann had agreed to do a big old-fashioned film musical together.

That dream never came to be, of course. In one of the ironies of Hollywood, he eventually found himself costarring with Kathryn Grayson, Ann's chief rival at MGM. As the years passed, Merv watched the rise and fall of his fellow singer, even when Ann raised eyebrows at the 1954 Academy Awards. Despite the fact that she was seven months pregnant, she appeared before the world singing Doris Day's hit, "Secret Love," from *Calamity Jane*.

Although the critics panned her, Merv loved her starring role in *The Helen Morgan Story* (1957), wherein she performed such hits as "Can't Help Lovin' Dat Man."

Ann was furious and humiliated when the studio decided to dub her own wonderful voice with that of another singer, the highly emotive Gogi Grant. To Merv, Ann's performance captured in perfect detail the kerchief-holding, liquor-swilling torch singer whose train wreck of a personal life seemed destined for celluloid.

It was with dismay that Merv in the 1970s watched Ann in TV commercials play the typical American housewife for Hostess in their Twinkie, cupcake, and fruit-pie commercials. "But," as he noted, "in show business, a gig is a gig."

That next guest at Roddy's party turned out to be a young actor, Darryl Hickman. Merv found him to be a captivating personality, although he would forever be confused with his better-known brother, Dwayne, who would one day achieve a cult following on TV for playing Dobie Gillis. Merv had seen both brothers emote in *Captain Eddie* (1945), in which Darryl had been cast as the aviator Eddie Rickenbacker as a boy.

Merv had first become aware of Darryl when he appeared in *The Grapes of Wrath* with Henry Fonda in 1940. Like Judy Garland, the performer had grown up in show business, having been discovered at the age of 13. Most recently Merv had seen the actor in

Ann Blyth (left) playing über-bitch to Mommie Dearest **Joan** (Mildred) **Crawford** (Pierce)

Any Number Can Play, starring Clark Gable.

Merv didn't know if Darryl was gay or straight, but he later confessed to Roddy that he almost made a play for him to see what might happen.

"Like a bolt of lightning, and just as I was about to put the moves on him, he let go with a startling confession," Merv told Roddy. "He said he was seriously considering abandoning acting to enter a monastery. Talk like that can really take the air out of a hard-on. Think Bette Davis in *Winter Meeting*."

In 1951, Darryl lived up to his promise, and did indeed enter a monastery. It didn't surprise Merv at all. But he predicted that Darryl's stay among the monks wouldn't work out. "When you've appeared with such stars as Barbara Stanwyck, Gene Tierney, Alan Ladd, Judy Garland, Mickey Rooney, Spencer Tracy, Katharine Hepburn, and Shirley Temple, how can you settle for some stinking old monks who aren't even allowed to jerk off?" Merv said. Lasting only a year in the monastery, Darryl returned to Hollywood once again to find his place in the sun, only to find that that sun wasn't burning too brightly for him.

Elizabeth Taylor was the last to arrive at Roddy's bash, and she made the grandest entrance. All eyes turned on her. Roddy introduced her to Merv at once—the star knew all the other guests—but it was an hour before Merv was able to corner Elizabeth alone.

He finally captured his "prize" when he saw Darryl leave her side to answer a phone call. "Alone at last," he said to Elizabeth.

"It's great to meet you," Elizabeth said, flashing her violet-colored eyes at him. "A coincidence, really, I'm going to the Cocoanut Grove next week to hear you sing. Lana Turner told me you really know how to deliver a romantic ballad."

"I'm surprised she noticed me with Frank Sinatra at her side," Merv said.

As Elizabeth talked to him, she would often tenderly take his hand. He looked directly into her eyes, which he considered the most enchanting he'd ever seen on the screen.

With those eyes, she seemed to take him into her confidence, as if allowing him to join her inner circle. But, for all he knew, she did that with everybody she met.

Both of them looked across the patio at Roddy moving gracefully among clusters of his guests. "When I first met Roddy," she said reflectively, "I felt he was my twin. That we'd been separated at birth. He conceals the loneliness of his childhood—something I know a lot about—with a spontaneous playfulness. He is Peter Pan."

Top Tomato:
Elizabeth Taylor

"Roddy told me that he's signed you up to our Sunday afternoon club," she said, smiling at him.

He'd later tell Roddy, "I don't know if she knows it or not, or what you told her about us, but Elizabeth seems the least judgmental of any person I've ever met. She seems to recognize that all people have needs—and that love takes many forms."

"Roddy might have grown into a man who loves women," she said, "if not for his mother, Winifriede. She doted on him almost obsessively. For years she even dressed Roddy like his older sister, Virginia. She wanted to make dolls out of them, not living, breathing children. My mother did that to me too. I think she came to regard me as a beautiful porcelain doll, not a little girl trying desperately to grow up in the spotlight."

"My mother regarded me as a fat, pudgy kid," he said.

She reached for his hand again. "Don't ever get fat. Once you've established a romantic image, fat is out. I gathered you didn't have a domineering mother like Roddy and me. That's good. It's easier to break away when you don't have apron strings tied in knots around you. Both Roddy and I are trying to establish independent lives." She looked across the patio once again at her friend. "What he's doing with these Sunday afternoon gatherings is trying to re-create a new family for himself. Welcome, kissin' cousin."

Without thinking of what he was saying, Merv blurted out, "Can I take you out some time? I mean . . . not like a real date. We could be friends."

She leaned over and kissed his cheek. "Of course, you can. Like a friend. Like the relationship I have with Roddy. We don't have to sleep together. We can find other people to perform that dirty deed." She leaned over close to his ear. "Sometimes I need an escort when I can't be seen in public with the object of my desire."

"You mean like when he's married or something?"

"Exactly. I'll tell you a secret. Don't tell anybody. You know who's picking me up three blocks from Roddy's house tonight? Robert Taylor." She giggled like the sixteen-year-old she really was.

"Don't let Barbara Stanwyck find out," he cautioned.

"That's not a real marriage," she said, wanting to dismiss the subject. "They just live together. I've just played my first real grown-up role in *The Conspirator* with Bob. I'm an American debutante, and he's a Communist spy. Just imagine: Here I am playing love scenes with a man who's thirty-eight. When we shot our love scenes, he always stuck his tongue down my throat. The only thing he doesn't like about me is my legs. He's threatening to shave the hair off them himself."

Merv rose to his feet as did she when they spotted Roddy coming across the patio to say something to them. "Louis B. Mayer told Roddy and me that both of us would be washed up by the time we turned seventeen," she said. "He cited Shirley Temple as an example. Both Roddy and I are determined to prove Mayer wrong. Another shit, Hedda Hopper, warned me about the perils of having been a child star. 'There is no second act for children in the movies,' she told me. 'What awaits a child star? A decline in fans. A dwindling bank account. Personal disasters in relationships. Booze. And, dare I say it, premature death. Most child stars can't adjust to life when the sound of applause no longer rings in their ears.' Charmingly reassuring, that Hedda."

A beaming Roddy appeared before them, looking fresh-faced and innocent, as if the past night with Merv had never happened. He kissed Elizabeth on the cheek, taking her arm. "Hot dogs are now being served. He turned to Merv. "I've got the most divine creature I want you to meet. You'll flip."

"I've already flipped over you," Merv said.

"By tomorrow morning, you will have forgotten all about me. Wait until you meet Richard Long. He should be arrested for being so handsome."

"Oh, you guys," Elizabeth said, leading the way across the patio.

***

Roddy flitted from lover to lover, breaking hearts along the way. But often he didn't leave his jilted lover completely deserted. He procured other loves for the young men he deserted. He never called it procuring, as some did, but preferred to say he hooked up former lovers with "new talent."

Such was the case when he introduced Merv to Richard Long. The face of this young actor had already enthralled Merv when he'd seen him in *The Egg and I*, playing Tom Kettle, whose movie parents were Marjorie Main and Percy Kilbride. Merv and Richard bonded over hot dogs. Merv learned that Richard feared he'd been trapped in the Ma and Pa Kettle hillbilly flicks since the studio was determined to make an ongoing series of them.

As the sun set in the West and Roddy's party was winding down, Merv remained at Richard's side. As Merv would later tell Johnny Riley, "If any man in the world could cure me of a broken heart after my one-night stand with Roddy, it is Richard Long."

Working it Out: **Rock Hudson** (left) with **Richard Long**.
In the background, keeping things safely hetero, is a publicity pinup of **Yvonne de Carlo**

Richard whispered to him as the other guests were leaving that Roddy had invited both of them to stay over for the night, using his guest room. Merv was thrilled at the prospect of getting to sleep with this good-looking and charming young man.

When Merv later met with Johnny, his friend was eager for all the details. "There's not a lot to tell," Merv claimed. "Unlike Roddy, who is all over you, Dick is a gentleman in bed. He does it the old-fashioned way. It's all very satisfying. I think I've fallen madly in love with him."

Merv was poised for another heartbreak. After only three sleepovers at Roddy's, Richard informed Merv of his decision. "I'm not a homosexual, and I don't care to be one. I've had some experiences in Hollywood with men, but I want to get back on the straight-and-narrow path. I plan to have a big career in Hollywood, and rumors of homosexuality would destroy that for me."

"But we could keep on seeing each other in secret," Merv protested.

"I'm sorry," Richard said. "I've got to cut this off. I think you're someone I could really care for, and I just can't let that happen."

To make matters worse, Richard even told Merv that he should start dating and being seen with attractive young women. "There's already been a lot of talk about you," he said. "You've got to change that and get involved with a woman even if it's not in your heart."

Richard was a man of his word. In 1954 Merv heard that he'd married Suzan Ball, a cousin of Lucille Ball. But she would die of cancer the following year at the age of 21. In 1957 Merv's former lover would marry the actress and model, Mara Corday, with whom he was living at the time of his early death of multiple heart attacks in 1974. Richard was only 47 at the time. Merv sent the largest wreath of flowers to the funeral but did not enclose a card identifying the source.

Merv thought seriously about Richard's warning about both of their careers. Even though he didn't want to start dating women, he knew it was a smart move. He didn't think Rock Hudson or Tab Hunter wanted to date women either, but it was what was expected of male heartthrobs. Dating a woman, he knew, didn't have to lead to the bedroom.

Richard had hardly exited from Roddy's front door before Elizabeth Taylor spotted Merv and beckoned him over. Standing beside her was a young woman.

"Merv," Elizabeth said, "I want you to meet Judy Balaban."

***

Merv later wrote that Judy, a bright, lovely young redhead, "was nineteen going on thirty-five." That was true. He also claimed that "we fell madly in love," and that was not true. He genuinely liked Judy and they began dating, but it was never a serious romance on his part.

Instead of "my one true love," as he claimed to his friends, Judy became "my best gal pal ever." She was smart, fun, amusing, a kindred soul, and she could make him laugh, which she did at every opportunity. Most of the time he spent with her they played practical jokes on their friends.

When Merv would take Judy home, he'd give her a quick kiss on the lips, and that was about it for heavy romance. He genuinely liked Judy and wanted to be with her as much as he could. As the days turned into weeks, she fell in love with Merv and wanted to go on the road with him and Freddy's band when their engagement at the Cocoanut Grove came to an end.

Normally, the bandleader didn't allow girlfriends or even wives to travel on the road with his musicians. For Merv, he made an exception, as he genuinely liked Judy.

Her father, Barney Balaban, was a powerful figure in the movie industry, operating out of offices in New York. Along with his five brothers from Chicago, he'd founded the Balaban and Katz Theatre Chain. In 1936, Barney had moved to New York where he became president of Paramount Pictures, a post he held until 1964.

He was eased out of Paramount as the studio came under the control of Gulf + Western. Before that, he was a man to be feared. He also was a deeply religious Jew and overly protective of his daughter, Judy.

Freddy Martin had not wanted to offend Barney by denying his daughter's request. It was only later that the bandleader learned that he'd made Barney furious by allowing his daughter to travel on the road with his band and a *goy*.

"I knew what Merv was doing," Freddy later said. "Merv was desperately trying to establish his credentials as a straight boy. There had been too much talk in the other direction. Dating Judy was a career move on his part. Throughout the rest of his life he'd have some gal on his arm. Since I didn't think Merv and Judy would be making the bedsprings squeak at night, I allowed her to travel with us."

As was obvious to the boys in the band, Judy was far more entranced by Merv than he was with her. Even so, their so-called romantic fling set off alarms in Barney, who referred to Merv as "that Irish Catholic son of a whore."

More publicity pinups:
Boy singer **Merv**

To break up their romance, he dispatched the famous New York show business columnist, Leonard Lyons, to see Merv and talk him out of dating Judy. Following strict instructions from Barney, Lyons met with Merv in New York, making his pitch that religious differences between Judy and Merv would doom a potential relationship and most definitely would "ruin" a marriage.

When Merv refused to listen to that line of reasoning, Lyons got tougher. "Barney knows a lot about you, Griffin. You wouldn't want me to publish some of what we know in my column. It's read by everybody in show business. It could destroy your promising career."

"Get out!" Merv ordered Lyons. He was furious that Barney would send the columnist to threaten him. If anything, it made him more determined than ever to stay with Judy. There was a rebellious streak in him, and he even began to seriously consider marriage.

However, Roddy warned him against it, pointing out that Lyons would not come out and say he was a homosexual in print, but could make veiled references. He cited several instances where Cary Grant was "outed" by columnists in the 1930s, long before that term was invented.

Merv felt that once he was safely married to Judy, rumors about his homosexuality would be laid to rest. Judy was in Los Angeles when he called her and asked her to fly to Las Vegas where he was booked into The Last Frontier. He promised her that at the end of his engagement there, he'd marry her in one of the local chapels.

Somehow Dorothy Kilgallen learned of this marriage proposal and broke the news in her column. Barney was traveling in Paris with his wife when the column appeared, and he canceled his vacation, flying home at once to prevent the marriage of his daughter to Merv.

When Judy went to the studio cashier at Paramount in Hollywood, the woman in charge refused to issue her a ticket to Las Vegas or to give Judy any spending money. "I'm sorry, Miss Balaban, but I have my instructions. No ticket, no money."

After his appearance in Las Vegas, Merv flew to Los Angeles to meet with Judy. He learned that her parents were en route to the West Coast for a showdown. Kilgallen continued to run several items in her column about their upcoming marriage, and about how it did not have parental approval. Merv later recalled that "Kilgallen treat-

Ferociously protective father,
Merv-hater,
and president of Paramount
Pictures :
Barney Balaban

69

ed the event like a scenario for a spy movement, tracking our movements from coast to coast."

A singing engagement caused Merv to fly at once to New York where Judy promised to join him soon. Without Merv, she confronted her parents who threatened to disinherit her. Still claiming that she was in love with Merv, she borrowed the money from a friend and flew to New York to join him.

But after only a few weeks there, reality set in. Perhaps she realized that Merv wasn't really in love with her, but wanted to use her for some welcome boy/girl publicity.

At the time, Merv's agent was an ambitious young man named Jay Kanter. Astonishingly, Jay functioned at various points of his career as the agent for Marilyn Monroe, Grace Kelly, and Marlon Brando as well. One night over dinner at a restaurant in Little Italy, Merv introduced Judy to Jay. It was love at first sight. Within the week, Jay, with Merv's approval, began dating Judy. Merv had already told Jay that, "I'm not ready for marriage," And in a phone call to Roddy in Hollywood, Merv told him, "My affair with Judy was the romance that never was."

At the marriage ceremony for Judy Balaban and Jay Kanter in 1953 Marlon Brando was best man, and Rosemary Clooney, the singer, was one of the bridesmaids. Clooney would go on to become one of Merv's closest women friends. Judy's marriage to Kanter would produce two children and end in 1961, the same year she went on to marry actor Tony Franciosa. In 1956, Judy was famously associated with Princess Grace of Monaco, when she served as one of her bridesmaids during her marriage ceremony to Prince Rainier of Monaco.

***

Back on the West Coast for a return engagement at the Cocoanut Grove, Merv discovered that he had had a loyal devotee of his singing long before he ever had a fan club.

It was the eccentric and elusive billionaire, Howard Hughes.

Before Merv actually met him, he'd read all the magazine stories and heard all the rumors going around Hollywood. Some of the aviator's story was known to the world, including how he became the richest teenager in America upon the death of his father. His exploits in aviation, including an around-the-world flight, had been highly publicized, as was his attempt to build his controversial "Spruce Goose," one of the great airline development failures of World War II.

His romances with such screen beauty queens as Billie Dove and Lana Turner were fodder for the fan magazines. Although he was believed to have actually gone to bed with Ginger Rogers, Merv had heard that his celebrated romance with Katharine Hepburn was more for public consumption than the boudoir. Rumor had it that she was "mostly dyke" anyway.

After her affair with Howard in the late 1930s, Bette Davis had spread malicious gossip about him, strongly suggesting that he was more homosexual than heterosexual. Gossip had it that on the set of his most notorious film, *The Outlaw*, Howard had pursued Jack Buetel, who played Billy the Kid, instead of busty Jane Russell.

Howard was known to stash a bevy of hopeful starlets in various apartments in Hollywood, promising each of them future stardom at RKO. But, or so it was said, he never got around to seducing most of them, although he paraded them out for public viewing at such clubs as the Cocoanut Grove. These women were trivialized as "arm candy," and Merv would later use Howard as a role model when he, too, arrived at public gatherings with a glamorous woman on his arm, most visibly Eva Gabor during his later life.

Every night at the Grove, Howard brought a different woman. Sometimes they were famous, including Jane Greer, but most of the time these young aspirant actresses were starlets destined never to find stardom. Many of them eventually became housewives, the highlight of their lives being their dates with Howard.

"He was a creature of habit," Merv later said. "During my entire engagement, I could always count on his being in the audience except for that rare night when he failed to show up. You'd think that a bigwig like Howard would have better things to do in life than listen to me sing. The waiters told me he always ordered the same thing, a big dish of vanilla ice cream. But not any ice cream. Howard didn't like the vanilla served at the Ambassador. So he sent over shipments of some ice cream he'd discovered so it would be available to him. He was also obsessive in his music tastes. Every night he requested the same song from me. A rhumba I sang in Greek called 'Miserlou.'"

Merv dutifully sang that song night after night, directing it toward Howard. For his kindness, Howard slipped him a one-hundred dollar bill every night. "This surprised me because Howard was not known as a big tipper, at least among the waiters who always complained about their gratuity. When Saturday night came around, I had made more from Howard's tips than Freddy Martin paid me for the whole week."

Wealthiest Man, Most Beautiful Woman: **Howard Hughes** with **Ava Gardner**

71

Other than requesting that one song, Howard had nothing to say to Merv and never invited him to table as did other big stars such as Clark Gable. That was why Merv was surprised when a waiter came to his dressing room one night with an invitation from Howard to join him and a lady friend at table.

"Apparently, Howard had heard that I was star-struck, and he wanted to thank me for singing all those 'Miserlous.' After my performance, I hightailed it to his table. There sat the very luscious and very drunk Ava Gardner. Other than Elizabeth Taylor, she was the most beautiful woman I'd ever seen. I could only imagine how great she looked when sober. Howard didn't have much to say, but Ava not only drank a lot but talked like a drunken sailor. She was the most vulgar woman I'd ever met, but utterly fascinating."

Seated at table with Howard, with Ava between them, Merv sensed at once that the battling pair had just had a big fight, perhaps moments before his arrival. At the time of his meeting with them, they were already famous for their feuds, many of their explosive arguments turning violent. The musician, Artie Shaw, Ava's former husband, had told Freddy Martin that, "Hughes regularly beats the shit out of Ava, and that bitch has sent our aviator friend to the hospital on more than one occasion."

Turning her back to Howard, Ava took Merv's hand and stared deeply into his eyes in her most seductive manner. "Howard here thinks he can buy me, but I ain't for sale, sugartit. He even offered Elizabeth Taylor a million dollars in gems, and still she said no. Liz and I are the only cunts in Hollywood who can't be bought. I'm more tantalized by the size of a man's cock than I am by the size of his bank account. Surely you agree."

"I wouldn't know, Miss Gardner," he said, startled at her bluntness. "I like girls. As for cock sizes, I don't think I've ever got around to measuring my own."

"Don't worry," she said, "I'll do it for you some night. So sorry if I offended you. But one of the boys in Freddy's band told me that you'd had him before I got around to him."

"Well, he lied!" Merv said, offended by her accusation. "Hollywood is known for its unfounded gossip. Isn't that how Hedda Hopper and Louella Parsons make their living?"

"Suit yourself, little darling," she said. "But you can ask your friend, Roddy McDowall. He'll tell you I'm very understanding about such matters. Even with Howard here." She turned and looked rather disdainfully at her host. "Howard may be my date for tonight, but you've got to understand that appearances are meaningless in Hollywood. He'll take me home and get rewarded with a kiss on the cheek—that's it. For all I know, morning will find him waking up in bed with Tyrone Power."

Howard sat in stony silence listening to her drunken tirade.

72

Since Ava had been provocative with him, Merv uncharacteristically decided to strike back. "If you care so little for Mr. Hughes, why do you date him?"

"Good question, honey chile. He makes life easy for me. If I want to go to Mexico, a plane is waiting. If I need a first-class seat to New York at the last minute, one suddenly becomes available, even if Howard has to bump Cary Grant. Speaking of Cary, dear Howard has 'bumped' him a lot."

Not surprisingly, she'd hit a delicate nerve in Howard. He became furious. In a voice dripping with sarcasm, he said, "Ava, would you shut your fucking mouth? You're a lush. If you keep on drinking, what beauty you now have will be gone in three years. Then you'll be just another broken-down old alcoholic broad, a has-been. The Hollywood Hills are full of them, talking about how big they were in 1933. When all you pussies are faded celluloid memories, the world will still be talking about Howard Hughes."

"Yeah!" she said with utter contempt, her face flashing her fury. "They'll be talking all right. They'll mock you for being eccentric. Read that crazy." Diverting her eyes momentarily to Merv, she said, "Know something, kid. The real reason I don't go to bed with Long John here is that Lana Turner told me he gave her syphilis." She suddenly stood up and reached for her drink. Impulsively she tossed it in Howard's face.

She stormed out of the nightclub, as a waiter rushed with a white napkin to help dry Howard off, but he shooed him away. Flabbergasted, Merv sat there, not knowing what to do. He wanted to flee to his dressing room, but Howard signaled for him to remain seated.

Without bothering to wipe his alcoholic-soaked face, he turned to Merv. "Pat DiCicco, Errol Flynn, and I are going to play a game of tennis tomorrow morning before it gets too hot. I've played with your Uncle Elmer. He's good. I hear you play well, too. Why not team up with me to stand off Pat and Errol? How about it? Give me your phone number. I'll call you in the morning about picking you up here at the hotel."

At first Merv couldn't believe that Howard would pick him as a tennis partner. "I'd be honored. But I must warn you: I'm not as good as my uncle."

"Neither am I." Without another word, Howard stood up and left the table. Within a minute, he was back. Please come with me," he urged Merv. "I need to go to the men's room to clean up. But the door is shut, and I never touch doorknobs. Too many germs."

"Gladly, Mr. Hughes."

***

On the tennis court that Sunday morning, Howard was growing impatient. Along with Merv and Pat DiCicco, he'd already waited forty-five minutes for that swashbuckler, Errol Flynn, to show up. Not a man to waste time, Howard made telephone calls to his staff. In those days if you worked for Howard, you had to make yourself available to receive his calls, not just on Sunday morning, but at three o'clock on any other morning as well.

Merv didn't mind the wait, as he was intrigued by the handsome but notorious Pat DiCicco, who was always appearing in the gossip columns involved in one scandal after another. With a suntan and in his tennis whites, Pat dazzled him. He would later confide to Roddy that, "Pat has the world's most beautiful legs, far better than Betty Grable's, at least for my taste."

Most tennis shorts in those days were loose fitting, but not Pat's. They were so tightly tailored that they revealed what looked like an ample endowment. Merv kept glancing at Pat's package. Once Pat caught him, but only smiled his approval. He scooted down on the bench, as his shorts rode higher, giving Merv an even better view. "In my business, it pays to advertise," Pat said. Merv wasn't sure exactly what business Pat was engaged in, and he pondered the nature of Pat's relationship with the mysterious Howard Hughes.

Several times that morning, Pat had called Howard "Lambie," which seemed to be his nickname for the aviator. Merv couldn't imagine a less appropriate name for Howard.

Pat had been famously married—first to actress Thelma Todd in 1932 and later to the heiress Gloria Vanderbilt in 1941. Both women had been former girlfriends of Howard. The oily Egyptian actor, Alexander d'Arcy, had once said, "Pat would fuck a rattlesnake if he thought it would advance his career." That pronouncement had spread among the gossips of Hollywood.

Pat's first wife, Thelma Todd, had died mysteriously on December 16, 1935, a year after her divorce from Pat, when she was discovered in a car parked in a garage. It was ruled at the time by the then-notoriously corrupt Los Angeles District Attorney's office that she'd committed suicide, dying of carbon monoxide poisoning. Merv had heard that the mob had ordered her murdered, and that Pat somehow was involved. But instead of making Pat a sinister figure to Merv, the notoriety made him all the more appealing.

Gigolo, stud, and
ace tennis player
Pat DiCicco

Finally a hung-over Errol arrived at the tennis courts. Even though worse for wear, he still looked dashingly handsome, though not as much so as when Merv had first met him in the 1930s at his Uncle Elmer's. At first Merv wasn't sure if the star would remember him, as there had been a long line of young boys and girls in Errol's life since their adventure. Merv had been young and pudgy when he'd first encountered Errol lying naked in his uncle's living room. Merv's appearance had changed drastically since then.

Errol came right up to Merv and kissed him on both cheeks. "You're looking great, pal," he said. "Trimmed down, I see. I'll be at the Grove next week to catch your act." As he turned to see Howard approaching the court, Errol hugged Pat, also kissing him on both cheeks. "C'mon, mate," he said to Pat, "let's beat hell out of these two fairies." He winked at Merv to indicate that he was only joking.

Maybe Errol was still drunk from the night before, but he lost the game for his team. Merv and Howard easily beat Errol and Pat. Howard seemed elated, inviting them for a plane ride that afternoon to Catalina Island.

On the way to the showers, Errol whispered to Merv, "Pat and I deliberately let him win. If Howard loses, he's furious for the rest of the day. He'd get back at us for winning, so we never win. Got that, sport?"

There were six shower booths with moldy plastic curtains. Still shy about nudity, Merv stripped off his tennis whites and took the first shower where he began soaping himself. He was about two minutes into his hot shower, when the curtain was pulled back. There stood Errol Flynn as nude as the first day Merv had met him. His body was not as lean and lithe as Merv had remembered, it, but he was still matinee handsome and seductively attractive.

"If I remember correctly what you like—and I do—I want you to know that here I am," Errol said. He stepped inside Merv's shower booth and placed a firm hand on the back of Merv's neck. Merv seemed to follow the command of that hand, finding himself on his knees on the floor of that still-running shower, servicing Errol as he'd done as a kid. "You've improved," Errol said, offering encouragement. "You must have been practicing."

Errol must have had a lot to drink the night before, because it took him a long time to climax. As Merv was getting to his feet and Errol was soaping himself, the shower curtain opened again. A nude Pat DiCicco stood there. "You may have seen him first, but I'm next!"

On the plane ride to Catalina, Howard honored Merv by letting him sit up front with him, while Errol and Pat occupied the seats in the rear. For the duration of the flight, Merv thought about only two things—the delectable taste of Pat DiCicco's cock, which he actually preferred to that of his former

Before Rainier and the French connection: **Grace Kelly** with **Bing Crosby**

75

idol, Errol Flynn, and his chance meeting with Bing Crosby.

Although just as sweaty as they were, Howard had not joined the men in the showers. Merv had heard that he was quite shy. As Merv emerged fully dressed with Pat and Errol, he saw Howard chatting in the corner of the court with Bing Crosby and a very young honey blonde who looked like a princess. He was astonished when he realized that the court was being taken over by Bing and this dazzling creature.

Unlike Sinatra, who seemed jealous of other singers, Bing was more confident and self-assured. "Freddy Martin tells me you're the best male singer he's ever had," Bing said, extending his hand. "I've been meaning to drop in to the Grove one night to catch your act."

"I'd be honored, Mr. Crosby," Merv said. "But it might take more guts than I have to perform before the world's greatest singer."

"You're far too kind," Bing said.

Merv was astonished that the singer did not introduce him to his demure companion. She smiled at Merv, and he smiled back—and that was the extent of their meeting. Years later, Merv would insist that Bing's companion at the time was Grace Kelly.

If Merv were correct in his identification of the starlet, that would mean that Bing and Grace had begun an affair long before it was generally assumed that they did and much before the 1954 release of their joint film, *The Country Girl*, for which she'd win an Oscar, beating out Merv's favorite, Judy Garland, who had competed with a spectacular performance of her own in *A Star Is Born*.

While still a model on the East Coast, Grace had flown to Los Angeles and could well have been in California at the time Merv first claimed that he'd seen her. How she met Bing Crosby so early in her career remains a mystery.

On Catalina, Howard had arranged for the quartet to stay in a private home. Whenever Howard needed a temporary residence, one always seemed to be made available to him. Pat and Howard shared one bedroom, Errol and Merv another, just as he'd done at his Uncle Elmer's. Later that afternoon Pat and Howard left without inviting Errol and Merv, though Howard agreed to be back in time to take them to dinner that night.

As Merv remembered it, Errol was drinking heavily that afternoon and complaining bitterly about the huge back alimony payments he owed to Lili Damita, a bisexual actress he'd married in the 1930s.

When he wasn't talking about Lili, Errol enthralled Merv with stories of the shooting of his latest film, *Kim*, in Jaipur, India. It was scheduled for release in a few months.

At the end of the shoot, or so Errol claimed, he'd invited all the men who'd worked on the crew—"all except our homo contingent"—to join him for a big private party on the sound stage. Spending money he could ill afford at the time, he hired the prop department to build a pyramid-like structure in the center of the stage and to paint it in gold.

The week before, he'd had his assistant round up the prettiest girls he could find in Jaipur. They were dressed in see-through gold lamé Turkish pajamas and arranged artfully on the pyramid. Errol's rule was that each of the young women had to make herself available for intercourse to any member of the crew attracted to her.

At the door to the sound stage, Errol had stationed two bare-breasted handmaidens to take all the clothing of the male crew, including their underwear. Errol told Merv that he'd spent most of the night watching the crew seduce the beautiful women before taking "the prize" at the top of the pyramid for himself. He described her as a fourteen-year-old virgin. "God, did she bleed that night."

At the end of the orgy, as dawn broke over Jaipur, Errol handed out gold medals to each man. Each was engraved with the words, "Flynn's Flying Fuckers." In time those medallions became highly prized souvenirs in Hollywood.

After dinner on Catalina with Howard and Pat that night, Errol and Merv shared a double bed, crawling in shortly before midnight. If Merv expected any more action, he was disappointed. As he would later tell Roddy, "The moment he hit the pillow, Errol was sound asleep and can that man snore. From the sounds coming from the next bedroom, Howard and Pat seemed to be having fun."

The next morning, Merv rose early and wandered the beach by himself. As he was heading back to the house, he saw Pat emerge from the bungalow, wearing only his underwear. Rubbing sleep from his eyes, he invited Merv to walk along the beach with him to look at the seagulls. Merv found himself wishing that he'd spent the night with Pat instead of his childhood idol.

Pat was extremely candid about his relationship with Howard. "The fucker knows I'm mostly a ladies' man but he likes to bang me to show me who's boss, as if I didn't know. I hate it. It hurts me. Our aviator friend is huge."

"Why do you put up with it?"

"I'm on his payroll, and have been for a long time," Pat confessed. "At some point I decided to hang out with the rich and famous, knowing that would make me their servant, subject to their bidding. If I don't like it, tough. If that means that on occasion I have to spread my cheeks for Howard for a few minutes of pain and humiliation, so be it. The financial rewards are great."

The two men strolled along in silence for a long time before Pat came to a stop and looked out toward the sea. "If you ever become rich and famous, enough so you can afford me, just call me up and I'll come running. I'm sure you'd be a lot more fun to be with than Howard. He's nuts sometimes. You see, I'm what is called a hustler."

By the time Merv became rich and famous enough to hire Pat, he was no longer appealing to him. But on that beach in Catalina, Merv determined that when he got older, and no doubt pudgy again, he would hire a string of Pat DiCiccos.

The prospect thrilled him because it meant he wouldn't have to depend on his youth, good looks, or even his waistline to have the sexual adventures with young men he craved.

***

Merv bonded with many men—only a few of whom became sexual relationships—over the course of his life. Along the way, he made a number of "to-the-grave friends," as he called them.

Marlon Brando was a friend of a then-unknown jazz vocalist, Harry Belafonte. Marlon had met Harry at the New School in New York in the 1940s and had formed a friendship. Since money was tight, Marlon and Harry sometimes bought only one theater ticket to a Broadway play, Harry sitting through the first half of the show, Marlon sitting through the ending—or vice versa—and comparing notes about the plot developments.

Marlon, of course, had found success on Broadway, but Harry was still struggling and going through a sort of identity crisis. Instead of a jazz vocalist, he had decided to become a Calypso singer, inspired by African and West Indian songs such as "Yellow Bird."

Marlon called Merv one night and invited him to hear Harry sing at a little dive along Bleeker Street in Greenwich Village. "He's a real good-looking guy, and you might fall for him, but I've got to warn you: He's not one of my fuck buddies. No way!" Puffing on a cigarette for emphasis, Marlon said, "Oh, in case it matters, he's black."

"Fine with me," Merv said. "I'm color blind."

Hearing Harry sing for the first time, Merv was immediately enraptured by his looks, his voice, and his style. He later told Marlon, "An electric bolt went up my spine when I heard the lyric 'Day-O.' Merv seemed to understand that Calypso could capture an American audience, although he could hardly have known that his "discovery," Harry Belafonte himself, would one day be dubbed the "King of Calypso."

Born in Harlem, Harry was the son of a cook from the island of Martinique. He later lived with his grandmother in her native Jamaica. Back in New York, he performed at the American Negro Theatre with Sidney Poitier, another rising star. Merv had already heard Harry's debut as a pop singer on the Jubilee Label in 1949, but on the night of their first meeting in the Village he told Harry that he could "scale a higher ladder" in the music world if he developed his talents as a Calypso artist. "You're the best, man."

"That's Mon!" Harry corrected him.

From the first night, Merv and Harry bonded so much so that Merv invited the singer to become "my first roommate in New York." Harry had recently separated from his first wife, Marguerite Byrd, whom he'd married in 1948. "He was very sad and didn't have a career going yet," Merv later recalled.

After his first week as Harry's "roomie," Merv called Marlon. "Harry Belafonte is the best reason I know for integration."

"Has he fed you any big black dick yet?" Marlon asked provocatively.

"Not yet—and maybe never," Merv said. "Sigh, I can dream, can't I? I don't think Harry swings that way, much to my regret. Since we're roomies, I can at least check him out to see what I'm missing."

Merv even went with Harry to Philadelphia where he sang an evening of Calypso songs, introducing "Matilda," which in time would become his first full release single after he recorded it on April 27, 1953. The song would remain his "signature" throughout his career.

"He bombed that night with 'Matilda,'" Merv said. "It was an all-white club and they couldn't relate to songs about Kingston Town and banana boats. In the middle of 'Matilda,' a fat drunk called out, 'Sing *Melancholy Baby,* nigger, or get off the stage!' Harry bravely carried on."

Although not the ardent civil rights champion that Marlon became, Merv as a TV talk show host would expose the world to a parade of black entertainers, followed later by the most important civil rights leaders, including Dr. Martin Luther King Jr.

Long after they were roommates, Merv stayed in touch with Harry and took pleasure in his success, especially when he became the first African-American to win an Emmy for his solo TV special, *Tonight With Belafonte* (1959).

***

Around the time he met Harry Belafonte, Merv also became a close friend of Robert Clary, the Parisian entertainer, who was about his same age. The two performers became close when Merv was performing on *The Hazel Bishop Show* and also appearing with Freddy Martin's band at the Roosevelt

Hotel.

Merv had met Robert in the summer of 1950 when "the little short guy" had come to see Freddy Martin's band at the Hollywood Palladium.

Robert was just getting known in the States because of his popular recording, "Put Your Shoes On, Lucy." Merv loved the song. At the Palladium, when he heard that Robert was in the audience, he went over after his act and introduced himself.

Robert (often known as Bob) was there with Red Doff, a publicist for Capitol Records, and he'd just signed a recording contract with Capitol. Merv congratulated Robert and praised his singing voice.

"I don't think I ever saw two men get along so well on first meeting," Doff said. "Before the night was over, Bob and Merv were in love with each other. Don't draw the wrong conclusions. In fact, the next day Merv would introduce Bob to Bob's future wife, Natalie Cantor, Eddie Cantor's daughter. Those two lovebirds, however, would wait until 1965 to get married. Eddie gave Bob's career a big push, but that wasn't the reason for the marriage."

Robert had long admired his future father-in-law, especially when he appeared in blackface as had Al Jolson before him. He was so impressed that he, too, performed in blackface in Paris between 1945 and 1947, long before it became politically incorrect for a white performer to come out with such makeup.

When Robert flew to New York for an engagement, he moved in with Merv at the Royalton. Merv later complained that, "I got little sleep because my new friend and I would sit up all night talking about our future plans for stardom for both of us. Today you'd call it a heavy rap session."

Merv became fascinated with Robert's horror stories about his childhood in Nazi-occupied France. He was the youngest of fourteen children, most of whom would die in concentration camps. As a young Jewish boy, Robert, too, would be deported by the Nazis.

"The whole experience was a complete nightmare," Robert told Merv and others. "The way they treated us, what we had to do to survive. We were less than animals. Sometimes I still have nightmares. I wake up in a cold sweat thinking the Nazis are coming for me. I fear they're going to haul me off to a concentration camp like they did my brothers and sisters."

"What a way for a kid to be introduced to life," Merv said. "You must hate them."

"I don't hold a grudge," Robert said. "Grudges are a waste of time. But I learned the hard way just how dark the human soul is. My fellow human beings can be more savage to each other than any animal who might kill you in the jungle and eat you. At least the animal is killing to survive, as nature intended. The Nazis killed for sadism, pleasure, and a psychotic political creed. When you meet a human being who is kind and generous, a friend like you, you cherish that person."

Merv also cherished Robert. The two men were seen walking down Fifth Avenue arm in arm. Sometimes, Merv would play- fully rest his elbow on Robert's small head. These were just some of the endearing moments the two friends shared with each other. Some members of Freddy's band, knowing Merv's sexual proclivities, assumed the two friends were lovers, at least to judge by their open displays of affection. But that does not appear to be the case at all.

"I adored Bob," Merv later said. "He brought a joy to my life, and he was a survivor. Except for getting kicked out of our house in San Mateo, I'd had it easy growing up. As his friend, I was always there to cheer Robert on, when- ever my schedule allowed, at one triumph after another."

That included the time Robert became an overnight sensation on Broadway when he appeared in Leonard Stillman's *New Faces of 1952* along with Eartha Kitt and other stars. Merv was also in the audience when Robert appeared on Broadway in *Seventh Heaven*, with such famous names as Ricardo Montalban, Gloria de Haven, Chita Rivera, Kurt Kazner, and Bea Arthur. Merv also watched every episode of *Hogan's Heroes* on TV, when Robert became a household word playing the quirky Louis LeBeauy. "Back in that concentration camp in the 40s, little did I know that I'd eventually play a prisoner of war in a Hollywood version of a Nazi stalag," Robert told Merv.

"Although I was a singer myself," Merv recalled, "I was never jealous when my friend sang such show stoppers as 'Lucky Pierre' or 'I'm in Love with Miss Logan.'"

***

Early in his career, Merv formed a friendship with another Robert. The two men would become bonded for life.

One of the unlikeliest of all his friendships—one definitely not sexual— was the bond Merv formed with an Italian-American actor from New York, the son of a shoemaker. Robert Loggia, five years his junior, was a character actor and leading man best known for playing crooks, thugs, and gravelly voiced cops. He even portrayed Joseph, the "stepfather" of Jesus, in *The Greatest Story Ever Told* in 1965, with Dorothy McGuire as the Virgin Mary.

It wasn't that film but the 1985 movie, *Jagged Edge,* with Glenn Close and Jeff Bridges that brought Robert his only Oscar nomination in the supporting role as a delightfully foul-mouth private investigator.

Loggia later told friends that it was Merv's philosophy of life that first attracted him to the singer. "My philosophy is that you have to constantly be turning the page," Merv said. "That prevents me from getting caught up in negative vibes. It's all about change for me. I just keep moving and enjoying the ride."

Over the decades, Merv and Robert would take sixteen long sails on Merv's yacht, including one that lasted three months. "Merv knows how to live and how to give," Robert later said of his friend. "His spirit and charm are unwavering. Every sail with him into unknown waters was a new adventure because Merv is as close to me as any brother I could have."

Robert, who probably spent more quality time with Merv than almost any other male friend, joined the chorus of those who praised Merv for, "Just being a great guy to be around. He's a storehouse of anecdotes and a walking history of show business in the 20th century. Bring up any name, and Merv will tell you about the weekend he spent with that celebrity in Cannes. My God, he even knew Pat Boone when both of them appeared in the 1950s on *Arthur Godfrey and His Friends*."

"Merv always told me that he'd never retire," Robert said. "His exact words were, 'You'll have to carry me off and beat me over the head at my funeral to make sure I don't rise up out of the coffin for one last show-stopping number.'"

Robert didn't have to do that, but he had the saddest face at Merv's funeral, when he, along with Merv's son, Tony Griffin, and others, had the painful job of carrying a dear, lost friend to his final resting place.

"Merv had a great life," Robert said, "one of the most fabulous of any show business personality who ever lived. It was my great pleasure to share in that life. During those long voyages at sea, I got to know one of the world's special people."

***

"I've got a lovely bunch of coconuts,
Every ball you throw will make me rich
There stands my wife, the idol of my life
Singing roll a bowl, a ball, a penny a pitch"

At long last, in 1950, Merv recorded a hit song, a puckish and rather silly novelty entitled "I've Got a Lovely Bunch of Coconuts." He recorded it despite the fact that he hated it, denouncing it privately as "fake and phoney." As its popularity grew, he would immediately turn it off when it came on the radio, as it did frequently over a period of several months.

Composed in 1944 by Fred Heatherton, an English songwriter, the ditty celebrated the traditional "coconut shy" (coconut toss) sometimes seen at English country fairs. What is rarely known today, and never mentioned in Merv's autobiographies, is that Danny Kaye also recorded his own, less popular, version of the same song in the same year, 1950, that Merv's version was defined as a hit.

Danny and Merv weren't the only two artists competing for sales of "Coconuts." Eventually, even Monty Python recorded it, and the song is still played over the public address system at Cambridge United football matches after home wins. It was sung on the *Magical Mystery Tour*, the special BBC broadcast by The Beatles in 1967, and it was heard in Judy Garland's last film, *I Could Go on Singing*.

The silly song became such a pop culture reference that the apes are seen singing the ditty in the Walt Disney film, *The Jungle Book*, and it appeared again in another Disney film, *The Lion King*, when Zazu is forced to sing it for the amusement of Scar.

Merv sang "Coconuts" with a Cockney accent, and it was such a big show stopper that fan clubs formed across America from New York to Los Angeles. He heard that a fan club had even been organized in Cleveland.

When Freddy Martin's Band returned to Los Angeles, the Cocoanut Grove could not meet the demand for reservations. Consequently, Freddy booked Merv and his band into the much larger Hollywood Palladium, a sold-out ballroom that accommodated 6,000 fans.

"Thousands of screaming girls chanting 'We Want Coconuts!' greeted me," Merv remembered. "It's an image I'll never forget."

After his first show, an usher told Merv that the president of the recently created Hollywood High School Merv Griffin Fan Club had arrived and wanted to meet him. He'd never personally met even one member of his fan clubs, so he told the usher to bring her backstage. He decided to stand outside the door to his dressing room to greet her. He expected some shy little girl with an autograph book and was surprised instead to encounter a rather ugly duckling in pigtails—"all skin and bones"—wearing glasses and a dress obviously purchased at the five-and-dime. Years later he would recall her "big voice and marvelous laugh."

President of her local
Merv Griffin fan club,
a then-unknown
Carol Burnett

"Hi, Merv," the perky girl said to him, extending her hand. She didn't seem shy at all, but bold and brassy. "I'm Carol Burnett, the prexy of your fan club." He liked her at once, finding her enthusiasm and spirit contagious. But he could hardly have known he was shaking the hand of one of the brightest stars of television in the future.

"My God," she said standing back and appraising Merv's figure, but not in a seductive way. "Wait till I tell the gals back at school. You're just a kid like us. They'll be so excited. From the sound of your voice on 'Coconuts,' we thought you were an old man like Bing Crosby."

The show was such a hit with fans at the Palladium that its organizers invited Merv and Freddy's band back for repeat performances. Carol promised to show up for every event. "Somewhere I'll find the money," she told him. "My Nanny and I are living on relief."

"You'll do nothing of the sort," he said. "I'm giving you a free pass to all the shows and ten tickets each night to distribute among my fans. I want to meet them, and I want you to keep me abreast of what you gals are up to. I'm not sure what a fan club really does. I assume the club is all girls."

"Well," she said, flashing a big-toothed smile. "A couple of guys. They're . . . you know."

"We're all God's children, and I welcome all fans wherever I find 'em."

"I couldn't agree with you more, but it makes it much harder for a gal like me to get a date."

True to her word, Carol and other members of Merv's fan club showed up for every performance. In time, he got to know her better, welcoming her bubbly personality and merry smile, which he later learned was a mere cover-up for the private tragedies in her life.

Living on welfare in a tiny one-room apartment with her grandmother, Carol was a spunky kid, bright and alert and always ready to make a joke about the bitter sweetness of life. Both of her parents were alcoholics. To escape that painful reality, Carol went to the movies at the rate of eight per week. One week, attending double features, she managed to sit through a dozen films, including two Tarzan flicks. Back at her small apartment, she practiced the Tarzan yell, which almost got Carol and her grandmother evicted.

Sleeping on Nanny's sofa at night, she dared dream the impossible dream, that she could become the next Betty Grable, her favorite star at the time. If not that, then at least Rita Hayworth. Sometimes her attractive grandmother tried to force Carol to face reality. "With that overbite of yours, you'll be lucky to get *any* boy to go out with you."

Carol wished she was as pretty as her Nanny, who was a Southern belle, a flirtatious and self-confident woman who, at the time of her death at the age of eighty-two, had a forty-year-old boyfriend.

As Merv got to know Carol better, she confessed to him that in addition to being the president of his fan club, she had "this crush" on Linda Darnell.

"Whatever happened to Betty Grable?" he asked. "Oh, *her*. I'm just crazy about Linda, although one of her nostrils is larger than the other. When I grow up, I'm going to become a big movie star like Linda. It'll be a challenge. Movie stars have to look like Marilyn Monroe and Tony Curtis. At the moment I look more like Tony than Marilyn."

In the years to come, Merv looked on in amazement as Carol's television career took off, as millions of viewers delighted in her wacky humor and self-effacing wit. "I always thought Carol was a more brilliant comedienne than Lucille Ball," Merv once said. "Lucy was broader in her humor, real slapstick, like the Marx Brothers. Carol was more subtle and ultimately more devastating. Take her character of Eunice, a brilliant send-up of a type of American housewife that has never been equaled. And, of course, she also knew talent when she saw it, namely, yours truly and that fan club."

For Merv's final performance at the Palladium, Carol presented him with a Christmas poem she'd written. He loved it so much he had it framed and for years carried it from dressing room to dressing room as a good luck omen.

Saccharine and campy:
Carol Burnett
as Shirley Temple

i wisht i was a xmas star
perched atop a tree
folks wood see me from afar
cuz of how brite I'd be
i'd shine all nite
i'd shine all day
a lovely site to see.

***

In the aftermath of the "Coconuts" success, Freddy Martin incorrectly assumed that he'd discovered, in Merv, "the next big singing star of the 1950s." He instructed his songwriters to create witty lyrics and music for Merv, beginning with "Back on the Bus," a clever song that mirrored Merv's own life of riding the bus every night with Freddy's band. Although audiences loved it, it came nowhere near becoming the hit that "Coconuts" was. Although as the years went by he valiantly attempted to duplicate his 1950 sensation, Merv would never have another hit song.

Ultimately "Coconuts" sold more than three million copies. Merv cut many other records, but only two became what might even be called a hit—"Wilhelmina" and "Never Been Kissed." Each of those records sold about 500,000 copies each, more or less.

"Am I in Love?" also enjoyed minor but very brief success. "I'm a one-hit wonder," Merv lamented to Freddy.

Months after his sudden fame, Merv spoke with bitterness about his success with "Coconuts," telling Judy Garland and Peter Lawford that, "All I got was a flat fee, a lousy fifty bucks." He was under contract to Freddy, who pocketed all the money from the royalties generated by the ditty. "Freddy could have written me a check for some of it, but he never did."

"I've been there," Judy chimed in. "The MGM Lion has been fucking me in the ass for years without lubrication."

Peter was more optimistic, reminding Merv that because of the song, RCA Victor had given him a recording contract. "You'll knock Sinatra on his ass."

"I'm not so sure," Judy cautioned. "I think Frank will be like me. Both of us will probably make three or four comebacks before we go Over the Rainbow for one final curtain."

At that point Peter grew impish. "Tell me, Judy, just how deep is the penetration from Frank? I've seen him nude, even semi-hard, but just what depth can he really reach in a woman?"

Peter's drunken bluntness embarrassed Merv, but didn't seem to faze Judy at all. She was used to his outrageous behavior. "He's got three inches more than you," Judy told Peter. "But he's lousy at giving head. In that, Ethel Merman is the world's expert."

"But I give great head," Peter protested. "As you know, it's my favorite thing."

"Merman has all of you guys beat, although I hear Marlene Dietrich has a certain flickering tongue, like a feather, that drives the girls wild."

Realizing she was shocking Merv, she turned to him and gently took his hand. "Forgive us, dear, but that's how show biz folk talk in private. Get used to it if you ever want to be a star."

Merv definitely wanted to be a star—"and I definitely got used to it," as he confided to Johnny Riley on his next trip to San Francisco. "After you've been worked over by the likes of Rock Hudson and Roddy McDowall, there isn't a lot more to learn. Sometime before the Fifties came to an end—and I'm not sure of the exact date—I buried that naïve little boy from San Mateo."

Chapter Three

When Freddy Martin told Merv that "I've booked my boys" into the St. Francis Hotel in San Francisco, Merv was elated. It meant he'd have time to reunite with family and friends, especially his three best pals, Johnny Riley, Paul Schone, and Bill Robbins. He'd spoken to all his buddies over the phone, especially Johnny, but he was particularly anxious to see firsthand how their dancing careers were going in post-war San Francisco.

His family welcomed him with their usual love and devotion but treated him differently. During his first evening home, he deciphered the subtle change: They were treating him like a big-time star, even though he was a long way from achieving that lofty ambition. What impressed his family the most was that he was "dating" Judy Garland and planned to marry her. Merv later wrote in his autobiography, "I always thought one day I would go to Hollywood and marry her." Later he confessed that he "misspoke" when describing the specific nature of his relationship with Judy.

"I had to say something," he later told Johnny. "What was I going to say to my family? That Rock Hudson fucks me up the ass or that I gag trying to go all the way down on Roddy McDowall's whopper?" He just hoped that word didn't travel from San Francisco back to Judy in Los Angeles that he was planning to marry her.

At this point he'd gone to bed with her, not just on that one night when he'd held her in his arms, but on other occasions when she'd been drunk, sobbing, and suicidal. There had been no sex. He'd never had sex with any woman, but was seriously thinking about it. If he had to do the dirty deed, he wanted Judy to be his first conquest. He instinctively felt she'd be understanding and compassionate even if he failed. After all, she'd had a long track record of sleeping with homosexual men.

His biggest disappointment came as a result of hanging out with his friends. Johnny got an occasional job in the theater as a chorus boy, but supported himself as a waiter. Bill too, had become a waiter and had found no work in the theater at all. Through a contact of his father's, Paul had found a job selling hardware in a store run by what he called a "tyrannical Jew." All three of the young men hated their jobs.

On the third night of going out with "the boys," it became apparent to Merv that all of his friends were genuinely excited by his "stardom." He also realized the degree to which their motives were selfish. Although none of them admitted it, each seemed to expect that when he became a really big star, he'd get them work in the theater. After two or three drinks, Merv more or less went along with this, making promises that he really couldn't keep, at least not at this point in his life.

Before he left San Francisco that month, Merv was acutely aware that the balance of power had shifted in his relationship with both his family and friends. He was no longer the fat, pudgy kid from San Mateo, but a romantic singing star who'd had one big hit record. He even had fan clubs, including one that had formed in the Bay area.

Before leaving his best pals and his family, he told his second biggest lie, one that topped the one about his romance with Judy Garland. He said that he'd been offered movie contracts at MGM, Warner Brothers, and Paramount, but had not as yet decided which studio he was going to sign with.

"I owe it to Freddy and the boys to keep singing with them for a few more months," Merv claimed. "After all, Freddy made me a star. At the right time, I'll split, especially when I get offered a really big musical."

In every reunion with family and friends, there is always an embarrassing moment you'd rather forgot, something that happens that makes you want to squirm later when you think about it. For Merv, that occurred when he invited Paul, Bill, and Johnny for a nightcap at his suite at the St. Francis.

Merv had promised to stay on for another few days and take a motor trip north with his pals, but he told them he'd been called back to Hollywood. Freddy had booked his orchestra, with Merv as the lead singer, to perform at a spectacular party for the columnist, Louella Parsons, celebrating her fiftieth anniversary as a Hollywood writer. Freddy had told Merv that "every big star in Hollywood will turn out to honor that witch, but not because they like her, but because she has the power to destroy most of their careers."

After kissing Paul and Johnny good night, he turned to Bill, who asked to stay behind. Bill had had too much to drink, and at first Merv thought he just wanted to sleep over, since he wasn't sober enough to drive home. He lived outside the city.

It took Bill another hour and two more drinks before he worked up enough courage to tell Merv what was on his mind. "I know you were always attracted to me, and I deliberately didn't pick up on the signals you were sending out."

Merv was flabbergasted. He'd never been attracted to Bill sexually, finding him far too effeminate for his tastes. He had a crush on Johnny, not on Bill.

Still, he listened politely to Bill's pitch.

"I've been thinking it over," Bill said. "I know you're going back to Hollywood and you're going to become a big star. I want to go with you. I want to become your boy." He slammed down his drink. "Now I've said it!"

At first Merv didn't know what to say. Finally, he blurted out, "But I told you, I'm going to marry Judy Garland."

Bill stood up on wobbly legs. "No you're not. Your family fell for that line, but me and Johnny don't buy that. Paul thinks you will but we don't. Let's face it: Judy can't do it for you. I can!"

As Bill moved toward Merv to kiss him, Merv stepped out of the way. "C'mon, buddy, I'm putting you to bed. We're not going to have sex. We're going to sleep. In the morning, let's forget this moment ever happened."

When morning came, Bill seemed embarrassed and did not press his case again. At the door, Merv kissed Bill good-bye after room service had served their breakfast. "We're friends, okay?"

"Okay," Bill said demurely, looking dejected.

"Bonded at the hip, right?" Merv asked.

"You got it," Bill said, hugging him one final time. "You'll call me when you get back to L.A. and tell me how that big party went."

"It's a promise."

Merv kept that promise and Bill never mentioned that night at the St. Francis ever again.

* * *

It was a night to remember as *tout* Hollywood gathered to pay homage to the self-styled "Gay Illiterate," Miss Louella Parsons. Merv had sung to movie stars before at the Cocoanut Grove, but never to such an assemblage. There "were more stars at the party than there are in heaven," press reports the next day proclaimed, parodying the words of Louis B. Mayer.

The gala was a private, invitation-only party held at the Grove. Merv had never met Louella and was terrified of her, knowing that a bad review of his singing tonight could jeopardize his hopes for a career in movie musicals. He was shocked to learn that one of the waiters had been instructed to place a rubber cushion under Louella's seat. When she got excited or agitated, she was known to wet her panties.

From behind the curtains Merv peeked out when word spread that Louella had entered the ballroom on the arm of the press baron, William Randolph Hearst, who was accompanied by his mistress, Marion Davies. For the occasion, Louella had swathed her corpulent body in black silk, whereas Marion was in white satin and sable. As for Hearst, he looked at least eighty-five years old and near the grave.

Freddy Martin had told Merv that Marion and Louella used to be "as close as sisters." But that was a long time ago. Somewhere along the way, Louella and Marion decided that they didn't like each other, but were forced into a position of keeping up appearances.

Marion had turned on Louella long ago when she learned that the columnist was a spy, reporting on her nocturnal activities with the likes of Charlie Chaplin or Clark Gable.

As the guest of honor, Louella sent word backstage to Freddy and Merv that she wanted to hear the song that was playing when she first arrived at the Cocoanut Grove in the 1920s. The band was playing "Yes, Sir, That's My Baby." Both men knew the song well and were glad to oblige.

Merv sang all his hits that night, including the Coconuts song, and each number was met with appreciative—not wild—applause. The biggest disapproval came from Hearst himself. One of the waiters overheard him telling Marion and Louella that Sinatra, not Merv, should have been booked for such an august occasion.

Marion shot back. "Frank's a has-been! World War II is over, duckie."

Even so, after his numbers, Merv went to their table to greet the honored guests. Hearst shook his hand firmly; Marion told him he "sang really nice," and Louella gushed that "you're going to be the biggest musical star in pictures."

Every evening has its embarrassments, and this gala was marred by Marion herself, who had obviously had too much champagne, thereby incurring the wrath of Hearst.

When Earl Warren, then governor of California (later U.S. Supreme Court Justice), rose to speak, he heaped more praise on Louella than she'd ever heard in her life. On and on he went, until Marion screamed at the stage. "Oh, sit down Earl and shut up! Enough ass-kissing for one evening." When Warren ignored her and kept on speaking, she cat-called to him again. "Bring on Freddy Martin," she shouted. "For God's sake, Earl, Willie and I made you the governor of California, and we can unmake you too."

Finally, the governor brought a quick end to his speech. By that time, Hearst had ordered two burly waiters to escort Marion from the Grove and into a waiting limousine to speed her on her way back to San Simeon.

The "gay illiterate,"
gossip maven
Louella Parsons

Back in New York, Merv achieved one of his dreams by singing at the fabled Starlight Roof of the Waldorf-Astoria. He was still with Freddy Martin's band, but each day he thought of breaking away and doing solo gigs. He was getting tired of being referred to as "the boy singer" with Freddy Martin's orchestra. On his opening night, Margaret Truman, the president's daughter, attended the club and was impressed with Merv's singing.

When she was invited to appear on "The Big Show," NBC's top radio show in America, she mentioned to its hostess, Tallulah Bankhead, that she should have Merv on her show to sing.

Perhaps as a favor to Margaret, Tallulah called Merv the next day. Back in those days, the diva actually made some of her own phone calls. When Merv came on the phone, she said to him, "I don't need to tell you who I am, dah-ling. The whole word knows my voice. Of course, I must admit that female impersonators do it better than your old Auntie Tallu."

He would later tell his friends, "Tallulah's voice had more timber than the Yellowstone National Park."

"It's an honor to talk to you, Miss Bankhead. I think I know why you're calling me, and I'm doubly honored."

"I'm calling to ask you a very specific question, and I don't want you to lie to me like all other men have done. I have a way of getting the truth out of men in such matters. Dah-ling, forgive me, but just how big is your cock?"

He was completely flabbergasted and didn't know what to say. His embarrassment made her cackle into the phone. "Actually, dah-ling, I want you to sing on 'The Big Show' tomorrow. A lousy singer herself, Margaret Truman, told me you were divine."

With that introduction, Miss Tallulah Bankhead of Alabama became a permanent fixture in Merv's life.

* * *

The radio variety program, "The Big Show," which began a two-year run on November 5, 1950, was NBC's attempt to save talk radio from the onslaught of television. With Tallulah as its hostess, it became a Sunday night feature across America. The show had superior scripting, but what gave it "a big bang" was Tallulah's notorious wit and ad-libbing.

In immodestly assessing her own success, Tallulah proclaimed, "I snatched radio out of the grave. The autopsy was delayed."

Merv was honored to join all the big names she'd had on the show, including Gary Cooper, Bob Hope, Gloria Swanson, Ella Fitzgerald, Frank Sinatra, and Louis Armstrong.

At the time of his first meeting with Tallulah, she was front-page news around the country. Not only was she the new "Queen of Radio," she was involved in a sensational trial that generated as much press and interest as the O.J. Simpson murder trial would in years to come.

Tallulah had sued her maid, Evelyn Cronin, a former burlesque dancer, for adding too many zeros to too many of her personal checks. The trial, before Harold Stevens, the first black man to sit on a General Sessions Bench, received more newspaper coverage than the ceasefire negotiations for the war in Korea.

Cronin's lawyer, Brooklyn senator Fred G. Morritt, played dirty, turning the embezzlement case into a personal attack on Tallulah, claiming she'd bought "booze, drugs, and sex."

"I've never had to stoop that low," Tallulah said. The charges against her were so vitriolic that she claimed, "The next thing you'll hear from the defense is that I have been vivisecting my fucking dogs!"

In spite of the many personal smears on her character, Tallulah would win the case. Cronin was found guilty on three counts of grand larceny and was given a one- to two-year prison sentence. The sentence was later suspended.

Fresh from court, where she'd been accused of being an excessive marijuana smoker, Tallulah was an hour late for rehearsals at NBC. Attired in a full-length mink coat for which she'd paid $2,000, she leisurely strolled into the rehearsal hall walking like Jeanette MacDonald in *Naughty Marietta*.

Meredith Willson was there rehearsing the NBC Orchestra, with 97 musicians. The music stopped and all eyes turned to look at Tallulah who sized up each man one by one. "Any of you cocksuckers got a reefer?" she asked. The boys in the band burst into hysterical laughter as she suddenly changed her movements. Instead of a demure Jeanette, she shimmied off the stage like the burlesque dancer, Gypsy Rose Lee, doing a mock striptease with her mink.

She walked into a room where Merv sat with the upcoming guests on "The Big Show." The cast included Ethel Merman, Phil Silvers, and Loretta Young. Rising to his feet, Merv attempted to introduce himself and shake Tallulah's hand.

Instead of a handshake, Tallulah gave Merv a big, sloppy wet kiss with tongue before seating herself at the head of the table. She didn't speak to the other guests slated to be on her show, but eyed each of them skeptically. It was obvious to Merv that she knew all of them very well, even their darkest secrets.

After surveying the table, she said, "What a motley crew. Not a virgin here." She cackled at her own appraisal.

She reached for Phil's hand and fondled it gingerly before kissing it as if it were the Pope's ring. "I love Phil dearly even though he's a manic-depressive and a compulsive gambler," she said. "We were once together in Las Vegas, and he told me he was broke and had no money to pay his bills. But to pay for our drinks, he pulled out a large wad of bills that would have choked the most sword-swallowing of cocksuckers. I said, 'Why don't you use that money to pay your fucking bills?' He told me he couldn't because that wad was his gambling money."

She abruptly dropped his hand as a harsh frown came across her face. "Why should I have all my sins published on every front page in America? I'm sure all of you do ghastlier things than my drunken brain could conjure up. Take Phil for example. Everybody in show business knows he gets off by going to men's rooms to watch guys urinate."

"Tallulah," he said, "you've got my number." He said that with a smile and didn't seem offended at her revelation, which had shocked Merv. "I may indulge here and there but I never invited three actors back to my suite where I stripped nude, got into a bathtub, and invited them to piss on me," he said, staring at Tallulah.

"*Touché*, darling," Tallulah said before turning to Ethel. "Ethel here licks more pussy from Broadway chorus gals than Flo Ziegfeld himself. George and Ira Gershwin sure knew what they were doing when they cast you in *Girl Crazy*. *Dah-ling*, you were never big on brains, but Judy Garland told me you give great head."

The final days
of the Golden Age of Radio:
Alabama spitfire **Miss Tallulah Bankhand**
emcees *The Big Show*

Without missing a beat, Ethel shot back, "Hattie McDaniel told me you were awful at it."

"Mammy was right. I almost suffocated when she locked those fat, black legs around me. A real death grip."

Throughout the exchange, Ethel, a voracious eater of peanut brittle, chewed away at her favorite snack. "Just for all that, I'm going to sing 'I Got Rhythm' on your show with a mouth full of peanut brittle." She lived up to her threat. Later

93

on the show, even with a mouth full, she managed to hold the high C note for a full sixteen bars.

At last Tallulah's attention focused on Merv. "Merv is too much an innocent for me to turn on him and tell you good folks what I learned that he does with his mouth when he's not warbling 'Coconuts.'" He flushed red with embarrassment.

Tallulah instinctively knew that such tough show business pros as Ethel and Phil could easily handle her provocative banter. She saved her final victim for last, knowing Loretta would be the tastiest morsel to be devoured at the table. She moved toward Loretta like a *Tyrannosaurus rex* returned to Earth to devour a juicy water buffalo.

"Now take Gretchen here," Tallulah said. Between 1917 and 1928, Loretta here appeared in pictures as Gretchen Young. "This WAMPAS Baby Star eloped when she turned thirteen. She was broken in earlier than any of us."

"I was seventeen," Loretta protested.

"All I know is that you appeared with your young husband, Grant Withers, in a movie ironically called *Too Young to Marry*. My sins are paraded in front of the press. But you cover up your dark deeds, like getting impregnated by Clark Gable when you two lovebirds made *The Call of the Wild*, and then later pretending to adopt the kid with the big ears she inherited from Gable."

"Oh, please," Loretta protested. "That was a mortal sin. Don't mock me for what I did. In an entire lifetime, I made one mistake. Otherwise, I've never betrayed any of my husbands, unlike you who could never be faithful to anybody. You should be ashamed of yourself. I read the newspapers. I know what you've been doing."

"Don't you dare lecture me on morality, you sickeningly sweet little phony. That's bullshit. You were unfaithful to all your husbands. Just ask George Brent, Louis Calhern, Douglas Fairbanks Jr., Norman Foster, Richard Greene, Wayne Morris, David Niven, Tyrone Power, Gilbert Roland, James Stewart, Spencer Tracy, and Darryl Zanuck. Dare I mention my own beloved Jock Whitney? He personally told me that the reason he broke from you was your demand that he perform anilingus on you?"

"I can't take this any more." Loretta rose to her feet and rushed from the room.

Tallulah got up and walked over to the chair vacated a moment ago by Loretta. "No one must sit here. It still has the mark of the cross on it."

She turned to Merv. "Better go and look after her before she jumps out of a building or something."

Unknown to Tallulah, Merv was relieved when she commanded him to go look after Loretta. It had already been agreed that after the rehearsal run-through, he was to escort Loretta to Fulton Sheen's suite for a dinner engagement. He found her in the hall weeping and tried to console her. After she went to the women's room to make emergency repairs to her face, he took her downstairs and hailed a taxi.

En route to the dinner with Sheen, neither Loretta nor Merv spoke of Tallulah but talked about their joint admiration for Sheen. At the bishop's apartment, Loretta requested that she meet privately in Sheen's study because she needed counseling after that attack from Tallulah.

A servant ushered Merv into the living room where he introduced himself to Irene Dunne sitting on a sofa.

"Miss Dunne," he said. "I'm honored to meet you. I can't believe how the Academy hasn't given you an Oscar. Nominated five times and no award. You deserved all five Oscars. What a shame!"

"It doesn't bother me a bit," she said. "I do not have the terrifying ambition of other actresses—take Joan Crawford for instance. I drifted into acting and one day I'll just drift out. Acting is not everything. Living is."

For the next thirty minutes, Merv chatted with Irene, finding her one of the warmest persons he'd ever met in show business. She was the complete opposite of Tallulah. He learned that they shared some of the same background, as she too had taken piano and voice lessons and sang in local churches and high school plays.

By the time Sheen emerged with Loretta, Merv felt he'd formed a warm bond with Irene. Sheen walked into the room and shook Merv's hand, avoiding his usual embrace.

When he surveyed the finery worn by both Irene and Loretta, Sheen changed plans. Suddenly, he didn't think it appropriate that he be seen at Twenty-One, having dinner with such gorgeous and spectacularly dressed actresses. "People might get the wrong impression." Sheen seemed to forget that he was also spectacularly dressed--right down to his red alligator shoes.

At 7:50pm, Sheen arose from his seat at the table and announced that the party was over. He always did this with his guests to get his sleep before beginning another nineteen-hour day. On the way out, Sheen whispered something to Merv. After he'd taken Loretta and Irene back to their hotel, Merv returned at 8:45pm and was ushered into Sheen's apartment. What happened between them that night is not known.

Merv was only mildly surprised when Loretta the following day showed up for her scheduled appearance on "The Big Show." On air, she and Tallulah, being the pros they were, greeted each other like longtime friends. No mention was ever made of Tallulah's drunken episode.

When Merv sang on the show, he was given another wet, sloppy kiss with tongue from Tallulah. "You were just divine, dah-ling," Tallulah announced to millions of Americans. "Let's all give a big hand to the next major singing sensation of America. Merv Griffin. Remember that name, dah-lings."

When Merv encountered Irene in 1957, president Dwight Eisenhower had appointed her one of five alternative U.S. delegates to the United Nations, recognizing her charitable works and her interest in conservative Catholic and Republican causes. She spoken to him of how important "keeping up appearances" was to Sheen.

She claimed that an angry husband had discovered a photograph of his wife, dressed only in a pair of shorts, getting into Sheen's car. The husband proclaimed to all who would listen that the monsignor was having an affair with his wife. "No one believed him," Irene said, "but our dear friend never set foot in Beverly Hills again until the husband died."

Years later Merv was asked to comment on Tallulah and "The Big Show." "It was big—the biggest thing on radio—but not big enough to kill TV. After all, TV had moving pictures and was free if you owned a set. I entered the Big Band era when it was dying. Tallulah entered radio in its dying gasps. Her Big Show was variety radio's last grand stand. Tallulah never had such a perfect forum to show her innate brightness and a razor-sharp wit that could make a Bob Hope sound like a dull carnival barker. If radio audiences wanted the best in grown-up entertainment in those days, they could always bank on Bankhead. I was honored to be a part of it."

* * *

In December of 1950 Merv found himself back in San Francisco with family and friends. Once again he was the boy singer with Freddy's band at the St. Francis.

As a special tribute to his increasing fame, Mayor Carrol M. Spears, along with 250 other citizens of San Mateo, drove to San Francisco and threw a gala in honor of Merv in the Mural Room of the hotel. Merv was given a gold key to the city, honoring the hometown boy who had made good.

Right after Christmas, Merv was in San Mateo at the Mills Memorial Hospital having his tonsils removed. He feared the operation would forever damage his singing voice, but, of course, that never happened.

As soon as he recovered, he drove to Los Angeles to make his motion picture debut in *Music by Martin*, a sixteen-minute short for Universal-International. Shot in only one day, the film did nothing to launch Merv into a movie career, centering mostly on Freddy and the boys in his band. Within the context of the short, Merv sang "Tenement Symphony," not one of his best numbers.

One night in Hollywood, as Merv returned to the Roosevelt Hotel, he was surprised to encounter Tom Drake, wearing sunglasses, waiting for him in the lobby. He looked as boyishly handsome as ever. He hadn't seen Tom since that night he first met him at the Cocoanut Grove with Judy Garland and Peter Lawford.

Tom wanted to talk to Merv in private, so he invited him up to his small hotel suite.

When they were alone in the elevator, Tom removed his sunglasses to reveal bloodshot eyes. He'd been up all night crying over Peter, who had broken off their relationship.

In his suite, Merv offered Tom a drink, which he accepted as he poured out his undying love for the errant Peter, who liked to maintain many relationships simultaneously, including those with women.

Merv tried to pass it off as a lover's quarrel, reminding Tom that Judy Garland had told him that Peter had kicked him out many times previously, but had then repeatedly taken him back.

Tom admitted that was true, but claimed that what was different from before was that this time, a drunken Peter had turned violent, threatening to kill him if Tom didn't quit stalking him. He also claimed that Peter had been spending many of his nights with the troubled young actor, Robert Walker.

Merv, later relating details of the evening to Roddy McDowall and others, claimed that Peter was someone you had an affair with--not someone you fell in love with.

As Merv later revealed to Roddy McDowall, he tried to assure Tom that he was still young and attractive and still loved by many people. Merv pointed out that Tom, like Merv himself, even had fan clubs.

But Tom countered that his fan clubs had reached their peak at the end of World War II, and that the members of those clubs had tended to have gotten married and moved to the suburbs to raise children.

Merv invited Tom to spend a few days with him at his hotel, where he would offer him comfort and friendship. He later claimed that he and Tom shared the same bed together, but Merv was doing so only as a means of offering comfort. He assured Roddy that no sex had ever taken place between them. Tom was just too depressed for that. "All we did was cuddle," Merv told Roddy.

Sometime during their discussions, Tom extracted a promise from Merv that he would go and see Peter the following morning, and beg him to take Tom back.

Falling in love with
the boy next door,
Tom Drake

Keeping his promise to Tom, Merv called Peter Lawford. Peter had been staying at Robert Walker's house, and he invited Merv to come over. All of Hollywood was gossiping about Peter's relationship with Robert, an emotionally unstable actor, and Peter's simultaneous affair with Lana Turner.

Robert had been married to Jennifer Jones, his costar in the 1944 *Since You Went Away*, until David O. Selznick stole her away. Robert later married Barbara Ford, daughter of director John Ford. When Peter was with Lana, Robert was said to be moving from bed to bed—Nancy Davis (Reagan), Ava Gardner, and Judy Garland herself, among his conquests.

Privately Merv had told Roddy that he envied the bisexual lifestyle of Robert and Peter and wished he could live as they did, but he could not bring himself to get sexually involved with a woman.

When Merv drove up to Robert's house and rang the doorbell, there was no answer. He spotted a note tacked onto the mailbox. It was from Peter, telling him that he and Robert had gone for a ride in the Hollywood Hills and would be back soon. Merv was told to go around to the back of the house where Robert had left the door unlocked.

Merv entered the darkened house and plopped down on the sofa. The whole idea of talking to Peter about taking Tom back was a wildly foolish dream. With Robert and Lana in his stable, what did Peter need with Tom?

As Merv dozed off, he heard a sound. Bolting up, he was startled to see a nude woman emerging from the back bedroom. She was dripping wet from the shower and was obviously searching for a bath towel. Seeing Merv, she screamed and ran back into the bedroom, slamming the door behind her.

He'd seen her for only a moment, but immediately recognized her as Nancy Davis (Reagan). He'd met her at the Cocoanut Grove with Clark Gable. So, the rumor mill was correct. Nancy was said to be having an affair with Robert. Roddy had heard talk that Nancy, Robert, and Peter often enjoyed a three-way together. Could this be true? He suspected that it was.

Starlet, pinup, and future First Lady
Nancy Davis (Reagan)

The roaring of motorcycles in the driveway distracted Merv. He went outside to the graveled driveway near the garage where he saw Peter and Robert pull into the yard while mounted on their bikes. In spite of the hot weather, both actors were clad in black leather jackets.

Merv had heard that Peter rode his Enfield to MGM every morning until Louis B. Mayer put a stop to it, after the press reported that Robert had had a minor accident on his motorcycle. "I have no roles for movie stars with broken necks," Mayer warned Peter.

When Robert invited Peter into his house, Merv wondered if Nancy would appear again. She never did. Merv suspected that she'd dressed hurriedly and fled through the front door when Merv went out to greet Peter and Robert. He never mentioned to Robert that he'd seen her.

At this point Merv still didn't know Peter very well, and had never seen him sober. Without the booze, he found him even more attractive than his 1930s idol, Errol Flynn. When Robert excused himself to take a shower, Peter stripped down to his underwear because the afternoon sun had made the living room very hot.

Merv appraised his tight physique which was hardly that of a bodybuilder but which was extremely sexy and appealing. His smile was one of the most dazzling of all the leading men in Hollywood, especially on that still boyish face of his. It was his sharp wit, his ever so polite demeanor, and that divine London accent of his that added to his almost irresistible charm. Little wonder that everyone from Noel Coward to Rita Hayworth had fallen for him.

Robert went to take a shower, as Peter watched him retreat. When he was out of hearing range, Peter asked, "Can you believe it? My two best friends are Robert Walker and Judy Garland. They view me as the steadying influence in their lives. No one except those two dears think I have a grip on reality. The fact that they turn to me for emotional support shows just how fucked up they are."

While Robert was away, Merv decided to accomplish his mission and get it over with. "Tom's heart is broken," he said. "He wanted me to come and see you today. To plead with you to take him back."

"That's not going to happen," Peter said, the soft lines in his face becoming harsher. He made his way to the bar for a drink. With his impeccable manners, he asked Merv to join him. "I'll see Tom once, maybe twice, a week. He's got a great little dick, made more for sucking than fucking, and I love it. But that's all. I'm not in love with him. I'm not going to live with Tom in some rose-covered cottage. Tell him he'll either take me on my terms—or not at all."

Robert came out of the same bedroom door from which Nancy had emerged. He too was stark nude and looking for a towel. "God damn it, Peter, you used up all my clean towels."

"A trick I learned from Sinatra," Peter said. "He uses five big fluffy towels to dry himself on."

"You'd think a shrimp like that could manage with a T-towel," Robert said.

"It takes three towels just to dry his dick," Peter claimed.

Forgetting to eat, Robert and Peter wanted to talk the night away with the bottle. Merv would have preferred some food. After three drinks, he stopped and switched to club soda. Peter and Robert continued to walk to the bar. Each actor seemed to have an unlimited capacity for alcohol. As the evening waned, Peter seemed to retreat into a zombie state, but Robert kept talking and was amazingly candid about himself.

"I can't live with my problems," he told Merv. "That's why I turn to alcohol. It's my only escape." At one point he launched into an attack on Selznick. "He had an obsession with my wife. He wanted Jennifer at all costs. I couldn't stand against a man as powerful as he was."

Later in the evening, he broke into sobs. Merv moved over toward the sofa where he sat and tried to comfort him. "I've been unloved and unwanted ever since the day I was born," he admitted.

"The world loves and adores you," Merv assured him.

When Robert spoke of his early days working on a banana boat in Central America, Merv found that he had a heart-grabbing, little-boy-lost appeal.

He surprised Merv when he told him that he was playing a homicidal homosexual in Alfred Hitchcock's *Strangers on a Train*, opposite Farley Granger. "Farley and I will know we're playing it homo, but only the hip ones in the audience will get it."

It was two o'clock that morning before Merv finally left Robert's house. Peter had already passed out.

Merv had an early rehearsal and suspected he'd wake up with a headache. At that point he didn't know if he'd continue to see Peter, Robert, or even Tom. All three men, especially Robert, seemed a little too self-destructive for him. He carried none of their baggage. In fact, Peter had told him, "You're the most happy-go-lucky guy I've ever met. Haven't you suffered? Don't you have any problems to drive you to drink?"

Actually, he didn't. His only dark secret was that he was a homosexual, but he seemed to be covering that up fairly well. At least he didn't plan to turn to drugs and alcohol to deal with his sexual preference. He was beginning to enjoy living in a secretive world and fooling the public. It made life more thrilling. He told Tom, "I owe the public a good performance, the best I can give them. I don't owe them a blueprint to my private life."

Merv was elated at what he viewed "as a really big break" when Freddy Martin told him that he'd signed Merv and his orchestra for a twenty-six gig, "The Hazel Bishop Show" in New York. The televised thirty-minute program would be aired on Wednesday nights at ten o'clock. Merv would appear live on the show as the boy singer.

In spite of his nationwide exposure, he later felt that the NBC feature did nothing to advance his singing or his film career, fearing listeners only tuned in to hear Freddy Martin and his orchestra. "Lawrence Welk did more with this type of show than we did," Merv later recalled.

The cosmetic queen, Hazel Bishop, was sponsoring the show, primarily to promote her new "lasting lipstick," which she advertised as "Won't smear off, won't rub off, won't kiss off." Merv was asked to do a commercial for the lipstick in front of a live audience. As pre-arranged, a beautiful girl came out in the middle of his song, ironically called "Never Been Kissed," and kissed him on the cheek.

Acting surprised, he reached for a white handkerchief to wipe off the lipstick. He was wearing a lot of makeup that night, and as he wiped his face a big gooey makeup stain appeared. In front of the black-and-white TV cameras, the stain photographed like a lipstick smear. Noting this, the audience burst into hysterical laughter which went on for two minutes. At the end, Merv claimed, "See, no lipstick smear!" His words were drowned out by more laughter.

It was his misfortune that night to encounter Hazel Bishop in the flesh backstage. She'd chosen this night of all nights to come to the studio to meet Merv and Freddy Martin for the first time. Merv later remembered Hazel "looking like a lesbian prison matron," not the beautiful lipstick beauty he'd imagined she'd be.

"You made a laughing stock out of me, Griffin," she charged. "You're fired. I'm telling Martin tonight to get another boy singer. Dick Haymes could have pulled that commercial off without a glitch."

"Just a minute!" he said. "It was an accident. A blooper. Okay, so your lipstick doesn't smear. Dishwashers in diners across the country are grateful to you for no more lipstick traces on coffee cups. But those samples you sent over to Freddy's band caused a lot of trouble. They gave the lipstick to their girlfriends or mothers, and it made their lips swell. They ended up

Merv with fag

101

with bee-stung lips like Mae Murray in those old silents."

She looked startled hearing his news, which astonished him. Surely some consumer had brought this to her attention before. She took his hand, all anger disappearing from her face. "Thank you, Merv, for telling me this. Don't tell another soul. I'll take care of it right away."

As she was leaving, he called after all. "Instead of lasting lipstick, why not kissable lipstick?"

That very night the chemist went back to her lab and isolated the ingredient causing the skin irritations. She forgot all about firing Merv, and he was able to finish his gig.

Her no-smear lipstick became the foundation for a multi-billion cosmetic conglomerate.

When she next encountered Merv in Los Angeles in 1955, she greeted him with a smile. "That year I met you, I took in $49,527 from my lipstick. In no time at all, I was raking in ten million a year. You were so right about that flaw."

On The Hazel Bishop Show, Merv made many close friends, who would later go on to hit it big in the entertainment industry. He was so warm and outgoing with people that he was almost universally liked. His capacity for friendship with people in all walks of life seemed almost limitless. In time, he became as close to women friends as he did to his straight male pals.

The director of the NBC show was Perry Lafferty, who in the 1970s created such hit TV shows as "All in the Family" and "M*A*S*H." For eleven years he would be head of West Coast programming for CBS, earning the studio number one ratings with such hits as "The Mary Tyler Moore Show" or "The Waltons."

In September 2005 when Merv sent flowers to Perry's funeral, he said that he had done more to awaken him to the possibilities of television than any other person in the business. "I was still day-dreaming about becoming a movie star when I met Perry," Merv said. "But he knew the future was on the small screen—not the big screen. When I failed many times in my early days in TV, I turned to him like a father confessor. He told me never to give up, that I'd be big one day in television. And so it came to be."

"Perry battled with censors most of his life, but he won out in the end," Merv said. "His 1985 *An Early Frost* won an Emmy for a TV movie. The brass had told him that straight America wasn't ready for a realistic drama about AIDS—one that wasn't a fucking lecture on morality—and Perry proved them wrong. Of course, he had to take that teleplay through a dozen rewrites. He was a pioneer of television, a real Renaissance man, and I loved him dearly."

Merv also became friends with Arthur Penn, the front stage manager. After making a name for himself as a director of quality TV films, Penn scored with such big-time movies as *The Miracle Worker* in 1962 and *Bonnie and Clyde* in 1967.

Bill Colleran, the backstage manager, also bonded with Merv during the gig. After working with Merv, he became associate director of "Your Hit Parade," a weekly TV variety show, and he also directed specials for Frank Sinatra and Bing Crosby, and was executive producer of "The Judy Garland Show."

Bill would later marry the actress Lee Remick in 1957. When their daughter, Kate, was born, Merv was asked to become the godfather. He would remain friends with Bill and Lee for life, even after their divorce. He faithfully called her with congratulations after her hits such as *Anatomy of a Murder* in 1959 and *Days of Wine and Roses* in 1962.

It was early in 1991 that he called on her for one last time, not recognizing her at first because her face was so bloated by chemo treatments. They spoke of the many good times they'd had together, often with such mutual friends as Robert and John F. Kennedy. He was startled that she was still even talking about a possible comeback in films. "I make movies for grownups. When Hollywood starts making that kind of film again, I'll start acting in them again."

After leaving her that cold afternoon in Los Angeles, he kissed her forehead. "Good night, sweet princess."

Her final words were, "Baby, the Rain Must Fall," a reference to a film she'd made in 1965. She died that July.

* * *

While appearing in New York, Merv picked up the phone to hear a famously seductive voice, even though it was coming from the throat of a teenager. "You said you wanted to date me," she said. "Well, big boy, hop to it."

It was Elizabeth Taylor. She'd introduced him to his only really serious girlfriend up to now, Judy Balaban, and Elizabeth must have heard that their so-called romance was over.

Breaking from the domination of her parents, a rebellious Elizabeth was in New York for her first extended stay. It was a city to which she would journey for the rest of her life.

When Merv arrived at Elizabeth's hotel suite, he brought her three dozen long-stemmed yellow roses. After smelling the flowers with that regal nose of hers, she kissed him. "How could you have known they're my favorites?" Smiling, she answered her own question. "How smart of you. You called Roddy McDowall."

It was a new and provocatively different Elizabeth Taylor he encountered that night. She was no longer the beautiful young girl he'd met at Roddy's party in Los Angeles. While still in grade school, she'd made *The Conspirator* with the bisexual actor, Robert Taylor. Rumor had it that she'd given him such a raging hard-on that he had to be shot from the waist up in their scenes together.

It took him a while to adjust to her new look. No longer did she depend on her beautiful face and those violet eyes to get her across the threshold of Hollywood. She was dressed seductively with a plunging *décolletage*. "Let's go dancing," she said. "I love to dance. Let's dance the night away."

At the Stork Club, she danced with him through three numbers before the orchestra took a break. At table he ordered champagne. If the waiter might have had any concern that she was too young to drink, he did not reveal that. As they talked, he admired the way she could speak candidly about herself, as if "Elizabeth Taylor" were a product she was selling to the public, not the actual person who sat before him.

She confided to him that the master portrait photographer, Philippe Halsman, had told her, "You've got tits, gal. 'Bout time you started cashing in on them."

"After just one session with him," she said, "I suddenly learned to become sultry like Ava Gardner and Lana Turner. I even know how to pose like Marilyn Monroe even though I don't feel the need to show my pussy. Incidentally, I like Ava and Lana. Can't stand Marilyn. Who does that slut think she is?"

At table, Elizabeth seemed self-enchanted. She kept turning one side of her face to him, then the other. "Philippe claims my left side photographs more mature than my right side which makes me look like a little girl. *Still*. What do you think?"

"Both sides look gorgeous to me," Merv said to reassure her. "I think Philippe is full of shit." One aspect of her body disturbed him, but he said nothing. For the first time, he noticed that her bare arms were peppered with tiny black hairs. It was unsightly and distracted from her otherwise stunning beauty, but he was certain that many makeup artists in her future would call this to her attention, with remedies of how to rectify it.

The occupants of the other tables couldn't stop staring at Elizabeth, who seemed to tune them out until she got up to go to the women's room. Then she was trailed by a retinue of adoring fans. Back at table she giggled and whispered to Merv, "I think the rubberneckers wanted to see me take a piss."

Several hours later, at the door to her hotel suite, Elizabeth kissed Merv gently on the lips but didn't invite him to come in, much to his relief. The following night he took her for dinner at Twenty-One. In the middle of the meal,

Clark Gable walked in with his new wife, Lady Sylvia Ashley, a willowy blonde with a peaches-and-cream complexion and Wedgwood blue eyes.

Nancy Davis (later Nancy Reagan) had failed to get Clark to marry her. Lady Sylvia pointedly ignored Elizabeth even though introduced. Clark shook Merv's hand, remembering him from the Cocoanut Grove, before leaning over and kissing Elizabeth on the cheek. The newlyweds departed quickly to their own table.

"I've had a crush on Clark for years," Elizabeth confided. "If he wants to take my virginity, he's welcome to it. Now that's a real movie star. That kiss on my cheek made me shiver."

"What did you think of Lady Sylvia?" he asked, eager for her response.

"That gold-digging bitch. I heard she got her start modeling bras and bloomers. You know, she was once a chorus girl in the seediest clubs in London's Soho."

That night, back in front of the door to her hotel suite, Elizabeth did invite Merv in for a nightcap, but for no other reason than to continue their talk. "I'm thinking about getting married."

"Well, I'm an available candidate," he said, not at all seriously.

She looked at him lovingly and smiled, showing more far wisdom about human nature than a teenager might possess. "Oh, Merv, let's not kid ourselves. You and I will always be friends, not lovers, and you know that better than I do." She quickly changed the subject. "For me, it's college or marriage. I've got to escape from my parents. Personally, I think marriage would be more fun than college."

"Who's the lucky guy?"

"I have five candidates in mind," she said. "I know I can take Bob Taylor from Barbara Stanwyck. She's a dyke anyway. I'm sure I can lure Clark away from that Ashley creature. But I've got other candidates in mind."

"C'mon," he said. "Tell me."

"You'll read about it in the papers," she said. "Now I've got to get my beauty sleep. Night, love, and thanks for a darling evening. You're sweet."

* * *

Without any particular malice toward Elizabeth, and with no harm intended to her, Merv became the source of the rumors going around Los Angeles and New York that he was having an affair with the young star. Throughout his life, he went to great trouble, including outright lies, to establish heterosexual credentials. Since he was seen dating Elizabeth at both the Stork Club and Twenty One, he felt here was a golden opportunity for him to get some straight publicity, even if nothing appeared in the papers, although Walter Winchell ran an item.

"In those days," Merv later said, "there wasn't a cockroach that walked across the floor of the Stork Room without getting Winchell's permission.

As was inevitable, those *faux* romance rumors eventually reached Nicky Hilton, son of Texas hotel magnate Conrad Hilton, whom the newspapers had dubbed "the man with 100,000 beds."

Widely known as a playboy and womanizer, Nicky had replaced Glenn Davis, the centerpiece of Elizabeth's summer of 1948 romance. Glenn, a West Point football star and Heisman Trophy winner, had been shipped off to the Korean front, and Nicky—after being introduced to her by Peter Lawford, had moved in to replace him.

Merv wanted all the gossipy news he could get about Nicky, and naturally he turned to his friends, Peter Lawford and Roddy McDowall. "From what I've seen of Nicky's pictures, he has a real animal magnetism about him," Merv told Roddy. "He's more than six feet tall and good looking, not to mention rich. I saw a picture of him in a bathing suit. Broad shoulders. Swimmer's waist. I couldn't believe the bulge. Too bad he's straight."

"Yeah," Roddy said sarcastically. "So straight he lets boys suck on that beer can dick of his. I hear it's not just thick but nearly a foot long."

"Is that just a rumor?" Merv said. "You know how the boys exaggerate."

"Why don't you call Peter Lawford and check it out for yourself?" Roddy advised. "He knows a lot more about Nicky Hilton than I do."

Merv did just that, learning that Peter regularly supplied Nicky with a steady stream of beautiful starlets, hoping to make it big in the movies. "He returns the favor by letting me go down on that tree trunk of his," Peter said. "He goes deep down the throat. I kid him and call him 'Deep Throat.'" Without knowing it, Peter had hit upon the name of what would eventually be the world's most famous porno flick, which would be filmed years later.

Both Peter and Roddy believed that Elizabeth should not marry Nicky. They knew too much about him. They didn't want to say anything bad about Nicky, at least for the moment, based on their fear of offending her.

Known for his volatile temper, a jealous Nicky had decided to confront Merv

Hotel heir **Nicky Hilton** with his wife, **Elizabeth Taylor**

upon his return to Los Angeles. Earlier at his hotel Merv had called down for room service. When he heard a knock on his door, thinking that it was a waiter carrying his dinner, he opened the door only to discover Nicky standing there, with bitterness and anger on his face. His clothes were rumpled from a night of heavy drinking.

Not knowing what to do, Merv invited him inside, guiding him to the sofa. "I'm sure he came to clobber me, but in that condition, he couldn't harm a fly," Merv told Roddy the next day. "He passed out right on my sofa. When dinner came, I enjoyed it while taking in the beauty of this man."

Merv later confided to Roddy that to make Nicky more comfortable, he had pulled off all his clothes—"yes, even his underwear. Peter had not exaggerated. It was the most impressive I've ever seen. I spent the night working it over while he slept it off. But it wasn't until ten o'clock the next morning that he woke up with a hard-on and gave me what I'd worked for for so long."

Around noon, when he was leaving, Nicky turned and smiled at Merv. "I'd heard that you were a fairy. Elizabeth always seems to gravitate toward fairies—take that Monty Clift, for instance."

The next day Merv called Elizabeth but didn't mention that he'd met her future husband. She tried to explain her reasons for marrying Nicky. Merv noted that at no point did she mention love.

"I love jewelry," she said. "Nicky's rich or at least his daddy is. His father gives him a new car whenever he wants one, even a private airplane. I bet Nicky can persuade his father to buy me all the jewelry I want."

No longer viewing Merv as competition, Nicky called him two weeks later and invited himself over. It was the beginning of a friendship that brought nothing but trouble. As attracted as Merv was to Nicky, he also experienced his dark side.

He was an extravagant gambler, never minding losing a fortune at a table in Las Vegas. But that wasn't the worst of it. He was not only an alcoholic—everybody who knew him knew that—but he was a secret heroin addict, as Merv discovered one night to his horror when he went into his bathroom to discover Nicky shooting up.

For Merv, getting acquainted with Nicky's fabulous endowment came at a price. "When he's sober, which is rare, he's a warm and generous person," Merv confided in Roddy. "But on liquor and drugs he turns violent. He's also quite a racist, ranting about 'kikes' and 'niggers' all the time. One night when he was sleeping over, he woke up and for no reason at all beat the shit out of me. I was black and blue for days. He didn't remember it the next morning."

On another night when Merv was staying at Roddy's house when the actor was out of town, Nicky pulled up around midnight in his black Cadillac convertible. Merv had never seen him this wild. Nicky carried a loaded .38

revolver. For fun, he began shooting out Roddy's lights until Merv wrestled the gun from his drunken hand.

When Roddy returned to Los Angeles, a check was waiting from Conrad Hilton to pay for the damage, with a suggestion that "It might be best for all parties to keep this out of the papers."

Seated in Roddy's living room that Merv had cleaned up, both men tried a little dime store psychology as it applied to Nicky. "He knows he'll never live up to his father's success, and his ego has been seriously battered," Merv said. "He's got to prove his masculinity every day of his life, not just with women, but sometimes with men. I think it builds up his self-esteem to have the boys worship that fabulous cock of his."

"Maybe it makes him a bigger man than he already is," Roddy said, surveying his living room. "But, for God's sake, don't invite him back here. Poor Elizabeth. What hell is she in for?" Should we warn her about him?"

"You can't tell a girl like Elizabeth what to do," Merv said. "She'll find out for herself. I have a feeling Nicky will be just the beginning of several husbands, all of them disasters."

"That's the curse of all of us who like men," Roddy said.

"Let's face it," Merv said. "They put us through hell, but we can't keep our hands off them."

"Proceed with caution," Roddy warned Merv. "Nicky sure must be attracted to those blow-jobs of yours. You are good."

"It's more than that," Merv said. "Nicky says I fry the best hamburger with onions in Los Angeles."

Even before his marriage to Elizabeth, Nicky on many a drunken night shared some dark secrets with Merv. He confessed one night of having had a long affair with his father's wife, Zsa Zsa Gabor. The duration of his affair with Zsa Zsa extended not only throughout the star's marriage to Conrad, but continued during her marriage to George Sanders and then into the period of Nicky's betrothal to Elizabeth Taylor.

Of course, at that time in his life, Merv's friendship with the Gabor sisters, both Zsa Zsa and especially Eva, lay far away in his own future.

* * *

For Merv, the 1950s looked like it was going to be his decade, as some of his friends had already predicted. Almost nightly someone he knew, including Ann Sothern, kept predicting he was going to make it big in show business.

Freddy Martin still wanted to retain Merv as his boy singer, and their appearances together at the Roosevelt Hotel in Los Angeles were usually sold out, in spite of the fact that each year the big bands of the 1940s waned in popularity.

With an RCA Victor recording contract in his pocket, Merv knew he needed another "Coconuts" song, a really big hit, but so far that had eluded him. One night he told Judy Garland, "I want to find my own version of 'Over the Rainbow.' Not some silly ditty like 'Coconuts.' A real romantic ballad that fans will request I sing every time I make an appearance."

Despite the fact that a hit song simply didn't materialize, more and more job offers were pouring in for Merv, and he accepted quite a few of them, even though he knew Freddy resented it when he did a freelance solo gig.

With all the excitement going on in his personal life and with his career, Merv almost forgot that there was a war raging in Korea. Many Americans blamed President Harry S. Truman for the conflict, and he was at the lowest popularity of his political career.

Simultaneous with the growth of Merv's popularity as an entertainer, his relationship with Tom Drake had graduated from the cuddly stage into something serious. Merv had flown with Tom to New York, and was sharing his hotel suite with him. While the handsome actor still slept, Merv got up before him and headed for the kitchen to make his morning cup of coffee. On the table lay the mail which the bellhop had already brought up.

One letter caught his eyes. Tearing open the envelope, he read greetings from Uncle Sam. He was being called up for the draft. He'd already transferred his records from San Mateo to New York. An awful sinking feeling overcame him. Even his beloved morning cup of coffee felt like lead on his stomach.

He'd had all those physical examinations in San Francisco during the war, and had been rejected as a candidate for active service every time. But now, weighing eighty-five pounds less, he was an entirely different, and healthier, physical specimen. Intuitively, he knew there was no chance for a deferment.

Without even waiting for the results of his latest physical examination, he marched down to Freddy's suite in the same hotel and told him that he was quitting his job with the orchestra and going into the Army for two years. Freddy was bitterly disappointed at the news. "We've been together for four years," the orchestra leader said. "I was looking forward to at least another four."

"There's no way," Merv said. "I just know I'm going to ship out. I have gut feelings about such things."

When his time came to report, he splurged on a taxi and rode down to 39 Whitehall Street in Lower Manhattan with Tom, who had agreed to wait in a coffee shop nearby until the exam was over.

Once again, Merv had an Army doctor juggling his balls and examining him thoroughly. It was three o'clock that afternoon when he learned the news. "Your draft board in San Mateo fucked up," the burly doctor told him. "You're not supposed to be here. You're over the hill. Too old."

"I'm only twenty-seven," Merv protested.

"The law changed six months ago," the doctor said. "Twenty-six is our limit for inducting a guy. Now get out."

Tom was waiting outside the induction center and did a hop, skip, and a jump of joy on hearing the news. Merv seemed more disturbed than happy. "Where do I go now?" he asked. "With my tail between my legs back to Freddy begging for my old job back."

"Here's your chance to break out on your own," Tom said, "To become a really big star. You don't need Freddy and his boys any more. Fly back to Hollywood with me tomorrow. I just know you can make it really big in the movies."

Merv made up his mind not to go back to Freddy. When Freddy learned that his star wasn't going to be drafted after all, and wasn't coming back, he was furious. "God damn him!" he told the boys in his orchestra. "The fucker just used me. A step on the ladder. I even had plans to become his personal manager when his contract was up. By tomorrow I will have signed another singer. They're a dime a dozen."

Despite the fact that he had staged this grand play in front of his orchestra, Freddy met the next day with his lawyer to see if he should sue Merv. After all, Merv had signed a five-year contract with a year remaining on the life of the contract. Freddy discussed the matter with his lawyer, who advised him not to press ahead with legal action.

Almost gleefully, Merv announced to his agent that he was free to accept singing engagements. The agent promised he'd work on it, but had no gigs for him at the moment.

Merv was sad to see Tom go when he had to fly back to the West Coast for an acting job. Merv had grown quite attached to him, although he knew he wasn't in love with him. Tom truly lived up to his movie billing as "the boy next door." He was easy to be with, comfortable to talk to, and a nice companion at dinner. In bed, Tom lacked the fire and passion of Roddy McDowall or Rock Hudson, but who could compete with them?

Tom Drake

Every day Merv called his agent. Still no jobs. He grew lonelier than ever and considered returning soon to Los Angeles before all his money ran out in New York. He missed Tom and his other friends.

One afternoon he bought a corned beef sandwich and ate it in Central Park. Cut off from steady work night after night, he didn't know how to fill his day, much less his nights.

All that would change when he got back to his hotel. The phone was ringing. Picking up the receiver, he was surprised to hear the familiar voice of Judy Balaban, his former girlfriend. She still seemed grateful to him for having introduced her to the "love of my life," Jay Kanter. She was in New York by herself, and she wanted to meet Merv for dinner. He readily agreed, welcoming the company. As an afterthought, she added, "Oh, I'll be with a friend. You'll adore him." She paused awkwardly. "Of course, sometimes he's a bit strange."

* * *

The friend turned out to be the young actor, Nebraska-born Montgomery Clift, with whom Merv would launch one of the most mercurial love-hate relationships of his life. The actor was extraordinarily handsome and gifted, as he'd proved when he'd starred opposite Elizabeth Taylor and Shelley Winters in *A Place in the Sun* (1951). The media constantly compared him to Marlon Brando, often referring to both of them as "The Bad Boys of Hollywood." But as Merv got to know Monty better, he came to realize just how very different the two men were.

Ever since Merv had seen Monty in the 1948 *Red River*, starring John Wayne, Merv felt that Monty was the most powerful, sensitive, and magnetic actor on the screen.

When Merv met Monty, the actor had already been nominated for an Oscar for his moving portrayal of a young G.I. in the 1948 movie, *The Search*. His second Oscar nomination had come for *A Place in the Sun*.

When Judy introduced Merv and Monty at Daly's Restaurant on Lexington Avenue, Monty's reaction to Merv did not suggest the beginning of a beautiful friendship.

"You're hot, kid," Merv said, "Really hot."

Monty was drunk and hostile. He'd obviously been drinking all afternoon. "Oh, Merv Griffin. The band singer!" He didn't bother to disguise the contempt in his voice.

Monty was obviously enjoying the attention he was getting from the other diners. His face, even during that early period of his career, was known around the world.

There was a claim made that Merv and Monty engaged in a food fight before the dinner was over and that both of them were ushered out of the restaurant by the manager. In his memoirs, Merv claimed that he shoved Monty's face into a lemon meringue pie after Monty started licking the meringue off it. But that is not how others in the restaurant remembered the evening.

In spite of (or perhaps because of) the hostility that was percolating between them, the two young men bonded on some level. After hailing a taxi for Judy and kissing her good night, Merv received an invitation from Monty to go for a night ride through Manhattan in Monty's car.

Alarmed at how drunk Monty was, Merv offered to drive. Monty wouldn't hear of that. "Get the hell in," he ordered Merv.

Later Merv confided to Roddy McDowall, "He was just too appealing. I couldn't say no. In the first thirty seconds after Monty roared off, I knew I was in a death machine. I'd taken my life in my hands."

Speeding away into the night, Monty appeared demonic behind the wheel as he raced through the nearly deserted streets of Lower Manhattan, running every red light he could. Amazingly, there was no squad car around to give chase.

Finally, Monty slammed on the brakes, coming to a screeching halt near a darkened pier where a lone sailor near a warehouse was obviously getting a blow-job from an older man in a trench coat.

As Merv gazed into Monty's eyes, lit by a street lamp, he appeared almost sober for one brief moment. The actor's eyes looked exactly as they did in the closing reel of *A Place in the Sun* when he confronts Elizabeth Taylor for one last time. Without warning, Monty lunged toward Merv, grabbing him into a death-like grip and kissing him so violently he caused Merv's upper lip to bleed.

"I need you," Monty said, "Desperately. Don't ever leave me. I'll die if you leave me."

The next morning, Merv told Roddy, "After that kiss, I fell in love with Monty. Who wouldn't? After all, he was the most beautiful man on the planet."

* * *

Much to the disappointment of Tom Drake, Merv did not immediately return to Hollywood, but stayed in New York. He felt he had a better opportunity to pick up solo gigs as a singer on the East Coast than in

Self-loathing and unstable:
Montgomery Clift

California, where there were fewer bookings. He still toyed with the idea of becoming a big musical singing star like Gordon MacRae or Dennis Morgan, but temporarily postponed that goal.

Roddy McDowall called to ask him to share the rent at an apartment he'd sublet in the Dakota, New York's most fabled apartment house. In years to come, John Lennon would be assassinated on the sidewalk in front. Merv gladly accepted.

After success as a child star, Roddy had entered a difficult phase of his career. Even though he was in his early 20s, he photographed like a lanky teenager. To save his career, he'd moved to New York to pursue work on the stage.

When Roddy and Merv moved in together, it was commonly assumed within New York acting circles that they were lovers. This was partially true. Gay actor Monty Woolley, who had starred with Roddy in the 1942 film, *The Pied Piper*, and who had continued his contacts with him, said, "Merv and Roddy slept together when they could find no other partners."

One night when Merv had dinner with Roddy and Monty, Merv reminded the aging actor of his first encounter with him when as a kid he was rudely dismissed. In his candid, often astonishingly blunt fashion, Monty responded, "I'll make it up to you by sucking your cock tonight." Merv turned down the offer.

Later, with Roddy, Merv lamented how disappointed he was at the sex that had transpired the previous night with Montgomery Clift. "He's no Rock Hudson," Merv said. "To me, it looked like a little piece of foreskin. There wasn't much I could do with it."

"You forget you're talking to your mother," Roddy said. "I've been there, done that. But only once. In spite of all that male beauty, guys tend to go to bed with Monty only once."

"In some strange way, I'm fascinated by him," Merv said, "and I hope to hang out with him in the future. But I think I'll steer him away from the bed."

"Believe it or not, our beloved Elizabeth is madly in love with Monty for reasons known only to her," Roddy said. "Surely, it's not for the sex. After getting pounded by Nicky Hilton, I don't think she could even feel Monty down there. Anyway, she's coming back to New York and wants to call on you. She wants you to take her out to a few places. You'll get your picture taken with her. It'll cool down all those queer rumors about the two of us."

"I'd love to be her escort," Merv said. "But I certainly won't talk about Nicky Hilton to her. She must never unravel some of our little secrets."

"I'm sure that every day of her life she grows wiser about what men are capable of once the lights go out," Roddy said.

Merv surveyed their temporary apartment and liked what he saw. "Let's throw a party to welcome her to New York."

"Great! I'll arrange it."

"Hey, I've got an idea," Merv said. "I met this sweet kid at RCA Victor," Merv said. "Eddie Fisher. He's also under contract there. Real cute. Jewish. I bet Elizabeth will go for him. I also hear he's got a big dick. Maybe not as big as yours or Nicky Hilton's, but very, very respectable."

"Invite him too," Roddy said. "We'll be matchmakers."

"If Elizabeth doesn't go for Eddie, I'll make a play for him." He sighed. "But I hear he doesn't swing that way. Oh, well. Maybe in my case he'll make an exception."

"Don't get your hopes up," Roddy cautioned. "Stick to the fairies. You've got to get over your obsession with straight guys. It's such a difficult struggle to get laid if you date hetero."

* * *

When Merv escorted Elizabeth Taylor into Asti's Restaurant in Greenwich Village, she was arguably at the peak of her beauty. All heads turned and stared at her, conversation coming to an end, as the maître d' showed Merv and Elizabeth to a table. Asti's was an odd choice of a restaurant to take a movie star. The Italian waiters not only served you pasta "like momma made," but sang opera to you.

Elizabeth ordered ravioli and some other side dishes just to sample them, not finishing one complete plate. As she ate, she chatted about her failed marriage to Nicky Hilton. "He spent more time in bed with other women than he did with me," she lamented. Merv didn't tell her that a few of those nights had been spent with him.

He arranged tickets to the Broadway Theater where Mae West was appearing in a popularly priced revival of *Diamond Lil*, which she had written herself and had first performed in April of 1928. In his memoirs, Merv remembered the play as *Catherine the Great*, which Mae had brought to Broadway in 1944. Ironically, the producer of that play was the flamboyant showman, Mike Todd, who in years to come would marry Elizabeth.

As Merv entered with Elizabeth, even though the lights had dimmed and the curtain was about to go up, a murmur went up from the audience. Word spread quickly that Elizabeth Taylor had entered the theater and was being ushered to her seat. Only the opening of the curtain silenced the crowd.

All thoughts of Elizabeth vanished as a usually blasé New York audience greeted Mae's appearances with applause and huzzahs lasting five minutes. In this mixture of comedy and melodrama, Mae seemed to take delight in reviving her "classic," still getting laughs from such now-familiar lines as "I'm one of the finest women who ever walked the streets."

Reviewers still called the play "pure trash . . . or rather impure trash," but through it all the buxom, blonde Mae prevailed in her Gay Nineties garb. She was still maintaining her reputation as "the world's wickedest woman." Ironically, in years to come, Elizabeth herself would be dubbed as such in the hate press.

Out of courtesy, Merv and Elizabeth went backstage to pay their respects to the star of the show. She was engaged in a noisy fight with producer George Brandt, and was furious that some critic had written of the "dromedary dip with which she walks," and she was demanding a retraction. The producer was patiently trying to explain to her that she couldn't force a reviewer to retract something like that.

Seeing Elizabeth, Mae, who had changed into a white satin robe, became all smiles. She was introduced to Merv, but apparently had never heard of him.

Elizabeth complimented Mae on her wisecracks. "They made the play for me. You are so Americana. You're in the great tradition of Charlie Chaplin, Buster Keaton, W.C. Fields."

"Please!" Mae protested. "Don't mention that old drunkard Fields to me. He once stuck his filthy paw up my dress to see if those stories about me were true. He learned I'm a real woman down there. Not a transvestite!"

The aging sex diva invited them back to her dressing room, which Merv claimed had more flowers than the funeral of a head of state. He remembered her "looking like a pagan love goddess, getting ready for the mating season."

After arranging herself, Mae advised Elizabeth "to stick to the movies—don't go on the wicked stage. The damn producers when they go on the road will try to book you into an outhouse and try to ruin your play, washing it right down the tur-let." Merv was surprised that she still spoke in pure Brooklynese.

Mae liked to give advice, and she had plenty of it for Elizabeth but nothing to say to Merv. "I know everything worth knowing about show business," Mae said. "First, you've got to insist to a director that at least one redheaded actor be hired. Redheads are good omens. I've got one appearing in this play with me. I run my fingers through his red hair every night before going on. Second, you've got to surround yourself with a real swish, maybe two. A woman always looks more feminine when she's got a swish hovering over her, doing her hair, her nails, tightening her dress."

"I'll keep that in mind, Miss West," Elizabeth said.

"Now the important part," Mae confided in a confessional tone. Before facing the camera or going on stage in front of an audience, select the husky of the crew. Demand that he give you an orgasm if he wants to keep his job. When I was doing *Catherine the Great* for that God damn bricklayer, Mike Todd, in 1944, I had this *sri*, who not only supervised my yoga lessons, but could give me an orgasm in thirty seconds. Some men can't do that after sweating over a woman's body all night. After orgasm, a woman looks more beautiful, more regal than ever. Don't you agree, Griffin?" She looked him up and down skeptically, as if seeing him for the first time. "On second thought, you're not a man to answer such a question."

About fifteen minutes later, Merv escorted Elizabeth out of Mae's dressing room. The blonde goddess stood at her door. Ignoring Merv, she gazed into Elizabeth's violet eyes. Mae was no longer impersonating herself but looked like a real woman for the first time tonight—not a caricature. She also looked fifteen years older.

She took Elizabeth's hand. "There was a time, dearie, when I was as beautiful a woman as you are tonight."

* * *

After leaving Mae's dressing room, Merv put Elizabeth in a taxi to haul her to the Broadway hangout, Lindy's, whose patrons looked like a cast of characters released from *Guys and Dolls*. All the comedians hung out here— even Bob Hope who dropped in whenever he flew in from California. On any given night you could see Jack E. Leonard trading insults with Jack Carter or Joey Bishop. Milton Berle was a regular.

As Merv entered Lindy's with his "arm candy," even this rather sophisticated Broadway crowd stopped eating and started rubber-necking. Martha Raye they were used to, not Elizabeth Taylor, the screen goddess. One awestruck young waiter, an aspiring actor, almost spilled a double order of matzo ball soup onto Mary Martin's table.

Since she'd already eaten a big dinner, Elizabeth had come here for one reason, and that was to sample Lindy's celebrated cheesecake. Frank Sinatra had recommended it as a "must" on her visit to New York, although he claimed his mother could make a better one.

As Elizabeth dug into her cheesecake, Merv looked up to see "Uncle Miltie" heading for their table. Milton Berle usually ignored Merv, but tonight greeted him like his best friend. "Baby, I've missed you. We've got to get together. After all, you're my favorite band singer."

Merv knew that this effusive greeting was just staged so that Merv would introduce him to Elizabeth. After being introduced to the "King of Comedy," Elizabeth merely smiled before digging back into a large dab of her cheesecake.

Knowing all eyes were on him, Milton sat down in their booth and attempted in vain to engage Elizabeth in conversation. She just wanted to eat the cheesecake and get out the door. Looking disappointed, he finally got up and left, returning to his own table.

"Why did you snub Uncle Miltie?" Merv asked.

"Never heard of him," she said.

"Don't you watch television?" he asked.

"Never," she said. "It bores me."

"But he's one of the most famous entertainers in the business, the King of Comedy."

"Since when did he dethrone Bob Hope?"

Before leaving, Merv excused himself "to go to the little boy's room."

Standing at the urinal, he was surprised to see Milton enter and stand beside him. He reached in and pulled out what looked like a foot-long cock, the biggest Merv had ever seen in his life—and it was still soft.

"What's with that stuck-up little bitch you're dating tonight?" Milton asked. He shook his penis. "She needs for me to stick this whopper up her cunt. I'll have her screaming all night for more."

Merv quickly zipped up and headed back to Elizabeth, who was surrounded by fans complimenting her on her fur coat.

As he was shepherding her into a taxi, she said, "Women usually compliment my beauty, not my fur. I'll have to get rid of it. No woman should have her apparel detract from her looks."

As she snuggled into the fur for the ride back to her hotel, she said, "That was the best fucking cheesecake I've ever had in my life."

* * *

When Roddy and Merv learned that Jane Powell was going to be in New York, they decided to throw a joint party for both Elizabeth and Jane at their sublet at the Dakota. In his memoirs, Merv claimed that the party took place at his suite at the Hotel Meurice, but Eddie Fisher accurately remembered in his autobiography that the venue was the Dakota.

Perhaps the ever-closeted Merv did not want his public to know that he was rooming with one of Hollywood's best-known homosexuals, Roddy McDowall. Merv especially wanted to conceal from the public that they were sometimes lovers.

Ever since he'd met Eddie Fisher at RCA Victor studios, Merv had wanted to get to know him better. Using Elizabeth as bait, he decided to call Eddie and invite him to the party.

Merv was jealous of Eddie as a singer, and knew their recording studio was predicting big success for him. Yet he also had a secret crush on Eddie, even though Roddy assured him that "You'll strike out with him. I know Eddie. He's a connoisseur of beautiful women."

117

"So is Nicky Hilton, and look what happened," Merv said.

"Regardless of what people say, lightning doesn't strike twice," Roddy warned.

When Merv called Eddie, the singer at first didn't believe that Elizabeth would actually be at the party, but he agreed to come over anyway. He arrived at 1:45pm although the invitation was for two o'clock.

"Oh, yeah, right," Eddie said skeptically. "I'm sure Elizabeth Taylor is going to show up at any minute."

"Actually," Merv said, "she's already here." He led Eddie into the bedroom which he shared with Roddy. Seated on a padded stool in front of a vanity mirror, she was applying the finishing touches to her makeup. Unlike Milton Berle, she knew who Eddie was. She gracefully turned around and smiled at him. At first he didn't know what to say.

He later recalled the moment. "I was awestruck by her extraordinary beauty. I mean, by that point I had been around a lot of beautiful women, but I'd never met anyone like her. I fell in love with her that afternoon. I can still close my eyes and see her sitting there."

Merv had disappeared to answer the buzzer for the apartment door, as Roddy was busy in the kitchen. It was Montgomery Clift at the door, another honored guest. For the first time in his life, the actor had arrived somewhere on time.

Rushing back to his bedroom, Merv announced to Elizabeth, "Monty's here." Taking one final look for reassurance in the mirror, Elizabeth rose and headed for the living room and Monty.

"She brushed right past me and went to the side of her co-star in *A Place in the Sun*," Eddie said. "At that point I might not have existed. I spent most of my time that day talking to Roddy and Jane, but I cast frequent glances at Monty and Elizabeth, who seemed engaged in some epic battle."

Merv later revealed what was going on between Elizabeth and Monty. "It was her final attempt to get Monty to marry her before he headed back to Hollywood. Even though Monty told me he'd never marry anyone, Elizabeth was persistent."

At the end of the party, Eddie went over to tell Elizabeth good-bye, but she was still engaged in her dispute with Monty. She brushed Eddie aside. He later told Merv that he saw her back in Hollywood when he was visiting the MGM lot. "She was obviously furious and talking out loud to herself. She walked right past me and didn't even look at me. At that time I could never have believed that one day she'd marry me. You figure."

Eddie Fisher

118

Weeks later, it was the better-informed Roddy who told Merv that it had been announced in Hollywood that Elizabeth was going to marry the British actor, Michael Wilding. Merv looked shocked. "That dime-store version of David Niven? It won't last."

"Poor Elizabeth," Roddy said. "Another rotten choice in a husband. Wilding's completely bi. I know that Noel Coward's had him. He and Stewart Granger have carried on an affair for years."

Still harboring his crush on Eddie, Merv called the singer's hotel to tell him the news. In some secret cell of his brain, Merv thought Eddie might be heartbroken. After all, he'd told him that he'd fallen in love with Elizabeth on first sight. Maybe, or so Merv "reasoned" with Roddy, he could get Eddie on the rebound, perhaps when he was sobbing his heart out for losing Elizabeth.

"Even Noel Coward with all his charm couldn't get Eddie," Roddy claimed.

"What do you mean?" Merv asked.

"Noel encountered Eddie in a steam room," he said. "I think it was on an ocean liner. Eddie was completely nude, and he's got a big one. But Noel didn't want to suck his cock but pat his ass. Eddie turned him down."

Despite these warnings, Merv called Eddie's hotel suite anyway. He didn't pick up the phone. A world famous woman's voice came over the wire instead. "Hello, this is Mr. Fisher's residence. I'm his maid. Mr. Fisher can't be disturbed at the moment. If you care to leave a message?"

Without saying another word, Merv put down the phone. How could he compete with *The Blue Angel* herself? That was Marlene Dietrich speaking.

He later confessed to Roddy how he finally got over his crush on Eddie, realizing how hopeless it was. Judy Garland flew into New York and called Merv. "Where in the fuck is Eddie Fisher?" she demanded to know. "I've been calling all over town for him."

"I'll try to get in touch with him," Merv promised.

"As soon as you do, tell that little Jew bastard to get over to the Royalton right away. I want him to fuck my brains out." She slammed down the phone.

* * *

Still hanging out in New York with Roddy, Merv had not uncovered any singing engagements, even though he contacted his agent daily. It was ironic that his first gig came from Freddy Martin. The orchestra leader and his boys were appearing for a two-week engagement at The Last Frontier in Las Vegas. Merv's replacement, another boy singer, had a family emergency that forced him to return to New York.

"Will you do it?" Freddy asked over the phone after making his pitch.

"I'm on the next plane," Merv said.

Even though he hadn't been away all that long, it was good being back with Freddy's boys again and playing Las Vegas, one of his favorite towns. The promise of a paycheck made it all the sweeter. Performing two shows a night, Merv sang to a packed room.

He was in his dressing room during the second week of the show when there was a knock on his door. What happened next is a matter of dispute. Merv confused the incident by presenting two different versions of what happened, one in a 1980 memoir, another in a 2003 autobiography. We'll go with a more reliable version promulgated by Marty Melcher.

When Merv opened the door, he was shocked to encounter a young boy who looked no more than ten years old.

"Hi, kid," Merv said, "give me your autograph book."

"I don't want your autograph, Mr. Griffin," the boy said. "My mother sent me backstage. She wants you to join our table after your next show."

"Sorry, kid, but no thanks. I'm tired tonight and want to get some shut-eye. Tell your mama to give me a raincheck."

"But, Mr. Griffin, she wants you to be her new leading man in her next big musical."

"Just who is this mother of yours?" Merv asked. "Judy Garland?"

"Doris Day."

Merv later told Freddy that he was so overwhelmed at the prospect of meeting Doris that his knees were knocking throughout that night's second act. Like himself, Doris had been a band singer. But now she was the newly crowned Queen of Warner Brothers and one of the biggest box office attractions in the country. Instead of concentrating on his singing, Merv's head was filled with dreams of becoming Doris's leading man, replacing Gordon MacRae.

"It was a crazy thing to do," Marty Melcher, Doris's husband, later said. "I should have gone backstage and introduced myself to Griffin instead of sending Terry. For the life of me, I don't know why I sent the boy. He was just a kid. And besides, Doris knew that Warner's at the time was planning future musicals with her and MacRae. They'd already filmed *Tea for Two* together. Frankly, she didn't like him. His heavy drinking had led to several fights on the set, and she wasn't hot to work with him again."

"At the time we heard Merv sing, I was scouting around for another boy singer," Marty said. "We needed a good-looking guy with a voice who could be a good second banana for Doris. Someone who would let Doris shine like the star she was without any interference from MacRae's colossal ego. Merv seemed like the ideal candidate, although I was considering a lot of other boy singers."

Marty later admitted that Doris wanted unchallenged star billing. Gordon, with his great baritone voice, seemed to think he was a much bigger star than Doris. "Doris wanted to get a virtual unknown for her leading man," Marty said. "That way, there could be no doubt as to who was the star of the picture."

After the show, a nervous Merv walked up to Doris's table and extended his hand. "Doris Mary Ann Von Kappelhoff," he said. "Why did you ever change it to Doris Day? Kappelhoff would fit better onto a marquee."

"Doris burst into laughter," Marty said. "Merv showed us that he could not only sing, but had a sense of humor."

After both Merv and Doris exchanged compliments about each other's singing, Marty got down to business. A waiter had already escorted Terry upstairs to their suite, as it was long past his bedtime.

"I want a new face," Doris said abruptly. "Jack Warner is planning to team me with the same actors again and again. Jack Carson has already taught me all the tricks he knows about how to be in front of a camera. Gordon MacRae and I are not compatible. I've got my own career to think about. It's not my job to keep all the contract boys at Warner's working full time. The films are coming at me fast and furious. Jack Warner doesn't even want to give me a week off to lie by my pool. His excuse? The sun would give me too many freckles."

When she returned to Hollywood, Doris promised Merv that she'd arrange a screen test for him at Warner's. "You'll find out for yourself," she said. "Appearing before a camera will be a lot more rewarding—and a lot more fun—than standing in front of a live audience every night singing 'Sentimental Journey' for the ten thousandth time. In your case, that 'Coconuts' ditty."

Mary Ann Von Kappelhoff
(Doris Day)
with **Gordon MacRae.**

The next morning, going down on the elevator for breakfast, Merv encountered Terry again. He was checking out of the hotel with his parents, who had already gone to the garage. "Isn't my mom a great lady?" he asked.

"My favorite singer," Merv said. "What a bubbly personality."

"When you become her next leading man, you'll find that she's wonderful to work with." As he stepped off the elevator, the boy turned to Merv, a frown crossing his brow. "Watch out for that Marty Melcher. He's a real son of a bitch and a crook. He'll steal you blind."

With that parting remark, Terry raced across the lobby. Even though he'd been given Marty's last name, Terry was the biological son of Doris's first husband, a trombonist, Al Jorden, who had committed suicide years before.

After Doris flew out of Las Vegas to return to Hollywood, Merv could hardly wait to finish his final appearances with Freddy's orchestra. "I was the little fat boy back in San Mateo dreaming dreams that could never come true. Hollywood star. Doris Day's leading man. I just knew we'd become the new Jeanette MacDonald and Nelson Eddy of the screen. I couldn't wait to go back to Hollywood. I left it as a boy singer with a band. I was returning to become a big-time star. Years later I looked back at how naïve I was. I did become a star but in another medium. The Hollywood I was about to enter in the early 1950s was dying on the vine, as television rose to challenge it. It was to become my baptism of fire. I don't want to get too melodramatic, but it became my season in hell. Even so, I had a lot of fun along the way and an occasional heartbreak."

Merv on the road to bigger things

Chapter Four

Back in Hollywood, and back in Tom Drake's bed, Merv's daydreams almost overpowered him. Stardom seemed only months away.

Tom warned that he'd felt the same way in 1945, only to be bitterly disillusioned. "I was hailed as the next Van Johnson, but Van is still going strong. You're hailed as the next Gordon MacRae even though he hasn't departed from the scene either. In fact, his career seems stronger than ever."

"Maybe," Merv said, not wanting the actor's pessimism to spoil his usually sunny outlook. "So maybe I won't replace MacRae. Yesterday, one of the trade papers predicted that I'd be the next Dennis Morgan. I hear Warners isn't going to renew his contract. Besides, I sing better than Dennis."

"I don't think you and I are going to replace anybody," Tom predicted. "Better that you find your own voice. Be yourself."

"Okay, okay," Merv said, slightly dismissive. Merv was already growing bored with Tom, finding him "too clinging," as he relayed in a phone call to Johnny Riley in San Francisco.

"When you get tired of Tom, ship him north to me," Johnny had said.

But on the way to his first meeting at Warner Brothers, Merv began to fear that Tom Drake and his pessimism might be right. He read a story about Warner Brothers in *Variety* that suggested the studio might be on the way down. In 1947, it seemed, Warners had earned more than $22 million. But in 1951 its earnings had plummeted to $9.4 million.. Dozens of personnel, Merv had learned, had been fired, including one quarter of the publicity staff.

Merv had grown up on movies made by Warner Brothers, seeing the entire output of such big stars as Bette Davis, James Cagney, Edward G. Robinson, John Garfield, Humphrey Bogart, and his special favorite, Errol Flynn.

For Warner's, 1952 was a crucial year. In 1946, a Federal court had ordered that the studio, and others, divest themselves of their theater holdings. That meant that Warners could no longer be guaranteed block bookings of its films, especially the duds. In the future, each movie would have to be sold on its individual merits.

Merv was confident, however, that he and Doris would produce an ongoing roster of musical box office hits. He was delighted that his name was recognized at Warners' security gate. The security guard there had even called him "Mr. Griffin." He was escorted to a rehearsal hall with a piano where he was told to wait for Bill Orr, the casting director. Bill was married to Jack Warner's stepdaughter, Joy Page.

At the time of Merv's acting debut at Warners, many of the stars that he had hoped to meet there had already told the studio good-bye, or vice versa. Bogart and Lauren Bacall had departed, as had flat-chested Ann Sheridan and "ballsy" Ida Lupino. The tough, cynical and edgy John Garfield was on his last legs and would die of a heart attack that May, reportedly nude and between the sheets with a starlet. He was only 39 years old.

Two of Merv's all-time favorites, Joan Crawford and Errol Flynn, were still on the lot, and Merv planned to look them up. He wasn't sure if Joan would remember him, but he was certain that Errol would. Joan was finishing *This Woman Is Dangerous*, and Errol was trying to launch *The Adventures of Captain Fabian*, which he had written himself.

The woman whom Merv referred to as "the demented screen goddess," Bette Davis, was long gone, following the disastrous release of *Beyond the Forest* in 1949. His encounters with Bette lay in his future.

Ronald Reagan and his former wife, Jane Wyman, were still on the lot, although they avoided each other after their divorce. Free-lancers such as Burt Lancaster came and went, appearing in such adventure epics as *The Crimson Pirate*. Patricia Neal had gained good notices after appearing with Ronald in *The Hasty Heart*. Much to Patricia's broken-hearted regret, her former co-star and lover, Gary Cooper, was appearing with that sexy ice blonde, Grace Kelly, in *High Noon*.

Cross-eyed Virginia Mayo, who was playing a burlesque queen in *She's Working Her Way Through College*, was co-starring with Ronald Reagan. Rumors spread around the lot that they were having an affair, even though Nancy Davis was hovering in the wings to throw ice on the fire.

Now that Errol was getting long in the tooth, and increasingly drunk, Merv felt that the sexiest man on the Warners lot was Steve Cochran, who had been Mae West's leading man on the stage in *Diamond Lil* and her off-stage lover. Steve had become known for playing sleazy pretty boys. "When it comes to menacing sexuality, no one does it better than Steve boy," Merv told Tom Drake

In the rehearsal hall at Warners, Merv was told to wait until Bill Orr appeared. The casting director had worked for Merv's Uncle Elmer at a night-club he owned on Sunset Strip. It was called The Sports Circle, and Bill appeared there as an emcee doing impressions. At Merv's instigation, Uncle Elmer had called Bill asking for him to "give Merv special consideration."

By the time the second hour rolled around, and Bill had not appeared,

Merv mumbled "some consideration" to his agent, "Bullets" Durgom, who stood around with a pianist from Warners.

During this time, Merv at least got to know his agent a little better. Up to now, Bullets usually had less than fifteen minutes to devote to conferences or talks with Merv. He was one busy agent, hustling jobs for other clients who included one especially big one (in more ways than one), Jackie Gleason.

The agent's real name was George Durgom, but he preferred his nickname of Bullets. Long linked to Tommy Dorsey and his orchestra, Bullets at one time also represented Glenn Miller, who had died during the war.

His newer, sexier stars included Natalie Wood, and, for a time, even Marilyn Monroe. During their wait, Bullets told Merv he wanted him to meet another artist he represented, Sammy Davis Jr. "He's terrific. You guys will get along fabulously."

Merv suspected Bullets was of some vague Arabic descent, perhaps Lebanese, but he didn't dare ask. A short, intense, rail-thin man, Bullets was balding and walked with a stoop. He always had a harassed look as if he were late for an appointment somewhere else. He'd earned the sobriquet Bullets in a Brooklyn schoolyard because he kept ricocheting his sentences from one subject to another without connecting them.

Finally, one of Bill Orr's assistants warned Merv and an increasingly impatient Bullets that "the boss man is on his way." His temper flaring, Merv was furious at having to wait so long, even though Bullets warned him "to cool it."

Merv knew it might blow his chances for a screen test, but he decided to get back at Bill.

Merv instructed the pianist to play the last notes of Cole Porter's "Night and Day." Just as Bill entered the hall, Merv sang the last refrain of the song before bolting for the door.

Even though Bill introduced himself, and apologized for being late, Merv snubbed him. "I've just done my act. I'm not doing it again. Don't get too grand with me, Orr. If you want to hear me sing, catch my next solo gig in Las Vegas."

Bill Orr could easily have walked away from Merv that day and never called upon him again. Merv was uncharacteristically rude and arrogant toward this major Hollywood player, and Bill himself told Jack Warner that "singers like Merv Griffin are a dime a dozen."

Bill would go on to forge a big career as a TV producer, associated with a string of westerns and detective programs, including *Maverick* (1957), *Cheyenne* (1955), *77 Sunset Strip* (1958), and *F Troop* (1965).

Before coming to Hollywood, Bill had served as an officer in the Army Air Force's First Motion Picture Unit, making training films with William

Holden, Alan Ladd, and Ronald Reagan. After the war, and after his marriage to Joy Page. Bill became in his own words "a big enchilada" at Warners. Behind his back, his co-workers claimed "the son-in-law also rises."

Elmer had arranged for hetero pornographic pictures of Bill to be snapped when the casting director worked for him at his burlesque club on Sunset Strip. Rumors still persist that Elmer threatened to present those pictures to Bill's father-in-law, Jack Warner, if Bill refused to arrange a screen test for Merv.

Somehow, and it isn't known how it happened, Jack Warner eventually saw those pictures, and got a rundown on the whole sordid blackmail attempt. In the wake of that, Warner allegedly told his confidants that, "Merv Griffin got his screen test and his Warners contract because that old fuck, Elmer, blackmailed Bill into granting them. What Merv didn't know was that I was planning to cast him as the lead in only one of our pictures—and nothing more. So, fine.....I'll give him a god damn contract to be in some pictures, but if I'm still here, I'll see that he's uncredited and with no more than 30 seconds of screen time in each of them. I'll show those fuckers they can't piss on Jack Warner and get away with it."

Amazingly, Jack later became friends with Merv and invited him on several occasions for Sunday afternoons at his palatial home. But in spite of this outward friendliness, Jack was "stubborn as a horse," according to Bill Orr, and stood by his original forecast about how he'd handle Merv. "Jack Warner and Bill Orr completely fucked my chances for a film career," Merv would later claim.

As the months went by, Bill and Merv "mended fences" (in Merv's words) and became confidants of a sort, even though Bill—perhaps the result of the remembered grudge— did almost nothing for Merv's film career. "I hung out with Bill Orr on a Saturday night but come Monday morning he always put me at the bottom of the cast—that is if he listed my name at all."

Merv told Roddy McDowall and Tom Drake that Elmer had showed him those pornographic pictures he had of Bill. "Orr is exceptionally well endowed. No wonder all the gals and closeted male stars went for him," Merv said.

Bill liked to gossip about the stars, and so did Merv. Bill claimed that the very closeted Edward G. Robinson had come on to him, as had "shorty," Alan Ladd. He also claimed that he'd had an on-again, off-again affair with Lucille Ball in the late 40s during her marriage to Desi Arnaz.

Because of the risks associated with his role as Jack Warner's son-in-law, Bill appears to have kept his bisexuality locked tightly in a closet. It seems that he did, however, have an occasional sexual involvement with a man, but mostly he pursued the ladies, with a rare exception every now and again.

126

"Bill's big mistake was in not recognizing what a big star I could have been at Warners," Merv later said, only half kidding. "I could have stayed at Warners and presided over the death of the movie musical with Doris Day at my side. Even though Bill never realized my potential, he did have a nose for new talent. Armed with the power of granting a contract from Warner Brothers, he pursued James Dean, Marlon Brando, and Paul Newman. Not bad, not bad at all. He told me that he got to fuck Dean on several occasions."

***

"I was shaking like a burlesque queen," Merv recalled, "when I arrived at the Warners lot for my screen test." A studio employee handed him a scene from John Patrick's play, *The Hasty Heart*. Merv had seen the 1949 film, starring Ronald Reagan, Patricia Neal, and Richard Todd.

Fully made up in a borrowed dressing room, Merv waited for two hours to be called to the set. "I just assumed that I'd make the test opposite Doris Day," he later said. "After all, the whole point of the test was to see if Doris and I had on-screen chemistry."

To his disappointment, he learned that he'd be appearing on camera opposite Phyllis Kirk. A former model, bright-eyed Phyllis was an attractive *ingénue*, not really beautiful and certainly not magnetic. Merv had not been impressed with her appearance in the 1950 Samuel Goldwyn movie, *Our Very Own*, starring Ann Blyth.

False harmonies:
Merv with **Phyllis Kirk**

In that film, instead of looking at Ann and Phyllis, he'd fallen for the good looks of Farley Granger, a homosexual actor who at the time was being groomed for big stardom.

As for Phyllis, Merv was dismissive, telling Bill Orr, "You can find dozens of Phyllis Kirks on any college campus in America."

"I had respect—not enchantment—for Phyllis," Merv later told Roddy McDowall. "She was hard working and rather personable, but rather full of her-

Life after Merv:
Cover girl **Phyllis Kirk**

self. To me, she represented a new breed of post-war woman appearing on the screens of the 1950s. Most of them would not survive that decade. These gals lacked the box office magic of the 1930s divas that lured us to movie houses—Marlene Dietrich, Joan Crawford, Bette Davis, Greta Garbo. These bubbly new personalities with their meager talents pop up on the screen like a bad dream. But I think most of them will end up as suburban housewives. Could you imagine anyone buying a movie ticket just to see Phyllis Kirk emote? I was furious, not that I had anything against her personally. I felt betrayed by Doris for not agreeing to do the test herself."

When Merv placed a call to Bill Orr to complain, he was told that Phyllis was going to become one of the studio's biggest stars. "Besides, Doris is too busy to make the test. Who knows? In the future, when you're not making a film opposite Doris, I might cast you in a picture with Phyllis. I think the two of you would make an ideal screen couple."

Merv suffered through the screen test with Phyllis, who proved competent in front of the camera, although it was obvious she had no great love affair with the lens the way Marilyn Monroe did. He thought Phyllis had about as much talent as Nancy Davis (Reagan), no great compliment. On screen, he sang, "I Don't Want to Walk Without You." It was not one of his best numbers and did not really showcase his singing talent.

Despite Merv's misgivings, Warners signed him to a contract at $250 a week after seeing the test. However, Jack Warner insisted that he change his name to Mark Griffin. "Merv sounds like a little old Jewish shopkeeper with a fat wife at home."

"I'm sticking with Merv," he stubbornly maintained. "I was named after my father, and it would be insulting to him to change it."

Jack Warner could have torn up the contract right at that point. But instead he invited Merv to come over to his home that Sunday afternoon. "Maybe we'll play a game of tennis."

The night after his screen test, Merv drove with Roddy to Rock Hudson's house for an all-male party. Tom Drake was in the back seat sulking, having complained earlier that Merv was not showing him enough attention. Merv secretly suspected that Tom was still daydreaming that he'd get Peter Lawford back.

At the party, both Roddy and Rock once again urged Merv to be seen in public with starlets, getting his picture taken with "arm candy."

"Those rumors about you being queer are all over town," Rock warned him. "That's why I date Vera-Ellen. You don't want to end up on the front page of *Confidential*."

Roddy joined Rock in urging Merv to publicly date women, and he looked over at a pouting Tom. "When you dump your date back at her door, you can always hurry home to Tom here. He'll be keeping the bed warm for you." Tom continued to sulk throughout the party.

Reluctantly, Merv called Phyllis the next day and asked her out on a date. She told him, "I'm very busy. Lots of appointments. But I'll try to work you in Thursday night."

From that unpromising beginning, Merv and Phyllis began to be seen all over town. "That gal had more appointments and more invitations than the Queen of England," he later said. "She was always rushing here, running there, and some of those appointments called for a male escort. That's where I came in."

Merv told Roddy that after three weeks of steady dating, all he'd done romantically with Phyllis was kiss her lightly on the lips at her doorstep. For publicity purposes, and without consulting him, she began to play up their dating as a big romance. She'd even vaguely hinted to gossip maven Louella Parsons that "marriage might be around the corner, though there's nothing official yet."

Merv shuddered when he heard this, as he had no intention of marrying Phyllis, or any other woman at that point in his life.

One night he invited her to an Italian restaurant, Dominick's. When he picked her up at her house, he knew something was seriously wrong. She almost didn't speak to him as he drove her to the restaurant. She was mad at him, and he had no idea why.

Over dinner, and to rescue the evening, he tried to get her to talk about herself, knowing that few ambitious young actresses could resist that temptation.

"You know," he said, "I've been hearing all this talk about us, and it occurred to me that I know almost nothing about you."

She addressed him as if talking to a newspaper reporter about her life. "My parents were Danish. I grew up in Syracuse, New York, as Phyllis Kirkegaard. I had several jobs slinging hash and once I sold perfume at a counter in a department store. I later became a model while studying acting under Sanford Meisner, a great coach. He helped me get cast in a Broadway play in 1949. I played a French maid opposite Jean-Pierre Aumont, who seduced me both on and off the stage."

She claimed that a talent scout had discovered her, which led to her going to Hollywood and signing a contract with Samuel Goldwyn, who'd cast her in *Our Very Own*." Goldwyn lent me out to MGM but didn't renew my contract," she said. "That's how I ended up at Warners."

The rest of their short evening was devoted to talking about her upcoming film. She'd been cast opposite Vincent Price, who played a maniac sculptor in *House of Wax* (1953).

She told Merv she'd been given the female lead, playing a character originally created by Fay Wray in the 1933 *Mystery of the Wax Museum*. "I'm being forced to do the role, but I don't want to become another Fay Wray. Hell, they'll remake *King Kong* with me doing love scenes with a big, hairy gorilla."

The film was to be shot in the revolutionary 3-D, which Warners was hoping would bring hordes back into movie theaters. "As far as I'm concerned," she said, "3-D is just a gimmick. I don't want to appear in a film that uses a gimmick to lure audiences in."

Years later she told a reporter, "I hated it when I was cast in *House of Wax*, although Vincent Price turned out to be a delight. The irony of it all is that throughout the rest of my life, this is the one film I am remembered for."

Merv listened patiently to her brief resumé, but still wanted to know why she was mad at him. He decided to be blunt and ask. "Just why are you pissed off at me?"

"With stardom on the way, I've got to think of my career and who I'm seen out with. A scandal could wreck my plans."

"What sort of scandal?" he asked, growing uncomfortable. "I mean, we haven't even gone to bed with each other. How could I knock you up?"

"I'll be frank," she said, sliding slightly away from him on the red leather upholstery. "I learned some disturbing news about you today. I won't tell you from whom. But I've got to ask you a question. Are you a homosexual?"

He looked flabbergasted, putting down his fork. "I definitely am not, and I resent such a question. I don't know what asshole told you that."

"Were you the lover of Roddy McDowall in New York, and are you the lover of Tom Drake here in Hollywood?"

"We're just good friends," he said, acutely embarrassed. He'd never been confronted with such a question from a woman before.

"I was told that you're dating me just to get publicity for yourself," she charged. "To fool the public into thinking you're straight. One of those Tab Hunter/Debbie Reynolds things."

"That's not true!"

"Then what are your intentions?" she asked. "Do you plan to marry me?"

"Well . . . marriage is something I haven't thought about. I think we should just continue dating like we've been and see what happens."

Suddenly, she stood up, flashing anger. "You're using me. I was falling in love with you until I learned the truth about you today. You're lying to me right now. You *are* a homosexual. I refuse to be a part of your sick publicity campaign to fool your public." She picked up her platter of spaghetti and tossed it over his head before storming out of the restaurant.

The many witnesses in the restaurant, fellow diners, spread word of this confrontation around Hollywood. Merv attempted a cover-up, claiming that Phyllis had discovered that he'd been seeing another woman.

In his memoirs, Merv came up with a completely different story. He claimed that Phyllis was always talking about her busy schedule, and that she carried an appointment book around with her at all times. At one point during their dinner, Merv allegedly told her, "Now, you're not going to read me all your appointments, are you?" He falsely maintained that it was because of that question that she picked up that platter of spaghetti and dumped it over his head.

***

Despite that episode, Merv did not hold a grudge against Phyllis and would occasionally encounter her on friendly terms in their future. He applauded her success when she was cast as Nora Charles opposite his friend, Peter Lawford, in the hit TV series, *The Thin Man*, which ran for three years (1957-59). Privately Merv confided to Peter, "Let's face it: Phyllis is no Myrna Loy." Merv might also have said that Peter was no William Powell.

Years later, Merv was saddened to learn that Phyllis had to abandon her film career. As a child she'd battled polio, and throughout the rest of her life, had trouble walking. During the early 1970s, she fell and broke her hip, which deteriorated even further her ability to walk without limping. Partly because of her walk, directors would no longer hire her.

During her final years—she died in 2006—Merv noticed that Phyllis was no longer as self-enchanted, and that she devoted much of her time to liberal causes under the banner of the American Civil Liberties Union. As he migrated more and more to the right, she went left. They especially differed in their beliefs about capital punishment, which he favored and which she adamantly opposed.

After Phyllis's break from Merv, he began to date Rita Farrell, a performer he'd met when he was appearing with the Freddy Martin Orchestra. Vivacious and irreverent, she appealed to him as a "fun gal" to date. They were seen around town together, and she later joined his act when he was booked for singing gigs by his agent. Rita and Merv made appearances together in Chicago, Houston, Reno, and even at a church benefit in Hartford, Connecticut.

Once Merv and Rita appeared on CBS's "The Jane Froman Show," singing "I Like the Look of You" with the fabled host of the show. Jane had been the subject of a hit movie, *With a Song in My Heart* (1952), starring Susan Hayward.

Romantically, Merv never took Rita seriously. She became another one of his "gal pals."

Merv was just filling in his time before he was cast in his first big musical at Warners. Bill Orr called him and told him that "it was almost certain that he was going to appear with Doris Day in her next picture, *Lucky Me*, the first CinemaScope musical. Phil Silvers, whom Merv had met through Tallulah in New York, had already been signed, as had Eddie Foy Jr. and Nancy Walker. One day on the Warners lot, Merv was introduced to actress Martha Hyer who had also signed to do the picture. A blonde, she was furious that the studio was going to force her to dye her hair red so as not to conflict with the blonde tresses of Doris herself.

Merv's hopes for his first big chance on the screen collapsed when the upcoming director of *Lucky Me*, Jack Donohue, saw Merv's screen test. "The kid's out of the picture," Donohue said. "Christ, he photographs like he's nineteen. Doris will look like his mother." The director cast Robert Cummings in the part instead, liking his "everyman appeal" and his bright speaking voice.

"Lucky Me, indeed!" Merv said. Despite the rejection, he added the song to his repertoire of night club standards. During his solo appearances, he'd warble: "Lucky me! Down the four-leaf clover highway, all the signs are pointing my way."

Just when he began to think he'd never be cast in any film, Bill Orr called with good news. *Lucky Me* had been postponed, and Doris was going to film *By the Light of the Silvery Moon* (1953) instead. She had seen his screen test, and thought he'd be ideal playing opposite her as her romantic interest. "She didn't think you looked too young at all—she thought you were just right," Bill assured Merv. Not only that, but she'd invited him for a face-to-face in her dressing room the following afternoon.

"I felt like I was the King of Hollywood that night," Merv said, "Bigger than Clark Gable. A better singer than Bing Crosby. The only thing I feared at Warners was running into Gordon MacRae. He was liable to make mincemeat of me when he learned that I'd replaced him opposite Doris."

As Merv later recalled, "And then who did I run into that very night at a Hollywood party?"

***

Bill Orr and his wife Joy were throwing a party at their house for some of the employees of Warners. The gathering was mainly for the behind-the-camera staff. At the party, Merv presumably would be meeting the technicians he'd be working with when he became the leading man opposite Doris.

"I invited the big diva stars but when they heard it was mostly for technicians, they cabled their regrets," Bill told Merv over the phone. "Doris is too

132

busy to attend, and Miss Joan Crawford has a headache. Actually, I know for a fact that she plans to spend the evening fucking Steve Cochran."

Before putting down the phone, Bill gave a stern warning to Merv. "The invitation is only for yourself. Don't bring Tom Drake. I figured the best way for you to meet your fellow co-workers is to sing to them. I'll have the piano ready. About five numbers should do just fine. Oh, yes, and don't forget the Coconuts ditty."

As Merv put down the phone, he was stunned with the realization that Bill knew about his affair with Tom. He called Tom to tell him that he was deliberately not invited to the party. In anger, Tom said, "Accept one of those sing-for-your-supper invitations if you must. At least you'll provide the evening's free entertainment. Jack Warner pulls those stunts all the time, even getting Judy Garland to sing at his private parties."

At the Orr house, Sammy Cahn, the lyricist and songwriter, befriended Merv. Merv was impressed with Sammy's previous output of Broadway songs, and the fact that both Frank Sinatra and Doris Day had recorded many of them, sometimes transforming them into hits. Sammy welcomed Merv to Hollywood and exchanged stories with him about working with the big bands.

Sammy was very interested to hear that plans were being activated for Merv to replace Gordon MacRae. "For all I know, if this changeover occurs, you and Doris might be recording my next big hit." In 1948 Doris had introduced "It's Magic" in her film, *Romance on the High Seas*, and in 1949 she'd performed the same honor for Sammy's hit, "It's a Great Feeling" in the movie of the same name.

Merv was anxious to get to know Sammy and become his friend. The lyricist had been born of Jewish immigrants from Poland and grew up on Manhattan's Lower East Side, but Merv believed that Sammy had amazingly captured the essence of American romanticism. He just knew that if he could convince Sammy to write a song for him, he might have another hit, even bigger than Coconuts.

"Ever since I was 13 and saw my mother pay the musicians at my bar mitzvah, I realized there was money to be made in producing music," Sammy told Merv.

"Don't you have another one of those Yiddish songs your mother taught you that you could adapt for me?" Merv bluntly asked. He was no doubt referring to a specialty number, *"Bei Mir Bist Du Schon"* ("Means That You're Grand"). The song sold more than a million copies for The Andrew Sisters.

"No Yiddish," Sammy said, "but I do have a song for you that I think could be a big hit. It's called 'Three Coins in the Fountain.'"

"Could I hear it?" Merv eagerly asked.

"I'm still working on it," Sammy said. "But drop by my house late tomorrow afternoon, and let me hear you sing it for me . . . at least what I've written of it so far."

Merv showed up the following afternoon, and thought "Three Coins in the Fountain" was one of the most romantic ballads he'd ever heard. He also learned that Jule Styne was working on the song with Sammy. After Merv sang for Sammy, the lyricist said, "We've got a hit. You were great!"

To Merv's great disappointment, he later read in the trade papers that Frank Sinatra had signed to record Three Coins, and that Frank would introduce it in the film of the same name. *Three Coins in the Fountain* eventually won an Academy Award. "If only it had been me," Merv told Tom Drake. "I dropped my coin in that fountain, but I came up empty-handed. That fucking Sinatra. All songwriters give him their best material first."

"Welcome to Hollywood," Tom said. "At MGM my case was even worse. Louis B. Mayer gave Peter Lawford, my lover, all the parts I wanted to play."

Back at the Orr party, Merv diverted his eyes from Sammy to see Gordon MacRae approaching. This was the moment he'd been dreading. He didn't know if Gordon had heard that he was going to be Doris Day's new leading man.

During their brief talk, Gordon gave no indication that he viewed Merv as a rival. Maybe he hadn't heard the gossip going around the Warner lot.

"So, what brings you to Hollywood?" Gordon asked with such innocence that Merv thought he might not have heard about what he'd just signed with Jack Warner.

"Don't you know?" Sammy asked. "Merv's in town to replace you in Doris's next picture."

Gordon looked startled before turning and walking away.

No sooner had Gordon left than Bill Orr approached Merv, telling him it was time to start singing. All the guests were assembling around the piano in the Orr's spacious living room. Before coming to the party, Bill had sent over the music and lyrics for five songs that Gordon had already recorded.

Merv had expected to sing them out of earshot of the star himself. He whispered to Bill that he wanted to change the music, but Bill practically pushed him into the spotlight, telling Merv that it was too late for that since he'd also hired five Warners musicians to accompany him.

Fearing disaster, and with

Public and private views of
Gordon MacRae

knees knocking, Merv entered the room and headed for the piano. He scanned the room but saw no sign of Gordon. Maybe, he thought, the Gods were merciful and the angry Gordon had gone home.

No such luck. After Bill introduced Merv to mild applause, Merv began to sing the first lines of "On Moonlight Bay." Suddenly, Gordon mysteriously appeared through the sliding glass doors from the garden. He took the microphone. "Ladies and gentlemen, I met Merv earlier this evening. He told me he wasn't in good voice tonight. So why not hear these songs from the star who originally recorded them?"

Humiliated and embarrassed, Merv was virtually shoved from the piano as Gordon launched into the song himself. Frank Sinatra had humiliated him in a similar way at the Cocoanut Grove.

Unknown to Merv at the moment, Judy Garland, late as usual, had entered the living room. Even though she'd married Sid Luft a few months ago, her husband was nowhere to be seen. Judy was accompanied by Peter Lawford.

Almost for protection, Merv gravitated to their side. Both Peter and Judy kissed him on the lips as Gordon finished his first number. Merv told Judy what had happened. Saying nothing, she kissed him once again for reassurance.

She was already formulating a face-saving device for Merv. At the end of Gordon's act, Judy strode forward, taking over the piano as Gordon bowed out to loud applause.

"As a special treat, I'm going to do 'Over the Rainbow' tonight for you," she told the audience, the news causing the guests to burst into the loudest applause of the evening. "Accompanying me on the piano and singing with me tonight will be Merv Griffin, the new musical sensation of Warner Brothers."

Merv joined her. He and Judy had never rehearsed the number, but Bill Orr later said that Merv and Judy delivered one of the finest and most tender renditions of this song he'd ever heard. "If only I had recorded it."

***

After leaving Bill Orr's party, Merv congratulated Judy on her wedding to Sid Luft, although he'd heard from songstress Peggy Lee that Sid frequently beat her, even before their marriage, which Merv didn't think would last. He also congratulated Judy on having turned thirty, and she apologized that Sid did not invite him to the celebration. Merv had also heard that Judy was pregnant, presumably with Sid's child, but he did not offer congratulations because she did not mention it.

Peter and Merv drove Judy home, and she kissed both men good night, a

135

very wet kiss for each of them on the lips. She promised to call Merv soon and had plans to see Peter tomorrow for lunch. Peter dropped Merv off beside the spot where, earlier, he had parked his car. Before kissing him good night, he bluntly asked, "How's life with my ex?"

"I won't kid you," Merv said. "It's not the most exciting spectacle. It has its dull moments. But he's a good kid."

"On Tom's tombstone, I think they are going to write, 'The Boy Next Door' was a good kid," Peter said.

"How's life with Mr. Robert Walker?" Merv asked.

"A thrill a minute," Peter said. "Not just the sex. It's the feeling that with him you never know what's going to happen next, including the possibility that he's going to commit suicide at any moment."

"He's a very attractive guy," Merv said, "and I envy you. You're a very attractive guy too. I think I missed out on something."

Before Merv got into his car, Peter stopped him and took his arm, squeezing it tightly. "You don't have to miss out on anything. Bob and I like three-ways. The first night you can get away from Tom, give us a ring."

"You're serious?" Merv said, not knowing at first if Peter were joking. The look on his face told Merv that Peter meant what he said.

"That's an offer I'd like to take you up on," Merv said. "After all, I'm in the most decadent city on the planet and not wallowing in filth like I should be."

Peter reached out and fondled Merv's genitals. Then, without saying another word, Merv got into his car and drove off into the night.

Before returning home to Tom, Merv called Roddy McDowall, giving him a play-by-play description of his encounter with Peter. Roddy's parting advice was, "Go for it!"

***

The next day Merv received a call from "the girl singer," Rosemary Clooney. She announced that she was back in Hollywood and wanted to get together with him. He'd met her on the road when traveling with Freddy Martin's orchestra and had been drawn to her wit, charm, warmth, and humor.

Actress Janet Leigh had told Merv that Rosemary was "one hell of a person," and he eagerly wanted to pursue a friendship with her and to become a part of her inner circle of friends. They included Frank Sinatra, Bing Crosby, Tony Bennett, and Billie Holiday. Merv had also heard from Roddy that Rosemary was seen frequently in the company of Marlene Dietrich, with whom she was recording some duets.

At the time, there was a lot of speculation about Marlene and Rosemary being an item, but Merv dismissed this as malicious Hollywood gossip, even though at parties, a drunken Louella Parsons often insisted that Marlene and Rosemary were having an affair. "She seems like a one-man woman to me," Merv told Roddy. "But who knows? It's Hollywood. If Marlene could fuck Eddie Fisher, she might be capable of fucking Rosemary Clooney."

Merv had first met Rosemary in Virginia Beach when she was singing at the Surf Club. Freddy Martin, with Merv as the lead singer, had been booked into the club following the closing of one of Rosemary's gigs. It was a long-standing custom there for the new entertainers to arrive the night before to hear the closing act of the previous group.

The club was positioned directly on the beachfront, and Rosemary strolled out between acts to breathe the ocean air. There she had encountered Merv for the first time, little knowing that he was destined to become one of her most loyal supporters and lifelong allies.

"He looked a little lonely that night, and I immediately gravitated to him," Rosemary later told Janet Leigh. "I think he wanted to be *in* love instead of singing about love every night. At the time, I knew nothing of his sexual preference. But intuitively, I realized he wanted a friend more than he wanted a hot *tamale*."

"We spoke and opened up to each other, sharing our mutual experiences of the hardships of the road," Rosemary later said. "It was a tough life in those days, and we'd both been wounded in various ways. Later, when I got to know Merv better, I came to realize that we both shared a tragic flaw. He and I were always falling in love with the wrong man."

Just before Rosemary was called back onstage, she kissed her new-found friend on the lips and agreed to meet with him later at the Cavalier Hotel where both of them were staying.

Merv came into the club to catch Rosemary's closing act. As she delivered her last song, he watched something remarkable happen. The band got up and paraded right off the stage and into the Atlantic Ocean, soaking their baby blue dinner jackets and their red Scottish plaid dress pants. Merv eagerly reached out to take Rosemary's hand as they headed for the cold waters with the rest of the band.

Merv later told Freddy Martin, "The waters were so God damn cold that night I think I got blue balls, but who would turn down Rosemary Clooney, Miss

Two views of
Rosemary Clooney

'Beautiful Brown Eyes?'" He was referring to her hit song that sold more than half a million copies.

After Merv agreed to see Rosemary, she called him two days later inviting him to "Come On-a-My House," referring to what would become her signature song, although she hated it and at first refused to record it.

She suggested to Merv that he bring a date, presumably a female, since she'd be with her new beau, the distinguished Puerto Rican actor, Jose Ferrer.

***

When he met Jose Ferrer, Merv did the obvious and congratulated him for the Oscar he'd won as Best Actor in his portrayal of Cyrano in the 1950 film version of *Cyrano de Bergerac*.

"Yes, thank you," Jose said sarcastically. "I celebrated by being subpoenaed to appear before the House Un-American Activities Committee as a suspected Communist. I'm not, incidentally."

When Merv first met Jose, he'd been Oscar nominated for the third and last time for portraying the French painter, Henri de Toulouse-Lautrec, in John Huston's *Moulin Rouge*. Jose was preparing to appear opposite Rita Hayworth in the 1953 *Miss Sadie Thompson*, a remake of *Rain*.

At the time of his first dinners with Jose and Rosemary, Merv was still dating Judy Balaban before she ran off with the agent, Jay Kanter. The first time the quartet got together, Jose did all the talking. "I was so in awe of him that all I could do was listen," Merv later said. "He was the first intellectual I'd ever met in show business."

Jose spoke seven languages fluently, and often reminded his listeners of that. He'd been accepted at Princeton when he was fourteen, and he'd studied at an exclusive boarding school in Switzerland. He could wax eloquently on seemingly any subject, from the literary output of Thomas Hardy to the plight of the underpaid workers at the time of the Industrial Revolution.

Jose always preferred to take his guests to a steakhouse where he'd discuss in precise detail how marbled he preferred his choice cut of meat. He'd even inspect the steak before it sizzled on the grill.

Love Triangle:
Rosemary Clooney with her husband **Jose Ferrer** and her friend **Marlene Dietrich**

When Judy and Rosemary headed for the powder room, Jose immediately took Merv into his sexual confidence, which Merv found incredibly indiscreet.

"I don't know if *Sadie Thompson* will ever be filmed," he said. "I'll be too busy fucking Rita Hayworth in her dressing room."

Merv had already heard that Jose was a first-rate womanizer. Later he'd tell Tom Drake, "I was stunned that Rosemary was planning to marry this rooster, even though he was the most talented actor in Hollywood. Here he was contemplating infidelity before ever putting the wedding ring on Rosemary's finger. Poor Rosemary."

Merv didn't think Jose had any sex appeal at all, and in some respects he struck Merv as downright ugly. "However, he could charm the pants off anybody with that mesmerizing voice of his," Merv recalled.

Even though he was fantasizing about his future infidelities, Jose seemed bitter and resentful about the perceived competition for Rosemary's affections.

"That god damn lesbian, Marlene Dietrich, is around our house day and night," Jose claimed. "I can't even walk around with my dick hanging out without encountering her. She even puts on an apron and scrubs our kitchen floor. A *hausfrau* at heart. If Rosemary gets a slight headache, Dietrich puts her to bed and hovers over her like a newborn infant. The Nazi bitch is always making buttermilk soup for Rosemary and she completely ignores me. Actually, Dietrich is bi. When not chasing after Rosemary, she's out fucking Frank Sinatra. Frank told me that Dietrich gives the best blow-job in Hollywood."

"If you've got to compete with Dietrich, I don't envy you," Merv said.

"Not only Dietrich but Marlon Brando," Jose claimed. "We run into him all the time, especially in New York. He always drags Rosemary off into a corner and spends the rest of the evening whispering some shit in her ear."

"Marlon always gets what he wants," Merv said enigmatically, "And I speak from experience."

Just prior to one of their scheduled rendezvous, Jose had to cancel with a stomach virus, and Merv took Rosemary out to dinner by himself.

En route to the restaurant, she asked Merv to stop at a newsstand. "Please go and buy the latest copy of *Confidential* magazine. It's for Marlene. Even though she hangs out with famous writers like Ernest Hemingway, she reads every word of *Confidential*."

"No doubt to find out the latest gossip they're spreading about her."

Merv returned in a few minutes with the latest issue of the gossip rag. "I feel so sleazy buying it, but I love it, providing no one's writing about me. I like to keep my secret life to myself."

Over their steaks that night, she told him that the conductor Mitch Miller had introduced her to a hot new male singer. "It was Guy Mitchell, and he said he knows you. 'Great guy' were his exact words to describe you. Guy said you and he used to pal around together in San Francisco."

"What else did Guy tell you?" a nervous Merv asked.

"Nothing, nothing at all." Finally, Rosemary slammed down her fork. "Listen, if we're going to be pals, we've got to be honest with each other. There's no way in hell we can have a friendship any other way. I know you had a crush on Guy. I know you and Tom Drake are lovers. Surely you don't think I have a problem with that? In the future, I'll tell you about the different men who've made love to me, and you can tell me about the men you've loved or will love."

"Okay," Merv said, biting into his steak. "You've asked for it. Gal, can we talk. Who goes first?"

Some of the details Merv related to his new confidante involved his sexual involvement with Peter Lawford and Robert Walker.

***

As related to Rosemary Clooney, Merv had accepted the invitation of Peter Lawford and Robert Walker to shack up with them as part of a three-way. He later told Roddy, "Until I met those guys, I was a bit of a square. They taught me tricks that only a whore in a bordello in Shanghai could have known."

In later years when Merv was rich and powerful, he staged many nights of debauchery himself with a paid "cast." He always credited (or blamed) Peter and Robert for liberating him. "Until I started hanging out with those guys, I was limited to just the missionary position," he once confided to Johnny Riley.

As Merv told Roddy, something the actor already knew, "Peter has only one physical flaw. A deformed right hand. He conceals it by hiding it in the pocket of his slacks or holding a jacket over his hand. Otherwise, he's perfection itself."

Merv related to several of his friends that Robert Walker had a profound effect upon the acting techniques of both Montgomery Clift and James Dean—both, according to Merv, were inspired by the rebel-misfit brand of sensitivity that Robert Walker had originally brought to the screen. The tortured souls he played on the screen, especially in Alfred Hitchcock's *Strangers on a Train*, mirrored his own life.

To Merv, Robert always spoke of "the demons haunting me," though he never specified exactly what those demons were. During the final months of his life, according to Merv, Robert seemed to be migrating toward deeper patterns of self-destruction.

Merv continued the *ménage à trois* with Peter and Robert for at least five more dates, taking great pains to conceal his sexual involvement from Tom Drake, who was still pining for Peter, despite his ongoing declarations of love for Merv. One evening, Robert told him that he had not been able to reach Peter for five days. He'd left several messages but Peter had not returned his calls.

Robert and Merv made love as part of a conventional twosome that night, relating to each other without the distracting presence of Peter.

To Roddy McDowall, Merv had high praise for Robert's friendship. "He's quiet, gentle, a lovely but very lonely man, at least when he isn't drinking. He's tender in his lovemaking. Very giving of himself. He always tries to satisfy his partner instead of selfishly thinking of himself." Merv would later lament, "If Robert had lived, I think I could have fallen madly in love with him."

With Tom out of his life, and Peter gone from Robert's life, Merv began to see Robert exclusively. But he hardly had exclusive rights to Robert, since he had to share him with Nancy Davis. At the time, Nancy was trying to get Ronald Reagan to marry her, despite the fact that he was dating a roster of other women who included Doris Day.

Often when Ronald didn't call, Nancy spent her evenings with Robert, although Merv never encountered her again the way he had that first day he'd visited Robert's home.

As he spent more and more time with Robert during the final weeks of his life, Merv came to know him quite well. Robert often spoke of Nancy, although it was obvious that he still carried a torch for his first wife, Jennifer Jones.

One night Robert revealed that he'd once proposed marriage to Nancy, and that she had turned him down. "Nancy likes that vulnerable little-boy-lost quality in me," Robert confessed to Merv. "When I'm around her, I turn that particular charm of mine on to the maximum."

"Then why didn't she accept your offer of marriage?" Merv asked.

"She told me that over the course of a lifetime, Ronnie would be the better provider," Robert said.

Nancy maintained enormous faith even then in Ronald as a prospective husband, even though his movie career at Warner Brothers was at low tide. A few months later, after Warners had dismissed him, Ronald was offered a job as emcee hosting a parade of big-busted strippers as part of a burlesque act in Las Vegas. He turned down the gig.

Once, after a night with Robert, Merv arrived back at his suite in the early

141

hours of the morning. He was startled to find Tom Drake packing his luggage. "I hate to do this to you, but Peter called," he said. "He's in Palm Springs. He's taking me back. I'm leaving you."

Merv was stunned, at first thinking that the reason Tom was deserting him was because he had learned of his ongoing *ménage* with Peter and Robert. At the very least, Tom had revealed to Merv where Peter was.

As Merv later told his intimates, "I was glad Tom was leaving. He never really loved me—always lusting for that fickle Peter—and I never really loved Tom, although he was mighty cute and adorable at times. But it was time to end it, and I let him go. We kissed tenderly—and that was that."

During the latter days of Merv's involvement with Robert, he suspected that the actor was on the verge of another breakdown. He'd had a highly visible nervous breakdown in 1949 and had checked himself into the Menninger Clinic in Topeka, Kansas. When he'd escaped and was arrested for public drunkenness, a picture of him in the police station had appeared on front pages across America.

As Merv would later recall to his friends, Robert would have good days and bad days. On a good day, he liked to drive Merv to little hidden, out-of-the-way places in Southern California. Once he took him to an enchanting Japanese garden teahouse, which could be reached only by climbing a mountain.

Long before the hippie communes of the late 60s came into vogue, Robert drove him to Laguna Beach for a long weekend. At this compound, they shared a Quonset hut. Young people in varying states of dress lived here and engaged in all sorts of sexual couplings. One long-haired young man told Merv that "one week I'm into girls, the next week I want to share my love with a boy."

On another weekend Robert drove Merv to an unpopulated spot near Big Sur, where he was contemplating building his dream house. He claimed that he wanted to bring his two sons, Bobby and Michael, here when they weren't in the custody of their mother, Jennifer Jones.

One night Robert invited Merv to The Blue Note, a jazz dive in North Hollywood. It was strictly an off-the-record joint where stars sometimes took tricks who weren't suitable for public viewing.

Just as Robert and Merv entered the club, Ava Gardner was leaving. With her was a studly garage mechanic wearing a uniform with the insignia of Howard Hughes Aviation. Robert had had an affair with Ava when they filmed *One Touch of Venus* in 1948.

The sultry beauty was dressed very casually and wore no makeup. After approaching Robert, she suddenly slapped his face with all her power, then headed out the door, trailed by the mechanic.

When she'd gone, Merv turned to Robert, who was rubbing his cheek still stinging from Ava's slap. "What was that all about?" Merv asked. "You told her you didn't like her last picture?"

"When Ava and I were filming *Venus*, I made a surprise visit to her dressing room and caught her fucking Howard Duff. He retreated and let Ava and me fight it out. In a jealous rage, I slapped her. I guess tonight she was returning the favor."

During the course of that weekend, Robert confessed that he'd once plotted to kill David O. Selznick for stealing Jennifer from him. "She's the only woman I've ever loved, even though I never felt I was good enough for her."

The following week, Merv arrived at Robert's house, opening the door with the key he'd been given. Before entering, he switched on the lights to discover Robert on the sofa making love to Peter. "The prodigal has returned!" Merv said to Peter.

"Come join us," Peter said in his most beguiling voice.

Before he left, later that night, Merv learned that Peter had dropped Tom Drake once again.

Peter himself had been dropped by Lana Turner, but he'd wasted no time finding a new female love. In addition to a sexual reunion with Robert, and with Merv as well whenever he wanted to join the twosome, Peter was also seducing Jane Wyman, who was in the recovery stage from her previous divorce from Ronald Reagan.

As the summer wore on, Robert began to drink more heavily. In the past, he'd usually waited until the afternoon to start boozing. During the final weeks of his life, however, he was often plastered before noon. Peter tried to help Robert, but during those days, Peter himself was often drunk before noon as well.

Merv didn't want to return to Tom, and he seriously debated dropping both Robert and Peter from his life as well. He had a movie career to pursue and didn't know how he could do that sitting around with two debauched actors in their underwear, refilling their drinks.

And then without warning, Robert was dead. He died on the night of August 28, 1951, when his maid encountered him in a distraught, highly agitated state. She'd called his psychiatrist, who arrived within the hour but could not calm Robert down. He'd been drinking heavily since early morning.

The doctor injected a dose of sodium amy-

Drunk, disorderly, and disheveled:
Robert Walker

143

tal into Robert's veins. He immediately suffered an acute allergic reaction to the drug and stopped breathing. Although the psychiatrist worked frantically, he could not resuscitate the actor.

Merv sent flowers to Robert's burial site at Washington Heights Memorial Park in Ogden, Utah, but did not attend the funeral.

One reporter, no doubt knowing about Merv's involvement with Robert, tracked him down for a quote. "You know," Merv said, "Robert was the original choice to play Judy Garland's boyfriend in *Meet Me in St. Louis* in 1944. But the role went to Tom Drake, despite protests from Judy." That was Merv's only comment about the death of his close friend.

With Roddy, Merv showed more sensitivity. "I'll always remember Robert standing in his doorway wearing only his underwear," Merv said. "Talk about a deer caught in the headlights. 'You know,' Robert once said to me, 'even as a kid I knew I was never meant to be born in this world. It was an accident. I've spent my life trying to escape this world, wanting to go back to the peace I knew before I entered it.'"

***

Merv's jaw dropped when Warners told him that he'd been cast in his first picture. It was hardly a musical starring Doris Day. After he read the script of *Cattle Town* (1952), Merv knew it was going to be a disaster. It was a low-budget "oater" (an early film nickname for a Western), and it was to be shot in black and white. "I thought I'd at least have one of the leads, but no such luck," Merv later recalled. "I got twelfth billing, playing Joe, the secretary of the governor of Texas."

On his first day on the set, Merv showed up hoping that the director would enlarge his part. Noel M. Smith informed him that the script was "locked up" on orders of Jack Warner himself. Between 1917 and 1952, Smith had helmed 125 films. *Cattle Town* would be his last effort, and he would face death in 1955.

Merv later recalled that Noel wasn't really directing the cast but "putting us through our paces. He had a faraway look in his eyes like he longed to be somewhere else. I hated the whole experience of being in that damn film. Right from the beginning, I knew in my heart that movies were not my calling."

Merv and the director did not get along. On his first day of actual shooting, Merv had to deliver a line, "The governor wants to see Shiloh," the name of a character role played by George O'Hanlon. Merv was supposed to exit but when he reached for the door handle, it fell off in his hand. "Cut!" the director yelled. With a certain annoyance, Noel called out as loud and as sar-

144

castically as he could, "You're gonna go far in movies, Griffin."

The next day Merv met the writer of that memorable first line of his, and he wasn't impressed. Not even when Tom W. Blackburn told him that he was also a lyricist—"not just a screenwriter." He was familiar with Merv's music, and had heard him singing with Freddy Martin's band.

Tom was working on "The Ballad of Davy Crockett." He played the song on a studio piano for Merv and asked him to try it. Merv refused, thinking it was just another silly novelty tune. "I could have beaten myself to a pulp when the Davy Crockett craze swept America," Merv said. "I could have made millions. I had forgotten that my one big hit, 'I've Got a Lovely Bunch of Coconuts,' was also a novelty song."

Merv was introduced to one of the female leads in the picture, the dynamic Rita Moreno. She was said to be suicidal over her ill-fated romance with Marlon Brando. He wanted to tell her that he too had gone to bed with Marlon, but hardly thought it was an experience to get suicidal about.

He bonded with the other female star of the picture, Amanda Blake. She was on the dawn of her greatest success when she'd play Kitty Russell in the hit TV series, *Gunsmoke*, which ran for 351 episodes beginning in 1955. He liked her immensely but on the downside blamed her for accelerating his smoking habit. "After trying to keep up with her, I found myself smoking two packages a day, a disgusting habit I kept up for far too long in my life. Poor Amanda contracted mouth cancer and underwent surgery in 1977. "That was a sort of wake-up call for me, but then I've been known to sleep through wake-up calls," Merv said.

Merv was saddened when he learned that Amanda had died in 1989 from AIDS-related complications. She contracted the dreaded disease from her last husband, Mark Spaeth, who also succumbed to AIDS.

Meeting actor Philip Carey, a former U.S. marine, thrilled Merv. He'd heard that Philip was straight and Merv didn't have a chance with him. "At least I could admire him from afar," Merv told Roddy McDowall. "I thought he was one of the handsomest men I'd ever met, and incredibly sexy. No wonder Joan Crawford went ape-shit over him."

The actor had finished *This Woman Is Dangerous* with Joan that same year. He was being groomed to appear with Doris Day in her upcoming hit, *Calamity Jane* (1953), a picture in which Merv also wanted to appear.

At six feet, five inches, Philip towered over Merv. He wished that he'd been ordered to share Philip's dressing room, but ended up instead having to dress with the extras. In 1958, Merv, with his passion still unrequited, gazed at the screen image of Philip as he starred in what became a cult fave, *Screaming Mimi* with Anita Ekberg and Gypsy Rose Lee.

Late one hot afternoon, when there was a long wait between scenes, Merv finally got to meet the star of the picture, Dennis Morgan. "It was a talk I'd remember for the rest of my life," Merv said. "Through Dennis I saw how the film factory sucked the young blood out of a performer and then discarded him when he got a little long in the tooth. It was a bitter lesson that Dennis was learning at the time I met him."

Launched near the closing years of World War II, the career of Dennis Morgan had peaked by 1949. Merv remembered him from his starring role opposite Barbara Stanwyck in *Christmas in Connecticut* and in another role with Ginger Rogers in *Kitty Foyle*. Even though Dennis was of Swedish descent, the star, like Merv himself, was known for his "Irish tenor voice."

Dennis acknowledged to Merv that he'd heard the rumor that Merv had been brought in to replace Gordon MacRae. "Believe it or not, Gordon was brought in to replace me as the singing sensation of Warner Brothers," Dennis said. "Before a guy even gets started, they bring in your replacement. *I* should right now be making movies opposite Doris Day, not Gordon. But here I am stuck in this stinker."

Dennis felt that his life mirrored the Bette Davis film, *All About Eve*. "Margo Channing is the reigning star. Eve Harrington wants to replace her. But at the end of the picture another eager young starlet is waiting to replace Eve Harrington. That's the movie business."

Dennis, like Philip Carey, had also appeared with Joan Crawford in *This Woman Is Dangerous*.

"What was it like working with Joan?" Merv asked.

"When she couldn't get Philip, she went for me and also for David Brian. Crawford's too much woman for me, but our other co-star, David Brian, handled her just fine. He told me that the one way to keep Crawford happy is to shove a big dick up either end of her."

Jack Warner still had a contract with Dennis but wanted him off the lot, because he was the highest salaried actor still left. To get rid of Dennis, Jack was sending him the worst scripts he could find, hoping Dennis would reject the latest offering and buy his way out of the contract.

"That's why I got *Cattle Town*," Dennis said. "This film should not even be made. Even though I know the screenplay is awful, I sent word to Jack that I loved it and couldn't wait to star in it. Do you think I'm going to pass up a weekly paycheck? I think my career in films is winding down, and I'm going to get every last penny coming my way, even if Jack Warner demands that I moon the camera in my next picture."

Later a reviewer commented on the numerous

Dennis Morgan

146

songs sung by Dennis in the picture. "We usually like to hear Dennis Morgan sing. But not this time. The songs come across as irritating."

As Dennis was called to the set for a retake, Merv asked one more question, "Any regrets?"

"Yeah," he said, "one big one. In 1942 I was set to play Rick Blaine in *Casablanca*. Damn you, Humphrey Bogart. And just for fun, I should have let Jane Wyman have her way with me when we worked together in *Cheyenne*, but I insisted on being faithful to my wife, a good woman I married back in 1933."

When Jack Warner saw the first cut of *Cattle Town*, he didn't like the scene of a barroom brawl, and he ordered footage from *Dodge City* (1938) thrown in instead.

Merv finished his small part in the film and felt a wave of great disappointment come over him. He invited Roddy to go with him for a long weekend in Las Vegas, but he was too busy.

Roddy told him to check into the Las Vegas Sahara Club, claiming that there was a well-muscled and incredibly handsome lifeguard there who was available to men or women. "You've got to pay."

"But I've never paid for sex in my life," Merv protested.

"Get used to it," Roddy advised. "Anyway I hear this guy is worth every inch. Speaking of inches, take along enough money."

"You've convinced me," Merv said. "I'm packing my bags right now, ready, willing, and able to meet this Adonis."

***

On the theory that the early bird gets the worm, Merv was at poolside at the Las Vegas Sahara Club when Gordon Werschkul reported to duty at ten o'clock. Later he would tell Roddy, "It was more like a snake than a worm."

Since no one else was at the pool, it was easy to strike up an acquaintance with this startlingly handsome athlete and his nineteen-inch biceps. He stood six feet, three inches tall and weighed 218 pounds. Merv pretended he didn't know how to swim, and Gordon volunteered to teach him. The way Merv figured it, this would allow him to come into a close encounter with all those muscles.

After one hour of instruction, Gordon, after enduring a lot of fondling, turned to Merv. "I get off for an afternoon break at two o'clock. What's your room number? We both know what you want. But it'll cost you fifty bucks."

"It's yours, all in tens," Merv said.

Merv would later tell Roddy that even before Gordon got out of his swimming trunks, he warned Merv that "you can have me only from the waist down. I like girls."

In the months ahead, Gordon, either in Las Vegas or Los Angeles, would earn many a fifty-dollar bill from Merv, who became obsessive about the bodybuilder's virility and good looks.

Months later Merv was astonished to read in one of the trade papers that the producer, Sol Lesser, had signed Gordon to a seven-year contract to play Tarzan. He was replacing the equally handsome Lex Barker, who had been married to Lana Turner.

Gordon Werschkul became Gordon Scott and a household name in America in the late 1950s. Gordon beat out 200 other male athletes to become Tarzan. Two of his more memorable pictures were *Tarzan's Hidden Jungle* (1955), co-starring the actress Vera Miles, whom he married, and *Tarzan's Greatest Adventure* (1959) with a young, pre-James Bond Sean Connery playing the villain.

After leaving the Tarzan movies, Gordon went to Italy to star in a series of "sword-and-sandal" epics, featuring handsome bodybuilders. In one, *Duel of the Titans* (1961), he teamed with Steve Reeves, an old buddy from his days at a gym in Oakland, California. Gordon was cast as Remus to Steve's Romulus. The film became a cult favorite among homosexuals, and remains so today.

A wealthy homosexual in England became so fascinated with Gordon and Steve that he invited them to his estate in Surrey where he convinced them to make a porno film, starring just the two of them. His obsession compelled him to offer a fee of $100,000, a vast sum of money in the early 1960s.

After leaving films, Gordon was unemployed for decades. For three years he lived off that fee for doing porno. Merv once heard about the film and went to great trouble to obtain a copy of it but to no avail.

Near the end of his life, Gordon was rescued financially by Roger Thomas, who had become obsessed with the star when he'd appeared in those long-ago Tarzan movies.

Roger used to spend his vacation time trying to track Gordon down. Eventually he located him and invited him to live in a back bedroom of his South Baltimore rowhouse. Gordon came for a visit and stayed for six years, mostly spending his days watching old black-and-white movies on TV.

Long before that happened, Gordon used to send word to Merv that he needed money. Merv

Gordon Scott
"Me Tarzan, You Merv"

148

would often send him a thousand-dollar bill, especially one time when he heard that Gordon was sleeping on a park bench.

The last time Merv ever spoke to Gordon on the phone, the former actor told him, "Years ago I never understood the attraction of you guys toward me when I became Tarzan. But I understand a lot more about it now. You guys still worship me when all those beautiful gals of the 50s have gotten old and forgotten me. After all, who wouldn't want to go to bed with Tarzan?"

***

In a surprise call, Merv picked up his phone receiver to hear the voice of Monty Clift, who had arrived unexpectedly in Los Angeles. In the early 1950s every major director in Hollywood wanted Monty to star in his next movie, despite rumors that he was emotionally unstable and very difficult to work with.

Monty told Merv that he'd signed to film *I Confess*, to be directed by Alfred Hitchcock. Based on Paul Anthelme's play, it was the story of a priest who is charged with murder after the real murderer had confessed the killing to him in confessional.

Monty was troubled by the plotline and wanted to meet with Merv to read him the script to see how plausible it was. "After all," he told Merv, "you're a practicing Irish Catholic, and you should know about such things. I bet you brought a whole list of sins to confessional to your priest, who probably molested you in return." He giggled. "I'm just joking, of course."

Monty may have been joking, but Merv realized how accurate his intuition was.

That night at Monty's, Merv met Mira Rostova, the impoverished Russian acting coach. He'd never encountered her before, although he'd been told that she and Monty were inseparable.

He seriously doubted if there was any great romance going on here, at least not on Monty's part. Mira, however, seemed in love with Monty and constantly referred to him as "my comrade." If only to get a drink for Monty from the bar, she moved through his living room like a great tragedienne. Her students in New York claimed "She is Duse and Bernhardt all rolled into one."

Merv was astonished to learn that even though the great Hitchcock was going to direct *I Confess*, Monty actually intended to take direction from Mira. She planned to send signals to him on the set. A pull on her left ear would mean the scene was no good and should be reshot. Monty carried out his threat. When *I Confess* was filming in Québec, Hitchcock might pronounce a scene "brilliant" and order it printed. But if Mira tugged on her left ear lobe, Monty would demand that it be reshot.

The reunion with Monty and his introduction to Mira occurred prior to Merv's screen test with Phyllis Kirk. The talented pair had given Merv acting tips before he'd shot that test. On the day that Merv's screen test was first shown on the Warner's lot to potential directors, Merv invited both Monty and Mira to the screening. Jack Warner had urged his directors to use contract players such as Merv whenever possible.

As the lights dimmed, Merv twitched nervously in his seat, glancing every now and then to see if he could determine the reaction of Mira and Monty in the light reflected from the screen. They remained respectfully silent throughout the brief showing, their faces emotionless.

At the end, Merv walked Monty and Mira to their car. Still no review from either of them. Finally, he asked, "Okay, guys, what did you think of Doris Day's future leading man?"

Mira remained silent, but Monty spoke up. "There was something up there on that screen," he said. "Maybe a bit raw. But definitely something up there on that screen."

With that enigmatic review, Monty drove off with Mira but not before inviting Merv to join them for a drive the following day down to Laguna Beach.

After that, Merv began to see more and more of Monty, usually with Mira. One day Monty complained that he found the noise at his hotel, Château Marmont, deafening. Merv invited him to come and live with him in a house he'd rented from his agent, "Bullets" Durgom. In the days and weeks ahead, Merv would regret that invitation.

One Saturday afternoon, Merv and Monty spent time alone together. Mira was nowhere to be seen, and Merv suspected that Monty was feuding with his "bound-at-the-waist twin," as he called her.

Monty had not had one drink that afternoon, but Merv noticed that he kept retreating to the bathroom. Merv walked out on the patio and dreamed of other conquests, as his on-again, off-again sex life with Monty was not adequate for him. He gave in whenever Monty wanted sex, but never pursued it.

In his unexpurgated version of *Hollywood Babylon*, filmmaker Kenneth Anger referred to Monty as "Princess Tiny Meat," and as a result, the actor had been deeply wounded that the size of his penis should be known to his public. "What is this going to do to my image?" Monty had shouted. "Jesus H. Christ. Is nothing sacred?"

When Monty emerged from the bathroom, Merv suspected that he'd been taking drugs, perhaps in pill form. Around seven that evening Monty abruptly announced that he had been invited to Alfred Hitchcock's house to meet with Olivia de Havilland to see if she'd like to take the female lead in *I Confess*. In 1949, both Monty and Olivia had made the highly successful film,

The Heiress.

Seeing Monty's condition, Merv offered to drive him there. He also had an ulterior motive. He wanted to meet Hitchcock, hoping he might have a role for him in the film. He also wanted to meet Olivia since *Gone With the Wind* had been one of his all-time favorite movies.

Monty adamantly refused, claiming he preferred to drive himself. Sensing what Merv really wanted, Monty agreed to use his influence and star power to get Hitchcock to offer Merv a role in *I Confess.*

At Hitchcock's house, as later reported by Monty to Merv, the actor bonded with Olivia. After nearly three hours of talking, and shortly before midnight, Olivia decided the part wasn't for her. "I would be horribly miscast," she told Hitchcock and Monty. The female lead eventually went to Anne Baxter.

Years later Olivia remembered that evening, recalling how "hyper-intense and overexcited" Monty was, his pupils dilated. "He talked very fast in an almost hysterical voice," she said. "Usually his speech pattern was much slower." At the time she believed he had had a strange reaction to the alcohol he'd consumed, not suspecting drug use.

Shortly before midnight, Monty called Merv from a phone booth. His speech was slurred. It seemed that he'd had an accident after leaving Hitchcock's house and had crashed into a tree. Although badly bruised with some cuts, he apparently didn't have any broken limbs. He gave Merv his location and begged him to come and pick him up.

About thirty minutes later Merv, only half dressed, arrived on the scene but couldn't find Monty. Getting out of his car, he searched the deserted neighborhood, eventually finding the actor wandering dazed in a park. He was limping, and his cheek was bleeding.

Although Monty had summoned Merv to the scene, he was hostile at first, even refusing to get into Merv's car. Merv forced Monty into the back seat where he collapsed in sobs. Before taking Monty back to Bullets' house, Merv drove nearby to the scene of the accident, getting out to survey Monty's smashed car. It was so badly damaged that Merv wondered how Monty could have escaped relatively intact.

Back at their rented house, Merv tucked Monty into bed after undressing him and putting iodine on his cuts. The moment he hit the pillow, Monty passed out. In his living room, Merv impersonated Monty's voice and called the police. "My car's been stolen," he said. "I wanted to drive it somewhere tonight and found it missing."

The police apparently were convinced by Merv's act and took down all the information. Merv went to bed beside Monty that night, thinking he had saved him from embarrassing headlines the next morning, and possibly time in jail.

Monty's smashed car was blamed on "joy riders" who had hot-wired his vehicle. Since the car could not be repaired, Merv went with Monty the next day to shop for what Monty called "new wheels."

Grateful to Merv for rescuing him, Monty kept his promise to get Merv cast in *I Confess*. At first Merv was thrilled until he learned what part he had, and then he was bitterly disappointed. If Merv thought his screen appearance in *Cattle Town* was brief, he learned what brief really meant in *I Confess*. He did not even appear on the screen. He was unseen but his voice was heard on the other end of a phone call.

He complained to Roddy, "Just as Monty gets the juicy role of the year in *From Here to Eternity*, I get to do voiceovers."

Two days later, Merv's luck changed, or at least he thought it had. He received a call from Bill Orr at Warner's informing him that he'd been cast in Doris Day's latest picture, *By the Light of the Silvery Moon*.

"I'll show Hollywood," Merv vowed. "Doris Day and I will knock Dwight and Mamie Eisenhower off the front pages."

***

Two weeks later Merv drove to the Kirkeby Mansion to meet Monty for a game of tennis. The home later became famous as the setting for *The Beverly Hillbillies*. Monty was nearly two hours late, and Merv was ready to leave. At the last moment Monty showed up, looking bedraggled and depressed.

He couldn't even finish one game, as his heart wasn't in it. He asked Merv to drive him at leisure through the Hollywood Hills where they might find a secluded place to talk. Merv willingly agreed. On the way to a lonely little hillside, Monty didn't say a word. Merv found a place with a beautiful view and retrieved a blanket from the trunk of his car, spreading it out for Monty.

No sooner had Monty sat down than he reached for Merv and burst into uncontrollable sobs. Merv held him tightly until he'd cried himself out. "Tell me what happened. It can't be all that bad."

Through tear-streaked eyes, Monty looked at him. "But it is. The worst humiliation of my life. What is it with me? I love women and want to be with them, but for sex I always turn to men."

Slowly, very slowly and with great hesitation and embarrassment, Monty revealed his story. Over the past few weeks, and much to the regret of Mira Rostova, Monty had developed an obsession with Greta Garbo. She had seen three of his pictures, including *A Place in the Sun*, and was equally fascinated with him.

If such a thing was possible for Garbo, she seemed flattered that such a handsome, brilliant young actor would show an interest in her, since she'd faded from the screen after the disastrous release of *Two-Faced Woman* in 1941. Her heyday in the late 20s and 30s was becoming more and more a distant memory, as each year passed and her once-loyal fans died in droves.

Monty had been introduced to Garbo by Salka Viertel, the once-famous Polish actress and writer who had moved to Hollywood in 1929 before marrying director Berthod Viertel. She had worked on such Garbo vehicles as *Anna Karenina* and *Camille*. Garbo was not only Salka's best friend, but they were said to be lesbian lovers.

Monty claimed that until the previous night, he had never had any sexual involvement with Garbo, except for a kiss on her perpetually chapped lips. "But last night that changed," he sobbed. "It was horrible. My thing never rose up beyond the size of a peanut, and I was faced with the Grand Canyon. I rushed to the bathroom where I threw up. I think she heard me. How unflattering for any woman. But for Garbo it must have been terrible, as it was for me. She'll never speak to me again."

That afternoon Garbo called and invited Monty for dinner. Impulsively he asked if he could bring a friend, and Garbo said yes. When Monty told Merv that he'd been invited to meet Garbo, he claimed it was a deliberate choice to avoid any embarrassment over discussing the previous night. Merv was delighted and accepted the invitation, although he wished that it had been extended under more favorable conditions.

Although her face had aged since Merv had last seen Garbo on the screen, he found that she was still a regal beauty with a thin, almost athletic body. In the years that lay ahead of him, he would become celebrated for the ease with which he dealt with celebrities, getting them to open up even in front of millions of people. Garbo, however, was not to be among his devotees.

Over the worst dinner of his life, cooked by Garbo herself, the diva wasted most of the limited number of words she uttered praising the merchandise at Hammacher-Schlemmer in New York.

Throughout the dinner, Monty did most of the talking. When not praising that department store, Garbo was mostly silent. When she got up to go to her kitchen, Monty whispered to Merv, "Isn't she terrific? My Sphinx Goddess."

After dinner, Garbo played a record on her phonograph and settled down in her favorite chair. To Merv's horror, Monty continued to drink heavily. He stood up only to take off his shirt and pants, retaining only his underwear. Lowering himself onto a position on all fours on her carpet, he began to crawl toward Garbo. At her feet, he removed her sandals. Once that was accomplished, he rubbed her big feet and then began quoting from *The Wanderings of Oisin* by William Butler Yeats:

The mist-drops hung on the fragrant trees.
And in the blossoms hung the bees.
We rode in sadness above Lough Lean,
For our best were dead on Gavra's green.

At the end of his recitation, he began to wildly kiss her feet.

Garbo claimed that Yeats had written her a fan letter after watching her emote in *Flesh and the Devil*. "He proposed marriage to me," she claimed. "He said that even though we'd engage in the 'tragedy of sexual intercourse,' we would still maintain the 'perpetual virginity of our souls.' I'm sure that must have been from one of his poems or something."

Over brandy consumed on her side porch, Merv sat with Monty and Garbo watching the fireflies. "God damn it, did I feel left out," he'd later recall.

Suddenly, a new excitement came over Monty, as he tried to revive Garbo's interest in appearing on screen as George Sand to his Alfred de Musset. Merv was not familiar with either the names or genders of these 19th-century French lovers, but his ears perked up when Monty said he wanted George Cukor to direct. Garbo suggested Salka Viertel for the screenplay, but Monty held out for the French existentialist, Jean-Paul Sartre.

Merv learned that the George Sand/Alfred de Musset affair had first been suggested in 1948 as the theme of Garbo's comeback picture. Apparently, Monty was hoping to rekindle hope for the production.

At one point Monty assured Garbo that she'd look great in the men's clothing that Sand wore. Merv wondered how Monty and Garbo felt they could bring a homosexual love story to the screen.

After Merv surveyed a reluctant Garbo and a hopelessly wrecked Monty, he would later tell Roddy McDowall, "That film with those two will never be made. Maybe if they would cast me as George Sand, it might have a chance."

"You'd have to do the role in drag," Roddy warned him. "George Sand was a woman."

***

Merv was disturbed that he still hadn't been shown a script for his upcoming movie with Doris Day. At Warners he had spare time on his hands, and he wanted to begin rehearsing the musical numbers

William Butler Yeats, **Greta Garbo, and** "the perpetual virginity of our souls" he'd perform with Doris.

He was also troubled that Doris hadn't asked to see him on the Warners lot. She'd been responsible for his coming to Hollywood, but she hadn't even placed a call to him. He decided to go to her dressing room, knock on her door, and reintroduce himself to her, as he hadn't seen her since that night in Las Vegas when she attended his show.

Bill Orr had instructed him never to go and knock on the door of a star. It was not proper etiquette, but Merv decided to defy the mandate. Although his knees were knocking, Merv stood before the door of Doris' dressing room, took a deep breath, and knocked three times. It was Doris herself who threw open the door, greeting him with such a bright smile that one would have thought she was welcoming one of her all-time best friends for a reunion.

"C'mon in, Merv," she said. "I've been meaning to call you. There are some friends I want you to meet." Taking his arm, she directed him inside where she introduced him to Steve Cochran and Ronald Reagan, two contract players at Warners, although both of them were being shoved out the studio door at the time.

Doris was having a get-together with friends she'd made while filming *Storm Warning*, a movie about the KKK. Merv had heard rumors that Doris had had an affair with Ronald before Nancy Davis snared him. Ronald was polite, friendly, and courteous, giving no hint that a grand friendship would one day form between Merv and himself.

As for Steve, Merv found him "about the sexiest thing walking on the planet," as he would later tell Roddy.

The conversation was mostly "shop talk," as Merv remembered it. He kept hoping that Doris would at least bring up the subject of working with him on *By the Light of the Silvery Moon*, but she said not a word about the upcoming picture. Finally, Merv himself built up enough courage to bring it up. Her only response was, "We'll have a grand old time making the film."

After a while, Ronald shook Merv's hand and kissed Doris on the cheek, as he had to leave for another appointment. Steve remained behind to talk with Doris and Merv. At one point Merv complained that he still hadn't been assigned a dressing room and was forced to dress with the extras.

The girl he didn't marry:
Ronald Reagan with **Doris Day**
in *Storm Warning*

155

"Jack Warner is such a cheap bastard," Steve said. "You're welcome to share my dressing room until you get one of your own."

Merv thanked Steve profusely, even though trying to conceal his eagerness to share the dressing room of the actor who'd been called "the male sexpot of Warner Brothers."

Doris abruptly shooed the men out of her dressing room, claiming she had to get dressed for a shot. She told Merv that she was looking forward to working with him and predicted that he'd become a big star at Warners.

Walking with Steve to his dressing room, Merv told him, "Getting to star opposite Doris is the big break of my life."

Steve stopped and stared at Merv, as if not comprehending what he'd just said. "Star? I ran into Gordon MacRae yesterday. He told me about starring once again with Doris."

"There must be some mistake," Merv said, utterly confused.

"Better clear it up, kid," Steve said. "That God damn Silvery Moon has been shining for two weeks of shooting on both Doris and MacRae."

***

On their first day of sharing the dressing room, Steve laid down the ground rules. If a yellow ribbon was tied around the doorknob, Merv was to idle away his time by having a cup of coffee in the commissary. The ribbon meant that Steve was engaged, seducing one of the female extras on the lot. "Sometimes I bed a big star, but not that often." He also confided that, "I have to have sex every afternoon. I often can't wait for the evening to roll around. If I don't shoot off in somebody, I get splitting migraines."

Merv had heard all the gossip about Steve, but later said, "seeing was believing" when he arrived at Steve's dressing room the following morning to see him emerge from the shower. "It hung all the way down to Honolulu," he confided to Roddy later that day. "Talk about meat for the poor."

Steve appeared amused that Merv kept staring at his appendage but seemed in no hurry to cover it up. Merv suspected that the B-movie bad boy might be an exhibitionist.

The Los Angeles crime writer, James Ellroy, had made more fans for Steve thanks to references to him in his novels *American Tabloid* and *L.A. Confidential*. Steve had one of the largest penises in Hollywood and was nicknamed "Mr. King Size" because of his endowment. In some of his

Steve Cochran

writings, Ellroy referred to Steve with the sobriquet "The Shvantz."

Virile and swaggering on the outside, Steve seemed deeply troubled to Merv, as if he possessed dark secrets that tormented his soul. The son of a lumberman from Wyoming, he exuded a rugged super masculine man-of-the-west appeal. He'd once worked as a cowpoke.

He'd had an ongoing affair with Mae West when he'd appeared on stage with her in *Diamond Lil.*

Steve told amusing stories about Mae, particularly one time when he had to administer an enema to her before she could go onstage. He grabbed his penis. "That's not all I administered to her. I made her squeal, and that from a woman used to taking the big ones."

Steve called his seduction of such big stars as Mae West "mercy fucks." He confided that he was still having an affair with Joan Crawford that had begun back when he'd appeared in her film *The Damned Don't Cry* (1950). "I don't fuck her because I have a hard-on for her. I keep plugging her, hoping she'll get me cast in her next picture."

Steve often drank in the afternoon while waiting to be called to the set. He drunkenly confessed that his dream in life was to have a harem composed entirely of thirteen and fourteen-year-old girls. "For me, that would be paradise—not Crawford or West. Those broads have seen their day!"

Every afternoon, Merv sat in the commissary pondering his fate, waiting for Steve to finish off his afternoon seduction. One day when he wandered back toward the dressing room to see if Steve had done his duty, he spotted two teenage girls emerging from Steve's dressing room. The rather beautiful girls looked thirteen at the most. When they were out of sight, Merv came into Steve's dressing room, finding the actor nude, sitting in a chair with an impressive semi-erection.

"Those gals looked like jailbait," Merv said.

"They are," Steve said, smiling mischievously. "The way I like them."

"Aren't you afraid of getting caught?"

"It's a risk worth taking," Steve said. "I have a lust inside me that must be satisfied at all costs."

At last Merv was allowed to meet David Butler, the director of *By the Light of the Silvery Moon*, which he called "old-fashioned corn." Merv was surprised that the director hadn't summoned him before.

Butler was a rugged Californian of the old school, although he still lived with his father and had never married. There were rumors. He'd even survived the San Francisco earthquake when he was eleven years old.

Merv wanted to talk about his role in the movie, but David deflected that, telling about his early days in silent films, including when he'd been hired to work as an extra for five dollars a day in *The Birth of a Nation* (1915). He told

Merv that it beat "scooping up camel dung." His first job on films was shoveling up shit dropped by camels appearing in desert pictures. "I've directed everybody from Rin-Tin-Tin to Errol Flynn and Bob Hope," David boasted.

Finally, Merv got up enough nerve to ask the big question. "Well, do you think you can make a star out of me?"

At that point David was called back to the set. Before leaving, he looked Merv up and down. "I'm still debating exactly what to do with you in the picture."

The next afternoon Steve seemed very agitated. "Some god damn bitch stood me up." He took Merv's arm and directed him toward their dressing room. "Count today as your lucky day," he said, once he'd entered the dressing room and locked the door. "I've got to have it real bad. Think you can handle it?"

Merv said nothing but was enthralled as Steve stripped down for him. He'd later tell Roddy, "Maybe Mae West or Joan Crawford could swallow that log, but I couldn't. I did my best and I got him off. From now on, I'll be begging for it every chance I can get."

"You are one lucky guy," Roddy said. "Every homo in Hollywood dreams of seducing Steve Cochran. If not Steve, then John Payne."

"He's available?" Merv asked.

"In Hollywood, if you didn't know it by now, all the handsome studs are available. It depends on how you approach them."

One day Merv returned to his shared dressing room and noticed that the yellow ribbon was not on the doorknob. Thinking he might get lucky again, he entered the room and walked in on Steve, who was standing completely nude searching for his underwear.

Joan Crawford in a robe emerged from the rear where she'd obviously taken a shower. She remembered Merv from Pebble Beach and greeted him warmly, not seeming in the least embarrassed that he'd caught her with Steve. As Merv later said, she was not Nancy Davis running and hiding at Robert Walker's house.

Joan was also not shy about exposing her own body, as she got dressed. After putting on his clothes, Steve wet-kissed Joan good-bye, as the diva continued to chat with Merv. She asked him if he'd escort her to a party Friday night, and he eagerly accepted. "Do you own a tux?"

"Do I ever!" he said. "I have two. Left over from all those years of singing with Freddy Martin's band."

After Joan made arrangements for him to pick her up, she kissed him lightly on the lips. Before departing, she turned and smiled at him. "Don't you think Steve is the best lay in Hollywood? What talent that guy has." And then she was gone.

Merv got lucky time and time again with Steve. He became better with practice and bonded with the actor. It was a sad day when Steve told him good-bye. He was leaving Warners to form his own production company, and he promised Merv he would get good roles for him when he started producing his own movies. In the weeks and months ahead, Merv waited and waited for the call that never came.

Encountering Doris Day on the lot of Warners, Merv confronted her about his role in the picture. He demanded to know from her when he was going to be called to appear on camera with her. She politely but firmly brushed him aside, assuring him that his big break would come soon. "I'll have a talk with Jack Warner," she promised. "Everything will be fine, you'll see."

By now Merv was growing leery of any promise from Doris. Then his luck changed, or at least he thought it had when he was summoned to Jack Warner's office. Perhaps Doris had come through for him after all.

In Jack's office, Merv was greeted warmly. "Griff, your time has come. I want you to play the male lead in *By the Light of the Silvery Moon*. Gordon MacRae's off the picture. We'll have to reshoot his scenes with you."

Merv was elated.

"For three days in a row, MacRae has been too drunk to go before the camera," Jack said. "I'm not putting up with any more of his shit. I fired him today and ordered him off the lot."

Merv was so overjoyed he couldn't sleep that night. He and Monty went out and got drunk—or rather Merv got drunk. Monty had already been drinking before Merv arrived home from work.

The next day a note from Jack Warner arrived for Merv at Steve's dressing room. "I learned that we're too far into the picture to change stars at this point," Jack wrote. "We've sobered MacRae up, and we think we can keep him dry until the picture is filmed. Be at my house Sunday night at eight for a big party. Bring a date. Someone with a title. Practically all my guests will be either a big movie star or royalty."

At long last David Butler decided how to use Merv in *By the Light of the Silvery Moon*. To Merv's great disappointment, he learned that he had only one line of dialogue.

Dressed in a mackinaw, with a large bullhorn, Merv was cast as an announcer near the final reel of the film. "All you figure skaters grab your favorite partner and let's skate to our favorite song." Naturally that song was "By the Light of the Silvery Moon."

Even though his role was small, Merv hoped for billing along with the other supporting players including Billy Gray, Leon Ames, Rosemary DeCamp, and Mary Wickes, the latter cast as a sarcastic maid. Merv's appearance was uncredited.

When he finally got to see the final cut of *By the Light of the Silvery Moon*, he found that his one scene was a disaster. He'd used a bullhorn to call out to the figure skaters, including Doris and Gordon, and that instrument practically obscured his face. His dream of movie stardom was growing dimmer by the day.

***

On the days Merv wasn't working, he drove Monty Clift around Hollywood, searching for the right trumpet that would be the mouthpiece of his character Prewitt. He was about to immortalize himself in that role in James Jones's *From Here to Eternity*, which was to be directed by Fred Zinnemann.

Merv was mildly disturbed to learn that Frank Sinatra had also been cast in the picture. "If the role calls for a singer, why don't you get Zinnemann to cast me? I'd be great."

Monty assured him that "Frankie doesn't get to sing in the picture. It's a war drama. Don't you ever read a fucking book?"

Monty just had to get the right horn, and Merv drove him to practically every store in Greater Los Angeles that sold musical instruments. Regardless of how many instruments he tried out, Monty could not find "the perfect fit." Finally, he came across a dusty old store in North Hollywood that had sold instruments to jazz musicians back in the 1920s. After trying out the worn trumpet, Monty claimed he'd found his instrument.

The role of Prewitt began to consume Monty's life. He virtually worked night and day with his coach, Mira Rostova, when she returned to his life after they'd had a serious disagreement.

Watching Monty's intensity as he worked with Mira made Merv realize that he'd never be a serious actor. "I just don't have the concentration," he told Monty. "Hell, you've rehearsed that one scene with Mira a hundred times, and she's still not satisfied. Neither are you. It's only a movie, for Christ's sake. Speaking of movies, I want to go out. Wanna come with me?"

"No, Mira and I have to rehearse," Monty said.

Monty even coerced Merv into going with him to a gym for workouts, something Merv had resisted up to now. In *From Here to Eternity*, Monty, in spite of his frail frame, was cast as a boxer. He had to get his body in shape for the role. He'd even flown to meet James Jones, the author of the book, who taught Monty how to throw his famous left jab.

Back in Hollywood at their gym, Monty tried out the punch on Merv and succeeded in loosening a front tooth. Merv had to rush to the dentist for emergency work.

"Monty is driving me out of the house," Merv told Johnny Riley in a phone call to San Francisco. He plays that God damn trumpet night and day to bugle sheet music. He's so off-key he's splitting my eardrums."

Taking his training seriously, Monty woke Merv at five o'clock in the morning so that Merv would drive him to the Hollywood High School athletic field. The actor's license had either been lost or suspended. Merv didn't know which. Catching up on his sleep, Merv would nod off at the wheel of the parked car, which actually belonged to his agent, Bullets Durgom. Occasionally, he would wake up at some traffic noise only to see Monty still marching around the track pretending to be a G.I. during the weeks before the Japanese attack on Pearl Harbor. Monty even wore a soldier's uniform.

One night Mira Rostova waited with Merv at his rented house until Monty showed up. Monty's invitation for drinks was at seven o'clock. By nine o'clock there was still no sign of Monty.

Suddenly, Merv heard him roar into the driveway. As Merv rushed out, Monty was crashing into the garage door. He slammed the gears into reverse. The car lurched across the lawn and crashed into a hedge concealing the mailbox. Finally, Monty came to a stop.

Merv and Mira rushed to his side, finding that he was not injured. The car was still in running order, but it had been badly damaged. Merv dreaded confronting his agent, Bullets, about the damaged car. While Monty's vehicle was being repaired, Merv had foolishly lent him Bullets' vehicle.

"Get in," Monty said. Mira refused and so did Merv. In his drunken state, Monty screamed, "You're nothing but shitheads. Shitheads." He backed the car up and pulled away, hitting the road again, with tires screeching.

From Here to Eternity: Wartime passion on and off the screen:
Left: Donna Reed with **Frank Sinatra;** *Right* **Burt Lancaster** with **Deborah Kerr**

Mira predicted that Monty would die in an automobile accident one day.

Two days later Bullets learned what had happened to his car and garage. Barely concealing his anger, he showed up at Merv's doorstep. He'd already inspected the damage to the mailbox, yard, and garage. Monty had sent the borrowed car to a garage for repairs.

After looking around at the debris and the wreck of his house, Bullets went into the kitchen where it looked as if the dishes hadn't been washed since Merv and Monty moved in. Politely but firmly, Bullets suggested that Merv and Monty should move out "sooner than later."

The next day Merv set out to find a modest rental since money was tight. He finally found a place called the Commodore Garden Apartments behind Grauman's Chinese Theater off Hollywood Boulevard.

Two days after moving in, Merv had seen most of his fellow tenants coming and going. "There's not an ugly among them," he told Roddy. "The most gorgeous guys and dolls I've ever seen in Hollywood. Or seen anywhere in one bunch for that matter."

Roddy was familiar with the Commodore. "No wonder they're so hot: that building contains the most high-priced hookers in town and the most expensive hustlers. Movie stars go there to fuck them on off-the-record nights."

Merv began to evaluate his fellow tenants. He kept an eye on two handsome young men who lived next door to him, but he'd never see them during the day. He agreed with Roddy that the male tenants at the Commodore were the most well built he'd seen in town. He suspected that all of them had come to Hollywood dreaming of becoming the next Rock Hudson, but had to hustle homosexuals as a means of supporting themselves.

Monty refused to move into the Commodore with Merv, but returned to his studio at the Château Marmont. Merv had heard that he was still seeing Greta Garbo, but Monty neither confirmed nor denied it.

Bullets called Merv to tell him that he'd found his second car in the garage, and all damages had been repaired, including those to his garage door, front yard, and mailbox. Monty had paid for all the harm he'd caused.

One night Monty arrived at Merv's door at the Commodore. He was drunk, and Merv showed him in. It took two hours of heavy drinking before Monty finally told him why he was here.

"I was getting too close to you and Mira, and I need my own space," Monty told him. "I know you love me, and, believe me, I don't get off on breaking someone's heart. I want us to remain friends. But one part of our life has to end. The sexual thing. I've met someone I've fallen in love with."

Merv appeared to be heartbroken, but never really was. He was Monty's friend but had never enjoyed one minute of their love-making. Monty slept over that night, and Merv put him to bed as he had so many times in their past.

162

But when he went to sleep beside Monty, he felt relieved that their so-called romance was over. After his first intimate night with Monty, he never wanted to repeat the experience, finding it completely unsatisfactory.

Before leaving late the following morning, Monty told Merv that he was going to fly to Honolulu with the cast of *From Here to Eternity* in a month or so, and that he wanted Merv to fly down to join him for a holiday. "I'll send you the tickets."

Merv thought that was a graceful exit line and never expected Monty to carry through on his promise. To his surprise, tickets for a round-trip flight to Honolulu did arrive on his doorstep. Merv cabled Monty he'd be arriving there in just ten days.

"Monty's a rotten lover," Merv told Roddy, "but I suspect he'll be a great friend."

Roddy agreed with that, but added an ominous comment. "He'll be a great friend until he kills himself."

***

When Merv got his next paycheck, he planned to sample some of the better-looking hustlers at the Commodore Garden Apartments. He'd already staked out the object of his desire, a handsome, lantern-jawed young man with a sculpted physique.

No doubt he was an actor, at least in Merv's mind, and probably hustled on the side to earn a living. Early every afternoon, he appeared on the roof lying on a chaise longue. A lot of the hustlers did that to keep their bodies tanned and ready for the next customer. Every actor wore a bathing suit except the young man who intrigued Merv. He wore the skimpiest of posing straps crafted from a gray velour that clearly outlined his genitalia.

On his first payday, Merv in baggy swimming trunks got up enough courage to make his move. Only problem was, he didn't know how much money to offer the actor. He finally decided that a twenty-dollar bill would do just fine.

"Hi," he said moving in as close as he could to the posing strap. "I'm Merv Griffin."

"Hi, yourself," said the young man, shading his eyes from the sun to get a good look at Merv. "I'm Charlton Heston."

Merv didn't feel comfortable initiating a dialogue, and felt nervous coming on to this handsome, athletic-looking man. Rather awkwardly, he said, "That swimming suit you're wearing is a bit brief. I would never be seen in that even in the privacy of my bedroom."

Charlton laughed. "It's not a swimming suit. In New York I posed for art

163

classes for $1.25 an hour. They didn't want me to show my dick, so I had to wear this strap. During all the days I spent posing nude, I got an erection only once. I had this problem. It gets pretty crowded down there."

After that remark, Merv's suspicion was confirmed. Charlton Heston was definitely a hustler.

"My wife sewed on the velour," Charlton said.

"Oh, I didn't know you were married," Merv said.

"My wife, Lydia, is an actress. She's out of town on a job."

On hearing this, Merv did not immediately abandon pursuing Charlton. He'd been in Hollywood long enough to conclude that all actors were at least bisexual.

Charlton did confirm that he was an actor and was actually appearing in a movie that was presently being screened at a nearby theater. He invited Merv to come and see it with him. "I've seen it ten times already. Each time by myself. It'd be good to get another opinion. "Are you an actor too?"

"Yes," Merv said rather proudly. "Jack Warner is grooming me to become Doris Day's next leading man."

After both men had dressed separately within their respective apartments, they met in front of the Commodore to stroll down Hollywood Boulevard together. At the movie house, Merv learned the film was *Dark City*, and was startled to see that Charlton was the actual star.

Noting his surprise, Charlton said, "I didn't get all that much money for it. That's why I'm still living at the Commodore Garden Apartments."

During the screening of *Dark City*, which was first released in 1950, Merv was impressed with Charlton's performance. He'd been cast as a war veteran opposite the sultry blonde, Lizabeth Scott, who was hailed in the press as a combination of Lauren Bacall and Veronica Lake. The press often referred to Lizabeth as "one of the baritone babes of Hollywood," hoping the reading public would draw their own conclusions from that.

In *Dark City*, Lizabeth played a nightclub singer, and Merv sat through five songs, later claiming that the movie was the only musical film noir he'd ever seen. "If this keeps up," he whispered to Charlton, "Humphrey Bogart will be singing in his next film."

At one tense moment in the film, Merv decided to go for it. He slowly placed his hand on Charlton's left knee and let it gradually move upward to his target, which had been so recently

The man who said "no."
Charlton Heston

164

encased in a posing strap.

With his own firm hand, Charlton took Merv's hand and slowly placed it back in Merv's lap. The actor leaned over and whispered into Merv's ear, "I'm not that kind of actor."

When the movie was over, Merv complimented Charlton on his performance. On the walk back to the Commodore, no mention was made of the groping.

At the door to Charlton's apartment, Merv shook his hand and congratulated him one more time. "Let's be friends."

"Sure thing," Charlton said, "providing we carry on that friendship outside of a dark movie house."

As Merv later sighed over the phone to Roddy McDowall, "Let's call him the man who got away. That package in the posing strap looked most promising."

In the trade papers, Merv was startled to read that Cecil B. DeMille had cast Charlton as one of the leads in his next big epic, *The Greatest Show on Earth*. The film would go on to win an Oscar as Best Picture and gross $40 million, the equivalent of $300 million at today's prices. Very quietly Charlton moved out of the Commodore, without telling Merv good-bye.

Charlton did not mention Merv in his autobiography, *In the Arena*. He told friends that when he'd moved into the Commodore, he didn't know "it was the hottest whorehouse in Hollywood. You never knew what movie star you'd run into there. Clark Gable slipping down the hallway to knock on the door of a high-priced hooker. Even Gary Cooper and Robert Taylor came to call. With all that money exchanging hands, I found the tenants, both men and women, a little sad. They'd come to Hollywood to become stars and ended up working the oldest profession in history."

In his own autobiography, Merv summed up his experiences at the Commodore this way. "So we had god in the front apartment, the boy singer upstairs, and hookers and con men everywhere else."

***

Dressed in his tuxedo from his days with Freddy Martin's band, Merv drove to Joan Crawford's house, not knowing what gala they'd attend. She hadn't informed him, and he didn't dare ask. It was only five o'clock in the afternoon, which struck Merv as a bit early to be attending some glittering function, which most often occurred at night.

For the occasion, Merv had borrowed a fancy car from Peter Lawford, who said it had belonged to his father.

Joan intimidated him, and he hoped he wouldn't make a faux pas and infuriate her, as he'd heard she had quite a temper.

Pulling into her driveway, he walked to her door and rang the bell. He was surprised when she answered the door herself, thinking she'd have a maid do that. She was fully made up and every bit the movie star in a black strapless gown and a white sable.

She marched him into her living room and poured a Scotch and soda, light on the soda. He was going to turn down the drink, because he didn't want to get drunk if he had to chauffeur her somewhere. She handed it to him and ordered him to deliver it to "the gentleman who requested it." She directed him to climb the stairs to her bedroom at the top. "The door is open," she said.

Walking up the stairs, Merv suspected that he'd encounter Steve Cochran in her bed. To his surprise, he walked in and found Clark Gable, lying apparently nude under the sheets.

"About time, kid," Clark said. "I thought I'd have to fuck somebody other than Joan to get a drink around this house."

"Mr. Gable, I'm Merv Griffin," he stammered. "We first met when I was singing at the Cocoanut Grove. You were with Nancy Davis."

"Yes, I remember her and I remember you," Clark said, sitting up in bed, exposing a chest that had looked a lot better in *It Happened One Night* back in 1934.

"Now give me that drink, kid, and get the hell out of here. After I down this drink, I've got to take a shower. Joan doesn't know this, but I've got another date tonight, and I hope I can get it up again for the lucky gal. Joan sorta wore me out this afternoon."

Excusing himself, Merv hurried down the steps where Joan was waiting impatiently. "I said deliver a drink to Clark, not take the time to suck his cock."

She directed him to carry two clothing bags to his car. "I'm taking you to a party," she said, "but before that, we're stopping off at Columbia. I have to meet Fred Zinnemann."

Merv immediately recognized the name, knowing that the Austrian director had cast Monty Clift in his upcoming picture, *From Here to Eternity*.

At the studio, Joan and Merv were ushered into the director's office.

Fred was just showing Burt Lancaster to the door. When Joan and Merv walked in, Fred finished his story with Burt before even acknowledging Joan. "Directing Ethel Waters in *The Member of the Wedding* was impossible," he said. "Every time I'd issue an order, she'd roll her eyes to the heavens and say, 'God is my director.' How can you argue with that?"

Burt kissed Joan on the cheek, and she introduced Merv to both Burt and Fred.

After flashing his by now-famous smile, and showing glistening Chicletwhite teeth, Burt excused himself and started to leave. He paused and turned toward Joan. "I don't know how I'm going to do that love scene with you on the beach without getting an erection. And me in skimpy swim trunks."

Merv was left standing awkwardly in the room holding two heavy clothing bags, as Fred and Joan engaged in a bitter argument which apparently had been ongoing for weeks. He learned from their shouting at each other that she'd been cast as the female lead in *From Here to Eternity* but was refusing to wear the drab clothes that an army wife might be seen in while her husband was stationed at Pearl Harbor on the eve of the Japanese attack.

Against Fred's wishes, Harry Cohn, the head honcho at Columbia, had cast Joan as the adulterous Karen Holmes, the faithless wife of an army officer in the film. From the beginning, Fred had opposed the choice.

Joan argued with Fred that she wanted everything in her wardrobe to be designed by her new costumer, Sheila O'Brien. To Joan's credit, Sheila had created a chic and high-fashion new look for Joan more in keeping with her mature years. Though she still insisted on wearing the famous Joan Crawford fuck-me shoes of World War II, Sheila had convinced her to abandon the shoulder pads, big bows, and other fashion excesses created by Adrian for Joan when she appeared in the pre-Depression films of the mid-1920s.

Joan ripped two or three dresses from one of the clothing bags and held them up in front of Fred. They were intensely glamorous, something that she might wear to a luncheon with the mayor of Los Angeles at Chasen's. Secretly Merv agreed with Fred but Joan was adamant.

After an argument that stretched out for more than an hour, Joan shouted at Fred. "If I can't wear this wardrobe designed especially for me, then I'm off the picture. You're trying to make me into a drab housewife. Joan Crawford is a movie star! She doesn't play a drab housewife."

"Then you're fired!" Fred shouted back at her. "Get out! You're off the picture."

At first Joan was stunned, as if it took a long time for Fred's words to sink in. She turned her back to the director and headed for the door. Suddenly, aware of Merv, she called, "Griffin, bring my clothes. I'll be directed in my next picture by a man capable of directing Joan Crawford, not this Austrian Nazi."

In the borrowed car, Joan ordered Merv to drive her back home. She was crying and claimed, "I've ruined my face dealing with that idiot." She said she could not face other Hollywood stars at a gala that night and just would not show up, even though the sponsors of the event were expecting her.

Back at her house, she asked Merv to carry her wardrobe into the living room. He felt embarrassed, not knowing what to say. He needed a drink like the one she'd mixed for Gable.

But she didn't offer one. While he sat on the edge of her sofa in her immaculate living room, she went into her spotless marble-clad hallway and made three or maybe four urgent phone calls.

"Griffin," she finally called to him. "Get the hell in here. At times like this, I need a good fuck. Clark's no good at it." She came up close to him, and without any warning her tongue was down his throat as she fondled his fly, feeling for his penis.

She pulled him down on top of her right on the marble floor. It looked clean enough to eat off. "I have to have it now!" she shouted. "There's no time to go upstairs and get undressed."

She raised her dress and tugged at her champagne-colored panties. At the same time she also managed to extract his penis and attempted to bring it to life. To his chagrin, it seemed to shrink to a record low.

He had no sexual desire for her at all, and, in fact, was in a state of panic. All of a sudden, he looked up. A little blonde-haired girl had emerged from her bedroom and was standing at the top of the steps looking down at her mother and him. He gasped when he saw her, realizing that Joan was unaware of her presence.

Breaking from Joan, he stood over her as she writhed on the floor. He stuffed himself back into his trousers and headed for the door.

He looked back only one time as a half-dressed Joan was trying to get to her feet again. "Fuck you, Griffin! I should have asked a real man to escort me tonight. Stick to sucking cock!"

Both Joan and Merv read in the trade papers that she was off the picture. Harry Cohn had been willing to pay her a $100,000 salary, although she'd have to take second billing to Montgomery Clift. But Cohn had offered her a sizable percentage of the box office profits. Since *From Here to Eternity* went on to become one of the big hits of the 1950s, Joan would have made a fortune.

She put up a brave front to the public when she heard that Fred Zinnemann had cast the rather demure Deborah Kerr in the role instead. Fred was definitely casting against type, because Deborah was known for playing well-bred ladies on the screen. "That's great for that stuck-up British bitch," Joan told William Haines, her gay friend and former star. "It's about time *somebody* got to fuck her!"

Years later when Joan made a glamorous appearance on *The Merv Griffin Show*, both she and Merv pretended to be meeting for the first time.

***

After fleeing from Joan Crawford's house, Merv drove back to the misnamed Commodore Garden Apartments. As he was walking across the courtyard, he noticed a man sprawled out on a chaise longue. He'd either passed out or was dead.

Merv moved closer to see if the stranger were all right. In the dim glow of the patio lights, he encountered Errol Flynn sound asleep with his mouth open emitting snores. Merv surveyed him closely. This world-famous actor was no longer the same man who was the focus of his sexual desires in the 1930s.

At long last a reckless life and endless abuse of a once-perfect specimen had caught up with Errol. He looked beyond tired, a dissipation that couldn't be erased even after treatment at the best spa on earth.

The night was getting cold in the way a Los Angeles evening can; and Errol wasn't even wearing a coat. When Merv tried to wake him up, he failed. Errol muttered something before entering what seemed like a deep coma.

It was at this point that Merv saw the two young men who lived next door to him enter the patio heading for their apartment. He signaled to them and asked them if they would help him "get my friend into my studio. He's had too much to drink."

Both of the young men agreed and practically carried Errol into Merv's studio after he'd unlocked the door. "Please put him on the bed and thank you so very much."

It was only then that Merv looked at the two young men, finding them incredibly sexy and appealing. One of them was especially handsome.

"I'm Merv Griffin," he said extending his hand.

"This here is James Dean, and I'm Nick Adams," one of the young men said. "We've seen you around."

"Sorry we didn't say hi before," James said. He looked at the body resting on the bed. "If I didn't know better I'd say that was Errol Flynn."

"He's a look-alike," Merv said. "When he was a bit younger, teenage gals used to come up to him and ask for his autograph."

"Yeah, he looks a little beat up for Errol Flynn," Nick said.

"We've got to go," James said. "Good night. Let's get together for a drink in the courtyard tomorrow."

"Great idea!" Merv said, eagerly wanting to make the acquaintance of these two striking young men. "At sunset, okay?" As the men were leaving, Merv seemed to want to prolong the contact. "Say, are you guys actors?"

"Yeah, we're terrific," Nick said.

"Let's be truthful with this man," James said. "We want to be actors. But right now we might list our profession as hustlers."

Errol Flynn

169

"I see," Merv said, startled at such candor. "You mean, love for sale, or are you referring to pool hall hustling."

"More like dick for sale," James said, before tipping his cap in a good night.

Nick winked at Merv before heading out the door.

After locking the door behind them, Merv turned to Errol on the bed. Slowly, almost sensually, he began to undress him. He'd never had the opportunity to examine the body of his teenage fantasy hero in detail. When he'd completely stripped Errol, he surveyed the body like a doctor in an examining room.

"No, he's not for me," Merv said in a whisper to himself. Errol chest had fallen and his stomach was paunchy. He still possessed that fabulous endowment, but that was no longer enough of an allure for Merv. He'd much rather be intimate with the two hustlers next door.

He stripped off his own clothes and got into the bed beside Errol, although his snoring kept Merv up for most of the night. This was the last time he'd ever sleep with the object of so many wet dreams of his past.

***

"A slouching stance, youthful rebellion in faded jeans, a cigarette in the corner of a kissable mouth, alienation, even outright hostility at times, and the most angelic face I've ever seen on a young man." That's the way many contemporary witnesses described James Dean at the time.

"This Dean guy is going to be a big star—maybe the biggest," Merv later claimed to such friends as Bill Orr. "I have this feeling about him. But he's got a lot of weird habits. He'll smoke a cigarette so far down that it'll burn his lips. Yes, actually burn them with intent. He gets off on being burnt. He's a hustler/actor and will let some johns crush out a cigarette butt on his ass. The first night I was with him, and even before I had sex with him, he pulled down his jeans and showed me the cigarette burns on a beautiful ass. Strange boy.

Rebels and starfucker buddies:
James Dean (left) and
Nick Adams (right)

But I adore the kid."

The evening that followed his meeting with Nick and James, Merv waited impatiently on the patio of the Commodore Garden Apartments. Nick and James were nowhere to be seen. Merv sat there until long after the sun had set before both of them came rushing into the patio to greet Merv.

"We had a john who wanted us to stay over for more fun and games," Nick said in the way of apology. To Merv's surprise, Nick gave him a light kiss on the mouth. James held back, saying nothing, until he somewhat bashfully invited Merv into their studio next door to Merv's own shabby apartment.

Dressed in a white Mexican shirt and jeans, James put on a pot of fresh coffee to welcome Merv. The whole place smelled like a dirty laundry bag. Yet Merv felt a sexual tension in the air, and this excited him. The prospect of having both young men strip down for his pleasure tantalized him.

As his eyes surveyed the studio, they drifted up to the ceiling where he was shocked to see a hangman's noose dangling. Following Merv's eyes, James said, "That's waiting for me when I decide to commit suicide."

Merv didn't know if James were joking or if he really meant that. While James poured the coffee, Nick stripped down and dangled his penis in front of Merv. "Now you know why I'm called Mighty Meat along the street." He headed for the shower.

Over coffee, Merv and James shared their experiences of surviving in New York. James told the best tales, especially about how he managed to live on twenty-five cents a day.

Merv suggested he should write a book. "All struggling actors coming to New York would buy it like a survivor's manual."

"Mostly I just hung around," James said. "Sometimes I'd get lucky, like when Marlon Brando would invite me into his place to fuck me and give me a meal. Often I'd sit on a door stoop for hours at a time. Once I sat on this bench in front of a barbershop for eight hours, needing a haircut real bad but I had no money to pay for it."

Ever the practical one, Merv asked, "But didn't you have to take a leak?"

James looked at him strangely, but didn't answer.

Nick emerged freshly showered and dressed only in a bath towel. He joined them for coffee and shared his experiences of trying to break in as an actor in New York and Hollywood. "Being an actor is like eating a shit sandwich every day. It's kiss ass…" He paused. "Sometimes literally. Waiting for the next job, not knowing if it's gonna come or not. Trying to get that job and having to compete with a hundred other starving actors. Congratulating your best friend when he got the job instead of you." He glanced furtively at James. "Waiting outside that producer's door. Even worse sometimes, getting invited inside the producer's door and having to submit to a blow-job from a disgusting piece of flesh. And then losing the job to the guy he planned to cast all along. Trying to get a job is half the job of being an actor—take it from me."

As the evening progressed, Merv was amazed that Nick seemed to be "tooting his own horn," often at the expense of James. It was clear to Merv that there was definite competition between the two actors. It was as if Nick sensed that James had far greater looks and more talent, and Nick was hellbent on convincing Merv that he, Nick—and not James—was the real star.

A latter day biographer, Albert Goldman, summed up Nick in ways that Merv felt but couldn't express at the time. "Nick was forever selling himself: a property which, to hear him tell it, was nothing less than sensational—'the greatest actor to hit this town in years,'" Goldman said. "In fact, he had very little going for him in terms of looks or talent or professional experience. He was just another poor kid from the sticks who had grown up dreaming of the silver screen."

When James learned that Merv had been living with Monty Clift, James entertained him with a dead-accurate impression. "Now I ask you: Who is better doing Monty Clift? The real thing or me?"

"You, of course," Merv said.

After that, he entertained Merv with an even deadlier impression of Marlon Brando. "Fuck, I do a better imitation of Brando than Jimmy," Nick claimed. Merv watched in fascination as Nick almost became Brando before his eyes. But he didn't dare tell James that Nick was better.

Right in front of James, Nick confessed that his friend would take much kinkier offers when both of them "hustled the queers along Santa Monica Boulevard."

"I turn down a lot of queens, but Jimmy here will go for anything," Nick claimed. Merv glanced over at James who did not seem in the least embarrassed at this revelation. "One night this weirdo wanted to eat my shit," Nick said. "I told him to 'fuck off,' but Jimmy went off with the creep in his car."

"Why not?" James said with a devilish bad boy look. "I hadn't had a good crap all day."

When Merv reunited with Johnny Riley, he would give him a blow-by-blow description of the approximately two and a half weeks he spent in the company of Nick Adams and James Dean in the months leading up to their getting cast in *Rebel Without a Cause*. "I had to borrow five-hundred dollars from Bullets to pay the freight, but it was worth every penny. Nick had the bigger endowment but Jimmy was better at love-making. It was the best sex I've ever had, even if I did have to pay for it."

***

The night of the big Sunday night bash at Jack Warner's was imminent, and Merv still didn't have a royal to escort to the party. Jack had warned him, "Don't show up with some low-rent piece of shit. Make sure she has a title. There will be plenty of royalty at my dinner, class acts who are visiting our town when they're not ruling over kingdoms in the east. Got that, Griff?"

Frantically searching his mind, Merv remembered that he'd once "dated" a woman named Lorraine Manville, the heiress to the Johns-Manville asbestos fortune and the sister of the much-married playboy Tommy Manville, who was always making headlines. Her brother had become a minor celebrity. In all, he'd eventually entered into 13 marriages to 11 women, winning him an entry in the *Guinness Book of World Records*.

Merv vaguely recalled that Lorraine had been married to some minor European count or something, which might mean that she could dust off her former title for the evening. When he called her, she told him that she had another engagement that night but was willing to cancel it, since she considered the Jack Warner affair the hottest ticket in Los Angeles.

Once again Merv borrowed a car from Peter Lawford to drive to Jack Warner's mansion for the grandest party he'd ever attended in Hollywood. As he recalled it, it was all flowing champagne and crystal bowls of caviar, with lots of minor European royalty, the stiff-collared men in tuxedos and the heavily coiffed ladies crowning their heads with diamond tiaras By request from Jack Warner, all the women were dressed either in black or white, perhaps a combination of the two.

As the butler was taking Lorraine's white sable, Merv felt a strong hand on his shoulder. "Griff, so glad you could make it." It was Jack Warner himself.

Merv introduced the studio chief to the Countess Lorraine Dumanceaux, using her former title.

"Glad to meet you, countess, but I regret to inform you, babycakes, that you're outranked tonight." He reached for the arm of a stunningly glamorous woman en route to the bathroom. "May I introduce Princess Aly Khan."

Rita Hayworth appeared before them looking as glamorous as she had in any of her screen appearances. She was one of Merv's all-time favorite movie stars from the 1940s. He'd seen *Gilda* three times. At one of Roddy McDowall's parties, he'd once put on a red wig and had performed an imitation of her "Put the Blame on Mame" number from that film.

At the dinner table, Lorraine was seated across from Merv, Rita by his side. He had little chance to talk to her, since she was busy being fawned over by other guests sitting near her and directing questions at her.

Jack presided at the head of a long table worthy of one of the Rothschilds.

It was set with Steuben glassware, antique silver, and gold and silver candelabra, everything lit by soft candlelight. Like an old time silent screen movie director, perhaps Erich von Stroheim, Jack shouted orders to his butlers and waiters. At the same time he managed to keep up a running dialogue about the filming of *Casablanca*. "That Ingrid Bergman looks so virginal on the screen, but Alfred Hitchcock told me she'd fuck a tree," Jack claimed.

At the end of the dinner, Jack rose to his feet. "I hope your worships…" he paused. "I hope you enjoyed this little spread we put out before you." The dinner guests clapped their approval. "Now it's time for the men to have some cigars and brandy and talk about their whores, while you ladies go and take a big piss."

Leaving Lorraine and Rita to talk to each other with absolutely nothing in common, Jack grabbed Merv's arm and took him on a tour of what Jack called "my waxworks," borrowing a designation from the film, *Sunset Blvd.*, wherein a bevy of geriatric silent screen stars arrived at the home of Norma Desmond as played by Gloria Swanson.

"I lost *count*—get it?—after being introduced to six counts," Merv said. "There were also nine countesses and at least three duchesses. I kept looking for the Duke and Duchess of Windsor, or at least the Queen of England, but they were no-shows. I did get to meet Princess Fawzia and even the Queen Mother Nawzli. Who in the fuck were they? I had no idea what kingdoms they presided over."

Hopefully out of earshot of royalty, Jack in a too-loud voice told Merv, "I'm farting countesses and duchesses out my ass."

After dinner, Lorraine attached herself to a minor count, perhaps a future husband, and wandered off into the evening, forgetting about Merv. He didn't want to join the men for cigars, brandy, and talk about Las Vegas prostitutes—it wasn't his kind of thing—so he wandered aimlessly to the deserted terrace, enjoying the night air and a break from all this royalty and pretension.

From the main room, he heard Jack announce that "the hot Scot with the lovable larynx" was going to sing." Merv knew that meant his rival, Gordon MacRae. Apparently, Jack and Gordon had made up after one of the singer's drunken bouts.

Merv had avoided Gordon all evening and

Rita Hayworth
"My husbands fell in love with Gilda,
and ended up marrying <u>me</u>:"

didn't want to hear him sing, so he remained on the terrace. It was hard for him to admit it, but he was jealous of Gordon's accomplishments and his success on *The Railroad Hour,* which was attracting 12.5 million listeners every week. Sales of Gordon's records were soaring, and at least one heavy bag of fan mail arrived for Gordon on the Warner's lot every day. Most of the letters were from female bobbysoxers, but a lot of the mail was from homosexual men attracted to the good looks and rugged virility of the star.

Newspapers had reported that Gordon's three-week appearance on the stage of New York's Strand Theater, where Merv had appeared, attracted audiences of a size unknown since Frank Sinatra had appeared there before his own screaming bobbysoxers during the war years.

Still on the terrace, Merv felt depressed listening to Gordon's powerful voice. He asked himself, "How can I compete with that?" The smell of an intoxicating perfume distracted him, and he turned around to stare into the beautiful, camera-ready face of Rita Hayworth.

They chatted pleasantly about nothing important for the first fifteen minutes. In person Rita was not *Gilda,* the sexy siren and sultry, flame-haired beauty who'd enthralled the world. She appeared sweet natured and rather homey, at least for a screen goddess and a princess. He'd read all about her fairytale marriage to Prince Aly Khan, the son of the Aga Khan III, the leader of the Ismaili sect of Shia Islam. From what he'd gathered that fairytale had turned into a grim nightmare.

"I'm back in Hollywood trying for a comeback," she confided. "Glenn [a reference to actor Glenn Ford] tried to re-create *Gilda* when we made *Affair in Trinidad,* but that old black magic just wasn't there. Reviewers called it a re-tread."

"I enjoyed it, and I thought you looked lovely," he falsely claimed.

"Thank you," she said. "You won't believe the latest script Joseph Mankiewicz offered me. It's a turkey called *The Barefoot Contessa.* The female lead is named Maria Vargas, but she might as well be Rita Hayworth. It's a ripoff of my own life. Mankiewicz stupidly thought I'd play myself in the film. I told him to give it to Ava Gardner."

"Sorry to hear about your marriage to the prince," he said. "You two looked like such a great couple."

"Oh, well, he spent too many days at the race track with his thoroughbreds and too many nights in the beds of other women," she said, sighing.

At one point Merv said, "I've always wanted to meet Rita Hayworth if only to put one question to her."

"Do you mean how's Glenn Ford in the sack?"

"No, not that," he said. "What did it feel like when you learned that your likeness was stamped on the first atomic bomb dropped on Hiroshima?"

"I'd say that was quite a blast."

At that point, Jack Warner emerged onto the terrace, obviously looking for Rita to bring her back into the party to be photographed with him. "I've been looking everywhere for you, gal." He possessively took her arm.

"Jack, I'll meet you inside," she said, "after I've repaired my face. After all, it's not 1944 anymore."

The studio chief remained behind. "Griff, I've been watching you out of the corner of my eye all night. I like the way you handle yourself. If only you could sing as great as Gordon. But you can't and that's that. However, just for the hell of it, I'm casting you as the lead in a big movie musical, maybe the biggest to come along in some time."

"You mean opposite Doris Day in her next picture?"

"Not quite," he said. "Doris stupidly turned down the picture. I'm giving the part to Kathryn Grayson."

"But she's starring in *The Desert Song* with Gordon MacRae," Merv said.

"She's going to drop Gordon in her next picture and star with you," Jack said. "You're gonna be big, really big. You're on your way up, Griff. Now get into my living room and sing for your supper. My guests are getting restless. Gordon did only one number. I want you to do three."

"Yes, sir, Mr. Warner," Merv said, eagerly shaking his hand. "Thanks for giving me my big break. I can't wait to read the script."

"Now get in there and sing 'I've Got a Lovely Bunch of Coconuts,'" Jack said. "I love that song. And, Griff, if you fuck up this big Grayson picture, I'll personally cut off your balls. Got that, kid?"

"I got you," Merv said, fleeing from the terrace and heading back into the party to entertain movie stars and mostly *faux* royalty.

Jack Warner with *real* Hollywood royalty:
Joan Crawford *(left)* **and Bette Davis**

176

Chapter Five

Someone in the administration at Warner Brothers had told Merv that a finished script of *So This is Love* wouldn't be ready for another two weeks, and that until then, he could go to Hawaii or anywhere else he wanted.

Soon after, Merv embarked for Honolulu on a ticket paid for by Monty Clift, probably wishing that he was flying there as a player in *From Here to Eternity,* and not just for a social call on an unreliable friend on his film set.

In Honolulu, brandishing a pot of espresso and a bottle of Scotch, Monty greeted Merv at the airport. He was staggering drunk and dressed as the soldier boy, Prewitt, the character that he played in *From Here to Eternity*. In a taxi on the way back to Monty's temporary rental, Merv realized that psychologically, the actor had virtually become Prewitt. He was living, breathing, sleeping, and eating the role. When asked a simple question, Monty would respond: "How would Prewitt answer that?" Before they arrived at the hotel, Monty confessed, "My character of Prewitt fucks me every night. I've become his bitch."

At Monty's apartment, Merv was introduced to James Jones, the author of the original novel, *From Here to Eternity*, upon which the film was based. Merv assumed that the writer was Monty's new lover. Jones exuded a macho sexuality in his tight-fitting blue jeans, even tighter, form-fitting white T-shirt, and a thick cowhide belt dyed a bright orange and held together by a silver Navajo buckle.

The author had witnessed the actual attack on Pearl Harbor when he was twenty years old. He'd later faced combat in Guadalcanal where he was wounded in action. James's second novel, *Some Came Running*, would also be filmed. Like *Eternity*, it too would star Frank Sinatra.

When Monty went to shower and get ready to give Merv a tour of Honolulu, Merv chatted amicably with Jones. "So how's your affair with Monty going?" he bluntly asked.

"There is no affair," Jones said. "For one reason and one reason only. He hasn't asked me. *I'm* willing. But he hasn't even admitted he's a homosexual."

During the course of the evening, Jones told Merv

James Jones:
"If only Monty
had asked"

177

that one of the reasons he was "hanging with Monty is to see that he gets through the picture. This movie means a lot to me even though that fucking Fred Zinnemann didn't use my version. Monty starts drinking at nine in the morning. By five in the afternoon, I often have to carry him bodily off the set."

On the second day on the set, Merv was introduced to the female star of the picture, a very ladylike Deborah Kerr. "I'm surrounded by men," she said. "All of them are a bit macho for me. I find Burt Lancaster very sexy, but so does everybody else. What woman in her right mind would say no to him? Or man for that matter. He's equally attractive to both sexes. As for Monty, I feel very protective of him. He came on strong to me, but I turned him down. I know he wants to love women, but sexually, he's attracted only to men. Sigh."

They were interrupted by the appearance of Burt Lancaster, who was dressed in a military uniform. Very politely Deborah introduced Merv to her costar, not knowing they'd already met. Burt recalled meeting him when he'd escorted Joan Crawford to Zinnemann's office.

After some pleasant chit-chat, Deborah excused herself to keep an appointment with her hairdresser. She told Burt to pick her up at eight o'clock that evening. After she'd gone, Burt flashed his toothy smile and invited Merv to go with him to a nearby gym for a workout.

At the gym, Burt confessed, "Zinnemann cast me as the film's beefcake. Christ, Frank Sinatra and Montgomery Clift look like they were just released from Auschwitz."

Burt had been cast as Sergeant Warden, "a man among men," who rallied his troops on the morning of December 7, 1941 as planes from the Empire of Japan rained unexpected hell down upon Pearl Harbor.

"Would you believe I was only second choice for the role I'm playing? Zinnemann, that prick, preferred Robert Mitchum. And instead of your buddy, Monty, Harry Cohn wanted Aldo Ray. And for the role being played by Sinatra, Cohn wanted Eli Wallach."

Burt Lancaster

Burt stripped off all his clothes and asked Merv to hold his ankles to the floor as he did push-ups. Merv was only too willing, enjoying the view of Burt's penis as it bobbed up and down with his push-ups. "I think he was teasing me, and I guess it was obvious that he had my full attention, but I knew I'd have to bide my time," he later told Roddy.

Burt had a long-established preference for working out in the gym in the nude during the late afternoon. When word of that spread around the set, every homosexual on the crew made up some excuse to visit the gym at five o'clock. As Merv later revealed, "Burt put on quite a show, especially in the shower when he paid extra attention to soaping up his genitals for a most appreciative audience."

After the gym, Burt invited Merv for a few drinks.

With liquor loosening his tongue, Burt admitted what had been obvious to Merv earlier that afternoon. "I'm having this thing with Deborah," Burt confessed. "We're getting ready for our scene on the beach with the waves washing up on our bodies. A scene like that takes a lot of rehearsals." He laughed at his own remark. "Tell you what: If she's busy one night, I'll give you your chance." He said that in such a matter-of-fact tone that Merv was stunned. The reference to sex was presented in the same voice Burt had used when inviting Merv for a beer.

It wasn't until his last night in Honolulu that Merv finally got lucky. After a final workout in the gym, Burt showered and invited Merv back to his hotel where they had a couple of drinks. In his suite, Burt confessed that his affair with Deborah was over. "It only lasted for the run of the movie. There will be other films to be made. Other pussies to conquer."

Suddenly, Burt stood up from his armchair and began to strip off his clothing in front of Merv. "You've been a great gym buddy, and it's been fun being with you. You deserve a reward, and I'm going to see that you get it. You've seen me soft many times, and I'm sure you've encountered a lot bigger looking. Now for your surprise: I'm a grower, not a shower. Come and get it, kid."

After Burt had climaxed, the actor told him, "When the world sees me on that beach making love to Deborah, no one will ever believe all those gay rumors about me ever again." Merv noted that he said gay instead of homosexual. The sexual (and sociological) meaning of the word had just come into vogue.

After Merv's return to Los Angeles, one of his first calls was to Roddy McDowall. "It finally happened. I've had Burt in all his uncut glory. He really enjoyed it too. This is the beginning of a great romance. I just know it."

"Don't get your hopes up," Roddy warned him. "Burt is fickle and very promiscuous."

Merv's friend turned out to be a prophet. When Merv phoned Burt the next day, the actor responded with, "It was great, kid, but it's over. Burt Lancaster doesn't do sequels."

***

In Hawaii, and in a pattern that would repeat itself throughout the rest of his life, it became increasingly obvious that Monty was addicted to a wide spectrum of drugs. Along with his daily bottle of Scotch, he swallowed barbiturates and tranquilizers like they were peanuts. Merv was increasingly alarmed by Monty's physical and mental deterioration, despite the fact that he seemed to be making the greatest film of his career.

During the filming of *From Here to Eternity*, Monty had found the ideal drinking partner in Frank Sinatra. "They didn't just drink," Merv said, "they poured it down their throats. It was frightening. Both of them seemed to want to drink themselves into oblivion. Monty was still conflicted over his sexual preference, and Frank drank because his marriage to Ava Gardner was in its death throes."

"Not only that, but Frank was at the nadir of his career," Merv later recalled. "Back taxes, maybe as much as $150,000. His $8,000 salary for *Eternity* wouldn't cover it. In fact, that paltry fee wouldn't even pay Frank's bar bills. Often Burt Lancaster and I had to carry both Monty and Frank back to their hotel, where we undressed them and put them to bed like little children. I personally took the responsibility of removing Frank's underwear to judge for myself if the legend was true. It was! Somehow Monty and Frank usually managed to pull themselves together to face the camera the following day, each giving brilliant performances," Merv said. "It was amazing."

When Monty sobered up and Frank sobered up, Monty actually managed to give Frank acting lessons. The singer later thanked Monty and claimed his help was the reason he got the Oscar for Best Supporting Actor that year.

Most evenings, Frank seemed to be always trying to place a call to Ava in Nairobi where she was filming *Mogambo* with Clark Gable and Grace Kelly. Word reached Frank that Clark and Ava had resumed their affair, which had been launched when they made *The Hucksters* years previously, back in 1947.

After the filming in Hawaii, Fred Zinnemann ordered the cast and crew back to Hollywood, where the final interiors for *Eternity* would be shot at Columbia Studios. Monty booked a suite at the Roosevelt Hotel in Hollywood and invited Merv to stay with him, at least until the end of the picture. "I can't stand to be alone."

Sometimes at three o'clock in the morning, Monty would hang dangerously out the window of his suite, tooting his bugle. There were endless complaints from other hotel guests and nearby tenants about the noise. James Jones was still on the scene, presumably to help the pieces and personalities he had originally created in his novel fit together in their film rendition, but Monty preferred to spend most of his time with Frank. Tough and gritty, the author of *From Here to Eternity* was a world-class drinker and would usually still be standing after Monty and Frank had passed out.

Years later, in 1965, Merv would tape an interview with James Jones, by then an expatriate living in Paris with his wife, Gloria Mosolino.

When he met her, Merv immediately bonded with the former actress. She amused Merv with her stories of being a stand-in for Marilyn Monroe on *The Seven Year Itch* (1955). "I stood for hours over that subway grate with my white dress blowing up to get the shot set up for Marilyn. When Marilyn finally appeared, the director couldn't use her first take. Marilyn's panties were see-through and showed pubic hair, which happened at the time to be black. We had to rush Marilyn back to the hotel where I helped her bleach her pubic hair."

"Shit," Merv said. "If only I could put *that* story on the air."

After meeting Gloria, Merv was almost tempted to do a TV show which focused exclusively on her and not on Jones. In Paris during that era, she had became the hostess of a literary salon the likes of which hadn't been seen since the days of Alice B. Toklas and Gertrude Stein. Her guests included Mary McCarthy, Romain Gary, William Styron, James Baldwin, and—just for fun—actress Jean Seberg and Merv's friend Peter Lawford.

Later, when Gloria moved with Jones to a farmhouse in Sagaponach, near the Hamptons on Long Island, such cultural icons as Norman Mailer, Peter Pattiessen, Kurt Vonnegut, and Arthur Miller showed up regularly at her gatherings.

During his time in Paris, Merv also interviewed another expatriate writer, Irwin Shaw, author of *The Young Lions* (1948). Like *From Here to Eternity*, it was one of the most famous novels to come out of World War II. Born in the Bronx to Jewish immigrants from Russia, Irwin expressed his extreme disappointment over the film adaptation of *The Young Lions* (1957). By coincidence, the movie, like *Eternity*, had also starred Monty Clift. This time, Monty played a sensitive Jew who becomes a war hero. He was cast opposite a blond-haired Marlon Brando, who played a Nazi officer. Irwin spoke to Merv with a well-articulated bitterness about America. He'd been placed on the Hollywood blacklist, having been accused of being a Communist.

Shaw and Jones jointly invited Merv out for a night of boozing in Paris. Merv suspected that the two authors would be intensely competitive rivals, since they'd both become famous for novels about World War II. Outside the literary arena, their competitiveness was at its most obvious when it came to drinking one another under the table. He compared their uneasy friendship to that of two other American expats who had lived in Paris forty years earlier, Ernest Hemingway and F. Scott Fitzgerald.

Merv tried to match them drink for drink. "A

Literary Lion:
Irwin Shaw

big mistake. That and jet lag nearly killed me." During the interview with Jones the next morning, Merv confessed that "I was a zombie." Away from the camera, he asked Jones just one question. "What's the most important thing you ever learned in life?"

"When fighting," Jones said, "never kick a man in the crotch."

Back in Hollywood, as the *Eternity* film was being wrapped, Merv confided to Roddy McDowall that he didn't believe Monty and Frank had become lovers, even though they had occasionally slept drunkenly nude in each other's arms. "I came in many times to wake them up, and saw them huddled together for comfort," Merv confided. "But I think it was more for the moral support they gave each other—not sex. What a contrast. There was Monty's peanut exposed only a foot from Frank's monster Italian salami."

Once, when Frank got drunk in a bar along Sunset Strip, the remainder of the evening became devoted to his ongoing obsession with Ava Gardner. "Frank was a womanizer," Merv said. "But at this point in his life, he wasn't interested in other gals. His rage about Ava consumed his life—that and his *Here to Eternity* role of Maggio. I kept urging him to get over her and get on with his life, but he wouldn't listen. After the release of *Eternity*, I predicted a big comeback for him but he was all gloom and doom. He claimed he was finished. He called my talk bullshit."

"He confessed to me that his vocal cords were hemorrhaged," Merv said. "He'd also received a devastating blow from MCA. His agents there informed him that 'no one wants you, Frankie, no more movie deals, no more night club offers.'"

"Every night," Merv said, "Frank threatened to commit suicide. It was Monty, as messed up as he was, who would talk him out of it."

One Saturday morning around four o'clock, Merv got up to go to the bathroom, which opened onto the hallway. Thinking Monty and Frank were asleep in the next bedroom, he turned the knob and walked into the bathroom. What he saw shocked him. A nude Frank lay sprawled on the tiled floor, an empty bottle of sleeping pills beside him.

Frank appeared to be dead. It seemed pointless to scream for Monty to help, because he was completely wasted. Merv ran into the living room and called the hotel desk, demanding an ambulance and the police.

Covered with sheets, Frank's body was hauled out of the hotel on a stretcher through the back entrance. In the back seat of a squad car, Merv followed the ambulance's flashing dome

Frank Sinatra:
Without Merv, he'd probably have died that night.

182

lights.

At the hospital, while Frank's stomach was being pumped, Merv put through an urgent call to Columbia's chief publicist, strongly advising him to get Harry Cohn involved. "Cohn knows how to keep stuff like this out of the papers," Merv said.

The call paid off. Within an hour, the PR staff at Columbia had launched itself into damage control. Cohn was an expert at keeping scandals about his stars out of the papers, and he managed to cover up Frank's latest attempt at suicide.

Three days later, a sober Frank returned to Monty's suite at the Roosevelt for a reunion with Monty and Merv. He thanked Merv for "saving my rotten life." His weight had dropped to 118 pounds, which Merv thought would make his interpretation of a defeated, burnt-out Maggio all the more convincing in *Eternity*.

He talked openly about why he'd tried to kill himself, claiming that Ava had flown to London where she'd had an abortion. "Her exact words to me," Frank claimed, were 'I killed your son.'" It is not known if Ava ever knew the sex of her unborn child. Perhaps by asserting that it was a boy, she hoped to cause Frank greater grief.

Frank and Monty learned no lessons from the singer's suicide attempt. Within three nights, Frank and Monty had resumed their heavy drinking, referring to their binges as "sloshing good times." Merv joined them on their nightly rounds, having little to drink himself because he knew he had to get both of them back to the Roosevelt intact.

The script for his first starring film, *So This Is Love*, arrived, and Merv read it eagerly. He was bitterly disappointed. Even though he was cast as the male lead, the role was meager, not what he'd wished for. "It's definitely going to be Kathryn Grayson's picture," he told Monty.

The next day, while Monty and Frank were at Columbia Studios, Merv quietly packed and left the Roosevelt. He'd found an apartment of his own. He went by the Commodore Garden Apartments to get his stuff, learning that Nick Adams and James Dean had moved out without a forwarding address.

One week later, Monty placed a desperate call to Merv, begging him to come over to his suite at the Roosevelt. Once there, Merv found that Monty had been severely beaten. Fortunately, he'd shot his last take at Columbia. He was far too beat up to face any camera. At first Merv assumed that Monty had picked up some rough trade along Santa Monica Boulevard, who had robbed and beaten him up.

When he wiped the blood off Monty's wounds and put iodine on the cuts, Monty related the details of what had happened. In a drunken rage, Frank had attacked him. Monty refused to tell Merv what had set Frank off.

The house doctor examined Monty, finding no broken bones. Merv called and ordered a male nurse to stay in Monty's suite and take care of him. That night he drove to Roddy's house to tell him what had happened.

Roddy had some ideas about what had caused the uncontrollable rage that had swept over Frank. "I bet Monty confessed to Frank that he'd fallen madly in love with him, and that was more than Frank could take. He sure as hell wasn't going to go from the arms of Ava Gardner into the arms of Monty Clift. No way! Not Frank."

"Frank and Monty are too rich for my blood, and frankly, they're just too complicated." Merv told Johnny Riley in a phone call to San Francisco. He was urging his friend to drive down to L.A. for a visit. "My big movie break is coming up, and I've got to think of myself. I can't get sucked into their whirlpool. I love the guys dearly, and I'll keep seeing them. But we were living in each other's crotches like The Three Musketeers. Our relationship got just a wee bit incestuous, and all of us need some space. The main reason I had to get out of the Roosevelt was that I'm not into self-destruction."

* * *

Kathryn Grayson, Merv's co-star in *So This Is Love*, was the reigning coloratura soprano at Metro-Goldwyn-Mayer, but had taken a short-term leave to work at Warner Brothers. Merv had thrilled to her 1951 film, *Show Boat*, in which she'd starred as Magnolia opposite Ava Gardner. At the time, both women were being pursued by Merv's friend, Howard Hughes. Kathryn later recalled the jealousies that ensued as Ava "shot daggers at me on the set with those Tarheel eyes of hers." Kathryn herself was a fellow Tarheel, having been born in Winston-Salem, North Carolina.

So This Is Love was a cinematic biography of the opera star Grace Moore. Nicknamed "The Tennessee Nightingale," she helped popularize opera by introducing it to a large audience. As a young kid, Merv had seen Grace's 1934 film, *One Night of Love*, for which she was nominated for an Oscar as Best Actress of 1935. He later said that, "I was too

Kathryn Grayson with **Merv Griffin**
in *So This Is Love (1953)*

young to appreciate her talent when my mother dragged me to see it."

On the morning of January 26, 1947, Grace Moore had boarded a KLM DC3 in Copenhagen, after a wildly popular concert that attracted hundreds of fans who demanded countless encores. She was sitting with Prince Gustaf Adolf of Sweden, father of the present king, Carl XVI Gustaf. They'd had an illicit affair in Denmark and were en route to Stockholm when the aircraft at an altitude of 150 feet stalled, crashed to the ground, and exploded. Unexpectedly, Elvis Presley so admired the operatic performances of Grace Moore that he named his beloved Graceland after her.

In *So This Is Love*, Merv was cast as Buddy Nash, the manager and fiancé of Grace, as played by Kathryn. For his role in the movie, Merv, a future billionaire, was paid $250 a week. Other cast members included players who at the time were well known: Marie Windsor, Walter Abel, Joan Weldon, and Rosemary DeCamp.

So many dire warnings had been issued to Merv about "that impossible diva," Kathryn, that he had trepidations about meeting her. There was a legend at the time that the worst thing that could happen to an actor was to get cast opposite Kathryn. Her former husband, Johnny Johnston, had warned Merv that "Kathryn will hog the camera and shove you out of the picture." Johnston had divorced the singing star two years previously.

To his surprise, Merv even received a phone call from Mario Lanza, who had starred with Kathryn in *That Midnight Kiss* in 1949 and in *The Toast of New Orleans* in 1951. "I despise the cunt, and so will you after making this picture," The Great Caruso warned Merv. "Those two big tits of hers kept knocking me down in every scene. She's a camera hog. She'll eat you alive." The actress was noted for having the largest bust measurements in Hollywood, putting Jane Russell and Marilyn Monroe to shame.

On the first day of the shoot, Doris Day showed up to wish Merv good luck. "You're gonna be big one day," she predicted.

"But when is that day coming?" he asked her.

"Just be patient," she assured him. "It'll happen. In fact, I'm considering casting you as the male lead in my next musical."

He smiled indulgently, having heard Doris's worthless promises before.

When Merv finally met Kathryn, she seemed to be the opposite of a monster. A pretty, petite brunette, she had a heart-shaped face and an engaging smile. Her co-star in *Show Boat*, Howard Keel, had described her as "the most beautiful woman in the history of movies."

Merv disagreed with Mario Lanza. "I found Kathryn a peach to work with," Merv claimed. "She gave me the most favorable camera angles, though she was known to nudge her leading man out of the scene. She encouraged me at every turn. In close-ups I had no problem with those big tits of hers because wardrobe had bound her breasts so she wouldn't project so much. After all, she wasn't trying to look like Jayne Mansfield. Perhaps Kathryn sensed I was a fish out of water, and she practically guided me through every scene."

The difficult point came in a kissing scene, which had to be shot nearly thirty times. At one point, Merv stuck his nose in her eye. To make matters worse, he had to act out the scene in front of the entire football team from the University of Texas. In town for the Rose Bowl, they were visiting the set that day. Practically to a man, every member of the team later claimed they could have done a better job of kissing Kathryn than Merv.

At one point the director, Gordon Douglas, insulted Merv in front of the homophobic team. "Griffin, just pretend Kathryn is Rock Hudson, and you'll do just fine." The team members cackled with laughter at Merv's humiliation, but he got through the next scene, and it was good enough for a print. The movie lives on today as a footnote in film history. It was the first major motion picture to focus on an open-mouth kiss.

Even though he received top billing alongside Kathryn, in the final version of the film he appeared onscreen for less than twenty minutes. He did get to sing, "I Kiss Your Hand, Madame," but it was one of his more lackluster numbers.

Kathryn found Merv "a nice guy," but feared he lacked the aggression and drive needed to become famous as a movie star.

Gordon Douglas later apologized to Merv for humiliating him on the set, and then promised to cast Merv in his next movie. Merv was excited at the prospect until he discovered it was to be a Western. To reinforce his reconciliation with Merv, Gordon singled him out for long talks between takes, and never insulted him again, even after he flubbed several takes. A native New Yorker, Gordon had had a long career in movies, beginning with those *Our Gang* two-reelers and graduating upward to Laurel and Hardy comedies.

After Gordon's death in 1993, after a career that had spanned nearly 50 years of filmmaking, Merv facetiously remarked, "He was the only filmmaker in the history of Hollywood to direct four screen legends—Frank Sinatra, Elvis Presley, Liberace, *and* Merv Griffin."

The press screening of *So This Is Love* was held at the Pantages Theater in Hollywood, and both Hedda Hopper and Louella Parsons were star guests. Merv remembered slinking down so low in his seat that he was almost hiding on the floor. He'd never seen himself in a feature-length movie before, and he was horrified at his image as projected on screen. He especially hated his big number, "I Kiss Your Hand, Madame."

In the lobby, Merv encountered Hedda, who kissed him on the mouth before exclaiming, "You're the next big star in Hollywood, maybe destined to be the biggest. I was flabbergasted by your performance."

In his attempt to escape from her clutches, he fell into the arms of Louella. "Frank Sinatra, Bing Crosby, move over. They've got nothing on you. That wop, Sinatra, can't even sing any more. Jack Warner should cast you in all his next big musicals, not Gordon MacRae. He's drunk all the time anyway." It was obvious to Merv and virtually everybody else that Louella herself was drunk that night.

"Before I fell asleep that evening, I deluded myself into believing those old bitches," Merv later said.

As part of the film's release, Jack Warner ordered Merv to go on a cross-country tour to promote the movie, even though the studio chief had serious misgivings about the film. "It stinks," he told Merv. "You stink in it. But I want to earn my money back."

On the road with Kathryn, Merv flew to Knoxville, Tennessee, the hometown of the ill-fated Grace Moore. Arriving at the airport, he was mobbed by teenage girls. Merv experienced "my first taste of being Tab Hunter. I was a romantic hero on the screen to these gals. The little fat boy from San Mateo had come full circle, or so I thought at the time."

"I even got to meet those hulking brothers of Grace Moore," Merv said. "Each of them insisted on slapping me on the back. No sadistic masseur ever delivered such blows."

Before appearing on stage before their fans that night, Kathryn and Merv rehearsed with the Kentucky Symphony. She went through her four big numbers and Merv did his solo. Later that afternoon, Kathryn and Merv rode in a convertible through the streets of Knoxville, waving at their fans. Rumors circulated that they were lovers. Even Governor Frank Clement of Tennessee turned out to greet them, inviting them to a reception after their performance that upcoming evening.

Hours later, with a beautifully gowned and made-up Kathryn on his arm, Merv paraded down the aisle of a packed auditorium. She suddenly gripped his arm. "I'm desperately tired," she whispered in his ear. "I can do only one number. You'll have to carry the rest of the show."

This was so unexpected that Merv was stunned. But ever the showman, he gallantly mounted the stage. After only one number, she retreated. The spotlight then shone on Merv, who clever-

Merv in Knoxville promoting
So This Is Love (1953)

187

ly won over the audience by singing "The Tennessee Waltz." After that, the crowd was his. Among others, he entertained them with his Coconuts song.

Later that night, after the governor's reception, Merv answered a knock on his hotel room door. It was a handsome young room service waiter, delivering a bottle of champagne from the governor. After uncorking the champagne for Merv, the waiter was invited to stay over to help Merv drink it. "That's great," the waiter said. "I just went off duty at midnight."

"That's what I call room service," Merv said jokingly.

In bed, the waiter told Merv he didn't know what to do. "I've never done it with a man."

"Good," Merv said, "I'll teach you."

The following morning Merv's ego was a bit deflated when the waiter begged Merv to "take me to Hollywood so I can become a bigger movie star than you."

Knoxville was Merv's last public appearance with Kathryn. For wider coverage, Warners split up the stars. Merv flew to Boston, checking into the Statler Hotel's presidential suite, an accommodation which had once been occupied by General Dwight Eisenhower.

Merv was delighted to learn that Freddy Martin's orchestra was appearing in Beantown. He called his former boss and invited all the members of Freddy's band to his suite after their final show. The musicians each predicted big stardom for Merv, as they devoured the champagne and caviar he'd ordered. "Warners is paying for this blast, so eat and drink like it's going out of style," Merv told them. He even made the suite's bedroom available to them, urging them to call their girlfriends, boyfriends, or wives.

One of the musicians, who had previously fooled around with Merv on the road, stayed over for the night. "No one handles 'Jimmy' like you do," the trombone player said before jumping into bed.

In the aftermath of that party, the accountants at Warners were furious that Merv's fiesta had run up a bill of three thousand dollars. In 1953, that was a lot of money.

Without Kathryn, the crowds diminished. By the time Merv reached Denver, there were fewer than one hundred fans who waved as Merv rode in a parade in a convertible along one of the city's main streets. Miss Denver got more applause than he did.

The publicists at Warners had arranged for the Colorado press to interview Merv at a reception within his suite at the Brown Palace. He was familiar with the questions that tended at this point in the tour to be routine: "Do you sleep in the nude?" and "What was it like kissing Kathryn Grayson?"

Around midnight, after a lot of alcohol had been consumed, there was a knock on the door. Uninvited, Peaches Browning burst into the room and kissed Merv on the lips. He remembered her from parties he'd attended in San Francisco during the war. She was the Anna Nicole Smith of her day, famous for being famous. Draped in furs and diamonds, the blonde, blue-eyed, buxom headline-grabber had married Edward W. Browning, a.k.a. "Daddy" Browning, as the tabloids called him.

The aging millionaire playboy had discovered Peaches in a ballroom in New York. Although at the time she was a fifteen-year-old Irish colleen, she soon became his bride. In 1927, after a few months of marriage, she filed for divorce, creating a media feeding frenzy by levying a series of fiery accusations—"degrading passion, depravity, and lewdness. One of the charges involved how he kept a big fat goose in their bedroom to arouse his erotic passion.

At Merv's reception, Warners' publicists didn't want Peaches horning in on their publicity, but Merv welcomed her and they posed together for pictures.

Merv was sad to learn of her death three years later. Peaches was found dead in her bathroom, and Merv always claimed that she had been murdered, although he had no evidence to back it up.

After Peaches, the tour dwindled down. Merv didn't remember the exact city where the publicity jaunt ended. "I blotted it out. By then, we'd learned that *So This Is Love* had bombed at the box office. On the last day of the tour, five fans showed up, and I'm exaggerating the number a bit. By the time I limped back to Hollywood, I feared my dream of stardom was eluding me once again. Yet hope bloomed eternal."

In 1953, instead of going to see *So This Is Love*, movie fans in America were lured away from their television screens to see such cinematic spectacles as *The Robe*, which 20th Century Fox had released in the new medium of widescreen CinemaScope. Briefly, Hollywood moguls believed that widescreen spectaculars would lure fans back into the theaters and away from TV programmers and their "nasty little boxes."

***

During the filming of *So This Is Love*, Merv had continued to play tennis with Howard Hughes, who was deep into his mostly unrequited obsession with Kathryn Grayson. Howard warned Merv not to tell her that they were friends or even tennis partners. Merv later said, "Howard had no real friends. He was the loneliest man in the world."

Howard was jealous of any person, male or female, he became involved with, and he spied on both his current lovers and even his would-be lovers.

As studio chief of RKO, Howard had hired Jeff Chouinard, a dashing ex-fighter pilot, to be the head of an elaborate spy ring, giving him a budget of two million dollars a year. Chouinard's specialty was somehow managing to install a "bugging radio" in the bedrooms of each of Howard's paramours.

Howard had organized a team of drivers—mostly college-age men—to infiltrate Los Angeles, trailing the beautiful women and handsome men upon whom Howard maintained a fixation at the time. When Howard learned that some of his drivers were actually encountering some of the women they were spying upon, and then seducing them, he fired all of them, demanding that henceforth, Chouinard hire only homosexual drivers.

One Sunday afternoon, while lunching with Merv after a tennis match, the aviator confessed that he had an army of some fifty detectives following such stars as Mitzi Gaynor, Barbara Payton (who later became a hooker), Gina Lollobrigida, Susan Hayward, and Zizi Jeanmaire, the French ballet star. His most sophisticated state-of-the-art eavesdropping devices were installed in the residence of Jean Peters.

Every morning at breakfast, Howard listened to the recordings derived from monitors positioned within the bedrooms of these stars. Howard was particularly fascinated by a tape of the Swedish actress, Anita Ekberg, making love to a former college football player.

Howard arranged for his sometimes lover, Pat DiCicco, to escort Elizabeth Taylor out on a date. Despite the fact that she'd repeatedly spurned Howard's advances, he was still fascinated by her. One of Howard's detectives climbed a telephone pole behind Elizabeth's apartment on Sunset Boulevard and reported that Pat didn't leave Elizabeth's bedroom until 8am the next morning. "I told him to escort her, not fuck her," Howard said. "For his punishment, I'm going to fuck that two-timing bastard until he bleeds," Howard told Merv. "That'll teach Pat a lesson."

By this point in their relationship, Merv had come to believe that Howard was completely deranged. He'd heard rumors that the billionaire had contracted syphilis from the actress, Billie Dove, a former love, back in the 1920s, and that it had never been cured, adversely affecting his brain and thought processes.

After the first day's shoot on *So This Is Love*, Merv went to bed early to get his beauty sleep before facing the cameras in the morning. At 3am, a mysterious call came in from Howard, who wanted to meet him in a parked car in a seedy neighborhood of Los Angeles. A sleepy-eyed Merv drove to the rendezvous point and met with Howard in the back seat of a twenty-year-old car that Howard used, since he believed that none of the press would believe that he was driving such a beat-up old jalopy.

Howard's proposal was blunt. The aviator wanted to spy on Kathryn during the shooting of the film, as he suspected that she was having a torrid affair with her handsome, dashing co-star in *Show Boat*, Howard Keel.

Merv found the idea of spying on someone distasteful. "But who was I to say no to Howard Hughes and live to tell about it?" he later said. For Merv's services, Howard agreed to pay him one thousand dollars a week, and Merv, who desperately wanted the money, agreed.

In Hollywood and later on the road, Merv dutifully recorded Grayson's every action, later submitting his written notes to Howard. One of Howard's obsessions involved wanting to know the exact number of times Kathryn excused herself to go to the toilet. In the past, Howard had been known to supervise the bowel movements of some of his conquests, both male and female. Cary Grant, for one, found that habit of Howard's "outrageously objectionable."

Howard kept his word, arranging for those thousand dollar checks to be sent to Merv every week. Once Merv and Kathryn split up their road tour campaign as a means of carrying the publicity into more cities, Merv suspected that the checks would stop coming.

But once Merv was back in Hollywood, Howard wanted to keep him employed, this time as a midnight driver. Howard was continuing his personal surveillance of Kathryn. He often did his own driving, but whenever Merv encountered him, he claimed to have blinding migraines that made it impossible for him to steer a car. Merv suspected that these headaches were brought on by all those airplane crashes he'd survived.

On his first night as Howard's driver, Merv drove him to Kathryn's Tudor-style mansion, parking a block away so as not to be detected, even though no one would have suspected that Howard Hughes was being driven around in Merv's old car. The pattern established on Merv's first night would be repeated frequently in the weeks to come.

Howard would stake out Kathryn's house from a lonely position in her rose garden, where he could look up at her bedroom window. One night she spotted him and informed her father the next morning. He threatened to take his rifle and "kill the whore-chasing son of a bitch." But Kathryn talked him out of it, claiming that such a scandal would destroy her career.

On the nights that Howard stalked the Grayson garden, Merv fell asleep at the wheel, waiting for Howard's return,

Dangerous liaison: **Kathryn Grayson** with her billionaire stalker, **Howard Hughes**

which was usually right before dawn.

On their third night of stake-out, Howard confessed what his real interest was in Kathryn. "It's her breasts, knockers from heaven. As you know from seeing Jane Russell in *The Outlaw*, I'm a breast man."

Seeing Howard wandering night after night alone in her garden, Kathryn in time took pity on him. She invited him inside and allowed him to sleep in her guest room, but not in her own bedroom. The Grayson home became the perfect hideaway for Howard and an escape from the press and the ever-increasing problems of Hughes Aircraft, RKO, and TWA.

Howard warned Merv one night that "both of us might be killed. I'm a marked man." He claimed that he was constantly pursued by process servers and, in fact, had a total of twenty-six lawsuits pending, some of them paternity actions. He was sometimes chased by jealous boyfriends.

Howard was eventually accepted into the Grayson household as one of the family. Even her father grew to like him. For Merv, this acceptance led to financial disaster. But whereas paychecks stopped, the tennis matches continued.

The relationship between Howard and Kathryn lasted on and off for eight tumultuous years. She finally tired of his games and abandoned him at the altar. Much that he did infuriated her, including when he appeared at her live show in Las Vegas. She was honored that he showed up to see her perform, but she later learned that he had stashed two of his other mistresses, actresses Jean Peters and Terry Moore, within different suites at the same hotel. Hughes would later marry Jean. Terry also claimed that Hughes married her, although no marriage licence has ever surfaced.

"I wish Howard had married me," Merv later told Johnny Riley. "Alas, he never proposed. Not only that, he never asked me to go to bed with him. I guess I wasn't his type. Once when I visited his suite at the Beverly Hills Hotel, I noticed that he had three bare-chested pictures of the actor John Payne photographed both in his boxing and swimming trunks. I made a mistake that night when I wandered into Howard's bedroom to take a leak in his toilet. He later had the bowl ripped out. I pissed off Howard Hughes by taking a piss. No one, or so I learned, uses the same toilet bowl as Howard."

In the years to come, Kathryn later recalled "a warm and wonderful relationship" with Howard. But Howard confessed that he'd once gotten violent with her. Merv suspected that her assessment of that warm and wonderful relationship was mere fodder for the tabloids, having nothing to do with reality.

In some ways, Merv was glad to escape from the clutches of Howard, as he found the job distasteful. He hadn't had a decent night's sleep in weeks. With Howard out of the picture except for Sunday tennis matches, Merv turned to the task of living his own life.

***

Throughout the early 50s, Merv made and maintained a friendship with Tony Curtis and Janet Leigh, two highly photogenic and congenial newcomers who were married on June 4, 1951. Having appeared on the cover of virtually every movie magazine in America, they were often headlined at the time as "America's Sweethearts." During the course of their bumpy eleven-year marriage, they would co-star together in five films, the best-received of which was *Houdini* (1953). During the era of their early friendship with Merv, Janet's career-defining role as stabbing victim Marion Crane in the Alfred Hitchcock classic, *Psycho* (1960), lay in her future.

Sometime during the period when they were still defined as newlyweds, Tony called Merv and asked if he'd join Janet and himself for a Halloween costume party at the home of Jerry Lewis. Merv agreed and told him that Marilyn Erskine would be his date that night.

Merv had only recently gotten to know Tony and Janet, both of whom he found to be open and candid with him, enough so that he felt he didn't have to keep secrets from them. Both Tony and Janet were already aware of Merv's homosexuality. And at least when they were separate from each other, both of the young stars were equally candid with him.

From the beginning of the friendship, Merv became aware that Tony was cheating on his wife. At the time, he didn't know whether Janet suspected that her handsome husband was "playing the field," as Tony described his lifestyle to Merv.

Without Tony, Merv and Janet frequently had lunch together to gossip about their romantic involvements. She delighted in telling Merv about how Errol Flynn had seduced her when they'd appeared in *That Forsyte Woman* (1949). "Yes, but I had him long before you did," Merv boasted to Janet.

"Well, at least I got to sample Joe DiMaggio before some of these other starlets," she said to Merv. She'd met the baseball great when he'd appeared in her movie, *Angels in the Outfield* (1951).

Later during Merv's friendship with Janet, she'd be cast with Robert Wagner in their rather laughable adventure film, *Prince Valiant* (1954). Merv confessed to her that he thought the stunningly handsome Robert Wagner was the sexiest man who'd ever lived. He begged Janet to go to bed with the young man, so "you can give me a blow-by-blow, inch-by-inch description."

"I'll get back to you on that," Janet promised.

Both Janet and Merv had slept with Peter Lawford, so Merv didn't need for her to spill any secrets about him. But he did want to know "all the details about that Tarzan stud, Lex Barker," who would go on to marry Lana Turner.

193

Merv also heard about Janet's involvement with the gangster Johnny Stompanato, who later would become involved with Lana and who would eventually be stabbed to death under murky circumstances in her home.

During the period Merv was hanging out with Janet, she was also being pursued by his friend, Howard Hughes. "I'd call it sexual harassment more than a romance," Janet confided. What surprised Merv most was Janet's confession that she'd married a student, Kenneth Carlyle, when she was only fourteen years old. That marriage was later annulled.

Knowing that for career reasons Merv needed to keep dating a string of beautiful women, Janet promised to arrange a date for him with her friend, Gloria DeHaven. Ironically, Tony Curtis had also dated Gloria.

With Merv, Tony was equally candid about his sex life. "I don't know what there was about me," Merv later said. "Perhaps I was just a Mother Confessor. But stars always wanted to tell me their secrets. I had this ability to get them to open up and talk. That certainly came in handy when I became a talk show host."

Tony revealed that he'd first ejaculated when he was eleven years old in a dark movie theater in the Bronx while holding hands with a girl from his neighborhood. "But it wasn't until I was in the Navy that I lost it in a whorehouse in Panama City," Tony said. "I was eighteen at the time."

Merv had continued to find accommodating young women to date, doing what was deemed necessary to keep up appearances and mask his private homosexual lifestyle. Marilyn Erskine, Merv's date, had been briefly married to the director Stanley Kramer in 1945, but after a few weeks this mysterious union was annulled. Around that time of her date with Merv, she was co-starring in *The Eddie Cantor Story* (1953). Merv and Marilyn jointly decided to dress up as drag versions of Shirley Booth and Burt Lancaster, who were appearing on screens across the nation in *Come Back, Little Sheba* (1952). Merv dressed in drag as Shirley's character of Lola Delaney, with Marilyn disguised as the male character played by Burt Lancaster, Doc Delaney. In synch with the cross-dressing choices of Merv and Marilyn, Janet dressed as Tony, and Tony appeared in drag as Janet.

"Marilyn and I looked like refugees," Merv later said, "but Tony and Janet had been professionally made up by people at the studio," Merv said. "They looked like a pair of high-class transvestites."

Behind the wheel en route to the party, Janet

Tony Curtis with then-wife **Janet Leigh,** London, 1957

194

roared out of her driveway, breaking all speed records until a motorcycle cop on Wilshire Boulevard pulled them over. He ordered all of them out of the car, proclaiming, "Jesus, Mary, and Joseph."

From beneath a wig of blonde curls, Tony tried to talk his way out of this embarrassing dilemma, but both Janet and he had left their drivers' licenses at home. At first the cop didn't believe, dressed as they were, that they were America's most widely publicized romantic couple. He looked with even greater skepticism at Marilyn and Merv. "But after I did my famous Cary Grant impersonation, he finally let us go," Tony said.

The policeman had tales to tell when he returned to his precinct. This was probably the source of those hot rumors that later distorted the actual events of the evening. By the next day, stories were going around Hollywood that Merv and Tony had been arrested dressed as drag queens. Not only that, but according to the rumor mill they were also having a torrid affair with each other.

Years later, during an encounter with Tony Curtis in 1960, Merv quipped, "You did better with your drag act than I ever did." In drag, Tony had completed the final scenes of *Some Like It Hot* (1959) with Marilyn Monroe.

Years previously, way back in 1949, while still a starlet, Marilyn had had a brief affair with Tony. Reminiscing about that affair, Tony often asserted that the gay costume designer, Orry-Kelly, a former lover of Cary Grant, had told him, "Your ass is tighter and better looking than Marilyn's."

When she heard this, Marilyn quipped: "But Tony's ass gets more work-outs than mine. I'm usually a front girl."

***

"Who are these unknown hookers you keep dating?" Jack Warner bellowed into the phone to Merv. "You've got to go out with name stars. Okay, so I understand why your thing with Joan Crawford didn't work out. Go for the starlets then. You'll never get your picture in the paper dating five-and-dime sales gals who give blow-jobs for five bucks a swallow." Then the studio chief slammed down the phone.

Even though Merv hadn't taken out any hookers, he agreed with his boss. Dating Rita Farrell was not a good way to get on the cover of *Photoplay* magazine like his friends, Tony Curtis and Janet Leigh. He searched around for suitable dates, focusing on women who needed publicity as much or more than he did. Through the intervention of Janet Leigh, Merv hooked up with Gloria DeHaven.

Despite roles which had included Mickey Rooney's sweetheart in *Summer Holiday* (1948) and Judy Garland's disagreeable sister in *Summer Stock*

(1950), and despite occasional film appearances alongside "America's sweetheart," June Allyson, Gloria had never made it big in MGM musicals

Though a competent and rather beautiful performer, Gloria just wasn't exciting enough on screen to join the upper echelons. In the mid-1950s, during the period when Merv was dating her, her career was winding down, fading into the sunset with the type of 1940s musicals in which she'd originally triumphed, as represented by *Two Girls and A Sailor* (1944). And whereas Gloria needed publicity to revitalize a career in decline, Merv needed exposure to jump-start a fledgling one.

Knocking on her door, he was startled when John Payne threw it open to greet him. "Come on in, kid," he said to Merv. Here was Howard Hughes' erotic fantasy in all his studly beauty, a heroic, muscled, and strikingly handsome hunk of All-American male. Like Gloria, John's major films were behind him, although he'd be known in decades to come for playing the leading role in *Miracle on 34th Street* (1947), which graces TV screens every Christmas.

Merv knew that John had married Gloria in 1944, divorcing her in 1950, a union that had spawned two children. "I'm babysitting tonight," John said to explain his presence in his former wife's home.

The actor didn't seem in the least jealous of Merv, perhaps realizing how harmless the date was. Merv later gave his impression of John to Johnny Riley in a phone call. "While I was waiting for Gloria to get dressed, and after he'd poured our second drink, I'd fallen madly in love with John Payne. He's my type. Forget Errol Flynn. I've left him in the dust. I had the hots for John the first moment I laid eyes on him, even though I remembered Roddy McDowall telling me how straight he was. Both Clifton Webb and even that mouthwatering beauty, Tyrone Power, had each failed to seduce John when they'd appeared with him in *The Razor's Edge* back in 1946."

It was with great reluctance that Merv tore himself away from John that night to escort Gloria to some event. Later he couldn't recall what function they attended, but the memory of John lingered.

John Payne had become famous among both horny women and homosexual men when he'd posed for a series of beefcake photos in the late 1930s, around the same time he was stripped down to a pair of tight-fitting boxing trunks for his co-starring role in *Kid Nightingale* with Jane Wyman. These two up-and-coming stars had a torrid affair, even though John was married at the time to actress Anne Shirley. When that affair cooled, Jane opted to pursue Ronald Reagan

Gloria De Haven with Merv's ex, **Tom Drake**

196

instead.

At the time of Merv's date with Gloria, John's career had been reduced to a series of forgettable Westerns and *films noirs* at Paramount, and seemed headed for oblivion.

Merv came up with a scheme. If he couldn't get John himself, "I figured I might earn brownie points with Howard," Merv later told Roddy. Merv called Howard and told him he'd met John Payne, and that the actor might be interested in flying to Catalina with him for the weekend. The aviator took the bait, inviting both of them to "Come fly with me."

Merv then transmitted the invitation to John, slyly suggesting that Howard might be intrigued by the idea of signing him to an exclusive contract when his present deal with Paramount ran out. John also took the bait.

The following afternoon, when John showed up at the airfield, Howard immediately informed John that he'd seen *Kid Nightingale* three times. John seemed flattered by the attention of such a famous and rich patron. During the flight to Catalina, Merv was assigned to the back seat while John sat up front with Howard, who manned the controls. Even though Merv knew that John was straight, he also suspected that few actors would reject the attentions, sexual or otherwise, of the great Howard Hughes.

As Merv later reported to Roddy, that rainy weekend in Catalina had been a dud for him, although John and Howard seemed to have a good time. "They were locked away in Howard's bedroom for most of the weekend, and I was on the sofa in the living room watching old Westerns on TV. My biggest thrill happened one night around one o'clock in the morning when John wandered into the living room for a cigarette. He was stark, raving nude as the day he was born. Quite a dangler on him. All I could do was drool and daydream. He knew what he was doing. He lingered long enough in front of the flickering light of the television to give me a grand view. Right then and there I decided to become a billionaire like Howard himself so I could entice the John Paynes of the future into my bedroom."

Films noirs and beefcake:
John Payne

As it turned out, Howard did nothing for John's career except to give him a great piece of career advice. Howard suggested that the actor acquire the rights to an Ian Fleming novel, *Moonraker*, and secure a deal to play the British spy in the book, James Bond. John followed this advice and took out a nine-month option at a thousand dollars a month on *Moonraker*. He decided to drop the option when he learned he couldn't acquire the rights to the entire James Bond series. Big mistake. For the rest of his life, he'd regret his decision to drop the option, as in the years ahead he watched the James Bond films make countless millions.

In May of 1961, John suffered extensive, life-threatening injuries when struck by a car on the streets of New York City. His recovery, which left him with facial scars, took two years. In New York at the time, Merv visited him, bringing a box of chocolates and flowers.

"Thanks, Merv," the grateful actor said. As they chatted, Merv understood how lonely John was. When Merv started to leave, John begged him to stay on longer, as he seemed starved for company. In their final hour together, John became confidential. "I should have taken care of you that weekend with Hughes on Catalina. I'm sorry I didn't. Forgive me. Considering how I look now, and what condition I'm in, I can't do much for you now either."

"No need for that," Merv assured him, smiling even though embarrassed.

"I sang and danced on screen with Alice Faye, Betty Grable, Carmen Miranda, and so many others, but you're the only celebrity to come and see me in the hospital. There's nothing more forgotten than a forgotten movie star."

***

Although Merv's earlier film, the 1953 film *So This Is Love*, had bombed at the box office, its director, Gordon Douglas, nonetheless opted to cast the perpetually willing Merv in yet another film, *The Charge at Feather River*. It was one of the first Westerns to be filmed in 3-D, and it starred that heartthrob of the 1940s, Guy Madison.

Merv eagerly looked forward to meeting Guy, one of "the boys" in the stable of Henry Willson, the notoriously gay talent agent who "created" a stable of newly minted male movie stars, renaming them with monikers like Tab Hunter and Rock Hudson.

On the set of *The Charge at Feather River,* Gordon ordained that the death scene previously filmed by another actor, a citizen of Poland, had to be reconfigured and re-shot. The original actor had returned to take a job in Warsaw, and "I was elected to redo the entire death scene," Merv recalled. "I was seriously pissed off at Gordon. What a fucker. I felt I'd been double-crossed by being given such a paltry role when I was dreaming of co-starring in the film with Guy Madison."

Gordon promised Merv that if "I ever direct a film that calls for a guy who can play the piano and sing too, I'll cast you."

"Yeah, right," Merv said.

Gordon, as director, later recalled, "Even though I didn't do much for the film career of Merv Griffin, I liked the kid. Like a politician, he sought out the stars of the film and ingratiated himself with them. He had the power to form instant friendships more effectively than any other actor I've ever known. And he was star struck. To Merv, a star meant anybody who got at least fifth billing in a film."

Merv didn't become friendly with Vera Miles, one of the stars of the film. But he'd already sampled the charms of her future husband, Gordon Scott, who became famous as one of Hollywood's sexiest (and most promiscuous) Tarzans. Merv did get to shake hands with the square-jawed, intense, no-nonsense Frank Lovejoy, born in the Bronx. "He brought the Bronx with him," Merv said. "In fact, Frank was the best thing in the movie."

Merv was no doubt referring to a scene where the actor "discouraged" a rattlesnake with tobacco juice and even aimed a squirt at the 3-D audience, who screamed at the prospect of getting tobacco juice in their eyes.

Merv claimed to have enjoyed meeting the other female star of the film, California-born Helen Westcott, who began her acting career at the age of four. He loved talking to her about her handsome father, Gordon Westcott, who had been cast in several Warner Brothers films until his early death at the age of thirty-two in 1935. Those films had included Gloria Swanson's ill-fated silent, *Queen Kelly* (1929), and Bette Davis's *Fog Over Frisco* (1934). "A lot of young actors were interested only in hearing about Rock Hudson or Marilyn Monroe," Helen recalled, "but Merv could listen for hours to tales about Hollywood during the silent days or during the early talkies. I liked that about him."

Near the end of Merv's association with *The Charge at Feather River*, Helen introduced him to a friend of hers, the gargle-voiced Aldo Ray who earlier had been a *protégé* of gay director George Cukor. Born Aldo DaRe to an Italian family, the former frogman for the U.S. Navy had been cast opposite the bisexual actress, Judy Holliday, in the 1952 *The Marrying Kind*.

According to Roddy McDowall, both Cukor and Spencer Tracy had enjoyed Aldo's considerable erotic charms when he was cast in *Pat and Mike* (also 1952), co-starring Katharine Hepburn. Roddy had told Merv that Aldo was "basically straight, but didn't object if some gay male wanted to service him."

"My kind of man!" Merv said.

Much of inside Hollywood was surprised at the almost instant friendship that developed between Aldo and Merv. Helen herself called them "the odd couple." After being introduced by Helen, Aldo and Merv were seen together frequently, especially when Aldo became involved with another of Merv's newly made friends, Rita Hayworth, with whom Aldo had co-starred in *Miss Sadie Thompson*. Another of Merv's friends, Jose Ferrer, was also a star in that steamy film of the tropics. "Jose planned to seduce Rita," Merv said, "but he was thwarted when Aldo got the Princess instead."

Merv was attracted to Aldo's husky frame, thick neck, and even his raspy voice, which made him perfect for playing tough, macho roles. At the time Merv met Aldo, his marriage to Shirley Green was coming to an end. On a few occasions Merv double dated with Aldo. "He was taking a girl out for serious purposes," Merv later told his friend Johnny Riley. "If Aldo would strike out with a woman, I'd get him later in the evening for sure. Okay, our so-called affair consisted entirely of me giving him a few blow-jobs, but in Aldo's case that was enough to satisfy me."

Aldo enthralled Merv with stories about George Cukor. "He did a lot for my career," the actor said. "So I felt there was nothing wrong with dropping my pants and letting the guy enjoy himself. I got pissed off at him, however, when he made me go to ballet school because he claimed I walked too much like a football player."

One night Aldo called Merv and asked if he could come over later. Merv eagerly invited his newly enlisted friend, hoping that this would be their first real "date." Aldo dispelled that notion when he asked if he could bring a friend.

When that friend showed up at Merv's door with Aldo, it turned out to be a recently acquired friend of Merv's as well. Rita Hayworth, who was starring in *Miss Sadie Thompson* with Aldo. They told him they would soon be flying to Hawaii for location shooting and wanted some place to escape from prying eyes for a few hours. "No one will think of looking for us at Merv Griffin's house," Rita said.

Merv immediately sensed that "two is party enough, three a crowd," as he put it, but Rita urged him to stay for a while to talk to them.

Merv knew that Rita, in the wake of her divorce from the Aly Khan, the then fabulously wealthy spiritual leader of the Ismaili Muslims, had gone back to playing the field. Amid torrents of international controversy, she resumed affairs with former loves who included Victor Mature and Glenn Ford, and also dated newer contenders who included Kirk Douglas. She was also seen increasingly with an Argentine, the crooner Dick Haymes, a rival of Frank Sinatra. Haymes was known among Hollywood insiders as "Mr. Evil" because of his record as a mean drunk with a penchant for beating up women.

After three failed marriages, Rita was very candid about herself and why she had returned to Hollywood. "I'm trying to reinvent myself, and that ain't

200

easy, dear hearts."

During their meeting, Merv noticed that she was distraught and kept asking for a refill of her drink.

"Rita and I are just having fun getting to know each other," Aldo interjected. "Both of us know we're not ideal candidates for marriage."

In spite of what she said, Merv suspected that Rita would impulsively race into another ill-fated marriage with yet another womanizer. She was the marrying kind, he'd determined. She looked disheveled, and he knew she was dissatisfied with her more mature appearance, and had been horrified at the way she'd been photographed in certain scenes in *Salome* (1953), her latest picture.

"*You Were Never Lovelier*," he assured her, quoting the title of her 1942 movie before disappearing for the night, after offering the couple his guest bedroom and making sure they had plenty of bath towels.

In the morning when he woke up, both Aldo and Rita had departed. "We've got to get back to our other lives," Rita had scribbled in her note of thanks. The ever-mischievous Aldo had written under it: "Why didn't you come and join us in the middle of the night? It would have been fun."

From that night forward, and until the end of his role as a player in 1950s Hollywood, Merv became accustomed to lending his guest room to off-the-record couples. Many times he wished he'd been the lucky one snaring the "hunk of the week," but he enjoyed having a lot of sexy men running around his house in their underwear. "Who knows?" he told Roddy. "Maybe the gal won't put out one night, and I'll get lucky."

Merv and Aldo remained friends for many years. In 1958, he accompanied Helen Westcott and Aldo to a screening of a film in which they had appeared together, the steamy drama, *God's Little Acre*. That film was based on a notorious novel by Erskine Caldwell which had sold more than fourteen million copies. In that film, Helen played Aldo's spurned wife.

By then, Aldo had long ago ended his affair with Rita, as she'd entered into another disastrous marriage, this time to Dick Haymes, who "used and abused her," in Merv's judgment. Aldo had lived up to his self-styled judgment that he wasn't a good candidate for marriage. He'd wed actress Jean Marie ("Jeff") Donnell in 1954, but divorced her two years later.

During the decades to come, as his own career took off, Merv watched with sadness as Aldo's own career began a long, slow, and painful decline.

Invitation to a three-way with
Aldo Ray

Hollywood's appetite for his particular brand of machismo had waned. Near the end of his career, Aldo even appeared in a porn movie, *Sweet Savage*. When he was dying of throat cancer in Martinez, California, Merv secretly paid a number of his exorbitant hospital bills that even Aldo's family didn't know about.

***

Although Merv had met most of the supporting players in *The Charge at Feather River*, he still hadn't been introduced to Guy Madison, the star of the film. To Merv, the handsome actor was the epitome of the post-World War II male sex symbol. "Ever since I'd seen Guy in *Since You Went Away* in that sailor uniform, I'd had the hots for him," Merv told Roddy. "I even had three beefcake pictures of him from the late 40s nailed to my bathroom wall. Guy's pecs did for me what Betty Grable's legs did for a lot of homesick GIs during World War II."

Incidentally, the word "beefcake" as it applies to a male sex symbol was actually coined by Sidney Skolsky, the Hollywood columnist, to describe Guy Madison.

At the wrap party that Gordon Douglas threw for the cast of his film, Merv, from across a crowded room, spotted Guy standing in the corner. The rest of the party was rather formally dressed, but Guy appeared in tight-fitting blue jeans and a white T-shirt which revealed the outline of his pecs. For Merv, it was love at first sight. On wobbly legs, he found himself heading across the room to shake Guy's hand. "I would gladly have eaten his toe jam as well," he later told Roddy. "In person he looked even more edible than in his photos."

"I'm Merv Griffin," he said extending his hand and holding onto Guy's just a bit too long.

"I'm Guy Madison," the icon said, flashing his famous smile. "My agent, Henry Willson, wanted to call me Guy Dunhill, but named me for my favorite baker, The Dolly Madison Bakery. Dolly was a bit much, so Henry came up with Guy."

"Hell, one newspaper referred to me as Mary Griffin."

"Maybe we should team up, Dolly & Mary, and take our act on the road," Guy said jokingly.

This secret language between them, so familiar to closeted gays of the 1950s, was music to Merv's ears. As he later predicted, "That Guy Madison hunk can be had."

That became more evident when Guy invited him to go with him to one of Henry Willson's notorious pool parties that weekend. As Merv related to

Roddy the following day, "In the case of Guy Madison and Merv Griffin, I think this is the beginning of a beautiful friendship."

Prior to his appearance in Hollywood, Guy had previously pursued several macho professions that appeal, at least in their fantasy versions, to gay men, including telephone lineman and a sailor in the U.S. Coast Guard. In the closing years of World War II, when he was on leave from active duty in San Diego, his striking good looks and manly physique had caught the eye of Henry Willson, who in addition to having a voracious appetite for handsome young men, was also head of talent for David O. Selznick.

Guy (actually Robert Mosely of Bakersfield, California) immediately fell, partially undressed, onto Henry's casting couch. After doing his duty for Henry and his career, he signed a personal management contract. The agent promised him, "I'll make you the biggest movie star in Hollywood." Guy (a.k.a. Robert) foolishly believed him.

After Guy finished his tour of duty in the Coast Guard, he joined Henry's stable of "Tom of Finland" stars, all of them marginally talented actors known for their stunning male beauty. Originally Henry was going to call his new discovery "Rock Madison," but decided to reserve the name Rock for some future actor.

Henry succeeded in getting Guy cast in a small part as a sailor in the sentimental 1944 tear-jerker, *Since You Went Away*, starring Claudette Colbert. Homosexual men and teenage girls, figuratively speaking, "fell out of the balcony" when Guy made his appearance in this Selznick film.

At the time Merv became romantically involved with the actor, Guy was married to the bisexual actress, Gail Russell, though their troubled relationship was heading for the divorce courts.

Guy arrived at Merv's house on a Friday night before the big pool party at Henry Willson's home on Saturday. "We didn't roll in the hay right away," Merv later told Johnny Riley. "Guy spent a good part of the evening talking about his failed marriage to Gail Russell. She was deep into her alcoholism whenever she wasn't involved with her affair with John Wayne or whatever hot female tamale she'd picked up on Santa Monica Boulevard."

In the course of their first evening together, Merv was astonished to learn the sheer numbers of male actors Guy

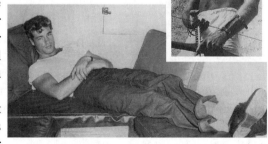

All Aboard!
Two views of beefcake **Guy Madison**

203

had slept with. They included Robert Mitchum, with whom he'd co-starred in *Till the End of Time* (1946). Guy also confessed to having conducted an ongoing affair with Rory Calhoun, another handsome young star in Henry's stable. The two actors had met on the set of *Massacre River* in 1949. At the time of his involvement with Merv, Guy surmised that Rory "will fall into the clutches of Marilyn Monroe." It had already been announced that Rory, Marilyn, and, ironically, Robert Mitchum would all be on location together, co-starring in *River of No Return* (1954), and Hollywood insiders were already speculating about the romantic and sexual imbroglios to come.

"I sympathize with you," Merv said. "It's hard to compete with Marilyn Monroe."

The actor complained that his career "as a serious actor" was going nowhere since he'd been cast in the hit TV series, *The Adventures of Wild Bill Hickok.*"

"That gut-belly on my sidekick, Andy Devine, grows bigger every day," Guy said, "and his voice sounds more and more like it needs oiling."

The following morning Merv dutifully reported the details of his night with Guy to Roddy McDowall in their ritual morning phone chat when they exchanged notes from their affairs of the previous evening.

"Unlike Rock Hudson, who can be brutal, Guy is a gentle lover," Merv said. "But I fear he's beyond my reach. The competition for him is too much for me. Guy's not only got a wife, but Rory Calhoun keeps popping in and out of Guy's life, that is if Marilyn Monroe doesn't steal him away."

"My dear boy, call it a fling and enjoy it for what it is," Roddy advised. "You don't have to install every guy you meet in a rose-covered cottage as the love of your life. Take delight, as I do, in playing the field."

On the morning of the day that Guy had offered to take Merv to Henry's pool party, Merv received a phone call from San Francisco. At first he thought it was from Johnny Riley. But it was from Bill Robbins, his San Mateo school buddy, whom he hadn't heard from in months. Bill and Merv's other friend, Paul Schone, had not been able to find much work as dancers in San Francisco and wanted to move to Los Angeles. Bill asked Merv if he and Paul could take over his guest bedroom until they found work. Without hesitation, Merv invited both of them to come down— "and stay as long as you want."

"We dance better than Gene Nelson," Bill said. "Like you, I think we're gonna take Hollywood by storm."

"I'm not exactly taking Hollywood by storm," Merv warned. "Instead of a tropical hurricane, it's more like a twenty-second summer shower."

Rory Calhoun

204

Guy Madison escorted Merv to the door of Henry Willson's house, where they were ushered inside by a maid and directed toward the pool. Here Merv was astonished to see at least fifty of the handsomest young men he'd ever seen in one assemblage in his life.

Most of the men were in the skimpiest of bathing attire, some in bikinis that were more like the flimsy *caches-sexe* "sex-hiders" then prevalent in St-Tropez on the French Riviera. Some of them were completely nude.

In a pair of conventional bathing trunks, Rock Hudson was the first to greet Merv, giving him a wet, sloppy kiss before introducing him to the actor George Nader. To Merv, George looked as well built as Rock and even sexier.

Guy ushered Merv over to meet the host, Henry Willson, before disappearing into a bedroom to change into his own swimming trunks.

At long last Merv was chatting amicably with the most notorious homosexual in Hollywood. At first Merv was intimidated by Henry and feared he'd say something stupid to the agent, which he did. "Mr. Willson, your reputation has preceded you."

"Don't believe those rumors that I'm a lecherous, dirty old queen," Henry said, smiling. "I take a bath every day—never alone, of course—so you can strike dirty from my list of credits."

Despite the tinges of awkwardness which marked the beginning of their conversation, Merv and Henry were soon talking with candor and animation as if they'd known each other for years. It was another example of Merv's ability to form an instant friendship with a kindred spirit.

Although the gay talent agent was known for his discoveries, including Rock Hudson, it was clearly evident from the beginning that he had no sexual designs on Merv. Merv was young and handsome at the time, but he hardly fitted Henry's concept of "the beefcakes" he preferred. It was obvious that Henry knew exactly what was going on in his stable of boys, because he complimented Merv on "seducing two of the most fuckable guys in Hollywood, Guy and Rock. You must have some hidden talent that's not immediately apparent."

With no need for pretense with Henry, Merv said, "I'm a great cocksucker. Word of a talent like that spreads fast along the Hollywood grapevine."

That made Henry laugh, and he patted the seat on the chaise longue beside him, inviting Merv to sit down "for some serious girl talk."

In the fading afternoon of a hot California day, that chat between Henry and Merv would become one of dozens they would share over the years that followed. Merv would later recall that "Henry was the ugliest man at poolside that day. Fortunately, his bulky bathing suit covered up a lot of sins." Henry had a hawkish nose which evoked a bird of prey sniffing out his next meal, and a protruding lower lip that implied a deep capacity for petulance. And like the famous New York-based Broadway columnist, Dorothy Kilgallen, Henry had no chin. Frank Sinatra had famously referred to Dorothy as "the chinless wonder," but the same appellation could easily have applied to Henry. Merv also noted Henry's "feminine hips" and sloping shoulders, with legs shorter than those of Elizabeth Taylor.

Sensing that Merv was evaluating him physically, Henry said, "I don't need male beauty to seduce a boy, gay or straight. In Hollywood you need power, and if you've got that, you can have virtually any actor, even if he's straight. You'd be surprised how many straight guys drop their pants and show you a hard-on if you've got a part for them in a movie."

Time after time, the press on Henry was the worst in Hollywood, and it had even been suggested by some of his critics that he "exuded evil." Even Merv's best pal, Roddy McDowall, had warned him that "Willson is like the slime that oozes from under a rock you don't want to turn over."

Rock Hudson had told Merv that "Henry operates the longest-running gay casting couch in the history of Hollywood." Since it was obvious that Merv wasn't Henry's type, he didn't have to face the possibility of going to bed with this rather repulsive creature and could get on with their friendship.

But for reasons he never fully understood, Merv liked Henry. Or, if not that, he was at least tantalized by the possibilities that Henry held out for him before the sun faded that afternoon.

"I'll toss you my rejects," Henry said, "and don't take that the wrong way. My rejects are some of the sexiest men in the world. I've got more handsome, beefy young guys in my stable than I can handle, and they're all horny and hot."

"I'm ready, willing, and able to host as many as you can send over to my bachelor pad," Merv claimed.

"I'm a flesh peddler, baby, and that's all I'll ever be," Henry said. "Before sending a guy out on a job, I always take a pound of that flesh for myself."

"My kind of guy," Merv said.

Henry Willson
courting Harry Truman's daughter
Margaret in 1954.
What would her father have said?

To this day, the question has remained unanswered: "What did Henry Willson see in Merv Griffin? His movie career was going nowhere, and instinctively Henry knew that Merv would never be one of the stallions in his stable.

Henry later told Rock Hudson, who conveyed the impression to Merv: "I sensed naked ambition in Griffin, although he disguises it as Mr. Nice Guy," Henry said. "I latched onto him like a dinosaur ready for lunch because I sensed that this boy one day is going to be big in this town. I bet he ends up a producer or something, perhaps the owner of a studio. I have this feeling the kid is going to be making billions one day, and that I'll be knocking on his door with my latest big dick discovery. He is not going to make it in front of the camera, but in back of the camera. I'm never wrong about these things."

On the afternoon he met Henry, Merv asked for career advice. "Do you think I could get better roles if I shed a few pounds?"

"Don't worry about it, kid," Henry advised. "Become a producer—that's where the money is. Hell, you can put one of these movie star boys under contract for $200 a week, maybe $300. There's no money in that."

You just named my present salary," Merv said.

"When a big dick on a great body is trying to break into films, they can be had for twenty bucks a night, ten if they're hungry. If you become a producer, you don't have to worry about your weight. Look at me. I like my liquor, good food and lots of it. Let Rock and Guy spend all day in a gym—not me. When I got into the business, I looked positively epicene. People said I looked like Vincente Minnelli—God knows what Judy Garland saw in that faggot. Now that I've put on a few pounds, they say I look like Alfred Hitchcock. It's not your weight, but your influence that matters in Hollywood."

Merv wanted to make the rounds of the party, like his "date" for the evening, Guy Madison, was doing, but something compelled him to hang out with Henry instead. "I'll invite you to go to Ciro's with me," Henry promised, "maybe the Mocambo. You'll meet plenty of pretty boys from Florida to Kansas, from Texas to Montana. I like to get them while the smell of hayseed is still on them. Not a bad life, huh?"

"Sounds great," Merv said.

"Just a word of advice, though," Henry said. "At midnight always promise a boy that you'll turn him into a movie star. In some cases you might even carry through on that promise when you become a big producer. But even if you don't plan to do that, always feed a boy in the morning after you've had him every which way. Not just toast and jam, but waffles, bacon, a three-egg omelet. Never let a boy leave your bed hungry and go out to face a day in the Hollywood jungle."

"That's good advice I'll carry with me until the day I die," Merv said.

The chat with Henry was interrupted by a blast of music. Merv recognized the recording at once. It was a recording of his friend Rosemary Clooney singing a duet with Marlene Dietrich. From a bedroom and behind beaded curtains emerged Rock Hudson and George Nader, each wearing only a pink bow tie with cherry-red polka dots.

Standing at the edge of the pool in front of the awed young men, Rock as Marlene and George as Rosemary lip-synched the Dietrich/Clooney song. At the end of the number, the bathers around the pool roared their approval.

For their finale, Rock and George waved their big dicks at the cheering audience.

***

In his description to Johnny Riley of the Henry Willson pool party, Merv remembered meeting the live-in lover of Rock Hudson, although he could not recall the young man's name. The handsome Korean War vet, still in his 20s when he met Merv, might have been "Jack Navaar," a pseudonym created by certain biographers to protect the identity and privacy of Rock's companion.

Jack, as he will be called, was engaged at the time in a hot, passionate affair with Rock and was jokingly referred to as "Mrs. Rock Hudson," even though it was suspected that he was actually bisexual, and may have married and fathered children later in life.

He could be seen driving around Hollywood in Rock's buttercup yellow convertible, and the movie star supported him financially. Ever faithful to Rock, Jack stayed home and cooked a hot dinner for Rock when he returned from the studio. In her own highly unreliable memoirs, Phyllis Gates, the only woman Rock ever married, referred to Jack by the name of "Bill McGiver."

It is doubtful if Jack Navaar is still alive today to set the record "straight" about his affair with Rock.

Sara Davidson, with Rock's blessing, drafted a memoir with him when he was dying of AIDS. She described Jack as "tall, lean and fit, with blond wavy hair, blue eyes, and a beautifully sculpted, heart-shaped face." This fits the description of the young man Merv met around Henry Willson's pool on that long ago day.

On the day of the party, Jack appeared so distraught that Merv asked him if anything was wrong. "Rock's gonna be a big star," Jack said. "Henry Willson and everybody else in Hollywood knows that."

"Yes, isn't it wonderful?" Merv responded. "I should be jealous."

"It may be wonderful for Rock," Jack said, "but not for me. Willson told me today that when Rock becomes a star, we can't live together any longer.

He's worried that *Confidential* will expose our relationship. That could ruin Rock's career before it gets off the ground. He loves me and I love him. He once told me he'd give up a fucking career in Hollywood to run off with me. But I don't think he meant it. It looks like I'm going to get my walking papers."

"That's the price of stardom," Merv said.

That response was just a little too glib and flippant for Jack, who turned and walked away. Merv never saw him again.

Jack's situation—he was eventually kicked out of Rock's house and cut off from any money—touched Merv in a deep, disturbing way. When he got to know Henry Willson better, Merv asked the agent if the Jack/Rock affair might have implications for his own life.

"Your safest bet is never to fall in love and never take in a live-in lover like Rock did," Henry advised. "It's too dangerous. If you want to become a movie star, get married to an understanding woman, the kind of gal who will let you slip around and get dick on the side, since obviously that's something she can't supply for you. Of course, you've got to provide for her financially so she'll keep her damn mouth shut. Hell, I was about ready to marry Margaret Truman until her father, that asshole of a Missouri mule, put a stop to it. He was on to me. Perhaps that nelly faggot, J. Edgar Hoover, gave him the low-down."

"The president's daughter," Merv said. "I'm impressed. You aim high. As for me, if I get married, it'll be to some gal the world has never heard of. I like to keep it quiet. I don't like a spotlight shining where it doesn't belong, I mean, one that's lighting up my private life."

"Keep it that way and you'll go far," Henry said.

In his impish way, Merv asked, "Tell me, have you managed to get that handsome hunk, Robert Wagner, to fuck you yet? I think he's the cat's pajamas."

"That, my dear boy, is for you to find out," Henry said. "In time, I'll tell you all the dirt as well as all the dirt on everybody else as well."

He was true to his word, and in his gossipy way kept Merv informed with a blow-by-blow description of his involvements, such as they were, with Troy Donahue, Rory Calhoun, Tab Hunter, Alain Delon, John Saxon, Mike Connors, Clint Walker, and an array of other handsome young men who never made it in show biz but ended up pumping gas and frying burgers.

"I decided to start pimping for Merv the first day I met him," Henry later told Rock, who passed the word along the grapevine. "I realized that he and I are attracted to the same hunky men. Both of us don't go for effeminate men. We want all-American hero types." Before the end of the 1950s, Henry was telling his boys that Merv's ultimate fantasy types were Tab Hunter and Troy

Donohue.

At a dinner party attended by Merv, a drunken Henry told his fellow guests, "Merv here doesn't go for the Continental types. A lot of guys thought Alain Delon was sexy and handsome when he first came to Hollywood." He held up a breadstick and broke it in half, holding it up in the air where it met with derisive laughter. "Delon just didn't have what it takes to make it in this town."

Weeks after Rock had starred with Jane Wyman in *Magnificent Obsession*, he drove over to Merv's house without previously announcing himself. Fortunately, Merv was home alone. It was very late, perhaps after one o'clock in the morning, but Merv was up listening to recordings. He liked to keep abreast of what the competition was singing.

Rock looked very distraught, and his eyes were bloodshot, perhaps from both crying and drink. Merv remembered that he and Rock sat up talking until dawn's light.

In the course of a long, drunken early morning, Rock confessed that Jane, the ex-Mrs. Ronald Reagan, had fallen in love with him. "I've got to turn her down," Rock said. "In bed she does nothing for me. I have a hard time getting it up. But her assurance that I'm so much bigger than Ronnie sort of turns me on."

"She's a big star," Merv said. "Let her down gently. And for God's sake, don't alienate her."

"Henry's convinced that after this movie, I'm gonna be the biggest male star in movies," Rock said. "After all, Gary Cooper and John Wayne are getting a little long in the tooth. But there's a price to pay. I've already had to kick Jack out. Henry forced the issue. I even pretended I hated Jack, and I love him. I called him a dirty, rotten faggot, all those names, anything to turn him against me. As a star, my life will never be the same again, and I know that. I'll be under intense scrutiny day and night."

"You could always marry me," Merv said, only half joking. "No one would ever believe that a guy with my ugly Irish puss could possibly be Rock Hudson's lover."

Even though still teary, Rock laughed at Merv's self-deprecating humor. "For me to marry you, you'd have to dye your hair blond. I'm partial to blonds, you know, and we're not talking Marilyn Monroe here." He smiled to soften the blow of what he was about to say. "And you'd have to add at least one or two more inches to your dick."

"Even if I did, it would never match that monster of yours," Merv shot back.

***

In 1953, it was mandated by Warners that Merv escort actress Dolores Dorn (sometimes known as Dolores Dorn-Heft) to the premiere of *The Charge at Feather River*, even though he was embarrassed by his limited involvement in the movie. Nevertheless, he and the glamorously dressed Dolores arrived in a stretch limo in front of Grauman's Chinese Theater on the night of the premiere.

They walked the long red carpet to the entrance where an announcer with a microphone awaited them. Hundreds of fans yelled for their autographs, although Merv was convinced that not one of them behind the ropes knew who Dolores was or who he was. After they each spoke briefly into the microphone to the cheering crowd, they disappeared into the lobby of the theater. Then, Merv shook Dolores' hand before she faded through a side door to meet her real date of the evening. Merv scribbled a note to the star of the film, Guy Madison, agreeing to meet him at midnight after the premiere.

In an autobiography, Merv wrote, "That was the first and last I heard of Dolores Dorn-Heft." Like many of the statements Merv either said or wrote about his own life, that wasn't quite true. In 1956, Dolores made front page news when she married aging actor Franchot Tone, Joan Crawford's discarded husband of the 1930s. On September 14, 1951 Tone had barely survived a beating from a jealous, heavily muscled actor, Tom Neal. Rushed to the hospital, Tone fought for his life. Neal had serious objections to that actor's plan to marry the drug-addicted actress/hooker Barbara Payton, who had also promised to marry Neal.

Merv had other, more private reasons to recall Dolores. He had had a brief affair with her future husband, the actor Ben Piazza. In 1969, Ben wrote and co-starred in a play he had created for his then-wife, *Khaki Blue*.

Merv had fallen for the Arkansas-born actor when Henry Willson had introduced the two of them around 1959 when Ben was appearing in *The Hanging Tree* opposite Gary Cooper. At the time Ben was being hailed in the press as "the new Marlon Brando."

As Merv later told Johnny Riley, "Our affair consisted entirely of three long weekends in Malibu, where I got very well acquainted with Ben's Italian sausage." Merv later admitted that he had a "one-night stand for old-time's sake" with Ben in New York in 1962, when he went to see him on Broadway. An accomplished actor, Ben had replaced the original cast member, George Grizzard, in the role of Nick in Edward Albee's *Who's Afraid of Virginia Woolf?* In 1973, perhaps for sentimental reasons, Merv ordered his staff to arrange for a private screening of *The Candy Snatchers*, a film in which Ben and Dolores appeared together as Avery and Katherine.

Merv encountered Ben two or three times after their brief affair. Privately, to friends, he expressed regret that the actor never lived up to his promise and certainly never became the next Marlon Brando. He was sad to learn of Ben's death on September 7, 1991, in Sherman Oaks, California, of AIDS-related cancer.

"God damn it, I'm gonna die too one day, but I swear it won't be from AIDS," Merv vowed to his close friend, Eva Gabor. This was not the first time he'd made such a declaration to her.

***

"My Hollywood career's going so great I don't even appear on the screen anymore," Merv sarcastically told anybody willing to listen. "I'm assigned to voiceovers." He was referring to such previous films as *Stop, You're Killing Me*," a comedy directed by Roy Del Ruth and starring such first-rate talent as Broderick Crawford and Claire Trevor. Merv was uncredited, his voice used as that of a radio announcer. The film was a funny farce about gangsters who'd gone straight.

"*Guys and Dolls* it ain't," Merv said, "but it is pure Damon Runyon all the way." Roy Del Ruth was old Hollywood, a former newspaperman who'd entered films in 1915 as a screenwriter and gagman for Mack Sennett. He'd also directed the worst sports biography of all time, *The Babe Ruth Story* (1948), but had fared better with Doris Day and Gordon MacRae in both *The West Point Story* (1950) and *On Moonlight Bay* (1951).

Audaciously, Merv told Roy that both of those pictures would have generated bigger profits if Roy had cast him in Gordon MacRae's roles. Roy seemed to like Merv and promised him he'd give him a "juicy part in my next picture."

In his next picture, Merv was also uncredited, cast as the voice of a football broadcaster in *Trouble Along the Way* (1953), a big-budget film starring John Wayne and Donna Reed. The director was the abrasive, much-dreaded, Hungarian-American Michael Curtiz, who'd achieved screen immortality thanks to his direction of the war-time tear-jerker *Casablanca* starring Humphrey Bogart and Ingrid Bergman.

Throughout the ups and downs of his long career, Merv was never afraid to meet and talk to the big names in movies and politics. The moment he met Michael Curtiz, he had the nerve to ask him for a bigger role.

"*Gree-fing*, this is a man's picture about football. A man's sport, Not girly-boy shit, not chorus boy shit from a big band crooner. I vant to hear you as the all-man voice of a football broadcaster. I vant you to sound like man on the air. With your stink of a talent, you're luck to get work. Who in hell do you think you are, keed? Bogie?"

"I just want to be in front of the camera sometimes, not just a voice-over," Merv protested.

"Tell you vhat, keed," Michael said. "I'll cast you in my next picture. A real he-man part, not she-male. I'll put you on a horse in a Western. Turn you into the next John Wayne. With one great big different. He's got small balls. I'll give you big balls in my picture. Make you big, bigger than Bogie. All the hot pussies will be scream out for Gree-fing dick."

"That's sure something to look forward to," Merv said. "I'll hold you to your promise. Say, I didn't know The Duke had a small dick."

"Yeah, not like Garee Coop," [Gary Cooper], Michael said. "When we did *Bright Leaf*, I pissed next to him. Big dick. Gals like men with big dick. Ingrid Bergman told me she goes to bed only with big dick. Bogie has big dick. Errol Flynn, son of a bitch, has big dick. But I married his first wife, Lili Damita. She said I was better fuck than Flynn."

Waiting for the next scene to be set up, Michael told Merv that he'd heard that he had fucked Joan Crawford. "I fuck her on *Mildred Pierce*. I fuck Bette Davis too. Those two are bitches. But they have the biggest dicks in Hollywood. Davis tells people I'm a god damn nothing no good sexless son of a bitch. I tell people she's a fuck lesbian who can't face truth about herself."

At one point before he was called to the set, the director said, "Get up! Let's go to toilet and make poodle together."

"Fuck a poodle?" Merv asked in astonishment. "I'm not into bestiality."

"Make poodle, you dumb stupid idiot," Michael said. "You don't speak English?"

"Oh, you mean make puddle?" Merv asked.

"C'mon get off your fat ass and come take piss with me. That way I'll see if your dick's big enough for my next movie."

Merv never told his friends what happened next or if he passed inspection. But he did relate a story about Michael's "conquest" on the set of *Trouble Along the Way*. The director had never been faithful to any of his wives, and he was known for having sexual involvements with female extras on the sets of his movies.

One such extra was a tall, strikingly beautiful "woman" who identified herself as Loretta Zotto. She was a dead ringer for Jane Russell with a bust to match. But there was something suspicious about her, and Merv noticed an Adam's apple that seemed inconsistent with the anatomy of a beautiful show-girl. He began to suspect that she was a drag queen. Every day at around noon, Michael disappeared with her into his studio office where they were together for at least an hour and a half.

One night Judy Garland and Peter Lawford called to invite Merv to a drag show in West Hollywood at a club called Tabu. Judy told Merv that, "I hear there's a drag queen there who does Judy Garland better than I do."

At the club, after sitting through three boring drag acts, the star of the show emerged singing "The Trolley Song" from *Meet Me in St. Louis* (1944). She was billed as "Stormy Weather," but Merv recognized her instantly as Loretta Zotto, Michael Curtiz's "girlfriend."

At the end of the show Judy graciously agreed that Stormy sang "Over the Rainbow" better than she did. Backstage, Peter got Stormy's telephone number and promised to call her for a date. "I'll find out what sex we're talking about here," Peter promised.

When Peter reported back to Merv that Stormy [i.e. Loretta] was, biologically speaking, a male, Merv kidded his director the next day. Instead of taking the teasing, Michael exploded. "*Gree-fing*, I know the different between dick and pussy. I fuck that gal every day. I should know."

"But do you go through the front door or the back door?" Merv provocatively asked.

"You sick pervert!" The director stormed off the set.

"God damn it," Merv later told Roddy McDowall. "I just blew my chance to get cast in Curtiz's next movie. Me and my big mouth!"

***

To Merv's surprise, he encountered James Dean on the set of *Trouble Along the Way*. Like Merv, James was also appearing in the film as an uncredited extra. Merv hadn't seen James since he had moved out of the Commodore Garden Apartments in the middle of the night.

James bonded with Merv like he was a long-lost buddy. He made no mention of Nick Adams, but said that he was planning to abandon Hollywood forever as soon as he finished his brief appearance in "this John Wayne piece of shit. How can you respect a town that would make that Nazi jerk a star?"

That same day, shortly after five o'clock, both actors headed for a drink at a bar near Warner Brothers. James quickly informed Merv of his new ambition. "I'm going to be a Broadway star. I've already appeared in *See the Jaguar*. I got rave reviews."

Merv had read in the trade papers that the play had closed after five performances. "I appeared on stage locked in a jaguar's cage," James said. "I bet Marlon Brando can't do that. I even got to sing, 'Green Briar, Blue Fire.' People raved about my singing." He smiled and winked at Merv. "Move on, baby—make room for the competition."

Over his second drink of the day, James confessed to Merv, "I've given up hustling. Before I hit it big on Broadway, I found an easier way to make money. Homosexuals in New York went crazy for me. They even sent me gifts

214

backstage." He paused. "An invitation for various things. I'm one pretty boy, or so the love notes said."

"So how are you turning that into money?" Merv asked.

"I posed for nudes in New York," James confessed. "Including one with a big erection. I sell these photos to my most ardent fans at twenty-five bucks a picture. It beats hustling. They get to look at what I've got and they pay for the privilege—and no one even touches me. Not bad, huh?"

"Sounds like a great way for an actor to make a living if these photos don't come back to haunt you after you've made it as a star."

"Like I give a damn about that," James said. "I've even set up some sessions with photographers here in Los Angeles. I've got a posing session around nine tonight. Wanna come with me?"

"I'd love to," Merv said. "There's more than a bit of the voyeur in me."

Just outside the photographer's apartment later that evening, James removed his denim shirt and blue jeans. He wore no underwear. He handed his apparel to Merv for safekeeping. "I like to arrive at the doorstep dressed for action." He chuckled at his own comment.

At the door, the shocked photographer hustled his visitors inside. "I've got two Eisenhower Republican old maids who live upstairs," the photographer said. "They might see you and have a heart attack. I don't want those old biddies to know what goes on down here."

That night, Merv assisted in James' photo shoot whenever and however he was called upon, fetching a glass of water or, in one case, holding a spotlight. But mostly he stared at the subject in fascination. As a nude model, James seemed to have no inhibitions at all. At one point he grabbed a black lace mantilla left over from a previous posing section and plucked a red rose from a vase, grasping on the stem with his teeth.

"That may be too girlish a pose for most of our clients," the photographer warned, but snapped the campy picture anyway. "But we'll do this one just for laughs."

At the end of the session, James put on his jeans and denim shirt but turned down the photographer's invitation for a three-way with Merv.

Back out in the open air, on the sidewalk with James, Merv asked, "What's next?"

"I want to go back to your place and fuck you," James said bluntly.

"A man after my own heart," Merv said. "Let's go!"

The pictures that James posed for that night—still in private hands—are a valued collector's item today.

***

215

On the Warners lot, Merv re-introduced himself to Donna Reed, John Wayne's co-star in *Trouble Along the Way*. He'd met her briefly in Hawaii when she was co-starring in *From Here to Eternity* with Monty Clift. They spoke only briefly, and she praised Monty as the "most sensitive actor on the screen today. But how long will it be before he destroys himself? Two years? Maybe three?" She raised an eyebrow. "Perhaps you can save him through your friendship."

"Only Monty can save himself," Merv replied.

"I don't think he will," she said, before turning to leave. At that point John Wayne walked up, kissing her on the cheek. She introduced The Duke to Merv before excusing herself to get ready for a scene.

John shook Merv's hand. "I heard you at the Grove one night. Nice voice. I like the old songs, the romantic ballads. Not this fucking rock 'n' shit coming out of Miss Elvis Presley. What a faggot!"

The Duke clearly intimidated Merv. He'd heard from Michael Curtiz that the actor had been grouchy and grumpy on the set that morning and was absolutely "merciless" with minor actors who blew their lines. Even though he was undergoing horrendous personal problems with the women in his life, he arrived camera-ready every morning, with all his lines memorized. He was taking his role seriously, playing a pool-shooting, divorced football coach at a financially strapped Catholic college.

The Duke invited Merv to his dressing room for a drink. Once there, Duke drank and talked, and Merv mainly listened. He was one of the most candid actors Merv had ever met. If he thought something, John didn't seem to censor his tongue before he spoke. "That Hungarian Jew, Curtiz, tells me you hang out with Rock Hudson," John said. "Better keep your pants zipped up around that cocksucker. God damn it, what I could have done with a face like Hudson's. Too bad it's wasted on a queer."

Merv and John chatted for about an hour before John was called to the set. "C'mon, walk with me." He handed Merv his flask. "Hang out this afternoon. When I'm not on camera, I'll slip over to join you, and I'll take a drink from my flask. Guard it with your life."

On the set, Merv encountered Curtiz, who seemed to inspect and assess the odd combination of tall John with short Merv. "Hey, kid," he said to Merv, "Wayne here walks like a fairy and gets away with it. You can't! If you're going to be in my next picture, you're going to have to learn to walk like a man."

John seemed to take a liking to Merv, who had no other work, as his meager part in the picture was finished. He spent the rest of the week hanging around the set as "John Wayne's flaskboy," as Merv later put it.

John was being smeared in the headlines by Esperanza Baur, his second wife. He'd met her in 1941 when she was working as a prostitute in Mexico and had married her in 1946. But by 1953, she was blackmailing The Duke to get "the largest alimony settlement in history," as she vowed.

Duke called her Chata. "She turned into a stark raving bitch," he told Merv. "She's trying to destroy me. She claims I beat the shit out of her. Maybe I've slapped her around once or twice, but the puta once tried to kill me." The Duke/Chata divorce resembled a soap opera, as she spread sensational and scandalous stories, with the expressed intention of destroying both his reputation and his career.

Merv lent a very sympathetic ear, especially when Duke confessed that Chata had hired private detectives to follow him everywhere. To complicate his life, Duke had met a Peruvian starlet, Pilar Palette Weldy, while scouting for a film location. He seemed quite taken with her, but was trying desperately to keep her hidden from Chata's detectives. There was more. Duke was also still involved with Gail Russell, with whom he'd launched an affair in 1947 when they'd made *Angel and the Badman*.

Merv turned red. Unknown to Duke, Merv was seducing Gail's husband, Guy Madison, although his marriage was also heading for the divorce courts.

On the last day of the shoot, Merv invited Duke to "use my spare bedroom if you want to slip away with one of your lady friends. Chata will never find you there."

Duke looked at him for a moment, as if mulling over the idea. "I think I'll take you up on that, kid."

After the movie was wrapped, days went by before Merv heard from Duke again. Every day Merv read a story in the papers about the steamy divorce. At one point Chata told the press that "John Wayne is an awful man—a drunk, violent, unfaithful." Merv worried that these allegations would harm Duke's career, but his fans remained faithful, turning against Chata.

Months after her contested divorce from John, Chata was found dead in a hotel room in Mexico, with dozens of empty liquor bottles scattered about. When she was sober enough, she had been writing a memoir. She told a Mexican reporter that her memoir would forever destroy John Wayne. "No one will go see one of the bastard's movies ever again. I'm also writing about how lousy the great John Wayne is in bed. And he calls himself a man."

At the time of her death, her incomplete manuscript, although viewed prior to her death by the Mexican reporter, had been stolen from her hotel bedroom.

Finally, a call came in one Saturday night from The Duke. "Kid, I've decided to take you up on that offer. Gail and I need to slip over for the night."

"I'm going out on a date, but I'll leave the key under the doormat," Merv said. "Stay as long as you want."

"I'll owe you one, kid," John said.

Merv turned down the offer to meet Gail Russell (a.k.a. Mrs. Guy Madison). Ironically, Merv's date that night was with her estranged husband, who at that point was living apart from his wife.

***

The next morning, while Merv was preparing his breakfast, he heard a loud noise coming from his guest bedroom, into which John Wayne had taken Gail Russell the night before. When Merv had returned home around three o'clock that morning after a hot night with Gail's husband, Guy Madison, he didn't bother to check the guest room. Duke's car was not in his driveway, and Merv just assumed that the lovers had already departed.

While still seated at his breakfast table, Merv looked up as the door to his guest bedroom was thrown open. Over his scrambled eggs, he encountered a bedraggled Gail Russell, staggering out of the room in a bathrobe that was split open to reveal all her goodies. He turned from the sight of her. The press often compared Gail's beauty to that of the screen goddess, Hedy Lamarr, but on this particular hung-over morning, Gail looked more like Harpo Marx after a bad night.

Merv had been following Gail's career in the newspapers, reading detailed and career-destroying accounts of her drinking problem. She'd been convicted of operating a motor vehicle while intoxicated, which led to Paramount dropping her after she'd filmed *Air Cadet* in 1951. She'd been offered no more movie roles after that. To make matters worse for her, she was in the midst of divorcing Guy, who at the time was her sole means of support.

All Merv could do was offer black coffee and sympathy. He had no intention of telling her that only a few hours before, he'd been sucking on her husband's cock.

"I'm Mrs. Moseley," she said, sitting down and tightening her robe to conceal her breasts. "As if you didn't know." He was aware that Moseley was Guy's legal name.

Angel and the Bad Man (1947):
John Wayne with **Gail Russell**

218

Behind her currently shattered face with its hung-over droop, he detected an incredible doe-eyed beauty. In spite of her failed life and out-of-control drinking habits, she still projected an image of innocence and vulnerability that he'd seen in such pictures as *Night Has a Thousand Eyes* (1948) with Edward G. Robinson and *The Uninvited* (1944) with Ray Milland.

Over coffee, she told Merv, "I ran into Jane Russell the other day. I knew the bitch when we attended Van Nuys High School together. I told the big tit cow that there was room for only one Russell in this town, and she'd have to change her name. Fans still come up to me and say, 'Jane, will you sign my autograph book?'"

Merv got up and squeezed Gail some fresh orange juice, inviting her into his living room. Her fragile appearance mirrored an even more fragile psyche. Yet he was blunt with her. "You've got to stop drinking and get your career back on track. You could be a bigger movie star than ever if you straighten yourself out."

"Thanks for the advice, but no thanks," she said. "I know how at ease you are with an audience. Not me, boy. I'm self-conscious because I know I have no real talent. I'm afraid. I started drinking on the set because I couldn't bear to face a camera. My insides feel like a fist is gripping my guts every time I see a lens. My face breaks into a sweat, and my hands grow clammy. Sometimes when I open my mouth to say my lines, my throat constricts. Nothing comes out. It's always been that way. Back in Chicago when my parents would invite company to our house, I'd run and hide under the piano."

"But you seem self-assured on the screen," he said.

"It's all an act," she said.

"That's why it's called acting."

"Don't get smart-ass with me!" she said, her face turning harsh. Up until then she'd been open and vulnerable with him, but perhaps his remarks had been too flippant. She suddenly looked threatening and hostile.

She deliberately dropped the glass of orange juice onto the tile floor, shattering it before storming off to the guest bedroom. In about half an hour, she emerged with a small night bag colored a shocking pink and chartreuse. She was wearing a white summer dress with red polka dots and had repaired her face as best she could.

With that angry look still on her face, she confronted him in his living room. "Call me a taxi," she commanded. "I'm going home."

"I'll drive you," he volunteered. "I have no work today."

"Welcome to the club," she said. "I have no work any day. That fucking whore The Duke married is dragging me into her nasty divorce trial against him. By using me, she's hoping to get more money out of him. And more God-awful headlines for me. Just what I need. As if things weren't bad enough for

219

me already."

"I'm sorry," he stammered, wanting her to leave as she was making him uncomfortable."

"Not as sorry as you're going to be, big boy," she threatened him. "Guess what I found hanging in the closet of your guest bedroom? Clothes belonging to my husband. I should know them when I see them. I bought them for him." Her eyes glanced nervously around his living room, as if seeing it for the first time. "So this is where the queer bastard has been spending his evenings now that Rory Calhoun's out of town fucking Marilyn Monroe."

Merv was acutely embarrassed that Gail had discovered details of his affair with Guy.

"Talk about getting messed up in a divorce," she said. "Like Chata with The Duke, I'm gonna take Guy for every penny he's making on that hit TV series. His fans wouldn't want to know that their favorite action hero takes it up the ass." She stood at his front door, looking back at him. "Oh, by the way, if Guy doesn't cooperate and meet my demands, I'm gonna destroy his career. Not only that. My revelations will destroy your career too—not that you have much of one."

As she slammed the door in his face, he experienced panic. She seemed like a very determined and very wronged wife. His first thought was that he hadn't called her a taxi, but then he figured she'd see the pay phone booth on the corner. He immediately went into his kitchen and called Guy at the studio to tell him about his confrontation with his wife.

"Oh, shit!" Guy said. "I've got to hang up and call my lawyer."

Fortunately for Guy, his attorney hired a private detective who during the two months leading up to the divorce proceedings managed to compile an extensive dossier on Gail's secret lesbian life.

"It was a Mexican stand-off," Guy later told Merv. "She had me, and I had her. If she wants to work another day in this town—and she does—she doesn't want to be branded a dyke. I reminded her what that did to Lizabeth Scott's career."

In time, Merv and Guy drifted off to other boyfriends, and much to Merv's relief, Gail never aired her explosive charges in a divorce court. The last years of Gail's life were spent in and out of sanatoriums.

Despite his ongoing affair with Gail, The Duke would deny until the end of his days that there had ever been anything going on sexually between him and the raven-haired beauty. Merv, however, knew differently.

In spite of her threats against him, Merv was still saddened to read about Gail's death on August 27, 1961. In her small one-room apartment in Brentwood, Los Angeles, her partially decomposed body wasn't discovered until a week after her death. She'd died from a heart attack attributed to alcoholism. In her apartment, police found thirty-six empty vodka bottles, which ironically represented every year of her young life.

***

When Merv drove up behind a yellow convertible parked in his driveway, he suspected at first that Rock Hudson had come for an unannounced visit. Then he spotted his old friends Paul Schone and Bill Robbins sitting on his stoop. They'd driven down from San Francisco with an enormous amount of luggage, which included three large stage trunks, each resembling something from the wardrobe department of a Hollywood studio.

Bill and Paul rushed to embrace Merv and kiss him as part of a long-delayed reunion. Suddenly, from out of the bushes jumped Johnny Riley, who'd driven his friends south to Los Angeles in that yellow convertible.

After the many setbacks of his on again, off again Hollywood career, Merv later recalled that "the reunion was one of the happiest days of my life. It was great being back with the old gang."

Those trunks, it turned out, belonged to Bill, and they were filled with stage gowns. In between his few-and-far-between dancing jobs, he'd become a nightclub entertainer who regularly appeared in drag doing impersonations of movie queens who included Mae West. "Bill was always the lady of our group," Johnny said, mocking him but not in a mean-spirited way.

All three men complimented Merv on his new looks, as he was suntanned and fit, weighing less than he ever had in his adult life. Whereas Merv was being appraised, he was also doing a quick evaluation of his friends. If anything, Bill seemed more effeminate than ever, while Paul and Johnny were movie star handsome, seemingly born for show business careers. He jealously suspected that either of them would project a more intense and more masculine screen presence than he did.

As the sun set that afternoon, Merv invited his rediscovered friends to the back yard for barbecue. All three of them emerged after showering wearing swimming trunks. Johnny and Paul were bare-chested, showing off their six-packs, but Bill demurely covered his frail chest with a white T-shirt. "My God, fellows, you guys would put Rock himself to shame." Merv obviously didn't include Bill in that appraisal. "Until you get jobs, I think I'll hire all of you out as hustlers."

Merv meant that as a joke but no one laughed. He scanned each serious face. For a moment, there was nothing but silence. "That's how I make my spending money," Johnny confessed. "That's how I bought that new convertible. It should come as no surprise to you, 'cause you know I was doing that back in San Francisco when I was just a kid."

221

Although Merv did indeed remember that, he was still surprised, since in all their long-distance calls, Johnny had never revealed that he was still hustling. "Of course, if I meet a guy who's really cute, I give him a freebie," Johnny said.

"What about you guys?" Merv asked, turning to Bill and Paul.

"I've turned a trick or two," Bill said. "Believe it or not, there are a lot of men out there—most of them married—who get off fucking a drag queen."

"Not me!" Paul said. He seemed adamant. "I can only get it up for good-looking guys with big dicks. I'm a size queen. I couldn't make it with some repulsive old queen."

"And you, Merv?" Johnny asked. "Confession time. How many casting couches have you worn out?"

"None, absolutely none," Merv said. "Maybe that's why my career has stalled. On Monday I'll take you to the studio and show you a film I was hired for, and then you'll see why I'm not setting Hollywood on fire."

By ten o'clock that night, all three of Merv's guests were sleepy and wanted to turn in early. Bill and Paul agreed to share the guest room, and Johnny said he'd sleep in Merv's bed "for old time's sake." Back in his living room, Merv called Roddy McDowall and asked if he could bring his friends over the following afternoon for one of his Sunday soirées. "All of them are great guys: Bill Robbins, Johnny Riley, and Paul Schone."

Roddy readily extended an invitation to Merv's three friends, saying "the more the merrier. I just hope they're handsome."

"Johnny Riley looks like a more masculine version of Tab Hunter," Merv said. "Eight and a half inches—and very, very thick. I've had him. Paul Schone looks like a young Gregory Peck. I don't know his measurements. I've never fucked with him."

"And your other friend, Bill Robbins?" Roddy asked.

"Oh, yes," Merv said. "Do you mind if he dresses up for the occasion?"

"I get it!" Roddy said. "I hope he comes as Bette Davis and does all the dialogue, especially that 'what a dump line,' from *Beyond the Forest*. See you tomorrow," he said. Before hanging up, he blew a "kiss-kiss" into the phone.

Chapter Six

Merv became almost jealous of how his friends in Los Angeles embraced Bill Robbins, Paul Schone, and Johnny Riley, taking these young San Franciscans directly to their bosoms. Bill was a hit at Roddy's Sunday afternoon *soirée*, thanks in part to his drag imitation of Marlene Dietrich in her *Destry Rides Again* costume. And throughout the course of the party, Johnny seemed to have three or four of the most attractive actors in a cluster around him. But despite the popularity of Merv's other guests, it was Paul that Roddy invited to sleep over that evening after the party ended.

When Merv's household woke up the following morning, Merv invited Johnny, Bill, and Paul to the Warner lot where he treated them to a showing of his uncredited appearance in *The Beast from 20,000 Fathoms* (1953). Based on a story by Ray Bradbury, the film's beast was a hibernating dinosaur. Awakened by an atomic test north of the Arctic Circle, it terrorizes New York City. In later life, Merv remembered his one line in the film, wherein he was cast as a radio announcer: "Well, folks, here's another of those silly reports about sea serpents."

Merv confessed to his friends that he'd fallen for the star of the picture, Paul Hubschmid, who had been defined by some press agents as "the most beautiful man in post-war German cinema," and who was billed in the United States as Paul Christian. The Swiss-born star had been a leading man in a number of Austrian stage and film productions.

"I made several plays for him," Merv confessed to his friends. "But I don't think he ever knew I even existed."

The Beast from 20,000 Fathoms—made for just $250,000—was a financial success, grossing five million dollars. It did nothing, however, to advance the American career of Paul Christian, much less Merv. The picture did go down in film history, however, as the first movie to deal with a prehistoric monster unearthed by an atomic explosion. As such, it spawned many other equally cheap imitations.

Just when Merv thought his film career had come to a grinding and permanent halt, Rosemary Clooney arrived at his doorstep with big news. She'd been cast in the film *Red Garters*, to be directed by George Marshall, and she'd be appearing opposite veteran actor Jack Carson, who'd be playing the male lead. "The third lead, the character of Reb Randall, is ideal for you Merv, and George has agreed to test you for the part," Rosemary said. "You ride into town—a singing cowboy like Roy Rogers—chasing the villain who murdered your brother."

"Hell's bells," Merv said, "I have to ride a horse? When Guy Mitchell and I used to go riding, I was always falling off."

"Oh, you just did that so he'd pick you up in his manly arms," she said. "You'll get to sing, baby, so don't worry about it. It's more of a musical than it is a Western. George thinks it'll photograph like a Broadway musical filmed in a theater. We'll do a number together."

"Will I get to wear a red garter?" Merv jokingly asked.

"No, but Edith Head is designing one just for me, sweetie," she said.

Each of Merv's friends predicted that *Red Garters* might do for him what *So This Is Love* with Kathryn Grayson didn't do—and that was to make him a star.

The director of *Red Garters*, George Marshall, gave Merv a screen test and concluded that he'd be ideal as the third lead. "All my disappointments have been worth the wait," he said in a phone call to Rosemary that night. He later told his friends, "I'm on my way up. You guys brought me luck. Stick around forever."

There was one nagging fear he had, although at the time he didn't share it with anyone. *Red Garters* was to be shot on the Paramount lot, where Barney Balaban still yielded great power. The studio honcho would have to approve Merv's contract, and he knew that Barney absolutely loathed him because of memories associated with his attempt to elope with his daughter, Judy.

Bullets Durgom, Merv's agent, was a good friend of Barney's and was convinced that he could talk the executive into signing Merv. "After all, Judy is happily married now. I bet he's forgotten all about it."

On the following afternoon, Bullets phoned Merv. "Barney's memory is long," he said. "His exact words were, 'Merv Griffin will never set foot on the Paramount lot as long as I'm around.'"

"Oh, shit!" Merv said, "my losing streak goes on and on. That really pisses me off. Who's getting the damn part. Gordon MacRae no doubt?"

"That singer, Guy Mitchell," Bullets said.

"I met him years ago and should have figured that he and I might be competing for the same role one day," Merv said. Later that night he called Rosemary. "How are you and Jose doing tonight?"

"Just sitting here all by my lonesome," she said. "Mr. Ferrer is out tonight fucking June Allyson. How you doing?"

"Crying in my beer," he said. "Thanks for all you did for me, but losing that part to Guy hurts like hell. Why did they have to cast my former lover in my part? That's salt on my wound."

"It's called show business and get used to it," she said. "I did what I could for you. I'm sure you'll get another part—an even bigger one—and soon."

"What are the Las Vegas odds on that?" he asked. "I'm not giving up, but I'm getting the hell out of this town as soon as I can. New York here I come."

"There's another side to show business," she said. "Just when you think you'll never work again, the phone rings with the break of your life. Just ask your buddy, Judy Garland."

Rosemary was a prophet. The very next afternoon, Bullets called him. Knowing how disappointed he was at losing the role in *Red Garters*, he'd come up with another part for him, that of the ensign, Willie Keith, in *The Caine Mutiny*, which Stanley Kramer was going to direct at Columbia.

"I'll take it!" Merv shouted into the phone.

"There's just one thing," Bullets said. "How shapely are your legs?"

"They're not like Betty Grable's," he said, "but I can walk on them."

"In one scene you've got to strip to your underwear, and there's a close-up of your legs."

"I can do that," Merv said, "providing the close-up is of my legs and nothing else."

Bullets promised to send the script over in three days. That night Merv boasted about his upcoming involvement in the film to his houseguests. As a diversion that evening, each of them piled into Johnny's yellow convertible and drove to a dingy little club in West Hollywood where Rosemary had secured a gig for Bill. That evening Merv was vastly entertained watching Bill impersonate Judy Garland, Peggy Lee, and Carol Channing, with only fifteen minutes to transform himself between the various impersonations.

A few afternoons later, after returning from a privately negotiated tryst with Henry Willson, Paul showed up at Merv's apartment looking bedraggled. "I did it!" he shouted at Merv and his friends. "I survived a night with that lecherous beast without throwing up. He started by slobbering in my ears and ending up sucking my toes. He must have wasted a gallon of spit on me. I have to get rid of all that slime." On the way to the bathroom, he called back to Merv, "If anyone asks, my new name is Lance Hart. Henry Willson re-named me. He's going to make me the next Rock Hudson."

When the script of *The Caine Mutiny* arrived, Merv tore the package open and feverishly read it before getting up off the sofa. He wasn't sure which role Jose Ferrer was going to play but the part of the ensign was a small one. Yet he felt it could be a career-maker. Hours later, when he was playing tennis with Howard Hughes, he told him of his lucky break, hoping Howard might use his influence to guarantee him the part.

Howard seemed familiar with the script and urged Merv to go for it. "You can't be doing voiceovers all your life," Howard warned him. That made Merv wonder why Howard hadn't gotten him cast into something before now. After all, he owned a studio.

After a game of tennis, a sweaty Howard rather nonchalantly asked Merv, "Do you have a copy of the script?"

"Right by my bedside," Merv said. "It's pretty dog-eared by now."

"There's a great kid in town I want you to meet," Howard said. "Robert Francis. I'm teaching him to fly. He's probably the best-looking piece of meat to hit Hollywood since Jack Buetel." He was referring to Jane Russell's co-star in *The Outlaw*. "Mind if I give him your number and have him give you a call?"

"Are you setting me up, Howard?" Merv asked.

"In this case, let nature take its course."

Merv returned home to hear his phone virtually ringing off the wall. Picking up the receiver, he heard, "Merv Griffin, this is Robert Francis." The voice sounded seductive. "I've been dying to meet you."

"Oh, yeah," Merv said, a bit cautious. "Howard mentioned that you might call, but I didn't expect it so soon."

"I couldn't wait," Robert said. "I want to see you. I'm sitting out here on my sundeck putting oil on the biggest hard-on of my career."

"That sounds exciting," Merv said. "I'm busy this afternoon but call me the next time you get out that oil."

"How about tonight?" Robert asked. "Have you got a date?"

"Not exactly a date," Merv said. "I'm joining friends for a drink."

"Great!" Robert said. "Then I'll be your date. If I show up at eight, is that okay? I know where you live. I drove by your house three times today."

"Yeah, I guess it'll be okay," Merv said. "I'll be ready and waiting." As he hung up, he had an ominous feeling. If Robert Francis was as good-looking as Howard had promised, no gay man would turn him down. On the other hand, he seemed a little too aggressive for Merv's tastes. But he figured that if he didn't click with Robert, perhaps Johnny, Paul, or Bill might.

After notifying his friends that his date would be joining them for the evening, Merv found himself taking extra care to make himself as attractive as possible. Almost exactly

Robert Francis

226

at eight o'clock, the doorbell rang. Nervously, Merv opened the door.

In a pair of white slacks and a white shirt that was unbuttoned to reveal his chest was a stunning looking man. "Hi, I'm Robert Francis. You must be Merv Griffin. Or, am I dreaming?"

As Merv later described it to Johnny, "There, right before my eyes, was the man I'd been waiting for all my life."

***

Clean-cut and All-American looking, Robert Francis had a swimmer's build and a fashionable 50s brushcut. Before he'd arrived at the Griffin household, Merv had already called Henry Willson for the lowdown on this rising star.

It was Henry who'd introduced Robert to Howard Hughes at one of his pool parties. "Robert's going to be one of the biggest stars in Hollywood," Henry predicted. "After all, Humphrey Bogart, Tyrone Power, Errol Flynn, and especially Bogie remind a lot of gay men of their daddies. I've got to recruit hot new guys to replace these old farts. Robert represents the brash new face of the 50s. The gals will go wild for him, not to mention some of us guys. I still haven't bedded him, but Howard raves about his performances after dark."

Up close and personal in Merv's living room, Robert was soft spoken, not like the aggressive personality Merv had heard over the phone. A native Californian from Glendale, he was gorgeous but wooden in his movements, a trait Merv considered ideal for military roles. Robert's good looks and warm, engaging nature won over Merv's friends as well as Merv himself. Once again Merv and his boys, this time accompanied by Robert, piled into Johnny's yellow convertible to see Bill's second and final drag appearance at that West Hollywood dive.

As an added bonus that evening, the club was also conducting an amateur all-male striptease. Merv was surprised when Robert volunteered as one of the contestants. The young actor seemed to have two sides to him—one of them rather reserved, the other with a streak of aggressive exhibitionism. Onstage, in front of the all-male audience, Robert began one of the most erotic and provocative stripteases that Merv had ever seen, not that he'd seen that many.

Under the glare of a spotlight, against a background of catcalls and screams of approval, Robert's personality seemed to radically change. He slowly removed his coat, his tie, his shoes, and his pants, revealing a tight-fitting pair of underwear with a promising bulge, beating the other men competing that night and walking off with first prize.

After Merv and Robert retreated to the privacy of Merv's bedroom later that evening, Merv learned just how promising that bulge really was. As he'd later confide to Paul, "Until I met Robert, men were mere boyfriends. Robert Francis, however, is husband material."

"Merv, you darling!" Bill said. "You have an endearing ability to fall in love with a guy after less than five seconds. It takes me at least an hour."

When Merv woke up the following day, he sleepily felt for Robert in bed, finding him missing. He eventually located Robert beside his pool reading the film script for *The Caine Mutiny*. "I hope you don't mind," Robert said, jumping up to give Merv a kiss. "I woke up early and wanted something to read."

"Feel free," Merv said. "My agent's getting me the role of Willie Keith."

"I've read that part," Robert said. "I bet you'll be terrific in it."

Merv spent most of that day in bed with Robert. As he later confessed to Bill, "Robert and I made love again and then made love again and then again. For me, it was a world record."

"Can I be a bridesmaid at the wedding?" Bill asked.

"What else?"

After a second night of passion, Merv woke up on Monday morning, reaching once again for Robert, but finding him gone, as before. Since he figured his new boyfriend was an early riser, he was not unduly alarmed. He took a leisurely shower and tried to spruce up his face, as he looked bedraggled after the weekend workouts. He put on coffee and, with two steaming cups on a bar tray, he headed for the pool where he expected to encounter "the new love of my life." Robert was nowhere to be seen.

A search of the house revealed no one—not even a note. Even a peek into the guest room turned up only Bill and Paul still asleep. Outside, Robert's car was missing from the driveway.

Settling in for the morning, Merv decided to read the script of *The Caine Mutiny* one more time. He searched for it but couldn't find it, even though he distinctly remembered placing it on his nightstand after Robert had finished going over it. A slight apprehension came over him. Had Robert taken the script?

By early afternoon, even though Merv had heard from Johnny, who was off in Laguna shacked up with a new conquest, Robert still hadn't called.

The next day Merv called Bullets, his agent, to report on the missing script and to ask if he'd arranged his screen test for *The Caine Mutiny*.

"Sorry, but I just learned that the role's already been cast," Bullets said. "I was about to call you. Van Johnson's been signed for one of the leads, and he's promoting this handsome young actor for the role of the ensign. Van got him a screen test, and he's got the part."

"Let me guess," Merv said. "Could that young actor be Robert Francis?"

"So, you've already heard?" Bullets asked.

"Yeah, something like that," Merv said, suspecting that Howard Hughes—not Van Johnson—had been instrumental in Robert's getting cast.

When *The Caine Mutiny* was finally released, both Merv and Rock Hudson agreed that Robert was a striking screen presence within it. Rock, in fact, viewed him as future competition, and Merv conceded that Robert had photographed beautifully and sexily, especially in that scene when he'd pulled off his sailor pants to reveal his shapely masculine legs.

Merv never encountered Robert again, although he heard he was being pursued by Spencer Tracy on the set of *Tribute to a Bad Man*. Despite feeling betrayed by the young actor, Merv was still saddened to hear that on July 31, 1955, his weekend lover had been killed when the small aircraft he was piloting crashed after takeoff from the Burbank Airport. The plane had suddenly lost power and exploded upon violent impact in an abandoned parking lot.

Merv skipped the funeral which was conducted two days later at Forest Lawn Cemetery, but showed up with Bill Robbins the following day with flowers for Robert's grave. "No hard feelings, old pal," Merv said to the newly dug grave. "You were great in *The Caine Mutiny*. Better than I could have done it. You could have been big in this rotten town." Just prior to his death, Robert had been voted one of *Screen World*'s "Most Promising Personalities of 1954."

***

When Johnny finally returned from his adventures in Laguna, he had to drive immediately to San Francisco after packing his clothes. There was no time to see Merv. "For your hospitality, I've left you a house-warming present," he told Merv in a call to the studio. "You'll find it in your bed with a red ribbon tied around it. Your surprise is waiting but you've got to enter the room exactly at six o'clock. The gift is perishable and has to be eaten at once."

"Okay, I'll be there," Merv promised. "Exactly at six. Perishable? Exactly what is this gift? A banana split?"

"Something bigger and tastier," Johnny promised before ringing off.

Keeping his word, Merv arrived home right at six. Finding no one in his living room, he headed for his bedroom and threw open the door to discover his surprise.

There lying in the middle of his bed was a good-looking blond-haired young man with a Davidesque physique. Like Johnny had promised, a red ribbon had been tied around Merv's gift, which in this case was a humongous erection.

In a seductive voice, the stranger said, "Hi, I'm Hadley Morrell—your

229

new live-in lover."

***

In the dawn light of another day, Merv studied Hadley's body as he lay nude on top of the sheets. His frame was long, lean, and well muscled without being of the beefcake "Henry Willson" variety. There was a gracefulness and undeniable masculinity to Hadley, as evoked by his strong chest, long arms and legs, and trim waist. To Merv, he was like some blond Olympian. He exuded sexuality.

Merv attempted to get to know Hadley better, since he showed no apparent willingness to leave. It just seemed to be assumed that after such a great night in bed, Hadley would be moving in. Merv wasn't even sure at that point that he wanted a live-in lover, and there was a slight resentment that his life was being directed by Hadley and, from afar, by Johnny Riley, who had instigated this setup in the first place.

As Hadley ate, he looked over at Merv's poolhouse. "While you were cooking, I checked that place out," he said. "It would make a great little live-in suite. An extra bedroom if you have company. I'd like to renovate it for you. After all, I've got to do something around here while you're away making movies."

"So you're good with your hands?" Merv said, suddenly realizing the implication of what he'd just said. "And I'm not referring to last night."

Merv's attempt to learn the details of Hadley's past failed that morning as well as during the days and nights to come. Hadley was almost obstinately vague about what he'd done during the first twenty-nine years of his life. He said he was from Minnesota, but at one point, Merv suspected that despite the fact that he spoke perfect English, he might be foreign-born, perhaps from Holland. Merv wasn't even sure that Hadley was his real name. Merv was left with the distinct impression that Hadley was running away from something.

In spite of these misgivings, erotic sensuality won out. Hadley, based on an unexpressed but mutual consent, was definitely moving in on Merv. What was agreed upon for the immediate present, however, was that since there was no work for Merv at the studio that week, Merv would drive with Hadley down to Laguna Beach to retrieve his meager possessions. They were stashed in a room at the motel where he'd previously been shacked up with Johnny Riley. With the understanding that Merv and Hadley would spend a few days together at the beach, they headed south in Merv's car.

With Merv at the wheel, they drove along the coast under a sky that shone brightly over deep blue Pacific waters. It was just assumed that from now on Merv would be paying Hadley's bills. He brought fabulous sex to the relation-

230

ship, but not a bank account.

The motel where Johnny and Hadley had had their torrid affair was the most sordid Merv had ever stayed in, even during his cross-country tours with Freddy Martin's Band. "So this is my honeymoon cottage?" he said, surveying the wreckage Hadley and Johnny had left behind.

"Who needs a great room when you've got me?" Hadley asked.

Merv felt he'd launched himself on a new adventure into the unknown with a perfect stranger.

Later that evening in Laguna, Merv and Hadley walked along the beach until they discovered an off-the-beaten-track bistro. From a seat inside, and for the first time, Merv really studied Hadley's eyes, which were large and blue, clear and intelligent, set in an angular face with spectacular bones and perfect honey-colored skin. As Bill later said, "When Merv got back to Los Angeles, he gave us a blow-by-blow description of his time away with Hadley. He didn't spare us the slightest detail."

After dinner they wandered the streets, stopping off at a club, The Thundering Surf, with a bright neon sign that flashed letters in fire engine red, sunflower yellow, and Halloween orange. Finding the club too raucous, and the music too loud, they wandered next door to a club called The Fighting Cock, marked outside with a neon red rooster. It was more intimate, the music more subdued.

Midnight found Merv in bed once again with Hadley. Their honeymoon in this tacky motel lasted three nights. By the end of the third night, Hadley was proclaiming undying love for Merv. Yet Merv held back. He wasn't quite sure he wanted to commit to Hadley. It was all too soon, all too fast. He needed more time to think. Hadley was virtually proposing that they live like a married couple.

On the way back to Los Angeles, Hadley promised eternal fidelity. But Merv said nothing. Back in Los Angeles, he talked privately to Bill and Paul, while the sound of hammering could be heard outside. Hadley was certainly industrious, having launched the restoration of the poolhouse.

"It looks to me like he could become the love of your life." Paul said. "If you don't want him, pass him on to me."

"And you can always slip away in the night and get fucked by Guy Madison," Bill told him.

"So much for serious advice from two horny queens," Merv said jokingly. "I'd better go and fetch my new husband a glass of something..."

***

When Bullets called the next day, the agent didn't disguise his enthusiasm. "You've finally hit it big. Roy Del Ruth liked you when he directed *Stop, You're Killing Me*. You've been cast as the male lead in *Three Sailors and A Girl*. Your buddy, Jane Powell, is the lead. The third lead is the guy I think she's having an affair with, Gene Nelson. What a dancer. And Jack E. Leonard has been appropriately cast as 'Porky.' And it's a musical, so you'll shine, baby, shine."

"What role will I play?" Merv eagerly asked. "Hopefully someone not called 'Porky.' I don't want to be reminded of my past blubber."

"Choirboy Jones."

"Choirboy?" Merv asked astonished. "Porky and Choirboy?"

"Gene Nelson plays Twitch," Bullets said.

"Who in the fuck named these characters?" Merv asked. "What character does Jane play? Cooze?"

"Penny."

"Are you sure you've nailed down this role for me?" Merv asked. "I've been screwed so many times."

"It's in the bag!" Bullets promised. "Who loves you, baby?" He hung up.

This time, Merv not only got the script and liked the role, but received a personal call from the director himself. "You don't have to test for it, kid," Roy Del Ruth said. "I know what your voice sounds like, and your acting is not all that bad. We start shooting in a week. In the meantime, drop fifteen pounds."

"How do I do that?" Merv asked.

"One lettuce leaf a day," Roy said, "without dressing."

When the script arrived, Merv, emerging from the shower, didn't even finishing drying himself off. He ran to a chaise longue by the pool and began to read. He even ordered Hadley to stop hammering so he could concentrate.

To Merv's surprise, he found the script oddly familiar. *Three Sailors and a Girl* evoked the film, *Born to Dance (1936)*, which, significantly, had also been directed by Roy del Ruth. It had starred Eleanor Powell and it had included a scene wherein Jimmy Stewart actually sang a song by Cole Porter.

Merv had been told to report to the studio the following Monday, and he spent the weekend rehearsing his lines and the music.

At six o'clock on Monday morning, as Merv was awakening for his anticipated first day on the set, there was a persistent ringing of his telephone. Sleepily he answered it to find Bullets at the other end. "Real bad news. Sammy Cahn— he's the producer—just signed Gordon MacRae as Choirboy. It was a last-minute casting change.

But don't worry. Del Ruth is still going to cast you as one of the sailors in the movie. Of course, the part is uncredited, but I know you'll be just great in it."

"Fuck!" Merv shouted into the phone, suddenly angry at Bullets for leading him on. "Here we go again. Of course, I should be used to getting dumped at the last minute. Riding high yesterday, shot down in flames today."

In disgust, Merv wanted to walk off the picture, but he had a contract and he needed the money. He not only had rent to pay but another mouth to feed.

Merv showed up the following day and shared a dressing room with other extras in sailor uniforms. As his bad luck would have it, he encountered Gordon MacRae the moment he appeared on the set.

The singing star rather sarcastically looked him up and down as if he was a piece of meat. "I must say, Griffin, I fill out my sailor's uniform better than you do, especially in the crotch area. Haven't you given up trying to be a star in Hollywood? You'll never make it in this town, kid." With that prediction, the romantic lead of the picture turned and walked away.

That night and for days after, Merv raged to Hadley that Gordon's mother should have smothered him at birth.

Merv quickly realized that Roy Del Ruth was using him mainly for set decoration. "Whenever I appeared on screen, I was always pictured standing behind Jack E. Leonard, who made Jackie Gleason look like a starving fashion model. People called him 'Fat Jack.' All through *Three Sailors and a Girl* it looked like Jack had a wart on his head—namely me!"

In spite of his resentment at being shuttled to the side as an extra, Merv bonded with the rotund, bespectacled, bald-headed comic. Merv defined him as "the funniest man I know—he was always breaking me up." Jack's *forte* was the comic art of the insult, and his most enthusiastic and devastating imitator became Don Rickles.

In years to come—during May of 1973 to be exact—Merv sat in the audience listening to Jack's hilarious performance at the Rainbow Room at New York's Rockefeller Center. "Good evening, opponents," Jack quipped as an opening line. "I see Merv Griffin is here tonight. He brought a girl for a change."

After the show, Merv headed backstage for a reunion with Jack. But a stagehand denied him access. Immediately after his performance, the comic had collapsed en route to dressing room. He was rushed to the hospital, where he died the following day from complications following emergency heart surgery.

***

On his final day on the Hollywood set of *Three Sailors and a Girl*, Gordon

MacRae—Merv's most clearly defined enemy—approached him again. "You've got a great future, kid," he said, "but not in this business." He turned and walked away. It was not Merv's nature to hate people, but in the case of Gordon, he was willing to make an exception. He simply could not stand the man or his put-downs.

Right on the spot he vowed he was going to steal Gordon's next big musical from him. That afternoon he called Bullets. "Find out what picture Gordon is up for next," he commanded Bullets. "And, also, the name of the director. If it's the last thing I ever do in Hollywood, I'm going to show that egotistical shit that he's underestimated Merv Griffin. I'll be making millions when he's a broken-down old drunk singing at roadside motels in Indiana." In his utterance of that prediction, Merv turned out to be a prophet.

As Merv later told Bill and Paul, "There was only one good thing that came out of his appearance in *Three Sailors and a Girl*. "I had a reunion with Burt Lancaster. He made a gag appearance as himself at the end of the film. We not only met up with each other, but I got to sample that delectable uncut meat of his one more time in his dressing room. I've hardly begun my affair with Hadley, and I'm already two-timing him. And I'm sure it'll happen again."

"Baby, you and me are fated to be two-bit whores," Bill chimed in.

***

Once again, the temperamental, almost psychotic Michael Curtiz cast Merv in a movie, *The Boy from Oklahoma* (1954)—"another God damn oater," as Merv described it to Hadley. Dressed as a cowboy, Merv showed up on the set, where Curtiz shook his hand. "It's not another *Casablanca*," he said. "I'm directing this turkey for one reason and only one reason. To pay my pussy bill from all my cunts."

"Sounds like a good enough reason to me," Merv said, secretly appalled at the director's phraseologies.

The stars of the film included Will Rogers Jr., Nancy Olson, and Lon Chaney Jr., none of whom had been scheduled for an appearance on the set that day. Merv spent most of the morning talking with such old-time actors as Wallace Ford and Slim Pickens.

With his hoarse voice and pronounced Western twang, Slim would later immortalize himself by riding an atomic bomb in Stanley Kubrick's *Strangelove or How I Learned to Stop Worrying and Love the Bomb* (1964). "All Curtiz needs to do is turn the camera on me and let me be myself," the former rodeo clown, bronco rider, and bullfighter told Merv.

Wallace Ford seemed disgusted with his role in the movie. "I've been in practically every film ever made—and now this piece of shit."

When called to the set, Merv sauntered over to Curtiz in an imitation of John Wayne. "I told you to stop walking like fairy," Curtiz called out to him in front of the entire cast.

That night Merv told Hadley: "Curtiz is a fucking sadist." Only hours before, the director had ordered him to lead a posse of three dozen men on horseback down a dusty hill. "I'm terrible on a horse," Merv protested.

"Gree-fing, get on the fucking horse," Curtiz ordered.

It turned out that all the extras were experienced horsemen who'd appeared in many Western films. Wardrobe positioned a ten-gallon hat on Merv's head, and it was far too large, repeatedly falling down over his eyes. Brandishing a bullwhip, and evoking memories of Erich Von Stroheim, Curtiz called for action.

The cowboys roared off on horseback down the hill. Although Merv was supposed to be leading them, the other riders left him in the dust. His oversized hat blew off his head, disappearing like a tumbleweed in a tornado.

At the bottom of the hill and at the rear of the posse he was supposed to be leading, Merv fell off his horse.

"Cut! Cut! Cut!" Curtiz shouted through a megaphone, snapping his bullwhip with his free arm. "*Gree-fing*, you stink on rotten horse. Go back to the top of the hill. We shoot fucking scene again, you dumb shit!"

After ten more takes, Merv still hadn't gotten it right. "*Gree-fing,* you no Garee Coop. I can't shoot no more. You'll never get it right. I'll order fucking editor to make you look like Gene Autry on his horse Champion."

The next day was even worse. The script called for Merv to shoot a gun. After the first take, Curtiz screamed at him: "You fire gun like fucking cunt. You blink eyes before firing. I want you to act like Garee Coop in *High Noon*."

By the ninth take, Curtiz had grown so exasperated with Merv that he cracked his whip very close to his face, narrowly missing his eye. "You god damn faggot," he shouted at Merv. "You're off the picture. I use only he-men in my future pictures, not pussy boy like you."

"Thank you, Mr. Curtiz," Merv said, trying to maintain what little dignity he had left.

Still on friendly terms with Jack Warner, Merv called the studio chief and told him he'd been fired. "You stay in the fucking movie," Jack said. "You're on the payroll. I'll call that pussy-chasing Curtiz and tell him who does the hiring and firing."

Merv stayed on the picture until the last day of the shoot, reporting to work in cowboy garb every day. Curtiz, however, never looked his way again and never used him in another scene.

In lieu of actually working in front of the camera, celebrity-struck Merv used the time to chat with the stars of the film. He found it ironic that both Will Rogers Jr. and Lon Chaney Jr., had each been cast as co-stars in the same film. Both of those actors had to live in the long shadows of their more famous fathers, neither of them expecting, or achieving, the fame of Will Rogers Sr. and Lon Chaney Sr.

Like his father, Will Jr. was quick with a rope. Merv got to chat with him several times, learning that he'd served as a Democratic congressman from Southern California between 1943 and 1944, when he resigned to join the U.S. Army. Merv had read about his heroic efforts to try to save the Jews of Europe during World War II and of the opposition he'd faced, even from President Franklin D. Roosevelt himself.

In later years, Merv would invite Will, Jr. as a guest on his TV talk show, but the actor always opted not to go on. He was in poor health and had suffered several strokes. His hip replacements were a source of constant pain.

In 1993, at the age of 81, as a means of ending his suffering, he drove into the desert and shot himself in the head.

Circumstances were somewhat different with Merv's other on-set friend, Lon Chaney, Jr. Although he resembled his father physically, he admitted, "I hate trying to cash in on his name just as much as I hate people constantly comparing me to my dad. He was an original. I'll never be as good as he was. I fail to live up to his reputation every single day, and I handle my disappointment by drinking myself into a stupor every single night."

Since he had nothing else to do on the set, Merv encouraged Lon's conversation. "My father pushed me out onto the stage when I was just six months old. When I was a teenager, he never gave me money, even though he was a big movie star. I had to earn my own money—a meat cutter's apprentice, a metal worker, a plumber, and at one point, a farm worker in the Midwest shoveling cow shit."

Left: **Lon Chaney** as himself
and (center) as Werewolf. Right: **Will Rogers, Jr.**

Lon was a secret drinker. He would disappear into the men's toilet every now and then to down booze from a flask. "Chasing the fame of one's father is never a good thing," Lon told Merv. You're lucky to have been born to an unknown father."

"Well, at least you've done what no other actor has accomplished," Merv said. "You got to play all four of the major monsters—The Wolf Man, Frankenstein's Monster, the Mummy, and Dracula."

A pathetic moment occurred near the end of the shoot. Around three o'clock one afternoon, Merv encountered Lon again. He was so drunk he could hardly stand up, but he seemed to recognize Merv. "Help me, my friend," Lon said. "I don't know where I am or why I'm here."

Merv escorted the drunken actor back to his dressing room and eased him down onto the sofa. There, Merv removed Lon's shoes and put a blanket over him so he could sleep off his intoxication.

***

Despite the fact that most of his energies were being devoted to being cast as a romantic lead, Merv retained an unshakable belief in the viability of his appeal as singer. And as the competition for singing roles got more intense, he cited a particular sense of rivalry with Eddie Fisher, upon whom he'd once had a crush. His feelings for Eddie had turned first to covert jealousy and later to occasionally expressed outrage at his success.

Merv couldn't stand hearing Eddie's voice on radio or TV, and would immediately switch channels if the young star came on.

"And to think I introduced Elizabeth Taylor to the bum," he told Hadley.

As Merv moved deeper into the 1950s, he spent time in recording studios when he didn't have movie work. Still under contract with RCA Victor, he recorded "Morningside of the Mountain," with the Hugo Winterhalter Orchestra. Very briefly, it appeared among the Top 40 hits, but soon after sank into oblivion.

In the mid-50s, Merv recorded "Once in Love with Amy," with high hopes for the song. Ray Bolger, in 1948, had had a hit with this song. But Merv's version failed to generate any excitement.

By 1956, RCA had decided not to renew his contract. Merv drifted from Columbia to Decca, but failed to turn himself into another Perry Como. In 1958, he recorded songs which included "Introduce Me to the Gal" and "You're the Prettiest Thing," both recorded with the Sy Oliver Orchestra. When the records were released, the public wasn't interested.

Still pursuing a recording career, Merv found himself at the relatively obscure Carlton Records in 1961, singing the disastrously campy "The Screamin' Meemies from Planet X."

Merv experienced a secret *Schadenfreude* when he learned that Eddie Fisher, too, had been dropped by RCA Victor. But that didn't happen until 1960. At the peak of Merv's TV successes a decade later, he read in the papers that Eddie, burdened with debts of more than a million dollars, had declared bankruptcy.

"So he married, in quick succession, both America's Sweetheart and America's *femme fatale*, and all that it got him was an addiction to methamphetamines," Merv said. "I hear that Debbie Reynolds also told friends that Eddie is lousy in bed. I'll have to check with Elizabeth for the real low-down."

***

Asleep with Hadley at four o'clock in the morning, Merv was awakened by the ringing of his telephone. In those days, he had only one phone, and it was in the living room. Arousing himself from bed, as Hadley mumbled something and rolled over, a nude Merv stumbled toward the phone.

Picking up the receiver, he heard a world-famous voice: "It's Judy. You've got to come over right away. I can't tell you over the phone. Promise me you'll come over NOW."

Merv somewhat reluctantly agreed. He was hesitant because Judy sounded drunk. He feared she might be making another suicide attempt. After scribbling a note for Hadley, he dressed and drove over to Judy's house. If they were in the house at all that night, her husband, Sid Luft, and the children were asleep upstairs. Merv encountered Judy looking distraught and wearing no makeup. She'd been drinking and looked far older than her years.

Once he was inside, she spoke to him in a soft voice. "It's Peter. A member of the vice squad arrested him in the men's toilet of a state park. The charge is lascivious conduct. I just found out about it tonight. He's supposed to be arraigned tomorrow. If the press finds out about this, you won't be seeing the name of Peter Lawford on any more marquees."

"Brother-in-lawford"
to the Kennedys
Peter Lawford

"Oh, my God," Merv said. "I'm so sorry to hear this, but what can I do?"

"You know Howard Hughes, don't you?"

"Of course," he said. "We're playing tennis together later today."

"Howard will know what to do," she said. "He

238

can get Peter out of jail and cover up this whole shitty mess. You'll go to Howard, won't you?"

"For Peter . . . anything," he promised.

Over badly made cups of coffee, Judy and Merv talked emotionally in her kitchen for about an hour, plotting what they could do to help Peter. Merv couldn't get Howard on the phone—no one ever could—but Merv told Judy that Howard always showed up faithfully on the tennis court exactly at nine-thirty every Sunday morning. Merv promised Judy he'd make the pitch to Howard then.

Before he left, he kissed her good-bye on the lips and headed out into the dark morning, as the first light of dawn pierced the sky over Los Angeles.

A few hours later, on the tennis court, Howard didn't want to talk business until he'd played a game. "I don't want to be distracted," Howard said. But during the game, Merv noticed that Howard seemed very distracted indeed by the sudden appearance of the startlingly handsome Hadley.

When Merv introduced them, he noticed that the aviator held Hadley's hand for a very long time during their initial handshake. Hadley was dressed in the tightest white tennis shorts Merv had ever seen, making his endowment rather obvious.

After the match, which Merv deliberately let Howard win, Merv called Howard to the far end of the court and told him about Peter's dilemma.

"Shit like this happens in Hollywood all the time," Howard said. "I'm an expert in covering up for stars. You won't believe the jam I got Robert Mitchum out of one night. I'll help Peter. Not because I like the boy, but he's getting connected with the Kennedys. That family might be very useful to me one day."

Changing into his street clothes, Howard agreed "to take care of business," but only if Hadley drove him where he needed to go. "I've got a blinding headache, and I don't trust myself behind the wheel. I might run over somebody who's got a good lawyer. That happened to me once, you know."

To Merv, Hadley seemed a little too eager to drive away with Howard. Although he hugged and kissed Merv good-bye, and promised to be back soon, Merv was consumed with jealousy watching his newly defined lover disappear into the late morning sunshine with Howard Hughes. "That's the last I'll ever hear from Hadley," Merv told his friends.

***

As Merv had anticipated, Howard managed to quietly secure Peter's release from jail. No charges were ever filed against him, and the story of the men's room arrest was kept out of the press. Merv tried to reach Peter by phone, but no one was picking up at his house. Hours after they'd taken off together, Hadley still hadn't returned from "driving Howard Hughes." Merv placed a call to Judy to tell her the good news about Peter.

She immediately pleaded with him to join her on a drive to Palm Springs where Peter was hiding out after his ordeal. Almost to defy Hadley if he did opt to return that weekend, Merv agreed to drive her, ordering Bill Robbins not to tell Hadley where he'd gone.

During the eastbound drive to Palm Springs, Judy was jittery and anxious, wanting the drive to be over. She drank from a flask she carried in her purse. "Don't be surprised when we get there," she said. "I mean, you'll meet Peter's new lover, and it may come as quite a shock to you."

"I read Hedda and Louella," he said. "I know about his fling with Patricia Kennedy, although I hear old Joe Kennedy is completely opposed to it. Apparently, Old Joe thinks all actors are faggots."

"He's probably right about that," she said. "Mr. Ambassador is completely opposed to Patricia seeing Peter, and he's persuaded that vicious drag queen, J. Edgar Hoover, to conduct a complete investigation. I hope Nelly Hoover doesn't discover Peter's fondness for tearooms."

"What do you mean tearooms?" Merv asked. "They seem harmless enough. It's his English upbringing."

"Oh, darling, you can be so naïve," she said, brushing his cheek lightly with her fingers. "A tearoom is gay slang for a men's toilet. It's called latrine sex. Some guys prefer that."

"Sex in a smelly toilet doesn't strike me as very romantic," he said.

"True, true," she said. "Incidentally, the lover you'll meet in Palm Springs isn't Pat. By the way, I'm having an affair with Pat's brother, and my philandering husband doesn't know about it. He's handsome and charming. Jack Kennedy, or John F. Kennedy if you want to get formal. I'll introduce you to him, but you can't have him. I saw him first. He calls me up sometimes late at night and asks me to sing 'Over the Rainbow' to him on the phone. Isn't that adorable?"

"You know I'm a bit of a voyeur, and I just have to ask," he said. "Is he great in bed? I heard that for years, his old man regularly fucked Gloria Swanson."

"Jack's no Frank Sinatra," she said, "but I adore him. He's got a bad back. Usually, I have to be on top doing most of the work."

Merv was absorbing all of this with the full intention of sharing every word, every sordid detail, with Roddy McDowall and Henry Willson.

At a beautiful Spanish-style villa in Palm Springs, Peter in bathing trunks greeted Judy and Merv at the door with wet kisses, inviting them in. Judy excused herself, rushing off to the nearest bathroom. When she was gone,

240

Peter profusely thanked Merv for interceding with Howard Hughes. "It worked out OK this time, but you'd better clean up your act," Merv warned him.

"Oh, what the hell," Peter said. "I'm just a tearoom queen and that's all I'll ever be. There's nothing more sexually thrilling than giving blow jobs to strangers in a men's toilet."

When Judy returned, Peter kissed her lips gently again. "I've arranged for you guys to have the master bedroom." Judy led the way, asking Merv and Peter to bring her luggage.

Merv lingered behind, tugging at Peter's arm. "Judy and I are sharing a bedroom?" he asked.

"Yeah," she told me about the romance you guys are having," Peter said. "Nothing serious. Just fuck buddies."

"She told you *what?*" Judy was calling from the bedroom for Merv and Peter to hurry up with her luggage. Entering the room with suitcases, Merv spotted white sheets already turned down. A sense of panic overcame him. Peter gave Merv another quick kiss on the lips before departing toward the pool patio. "After you guys settle in, come and join Smokey and me on the patio."

"Smokey?" Merv was bewildered. He wanted to ask Peter who Smokey was.

Judy began undressing before him the way she'd done in front of dozens of people in the MGM wardrobe department. "C'mon," she urged him. "Shuck those duds." In Palm Springs all the stars go skinny dipping. Even Marlene Dietrich and Greta Garbo show off their pussies to each other."

He stripped down but turned his back to her when he slipped into his bathing suit.

"Nice ass," she said before rushing out of the room. "Last one in is a rotten egg!"

Ignoring the invitation to go nude, Merv came onto the patio in his bathing suit. He immediately noticed that Peter had peeled off his trunks and was lying nude on the chaise longue. "Sammy, meet Merv," he called to a black man in the pool who was frolicking with Judy. She too had ripped off her bathing suit.

Merv had been promised an introduction to Sammy Davis Jr. but hadn't expected it to come like this. "Hi, kid, pull off your suit and come join us chitlin's," Sammy yelled to him.

"Yeah, Merv," Peter urged him. "After all, you're not Princess Tiny Meat."

"But to get naked with a black man" he whispered to Peter. "I'm not sure I can compete."

"It's not a competition," Peter said.

241

Hurriedly Merv pulled off his trunks and made a running leap into the pool.

Sammy swam over to him. "You can shake my hand or else grab King Kong," he said. "Whatever turns you on."

After that introduction, Merv soon overcame his shyness, finding Sammy enchanting and charming. They continued chatting even when the pool splashing ended. Peter and Judy donned robes and moved toward the bar to begin the heavy drinking of a fading afternoon. Dressed in a robe, Sammy lounged by the pool with Merv.

"Peter used to be a part of our Rat Pack," Sammy said, glancing over at Peter and Judy at the bar. "I keep begging Frank to take him back, but he's too stubborn. Ever since Louella Parsons wrote that Peter was seen out on the town with Ava Gardner, Frank cut him off. The Rat Pack's not the same without him. Judy's only a sometimes member. Before Peter was banished, the Rat Pack consisted of two dago singers, a kike comic, a limey swell, a hot puta with red pussy hair, and a slightly off-color entertainer—the best in the business." He was, of course, referring to Frank Sinatra, Dean Martin, Joey Bishop, Peter Lawford, Shirley MacLaine, and himself.

Sammy looked over at Peter and blew him a kiss before asking for a drink. "Don't get the idea I'm gay," Sammy said. "I'm not! I've fucked more blonde showgals than Frankie himself. I've even fucked Ava Gardner. But don't tell Frankie that. He'd have some of the boys in the mob cut off King Kong if he knew that. But I like a little gay action on the side for variety. After all, you know yourself that Peter is the best cocksucker in Hollywood. That boy's got a very deep throat."

Drinks and more drinks preceded and followed a patio barbecue presided over by Sammy. "We niggers know our barbecue," he said. Shortly before midnight Sammy and Peter disappeared into the bedroom, leaving Merv alone with Judy.

She urged him to join her at the piano. "Let's sing some songs together," she said. "You're the only person in Palm Springs who knows as many songs as I do." Merv sat and sang with her until around two o'clock that morning, as both of them were drawn to good lyrics and well-written melodies.

"You know," she said, finally rising to her feet, "we should take our act together on the road."

Reaching for his hand, she led him to the master bedroom, shutting the door behind them.

King Kong and Rat Packer:
Sammy Davis Jr.

Unfastening his robe, she also dropped hers at her feet. In bed she pressed her nude body against his. "There's always the first time," she said. "Didn't you tell me that as a little fat boy growing up in San Mateo, you told all your friends that you wanted to marry Judy Garland one day? Well, just imagine that this is our honeymoon night."

***

Late the following morning, Frank Sinatra called and invited Judy and Sammy as his house guests to a home he'd borrowed from a friend in Palm Springs. Although he knew that Peter was within earshot, he pointedly didn't invite him. So after Judy and Sammy checked out, that left Merv alone with "the outcast," Peter. Merv agreed to drive Peter back to Malibu where he was to hook up with Patricia Kennedy.

En route to the coast, Merv learned that Peter's marriage to Patricia was imminent. Peter had little to say about his future bride, although he made it clear that he did not plan to give up sex on the side once he'd married "this Roman Catholic school girl who needs some breaking in about the way we do things here in Hollywood."

Until he actually met her, all that Merv knew about Patricia was that she was the sixth of nine children born to Joseph P. Kennedy and Rose Elizabeth Fitzgerald, and that her brother was a rising politician in Massachusetts. Peter claimed that Patricia was the most beautiful of all the Kennedy siblings, "although Jack is pretty cute—I'd like to fuck him too."

"I talked to Rose the other day," Peter confided. "She's not as opposed to the marriage as that monster she's married to. Once I assured her that our kids would be raised Roman Catholics, she became more at ease about her daughter's upcoming marriage. Pat is clearly not her favorite child. She told me that her daughter had a fine physique and a good mind, but then Rose complained that she puts neither of them to any particular use. 'She's not competitive like my other children,' *Mamma Mia* told me. 'Pat won't really succeed at anything,' she said. She told me that Pat's major accomplishment in life might involve marrying a movie star."

At Peter's house in Malibu, Merv was introduced to Patricia, discovering that she had a certain regal bearing like her mother Rose. Lithe and athletic, she seemed the epitome of grace and East Coast charm school breeding. Also in attendance that day was Lady May Lawford, Peter's mother. Rather formally dressed for a hot afternoon, Lady May sat under a large umbrella protecting her fair skin from the harsh rays of the California sun.

It was obvious that Lady May did not approve of her future daughter-in-law. She seemed to endure her presence. Peter and Patricia quickly excused themselves for a walk on the beach, leaving Merv alone with the stern and rather judgmental Lady May.

Never in his life had Merv met a more outspoken woman. He didn't know if Lady May meant what she said, or whether she merely uttered scathing observations as a means of shocking people. No sooner was Patricia out of sight than she launched into an attack on the Kennedys. "They're nothing but a bunch of barefoot Irish peasants," she claimed. "By marrying Peter, that bitch hopes to link herself with the British aristocracy. My God, the next thing I hear, old Joe Kennedy will be buying a title for her. There are a lot of them for sale these days. I like her brother Jack, but he always has his mind down between his legs. I told Peter he should have married Elizabeth Taylor. She's always been in love with him. Besides, Elizabeth is going to make a lot of money one day, and then Peter and I could live in the style to which we were once accustomed."

Lady May asked Merv if he'd get up "and fetch me another gin and tonic. I share my taste in drinks with the Queen Mother."

When Merv came back onto the patio, Lady May, a bit tipsy, wanted to continue with her revelations. Like the TV talk show host that he was to become, Merv was all ears.

"Peter told me that Kennedy gal was a virgin when they met. Jack Kennedy introduced Peter to her in Palm Beach, and she fell madly in love with him right away...and started pursuing him that very day. She might have been a virgin when she first met Peter, but she's not a virgin now. I found contraceptives in their bedroom. Old Joe gave the gal ten million dollars, but I've warned Peter he'll have to pay all the bills after they get married. That bitch holds onto every last red cent she's got."

Before she'd completely downed the gin and tonic Merv had brought her, and before she requested a refill, Lady May launched into an attack on the Rat Pack.

"I'm glad Peter is no longer fraternizing with that dried-up piece of spaghetti, Frank Sinatra. He hates me

Above: **Patricia Kennedy** with her brother, **JFK.**

Left: Her toxic mother-in-law, **Lady May Lawford** as displayed on the cover of her 2006 autobiography

as much as I hate him. But Peter's still seeing that queer Van Johnson. Johnson is the one who got Peter to wear those damn red socks. One night at a party I saw Peter and that Pat Kennedy kissing that darkie, Sammy Davis Jr. They call him 'Chicky.' I'd call him a nigger and tell him never to get within ten feet of me."

Merv sighed, wondering how Lady May would react if she knew what her son had been doing with Sammy only the night before. Certainly a bit more than kissing.

Just before sundown, after Peter and Lady May went upstairs to get ready for the evening, Patricia sat with Merv on the patio watching the sun go down. Still in her sports attire, she looked tan and lovely, and Merv was enchanted by her New England accent. "May must have filled you in on a lot of things—her version of things, that is. I find it rare that a so-called lady of breeding would be so uncouth. When Peter and I get married, we'll have to muzzle her, especially if Jack continues his career in politics. We definitely have to keep May away from the press. Her class prejudice went out of style with Queen Victoria."

Patricia would later express the same sentiments to dozens of her friends and, once, in a letter to Lady May herself.

Before she went upstairs to get dressed for dinner. Patricia turned to Merv. "Did Lady May tell you that she used to dress Peter as a girl until he was ten years old?" With that startling remark, she turned and left.

Merv felt the need to excuse himself from further contact and dinner that night with this dysfunctional trio. He wanted to get home where perhaps he would learn some news about Hadley.

As Merv was leaving, Patricia rushed down the stairs and kissed him on the cheek. She even extended an invitation to him to visit the family compound at Hyannis. "You'll love my brothers, especially Jack. He's got more personal charm than any of the other Kennedys. Only Peter has more charm." As an afterthought, she said, "I hope you're athletic. The whole family is athletic, especially me. The only reason I was still a virgin when I met Peter was that I could outrun my brothers."

***

After his return to L.A., Merv opened the door to his living room to find Hadley sitting there in his boxer shorts. "What went wrong?" Merv asked. "Howard Hughes got tired of you? I could have told you that would happen."

"C'mon, baby, and give your daddy a big, sloppy kiss," Hadley said. "Sexual fidelity was invented by heterosexuals, and even they can't play by their own rules most of the time."

"You want me to take you back?" Merv asked.

"I never really left, not in my heart," Hadley said. "For me, you are the man."

"I'm not sure I believe that," Merv said. "You fly away with Howard Hughes and then you just show up whenever you like. I'm not sure I'm taking you back."

Hadley rose from the sofa. "I think I have something here that will make you change your mind." He unfastened his shorts and let them fall to the floor. Merv could not resist the temptation.

Sitting in an adjoining, plant-filled garden room, Bill Robbins heard every word but remained stonily silent during the interchange. He was later to confide to his friends that that afternoon set the tone for the future relationship of Merv and Hadley. "It was an agreement to betray each other any time their little ol' cheatin' hearts desired it."

That night Merv and Hadley, after making love, had dinner with Paul and Bill. Paul was still dreaming of stardom, which he insisted would be brokered by Henry Willson. "I love Henry dearly," Merv said, "but don't you think his promises are just bullshit?"

"No way!" Paul said defensively. "I know he's told dozens of Hollywood hunks he's going to make a star out of them like Tab Hunter or Rock Hudson. But there's one big difference in my case. Henry's fallen in love with me. I'm going to hold out and endure all that slobbering over me until I hit it big. When I do, I'll say 'adios forever' to Henry."

Merv sighed as he sipped a cocktail. "I'm not sure the scenario will work out that way. But good luck, kid. Tread lightly into that pit of vipers. They bite. They sting. They kill."

"I know how to take care of myself," Paul said. "Just you guys wait and see."

***

It was the last big gathering Merv would ever attend at the home of Jack Warner, to whom he was still under contract with a movie career going nowhere. Hadley had wanted to come to the party as Merv's date but Merv rejected the idea. "How in the fuck do you think it'd look if I showed up with you on my arm?"

At Jack Warner's mansion, Merv was greeted by the studio chief himself. "Hi Griff. Great news. I'm getting you cast in the *Phantom of the Rue Morgue*. Great part. Great cast. A 3-D horror production. It'll be bigger than *House of Wax*."

"Do I get to play the lead?" Merv asked.

"Not exactly, but it's a great part. You'll be a French student at the Sorbonne in Paris."

"Me, playing a Frog with my night-train-to-Dublin puss?"

"You'll be great, kid," Jack promised. "Do I see an Oscar for best supporting? Now circulate. I've got more MGM stars here tonight than that fart, Louis B. Mayer, ever had in heaven back in the creep's heyday."

"Do I have to sing for my supper tonight?" Merv asked.

"If Judy Garland, Gordon MacRae or Doris Day had showed up, I'd never have asked. But none of those pussies are here."

"Can I quote you about MacRae being a pussy?"

"What I mean is that he's usually so drunk he can't get it up. The only way he can have sex is if somebody shoves something up his ass. But you can forget about singing tonight. We've got Mimi Benzell who's about to go on."

Merv joined the others in the large living room, waving at Elizabeth Taylor with her second husband, Michael Wilding. He noticed Robert Taylor with his sultry new wife, Ursula Thiess, although Merv would forever remember him as the husband of Barbara Stanwyck.

Humphrey Bogart was also standing nearby, but not with Lauren Bacall. Merv hadn't seen Bogie since staring at him nude in the shower at his Uncle Elmer's sports club. Merv introduced himself again to Bogie, who in turn introduced him to an attractive brunette named Verita Thompson. Bogie claimed that "Verita here is in charge of my toupées." But Merv already knew that Verita was Bogie's long-time mistress, an affair that pre-dated Bacall and which had lasted through the course of the marriage itself.

Mimi Benzell had never been Merv's favorite singer, although the American soprano had performed at New York's Metropolitan Opera and was a Broadway musical star as well as a performer on television and in nightclubs.

In front of Jack's invited guests, she went through her familiar repertoire, ranging from *Roberta* to *The Vagabond King*. Not ending it there, she delivered renditions from Mozart's *The Magic Flute* and Met credits that included *La Bohème, Rigoletto*, and *Der Rosenkavalier*. As she was deep into her sixteenth number, Jack approached Merv, whispering in his ear, "Griff, get this fucking broad to sit down."

Studio Chief **Jack Warner** with opera diva **Mimi Benzell**

"Griff, get this broad to sit down!"

Merv was surprised that Jack, the host, didn't take it upon himself to bring an end to Mimi's concert. At the end of her latest number, Mimi asked the audience, "Any special requests?"

Merv piped up, "How about 'Tippy Tippy Tin?'" As the other guests burst into laughter, Mimi fled from the room in tears. Later Merv felt bad about having embarrassed her in such a way.

Jack came up to him. "Great, Griff. You were just great. I'll owe you one. Perhaps I can arrange for you to fuck Hedy Lamarr."

Wandering down to the terrace overlooking the garden, Merv encountered Robert Taylor smoking a cigarette. Although Merv felt that Robert in the 1930s had been one of the three most handsome men in Hollywood, ranking up there with Tyrone Power and Errol Flynn, he clearly saw that time had taken its toll. Robert had moved deep into middle age and was a bit jowly.

At the time Merv met Robert, he was trying to hold onto his box office allure with epic pictures, including the Biblical spectacle *Quo Vadis?*, which had brought a temporary reprieve for the fading star.

Even so, despite the passage of time, Merv was still thrilled to meet one of his schoolboy crushes of the 1930s, even if Robert no longer looked as he did when he played opposite Greta Garbo in *Camille*.

Hoping to ingratiate himself with Robert, Merv immediately mentioned his mutual friendships with Howard Hughes and Errol Flynn. He knew that Robert, a bisexual, had engaged in sexual dalliances with both of them. "They've both told me a lot about you, and I've been dying to meet you."

Merv knew at once that he'd said the wrong thing when anger flashed across Robert's face. "I don't know what in the fuck they told you, but I haven't seen either of them in years. Everything they say is a pack of lies."

"Oh, no," Merv said, "they spoke of you only with the highest respect."

"Yeah, I bet," Robert said. He moved menacingly toward Merv. "Get this and get it good. I'm not a God damn faggot like you guys. All you pansies run up and down Hollywood Boulevard trying to slander every straight actor in town. In my case, you're barking up the wrong tree." The actor stormed off the terrace.

"What a son of a bitch!" Merv said out loud.

"I've been called many things in my life, but not that, although I'm sure I deserve it." Merv whirled around to see who he was talking to. The voice came from Michael Wilding.

"Whenever I get mad at Michael, I call him a cocksucker," came a woman's voice behind Michael. It was Elizabeth herself, looking beautiful in the moonlight. She was glamorously attired in purple. Moving in on Merv, she kissed his cheek.

Merv shook Michael's hand, gazing into his handsome, intelligent face. "I've been dabbling in Hollywood for a spell, but the results so far have been less than sterling," Michael said. "Did you see me in *Torch Song?*"

"Who could forget Joan Crawford in black face?" Merv asked.

With Elizabeth between them, both Merv and Michael escorted her back into the party. "You've got to drive up and visit us one night for dinner," Michael said.

"It's a deal," Merv said. "But I've got to warn you. Not so long ago, your wife and I were having a torrid affair."

"That's right, darling," Elizabeth chimed in. "Merv could go all night, sleep an hour or two and then start all over again."

"That's certainly more than I can do," Michael said, smiling. "Of course, a woman as beautiful as my bride can inspire a middle-aged man to great glory. Wouldn't you say so, Merv?"

"I would indeed," Merv said. He never expected Michael to call him with that promised dinner invitation, and he forgot all about it as he entered the foyer to hear the familiar voice of Jack Warner.

"Griff, get your fat ass over here," Jack said. "I want you to meet the great, the one and only French dwarf, Claudette Colbert."

Jack laughed at his own line, but was greeted with a stony silence from Claudette.

"Since both of you arrived stag tonight, I want you to be Claudette's escort," Jack said.

"An honor, Miss Colbert," Merv said, bowing to kiss her hand.

"How gallant," she said to Merv, as Jack rushed off to greet arriving guests. "Far more gallant than Jack Warner. He's the rudest man in Hollywood. I only show up because he throws the greatest parties in town."

"I loved you and Gable in *It Happened One Night*," he said.

"That was so long ago," she said. "I wish you'd have congratulated me for *All About Eve*. I was set to play Margo Channing until I hurt my back. Bette Davis ruined that picture."

"You'll make bigger and better pictures than *Eve* in the years to come," he said.

Suddenly Jack Warner appeared again with a studio photographer. "Quick," Claudette said, taking Merv's arm and altering his position. "You stand on the right side of me. I can only be photographed from the left side."

Claudette Colbert

As an actor, Merv always considered Michael Wilding a poor man's James Mason. He had a facile British charm and impeccable manners. Merv found him likable during the three or four occasions he was invited to the home Michael shared with Elizabeth Taylor and their housemates, Stewart Granger and his wife, Jean Simmons.

Having been sexually involved with Elizabeth's first husband, Nicky Hilton, Merv, after evaluating her second husband, concluded that as a sex object Michael was a flame that flickered at a lower voltage.

After Elizabeth's firsthand contact with the mental cruelty, the womanizing, the drinking, and the hard fists of Nicky Hilton, Michael must have seemed like a relatively comfortable father figure. But during Merv's second visit, he sensed the tension between Elizabeth and Michael, to whom she was barely speaking. Monty Clift acted as intermediary between the newlyweds, seeming to hover protectively over the marriage. In their discussions, Monty confided to Merv, "I'm Elizabeth's platonic husband. She's the other half of me, the only woman who ever turned me on."

Merv found Stewart Granger dazzlingly handsome—easily as seductive as the swashbuckler he played in movies such as *King Solomon's Mines* (1950). With Errol Flynn frequently drunk and going to seed, Stewart seemed his heir apparent in adventure movies.

Merv had casually mentioned to Michael that his new friend, Hadley, had remodeled his pool house into a nurturing safe haven and love nest for overnight guests. The very next day Michael called him. At first Merv misunderstood the call and got rather flirty with Michael.

"Elizabeth is fucking Victor Mature," Michael said with anger and an uncharacteristic bluntness. "Do you mind if I borrow your poolhouse for the night?"

Merv was filled with anticipation at the prospect of seducing the second husband of Elizabeth. But he sensed a hesitation in Michael's voice. "And, oh yes, dear chap that you are, you don't mind if I bring a guest."

Even before Michael arrived with his guest, Merv knew who it would be. None other than Stewart Granger. Roddy McDowall had already told Merv that Michael and Stewart had been engaged in an ongoing affair for years.

In Merv's living room, Michael excused himself to go to the bathroom, leaving Merv sitting opposite Stewart and taking in his muscular figure. He knew of the actor's past affairs with the likes of Hedy Lamarr and Deborah Kerr, and he envied Michael for having such an appealing lover. Sitting on Merv's sofa, the actor was complaining about Michael. "He eats my food, he drinks my expensive wine, and he even fucks my women. Yet he won't do press-ups with me."

"Maybe he'll do something else tonight," Merv said provocatively.

"He's always willing to do that," Stewart claimed. "Don't get the wrong idea about me. I'm the top."

"I could have guessed," Merv said. "Michael is so passive, and you look like you're charged with testosterone."

"That I am, my dear boy," Stewart said. "Perhaps you'll get lucky one night and learn what the excitement is all about."

When Michael returned, Stewart said, "My bloke here should have married Marlene Dietrich, not Elizabeth Taylor. Marlene still adores him. She's just a *hausfrau* at heart and would have taken wonderful care of Michael's health, which has never been good. Marlene would make a wonderful wife, smothering him with good food and love. She once told me, 'Tell Michael he needs me, since he's too stupid to figure that out for himself.'"

"Marlene would be too much woman for me," Michael said. "Besides, she'll never divorce her husband, and I could never marry a woman who sleeps with more beautiful women than I could ever attract."

"What a thing to say," Merv chimed in. "For God's sake, man, you're married to the most beautiful woman in the world."

"Beware of what you think you want," Michael said. "My marriage was a ceremony performed in hell."

In the weeks leading up to Merv's departure from Hollywood's film industry, Stewart and Michael shared his poolhouse on at least three occasions. Hadley was disappointed that he wasn't invited to join "the two limeys."

On a Saturday night, Michael called late and asked to use the poolhouse once again. Merv agreed and Michael arrived about an hour later. Instead of Stewart, Michael had Marlene Dietrich on his arm.

Talented British blokes shacked up together
chez Merv in Hollywood
Stewart Granger (center) and **Michael Wilding** (right)
Left photo: **Marlene Dietrich** as temptress

Merv sat briefly with the blonde goddess in his living room. She was wearing a pink dress and black hosiery that highlighted her fabulous legs.

With candor, she chatted. "Taylor and I are forced to share Michael. Right now Taylor and I are also sharing Sinatra. Every time we make love, Michael tells me he cannot live without me. And then he goes home and fucks that Taylor bitch. It must be those huge breasts of hers. Michael likes them to dangle in his face." She raised the hem of her dress slightly. "Of course, Taylor has short, dumpy legs, the legs of a peasant. Not like mine at all."

"Miss Dietrich, your legs are legendary around the world," Merv said. "I heard that even Hitler wanted them wrapped around him."

She crushed out her cigarette with a certain fury, flashing her anger. "Hitler was a homosexual."

Getting up early the next morning, Marlene had apparently forgiven Merv and had prepared him the best scrambled eggs of his life. At the door that morning, he kissed Marlene and Michael on their cheeks and invited them to use his love nest any time they wanted.

An hour later, Hadley arrived without telling Merv where he'd been all night. He expressed regret at not getting to meet Marlene and then informed Merv that he was exhausted and didn't want to be disturbed for the rest of the day.

On yet another occasion, Merv wasn't surprised to hear Michael's horny voice on the other end of his phone line. "Mind if I show up with a blonde goddess?" Michael asked.

"Bring her on," Merv said, assuming that Michael had another date with Marlene.

At the door he was surprised to encounter a leggy and voluptuous blonde starlet. He recognized her at once, although he'd only seen one of her pictures and that was a piece of fluff called *Getting Gertie's Garter* back in 1945. Kentucky-born Marie McDonald—a.k.a. "Miss New York of 1939"—was known in Hollywood as "The Body" and the description fit her perfectly.

Michael went to check out the lighting within the poolhouse. When he returned, Marie looked him up and down and said in front of Merv, "I like my men rich and handsome. In Michael's case, I had to settle just for the good looks. Unless, of course, he can shake some money from Taylor's piggybank during their divorce."

Michael shocked Merv when he told him that he planned to divorce Elizabeth and marry Marie. As it turned out, however, Elizabeth divorced Michael, and he never married Marie.

"The Body"
Marie McDonald

Marie faded from Merv's life as fast as she'd entered, but her memory lingered. Years later he got an idea for a film script. He wanted to base a movie on Marie's tumultuous life, calling the film *The Body*.

He even hired a script writer to develop it, suggesting that real-life fragments from the experiences of other "popcorn blondes" might be incorporated, including Lana Turner, Betty Grable, Betty Hutton, Marilyn Monroe, and Jayne Mansfield. Merv had followed Marie's career as she went from a pin-up girl in World War II through seven husbands, addictions to alcohol and prescription drugs, arrests for drunk driving, and various suicide attempts. In 1957, she faked her own kidnapping, generating headlines worldwide when the plot unraveled.

As the years went by, Merv avidly followed the tabloid accounts of Marie's various scandals. They included a prolonged affair with the notorious gangster Bugsy Siegel. She was twice married to the shoe tycoon, Harry Karl, who went on to marry Debbie Reynolds and to lose both his and her fortunes. In her final film, a failure of a comedy entitled *Promises! Promises!* (1963), a forty-year-old Marie co-starred with Jayne Mansfield, whom she bitterly disliked.

As a means of showing Marie and the rest of the world who had the better body, Jayne opted to appear topless.

The producer of that otherwise forgettable film was Marie's seventh and final husband, Donald F. Taylor. In 1965 Marie presumably killed herself with an overdose of Percodan. Taylor was suspected of murdering her, but he committed suicide shortly after her death and never went on trial.

***

The ongoing poolhouse trysts between Stewart Granger and Michael Wilding would lead to embarrassing repercussions in the years ahead. In 1962, Hedda Hopper published her candid, self-congratulatory memoir, *The Whole Truth and Nothing But.* Although within its pages she protected her friends and protégés, she used the autobiography as a mouthpiece for the airing of decades of private grudges and vendettas. She loathed Michael Wilding and outed him as a homosexual in the book. He threatened a retaliatory lawsuit.

Reacting to that, Hedda summoned Merv to her house, offering him a glass of champagne.

True to her style, the gossip maven got right to the point. "I want you to testify in court that Michael Wilding is a homosexual. I know about those hot nights the cocksucker spent in your poolhouse with Stewart Granger."

"Hedda, be reasonable," Merv pleaded. "I can't do that."

"You *can* do it and you will in exchange for favorable mention in my column," she said. "I'm still powerful enough in this town to destroy a performer, especially one with your mediocre talent."

"You didn't hear me," he said. "I can't do it."

"You know what I wrote is true," she said, increasingly agitated.

"That's beside the point," he said. "I not only can't do that for you, I won't do it!" He rose from his armchair and handed her a half-empty glass of champagne. "I didn't finish it. You can have the rest of it. I'll show myself out."

That night Merv told Hadley, "Now and forever more, I'm officially on Hedda's Hopper's shit list."

In the days to come Hedda would reach out to other performers, including Eddie Fisher, with the same request. Each of her prospective witnesses rejected her request to testify against Michael Wilding, even though at least some of them knew that Hedda's accusations were true.

During the months which followed, thousands of copies of the book were sold for $4.95 each to a public which demanded to know what Hedda had to reveal about the inner secrets of Hollywood's elite.

Stewart Granger weighed in with the last word. He dialed Hedda's number and shouted into the phone: "You monumental bitch! How bloody dare you accuse a friend of mine of being a queer, you raddled, dried-up, frustrated old cunt."

***

In the early 1950s, just as the 3-D vogue was dying, Merv was cast in the doomed 3-D version of *Phantom of the Rue Morgue,* which was eventually released to lackluster sales in 1954. The film would mark the end of his career as a Hollywood actor, although later he'd make several final desperate and unsuccessful attempts to salvage his dream.

Cast in the role of Georges Brevert, Merv once again was directed by Roy Del Ruth, who had helmed *Three Sailors and a Girl,* in which Merv had made a minor impression in his sailor uniform. Based on a short story by Edgar Allan Poe, the *Rue Morgue* film starred Karl Malden, Patricia Medina, and Steve Forrest. Although years later Merv would write that the only time he ever met or saw Dolores Dorn was as part of their arranged "date" one night at a premiere, she too was cast in the film as Camille.

After it was released, the public understandably confused it with the previously released and roughly equivalent film *Murders in the Rue Morgue.* (Warner Brothers had used many of the same sets for both of the Rue Morgue pictures.)

Briefly during the context of the film, the character played by Merv became a suspect as the serial killer. Ironically, even the film's director, Roy Del Ruth, doubted the wisdom of the casting, saying, "No one would believe Merv playing the role of a serial killer." The director was right.

During chats with Karl Malden, Merv jokingly referred to his part as "type casting." He knew the actor was a close friend of Marlon Brando, having appeared with him in *A Streetcar Named Desire*. Karl, a Serbian, would also appear that year in Marlon's second greatest picture, *On the Waterfront*. In reference to his role in *Phantom*, he told Merv, "Sometimes an actor has to pay his bills. To be honest, I love every movie I appear in—even the bad ones. I'm a workaholic. As long as I work, I'm happy. At least in this turkey I can camp it up as an evil mad scientist with an ape as my sidekick."

Merv also met the female star of the picture, Patricia Medina, a voluptuous, exotic-looking leading lady who was born in Britain. She didn't look British at all, having inherited her sultry looks from her Spanish father. A veteran, she'd worked in movies since 1937 and had been famously married to the handsome English actor, Richard Greene. Patricia had already divorced him by the time she met Merv.

Within six years of their picture together, Patricia would marry Joseph Cotten, who'd starred in Merv's all-time favorite movie, *Citizen Kane* (1941), directed by Orson Welles.

In years to come, Merv would become friends with Orson and would invite him for frequent appearances on *The Merv Griffin Show*. In one confidential moment backstage, Orson told Merv that "Joseph absolutely hates you. He keeps urging me not to go on your show."

"Why?" an astonished Merv asked. "I never put the moves on Patricia Medina."

"Maybe you should have," Orson said. "Joseph calls you half a man. That's how he refers to men he suspects of being homosexuals. I know in your case you're not gay, but Joseph is convinced."

"Joseph Cotten, a homophobe?" Merv said. "I can hardly believe that."

Orson chuckled as if he knew a secret. "Some men with a gay past feel they can cover their tracks by attacking gays. That way, they think no one will ever suspect them."

***

Shamed by the failure of the *Rue Morgue* picture, Merv made plans "to get out of Dodge," as he put it. But dreams die hard, and Merv seemed fated to make a few final attempts before abandoning his hopes for a career in films as a romantic lead.

Merv's great ongoing hope had involved starring as Curly McLain in the film version of *Oklahoma!* *(1955).* When he heard that Fred Zinnemann had been hired as its director, he requested a meeting. He'd known Fred when he'd directed *From Here to Eternity.* Receiving Merv, Fred was gracious and spared ten minutes of his time. He was quick to share the names on the list of actors he wanted to play Curly.

"To be frank, I found an up-and-coming actor who is the exact type for Curly," Fred said. "Paul Newman. But regrettably, he lacks the singing voice needed."

"I can sing," Merv said. "And all my many girlfriends tell me I've got the looks."

"Maybe. But I've got my hopes riding on another young actor who, physically at least, would be ideal." Fred said. "James Dean."

"You've got to be kidding," Merv said. "I mean Dean can do the acting part, but what about the singing? You plan to dub him?"

"We'll see," Fred said. "But under no circumstances am I going to let you play Curly. Better luck next time, kid. I know a guy who's working on a script called *The Alligator People.* Would you allow make-up to transform you into an alligator?"

"Any day now," Merv said, heading out the door.

A few weeks later Merv called James Dean, not telling him that he, too, desperately wanted the part of Curly. James had just flown in from New York after testing for the role. He told an amusing story of getting kicked out of the lobby of the snobby Hotel Pierre because he showed up "dressed like an old cowboy wino." He wasn't allowed to pass through the main entrance of the hotel but had instead been directed to the rear service entrance, where he took a freight elevator up to Fred's suite.

"Zinnemann loved my 'Poor Jud Is Dead' number with Rod Steiger," James claimed. "Zinnemann said it was the best screen test he'd ever shot."

"And your singing?" Merv asked. "You can sing?"

"I'm not sure yet, but I might become a singing star in film musicals if I pull this one off," James said.

Eventually Fred decided against James, offering the *Oklahoma!* lead to a real singer, Frank Sinatra, instead. Rising from the depths of the depression he'd reached during the filming of *From Here to Eternity,* he'd leveled off in his drinking and was making a comeback. He'd signed a contract with Capitol Records, and with his more mature voice he'd go on to record a string of albums that would display his brilliance as a pop singer for decades to come. And after its release in 1955, his riveting performance as a junkie in *The Man With the Golden Arm* would eventually earn him another Oscar nomination.

When Merv called to congratulate Frank, he was shocked to learn he'd just turned down the role. "I learned the God damn thing is going to be filmed in CinemaScope and then again in Todd-AO," he said. "Frank Sinatra is known as one-take Lulu. I said no way." [Partially owned and heavily promoted by Mike Todd, Todd-AO was a high-definition widescreen film format developed in the mid-1950s by the American Optical Company in Rochester, New York. Todd memorably characterized it as "Cinerama outta one hole" because, unlike Cinerama, Todd-AO required only a single camera and only one set of lenses.]

Later that day, Merv learned that other actors were rejecting roles in *Oklahoma!*, including Betty Hutton, who'd refused the role of Annie, which would have jump-started her comeback. Eventually, tone-deaf Gloria Grahame got the part, singing without dubbing, which meant that her songs had to be edited together from recordings made almost literally note by note.

In quiet desperation, and without alerting Frank, Merv contacted Fred again, asking for a second chance at the role of Curly. "Too late, kid. This very morning I cast Gordon MacRae. He's got the right baritone voice. Only problem is the bastard refuses to curl his hair. Curly got his nickname from his curly locks. Gordon refuses to get a permanent. But his wife Sheila has agreed to finger-curl his hair every morning."

"Ain't that wonderful?" Merv said. "I'm about as crazy for MacRae as Bette Davis is for Miriam Hopkins and Joan Crawford."

***

Even though he didn't get the role of Curly, Merv was still determined and tried again. He wanted the role of Billy Bigelow in the Rodgers and Hammerstein blockbuster musical, *Carousel (1956)*. It was to be directed by Henry King, a Virginia-born native who'd gotten his start in girly burlesque shows before breaking into "flickers" in 1912. Still going strong in the 1950s, he'd directed such previous hits as *Twelve O'Clock High (1949)*, *I'd Climb the Highest Mountain (1951)*, and *The Snows of Kilimanjaro (1952)*.

In jockeying for the role, Merv used his influence with Henry Willson, who called the director and arranged a face-to-face interview for Merv. As the interview unfolded, Merv was carefully studied by a skeptical Henry. "Just what role do you think you can pull off in this film?"

"Billy Bigelow, of course," Merv said defensively. "I know all the numbers. Can I perform for you right now or else be screen tested?"

"The only song you could sing from *Carousel* is 'You're a Queer One, Merv Griffin,'" Henry said.

"Are you insulting me?" Merv asked.

"A mere slip of the tongue, my laddie," Henry said. "I meant to say, 'You're a Queer One, Julie Jordan.' Sorry but I've already cast the leads. I'm

257

going to ask Frank Sinatra to play Billy. The female lead's going to Judy Garland if she can hold herself together."

That night Merv called Frank once again to congratulate him on being cast as the lead. "I've turned down the God damn part," Frank responded. "The same way I turned down *Oklahoma!* This fucking picture's being shot twice—once in 35mm and again in 55mm. But not with me in it."

Three weeks after Frank had prematurely rejected the juicy role, and too late for him to recoup it, studio technicians found a way to film only in 55mm, which could then be transferred onto 35mm.

In the final hour, Merv made one last, desperate plea, virtually begging Henry for the role of Billy. "You're too late, Griffin," Henry said. "I came to my senses and offered the role to . . ."

Merv interrupted him, "Gordon MacRae."

"How did you know?" Henry asked. "I haven't told anybody."

"At night I moonlight as a fortune teller," Merv said before putting down the phone.

Even though he'd been disappointed, Merv wanted to appear sporting about his rejection and called Judy Garland to congratulate her for being cast in *Carousel*, which he thought might be an appropriate follow-up to *A Star Is Born*.

"Don't congratulate me," she said. "I'm off the picture. Henry King thinks I'm not—in his words—'emotionally stable enough.' He fears his God damn picture will run over budget. He cast Shirley Jones instead."

"You've got to be kidding," Merv said. "With you as the star, King would have had a great picture. With Jones, he'll get a mediocre one." He failed to mention that he had secretly sought the role of Billy Bigelow for himself.

The only news emerging from the set of Carousel that delighted Merv came weeks later when he heard that Gordon MacRae had been arrested for drunk driving.

***

Despite of the ongoing rejections, Merv continued reading the trades, hoping for one last chance. One morning he read that one of his former directors, Gordon Douglas, had been designated as director of *Sincerely Yours*, a schmaltzy film about a piano player. Previously, Gordon had half-jokingly promised him the lead if he ever made a movie about a piano player.

Before his rendezvous with Gordon, Merv told Hadley, "I'm still gonna be big in Hollywood." He paused. "Or maybe not. Wish me luck."

"Aren't you show-biz people supposed to say 'break a leg' or something?" Hadley asked as Merv headed for the door.

Face to face with Gordon Douglas, the helmer gave it to Merv straight. "Don't make me laugh, Griffin. You, the lead in *Sincerely Yours*? Haven't you heard? The God damn sappy picture is a vehicle for America's leading faggot, Liberace."

"Oh, I see," Merv said. "Hollywood's first big gay picture."

"Don't be an asshole," Gordon said. "I've got to make Miss Sequins look straight as an arrow onscreen, with two hot pussies, Joanne Dru and Dorothy Malone, chasing after him. Joanne Dru has been fucked regularly by John Ireland, and he's got the biggest dick in Hollywood. How can I make movie audiences believe that a woman getting plowed by Ireland would go for Liberace? Much less that little hottie, Dorothy Malone. I wouldn't mind plugging that bitch myself. Frankly, I don't know what any woman would want with Liberace. Or any man for that matter. He's not my type. If I were gay, I'd rather fuck you than Liberace." He answered a call from his secretary. "Say, if you stick around for fifteen minutes, I'll introduce you to the piano player himself. Seeing this guy still isn't believing it."

"No thanks," Merv said. "I'd better go. Sorry to take up your time."

"It's okay, kid," he said. "Don't feel too bad. Some guys aren't suited to make it in the movies, and you're one of them. You're too much of a nice guy. Too weak. No charisma. Not ruggedly masculine enough. John Wayne and Gary Cooper, even Clark Gable, allowed guys to suck their dicks when they were young and trying to get ahead. But they project a sense of macho on screen. You just can't do that."

"I'm a singer, not a cowboy," Merv said.

"Why don't you consider doing lounge acts in night clubs?" Gordon said. "Forget that big band shit—those days are over. You can still sing, right?"

"Better than ever, and I'm about to open in Las Vegas," Merv said defensively. "My opening is gonna get national coverage."

"Sure, kid," Gordon said, looking down at his papers. "Don't slam the door on your way out."

Heading for his car, Merv stopped to watch a purple-colored Lincoln Executive limousine pull up. From behind the wheel emerged a startlingly handsome and very tall chauffeur in a pink uniform, tall black boots, and a gold hat. He grandly opened the rear door. Out emerged the flamboyant showman himself, the one, the only Liberace, darling of blue-haired grannies from coast to coast.

From the blasting radio in front came the song "Mr. Sandman" by the Chordettes with the line, "wavy hair like Liberace."

Emerging from the limousine, Liberace reached back for his white cape, as the chauffeur excused himself to go to the studio's men's room.

Not meaning to stand there staring like a rubbernecker, Merv resumed his steps without acknowledging the showman. "Hey, I know you," Liberace called out. "You're Merv Griffin. I once heard you sing with Freddy Martin's band. I love your voice. Do you want to come on my show? We could do that CoconutsI number. I'll even rent a monkey and dress him in sequins. It'll be a laugh riot."

Merv was flabbergasted that this flow of words—even a job offer—would come from the syrupy mouth of this show-biz eccentric before he'd even said a word. "Hi, indeed...I'm Merv Griffin, as you said." He reached to shake the entertainer's hand.

Liberace withdrew his paw as if it were burned on the stove. "I can't shake hands," he said. "I have to protect my mitts for the piano." Merv looked down and was astonished to see Liberace wearing seven rings, each of them as large as a fat escargot.

"I was born Wladziu Valentino Liberace," he said, "but I've been billed as Walter Busterkeys, Walter Liberace, Lee Liberace, Liberace Chefroach, or else The Glitter Man. My friends call me Lee. You can call me Lee."

"Where in hell did you come up with a name like Chefroach?" Merv asked. "I don't know you well enough to call you Lee, but I do admire your work. I've watched every one of your shows. I must say I'm a bit envious. I too play the piano, but not like you."

"No one does, you dear sweet thing," Liberace said. "I'm unique." He leaned over to whisper something in Merv's ear. "I hear we share someone in

Onstage and over the top with **Liberace**

260

common."

"Who, pray, might that be, other than the piano?"

"We've both known Rock Hudson as David knew Bathsheba," Liberace said. "I got Rock back when he was a struggling actor and playing an Indian in the movies. Quite a tomahawk he carries around."

"I know." Merv was taken back that Liberace knew any detail about his private life.

"We have even more things in common," Liberace said. "Rosemary Clooney told me about your new boyfriend, Hadley Morrell. That darling boy lived with me once for three weeks, but I had to get rid of him. Too clinging. I need my freedom."

Merv was astonished. "You and Hadley? He never said anything."

"Hadley's paying you a great compliment in linking up with you," Liberace said. "He's a star-fucker. If he's hitched his wagon to yours, it means he thinks you're going to the moon. He thinks you'll be big." He glanced at his rings. "And rich." Then he checked his diamond-studded watch. "I think I'm going to be late for my appointment with Mr. Douglas. He's directing my new picture. It's called *Sincerely Yours*."

"I've heard about it," Merv said in a soft voice.

"Say, I have this great idea," Liberace said. "I'm throwing a little dinner party tonight for the Queen of Hollywood. No, I wasn't describing myself, you darling. I'd like you and Hadley to be my guests. It'd be a delight to see that stud one more time."

"Oh, I don't think so," Merv said, "but thank you anyway. Just out of curiosity, who do you mean, the Queen of Hollywood? There are so many who fit that description."

Liberace laughed. "Mae West, you dear thing," he said. "If you doubt it, ask her."

"Hot damn," Merv said. "I'd swim a moat filled with alligators and crocodiles to meet Mae West. I think she's the cat's pajamas."

"Darling, you've got to update your vocabulary. *Cat's pajamas* was something to say back in the days when Clara Bow was fucking that divine Gary Cooper."

At that point the chauffeur came back from the men's room. "This is my driver, Paul Richardson," Liberace said. The driver shook Merv's hand and smiled smugly as if he knew all about Merv.

Before his exit, Liberace whispered in Merv's ear, "He's hung down to his knees."

After Liberace's departure, Paul made arrangements to pick Merv and Hadley up at seven-thirty that evening.

As Paul drove off with Liberace in the back seat, Merv stood staring at

261

their dust. That scene with Liberace had happened so fast he suspected that it might have been a mirage. The Los Angeles sun seemed to be frying his brain. *Liberace and Hadley.* It was a mind-boggling concept.

Merv drove home, his heart beating fast. He had a few things to discuss with Hadley before the evening's upcoming dinner party.

As he steered his car down the street where he lived, he said, almost as a whisper to himself, "Mae West! My God. I don't have a thing to wear."

***

In red silk lounging pajamas, Liberace received Merv and Hadley at his spectacularly over-the-top home. He kissed both Merv and Hadley on the lips and told Hadley that he'd missed him but was happy to learn "you've found a good home with Merv here."

"You make me sound like some stray dog being passed around from master to master," Hadley said defensively.

"When you work the kennel, that's how the game is played, my darling boy," Liberace smirked, inviting them inside.

Hadley preferred to anchor at the bar, while Liberace shared his house treasures with Merv. After all, Hadley had seen it all before. During the tour, Liberace showed off an exquisitely crafted desk that he claimed had been the property of Louis XV at the Court of Versailles. Merv even got to bounce up and down on a bed once slept in by Rudolph Valentino and one of his lesbian wives. Back in the living room, Liberace invited Merv to play a piano which had once belonged to Fréderic Chopin.

Paul Richardon had gone upstairs to change out of his pink chauffeur's uniform. Coming down the stairs to take drink orders, he emerged this time as the waiter. He wore some Basque-like outfit with a white shirt open to reveal his six-pack stomach and tight black trousers with a red sash fastened around his waist. He even wore a pink beret, a gift from Liberace. When Paul was out of earshot, Merv whispered to Liberace, "You really know how to pick 'em."

"You should see my rejects," Liberace said.

"If only I could be so lucky."

At the ring of the doorbell, Liberace became hysterical. "My God, it's Mae. She's right on time." Standing in front of a full-length mirror, he asked everybody, "How do I look?"

"Lover-ly," Merv assured him.

Paul tried to answer the door, but Liberace blocked his movement, preferring the honor for himself. Merv, who would later describe every nuance of the evening to his friends, said that "Mae West really knows how to make a grand entrance."

"Hello, boys," she said. "Feast your eyes on a real woman!" She stood under the glittering hallway chandelier for an inspection. Pink was her color of choice, from her satin gown to her satin shoes, and of course, for her fluttering feather boa as well. She also wore an ermine stole and diamonds—more than enough to justify those cliché-ridden comparisons to *Diamond Lil.*

Before her introduction to Merv, Mae sized up both Paul and Hadley, beginning at their toes and spending far too long evaluating the potential of their crotches. "I've had the Montana Mule, Gary Cooper. And Mr. King Size, Steve Cochran. Oh, yes, and Mickey Hargitay, Mr. Universe as you know. If I recall, "beer can" David Niven had the time of his life, and even though he denies it, I've had everything that Anthony Quinn has got. There was Black Snake George Raft, and Bugsy Siegel carried his gun in the right place. A few moons ago, Mr. America, Richard DuBois, fell big for me. Even Harry Houdini didn't escape Mae's trap." Mae had the habit of sometimes referring to herself in the third person.

After a final once-over of both Paul and Hadley, she said, "Unless Mae is very, very wrong, and I'm never wrong about such things, I'd say you two studs have all those boys I mentioned beat. I bet I could take you two hunks from these two queens quicker than it takes Cary Grant to ejaculate. He was always premature, you know." She smiled as Paul eased her fur from her shoulders. Putting one hand on her hip, she said, "Mae never has to take her clothes off in front of the camera like the Marilyn Monroe or the Jayne Mansfield sluts of today. Men can imagine what's underneath. Adolph Zukor once said, 'When I look at that dame's tits, I know what lust means.'"

"Mae, when I look you over, I know that you're the only woman in the world who could convert me," Liberace gushed.

She cast a skeptical eye toward him. "At least you're dressed for me. I hear you play the organ. Just how well do you play the organ?"

"Just ask Paul or Hadley," he said. "Either boy. They can give eyewitness testimonials to my talent." Giggling, he reached for Merv's arm. "Oh, yes, Mae West meet Merv Griffin."

"Oh, yeah, the big band singer." She sounded a bit dismissive. "I've already had two of the boys in the Freddy Martin band. But I'm sure you beat me to 'em."

Embarrassed at her candor, he said, "Miss West, the greatest honor of my life. To me, you'll always be *My Little Chickadee.*"

"Dream on, sugartit," she said. "I'm too much woman for you. I could take on Paul and Hadley both, leave them exhausted, as I screamed for round two to come on. But if you guys love me so much, you could do Mae a big favor. Get Rock Hudson to ball me. I haven't sampled him yet. Have you both had him?"

Liberace confirmed that they had.

"Well, I hear he likes to fuck Golden Age stars. Jon Hall. Errol Flynn, Tyrone Power. Even that slutty dyke Joan Crawford. I'm sure Marlene Dietrich is running after that alleged ten and a half inches. Marlene tried to get my honeypot, but Mae doesn't make it with lesbians. Don't forget. Get Rock to come up and see me sometime."

"Mae, I'll see that he's delivered with a pink bow tied around it," Liberace promised, as he ushered Mae into his candlelit living room. Paul took her order for green tea, as she said she didn't "touch the hard stuff, unless it's attached to a man."

Then, before the evening had really begun, she warned Merv and Liberace, "Mae works solo. Not even W.C. Fields could steal a scene from me. If there are any one-liners to be delivered tonight, Mae herself will do the honors."

As Merv would later tell his friends, "Lee might wear more elaborate costumes on stage, but for sheer flamboyance, no one topped Mae West. She might call herself a real woman, but I've had my doubts. I think all those rumors about her being a drag queen are true. She's the mother of all female impersonators. In fact, I think she invented the gig just for herself."

Within the hour, Liberace bounced up out of his chair, announcing that he was to be the chef of the evening. "All the recipes are from my book, *Liberace Cooks!*" he said.

"I'm glad you're the chef," Hadley said. "Merv's idea of cooking is to overboil spaghetti, then heat up catsup to pour over it."

"I'm sure the dear boy is good at other things," Liberace said, leading the way to the kitchen with an impish wink.

Merv was going to escort Mae, but Paul beat him to it. Looking up into his eyes, she said, "I've always had a healthy appetite both for the well-endowed male like yourself and for food that is aphrodisiac. Ever since Eve gave that apple to Adam, women have known down through the centuries what foods they should feed men to stimulate them sexually."

"I never knew that," Merv said.

"Tonight Lee and I will share some of our secrets in attracting men, other

Rhinestones, kleig lights, and Über-camp
Mae West with **Liberace**

264

than our stunning good looks," Mae said.

Mae was speaking strictly privately. In the more public forum of her 1975 book, *Mae West on Sex, Health, and ESP*, she claimed, "I've never relied on food to turn on the guys in my life!"

Propped on a stool, she suggested that there was something to the ancient belief that a man could stimulate his sex drive by eating the sexual organs of animals, especially those of a bull. "I once hired a Spanish chef from Barcelona, who prepared the most divine bull's testicles. I fed them to my men and found that after eating them they could go all night. Of course, in the case of Steve Cochran, he didn't need any stimulation at all." She turned to Merv, "But, dearie, I'm sure you know that already after sharing that dressing room with him."

Merv was surprised that Mae even knew his name, much less the identity of a man he'd seduced.

Sensing his surprise, she said, "I might not have made a picture since 1943, but Mae knows what's going on in this town. A cockroach doesn't cross Hollywood Boulevard without getting Mae's permission."

As Liberace, wearing a red apron, stood over his range, putting the finishing touches on dinner, Mae warned him to "cool it with the spices. I don't believe in using too many, perhaps a bit of curry. I have discovered, however, that a bit of freshly ground pepper in a dish can get a man's sexual glands working overtime."

Over an elaborate dinner table set with gold tableware, Mae claimed she always enjoyed an evening out "with the boys. Ever since my days in vaudeville, you boys have always adored Mae. I've always been your champion. I remember when the cops on Broadway in the 20s launched a clean-up campaign in the district and started roughing up you boys. I called the flatfeet together and gave them a piece of my mind. I reminded them that when they were clubbing one of you, they actually were beating up on a lady. After that, they let up on you homosexuals."

"Mae is an expert on homosexuals," Liberace said with a touch of mockery in his voice.

She did not pick up on this subtle put-down, accepting it as gospel. "That's because I understand you boys," she said. "Homosexuality comes from the soul. When a man is born with a female soul, he becomes homosexual. When a male soul is trapped in a woman's body, she becomes a lesbian. It's an accident of nature. I have nothing but pity for you homosexuals."

"I'm sure some of us don't want your pity," Hadley said. "We're having too much fun."

For the first time that evening, she seemed insulted but she carefully masked it. "Some homosexuals—obviously not the brightest—just think

265

they're having a good time. They're deluding themselves. In fact, gay sex is only a form of masturbation. In the end, it doesn't satisfy."

Merv laughed at the *double entendre*, even though she didn't seem to realize why.

"Only sex between a man and a woman can satisfy," she went on. "Also gay sex is only transitory. Most gays end up sad old aunties."

Mae's pronouncements were met with stony silence at table. She got up to excuse herself to go to the toilet to repair her makeup.

After she'd left the room, Merv in a soft voice said to Liberace, "I can't believe what I just heard. Mae West a homophobe? What if her millions of gay fans knew that? They'd turn against her, and they're the only fans she has left."

"The poor dear was born back in the Stone Age of 1893," Liberace said. "For a woman of that century, Mae is considered enlightened. After all, she wrote that play *Drag* in the 1920s."

"I'm sure drag is something on which she is an expert," Merv said sarcastically.

Later that evening, the entire party went once again to Liberace's kitchen where he served Mae's favorite dessert, rice custard. Over her second helping, she talked about her novel, *Babe Gordon*, which had first been published in 1930. With the help of some collaborators, she had adapted it into the Broadway play, *The Constant Sinner*. "I deliberately set out to offend public taste. Let my critics scream, but I had them lined up with erections for me at the box office. I based the character of Babe on myself. Call me a daughter of joy. The French, or so I was told, call women like me *les femmes amoureuses*. We're not talking street walkers here. Daughters of joy might be the lowest tramp on the street or a queen in the fanciest of boudoirs. People have called Mae immoral. How wrong they are. Like my character of Babe Gordon, I'm non-moral."

Before departing that night—"I've got to get my beauty sleep"—Mae gave Merv some unsolicited career advice. "If you want to succeed in show business, you've got to have a gimmick, a personality that audiences can immediately identify. With me, all I have to do is flash some diamonds. Perhaps walk across the stage in my distinctive way. I have my costumes— my spectacular hats, my hip-swirled gowns. Lee here takes after me. All he has to do is swish out onto the stage in bejeweled drag and seat himself at his glass-topped piano with his flickering candelabra. The world will get to know you, Griffin, if you find a gimmick. That's what show business is all about. Jean Harlow was nothing until she discovered peroxide. Monroe followed her example. Veronica Lake had those peek-a-boo bangs. When she cut them off, her career was over. You've got to create a vivid personality to get the suck-

266

ers to part with their greenbacks. Get a gimmick, for God's sake. Being a bland Mr. Nice Guy doesn't make it in show business. Maybe in hardware. It's okay to sing those romantic ballads. But crooners are a dime a dozen. You've got to get a sound like Frank Sinatra. Hell, you don't need a great voice to become a sensation as a singer. Billie Holiday, when she wasn't drugged, thrilled audiences and she couldn't sing a note. But we listened to her. Take Louis Armstrong and that foghorn voice. See how far you can go even with no talent."

"I'll take your advice, Miss West," Merv promised.

And suddenly the evening came to an abrupt end, Merv remembering Mae's departure as a vision in pink encased in ermine. That vision would remain in his memory forever.

***

"Ain't Mae grand?" Liberace asked, settling himself later on a chaise longue by his piano-shaped pool.

"Narcissistic as hell and maybe touched in the head with some of those opinions, but completely adorable," Merv said.

As Hadley and Paul came out onto the patio, Liberace asked the two men to take off their clothes and go skinny-dipping in his pool. "That would amuse Merv and *moi*," he said.

Without the slightest hesitation, Hadley stripped down like he'd done so many times before and jumped into the pool. Like a professional stripteaser, Paul slowly removed his Basque outfit. Standing before the two voyeurs, he took off his white shirt, revealing a powerful chest—long, lean, and beautifully muscled. A thin line of golden hairs trickled from the center of his chest to his navel, contrasting with the rich tan of his entire body. His broad pectoral muscles tapered to a slim waist. Merv looked on with anxious excitement. The pathway of Paul's golden hair led to a curly, lustrous bush of golden pubic hair. His extremities—legs, fingers, and arms were lean, his cock long and thick. After he was assured that both had taken a satisfying look,

Alone at last:
Liberace at home

267

he ran to the edge of the pool, jumping in to join a nude Hadley. The two men yelled and splashed about in the water.

"That is some piece of meat," Merv said.

"Let's make a deal," Liberace said. "I can have Paul any night, but I'd like to shack up tonight with Hadley for old time's sake. You can take Paul to my guest room for fun and games. A deal?"

"You're on, buddy" Merv said. "There are side benefits to our friendship that I am only now beginning to realize," Merv said.

"You ain't seen nothing yet, Fannie Mae," Liberace promised.

Merv would later confide to Paul Schone and Bill Robbins. "Paul Richardson took me into dreamland. I'd been a good boy until I met Liberace. But I have a feeling he's going to teach me how to live. You can say that that night at his house officially launched me into my Age of Decadence. Incidentally, my new nickname for him is Sadie. He calls me Fannie Mae."

***

Merv appeared on the set of *East of Eden,* released in 1955, for a reunion with James Dean. The two men had talked and smoked cigarettes for only fifteen minutes during a break in filming before they noticed two other men walking toward them.

Merv immediately recognized both figures. One was Humphrey Bogart, the other was Solly Biano, head of casting at Warner's. Under his breath, Merv whispered to James, "I hope Solly does more for your career than he did for mine."

Ignoring Merv, Solly introduced Bogie to the rising young star, who completely avoided eye contact with the screen legend. Solly had thought that Bogie and James would hit it off, because both of them were graduates of the "I Don't Give a Fuck" school.

"They say you're the hot new rebel in Hollywood," Bogie said. "I remember when they said the same thing about me. Welcome to the Rebel Club." Bogie shook James' hand, but the young actor did not look him in the eye. Still the gentleman, Bogie complimented James on his acting technique. That brought no response from James at all and he continued to stare at his own feet.

"They say you're great, kid," Bogie said.

"Yeah," James said. "So they say, whoever in the fuck *they* are. As if I give a good God damn rooster's asshole what people think of me."

That was too much for Bogie. He grabbed James by his jacket and yanked him around. "Look me in the eyes, you little cocksucker! When I talk to you, show some respect. I was wrong about you. You're just another stupid little punk with skid marks on your underwear. Another Brando clone. Just what Hollywood doesn't need. In two fucking years from now, no one will ever have heard of you." He shoved James back, nearly knocking him down.

Merv stood with Solly, as both of them looked perplexed as Bogie in a rage stormed off the set. James watched him go with a stunned expression on his face. "I never saw *Casablanca*," he said, "and I don't intend to. But I hear that Mr. Bogart plays a queer who ends up with Claude Rains and not Ingrid Bergman." He turned and walked away. That was the last time Merv ever saw him.

***

Even though his contract had less than three months to go, Merv wanted out. From out of nowhere, he'd received a surprise call with the offer of a gig, but was told "to keep your mouth shut until I announce the damn thing myself." To deal with his hurt pride, Merv had mentioned the gig only once to Gordon Douglas, but hadn't filled him in on any of the details.

Since his days in Hollywood were obviously numbered, Merv, along with Hadley and his other friends, began to throw a number of farewell parties. In many cases he invited men (and often their wives) with whom he'd enjoyed brief affairs.

One Sunday afternoon Jack Warner arrived on his doorstep without an invitation. Merv was astonished to see him. "Griffin, you've been to at least two dozen parties at my house, and you've never invited me once to one of your parties. Can I come in?"

When Jack was ushered into Merv's living room, the other guests, including Peter Lawford, Aldo Ray, Rock Hudson, and Janet Leigh were stunned. They became subdued in the presence of such a powerful studio mogul. After all, each of them might be up for a Warner Brothers movie in the future. But Jack put everybody at ease and became the life of the party, playing "Tea for Two" on Merv's old piano or else tap-dancing like Ann Miller on the black-and-white tiles of the kitchen floor.

At one point Merv and Jack sat by his pool devouring barbecue. The studio chief spotted Merv's Uncle Elmer across the way. "Who's the fatso?" Jack asked.

"That's my Uncle Elmer," Merv said. "The best tennis player in Los Angeles."

"Oh, yeah?" Jack said. "What am I? Chopped liver? I'll challenge him to a game next Sunday at my place. I'll give him Bill Orr—he's a really good partner—and I'll take Solly Biano. You can call Bill and Solly and make the arrangements," Jack said. "I'm too busy turning down script proposals from

Joan Crawford. I hear even that old broad, Bette Davis, wants me to take her back."

Before the tennis match that Sunday, Jack called two dozen of his friends, inviting them to "watch me beat the fat ass off Merv Griffin's uncle. He's Jackie Gleason plus two. I'll clobber him."

At the actual game, Merv sat under the shade of a giant peppermint-striped umbrella with Doris Day and Judy Garland, sipping sweet ice tea. Judy spiked hers from a flask in her purse. Doris complimented Judy for her performance in *A Star Is Born*, and then concentrated on the game and seemed genuinely interested. Merv later claimed that "Judy looked as amused as she would have been at a lecture on the mating habits of caterpillars."

The aging Uncle Elmer defeated the studio chief six love. No one did that and still drew a paycheck at Warners. Upon losing the game, Jack was in a steaming rage, so angry in fact that he threw his tennis racket across the court at Merv, narrowly missing his head.

The next day Merv showed up at Jack's office and told him he wanted out of his contract. "I mean, all your stars are gone. Who have you got left under contract these days? Doris and me? You need her. You don't need me."

"Five thousand and you're free as a bird," Jack said.

Merv wrote him a check on the spot. In front of Merv, Jack tore up the check after extracting a promise from Merv that he would not work for another studio for the next two years.

"I'm heading for New York and a live audience once again," Merv said.

Later that night he told Hadley that he'd counted on Jack tearing up that check. "Let's face it. We don't have five thousand dollars in the bank."

That same night Merv also told Hadley, "We're going to Vegas." Only a few nights before, he'd received a drunken phone call from Tallulah Bankhead, who remembered him from his appearance on *The Big Show*, her NBC radio program back in 1951. She didn't request but demanded that he be her opening act for her upcoming debut at the Sands Hotel.

Jack Warner would appear one final time in Merv's life when he gave his only television interview on December 14, 1972, on *The Merv Griffin Show*. He and Merv talked about the good old days in the heyday of Hollywood. Merv's former boss told anecdotes about Bette Davis, Errol Flynn, Humphrey Bogart, and even Al Jolson. As one of the prime players in Golden Age Hollywood, he embarrassed Merv by launching into what Merv later called a "Queegian rant" (a phrase inspired by the tyrannical Captain Queeg in *The Caine Mutiny*) about the new standards of Hollywood.

Jack attacked the new permissiveness and even defended the honor of the American flag against "pinko Communists." The studio audience applauded his John Wayne politics and Jack's stand for the American way of life, motherhood, and apple pie. Even though the audience cheered the patriotic comments, the old showman seemed to realize belatedly that his remarks would be condemned by much of young America. The appearance was his last and only television interview.

In the few years that remained, Merv heard that Jack was slowly fading, the once-mocking, buoyant "Prince of Hollywood" ending up sitting lifeless in a wheelchair, his eyes vacant, no longer knowing the old stars who came to call. Eventually he was shut off from even those visitors.

At the Cedars-Sinai Hospital, he died on September 9, 1978, at the age of eighty-six. "I'll miss the old fart," Merv said upon hearing the news. "In some hidden place in my heart, I sorta loved the monster. At least he gave the most fabulous parties in Hollywood. People don't know how to give parties like that any more. The party's over."

***

Merv left Hadley behind in Hollywood to pack up their possessions and close down the house, perhaps sprucing it up for the next rental. No one wanted the owner to assess damages to the property in the wake of the residency of Merv, his friends, and their many wild parties.

"While I'm doing the gig in Vegas, I don't want you to be the Slut of Hollywood," Merv warned Hadley. "Don't pick up something you can't get rid of, and, if you do, don't pass it on to me."

Hadley promised to be a good boy, although Merv heard that on only the second night of his stint in Vegas, Hadley was already in bed with Henry Willson, who was promising to make him a bigger movie star than Rock Hudson.

Henry had tactfully asked Paul Schone to move on. "Stardom isn't in the cards for you, kid," Henry had told the terribly disappointed young man.

"I noticed you waited to tell me this until after you'd sucked me dry," Paul said in protest.

"Nature has a marvelous way of replenishing the *leche* I drained," Henry assured him.

Disgusted with Hollywood agents and their promises, Paul took a job as a waiter in West Hollywood to earn enough money to resettle in New York along with Merv.

Bill Robbins was also disappointed that his career as an impersonator wasn't taking off. On the final night of his previous gig, he'd worked for no salary—only tips—netting only ten dollars. He'd promised Merv that he too would be joining him in New York as soon as he got some money together. "It's a known fact," Bill said, "that New Yorkers appreciate female imperson-

271

ators more than the idiots who inhabit the hills of Hollywood."

In a good-bye call to Johnny Riley in San Francisco, Merv learned that his long-time friend was fed up with "going nowhere day after day." He wanted Merv to rent an apartment in New York "with a spare room for me." He promised that he'd be joining Merv and Hadley in New York in just a few weeks. "I should have been a star by now," Johnny said.

"Tell me about it!" Merv said.

"In New York, I bet all of us will hit it big," Johnny said.

"Something like that!" a more skeptical Merv replied.

In a final call to Merv before flying to Las Vegas, Tallulah had told him, "Bette Davis got to play me in *All About Eve*. But at least I got to play Margo Channing on radio, and everybody told me I was better than that Davis bitch. Patsy Kelly and I went to see Jane Wyman, another bitch, in *Magnificent Obsession*. Wyman, so I'm told, got to fuck Rock Hudson. I decided after watching that damn stinker that I too wanted to fuck 'The Rock.' During all those years in bed with Ronald Reagan, I'm sure Wyman didn't learn anything about sex. I decided the next time I head west, I'm going to hit the Rock pile. I'm sure he'll know how to get my rocks off. After all, the only reason I came to Hollywood in the first place in the early 1930s was to fuck that divine Gary Cooper."

Her chance to snare Rock occurred when she'd signed with The Sands in Las Vegas for *An Evening with Tallulah Bankhead*, for which she was to be paid $20,000 a week. That was far less than Marlene Dietrich or Liberace could pull in, but Tallulah welcomed the $60,000 for a three-week stint. "I'm glad to see some hard cash flowing in," she told Merv. "The wolf is always at my door, dah-ling."

According to her agreement with The Sands, she had to appear on stage for only 45 minutes. She'd liked Merv's singing when he'd appeared on *The Big Show*, and she told The Sands she wanted him to open her act. "He's harmless enough, dah-ling, and won't be so sensational as to take the attention away from the *real* star of the show," Tallulah told Jack Entratter, the entertainment director. "He likes to suck cock, and I'm sure you can fix him up with some of your better-hung waiters."

Also appearing as warm-up acts were the Clark Brothers and the singer Virginia Hall. These performers, along with Merv, would be backed up by the Ray Sinatra Orchestra.

From Los Angeles, he migrated to Las Vegas, checking into a suite of his own at The Sands. He called Tallulah for a reunion, and she invited him to come up at once.

He was ushered into her suite by Patsy Kelly, one of the screen's best low-brow ladies of mirth, always good for a biting barb and a disgruntled look in

272

any film in which she was cast. Merv had heard that Patsy and Tallulah were lesbian lovers when they couldn't find more enticing partners. The fading actress was hung over. "Go on into Tallulah's bedroom," she told Merv. "She's expecting you. I'm going back to bed. I feel like shit."

In Tallulah's bedroom, Merv didn't see the fabled star. "Tallulah," he called out. "It's Merv."

"Come on in, dah-ling," she called from the bathroom.

Figuring she was applying her makeup, he stepped into the bathroom only to discover her sitting stark naked on the toilet, taking a big, smelly dump. "Don't be afraid, dah-ling," she called to him as he started to make a speedy exit. "Receiving you this way is a sign of affection. It's also a power play to show you who's boss. Lyndon Johnson has business conferences with his fellow senators while sitting on the can. I learned the trick from him. Don't tell Lady Bird, but Lyndon fucked me one night in Washington after a reception. He's got the biggest dick in Texas."

"Let's talk when you get dressed," an embarrassed Merv said.

She held up her not altogether fallen breasts for him to inspect. "These jugs in their day used to drive John Barrymore crazy. I just had them lifted, and I had to show someone. You're it, you lucky pervert. You're the first man who's seen them other than the surgeon."

"I'm honored . . ." he stammered.

"Tell all your straight friends, if you have any, that Tallulah Bankhead's in town and ready to receive. Spread the word that my tits look like those of a sixteen-year-old virgin. That'll have the boys knocking on the door to my boudoir at all hours of the day and night."

For her opening night, some of the biggest stars in Hollywood showed up. The most honored guests were the most famous couple of television, Desi Arnaz and Lucille Ball. Wearing a gold lamé dress and looking stunning, Marlene Dietrich sat beside the nation's most celebrated redhead and the Cuban bandleader. Friends of Merv's, Montgomery Clift and Jane Powell, were seated in the front row.

Tallulah
("What's left of her, *daaahling*")
Bankhead

Before the show, Monty had stopped by Merv's suite for a big kiss and a hello. "I couldn't miss the chance to see Tallulah fall on that well-worn ass of hers," he said. "I met the bitch in the late 40s. No good memories there. She groped me frantically. 'Where do you hide it, dah-ling?' she asked me. 'I can't feel a thing.'" He did a perfect imitation of Tallulah's voice. "A man doesn't forget a put-down like that."

With shaky knees, Merv got through his opening numbers. He felt rusty appearing again before a live audience.

The crowd rose to its feet when Tallulah belatedly made her appearance. Heavily made up to cheat on time, she looked stunning in a sparkling white Hattie Carnegie gown. In her best baritone drawl, she sang "What Do I Care?" and "You Go to My Head." At the end of those numbers, she tapped the microphone. "Dah-lings," she said, "it's the mike that's flat—not me."

Her singing was followed by dead accurate impressions, including a devastating one of her favorite actress, Ethel Barrymore. Tallulah brought screams of laughter, especially from her gay male fans, when she imitated Bette Davis in *Beyond the Forest*.

"Tallulah's 'What a dump!' line was better than a thousand female impersonators," Merv later said.

"Bette impersonated *me* in *All About Eve*," Tallulah told the first-nighters. "So it's okay for me to take my revenge."

Knowing that Marlene was in the front row, Tallulah performed a caricature of her slutty appearance in *The Blue Angel*. Later that evening, Lucille Ball told Merv, "Marlene wasn't impressed."

Tallulah was less caustic and more sympathetic quoting Dorothy Parker's "The Waltz." She ended her performance with a tender and rather nostalgic "I'll Be Seeing You," which brought the sold-out room to its feet.

For her curtain call, Tallulah stepped in front of the audience and delivered her favorite lines of poetry, which happened to be from Edna St. Vincent Millay.

> *My candle burns at both ends;*
> *It will not last the night;*
> *But ah, my foes, and oh, my friends,*
> *It gives a lovely light.*

***

Backstage, Tallulah in a makeup-smeared white robe greeted her well-wishers. When Marlene came into the overcrowded room to kiss Tallulah, she opened her robe to expose her newly lifted breasts to her. In a loud voice Tallulah told Marlene, "Dah-ling, I know you're ashamed of your breasts, and I don't want to make you jealous. But let's face it: Marilyn Monroe doesn't have knockers like this pair."

"Oh, Tallulah," Marlene said. "It's true that in America no one with good taste ever succeeded in show business."

Privately smoking a cigarette with Desi Arnaz, Merv recalled their meeting in San Diego with Cesar Romero. "Just between us fellows, you look great tonight," Merv said to Desi. "You look even better without your pants on."

"Maybe you'll get lucky one night when I don't have any other place to put it," Desi said. "Perhaps I'll let you sample the goodies if I'm drunk enough. I like to throw you girly men a bone every now and then."

"I can't wait," Merv said.

On the second night, Merv could not appear because he'd lost his voice. "It's the God damn desert virus," Jack Entratter told him. "I book acts into The Sands all the time. It's amazing how many performers—both men and women—come down with this sore throat."

Merv appraised Jack from head to toe, finding him the most physically rugged and the biggest man he'd ever seen in Vegas. "I bet before you became an entertainment director, you were a bouncer. Am I right?"

"Cut the shit," Jack said. "I've seen the way you've been checking me out. Cool it! I don't go that way. Just get your voice back by tomorrow night, and everything will be fine."

With his voice back the next night, Merv finished the engagement and later pronounced it, "the most exciting gig of my life." He would talk privately for years with his friends about all the fun he had hanging out in Las Vegas with Tallulah, the tempestuous heroine of the Broadway stage, several bad films, and one good one—*Lifeboat* (1944) directed by Alfred Hitchcock.

Three days went by before Tallulah invited Merv to her suite again. She had avoided him when he had laryngitis, because she said she always picked up the symptoms of anyone sick. "Not only that," she said, "but if a person stutters around me, I stutter; if he's got a tick, I involuntarily pick up that tick, even though I don't mean to mimic. Just fifteen minutes with Louis Armstrong, and I'm speaking in foghorn."

Invited for morning coffee, Merv was ushered into Tallulah's suite, where he was greeted by Patsy, who was hung over once again. She directed him to the sofa in the living room. "Make yourself at home," she said. "Jerk off. Do what you want. I'm hitting the sack again till mid-afternoon."

Staring at the walls, Merv heard sounds coming from the bedroom. The door opened. Instead of Tallulah, out emerged Rock Hudson with an impressive erection at half-mast.

"Rock!" Merv said in total surprise. "You and Tallu?" I can't believe it. President Eisenhower in that bedroom I could believe, even Queen Elizabeth II. But Tallulah Bankhead!"

"Stranger things happen during the Hollywood mating season," he said, moving toward Merv. "Now gimme a kiss and be quick about it."

Jumping up from the sofa, Merv attempted to kiss Rock on the lips. "Not there, dumb-dumb," Rock said. He took his big hand and clasped it around the back of Merv's neck, lowering him to the floor. His erection was now at full mast.

Rock had been shacked up with Tallulah only for the weekend and had to return to Hollywood that Monday afternoon. After kissing both Merv and Tallulah good-bye, he wished them the best of good luck during their return to New York, where they'd each pursue their separate goals. Tallulah would have to face a fading career, and Merv would have to confront no career at all.

Tallulah immediately spat on the carpet, then explained her bizarre action. "Any time someone wishes me good luck, I spit. Wishing someone good luck is a bad omen."

"The next time you're in Los Angeles, I'll be your escort," Rock told her before turning to Merv. "I'll call you in New York. Sing to make Frank Sinatra lose his hard-on."

After stepping into the hall, he stuck his head back in the door. Addressing Merv, he said, "Speaking of the devil, I ran into Sinatra last night in the casino. He wants to hook up with you. Give him a call."

"What about your mama here?" Tallulah asked. "Doesn't Frank want to fuck *me*? I'm not Ava Gardner, but hardly buttermilk either."

"Next time I see Frankie, I'll run that offer by him," Rock said with a departing smile.

After Rock's departure, Tallulah evaluated him to Merv: "I'm sure you've had him too. You boys in Hollywood always pass around the big meat. Rock is a walking streak of sex--pure testosterone. He's more masculine than any of those faggots—Clark Gable, Burt Lancaster, Robert Mitchum. They exude masculinity on the screen, but I know their past histories. All of them have taken it up the ass, at least when they were breaking into the business. Rock may be a big homo, but he's more man than any of those limp-wristed faggots."

"I wouldn't exactly call Gable, Mitchum, and Lancaster limp-wristed faggots," Merv said.

"So I exaggerated to make a point," she said. "It's the first time in my life I've ever stretched the truth. I'm from Alabama. One mark of a Southerner is that he always tells the truth—no tall tales." She cackled and reached for her drink.

Rock's friendship with Tallulah didn't end at The Sands. He would remain a fixture in her life and would continue to see both Merv and her. When Tallulah flew into Los Angeles, Rock was often her escort as he'd promised. She was one of the first visitors to arrive at his new home, which he'd christened "The Castle."

When her driver pulled up at his mammoth gate, she was surprised that it was left open. Ushered into his living room, she asked, "Why the open gate, dah-ling? I mean I know you're glad to see me. But aren't you afraid your fans will camp out on the grounds?"

"The reason is simple," he said. "If some good-looking stud wants to break in and fuck me, I don't want him to get all exhausted climbing some high fence."

At a premiere, a reporter asked Tallulah why she was seen so frequently with Rock. "I have learned that he carries a magic weapon," she shot back, parodying a line from his Arabian nights fantasy, *The Golden Blade*, a picture released in 1953 and now a gay camp classic.

In the years to come, Tallulah did more to establish the heterosexual credentials of Rock Hudson than any other actress in Hollywood. As quoted in David Brett's biography of the tumultuous star, she told all who'd give her an ear: "This divine young man is hung even better than Gary Cooper—and, believe me, dah-lings, Rock sure knows how to handle that two-hander of his."

***

When they weren't performing or drinking in lounges, the fifty-two-year-old Tallulah and the twenty-nine-year-old Merv were seen together on the town. Most observers thought Merv was Tallulah's latest trick, and, wanting to maintain his straight image, he didn't deny it to anyone who asked.

On some occasions she invited the most handsome and masculine of bartenders to feel her new breasts, following her mammoplasty. "Unlike some of those Vegas showgals with their plastic bobs, dah-ling, these jugs are real. All me! And a good place to lay that beautiful head of yours tonight."

Many of these bartenders accepted her offer. If she later discovered that they were gay, and had only come to her suite to "hang out with the legendary Tallulah Bankhead," she generously handed them over to Merv so he could service them. On one such occasion, she held up her fingers. "Thank God for masturbation," she said. "The practice has saved my life on many a dark night."

At times, the star, being Tallulah, made a drunken nuisance of herself. She asked Merv to accompany her to the hotel lounge across the street to hear Bobby Short perform. Once seated, she talked loudly through his entire performance. When Merv gently chided her to keep quiet, she answered in a loud voice, "I've always respected darkies, even as a young gal growing up in nigger-hating Alabama. I even went down on both Hattie McDaniel and Billie Holiday so that proves there's not one bone of prejudice in my body."

When she wasn't watching other performers, Tallulah was fascinated with Las Vegas gangsters, with names like Slasher, Lefty, Louis, Wingy, and Cincinnati. "Oh, dah-ling, I just love men who wear their hats indoors. Bugsy Siegel told me that all gangsters in Vegas are built like brick shithouses and hung like tyrannosaurs."

During her final week in town, Tallulah ordered Merv to invite five of the sexiest gangsters she'd met to her suite for a private party. On the afternoon before the party, she'd been drinking heavily. True to form, the five gangsters arrived and after checking out the rooms for a hidden assassin, they filed in.

Tallulah divided her time among the gangsters, sitting on each of their laps as she tongue kissed them, followed by a clinical grope. And in spite of her age and booze consumption, she even performed cartwheels for them. During the cartwheels, she revealed to the men that she wore no panties.

Before midnight, she whispered to Merv that she wanted him to usher each gangster—there were five in all—one by one into her suite at forty-five minute intervals. "That's half an hour for them to do their business, with fifteen minutes left for me to freshen up between bouts. After all, a lady wants to look presentable for her next suitor."

In later years, Merv swore that this gang-bang actually happened and wasn't just another one of those apocryphal Tallulah stories.

In her suite that night, Cincinnati was mobster number two to enter Tallulah's bedroom. She later invited him to spend the night for an encore.

When Merv arrived for coffee the following morning, Tallulah called for him to come into her bedroom. He discovered her lying nude in her bed with Cincinnati, who was just waking up. Seeing Merv, she pulled back the sheets to reveal the gangster in all his glory. "Take a sneak preview of that three-hander. Not since my honeymoon with John Emery have I encountered a billy club like this."

***

Dining at The Sands at the best table, near the end of their three-week gig, Tallulah and Merv were having a gay old time. She'd told the handsome waiter to take back her chicken and tell the chef to cook it more. "Dah-ling, we Southern belles like our fried chicken well done—not a rosy pink like the head of Sir Winston Churchill's big prick."

After the waiter left, a tall, slim, well-built young man approached their table and introduced himself as Truman Herron. "Actually, my professional name is Mark Herron."

"And what profession is that, dah-ling?" Tallulah asked. "Other than an answer to a maiden's prayer. Smart thinking to change that name. Truman's

278

already taken, both by our beloved president and that squeaky voiced Capote."

She introduced him to Merv and invited him to sit down between Merv and her. "That way I can grope you, dah-ling. I always like to check out a man before going to bed with him. I don't want any unpleasant surprises later. By the way, I have to warn you. Merv, that dear, dah-ling boy, gets my sloppy seconds. So it may be a long night for you. I just hope you know how to perform at both ends of the stage."

"I always rise to any occasion," Mark assured her. He launched into a rave review of their show, although he paid far more attention to Tallulah than Merv. Even so, he managed a flirtatious glance or two at Merv. He called Tallulah "the Queen of the American theater."

"Don't tell that to Katherine Cornell or Helen Hayes," she warned.

As the dinner progressed, Merv found himself increasingly attracted to Mark, although Tallulah seemed to have booked him for the night. He was good-looking but not extraordinarily handsome. Later when Tallulah discussed Mark in private with Merv, she claimed "he looks like a model for an Arrow shirt commercial. It's what Ronald Reagan should have looked like but didn't."

Under a head of deep brown russet hair, Mark had the most inquisitive brown eyes Merv had ever seen. He listened to what each of them had to say as if one of them were delivering the Ten Commandments, which he was hearing for the first time and would obey religiously. Not only that, but he had a quick wit and a bright mind. Merv thought that as a pet to have around, he'd beat any dog.

Almost immediately Tallulah picked up on his slight Southern accent. He told her that he was from Tennessee.

"I detected just a scent of the magnolia," she said. "A true Southern gentleman like my Daddy. I should have known you were from the South. It's the only place in the country where a gentleman knows how to treat a lady."

"Are you an actor?" Merv asked, suspecting that gigolo was his actual profession.

"How did you guess?" Mark asked. "I was voted Best Actor of the Year in 1952 at Los Angeles City College."

"And I was voted the worst actress of the year by the New York Film Critics when I barged down the Nile in *Antony and Cleopatra* back in 1937. That was

Judy Garland and Merv shared a common love interest: Her husband, **Mark Herron**.

279

centuries before you were born, dah-ling."

"Not quite," Mark said. "I was about nine at the time."

"Oh, please, dah-ling, people are eating!" she said.

"I'm sure you were magnificent as Cleopatra," he said, "and I wish I had been there to see it."

"Tell that to my critics," she said.

After dinner and after drinks in Tallulah's suite, the star motioned for Merv to get lost. Fortunately, he'd already arranged a midnight rendezvous with the waiter.

Merv showed up for coffee at his usual time the following morning and was greeted by the sight of Mark in his underwear. The young actor explained that Patsy Kelly was still "sleeping one off." In the living room seated opposite Mark, Merv had a chance for a more detailed exploration of his body, which he found very sexy. As if realizing he was being appraised like a hunk of meat, Mark said, "I look even better without my drawers."

"I'm sure Tallu found that secret out last night," Merv said, flirting with him. "She got the goodies while I was left out in the cold."

"Don't kid me," Mark said. "I saw you slip that note to our waiter. Just because Tallulah has invited me to fly back with her and live with her doesn't mean I've entered a convent. She said you're going to New York too for a new start. There's no reason we can't get together. Why don't you call me at Tallulah's?"

"That can be arranged," he said. "But I must warn you, I already have somebody."

"Hell!" Mark said. "We're not getting married. Only shacking up on the side. Guys as good looking as we are have already been taken by somebody."

"Let's keep this a secret," Merv said. "I don't want to make Tallu angry."

"She's hardly branded me," he said. "Realistically, I'd give this thing with the temperamental bitch three weeks, a month at the most. But I'm sure I'll get at least a thousand dollars—maybe two thousand—out of the gig before she kicks me out on my arse."

"A gig?" he asked. "Strange way to refer to it."

"You see, babycakes," he said, "I'm a star fucker. My goal is to marry one of the biggest stars in Hollywood. I mean, *big*."

"Who did you have in mind?" Merv asked.

"It doesn't matter. Lana Turner, Ava Gardner, Marilyn Monroe, even Judy Garland, although I hear she's a mess. Even if one of those pussies already has a husband now, how long will it last? Divorce lawyers make more money than movie stars in Hollywood."

"I'm not a big star, but I'd love to get fucked by you," Merv said.

"You don't have to ask," Mark said. "I do men for the fun of it."

"So I figured," he said.

"With women, I do the dirty deed for career advancement. Sometimes it turns my stomach and I have to go to the bathroom and throw up. I turn on the water in the faucet real loud and flush the toilet. That way the bitch in the bedroom can't hear me vomiting."

"How romantic!" Merv said.

Suddenly the husky voice of Tallulah bellowed from her boudoir. "Would one of you queens bring this real queen some fucking black coffee?"

***

Before he left Las Vegas, Merv got through to Frank Sinatra, who invited him for a night on the town. Frank promised him he'd fix him up with some of the "hottest pussies in Vegas."

"I'd rather not," Merv said. "But I'd like to spend an evening with you."

"Okay, I get it, pal," Frank said. "That's fine with me. We'll go on a binge like we did in Honolulu."

Merv later told Tallulah that Frank was still very grateful for Merv's having rescued him after he'd overdosed on sleeping pills. "He thinks he owes me something, but he doesn't owe me a damn thing. Frank doesn't like to be in debt to anyone."

"I'm proud of you, dah-ling," Tallulah said. "You saved one of the great musical talents of the 20th century. But did he fuck you? That's what I want to know. And, if so, is it as big as Ava claims?"

"No, regrettably," Merv said. "But we did end up in bed together last night. Both of us completely wasted. I should have held back on the booze and let him get sloshed instead. At least I can say, like Monty Clift, that I slept with the great Frank Sinatra."

"Dah-ling," she said, "Tallulah is never wrong about these things. If you play your cards right, Sinatra can be had. Go slow at first. Plot your moves carefully. I've developed a theory based on my wide knowledge of the subject. All the big-time womanizers can be had by a man who's a skilled seducer. Your day—or night I should say—will come. When he's in a weak and vulnerable moment, make your move like a coiled snake ready to strike its victim."

"That sounds pretty gruesome," Merv said, "but I'll take your advice."

"Now, let's get ready," she said. "It's our last night in Vegas, and I think we should gamble away all our earnings."

Tallulah meant what she said. Entertainers at The Sands were forbidden to gamble, but since when did Tallulah ever play by the rules?

Drinking heavily before hitting the tables, Tallulah told him that she'd heard about "a new tropical punch—it's called a Zombie, dah-ling." When the waiter served it, she was disappointed. "What is this? Kool-Aid?" Nevertheless, she drank it, and Merv also downed his Zombie.

Not realizing how lethal it was, she decided to order another round for them, and both of them drank their second Zombie. "I can't feel a thing. Let's switch to daiquiris." And so they did, having two daiquiris on top of the Zombies.

Not too steady on his feet, Merv practically had to hold Tallulah up as he escorted her to the blackjack table.

At the table, she told him she had two thousand dollars in "my lady's handbag—it's black, dah-ling. A true lady never wears brown at night. Merv had just cashed his paycheck that afternoon and had one thousand dollars in one hundred dollar bills.

Amazingly, they won the first round and kept on winning. "I'm on a roll, dah-ling," Tallulah shouted at the crowd that had formed a half moon around them to oversee their plays. The winning streak continued throughout the night, as Tallulah ordered the waiter to keep those drinks coming.

Before dawn, Merv later recalled, "both Tallu and I had a mountain of chips piled up in front of us."

A member of the staff alerted entertainment director Jack Entratter. Rising from his bed, he half dressed as he rushed downstairs to bodily remove Merv and Tallulah from the blackjack table, where some of the morning onlookers were standing around in their bathing suits. Jack cashed in the soggy pair's chips for them. Almost carrying them up the steps like they were ragdolls, he had Tallulah on his strong left arm, with Merv dangling from his right.

As predicted, Tallulah just had to have an exit line. Turning to the audience, she yelled, "Which one of you lucky bastards gets to fuck me tonight?"

Jack dumped Merv in the hallway while he put Tallulah to bed in her suite. Returning to the hallway, he retrieved Merv, then and hauled him away to Merv's suite.

All Merv remembered was the feel of hundreds of dollars stuffed into his trouser pockets. In the center of the darkened hotel suite, Jack turned on a light. Sitting in an armchair in the corner was a tall, dark man smoking a cigarette.

Leaving Merv on wobbly legs in the center of the room, Jack left but only after politely greeting the stranger. "Good evening, Mr. Hughes."

Merv passed out.

Chapter Seven

In his highly unreliable autobiographical writings, Merv claimed that he drove cross-country to New York with a former girlfriend. Johnny Meyer, the "public relations man" (read that as "pimp") for Howard Hughes had a completely different version. He claimed that Howard Hughes flew Merv from California to a small airport on Long Island.

Meyer said that he and his boss had attended the last show at The Sands featuring Merv as the warm-up and Tallulah Bankhead as the star. "Neither Bankhead nor Griffin knew Howard was in the audience that night," Meyer said. "Howard learned that he was going to lose his favorite tennis partner, Griffin, who announced that he was going to New York for a new start. Since Howard was flying east the next morning, he decided to take Griffin along for the ride."

According to Meyer, Howard got the manager of the hotel to let him into Merv's suite. When Howard discovered Merv "falling down drunk," he had him carried out of the hotel by two bellhops and placed in the back of his car. Meyer packed Merv's luggage.

Piloted by Howard, the private plane flew Merv and Meyer across the country. "When Merv finally woke up, we were somewhere over the Middle West," Meyer said.

Merv did remember waking up with a mouth that was so dry it was like it'd been stuffed with cotton. He also recalled the most pounding headache of his life. But in Merv's account, he claimed he woke up in a car being driven to Los Angeles. He did say, however, that the driver of that car was a friend called "Howard." Merv gave no last name.

Meyer had stuffed Merv's winnings in his shoes because "he had hundred dollar bills falling out of his pockets."

On the plane, Meyer told Merv that he'd won $15,000 at the blackjack table. Merv was elated. This was enough for a nest egg for re-launching himself in New York.

After counting his money carefully in the back of the plane, Merv settled in for a smooth ride. After all, he was being flown by the world's greatest aviator.

After their airplane landed, Merv had recovered to the point where he could play a game of tennis that afternoon with Howard on a lavish estate on Long Island. Howard had rented the estate in Southampton for the summer. After Howard had beaten Merv at tennis, he lent him a car to drive into New York City.

On the Lower East Side, Merv was reunited with Hadley, who'd driven cross-country with their luggage. Their living standards had changed drastically, going from a rented house with a pool in Los Angeles to a sublet in a cramped and tacky, cockroach-filled, fifth-floor walk-up apartment in Manhattan.

After a reunion in bed with Hadley that lasted for most of the night, Merv woke up groggy but sober enough to place a call to his agent. He urged his agent to find him work—"any kind of work so long as it's not as a dishwasher."

Before leaving Los Angeles, Merv ended his association with Bullets Durgom, his longtime agent. Merv knew that Bullets was devoting most of his time to his top-grossing client, Jackie Gleason, and had little time or energy left over for him. Bullets also devoted time to the careers of both Marilyn Monroe and Sammy Davis Jr.

Needing a new agent based in New York, the thirty-three year old Merv signed with Marty Kummer of MCA, who predicted big things for Merv in his future career. Marty not only worked for the largest talent agent in the country, but he also handled Jack Paar and Ed Sullivan. Merv told Marty, "I want either of their jobs. This big band singer shit is yesterday. I want to be an emcee on TV."

"Don't you watch *The Eddie Fisher Show*?" Marty asked. "Eddie is fine singing about his pa-pa or that lady in Spain, but he can't talk. He's a fucking train wreck."

"But I can sing *and* talk," Merv protested.

"I'll do my best for you, kid," Marty said. "But let's start at the bottom before we knock Paar off the air." Merv later had only the highest praise for Marty, claiming that he paid as much attention to a client if he "were making ten dollars or ten thousand dollars" on a job.

Within a week, Marty came through for him with a summer telecast for CBS. *Summer Holiday* was broadcast in two fifteen-minute segments on Tuesday and Thursday at 7:45pm. In winter the show was very popular, featuring stars who included Perry Como, Jo Stafford, and Dinah Shore. Merv and singer/actress Betty Ann Grove were the summer replacements.

A petite redhead with a powerful voice, Betty never made it big on Broadway, although she'd starred in Cole Porter's *Kiss Me Kate*. She would achieve her greatest fame appearing on *The Bert Parks Show*, where she worked well with that star's manic, eye-batting vitality.

Before she left for the summer, Jo Stafford greeted Merv and wished him well. In San Francisco during World War II he'd listened to her wistful singing voice. She was nicknamed "GI Jo" by American servicemen and was viewed as the vocal embodiment of every GI's dream, the voice that kept the home fires burning while the men were fighting overseas.

Merv was impressed that her recording of "You Belong to Me" had sold two million copies in 1952. He envied her success. For her finale on the show, she invited Merv to join her in a duet with her standard, "I'll Be Seeing You." Their voices blended harmoniously, and she invited him to join her for dinner. Since she was one of Hadley's favorite singers, Merv asked if his friend could come along too. Jo graciously extended the second invitation.

Over dinner Merv told her how his voice had deserted him in the sandy winds around Las Vegas. "I don't think I'm going to depend on my voice to put bread on the table," he said. "It's too unreliable. I want to do something else."

Instead of urging him to stick to singing, she encouraged him to go in another direction. "Sinatra . . ." She paused. "I'm meeting him later tonight. Don't say a word about it or I'll cut off the balls of both you boys. Sinatra and Judy will probably go on until The Grim Reaper comes to call. At this point they're icons. Not little ol' me. I fear my days as a pop singer are coming to an end. Of course, I can always work the market of GIs nostalgic for the songs they heard during the war. But my kind of music—your kind of music—may be over. I'm not sure America will be listening to romantic ballads in 1965. Haven't you heard 'Shake, Rattle & Roll'? There's a new sound in the air. A new kid on the block. His name is Elvis Presley."

On *Summer Holiday*, both Merv and Betty were to simulate trips to various places in the world. On his first day on the show, Merv met the producer, Irving Mansfield. Today Irving's claim to fame is his marriage to the best-selling novelist Jacqueline Susann, a failed Broadway actress who would write *The Valley of the Dolls* (1966), one of the best-selling novels of all time.

Irving invited Hadley and Merv to dinner where they met his sultry wife. Merv had heard all the gossip about the bisexual actress, who'd had an affair with Carole Landis when she appeared with her on Broadway in *A Lady Says Yes* in 1945. Landis would later commit suicide in 1948 by overdosing on sleeping pills. She was said to be despondent over the break-up of her affair with Rex Harrison, whom Merv called "Sexy Rexy."

The gossip circuit along Broadway also claimed that Jacqueline was having an on-again, off-again affair with Ethel Merman. In 1959 Jacqueline would also have an affair with the fashion designer Coco Chanel.

After dinner that night with Mr. and Mrs. Irving Mansfield, Merv and

Jacqueline Susann never became friends, Merv preferring to speak of her privately as "my old acquaintance," borrowing the title from the Bette Davis/Miriam Hopkins movie. He would know her until the day of her death on September 21, 1974. At the age of sixty-six, Susann succumbed to cancer.

Merv and Susann never liked each other, but each of them figured they'd have some use for each other in their futures. Behind his back, Susann called Merv "a faggot." On the other hand, he was delighted when Truman Capote appeared on *The Tonight Show* and claimed that Susann "looks like a truck driver in drag."

When she started writing novels, and Merv was a successful talk show host, he claimed that the bubble gum author was the first to effectively exploit the TV talk show circuit to promote a novel.

When he heard that she was in the hospital, Merv in 1974 visited her, hoping that she'd make a final appearance on TV with him. But he discovered that she was "too eaten up with cancer, too weak." She told him she was unable to complete her last novel, *Dolores*. After her death, the movie critic Rex Reed completed the final chapters, which was to be Susann's take on Jacqueline Kennedy Onassis.

Upon hearing of her death, Merv told a reporter, "Jacqueline Susann was the Joan Crawford of novelists." In time Susann became a gay male pop culture icon.

***

Mark Herron had seen it coming: after only three nights with Tallulah Bankhead in her New York home, she asked him to move on. Merv had arranged through his agent, Marty Kummer, to give Mark his telephone number should he try to contact him.

Mark called Merv and invited him for lunch in his suite at the Plaza Hotel.

"The Plaza?" Merv said. "Our dah-ling Tallulah must have taken care of you very well."

"Not at all," Mark said. "Not a cent. But I've got another gig. Come on over and I'll tell you all about it."

A handsome six-footer, Mark greeted Merv in his suite and gave him a long, passionate kiss on the lips. "I've been hot for you, baby, ever since that first night," Mark said. "I know you've been dying to see what's in my underwear."

"I want to do more than see it," Merv said as he looked around the suite. It was filled with gowns, high-heel shoes, make-up kits, and recent shopping purchases. "Your new 'gig' must be some super glamorous puss . . . and rich."

"She is," Mark said smugly. "You know her as Lana Turner. Right now she's shopping on Fifth Avenue and plans to spend the early evening getting plowed by Frank Sinatra."

"I didn't know either of them was in town." Merv gave Mark a congratulatory kiss. "I've got to hand it to you, boy. First, Tallulah Bankhead. Then Lana Turner. Who's next?"

"I can't decide," Mark said. "If you make it big on TV, it'll be Merv Griffin. I'm trying to hook up with Marilyn, but so far Miss Monroe has evaded my butterfly net. She won't even return my calls. Maybe I'll switch to redheads. I'm thinking about Arlene Dahl right now—she's beautiful. I've fucked Cary Grant, and he's got the hots for me. But, so far, the tightwad hasn't set me up in my own apartment. I've got two other prospects crazy for my ass. Henry Brandon, for one."

"You mean Acacius Page from *Auntie Mame?*" Merv asked.

"One and the same," Mark said. "And get this. Charles Laughton has taken a more than fatherly interest in me."

"He's a brilliant actor, but the ugliest man on the screen. We're talking *The Hunchback of Notre Dame* here."

"I don't just fuck beauties or little cutie pies like you," Mark said. "I screw anybody, male or female, beast or beauty, if they're a star."

"Let's quit talking about fucking and do some of it," Merv said.

"You're in for a treat," Mark said. "I'm good."

Two hours later, with both men sitting in their underwear in the living room of Lana's suite, Merv agreed. "You're good. You motivate me to really make it big so I can have you full time."

"I'll be ready whenever you are," Mark promised.

Suddenly, the door to the suite opened and in barged Lana Turner, accompanied by a bellhop loaded down with packages. "Don't bother to get up or get dressed for me, gentlemen," she said when she saw them sitting half dressed on her sofa. She kissed Mark on the lips and shook Merv's hand. "I know you. Frank took me to the Grove to hear you sing."

"I remember it well," Merv said, feeling embarrassed to have been caught like this in front of the screen legend.

"Speaking of Frank," Lana said, "that God damn wop fucked up my plans for the night. Would you believe it? My darling gal pal, Ava Gardner, winged into town on her broom, and Frank's hard-on tonight is reserved for her. Of course, they invited me to join them in a three way, but I wasn't up for it. I tried three ways with Tyrone Power and Howard Hughes. Those two paid more attention to each other than to me. Then I figured that in a three-way with Ava, Frank would pay more attention to his lady love than to me. I never like second billing. So I told them I didn't want any part of their fun and games." She checked out the male bodies on her sofa. "Did you boys have fun this afternoon when mama was away?"

"Lover-ly," Merv said. It seemed that she didn't have a jealous bone in her body. Years later, Lana's daughter, Cheryl Crane, revealed to talk show host, Larry King, that her mother, for a woman of her time, was remarkably sophisticated about homosexual relationships.

Merv excused himself to get dressed in the satellite bedroom where Mark and he had so recently made passionate love. Lana retired to her boudoir to get dressed for dinner. Back in the main living room, Merv looked for Mark but didn't see him. He assumed that he'd retired with Lana to her boudoir.

About half an hour later, as Merv was pouring himself a drink, Lana emerged from her boudoir. A vision in white satin, she'd never looked lovelier. "I want you to escort me to dinner tonight," she said, almost as if issuing an imperial command. "My darling Mark was called away to spend an evening with Charles Laughton, who is also in town. Mark is Laughton's new *protégé*, you know."

Merv eagerly agreed to escort Lana, calling Hadley to tell him that he didn't know when he'd be home. He was proud to be seen on the town with Lana, and he hoped that Walter Winchell would write it up in tomorrow's column. He'd been dazzled by Lana ever since he'd seen her on the screen in *The Postman Always Rings Twice* (1946).

When Lana made a spectacular entrance into Sardi's every head at every table turned to take her in. She was, after all, one of the most glamorous stars of Hollywood's Golden Age. Even though she held her head high, Merv sensed Lana's nervousness. She held onto him too tightly. She was really scared, although she relaxed a bit after she was seated and after her drink had arrived. She looked fabulous, yet was sensitive about her appearance. She had reached *that* certain age—in her case, her mid-thirties.

To make the moment a complete disaster, two elderly ladies passed by their table, stopping to gaze upon Lana. "Honey, you sure don't look like you did when you were in the movies with Mickey Rooney."

"Who in the fuck does?" Lana shot back. The ladies hastily retreated, one of them saying, "Well, I never . . ."

"Lana you look great," Merv immediately reassured her. "The hottest woman in New York. In the whole world as far as that goes."

She merely smiled at him before ordering another drink. He noticed that her hands were visibly shaking. "But how long can I go on looking like this? How long will it last? Every day I stare for an hour at my face in the mirror, looking for telltale changes. New blondes are coming along—take Marilyn Monroe for instance. One night Betty Grable and I had a long talk about what was going to happen to pin-ups like us from World War II. Rita Hayworth is facing our same problem. Those glory days of World War II are long gone. I meet young GIs from 1945 who are now bald and pot-bellied."

"You'll go on forever," he said, not really meaning it.

What happened later in that evening became fodder for a Hollywood legend. Lana herself, of course, never addressed the rumors spread about her that night. Merv, to protect the lady's privacy, never commented either. Years later, Mark Herron claimed that the legend was true, although he was not with Merv and Lana that night.

The rumor may have been apocryphal, an urban legend.

After Merv's "date" with Lana, a story spread from the New York islands to the coast of California. According to an unverified report, Merv took Lana to the Cotton Club in Harlem that night. After one long drunken evening, Merv reportedly was put in charge of guarding the entrance to the men's room.

Presumably inside the toilet, Lana was said to have performed fellatio on five "Mandingo types" that had been pre-selected by her earlier in the evening. It was claimed that Merv allowed the lucky men in one at a time.

In her autobiographical writings, Lana denied her interest in oral sex, especially with Howard Hughes, but many of her lovers claimed that she was a skilled oral artist in the boudoir. Lana's antics that night in Harlem even made the newspapers, but only as part of veiled references.

When cornered by Hadley for the sordid details, Merv said, "That's one secret I'll take to my grave."

***

Late the following morning, Merv had brunch with Charles Laughton and Mark Herron. If Merv revealed secrets about what had happened the previous evening with Lana in Harlem, they'd have been told to Mark, in private, following brunch with the great actor.

When he met Charles, Merv exclaimed, "Oh, my God! Captain Bligh and Henry VIII all rolled into one."

"The honor is mine," Charles said, seating himself on a banquette between Mark and Merv. Merv later swore that the actor kept groping both of them throughout the course of brunch. Skipping the bacon and eggs, Charles demanded that the chef prepare cucumber sandwiches—"light on the mayonnaise and with the crust cut off the bread."

Fleshy, with a jowly face and beady eyes, Charles was a star in spite of his looks. He was versatile, inimitable, and unforgettable. Knowing that Merv had appeared with Tallulah Bankhead, Charles related stories about her when they'd made *Devil and the Deep* back in 1932. "Both of us were pursuing Gary Cooper, but Tallulah got him," Charles claimed. "How could I compete

289

with a tornado like her? I'll always remember her first words to me. 'Gary Cooper is a divine man,' she told me. 'But you, *Charlotte*, are a repulsive, fat mess of glop!'"

The paunchy actor was the first to admit, "I know I'm no Tyrone Power. Let's face it: I have a face like the ass of an elephant."

Over his delicate sandwiches, Charles also related stories of the filming of *Night of the Hunter* (1955), in which he'd directed Robert Mitchum. "I came to his dressing room and begged him to let me see him in the nude. I confessed that there was a strong streak of homosexuality in me. Mitchum is never known to be shy about dropping his trousers. He stripped for me and put on quite a show. Even got it hard. But he refused to let me play with it."

Merv was all ears during the brunch, letting the actor do all the talking. But he did interrupt Charles's dialogue long enough to find out how he'd met Mark. It seemed that the aging actor had become so fascinated with Mark at a tryout in Hollywood that he'd taken him East to appear in the Broadway revival of George Bernard Shaw's *Major Barbara*. He'd gotten Mark cast as Barbara's stuffy brother, Stephen.

During a tryout in Boston, however, the backers of the show decided that Mark wasn't up to the role. Defying Charles's protests, they fired him.

"What chance did I have?" Mark asked defensively. "I was up against a cast that included Glynis Johns, Eli Wallach, and Burgess Meredith."

Charles placed his hand lovingly over Mark's, which was resting on the table. He assured him that he'd secure bigger and better roles for Mark in the future. Merv felt that Charles was just using promises of future work as a tool of seduction, which, of course, he was.

At the end of the brunch, as Charles heaved himself up from the table, he patted both Merv and Mark on their cheeks. "Both of you charming boys will have to excuse me but I have an appointment with that darling Tyrone Power this afternoon at his hotel."

"My final advice to both of you precious chaps is this. If either of you make the horrible decision to get married, believe you me such a marriage can survive the obstacle of homosexuality. Of course, there will be pain from time to time on the part of the wife."

Charles Laughton

Since Lana was entertaining Frank Sinatra and Ava Gardner that night in her suite, Mark scheduled a date with the German-born veteran actor Henry Brandon. He usually played villains in films and had just completed what was to be his most memorable role, that of Chief Cicatrice in John Ford's *The Searchers*. In spite of a famous marriage that lay in Mark's future, he and Henry would become lifetime companions until Henry's death of a heart attack in Los Angeles in 1990.

When Frank heard that Merv was in town, he asked Lana to include him as one of her guests that night. Merv was the first to arrive at Lana's hotel suite, and was greeted by the smell of chicken frying. "It's Ava's favorite food," Lana said. "I have this small kitchen, so I hired one of the hotel chefs to cook dinner for us tonight. It'll be *intimate*. Frank and Ava aren't here yet."

Within thirty minutes, Ava arrived wearing a red dress and a mink coat. "Where's that son of a bitch?" she asked before greeting Lana and Merv. "The fucker told me he'd be on time for once in his wasted life."

After settling in for drinks, Ava an hour later claimed she was starved for some of the fried chicken she'd been smelling all night. Even though Frank still hadn't appeared, she begged Lana to order dinner served. "If the bastard shows up, I'll call room service to bring up some spaghetti. That's all Ring-a-Ding-Ding eats anyway other than pussy."

When the chicken was placed on the beautifully set table, Ava looked horrified. "Where's the fucking gravy? What's fried chicken without gravy?"

MOVIE STARS!
Left, **Frank Sinatra** with **Ava Gardner**
Right, **Frank Sinatra** with **Lana Turner**
Inset: **Merv**

Though wearing an expensive dress, she went into the cramped kitchen where she emerged later with the gravy. "This Tarheel Bitch is the best God damn gravy maker on God's green earth," she said.

After tasting it, Merv agreed that it was the best he'd ever eaten. Ava had demanded both cornbread and hot biscuits, and she got her wish. The freshly baked apple pie she'd requested was sent up by room service from the hotel kitchen below.

After dinner, when Frank still hadn't arrived, Ava rose from the table, a bit wobbly on her feet. "I'm out of here. If Frank shows up, tell him I'm fucking Mickey Rooney tonight for old time's sake."

An hour later Frank came into the suite, with apologies to Lana. When he asked where Ava was, Lana gave a weak excuse, suggesting she might have given her the wrong date.

"Fuck her!" Frank said. "We'll party without her." He warmly embraced Merv. "Here's the guy who saved my life. I owe him one."

"You don't owe me anything," Merv protested to him once again. "Payback is hardly necessary."

What happened later that night may never be known. All three participants—Frank, Lana, and Merv—are dead, and none wrote about the night in their memoirs. Mark Herron later provided the most speculation, but he wasn't there in the suite until three o'clock the following morning.

According to Mark, Frank finally let Merv give him that blow-job while he was kissing Lana and fondling her breasts.

It is for that reason that Merv appears today on those international lists of Frank's lovers. A typical list—say, one compiled by Mark Winburn—includes Lauren Bacall, Doris Day, Marlene Dietrich, Zsa Zsa Gabor, Shirley MacLaine, Marilyn Monroe, Grace Kelly, Jacqueline Kennedy, Nancy Reagan, Elizabeth Taylor, Gloria Vanderbilt . . . and Merv Griffin.

A tantalizing show business hierarchy.

***

The gigs, around 1953, were few and far between, and bookings to sing were so insignificant that Merv had difficulty recalling them in later years.

He became accustomed to last-minute appearances on radio and TV, especially if someone got sick and had to fill in. "I was a utility singer," Merv told *The Miami Herald*. "I knew every song that was ever written. If someone couldn't do their number singing in front of a waterfall, everybody would say, 'Call Merv—he knows all the waterfall songs.'"

His reviews were never raves, but pleasant. *The New York Herald Tribune* referred to him as "a glib, likable, singing emcee type."

Of those days, Merv said, "I did anything that was offered to me. I just loved the feeling of a live audience."

Suddenly, as if to break Merv's monotony of a stalled career, Monty Clift showed up in New York. He'd filmed *Indiscretion of An American Wife* with Jennifer Jones. It was produced and directed by Vittorio De Sica, with extra dialogue by Truman Capote.

Over the phone, Monty told Merv that he was having a brief affair with Truman Capote and asked Merv if he could bring the author over for dinner. In response, Merv invited both Truman and Monty. "I'm eager for you guys to meet the one true love of my life." Merv, of course, misstated the depth of his romantic attachment to Hadley, which was far more casual than what he was suggesting.

He was shocked when a dissipated and underweight Monty arrived on his doorstep. He was gaunt and disheveled, his clothes looking as if he'd slept in them for the past four nights. Truman seemed as drunk as Monty but was immaculately groomed, wearing a white sports coat with a chartreuse lining.

It was obvious that Monty was still taking too much Demerol. Merv had heard that the drug made its victims increasingly paranoid. Truman appeared not to care, but it was obvious to Merv as the evening progressed that Monty felt everyone was out to get him...everyone except Hadley.

Seated on Merv's sofa, Monty was almost on top of Hadley, virtually ignoring Merv and Truman. "At last," Monty announced, "I've found a man who understands me. A kindred spirit. I have the same kind of feeling when I'm with Elizabeth."

Intoxicated though he was, Truman still had his eagle eye, and he kept glancing at Merv for signs of jealousy. At that point in their relationship, Merv had gotten used to sharing Hadley, so he wasn't particularly jealous of Monty's interest in his boyfriend.

Merv's dinner of beef stew, cooked by Hadley, was interrupted that night by a phone call. The call upstaged Truman just as he was relating the most tantalizing story about the night Errol Flynn fucked him.

"I'm Monty's friend," came a rather ominous voice on the phone. At first Merv thought the call was for Monty, but the strange voice claimed he wanted to speak to Merv.

Earlier in the evening, Monty had told Merv that he'd given out his number to three different friends, any of whom might be calling. "You don't love him!" the mystery voice said to Merv.

Terrible Truman

293

"I do! You hangers-on just use Monty. You're trying to destroy him. You'll pay for what you're doing to him. I'm going to follow you down streets on dark nights. You're fucking with the wrong person when you're messing with me. One foggy night I'm going to stab you in the back." He slammed down the phone.

At first, Merv thought that Monty had been playing some cruel joke on him, as he'd been known to do such things in the past. But the voice had sounded too real, too upset, and too psychotic to be a joke.

At the dinner table, Merv interrupted Monty's fixation on Hadley and Truman's heavy drinking to tell about the phone call. "A weird friend of yours called," he told Monty. "He's threatening to stalk me. Stab me in the back on one Jack the Ripper night in New York."

"Oh, that's just Manfred," Monty said. "He's perfectly harmless—just had too much to drink. He tries to possess me, and he never will. He's a personal friend, a plastic surgeon by profession. As a side line, he's a necrophiliac."

"What's that?" Hadley asked.

"A person who gets off having sex with dead bodies," Truman said.

"That's disgusting!" Hadley said. "I like mine live and kickin'."

"Necrophiliacs have always fascinated me," Truman said. "Monty has promised to take me to his friend's next sex party. These parties are staged spontaneously. You have to wait until some young hot body—preferably male—dies, perhaps in a car accident. The body is taken to this morgue where they have a deal. I want to observe how one makes love to a dead corpse. I'm considering writing a short story about it. Perhaps I'll call it *Dead Bodies and Other Delicious Indulgences.*"

"Monty, I always thought you liked live people," Merv said. "Is this some new kick?"

"Don't be an ass!" Monty said. "I go to their parties because, unlike you, I'm not judgmental. I believe an artist must take the blinders off and look at all forms of human behavior, even love that takes a bizarre twist. I don't condemn people like you do. That's why I love Elizabeth so much. She tries to understand human foibles, not apply some stupid, smug condemnation to desires."

"But dead bodies?" Merv protested. "Come on. As Tallulah would say, 'Please, *dah-ling*, people are eating.'"

At that point, Monty indulged in one of his food attacks, for which he was becoming known around town. He picked up his plate of beef stew and tossed it into Merv's face. Sitting silently, Merv looked down as the stew beef, carrots, and onions oozed down his white shirt.

"C'mon," Monty said to Hadley. "Let's get the fuck out of here."

Hadley rose to his feet, as Monty almost collapsed into his strong arms.

The actor stood on wobbly legs, almost too drunk and drugged to leave the room without bodily help. "I hope you won't mind," Hadley said to Merv. "I'd better see that he gets home safe. I'll be back real soon."

"Yeah, right," Merv said. "You are, after all, a star fucker, and there's no doubt that Montgomery Clift is a genuine star."

As Hadley helped Monty to the door, Truman under his breath said, "Yes, a fallen star."

After they'd gone, Truman turned to Merv. "Now we gals can get down to some serious gossip. I'll tell you about the time I went down on Humphrey Bogart when we were making *Beat the Devil* in Italy. He said he'd let me suck him off, but absolutely forbade me to swallow his semen. He told me I had to spit it out. But after the son of a bitch came in my mouth, I swallowed it down to the last drop."

***

That fall, with no local television jobs available in New York, Marty booked Merv in nightclubs and hotel lounges in the East, principally in Ohio, Pennsylvania, and New Jersey. Merv remembered these gigs in what he called "dives, blood buckets, and seedy motels."

Still dreaming the dream of being an emcee on television, Merv sang "I've Got a Lovely Bunch of Coconuts" every night to drunken, smoke-filled rooms, along with many of the songs he'd performed in the 1940s while touring with Freddy Martin's band.

Both Hadley and Merv tried to hold onto their diminishing nest egg, which had dwindled to less than $10,000. On some nights, the money Merv made didn't pay for the gas and the motel room. To economize, Hadley shopped at local grocery stores. Before leaving New York, he'd purchased a hotplate on which he fried hot dogs or scrambled eggs. He recalled that some of their motel rooms were "so small that mice had to go piggy back to cross the floor."

To add spice to their sex lives, Hadley sometimes managed to lure a handsome young waiter or a bellhop to their bedroom. Before heading on tour, Liberace had given Merv a list of so-called gay bars in some of the towns where he'd already played.

"Everything was very discreet in those days," Hadley said. "There were gay bars but they were risky. Any bar filled only with male patrons could be raided at any time by the police. Still we found some secret hideaways, and many of them had pianos. After singing all night in a club, Merv often entertained the boys at these tawdry bars with his singing. He was also a great hit in these bars, and often we'd pick up something on the hoof for the night. It was fun, really. In those days Merv always threatened that he was going to give up singing. But he'll be singing when he's eighty. Merv Griffin is a total ham, but I find that quality in him adorable."

When Merv learned that his old friend, Marlon Brando, was sailing to Europe, he called Marlon and asked if he could sublet his apartment, the one where the star had lived with Wally Cox and his pet raccoon. Marlon was relieved to have Merv as a tenant and asked that only one closet be reserved for his personal items—"and kept locked at all times."

Once in residency, Merv could not resist the temptation to see what the mystery closet held, thinking it might contain pornographic pictures of Marlon with various stars, male or female. To his surprise, the closet mostly seemed to hold the wreckage of an electric toy train. Nonetheless, he went to the hardware, as he'd promised Marlon, purchased a lock, and securely locked the closet, leaving the key for Marlon upon his return.

The apartment still reeked of Marlon's pet raccoon, which had long departed. The animal had never been potty trained. When Shelley Winters once visited the apartment to get seduced by Marlon, she said, "the raccoon smelled like it'd just let eighteen farts." When Merv and Hadley moved in, it took them nearly a month to erase the lingering odor of that raccoon.

Marty tried to get work for Merv on Broadway, and even advised him to wear platform shoes so he'd look taller on stage. Merv auditioned for Richard Rogers and Oscar Hammerstein II, hoping to secure the part of Prince Charming in their TV production of *Cinderella*. Before these music men, he sang "It Might As Well Be Spring."

Before he could finish the number, Rogers called for him to stop singing. "Let me get this straight," he said to Merv. "Are you impersonating Margaret Whiting or Frank Sinatra? Dismissed. Next!"

Max Liebman agreed to audition Merv for a role in his TV special, *The Desert Song*. Merv walked on stage a bit wobbly in his elevated shoes. "What are you trying to be? A comedian?" Liebman asked. "What makes you think you're right for the role?"

"You got me there," Merv said. "Frankly, I think I'd be lousy in the part."

"Then get the hell out," Liebman said. "You're wasting my God damn time."

Marty was furious when he heard what Merv had said. He warned him, "Don't pull that shit again. Who do you think you are? James Dean?"

He eventually got over his fury at Merv and once again set about getting work for him. A break came when Marty found Merv a job filling in as host for Barry Gray. The smooth-talking but tart-tongued Gray in time became known as "The Father of Talk Radio." His shows were broadcast from Chandler's Restaurant on East 46th St. between midnight and 3am.

At first, sponsors didn't believe that listeners would stay up that late. But they did. Not only that, but Gray began to book top talent onto his show, including Danny Thomas, Phil Silvers, and Eddie Cantor.

When Merv filled in for Gray, he could not have known at the time that he was beginning a career as a talk show host that would bring him fame and fortune in the years to come. Instead of radio, it would, of course, be on television.

When Merv took over the show, the columnist Walter Winchell was still feuding with Gray over an incident involving Josephine Baker at the Stork Club. She'd claimed on Gray's show that the club owner, Sherman Billingsley, had refused her service.

One of Billingsley's best friends, and a regular at the Stork Club every night, Winchell counterattacked. He denounced Gray as a "pro-Communist" and made veiled references claiming that the announcer was also a homosexual. He spread the word at the Stork Club that Gray sucked off men in subway toilets. The feud between Winchell and Gray became so intense that both men began carrying pistols threatening to kill each other.

When it was announced that Merv was going to be a substitute host, Winchell placed a secret call to him one Saturday around two o'clock in the morning. "I know you're trying to get a career jump started," Winchell said to him in an ominous voice. "Hedda Hopper has given me the goods on you. There are two things your listeners might want to know about you."

"What's that?" Merv asked.

"First, that you're a cocksucker. Hedda gave me the full report. Second, that you joined the Communist Party in Los Angeles as an active cell member."

"That's a god damn lie," Merv said. "I'm not a homosexual, and I don't even know what a Communist smells like."

"Go on the show and I'll ruin your career." Winchell slammed the phone.

Defying Winchell, Merv subbed for Gray whenever he was needed. As a favor to Merv, Frank Sinatra once came onto the late show. He was accompanied by a blonde showgirl but didn't introduce her. "We stay up late, you know," Frank said. "As the song goes, Broadway babes don't get to bed until the dawn. Until the milkman comes. Shit, I forgot the fucking words."

Winchell did not attack Merv in his column, but Merv later claimed that Winchell hired "a goon" to mug him as he was walking back to Marlon's apartment in the pre-dawn hours. Merv's wallet was stolen and his eye blackened, and he always blamed Winchell for the assault, even though it could also have been a routine mugging.

At long last, in 1954, a big break came when Marty got Merv cast as one of the male leads opposite Helen Gallagher in a revival of *Finian's Rainbow* by the New York City Center Light Opera Company. Cast opposite them was Will Mahoney, who would be nominated for a Tony as Best Featured Actor in a Musical.

Even though he'd emerged as a Broadway "star," Merv was disappointed to learn that his salary would be only eighty-five dollars a week. "I made more singing with Freddy Martin's band in the 40s," he told Hadley.

It didn't help Merv's ego when Will Mahoney told him that at the peak of the Depression in the early 1930s, this vaudeville and musical comedy star was pulling in $5,500 a week, the highest paid variety star in the world.

As Woody Mahoney, Merv played the romantic lead in this play of whimsy, romance, and political satire. His big number was "Old Devil Moon," Merv's rendition meeting with hostility from the orchestra conductor, Julius Rudel. "You sing like Sinatra in a recording studio. This is the stage, Griffin. Project your voice, dumbass."

For reasons not known to Merv, the star of the show, Helen Gallagher, took an instant dislike to him. Reportedly, she was "seriously pissed" when Merv went to the director, William Hammerstein, and asked him if he—not Helen—could sing the show's hit song, "How Are Things in Glocca Morra?"

Multi-talented, Helen was a singer, actress, and dancer, but was known on Broadway for her fiery temper. Before meeting Merv, she'd won the Tony in 1952 as Best Featured Actress in a Musical, appearing in a revival of *Pal Joey*. After their first day of rehearsal, she told Merv, "I've worked with some of the most talented people on Broadway. You're not one of them. It's a drag working with bad people."

In the first week's run, she got the idea that Merv was upstaging her during one of her big numbers. She kicked him into the orchestra pit. Fortunately, he escaped without injury except for some bruises. He got even with her the following night by squeezing her so hard in one scene that she was breathless for her big number.

On opening night, critic Darlene Stafford wrote: "What can you say about Merv Griffin? His voice is better suited to a hotel lounge than Broadway. Miss Gallagher makes mince meat pie out of him whenever they appear together. The original 1947 cast of Ella Logan, Albert Sharpe, and David Wayne were far superior to the present cast except for the always superior Miss Gallagher and Will Mahoney. Again, I ask, what can you say about Merv Griffin? He was supposed to be romantic, although when he was with Miss Gallagher he looked more like Hitler calling on Churchill for tea

A Merv-hater:
Helen Gallagher

than a romantic star of the stage."

Another comparison to a World War II dictator was made when Merv told the director, "I'd rather be locked into an embrace with Josef Stalin than Miss Stage Hog."

Will appeared on stage in *Finian's Rainbow* bedecked in a green felt hat, a plaid scarf, and a checkered vest, playing a bibulous rascal who makes off with a pot of gold. "How can I compete against Will?" Merv asked. "He steals every scene. What he doesn't steal, and what Gallagher doesn't hog, goes to a beloved leprechaun." Merv was referring to the role of "Og," as played by Donn Driver.

In 1968 Merv heard that Francis Ford Coppola was making a film version of *Finian's Rainbow*, starring Fred Astaire and Petula Clark. Rather facetiously, he sent a telegram to Francis. "If I couldn't make the damn thing work, nobody can. So don't even try. Besides, haven't you heard? The big movie musical is over."

The public seemed to agree with Merv's own assessment, "a Broadway star I'm not. Nor will I ever be."

***

A former bootblack, Anthony L. Aste, founded Griffin Shoe Polish to rival sales of Esquire, which had been the nation's best-selling shoe polish since World War II. Esquire had been founded in 1938 by two brothers, Albert and Sam Abrams, from Long Island. Their greatest success came when they hired Kate Smith, a robustly large entertainer from Virginia, to host *The Kate Smith Hour* on television.

She was dubbed "The Songbird of the South," but she was more than that, of course. During the war, she became a true American icon, singing her inspiring rendition of Irving Berlin's classic "God Bless America."

She had heard Merv's voice in *Finian's Rainbow* and asked him to appear on her show several times. He later recalled that she was a "plump, jolly, double-chinned fat lady with a great soul." He remembered that one night, as he stood in the wings listening to Kate sing "When the Moon Comes Over the Mountain," he stepped on the foot of Tennessee Ernie Ford.

Over Kate's objection, Merv was fired from the show when the executives at Esquire finally took notice that his last name of Griffin was the trademark of their rival. But Kate, who'd objected to his firing, invited him to a cast party. At the party, the only remotely bitchy remark he ever recalled her making was when she said, "both Gene Autry and Bing Crosby tried to record 'God Bless America,' but they just didn't have the voices to pull it off. It takes a big gal like me to sing that song."

She ended the party with a touch of self-mockery when she sang "Pickaninny's Heaven," which she'd performed on live radio back in 1933. "I don't mean to be insensitive," she said. "I sang that number just to show how far we've come since 1933."

Merv always carried a fond memory of Kate and was instrumental in getting his friend, Ronald Reagan, to award her the Presidential Medal of Freedom Honor in 1982.

Later in life, he tried to get her to come on his show but found out that she was wheelchair bound and was suffering brain damage as the result of a diabetic coma.

One of Merv's young staff members had asked him, "Who is Kate Smith?"

"My God, kid, in 1942 she was the second most popular woman in America after Eleanor Roosevelt," Merv said. "Now she's remembered only by grandmothers with first names that no longer are popular—Sadie, Viola, Mabel, Edna, Maude, and Gertrude."

Upon her death in 1986, Merv told reporters that Kate Smith was the origin of the expression, "It's not over till the fat lady sings."

From fat lady to fat man, Merv's next assignment was with "The Great One," Jackie Gleason.

Although Merv had parted company with his agent, Bullets Durgom, they'd remained friends. Bullets asked his best client, Jackie Gleason, if Merv could sing on two or three of his shows, and "The Great One" agreed.

Merv was granted the rare honor of actually meeting Gleason in person before the show. Sometimes even his writers didn't get that chance and had to slip their manuscripts under the door of what Gleason called "my sable-lined dump" on Fifth Avenue.

One night at around ten o'clock, Merv was ushered into Gleason's penthouse apartment by a bellhop who told him to wait in the living room. It was decorated with memorabilia, including a framed photograph of Gleason as Reggie Van Gleason in a World War I outfit.

Off-camera, he was anything but jolly:
Jackie Gleason

Gleason kept Merv waiting for about an hour until he finally emerged from his bedroom wearing baggy underwear and looking hung over even before the night had really begun. There were no introductions, no handshakes. His first words to Merv were, "Bullets told me Marlene Dietrich used to slip in and out of your house in Los Angeles. Were you fucking her?"

"Never had the privilege," Merv said. "I fear Marlene's interests lay elsewhere."

"Too bad," he said. "I've always wanted to fuck Marlene. The closest I've come to that is insisting that Frank Sinatra share every detail with me. Hearing about his plugging the Kraut practically makes me cream in my pants."

"The next time I see her, I'll tell her of your admiration," he said.

Gleason looked skeptically at Merv. "Don't do me any favors, kiddo," he said. "Around this joint I dispense the favors. In fact, as a favor to Bullets, I'm gonna let you sing on my show. You can even do my theme song, 'Melancholy Serenade.'"

"Thanks, Mr. Gleason."

At that point a scantily dressed blonde showgirl type emerged from the bedroom and headed for the kitchen, but Gleason didn't bother to introduce her.

After chatting briefly with Merv about the numbers he wanted him to sing on the show, Gleason got up and went over to the bar and poured himself a hefty whiskey. Looking over at Merv, he said, "Help yourself. I'm no God damn bartender."

"I'm fine," Merv said.

"What's the matter with you, boy?" Gleason asked. "I've never known an Irishman to turn down a drink." After a big gulp of whiskey, his face lit up. "I've got a great idea. I'm taking you to my favorite saloon. There's this terrific one-armed trombone player you've got to hear." He didn't ask Merv if he wanted to go, but merely assumed it. "I'll even take Blondie if she ever comes out of the fucking kitchen. You can call your boyfriend to join us. Bullets gave me the full scoop."

"Thanks," Merv said, "but I don't have a boyfriend. I date gals."

"Sure, kid, whatever turns you on," Gleason said. "But I'm from Missouri—actually Brooklyn—and I'll give you a chance to prove what a lady's man you are tonight." He bounded up from the sofa to get dressed. "Don't believe all that shit you read about me in the papers. That I drink six quarts of Scotch a night, dine at a dozen different restaurants every evening, and fuck three dozen women before the rooster crows. The jerks in the press make one big mistake in writing about me. I fuck fifty-five women before the rooster crows—and that's every night."

In the elevator on the way down, Merv checked out Gleason's date, who looked like Alice Faye on a bad night. The hotel desk had ordered a limousine for them, and it was parked outside, a uniformed driver holding open the rear door for them.

When Gleason looked inside the limousine, he refused to get in. Turning to the driver, he said, "You're supposed to haul celebrities around town. Who in the fuck did you have in here last night?"

"Frank Sinatra and some of his girlfriends," the chauffeur said.

"I think one of Frank's bimbos threw up in the backseat," Gleason said. "Tell your company to send a vomit-free car."

On the sidewalk, Merv waited with an increasingly agitated and impatient Gleason for nearly half an hour before another limousine pulled up to the curb. Merv still hadn't been introduced to Gleason's girlfriend, but she took advantage of the wait to file her nails.

When Gleason wasn't cursing the limo company, he shared vignettes from his life with Merv. "I've never fucked Marlene, but I once plowed Ann Sheridan when we made *Navy Blues* together. She complained that she couldn't find it beneath all my blubber. I told the bitch, 'Shut your face. You've got no tits, so let's call it a Mexican stand-off.'"

When the new limousine came, Gleason, Merv, and the gum-chewing bimbo piled into the backseat. Merv was astonished that the driver had to go only one hundred feet before letting them off at a seedy saloon.

Gleason must have been a regular, because the manager and the waiters hovered around him, treating his arrival like the big star that he was. Gleason was known as the biggest tipper in New York City. At the bar Gleason ordered a whiskey and placed five one-hundred dollar bills on the bar.

He asked Merv for his wallet. Astonished at the request, Merv nonetheless handed his wallet to Gleason, who removed all his money right down to the last dollar. He threw Merv's meager cash on top of his and shouted to the other patrons, "Drinks on the house!" There was a mad rush to the bar.

After the round of drinks, Gleason, Merv, and the blonde sat at the head table, listening to a one-armed trombone player, Finger Lickin' Bollweevil. "I have this thing for one-armed trombone players," Gleason confided. It started back in 1943 when Sinatra and I discovered one, Wingy Manone. We used to go to this jazz joint every night and listen to the amputated fucker."

"I wouldn't think that there would be a lot of one-armed trombone players around," Merv said.

"There aren't," Gleason admitted. "That's why we've got to respect them. That's why I'm so devoted to Finger Lickin'."

Before midnight Gleason made a call to his hotel and sent Merv back to the desk to pick up another five one-hundred dollar bills. By the time he came back into the bar, Gleason was already deep into his second bottle of Scotch. Three other blondes had joined their table. Again, Merv was not introduced.

As the night progressed, Gleason placed a hundred dollar bill in Finger Lickin's pocket. "Play 'That's a Plenty' for me," he requested. The comedian did that five times, requesting the same song, until all the money was gone.

For his finale, Finger Lickin' announced to Gleason and the audience, "my swan song for the night is dedicated to 'The Great One'—and it's on the house." The trombone player must have realized that Gleason had run out of hundred-dollar bills.

Before the saloon closed, Gleason turned to Merv, after surveying each of the blondes at table. "All these dames have trained their vaginal muscles to suck a man dry. Take your pick. Any one of these gals will make you swear off cock sucking for life. Trust me on this one."

"Thanks for the offer but no thanks," Merv said, getting up. "I've had it for the night. I'm out of here." For his departure, Merv did an impression of Gleason's famous exit line, "Away we go."

Without looking back, he raced for the door.

***

The summer of 1955 brought Merv his long-awaited emcee job but it wasn't what he'd been expecting. He was astonished when Marty told him he'd be hosting a Sunday morning religious program for CBS called *Look Up and Live*. The job paid only $120 a week, and the gig was for thirteen weeks. Having no other work, Merv, at Hadley's urging, accepted the gig. Although Merv was a Catholic, the show's producers thought he was a Protestant. The Catholics would get their thirteen weeks after the Protestants went off the air.

Even though the idea of hosting a religious program appalled Merv, he had vowed to Marty that he would "take any talk show host job." He kept his word. On the show, the script was fed through a TelePrompTer. In those days of early television, the instrument often chewed up the rolls of paper feeding into it.

During his second show, the machine broke down, forcing Merv to ad lib his way through the rest of the broadcast. "I'm not a pastor or minister," he later said. "But I'd read books by my good friend, Fulton J. Sheen, so I just borrowed material from my memory of his writings until we went off the air."

Merv had to introduce a string of boring pastors but he also met gospel singers. His favorite, of course, was the greatest gospel singer of them all, Mahalia Jackson. He was without racial prejudice, and in later years Merv would do more than any other TV talk show host in introducing black performers to audiences numbering into the millions.

"Getting to know Mahalia Jackson was one of the highlights of all the jobs I held down in the 50s," Merv later said. Born in the Black Pearl section of New Orleans, Mahalia grew up in a three-room dwelling that housed thirteen people.

Merv listened in fascination as Mahalia told him stories of her early life, especially how her aunt used to beat her with a "cat-o-nine tails" for the smallest infraction when she went about performing her sun-up to sun-down household chores.

Backstage, Mahalia talked music with Merv, uttering such startling remarks as "Elvis Presley stole rock 'n' roll from the black churches."

On Merv's show, Mahalia in her grainy, full-throated soprano sang her signature recording, "Take My Hand, Precious Lord." The artist seemed to save all her love for the Lord, as she had little use for men. She'd married Isaac Hockenhull in 1936 but had finally divorced him. "All during my marriage to him, he kept pressuring me to grant him that divorce," she told Merv. "The devil finally got his wish. Frankly, I don't think most men are worth messing up your mouth with."

One morning Merv asked her to sing the William Herbert Brewster song, "Move On Up a Little Higher." That recording had sold eight million copies. She also sang Merv's favorite, "Go Tell It On the Mountain," her big 1950 hit.

In 1961, Merv watched with pride as Mahalia sang at the presidential inauguration of John F. Kennedy. Before 250,000 African-Americans, she also went to Washington again in 1963 to sing "I've Been 'Buked, and I've Been Scorned." Martin Luther King Jr. listened intently before he too appeared before that rally to deliver his famous "I Have a Dream" speech.

Mahalia died on January 27, 1972, suffering from heart failure and diabetes complications. She was only sixty years old. Merv sent flowers to her funeral at Providence Memorial Park in Metairie, Louisiana.

Harry Belafonte had been Merv's roommate at one time in New York. On the *Look Up and Live* show, Merv also got to meet Sidney Poitier, another black performer on his way to great fame and achievement. At the time, Sidney ran a drama school in Harlem.

Like Mahalia, Sidney told Merv fascinating stories of his early life. Although born in Miami, he grew up on Cat Island in The Bahamas, where his

(Left to right)   The Defiant One, The Queen of Gospel, and Yellowbird:
Sidney Poitier, Mahalia Jackson, and Merv's roommate, **Harry Belafonte**

father had been a tomato grower. When Sidney came to New York to try to make it as an actor, he was so poor that he often had to sleep in the bus terminal. He finally found a job as a dishwasher in Harlem.

Even though appearing on a Christian TV show, Sidney privately told Merv that he'd been "involved" in local voodoo traditions on Cat Island where he was also a juvenile delinquent. "I was once arrested for vagrancy in New York," Sidney confessed.

Merv had not seen Sidney's major film debut in the anti-racist *No Way Out* in 1950. Sidney told him that it was deemed too explosive to be shown in its entirety by the colonial government of The Bahamas. The butchering of this explosive film for its presentation before a Bahamian audience caused such a protest that it gave birth to the political party that eventually overturned British rule.

Hadley was in the studio on the day that Sidney first appeared. He later told Merv, "I don't give a damn about all his racial politics. I'd be satisfied if he'd throw me one good black dick fuck. I think Sidney Poitier is the best reason for integration that I can think of."

***

In 1955, Merv joined a parade of gay New Yorkers attending the premiere of the Broadway play, *The Desperate Hours,* starring a young Paul Newman. The word "gay," as it relates to male homosexuality, had just come into vogue.

Those gay men who had seen the preview of the play made a collective pronouncement: You couldn't call yourself a gay man if you hadn't seen the film *Sunset Blvd,* starring Gloria Swanson, or the new play, *The Desperate Hours,* starring Paul Newman. Paul's stunning appearance on the New York stage made him, almost overnight, the poster boy of gay New York.

Co-starring as his kid brother, another handsome young actor, George Grizzard, was making his Broadway debut in this play. Both Paul and George appeared as jailbreaker brothers who invade a home and terrorize its occupants, as portrayed by Karl Malden and Nancy Coleman.

Invited to the cast party, Merv met Paul Newman and later told Hadley, "He was the most dazzling creature I ever feasted my eyes on. I could look into his dreamy blue eyes forever." In reference to that night, Merv also claimed that "gay boys were clustered around this hunk like bees in a honey tree. I couldn't get near him."

Merv's reject:
George Grizzard

305

Merv turned his attention to George, a native of North Carolina. "He seemed a little frightened. Although he was only three years younger than me, he had the look of a lost kid who was definitely out of his element with this fast-moving Broadway crowd."

Before the night was over, Merv learned that Paul Newman had seduced the young actor on several occasions before dumping him. Perhaps following Paul's example, Merv later did the same thing to George.

One night in the 1970s at Ted Hook's Backstage Bar in New York City, George told Darwin Porter, "Merv and I hooked up pretty well, at least I thought so. The sex was vanilla, and he was a bottom, but that was okay by me. I thought he was my new boyfriend. My thing with Paul had gone nowhere, especially after he told me he was straight. Merv, on the other hand, was gay as a goose. I didn't see anything wrong spreading the word he was my new BF. That was the worst mistake I ever made. Word soon got back to Merv, and he dropped me like a hot potato. I ran into him again in 1962 when I was starring in *Who's Afraid of Virginia Woolf?,* and that devil pretended to his friends that we were meeting for the first time."

***

When Merv and Hadley found an apartment on 57th Street they liked much better than Marlon's place, they decided to move out. Merv called Marlon's agent, his old friend, Jay Kanter, and asked if he could find a sublet for Marlon's apartment, which no longer smelled of raccoon piss.

Within an hour, Jay called back and said he had a prospective renter, although mysteriously he provided few details. Merv suspected that the client might be another celebrity.

That night Merv hit the bars with Hadley, forgetting all about the appointment the following morning.

Arriving drunk back at Marlon's apartment at four o'clock that morning, Hadley threw some clothes into a suitcase. He told Merv that he had to catch an early morning bus to go to Philadelphia for a family reunion.

"But I thought you said your relatives lived in Minnesota," Merv said.

"They do," Hadley said, "but a lot of them live in Pennsylvania." He kissed Merv good-bye, promising to call, although he never did.

After drinking all night, Merv collapsed in bed until there was a loud pounding at the door. Marlon had long ago disconnected the doorbell. Merv had forgotten about the nine o'clock appointment he had with Jay Kanter and the prospective renter. Throwing Marlon's tattered and smelly bathrobe around himself, he stumbled to the door to find Jay and his client.

He was startled. With a kerchief tied around her hair, the client had enclosed one of the world's shapeliest bodies into a dull raincoat dyed a battleship gray. Even without her customary makeup and in this disguise, Merv knew at once that it was Marilyn Monroe. Anybody could have recognized her. She was at the time the most photographed face in America, as well as the model for the country's most famous nude calendar.

After the first thirty minutes, it became apparent that Marilyn had no intention of renting the apartment. She just wanted to see where Marlon lived. Merv knew that she and Marlon were on-again, off-again lovers.

Jay soon excused himself to rush to an appointment, leaving Marilyn in the apartment alone with Merv. Just because she insisted, Merv even unlocked the secret closet, showing her the wreckage of Marlon's electric train, which for some reason seemed to fascinate her.

"This closet is all I'll need for my wardrobe" she said. "I don't have many clothes. A few sweaters, two pairs of jeans and some tight Jax slacks. My most valuable possession is a mink coat Joe gave me for Christmas."

"You're always photographed in glamorous clothes," he said.

"They're not mine," she claimed. "They're borrowed from the studio."

Merv invited her into Marlon's kitchen for coffee. He noticed that she wore no stockings, and there was a big, ugly pimple above her left ankle. She wore a white silk blouse and matching slacks. Sipping her coffee, she surveyed the bleak kitchen. "Did I ever tell you my secret name for Marlon is Carlo?"

She settled in a bit and showed no sign of leaving that morning. Removing her kerchief, she revealed unkempt hair to him. She looked as if she'd suddenly risen from bed without combing her famous blonde tresses.

Returning to the living room, she focused on Marlon's piano. "Please, pretty please," she said, "play something for me."

They ended up at the piano for more than an hour, as he played her familiar songs. They began to sing duets together before she tired of that. She plopped down on the sofa, placing her feet under her body. After bringing her some cheap red wine Hadley had left behind, he settled in with her, just knowing that it would be a gossip fest about Marlon.

Gorgeous, glam, and gossiping about Marlon:
Marilyn Monroe

"Marlon doesn't really respect women," she said. "He makes love to them—to men as well—but he lacks the maturity to go the long haul in a relationship, unless you call his long friendship with Wally Cox a relationship. I'm a bit of an exception in that I'm blonde. Marlon usually lies to fuck dark-haired Latina putas. Even so, we make love from time to time. He's a far better friend than a lover. As a friend, he's gentle and caring. As a lover, he thinks he has to be Stanley Kowalski."

"You mentioned that Marlon likes to have sex with men," Merv said, feigning innocence on the subject.

"Oh, Marlon does have sex with men just to be daring," she said. "He probably doesn't really enjoy it. He does it because it's part of that rebel image he so carefully cultivates. Since society doesn't approve of homosexuality, Marlon thinks he has to be the sexual outlaw. Even with women he's got to flaunt convention. If men are supposed to enter women through the front door, Marlon always insists on knocking on the back door."

Tiring of the sofa, she rose to her feet. With wine glass in hand, she moved throughout the room. "Marlon is a lost cause. I've decided that Monty Clift is the one for me." She noticed a look of disbelief on Merv's face. "Don't believe all those stories about Monty being a homosexual. I know you two guys used to live together—and all that. But he's not gay. He just hasn't found the right woman to love him."

"Are you absolutely sure that's the case?" he asked.

"Of course, I'm certain," she said defensively. "For the life of me, I can't picture two men in bed together. Maybe in those bunks in the military when there are no women available. What man in his right mind would settle for another man when he could have this?" She ran her hands lovingly along the contours of her body. "Don't tell anyone, but I've always found the idea of two men seducing each other weird. I mean, if you think about, it's a bit creepy. Bumping two pricks together. How ghastly!"

"Marilyn, if millions of your gay fans could hear this talk, they'd desert you in a minute," he said. "C'mon, you've been in Hollywood far too long to be this naïve. For God's sake, you're sounding like Mae West. She's got plenty of strange ideas about homosexuality."

"Don't get me wrong," she said. "I adore the gays, like Tennessee Williams and Truman Capote. But, as I said, Monty is not a homosexual. He told me he loves women. He also told me that the finds sex with men dirty. I know for a fact that he's fucking Elizabeth Taylor, although what he sees in that cow I don't know. If I don't marry Monty, I'm certain that Frank Sinatra will marry me. If either of them wants to marry me, I'll divorce whoever I am married to at the time. Of course, bitch Taylor is also chasing after Sinatra. I wish the cow would leave my men alone."

Marilyn's talk quickly turned from men to her own career, which she seemed to think was about to take a new and daring step forward. "I just talked to Tennessee today." She was, of course, referring to the playwright Tennessee Williams. "It's almost set with him and Elia Kazan that I'm gonna play *Baby Doll* in their new movie. Elia is a little bit hesitant, but Tennessee is behind me all the way. Elia claims that I'm too old to play a teenager. Marlon has almost agreed to appear opposite me in the role of Silva. *Baby Doll* will give new meaning to my career. It'll show those assholes in Hollywood that I'm more than a dumb blonde."

***

When Merv read in the papers that Elia Kazan had turned down Marilyn for *Baby Doll*, he called her to console her, finding that she was bitterly disappointed. She sounded like she'd been drinking. "I'm not giving up," she vowed. "Somewhere in some dark attic in America a guy is writing a magical script for me that will change the direction of my career. I just know it." Before she put down the phone, she invited him over. "If you'll come and sing to me, it might cheer me up."

"Do you mind if I bring a friend?" Merv asked. "Hadley Morrell. He thinks you're the greatest thing since the invention of ice cream."

"The more the merrier," she said.

Later, he and Hadley found her occupying Rock Hudson's secret hideaway in New York. It looked like a hurricane had blown through. During her short term in residence, she'd completely wrecked the apartment. Dirty pizza boxes were found in the corner, the dishes looked like they hadn't been washed in a month, and empty champagne bottles littered the floor.

She found Hadley extraordinarily attractive. "Merv, you selfish boy," she said, "keeping this hunk for yourself when he should be shared with the world. Don't tell me he's gay, too. I refuse to believe it. He looks like he can handle any woman and call for reinforcements."

Hadley beamed hearing such praise of his manly charms, although Merv was growing jealous, realizing how foolish it was to take a lover to meet Marilyn Monroe. She could seduce any man, gay or not.

Once settled in, she offered them champagne, her favorite drink. "Do you know what that fucking Kazan told me? He said that I have a nigger butt. Can you imagine him saying that to me? I want both of you to judge." In front of Hadley and Merv, she lowered her jeans and exposed her ass, revealing that she wore no underwear. "Judge for yourself, fellows."

"That is the most beautiful ass in creation," Hadley said. "There is no ass in the world more fuckable."

"Hear that, Kazan," she said, "you old meanie." She looked at Hadley as she turned around. "I hope you're not another Marlon, always wanting to enter a woman through the back door." In front of him, she lowered her jeans, revealing that she'd dyed her pubic hair blonde.

What happened next depends on how reliable a witness Hadley is. He later claimed in a proposed memoir that he had sex with Marilyn right on Rock Hudson's carpet and that Merv hovered over Marilyn like a voyeur but did not actually penetrate her. In Hadley's words, Merv merely felt her breast while goading him on to action.

If an actual seduction took place that afternoon, it cannot be verified. Hadley later claimed that in a taxi back to their apartment, Merv turned to him in bewilderment and said, "I didn't know you were bisexual."

***

Upon its release, Merv and Hadley went to see *Baby Doll*. Instead of Marlon and Marilyn, it starred Eli Wallach and Carroll Baker. In Merv's own review, he said, "Tennessee was right in pushing for Marlon and Marilyn. Marlon would have eaten up the scenery, and Marilyn would have made it a classic. With Wallach and Baker, Tennessee has ended up with a merely mediocre film."

Months later Marilyn called Merv. "I've found the great script I've been waiting for all my life. At least with this script I'll be taken seriously as a star. You've got to read it."

Without telling Hadley where he was going, Merv went to Marilyn's apartment, which was no better kept than Rock Hudson's dive. Clothes were thrown about, along with remnants of long forgotten meals. When Merv excused himself to take a leak, he found a used condom on the bathroom floor.

Seated on the sofa, he read the badly written script with all its typos. She didn't leave the room for one minute as he read, and kept bouncing up and down on the sofa, her robe opening at times to reveal her vagina. Unlike that time with Hadley, he noticed that she hadn't bleached her pubic hairs.

As he put down the script, he looked at her in astonishment. "Who wrote this screenplay?"

"A gay friend of mine," she said. "Dickie Knight. He's a chorus boy on Broadway."

"This is a rip-off of Judy's *A Star Is Born*. You said earlier you wanted me to play the role of your husband. A big band singer from the 40s whose career in Hollywood is going nowhere. That's a little too close for comfort. You're a star on the rise, trying to hold our marriage together with this has-been, who happens to be a drunk and who happens to walk into the sea at the end of the picture and drowns himself. James Mason is a tough act to follow."

"You don't understand," she said. "In *A Star Is Born*, Judy was a singer. As Lola Velez in this new script, I'm a dramatic actress who gets nominated for an Oscar. In *A Star Is Born*, Mason played a has-been movie star. In this script, you're not a movie star but a failed singer. Don't you get the difference? Dickie has come up with a lovely flashback. You could be made up to look younger. In the flashback, you could be shown in your heyday singing 'I've Got a Lovely Bunch of Coconuts.'"

"I'd do anything to play opposite you on the screen," he said. "But you've got to come up with a better—read that original—script than this piece of shit."

"You won't be so nasty when I walk away with an Oscar for this script," she said. "And if you don't want the part I can always offer it to Frank Sinatra."

"I'm sure Frank would love to play the role of a failed singer from the 40s," he said.

"Frank will do what I ask him to do," she said. "He's madly in love with me and still fucking me—and doing a better job of it than you did. So there!"

When Merv encountered Marilyn months later, she made no mention of the script that would have co-starred them. He didn't bring it up either.

At the time, Marilyn was being considered as the lead in a new movie called *Some Like It Hot*. But, at least in Merv's opinion, she still had bizarre casting ambitions associated with Frank Sinatra. She'd been delighted to hear that the director, Billy Wilder, hoped to cast Frank Sinatra in the movie. It seemed that Billy wanted Frank for the cameo role of the gangster "Spats," but had to settle for George Raft. Marilyn had misunderstood, thinking Billy wanted to cast Frank as the male lead, with the understanding that he'd have to appear in drag for some of the pivotal scenes. The role eventually went to Marilyn's former lover, Tony Curtis.

Later, when Merv read a copy of the script, he told Hadley, "Frank Sinatra doing a movie in drag? Fat chance. At times I think Marilyn is out of her mind. There's about as much of a chance of Frank playing the part in drag as there is of Eisenhower getting caught in a love nest with Tab Hunter."

***

Merv had long ago forgiven Monty Clift for the beef stew attack, and the two old friends spoke occasionally on the phone. Monty revealed to Merv that he had been spending many of his nights with either Roddy McDowall or Libby Holman, who had been accused of murdering her twenty-year-old gay husband, Zachary Smith Reynolds, the tobacco heir.

"In many ways, Roddy is the only person I've found worthy of being my mate," Monty told Merv. "We spend a lot of time in bed together, but, as hard as we try, we can't work up a lot of passion for each other."

A few weeks later, Monty mailed Merv a script for a film adaptation of William Inge's hit Broadway play, *Bus Stop*. It was being readied as a vehicle for Marilyn Monroe. At one point Elvis Presley was suggested as the cowboy lead, but Col. Tom Parker, his manager, turned down the offer, which promptly went to Monty. After reading the script, Merv called Monty, telling him, "this could be a classic." He urged him to sign to do the movie with Marilyn. After mulling it over, Monty turned down the role as "not worthy of me. How dare Hollywood cast me as a dumb cowboy playing opposite a dumb blonde."

One afternoon in New York, Monty showed up at Merv's apartment unannounced, which is the way he often preferred to call on his friends. "I want to catch people like they really are—not gussied up for company," he said. He asked Merv to accompany him to a five o'clock showing of *Guys and Dolls*. "Frank Sinatra and Marlon Brando singing in a picture together," Monty said in amazement. "What a riot!"

On the way to the theater, Monty confided to Merv that a few days before, he'd gone with a friend to see the first screening of *Guys and Dolls* at Loews 86th St. Theater. He'd been drinking heavily and had screamed at the screen: "Brando's vomitable! Sinatra's a pansy in this shit-stinker!"

An usher asked Monty to leave. Escorted to the lobby, Monty was furious. With his bare fists he smashed a display case, advertising the movie. Shattered glass littered the lobby, and he'd badly lacerated his hand. Blood was dripping onto the shards of broken glass. When the manager rushed out and saw that the damage had been caused by one of Hollywood's biggest stars, he called an ambulance to rush Monty to the hospital.

This time around, at the same theater, Monty sat through the entire movie without saying a word. Later, in a nearby bar, he reviewed the movie for Merv. "Brando used to have something on Broadway back in 1947," Monty claimed. "Whatever talent he once had has been ruined by Hollywood. What a dirty, corrupt town that is. Marlon Brando is a horse's ass in this stinker. As for Sinatra, *Eternity* showed he could be an actor, but he's made all the wrong career choices since then. Like Brando, he's throwing everything away. Incidentally, Sinatra and I aren't asshole buddies any more. He kicked me out of his party in Hollywood. I got a little drunk and came on to Dean Martin. I'd heard that he has a big one, and I wanted to try it out for myself."

After that, Merv didn't see Monty for several months. One early morning at around three o'clock, a call came in from Hollywood. It was Monty, who sounded drunk. He professed his undying love for "Bessie Mae," his nickname for Elizabeth Taylor. He told Merv that her divorce from Michael Wilding was imminent and that he planned to marry her. "We are going to learn how to be as intimate as two people can be without sex," Monty said. He then revealed plans for their upcoming film together, *Raintree County*, where Elizabeth would play a neurotic, predatory Southern belle.

The next news from Monty came not from him but as part of a desperate early morning call from Elizabeth in Los Angeles. In a teary voice, she informed Merv that after a dinner party at her house Monty's car had gone over a ravine as he tried to maneuver it down a winding hill to Sunset Boulevard. "When I ran down the hill and got to him, his face was a bloody pulp," she almost screamed into the phone. "It was gone!"

She burst into hysterical sobbing and had to put down the phone. Merv later learned that she'd raced from her house down the hill to the wreck where she'd discovered Monty choking to death. In desperation, she'd reached deep into his throat and removed his two front teeth, which had been rammed into his throat by the impact of the accident.

Like one of the movie heroes he played, Rock Hudson, also a guest at Elizabeth's house that night, had raced down the hill. After struggling for half an hour, he managed to extricate Monty from the wreckage, which looked like a crumpled accordion. An ambulance called by Michael Wilding finally arrived.

Merv was deeply saddened by the news and wanted to fly to Los Angeles to be at Monty's bedside. But he'd already committed himself to a number of gigs and couldn't get away. When Merv finally got through to Monty on the phone, the fallen star had left the hospital and was living in someone's house on Dawn Ridge Road.

"They've made a new face for me," Monty told Merv. "Remember that movie you made about the Rue Morgue? I could star in it now. Those magazines that used to say I had the most beautiful face of any male star in Hollywood won't be writing such shit about me any more."

In his first autobiography, Merv relates an incident involving Monty's return to New York after his accident. The disfigured star went from the house of one friend to another to see if he would be recognized with his remarkably altered face, the creation of plastic surgeons. One night after midnight, Merv had to get up to answer the urgent ringing of his doorbell. With his dog, he made his way down the steps since his intercom was out of order.

Montgomery Clift
after the rebuilding of his face.

He dared to open to the door just a crack to see who it was, thinking it might be an old drunk or else a serial killer. A mysterious stranger was standing on the stoop, wearing a black overcoat, a wide-brimmed black felt hat, and sunglasses in the dim light. Sounding as ferocious as he could, Merv demanded to know who it was. In his book, he quotes the stranger as saying, "You don't know me, do you?"

Merv knew Monty's voice at once and apologized for not recognizing him in the darkness. It was too late. Even though Merv called for Monty to come back, he disappeared down the street, as if running away from himself.

***

Merv's next job was for CBS on *The Morning Show*, which was that network's answer to the challenge imposed by NBC's popular *Today* show. "I took the job—first, because I needed it, and, second, because this was the show where Jack Paar got his start, and I wanted to be the next Jack Paar."

On the show, Merv was to sing and talk with Paar's replacement, Texas-born John Henry Faulk. The TV talk show host was later blacklisted because of the long arm extended from the McCarthy era of the 1950s. Faulk was falsely accused of being a member of various Communist front groups.

Faulk later sued Aware, Inc., an organization that screened performers for the television industry, systematically exposing anyone alleged to have affiliations with various Communist-tainted front groups. In his case, Faulk was represented by famed attorney Louis Nizer.

After a six-year battle in the courts, Faulk was awarded the largest libel judgment in history to that date, $3.5 million. His suit, and his subsequent victory, was largely responsible for breaking the "Blacklist" within the television industry.

Merv bonded with Faulk and sympathized with his dilemma, later praising the Emmy Award-winning TV movie, *Fear on Trial*, made in 1975 and shown on CBS. It starred William Devane as Faulk, with George C. Scott playing his lawyer, Louis Nizer.

On air, the sponsor of *The Morning Show*, American Airlines, served Faulk and Merv a large breakfast of flapjacks, scrambled eggs, and sizzling bacon with hash brown potatoes at seven o'clock every morning. Both Faulk and Merv had to eat the same mammoth breakfast at nine o'clock for their California audience. There was no tape in those days, so the show and that breakfast had to be repeated in its entirety. Merv grew so bored with the show that one day he set the weatherman's report on fire.

Faulk became too much of a "hot potato" for CBS and was let go. "When I left the show, I recommended to CBS that they promote Merv as my direct replacement, elevating him from the #2 'co-host' role," Faulk said. "He was easy to work with and came across as very amiable on camera. He was witty and a skilled interviewer, though he never asked embarrassing questions. Sometimes we sat chatting on air with each other and often couldn't remember the name of our next guest or why he'd been booked on our show."

CBS rejected the idea of promoting Merv as the show's frontman, hiring instead a struggling young newcomer, Dick Van Dyke, who'd previously worked as a disc jockey in New Orleans. Before getting this break, Dick had found show business a hard road. At one point, he and his wife, Margie Willett, were so poor that they had to live in their car.

Minutes before the taping of Van Dyke's debut show, the director had waited until the last minute for Dick to show up. Only one minute before air time, he informed Merv that no one had been able to reach Dick and that Merv had to go on alone as the host of the show.

With no preparation, Merv more or less ad-libbed his way through the show. As the show was going off the air, Dick called the studio. He'd overslept.

To Merv's surprise, Dick went on to great success. Merv was always a bit jealous of Dick, viewing him as a rival. But whenever he encountered him in the years ahead, he masked that feeling. There was always a friendly banter between these two performers.

Unknown to Dick, Merv had been one of several competitors for the role of Rob Petrie on what later became *The Dick Van Dyke Show* (1961). Merv lost the role, initially to Johnny Carson, who, at least in the talk-show circuit, eventually become Merv's biggest rival. Merv later read in *Variety* that Johnny's bid for the role of Rob Petrie was rejected at the last minute in favor of Dick Van Dyke, who went on to achieve phenomenal ratings in a show that ended up bearing his name.

Merv went to see Dick attempt a Cockney accent in *Mary Poppins* (1964), and he ran into him later at a party. "That was the worst attempt at a Cockney accent I've ever heard," Merv jokingly chided him. "If you want to know what Cockney sounds like, listen to my recording of 'I've Got a Lovely Bunch of Coconuts' day in and day out."

"Some day, Alice, to the moon," Dick said.

The Morning Show became Merv's best rehearsal to date for his future as a talk show host. He was on for about six months before CBS let him go. The executives decided to give the host job to Will Rogers Jr., with whom Merv had worked on the film, *The Boy from Oklahoma*. An executive at CBS told Merv that he was competent and qualified for the host job, but lacked the folksy, homespun quality that Will Jr. could bring to the show. "If Will runs out of something to say, he can always twirl a rope," Merv said.

A hot new talk-show host:
Merv

Merv's ever-faithful agent, Marty Kummer, almost immediately came up with another job offer wherein Merv would fill in for Bob Smith, the emcee of TV's popular children's program, *The Howdy Doody Show*. Smith, a beloved pioneer of that program, had had a heart attack, and Merv was offered a role as his replacement, with the understanding that it was only temporary, and that it would end when Smith recovered from his near-fatal stroke. Bob went under the name of Buffalo Bob Smith and wore an Indian costume, claiming that he was a descendant of the Native American chieftain who had once worn the same costume.

Merv needed a job, but he was hesitant about filling the shoes of a TV personality who had won the hearts of millions of America's baby-boomer children. Merv also protested to Marty that "I'm not an Indian."

After mulling it over, Merv finally turned down the job. "Howdy Doody, a god damn puppet, would steal every scene from me," he told Marty. "Get me another job—and quick. My bank balance is dropping even as we speak. Besides, I think Howdy Doody is a sissy."

***

The Robert Q. Lewis Show was a popular TV series that was broadcast over the American airwaves between 1954 and 1956. Its bespectacled host and namesake was a well-known and highly eccentric radio and television comedian, Robert Q. Lewis. Irving Mansfield, husband of the best-selling novelist Jacqueline Susann, was responsible for scouting new talent for the show.

When the producers brought Irving in, there was immediate tension between Irving and Lewis, who wanted to be in charge of the selection of talent for his show himself.

Irving had learned that Lewis needed a summer replacement for his juvenile singer, Richard Hayes, and Irving also knew that Merv was out of work and in desperate need of a job.

Irving pitched an offer to Merv's agent, and Marty called Merv with the details. The gig paid five hundred dollars a week. Although Merv would have preferred the job held by Lewis himself, he gratefully accepted because he direly needed the money.

Although a forgotten name today, Richard Hayes was a pop music star in what is now called "the Interlude Era," between the crooners of the mid-1940s and the rockers of the mid-50s.

Merv was leery of replacing him, since he knew that he was Lewis's favorite singer. "That fucker, Lewis, is going to hate me before I even open my mouth," Merv had told Marty, and was amazingly accurate about that assessment.

Lewis was known for his fondness for show business nostalgia, and in general he liked the numbers Merv selected to sing. "I love the songs, hate the singer," Lewis told Irving Mansfield. But instead of reinforcing Merv, he ridiculed him, telling associates, "That creep Irving Mansfield forced Griffin onto me. I didn't want him on my show. He doesn't really have a voice. He takes a great number like 'That Old Black Magic' and completely fucks it up."

Actually, Lewis suspected that Merv would make a terrific emcee of the show and as such, might represent a serious threat. In time, and as Merv's reputation as a competent talk show host grew, Lewis substituted for—and ultimately replaced—Merv as host of *Play Your Hunch*, a TV show that lay in Merv's future.

Before actually meeting Lewis as part of a confrontation Merv dreaded, he tried to learn all he could about his new boss. Lewis, who was born with the name of Goldberg, was associated with distinctive horn-rimmed spectacles, which became a virtual trademark on his TV programs. Lewis frequently sat in for TV host Arthur Godfrey when he was ill or otherwise unable to perform.

Godfrey, however, eventually turned on Lewis for reasons which aren't clear. In front of their associates, Godfrey claimed that the "Q" in Lewis's name actually stood for "queer." On the air he made veiled references to Lewis's homosexuality, and in private, Godfrey called Lewis "a faggot." At one point Godfrey, getting it all wrong, even spread a story that Merv and Lewis were having an affair.

Actually the "Q" in Lewis's name stood for nothing, and certainly not his middle name. He'd borrowed it from a fictitious radio character, "Colonel Lemuel Q. Stoopnagle," which originated as part of a comedy routine developed by radio comedian F. Chase Taylor in 1942.

Lewis had scored his biggest hit in 1951 with a dialect novelty song, "Where's-a-Your House?," an answer to Rosemary Clooney's hit, "Come On-a-My House." For a brief period, Rosemary became romantically involved with Lewis. She was dating him at the time she met her future husband, Jose Ferrer, who was appearing on Broadway with Gloria Swanson in a revival of *Twentieth Century,* a play which had made its debut back in 1932.

Merv called Rosemary as a means of finding out what she might reveal about Lewis. "He's a real pain in the ass to work with," Rosemary said. "He likes to control everything. Our romance never got off the ground. He's really gay, but he gets hysterical if someone suggests that. That's why he hates Arthur Godfrey so much. Godfrey's a prick, but he knows the truth about Robert. To deflect suspicion about himself, Robert calls you the gay singer, and he hasn't met you. When Irving booked you on the show, Robert called me and asked me if you were gay. I told him you weren't—that you chased after showgals all the time. I don't think he believed me."

Merv wanted to meet the orchestra leader of the show, Ray Block, and he went up and introduced himself to the diminutive and bespectacled music man. "I don't think I can ever forgive you for ruining my Hollywood career," Merv said with a smile.

Block looked astonished, not really knowing what Merv meant.

"You were the vocal coach for Gordon MacRae—don't deny it," Merv said. "Had it not been for MacRae, I would have been the one romancing Doris Day on screen."

By the second day on the job, Lewis still hadn't spoken to Merv, but Merv nonetheless saw a display of Lewis's temper up close. Lewis became so mad at the way Block was conducting a number that he picked up a chair on the sound stage and tossed it at him. The chair narrowly missed Block, landing in the otherwise empty orchestra pit.

A particularly dynamic entertainer who appeared regularly on the *Robert Q. Lewis Show* was Colorado-born Jaye P. Morgan. Her rich singing voice and wholesome appeal captivated audiences, and she helped improve Lewis's sagging ratings. By the time Merv met her, she'd evolved into one of the top recording artists of the 1950s. Merv bonded with her the moment they were introduced. They began "dating" on an irregular basis, with Jaye becoming another of Merv's "gal pals." It was not a serious romance, and the friendship which formed in the 1950s endured into the 1970s when Jaye became a regular on *The Merv Griffin Show*.

"I loved the way she laughed," Merv recalled, "and she had an outrageous sense of humor." These characteristics would later be showcased on *The Gong Show* where Jaye was a resident female celebrity judge.

She'd started singing at the age of three, and later took the nickname Jaye P. from the banker, J.P. Morgan. Merv had wanted to record a duet with Jaye. It was called "Chee Chee-oo Chee," but Perry Como beat him to it. The song became a smash hit with Perry and Jaye. "It would have sold more millions," Merv said, "if Jaye had let me do it."

Early talk-show monsters: **Arthur Godfrey** (top), and **Robert Q. Lewis**

Like Rosemary, Jaye warned Merv about Lewis's temper. In an autobiography, Merv quoted Jaye as saying: "Lewis will scream at you in rehearsal, he will throw things. He just goes into fits and there's hell to pay. You'll know he's about to blow when his face gets red and his nostrils flare and his eyebrows go up to his hairline—that's when to duck."

In Merv's second autobiography, published after Lewis's death, Merv claimed that Lewis was "insane," citing the talk show host's lack of humor and comparing his looks to a "dyspeptic accountant."

During his days on *The Robert Q. Lewis Show*, Merv officially "dated" Jaye P. Morgan, unofficially going home to Hadley after midnight. In his column, Walter Winchell, even though he knew better, wrote that "wedding bells will soon be ringing for two singers, Jaye P. Morgan and Merv Griffin."

Such was not to be the case. Whereas Merv struck out with Lewis, he formed a bond with Lewis's secretary, Julann Elizabeth Wright. They became friends and eventually dated in a rather casual way, not exclusively. The friendship between Merv and Julann led to their marriage in 1958. Their union produced a son, Anthony Griffin, nicknamed "Tony," who was born December 8, 1959.

Time and distance would drive the Griffins apart, their divorce becoming finalized in 1976 after a difficult financial settlement. During his marriage, Merv continued to lead a private and closeted life, far removed from his family, and presumably even beyond the knowledge of that family. Tony eventually married and gave Merv two grandchildren, daughter Fatah and son Donovan Mervyn.

After his departure from the Robert Q. Lewis show, Merv accepted an offer as emcee of a travelogue and variety show, *Going Places*, whose weekly broadcasts emanated from different venues within Florida, including the Jai-Alai Fronton or Cypress Gardens.

Merv and Hadley flew to Florida every Friday afternoon, returning the following Sunday night. Hadley loved Florida, and sometimes stayed there after Merv's Sunday departure, remaining on site and at leisure for the entire week.

The show was covered by the local press, but Merv was still so unknown that few of the local papers spelled his name right. He was variously known as Herb Griffin, Mirth Griffin, and Mark Griffin. *The Miami Herald* called him Mary Griffin. "A paper in California also called me Mary Griffin," he told Hadley. "Maybe these newspaper boys know me better than I want them to."

The low point of the TV series came in Cypress Gardens, where three minutes before air time, Merv took a call from his sister Barbara in San Mateo. She informed him that their father had died of a heart attack at the age of fifty-five.

Merv had spoken to his parents only the week before and had no clue that

Merv Senior's health was in any jeopardy. Before putting Merv's mother on the phone, his father had uttered his final words to his son. "Keep up the good work—I'm proud of you—and keep your nose clean."

"After I put down the phone, I don't remember what happened next," Merv told Hadley later that night. "The TV cameras were on me. I remember that much. I must have said something, but I don't recall the show at all. I was in complete shock."

That very night, Merv flew to San Francisco with Hadley. To Hadley's disappointment, he was stashed in a room within the same hotel that Merv had occupied in the 1940s during some of his performances with Freddy Martin's band.

When Merv told Hadley that he'd be renting a car and driving to San Mateo alone, Hadley exploded in anger. This led to a bitter fight between the two men. "I'm your lover," Hadley said. "I have a right to be there. To meet your family. What are you trying to do to me? Lock me in a closet or something? Pretend I don't exist?"

"You're everybody's lover," Merv angrily charged before heading toward the door.

"You're right about that," Hadley said, his fury bubbling. "You might as well know. Robert Q. Lewis sucked me off in the men's room one afternoon. He liked it so much he's promised me he'll rent me an apartment in New York and take care of me."

Merv stopped at the door. "I'm not surprised. You are, after all, a known star fucker, although I wouldn't exactly call Robert Q. Lewis a star. Did you get cum on his horn-rimmed spectacles when you shot off?"

"I won't be here when you get back from the funeral," Hadley warned.

"Good riddance!"

In San Mateo, Merv had a tearful reunion with his family, to whom he had not paid much attention in recent months. After his father was laid to rest, Merv held his mother in his arms. "I loved my father," he told her. "But I never got to know the man."

"It was his loss," his mother assured him.

Back in San Francisco, Merv learned that Hadley had forged his name on three of his paychecks and had cashed them. He'd checked out of the hotel after running up a big bill, leaving no note, no forwarding address.

In his moment of despair, and like a show business cliché, the phone rang, a call from Marty, his agent in New York. In a futile effort to restore the glory days of radio, ABC was going to invest six million dollars into a radio variety show.

The executives wanted Merv to host the show, singing and talking. The TV broadcast was slated to be on the air for forty-five minutes and might later expand to one hour and forty-five minutes if Merv could find an audience.

Bruised from both *The Robert Q. Lewis* fiasco and the dismal *Going Places*, but eager for another gig, Merv accepted. He was delighted at the pay, knowing that he would be solvent once again.

After accepting, he put down the phone, then picked it up again to call Johnny Riley in Los Angeles. It took only a few minutes of talking before Johnny agreed to abandon his job as a waiter. He flew to San Francisco that night and joined Merv for a reunion.

They slept in the same bed that night, but there was no sexual contact, even though Merv made it abundantly clear that he was still physically attracted to Johnny, just as he'd been in San Mateo years before.

That following morning, Johnny sat beside Merv on a flight to New York. He assured Johnny that it was all over between Hadley and himself. En route across country, Merv and Johnny plotted their new lives and anticipated the arrival of Paul Schone and Bill Robbins in New York. "We can all live together, at least for a while" Johnny said. "The boys will find work and get their own places. It'll be like the old days in California all over again. New York here we come. Ours to conquer."

Before the plane landed in New York, Merv made a very determined decision. Whatever he did in his future, he planned to keep his world with "the San Mateo Gang" separate from his newly acquired straight friends. Only in rare exceptions, such as his friendships with Monty Clift or Liberace, would he allow his two separate worlds to come together.

With his new salary, he was even contemplating renting a secret hideaway address, now that he was getting better known. Only the other day, a newspaper critic had claimed, "Merv Griffin, for my money, sings better than Perry Como and with a lot more feeling."

More than love, Merv craved success. He was still wounded by his failure to become a Hollywood star, and he wanted to show Jack Warner and the rest of Hollywood that he had the talent to make it big.

When he discussed with Johnny his plans for maintaining a "compartmentalized" life, his friend said, "Sounds to me like you want to have your cake and eat it too."

"Exactly," Merv said. "Who's to say a guy can't do that? It's never been tried. I'm going back to New York to make it—and make it big. Pretending you're straight is part of the game for making it big. It's in the rule book. Name one big star who's openly gay?"

"Liberace."

"Are you crazy?" Merv said. "Liberace tells the world he's straight."

"Is there anybody in his right mind who believes that?" Johnny asked. "If Liberace can convince the world he's straight, then anybody can. As for your being straight, does that mean birthin' babies and all that shit? If so, count me out. I don't know nothin' 'bout birthin' babies, Miss Scarlett."

"Yes, I'm going to enter the breeding grounds for procreation purposes," Merv said. "People will think I'm as straight as Ronald Reagan. What I do behind closed doors, and in the privacy of the various hideaways I'll have over the years, is my own damn business."

"Have it your way," Johnny said. "Just keep me informed, leaving out no sordid details."

"It's a deal," Merv said. "You've been working as a hustler. Well, hustlers have to put out. If I'm going to be paying all your bills, keeping you in New York, I want some action."

"You got it, boy," Johnny promised.

***

Ultimately, Merv's radio show collapsed. At the peak of its limited success, it attracted ten thousand fan letters a week. "ABC failed to bring back the great days of radio," Merv later said. "If Tallulah Bankhead and all those famous guests on *The Big Show* couldn't do it, what chance did I have?"

After the failure of that show, my phone stopped ringing," Merv said. "Marty Kummer couldn't even come up with a gig for me in some seedy lounge in South Trenton."

Before landing in New York, Merv had agreed to take care of Johnny Riley, but for several months Johnny took care of Merv.

"Johnny always seemed to have money in his pockets" said Bill Robbins, who had found work as a waiter after moving to New York. Occasionally Bill got a booking as a female impersonator at some dive in Greenwich Village. "Paul Schone and I knew how Johnny was making his money," Bill said. "I believe Merv knew too but nothing was ever said."

After Paul had also moved from Los Angeles to New York, he found no work as a dancer in Broadway shows and once again, like Bill, took a waiter's job.

Through the darkest days of his career, Merv continued to hold onto his famous friends such as Rosemary Clooney, Roddy McDowall, and Liberace. "When it came to friends, Merv had the Midas Touch even before he became famous himself," Bill said. "Not only that, but he often met and befriended people who were on the dawn of fame. It was a special gift he had, which became more evident when he was a talk show host. He discovered major talent before the world had a clue."

Such was the case with a young songwriter who lived across the street from Merv's apartment on 57th Street in New York. His name was Burt

322

Bacharach, and he and Merv bonded from the first time they were introduced by a mutual acquaintance. Burt was just starting to date again after his failed marriage to the singer, Paula Stewart. As a pianist, he used to accompany her, as he had far better known entertainers such as Imogene Coca, Mel Tormé, Vic Damone, the Ames Brothers, Steve Lawrence, and Polly Bergen. When Merv met Burt, he was dating Rose Tobias, an assistant to producer David Susskind.

Merv was seen frequently on the town with Burt when Johnny was otherwise engaged. One night in a club, Merv saw Robert Q. Lewis in an adjoining booth, sitting with Hadley Morrell. Hadley did not speak or acknowledge Merv. Neither did Lewis. Although Merv had no proof, he always suspected that it was Lewis who spread the false rumor around town that Burt and Merv were lovers.

Burt came up with the idea that if Merv, Rose, and Robert Barry, an agent, would pool their meager funds, they could rent a beach house on Ocean Beach (Fire Island) for the summer. The little resort had a reputation as an artists' colony, and there was a local bar where Burt could earn extra bucks playing the piano.

Merv agreed, but was reluctant to invite Johnny, as he didn't want to appear as part of a male/male couple. As it turned out, Johnny didn't want to spend weekends on Ocean Beach, but preferred another part of Fire Island, Cherry Grove, which had become a notorious homosexual hangout. Somewhat reluctantly, Merv agreed to spend his weekends apart from Johnny, while Johnny pursued whatever he was after in the Grove.

At Ocean Beach, this hastily assembled house party wasn't congenial. Burt's dog fought constantly with Poochie, Merv's dog. When the dogs weren't fighting, Rose Tobias was arguing with Burt.

One night Burt invited a troupe of Spanish dancers to their house for a party with wild music. Having had more than his share of drinks, Merv wanted to dance the fandango along the top of a stone wall. He was in no condition to do that. Losing his balance, he fell off the wall, his head almost colliding against a large rock. He landed in a bed of poison ivy and seriously injured his back. He had to be hauled away in an ambulance, and although he never returned to Fire Island, his back injury was to plague him for the rest of his life.

A few weeks later, Burt also left Fire Island, flying to Los Angeles for a gig. When he returned, he called Merv. "I got this cold out there," Burt said. "Guess who cured me?

Composer
Burt Bacharach

323

Marlene Dietrich herself, the femme fatale of the 20th century. And doctors claim there is no cure for the common cold. Those doctors haven't met Miss Dietrich."

Suspecting something, Merv asked, "And what else did Marlene teach you?"

"We made fantastic love together," he said.

"But you're twenty-eight years her junior," Merv said.

"How lucky for me," Burt said. "That means she's had all those years to perfect her technique. I'm the lucky beneficiary. Not only that, but she's asked me to be her accompanist during her world tour."

"Congratulations," Merv said. "But don't get burned. Marlene is terribly fickle. The last I saw of her, she had the hots for Michael Wilding."

"She's forgotten all about him," Burt said. "I've seen to that."

Merv watched in amazement and from afar as the affair between Marlene and Burt heated up. She was soon telling her friends that "Burt takes me to seventh heaven. I even wash his socks and underwear. He's my Lord and Master."

In the years to come, Merv saw little of Burt although he followed his career with a sense of pride but also with a touch of jealousy. "I shouldn't have lost him as a songwriter," he said. "I mean, I could have recorded 'What's New, Pussycat?,' not Tom Jones. I could have recorded 'Raindrops Keep Falling on My Head,' not B.J. Thomas."

Merv was intrigued to learn of Burt's marriage to actress Angie Dickinson in 1965, following her celebrated affair in the early 60s with President John F. Kennedy.

Merv one dull afternoon decided to take the rest of the money he had in the bank and fly on a vacation to Jamaica with Johnny. He'd already asked Burt if he could get Marlene to arrange a meeting with Noel Coward, who was in residence on the island.

Paul warned Merv that if he spent all his money, he'd have nothing left for groceries and the rent. "Oh, I'll be like Scarlett O'Hara and think about that tomorrow. Besides, why should I worry? Johnny always manages to come up with grocery money."

Before flying to Jamaica, he called Rosemary Clooney. On the phone she'd never sounded so bubbly, even though her marriage to Jose Ferrer was still as troubling as ever. Alhough Jose's affair with June Allyson had ended, his womanizing had continued.

"I've fallen in love," Rosemary confided to him, "for the first time in my life. He's wonderful, the man I've always wanted. But there's one big problem. He's married."

"Jose is married to you, and that doesn't stop him," he said. "What's good for the goose is good for the gander."

"I'm glad you see it that way," she said. "I need a big favor. My new beau is very famous, and we have to slip around and see each other in secret. We need a place to hide away where no one would think of looking for us. How about your apartment?"

He readily agreed, advising that he and Johnny were flying to Jamaica but that he could arrange for Bill Robbins to deliver her the key. "When I get back, can I meet this Mr. Wonderful?"

"I'll introduce the two of you," she said. "You'll adore him."

"Can't you tell me who he is?" he asked. "A famous actor, no doubt."

"Not at all," she said. "But I'll give you a clue. He plans to run for President of the United States in 1968 after his older brother has served his two terms in the White House. It'll be the beginning of a dynasty."

***

Waiting in the lounge of New York's Idlewild Airport for the departure of their flight to Jamaica, all Merv and Johnny could hear was Elvis Presley music. Merv turned to Johnny. "Both of us will be in our mid-30s sooner than later. Do you agree with those who say that's the beginning of middle age?"

"We're certainly not schoolboys from San Mateo any more," Johnny said.

"I think I'm washed up," Merv said, as another song came on from Elvis. "Rock 'n' roll is here to stay."

Showing an amazing gift of prophecy, Johnny said, "Don't worry about it. Next summer, or maybe a summer or two after that, you're gonna be the biggest talk show host on TV. The next Steve Allen. You're a born entertainer."

In Ocho Rios, a room had been reserved for them at the distinguished Jamaica Inn, where Sir Winston Churchill had stayed, capturing the local landscapes in watercolors during his retirement years. For reasons not fully known, Errol Flynn had been forcibly ejected from that hotel one early morning at three o'clock.

Merv stayed in bed until noon of the following morning. When he finally woke up, he found Johnny still asleep. After a shower and after dressing, he wandered down to the main lobby, after checking out the beachfront.

Mad about the boy:
Noel Coward
at the posh and venerable

JAMAICA INN

The weather that morning was uncharacteristic for Jamaica at that time of the year. The north shore was steamy, and there was a dull gray mist that hung in the air.

Merv didn't know whether Marlene Dietrich had previously called or written Noel Coward, announcing his arrival in Ocho Rios. At the desk of the concierge, Merv asked if he could put through a call to Noel's residence. He'd read that whenever Noel was in Jamaica, he was a frequent luncheon guest at the Jamaica Inn.

"You're in luck," the courtly black concierge told him in accented English. "The great man is in the lobby today, sitting in his favorite peacock chair."

Merv walked into the lobby and spotted Noel at once, but was too shy to approach him. He sat near him. Noel seemed to be struggling through a cross-word puzzle. Merv viewed himself as an expert on crossword puzzles.

"Bloody difficult," Noel said out loud. "Eight letters for the first word, five for the second." When Merv heard that, he used that as an opening to introduce himself to Noel. Years later Merv could not remember the word he came up with, but it had fitted the puzzle perfectly. As Merv introduced himself to Noel, he seemed appreciative to have received help in solving the puzzle.

"Come and join me for a drink, dear boy," Noel said. "They make the best mint juleps in Jamaica here."

Over drinks, Noel told him that he was waiting for the arrival of Miss Claudette Colbert, who was to be his guest for lunch. "Forgive me for name dropping—of course, I know half the people in the world, and the other half isn't worth knowing."

Trying to sound important, Merv said that he too knew Claudette Colbert and had been her escort at a party thrown in Hollywood by Jack Warner.

"By the way, who are you?" Noel asked. "You seem to be in show business—an actor, no doubt."

"A failed actor," Merv said. "I'm really a singer—radio, TV. Nothing that has shaken the world. I love singing your songs."

"Good," Noel said. "That shows you have taste. I hope you send me royalties."

At that point a sleepy Johnny in tight white pants emerged. Merv introduced him to Noel. "One of the world's great beauties," Noel said, inspecting him head to toe. "Human perfection if I ever saw it."

"A great fan of yours," Johnny said, extending his hand to Noel for a shake. He had a little difficulty getting his hand back.

"As for you, Griffin," Noel said in a slightly accusatory voice, "You have somehow managed to capture this prize specimen of manhood. Ivor Novello, at the height of his male beauty and charm, would pale in the luminosity cast by one of such pulchritude."

"I don't know what pulchritude means, but I'll take it as a compliment," Johnny said.

"A boy like you should lie on satin sheets and have mere mortals like me bring you gifts all day. The evening would be spent worshipping you."

At that point a white-jacketed attendant arrived to announce to Noel that "Miss Colbert's car has arrived."

"I hope you weren't exaggerating, and that Miss Colbert does indeed know you," Noel said to Merv.

"I'm sure she'll remember me," Merv said. He paused. "At least I hope she will."

Indeed Claudette did remember Merv fondly, and the four of them had an enchanting luncheon that lasted for three hours. When Claudette had to excuse herself, Merv, Johnny, and Noel remained at the table, finding it almost impossible to move. All those mint juleps. The steamy afternoon had gotten even hotter, and their clothes, even though lightweight, seemed to cling to their bodies.

"My friend, Graham Payn, will be arriving soon to pick me up and drive me back to Blue Harbour," Noel said. "He'll be sorry that he couldn't join us today. But I'm inviting both of you for a mid-afternoon swim and dinner tomorrow. The concierge will give you the directions to my little hideaway."

"We'd be honored, Mr. Coward," Merv said.

"Call me Noel," he said. "I'm sure by tomorrow night we'll know each other intimately enough to be on a first name basis." He turned to Johnny. "You, dear boy, deserve a long, lingering, and wet kiss on those succulent red lips of yours." He proceeded to plant one before turning to Merv, who was puckering up. "You, Griffin, at least deserve a firm handshake for bringing this beam of sunshine into the dreary life of a songwriter and playwright on a rare gray day in Jamaica."

The next day at Noel's vacation home on a hilltop above Blue Harbour, which he said he reserved for "my bloody loved ones," he introduced Merv and Johnny to his lover, Graham Payn, a British actor. Merv found Graham handsome to the point of being mesmerizing. Noel invited them to put on their swimming suits and join Graham and him in the pool. Johnny had forgotten to bring his. Noel agreed to take him back to the house to find one to fit him.

As Graham and Merv frolicked in the pool, Merv noted that Johnny and Noel were gone for a long time. Johnny emerged in a tight-fitting white bathing suit, almost a bikini, that made things rather obvious.

After a swim and over drinks, Noel told them how he came to buy land in Jamaica. "I came here back in 1944 and fell in love with the place at once.

Before I bought land, I rented Goldeneye from Ian Fleming. Can you believe that old sod charged me fifty pounds a week? Extortion. He left us with Violet, his housekeeper, who cooked for us."

"Salt fish and ackee every night except Sunday," Graham said. "Then we were treated to curried goat. The pud was the same every night. Stewed guavas and coconut cream."

"Violet's cooking tasted like armpits, except for the succulent armpits of Graham, which always taste divine," a slightly tipsy Noel revealed.

As they lay on *chaises longues* in a fading afternoon, Graham laughingly recalled how he first had met Noel in London. "I was only fourteen at the time and with my mother, Sybil. I had no idea that Noel was a pedophile."

"I'm not, dear heart," Noel interjected. "But I've always believed that nature intended young men to start having sex when they are able to ejaculate."

"Sybil took me to an casting call for a revue called *Words and Music*," Graham said. "She insisted I sing 'Nearer My God to Thee' to show off what she called the purity of my boyish treble. She also ordered me to tap dance like Ann Miller while I sang the song."

"I wasn't really impressed," Noel said, "but rather astonished at the versatility. I cast Graham as an urchin street singer in *Mad About the Boy*." He reached over to pat Graham's hand. "I've been 'Mad About the Boy' ever since."

"That might be so," Graham said, "but he still called me his illiterate little sod. But I learned fast. Soon I was hanging out with Larry and Vivien, Katharine Hepburn, John Gielgud—who made a pass at me, Gertrude Lawrence, Tallulah, of course, Marlene, and inevitably, the Queen Mother."

"Graham is certainly good looking enough," Noel said. "He has humor and a sense of fun. I've always found that a bubbly personality makes up for a barrage of other failures. And he's hung as well as any man should be without being a grotesque like Rubirosa. But do you know why I've stayed with him all these years?"

"We're all ears," Merv said.

"The dear boy has never refused to perform any act in bed that my perverse mind can conjure up," Noel said. "And I do have a very active mind."

As twilight fell, Noel seemed particularly intrigued by Merv's appearance with Tallulah Bankhead in Las Vegas. He speculated at length and wanted to hear Merv's opinion about Las Vegas being a proper venue—or not—for either his own one-man show or perhaps a stage for Marlene.

Noel told about going to Chicago in the 1940s to introduce Graham to Tallulah when she was appearing there in his *Private Lives*. "We took Tallu to Chez Paree to hear Carmen Miranda in cabaret. Both of us loved the show.

Later Carmen joined us at table. Tallulah got loud and drunk and propositioned her. Carmen eventually went back to the hotel with Tallulah. I knew all about Tallu's escapades but until that night I didn't know the Brazilian bombshell was part dyke."

"Tallulah can be so naughty, yet she is so generous," Graham said. "When Noel and I went to check out of our hotel in Chicago, we found out that she'd paid the bill for us."

Merv, hoping to appear like a show business insider, brought Noel up to date on the latest gossip about Marlene, telling him that she'd hooked up with Burt Bacharach. "My dear Marlene," Noel said. "God certainly had a talent for creating exceptional women."

Over a dinner of salt fish and ackee that night, Noel grew increasingly intoxicated and even more indiscreet. "I lost my virginity at the age of thirteen to Gertrude Lawrence. She was only two years older than me. The seduction took place on a moving train. All that open plumbing revolted me. Being in bed with a woman is like feeling the skin of a snake."

As the drinks kept coming, and the party grew more intoxicated, the revelations became more lurid. Merv, like the skilled interviewer that he was to become, goaded Noel into more indiscretions.

"Roddy McDowall has presented me with a fairly detailed list of your seductions," he said to Noel. "*Impressive* I might say. Richard Attenborough. Louis Hayward. Cary Grant. Laurence Olivier. Tyrone Power. Michael Wilding, whom I know. Peter Lawford who claimed to me personally that you seduced him. But tell us the most unlikely men you ever seduced?"

"First, I'll confess to two that got away. Years ago I was a guest of John Gilbert in Hollywood while I was waiting for a boat to take me to the Orient. His affair with Greta Garbo was going nowhere. Sitting on a sofa in front of his fireplace, we enjoyed a nightcap together. I let my hand creep slowly upward until it landed on his crotch which felt promising. He jumped up, ran up the stairs, and locked himself into his bedroom, with me, obviously, on the other side.

Once on an ocean liner sailing from Southampton to New York, I found myself in the nude in the steam room with that divine little piece of ass, Eddie Fisher. I ran my hands over his smooth buttocks. He too fled from me."

"Those are great stories, Noel, but we want to hear the two most unlikely conquests," Merv said. "Those who didn't get away."

"Okay, but you are a dirty bitch for prying into my private affairs," Noel said. "I will tell you if all of you promise not to tell the Queen Mother."

"It's a deal," Johnny said.

Finishing his drink, Noel settled back onto his *chaise longue* prolonging the suspense. "James Cagney and Leslie Howard. As God is my witness."

After that, there was silence. No one could top that.

Before the dinner party broke up, Noel suggested that Merv and Johnny spend the night, as the winding, rutted, steeply inclined road back to Ocho Rios was dangerous in the pitch blackness.

As Noel staggered to his feet, he placed a possessive hand on Johnny's shoulder before running his fingers through his hair. "I'll protect this dear boy from all harm tonight," he said to Merv. "And you can sample Graham's undeniable charms."

"Sounds like a fair trade to me," Merv said. "I would be honored to sup at the trough where the great Sir Noel Coward has fed."

"Inelegantly put but to the point," Noel said. Taking Johnny's hand, Noel guided him to the house.

There was a long moment before Graham put his hand on Merv's knee. "You're not going to be like John Gilbert and escape from my clutches tonight, are you?" Graham asked.

"Breathe in my ear and I'll follow you anywhere," Merv said.

The two men rose from their chairs and headed toward the guest room. "Something tells me we're not going to arise for breakfast before noon," Graham said.

In 1963 Merv called Noel again when *Doctor No,* with Sean Connery, was being filmed on location in Jamaica. Merv had seen pictures of Noel posing with his arms around the Scottish hunk, and he wanted Noel to use his influence to arrange an on-island television interview.

On the phone, indiscreetly, Noel confided that "my lifelong ambition is to commit an immoral act of fellatio on this divine Scotsman and to discover what's hiding under his kilt. Tallulah is still raving about Gary Cooper from back in 1932, but for my quid, Sean is the sexiest man alive. I hear his endowment is twice or even three times that of an ordinary man. John Gielgud disputes the point with me. He claims that Louis Jourdan is the best hung man in Hollywood. His opinion is not based on any close personal encounter with the French God, but on what Louis Jourdan revealed on screen when he wore those tight trousers in *Gigi*."

Months later, when Merv re-encountered Noel face-to-face in New York, Noel sighed, "Alas, Sean Connery can be added to my list of the men who got away."

Bosom buddies:
Sean Connery & Sir Noel
in Jamaica

***

The following day when Merv and Johnny returned to the Jamaica Inn, a cable was waiting from Merv's agent, Marty Kummer. Mark Goodson and Bill Todman, the producers of such hit TV shows as *What's My Line?*, *I've Got a Secret*, and *To Tell the Truth*, wanted Merv in New York for an audition. They were putting together a new show, *I've Got a Hunch*, which was heavily inspired by *To Tell the Truth*. Merv and Johnny flew back to New York the next day.

Merv arrived at Idlewild in time to make it to the Goodson-Todman production offices for a seven o'clock appointment. A secretary told him he'd have to wait. From the next room, Merv heard the sound of hysterical laughter from an audience. He thought that Johnny Carson might be auditioning for the same show.

Marty was supposed to have shown up to go into the audition with him, but he was nowhere to be seen. After waiting an hour, Merv said, "to hell with this." He headed for the elevators just as Marty was getting off. He urged Merv to stay, claiming, "We're almost ready to close the deal if the audition goes well."

Ushered into a large room, Merv discovered himself in front of an audience of Goodson and Todman employees. "You're on," Mark Goodson called out to him. Suddenly, Merv found himself as the emcee of a trial run of *Play Your Hunch*. Using all his skills, he sang, he danced, he performed skits, he interviewed guests hastily summoned to the stage.

At the end of the show, Mark Goodson led the loud applause, as Bill Todman sat in a front row seat, seemingly unmoved. Mark asked Merv to come with Marty to his office. Bill Todman left the room.

"Where's Todman?" Merv asked. "I don't think he liked me."

"I thought you were terrific," Mark said. "Don't worry about Bill. What does he know about show business? When I met him, he was selling insurance door to door. We have a love/hate relationship. If I like a performer, he hates him—and vice versa. If we agree, we know that one of us isn't doing his job."

"So, did you call me in here to tell me I don't get the job?" Merv asked.

"You're hired," Mark said. "We've got to do a pilot and sell it to CBS." He paused and looked sternly at Merv. "You're not a Communist, are you?"

"I don't even wear the color red," Merv claimed.

Merv made the pilot, and even Bill Todman approved of it. The problem remained for the show to win over what Merv called "the suits at CBS." It took six long months for CBS to make up its mind to go ahead with the show. In the meantime, Merv took any job Marty tossed his way.

Taking over for Carl Reiner, an emcee on ABC's *Keep Talking* show, Merv proved that he was a skilled ad-libber. "I was paid $1,500 per show, which allowed me to stay ten paces ahead of my creditors."

The show had two teams of celebrities competing in improvised comedy bits. For Reiner's last show, Merv was asked to sit in and watch to see how the series was filmed.

Backstage he encountered Reiner, a self-styled "Jewish atheist," who gave him the same advice he shared with nearly all rising comedians. "You have to imagine yourself as not somebody very special but somebody very ordinary. If you imagine yourself as somebody really normal and it makes you laugh, it's going to make everybody laugh. If you think of yourself as something very special, you'll end up a pedant and a bore. If you start thinking about what's funny, you won't be funny, actually. It's like walking. How do you walk? If you start thinking about, you'll trip."

Merv later claimed he took that advice. "It was the secret of my success, and I owe it all to Carl Reiner." It's not clear if Merv was serious, or merely joking.

On *Keep Talking*, Merv found himself working with such familiar TV faces as Morey Amsterdam, Peggy Cass, Pat Carroll, Orson Bean, Ilka Chase, Audrey Meadows, Elaine May, and Joey Bishop, who would later become Merv's rival for TV ads and audiences.

In a few weeks, Merv met with Bud Collyer, the host of *To Tell the Truth*, with the understanding that Merv would be taking over for him during a temporary leave of absence. Merv wore a bow tie in honor of the one Collyer often wore on TV. "I remember as a kid screaming at the radio, 'this looks like a job for Superman!'" He was recalling Collyer's job in the early 1940s when he supplied the voices of both Superman and his alter ego Clark Kent. "I never missed a program," Merv claimed.

He might have taken Carl Reiner's advice, but Merv did not take Collyer's advice, which was to contribute ten percent of his winnings to the Christian church. After meeting Merv, Collyer shook his hand and proclaimed, "God and I will be watching you." Collyer was extremely religious and often delivered pronouncements which he said had been revealed to him directly from God, having claimed to have talked personally with Him the night before.

On *To Tell the Truth*, Merv got to deliver the show's most famous and most oft-repeated line: "Will the real [*person's name*] please stand up?"

On one episode of *To Tell the Truth*, Merv met a panelist, Johnny Carson, a comedian who at the time was hosting a rival show, *Who Do You Trust?* This was Merv's first meeting with the star who was destined to become the most successful entertainer in the history of television.

Earlier, backstage, Merv had introduced himself to Johnny. The first question Merv presented to the TV host bombed. "Johnny, how does it feel to be a WASP in a field filled with Jewish comedians?"

"I don't want to talk before going on the air," Johnny told Merv. "It destroys my concentration."

"And that was that," Merv said. "I found Carson cold and distant: I didn't like him at all, and I think he viewed me with as much excitement as stepping on a mule turd in Nebraska. Maybe we both sensed in that brief meeting that in a few short years we'd become bitter rivals."

CBS finally came through and at long last offered Merv the job of hosting *Play Your Hunch*. The show did more than any other at the time to make Merv Griffin a household word. But the survival of *Play Your Hunch* would soon devolve into something akin to a twisting, high-anxiety ride on a rollercoaster. As it staggered through its many permutations, it became known as "The Game Show That Would Not Die." After six months with Merv as the host, CBS killed it. ABC picked it up with options, but after six months, it too canceled the show.

Finally, the game show found a relatively secure home at NBC, where it would last for four years—mostly as a daytime TV show but with occasional brief forays into prime time.

Its formula was simple: Usually a husband and wife would face another team of contestants and be presented with a puzzle which involved associations with the lives of up to three celebrity guests, or with something associated with up to three veiled objects. The competing teams would be given three choices marked X, Y, and Z, and the winner would be whichever team opted for the correct choice.

Between 1958 and 1962, Merv would be the show's longest running host, although the show sometimes brought on other announcers as well, including Johnny Gilbert, Don Pardo, and Johnny Olson. Olson would go on to additional fame as the first announcer for the Bob Barker version of *The Price Is Right* and, eventually, the announcer and host of *The Match Game*.

During Merv's tenure as host of *Play Your Hunch*, many celebrities appeared, the most famous of whom was Bob Hope. Merv wanted to ask Bob some really tough questions, including some about a rumored affair he'd had with Milton Berle when they were both young. Other, somewhat less controversial leads which Merv wanted to pursue involved Hope's seductions of such stars as Paulette Goddard, Betty Hutton, Marilyn Maxwell, Dorothy Lamour, and countless Las Vegas showgirls.

Bob's whoring had remained a relative secret until *Confidential* magazine exposed his sexual liaison with blonde starlet, Barbara Payton, who later became a prostitute and drug addict after her star had fallen from the Hollywood sky.

When Merv was talking on the phone with Marlon Brando, and informed him that Bob Hope was scheduled to appear on his show, Brando wasn't impressed. "Bob Hope will go to the opening of a phone booth in a gas station in Anaheim, provided they have a camera and three people there."

As always, Bob was a success on the show, using such familiar lines, as "The other day I was asked why I didn't run for President of the United States. I thought about it. But my wife said she wouldn't want to move into a smaller house."

A more unusual booking came in the form of an Englishman, Boris Karloff, Frankenstein himself. Merv told him, "I didn't recognize you without your neck bolts and asphalt spreader's boots.

Boris did not find that amusing, confessing to Merv that he suffered from chronic back trouble as a result of the heavy brace he had to wear as part of his Frankenstein costume.

One of Merv's favorite guests was the comedian and improvisational genius, Jonathan Winters, who'd just been released from a mental institution where he'd been sent after suffering a nervous breakdown. Seemingly well again, and appearing frequently on the shows of Merv's rival talk-show hosts as well, Jonathan shone brilliantly.

Backstage after the show, Merv lamented to Jonathan about how difficult it was for him to find a proper niche in show business. The comedian's response? "If your ship doesn't come in, swim out to meet it."

Merv's most anticipated moment came when he got to meet the gloriously lowbrow Three Stooges. He told the comedians that he'd gone to see all the movies made by the Stooges in the 1930s. "Later, with some local kids, I staged re-creations of your films on my back porch in San Mateo and charged admission. I could face slap, pull hair, and yank noses with pliers with the best of them," Merv said.

The cranky, sour-faced Moe Howard told Merv, "You little fucker! We should have charged you royalties." Merv didn't bond with the comedians the way he'd hoped, and they quickly went on their way.

Merv seemed insulted by their dismissal of him. In the wake of Curly Howard's death in 1952, Merv told his producer that as far as he was concerned, "the group was never the same again. They're on their way out. Without Curly, they're nothing." But for years, Merv imitated Curly's fabled "*nyuk-nyuk-nyuk.*"

Arthur Veary Treacher, a celebrity guest hosted by Merv on *Play Your Hunch,* would have an enormous impact on Merv's subsequent television career. Born in England in 1894, he played an eccentric English valet better than virtually anyone had before or since. "She denies it," Arthur said, "but Mae West and I are about the same age."

Standing six feet four, he towered over Merv, who had seen all three of the movies in which he'd appeared with Shirley Temple—*Stowaway* in 1936,

Heidi in 1937, and *The Little Princess* in 1939.

Before Arthur left the studio, Merv cornered him. "If I ever get the gig as host of *The Tonight Show*—or some other talk show—I want you to be my Jeeves." He was referring to Arthur's creation of P.G. Wodehouse's perfect valet character of Jeeves in two movies—*Thank You, Jeeves!* in 1936 and *Step Lively, Jeeves!* in 1937. Arthur had also played the perfect valet or butler in several other films, including *Curly Top* in 1935.

Obviously believing that such an offer would never come through, Arthur patted Merv's shoulder affectionately. "You dear little man," he said before going on his way.

It was while hosting *Play Your Hunch* that Merv had another chance encounter that would have an enormous impact on his career. At Radio City Studios, the audience participation show was broadcast live every morning. Later in the day, the set was altered for Jack Paar's late-night TV appearance.

After a nightmare he'd had about falling to his death in an elevator, Paar refused to take one. His habit of reaching his office via a labyrinth of stairwells, corridors, and short-cuts had become virtually an obsession.

He usually arrived at his office at noon. One morning he arrived early and followed his usual series of stairwells and short-cuts, unaware that *Play Your Hunch* was being broadcast.

Thinking it was a planned appearance, Merv's audience went wild when Paar suddenly appeared from behind the curtains. Seizing the opportunity, Merv locked a vise grip on Paar's arm and lured him into a spontaneous interview. Paar already knew Merv, who had sung a few times on his *Tonight Show*. "So this is what you do in the daytime," Paar quipped to Merv.

Paar would later recall how Merv had cleverly "milked" the incident to its maximum effect. Later, when Paar was scouting around for a substitute host to fill in for him on *The Tonight Show*, he thought once again of Merv.

Merv noted with a certain glee that his enemy, Robert Q. Lewis, had functioned as the host of *Play Your Hunch* during a low point in the show, just before it went off the air. "Lewis just wasn't Merv Griffin," Merv himself said. "Four Eyes just didn't have what the public wanted. I did."

***

Merv kept an "official" apartment in New York City, as well as a "secret hideaway" in Greenwich Village where the rent payments were split among himself and his friends, Johnny, Bill, and Paul. In addition to those two apartments, he maintained a twenty-acre farm in Califon, New Jersey, for his family. He retreated there whenever he could, although legitimate business and his continuation of a secret life kept him away from them for much of the time.

The farmstead in New Jersey had been the setting for a famous murder, which later became the subject of a book. A former occupant, the pastor of a local church, had injected small dosages of arsenic into apples and fed them to his wife. "It was a twist on the Adam and Eve story," Merv said. "Talk about forbidden fruit." The minister was later tried and convicted on a murder charge, and became the last person in the history of New Jersey to be publicly hanged.

Once, after a weekend on the farm and somewhat bored with his stalled career, Merv returned to New York to discover a surprise in the mail. An invitation to visit Liberace and a roundtrip ticket to Palm Springs awaited him. Liberace had enclosed a tantalizing note: "Come for the weekend. I want you to meet my mystery guest. Hint: he's the most famous man in America."

Johnny begged Merv to take him on the trip to Palm Springs. Merv turned him down, citing the fact that Liberace had sent only one ticket.

In Palm Springs, Merv was dazzled by Liberace's estate, with its Valentino Suite, its Marie Antoinette room, and—for orgiastic fantasies—its Persian Tent Room. After a long trip, Merv had to visit the bathroom. In all his life, before or since, he would never see such a bathroom. The giant bathtub, big enough for eight, had mirrored walls and ceilings with shower curtains depicting gay porno scenes. Merv took it all in as he sat on a Louis XVI gilt-and-mahogany commode. "What a place to take a shit," Merv later told Liberace. "I felt like a queen on my throne."

"That you were, Fannie Mae," Liberace said.

A handsome, shirtless Paul Richardson emerged to greet Merv with a kiss. Paul had remained Liberace's lover and bartender. Merv embraced him warmly, with fond memories of their previous intimacies.

Like all of Liberace's paid lovers, Paul would be no exception. His days with Liberace were numbered. But it is because of him that the details associated with this infamous weekend at Liberace's Palm Springs estate have not been lost.

After Liberace released Paul with only one thousand dollars in cash, Paul went to publisher Robert Harrison of *Confidential* magazine with explicit details about this secret weekend. Harrison wanted to run the story, but the magazine's lawyers turned him down since Liberace might sue—and win once again—on a charge of libel.

In London in 1957, "Cassandra" (actually journalist William Connor) wrote in *The Daily Mirror* that Liberace was ". . . the summit of sex—the pinnacle of masculine, feminine, and neuter. Everything that he, she, and it can ever want . . . a deadly, winking, sniggering, snuggling, chromium-plated, scent-impregnated, luminous, quivering, giggling, fruit-flavored, mincing, ice-covered heap of mother love." Liberace sued for libel, claiming in a

London court that he was not a homosexual—and had never taken part in any homosexual acts. Amazingly, he won the suit on the basis of the term "fruit-flavored," which was held to impute homosexuality. Liberace received eight thousand pounds in damages from *The Daily Mirror*.

As Paul served drinks, Merv seated himself in a comfortable chair in a courtyard which contained a fountain in the shape of a well-endowed boy embracing a white swan.

The courtyard also contained an Olympic-sized pool. Liberace dazzled Merv with stories about the notorious pool parties that took place here. "It's the talk of Palm Springs," Liberace said with a certain glee. "I invite all the big male stars, and you'd be surprised how many show up for these private all-boy parties. Naturally, Tyrone Power and Errol Flynn wouldn't miss them. Even Gary Cooper shows up, and Clark Gable has become a regular."

"You don't mean Clark Gable as in Rhett Butler," Merv said, totally shocked.

"One and the same," Liberace said. "He's one kind of man in Hollywood, quite another in Palm Springs. All the Palm Springs insiders are on to Gable's gay streak. Someday his biographers will write about his exploits which began in Hollywood back in the 20s. Of course, all the boys were putting out then, not just Gary Cooper, but guys like John Wayne. John Ford sucked that one's dick on a regular basis."

Later Merv sat at Liberace's Louis Philippe rosewood piano, and the two of them sang their favorite duets. "The party favor's late tonight," Liberace said. "You can wait around or else I can arrange a stud for hire. Or perhaps you want to sample my darling Paul again."

Liberace disappeared into an adjoining salon and emerged a minute later with a six-foot stuffed male doll with an erect penis. "Or else I can give you my adorable Adonis—that's his name—to keep you company."

It was shortly before midnight that the guest of honor arrived. Merv was astonished when Liberace introduced him to Elvis Presley in person. Merv was used to meeting stars, and never seemed in awe of them. Elvis was different. Merv was so awed by his sudden presence that for the first time in his life he was at a loss for words.

Elvis wore a pink shirt and a pair of simple blue jeans that were skin tight like Marilyn wore them. Merv couldn't help but notice Elvis's trademark blue suede shoes. He turned down a drink from Paul, who seemed dazzled by Elvis. The singer did ask Paul to prepare him a midnight snack. He told Liberace that he wanted to go for a midnight swim, and he emerged about fifteen minutes later in baggy white swimming trunks with a red stripe on each side. He joined Merv and Liberace in the courtyard, allowing both men to inspect his then thin body, before jumping in the pool to swim four laps.

After the swim, Elvis emerged from the pool where Paul held up a white terrycloth robe for him to wrap around himself. He sat beside Merv as Paul handed him a peanut butter and banana sandwich with fried bacon.

Paul sat nearby listening to every word, although ostensibly available for any drink orders. He got up to answer a telephone call, only to come back onto the patio. "It's urgent," he said to Liberace, who heaved himself up from his chair and excused himself.

With Paul back in attendance, Merv turned to Elvis. "I didn't know you and Sadie—that's my pet name for Lee—knew each other. In fact, I read in some gossip column only the other day that every time you see Sadie on TV, you throw something at the set."

"That's just for public show," Elvis said. "Actually, we see a lot of each other, but we do it in private because of all that publicity we received when we first got together. We like to keep our friendship a secret."

"Personally, I like to keep my friendship with Sadie a secret too," Merv confided.

Elvis claimed that when he'd first opened in Las Vegas at the New Frontier in 1956, his show had bombed. "I was a teenage heartthrob, but my act didn't go over with more mature audiences. Read that drunken audiences."

Liberace returned to the patio and immediately picked up on their conversation. "It was actually Colonel Tom Parker who set up a meeting between Elvis and me," Liberace said. He came backstage one night when I was appearing at the Riviera where I was making $50,000 a week, and poor Elvis was taking home only $7,500."

"'My boy is appearing across the street and he's having some problems,' the colonel told me. 'I think you're the man to help him. He admires you so much. He thinks you're a great showman.' I went over on my free night and caught Elvis's act. I loved his movements and his voice, but not his costumes. I advised him to put more glitz in his act."

"Lee here has been practically dressing me ever since," Elvis claimed.

"Or undressing as the case may be," Liberace said. "Since he started dressing the way I told him to, Elvis became hot as a tamale fart!"

"Could you put that more elegant?" Elvis asked, cracking a smile. "The first night I met Lee he gave me an autographed picture to take home to my mama in Memphis," Elvis said. "She adores him and never misses one of his shows."

Since Liberace had attended Elvis's show at the New Frontier, Elvis returned the favor, appearing on November 14, 1956 at Liberace's opening night at The Riviera. In snowy white tails, Liberace welcomed Elvis, as the house lights went up to reveal Elvis in a wide-striped jacket in the front row.

Later that night Elvis went backstage to congratulate Liberace. Ever the showman, Liberace in front of cameramen suggested that they exchange jackets and entertain the press. Wearing Elvis's striped jacket, Liberace played Elvis's guitar, while Elvis himself sat at Liberace's piano wearing his gold sequined tux jacket. The odd couple sang duets for about twenty minutes. "I'll Be Seeing You." "Deep in the Heart of Texas." And, of course, "Hound Dog." "Lee did a better 'Hound Dog' than mine," Elvis said.

"I told the press that Elvis and I may be characters—me with my gold jackets and him with those sideburns—but, as I said, 'both of us can afford to be characters,'" Liberace chuckled.

"I got really pissed off the next day by the press coverage," Elvis said. "One jerk said that up against Lee I was 'just a jug of corn liquor at a champagne party.' Those photographers did all they could to make us look like the two biggest queens in show business. In one picture Lee looks like he's practically drooling over me."

"I was," Liberace confessed.

It was Liberace who first suggested that Elvis have his tailor, Nudie Cohen, famous for his rhinestone-studded Western gear, make a simple pair of black trousers to better show off Elvis's sparkling gold coat. In time, Liberace would be the inspiration behind several of Elvis's outfits, including a famous white Bill Belew extravaganza, an outfit encrusted with rhinestones with a matching thigh-length cape that weighed an astonishing forty-two pounds. The similarity between the wardrobes worn by Elvis and Liberace did not escape detection by the press.

It was an exposé in the scandal magazine, *On the QT*, that led to Elvis and Liberace going underground with their friendship. The article, published in

left Fashion advice: **Elvis** and **Liberace**
right Singing in public, stripping in private

1957, was about "Presley's Powder-Puff Pals."

"The suggestion was clear that I'm a queer," Elvis angrily said. "The article practically had Lee sucking my dick. They published photographs of us, calling Lee and me the most prominent bachelors in the entertainment business. The fucker who wrote the article suggested that Lee and I would never be able to find the right gals to settle down with because our interest lay elsewhere."

"It's better to be compared to Liberace than a comparison I recently read," Merv said.

"Yeah, I saw that piece of shit too," Elvis said. "Some asshole compared my performance to an appearance of Zsa Zsa Gabor."

Liberace advised Elvis that he should sue *On the QT*.

"Like hell I will," Elvis said, "and have a court case airing charges of me being a fag."

"Well, I once sued and cried all the way to the bank," Liberace said.

It was three o'clock on a Palm Springs morning before a famous duet and a well-known performer, Merv himself, began to break up their party. Paul had spent the night serving drinks. To cool off, Elvis wanted a final dip in the luxurious pool.

It was Liberace who persuaded Elvis to remove his bathing trunks and put on a show for them. At first Elvis was reluctant. Finally, he said, "What the hell." He pulled down his trunks, exposing himself, and jumped into the pool.

Elvis was gone the following morning when Merv woke up. Over breakfast Liberace claimed that Elvis allowed him to give him a blow-job, "as he has several times in the past."

Merv didn't know if Liberace actually did that or was merely indulging in wishful thinking.

"I did give the boy a special gift," Liberace said. "A stunning and frightfully expensive gold watch studded with diamonds and rubies."

When Merv went to see Elvis's next live show, he saw him wearing just such a watch. Maybe, or so Merv thought, Liberace might not have been exaggerating about his conquest.

One night when Merv was talking to Liberace on the phone, he said that he'd seen a picture of Graceland covered in snow with five Cadillacs parked in the driveway. "I went at once to Tiffany's and ordered a silver-plated snow shovel for Elvis," Liberace said. "Before I sent it to him in Memphis, I had Tiffany's gold plate it."

Liberace also revealed that during his latest opening in Las Vegas, Elvis sent him a guitar made of flowers. "He enclosed a note," Liberace said. "It read: 'I only send this special guitar to people I love.'"

When Elvis died on August 16, 1977, Liberace was among his chief mourners. Even so, he was very guarded in a statement to the press. "A lot of Elvis's troubles were self-inflicted," Liberace claimed. "I knew him very well. He always felt somebody was after him. When you have that kind of fear, that kind of attitude, you attract people who want to do you harm."

In a private call to Merv, Liberace said, "to borrow a line from Noel Coward, I was mad about the boy right from the first time I met him. Of course, it was a completely one-sided love affair. He had all those young girls. What would he want with an old queen like me? Yet on many a night he came to me and let me hold him in my arms. Sometimes he cried like a baby. He seemed to know how fucked up he was at the end. One thing I never told him, as it would have frightened him and made him run away. But he was the love of my life. And now he's gone."

***

Back in New York, Merv was invited to sing on *The Arthur Murray Party*, a popular TV series that stayed on the air for a decade, beginning in 1950. It was basically devoted to ballroom dancing, plus songs, comedy, and dance contests. Merv sang a song he'd written, "Eternally," which was recorded with the Hugo Winterhalter Orchestra.

Hugo and Merv had known each other for years, and the orchestra leader had scored countless hits with such stars as Perry Como, Eddie Fisher, Billy Eckstine, and Tony Martin. But "Eternally" was a bomb for Merv as was "Hot-Cha-Cha," which he'd recorded with Mitch Miller and his orchestra.

Frank Sinatra had warned Merv not to work with Miller. "He and he alone is to blame for my fall from the charts when I was recording for Columbia. He forced me to sing such shit as 'Mama Will Bark' and 'The Hucklebuck.'"

When Merv talked about this with Miller, he said, "that's bullshit. The contract signed by Sinatra gave him the right to turn down any song. He's blaming me for his own failure."

Mitch and Merv worked well together. They remained friendly acquaintances. When Miller turned 89 at the millennium, Merv sent him a telegram. "You'll be one hundred before I reach that mark." In the year 2008 Mitch, born on July 4, 1911, was still alive.

Merv had greater luck with two other songs, "Banned in Boston" and "Charanga," both of which hit the top twenty on the charts. "Even so, they had the life of sickly butterflies," Merv said. "At any rate, I didn't make Elvis quiver in his blue suede shoes. The King still sat safely on his throne—that is, until the Beatles came along to unseat him."

Merv was grateful to Arthur and Kathryn Murray to allow him to showcase his music on their *Arthur Murray Party*, even though the TV show exist-

341

ed mainly to publicize their chain of dance studios. The show would always end with the famous dancing couple—the Fred Astaire and Ginger Rogers of television—performing a Johann Strauss waltz. Years later Merv said his chief memory of the show was not his failed music but of Ann Sheridan, a fellow guest, "teaching me to jitterbug."

Merv's next gig, *Music for a Summer Night*, started as a summertime replacement on TV in June of 1959. The show was not successful and went off the air in 1960. It came and went so fast in Merv's career that he hardly remembered what happened except for one episode. "I encountered Dick Haymes, a singer whose voice I used to admire and imitate."

He came up to Merv and said, "You're a stinking piece of faggot shit."

"Why Dick, it's so good to see you again," Merv said. He later speculated that the crooner had learned that Rita Hayworth and Aldo Ray had used his home in Los Angeles as a venue for their trysts.

Merv made yet another attempt at a TV show when he not only directed *Saturday Prom*, a weekly series, but co-hosted the show with Hugh C. Daly. Beechnut Gum was the sponsor, and Merv spent a lot of air time chewing gum and trying to imitate Dick Clark's more successful *American Bandstand*.

In a game of one-upmanship with Dick Clark, Merv persuaded the network to hire a live orchestra directed by Bobby Vinton, who was just on the dawn of his great success which would come in the 1960s. Ironically, Bobby got some of his greatest exposure on *American Bandstand*, not Merv's *Saturday Prom*.

Merv thought Bobby was a musical genius and envied his talent. Like Merv he could play the piano. Unlike Merv, Bobby could also play the clarinet, saxophone, trumpet, drums, and oboe.

In the years ahead, Merv watched in awe as Bobby plucked a hit single from the reject pile and recorded "Roses Are Red (My Love)," which spent four weeks at No. 1 on the *Billboard* Hot 100. His most famous song, however, was to be the 1963 "Blue Velvet," which had originally been a minor hit for Tony Bennett about a dozen years previously, in 1951.

During the course of his career, Bobby would sell more than 75 million records and became, in the words of *Billboard* Magazine," the all-time most successful love singer of the Rock Era. From 1962 to

Merv:
Smirking host/enabler
of illicit trysts

1972, he would have more *Billboard* Number One hits than any other male vocalist, including Frank Sinatra and Elvis Presley.

Merv later lamented, "If I'd been successful in my singing, I would have wanted a career like Bobby Vinton had in the 1960s. Alas, it was not meant to be. But even Bobby could not stave off the British Invasion, although he made a spectacular comeback with 'My Melody of Love' in 1974—singing partly in Polish. Who would have thunk that?"

In many ways, *Saturday Prom* was a traumatic experience for Merv, making him feel "like yesterday's spaghetti." He came face to face with "tomorrow's competition" on live television. Some of the most popular rock 'n' roll performers of the time appeared on camera—The Shirelles, Brenda Lee, Hank Ballard, Chubby Checker, Sam Cooke, The Playmates, Jo Ann Campbell, and Johnny and The Hurricanes. No lip sync was permitted. High school kids made up the studio audience. But whenever the cameras rolled, members of the relatively wholesome NBC Teen Workshop stood around Merv and his fellow performers so that no punk would present "the bird" to the camera.

***

Marty secured a booking for Merv on the *DuPont Show of the Week* series. He'd be appearing on TV in a segment called *The Wonderful World of Toys*. The setting would be New York's Central Park, where on the first day of filming he met one of the stars, Harpo Marx.

Merv had always been fond of the Marx Brothers when he'd watched their movies in the 1930s. He was eager to meet Harpo. At first, though, he didn't recognize him. When Harpo shook his hand, he encountered a bald man. Harpo had always been seen on screen with his poofy, curly red hair. It was a wig.

As they talked, Merv learned that Harpo, the silent one on camera, was actually very articulate. He told Merv that he too had wanted to learn to play the piano when he was a kid. "My family could afford to give lessons to only one of us," Harpo said. "My brother Chico was selected. I *mastered* the harp instead."

While waiting for the cameras to be set up, Harpo enchanted Merv with stories of his life, and those of his brothers. He said that Chico once appeared on TV as Harpo in wig and costume on *I've Got a Secret* in 1952. "Chico fooled all the panelists, including one in particular—Groucho himself."

Harpo said that he was once vacationing in Nice on the French Riviera and enjoying sunbathing in the nude. "An elderly man and woman approached. I grabbed my bath towel from the Carlton and wrapped it around my genitals. The man yanked the towel from me, exposing me. He reached to

343

shake my hand. 'Good afternoon. I'm George Bernard Shaw. This is my wife, Mrs. Shaw.' It was the beginning of a lifelong friendship."

Appearing before the cameras in Central Park, Merv launched into his song, "Hot-Cha-Cha." Just as he did, a pigeon with diarrhea flew over and dumped on his head.

"That God damn pigeon got to me before the critics crapped on me," Merv said.

During the filming, Merv had a reunion with co-star Carol Burnett, who was no longer the president of his fan club in Hollywood. In fact, Merv no longer had fan clubs anywhere.

Merv was also surprised to encounter Milton Berle playing himself in the show. He hadn't seen Milton since that night in New York when Merv was escorting Elizabeth Taylor, who claimed at the time that she didn't know who Milton Berle was. "Has the bitch heard of me by now?" Milton asked Merv.

"She's not only heard of you, but thinks you're twice as good as Bob Hope. Elizabeth told me the other night that you're an original. She heard that Hope without his writers wouldn't know what to say."

"The whore got that right," Milton said, still obviously offended by Elizabeth.

When Merv was introduced to Audrey Meadows, another star of the show, he said, "You don't have slanty eyes at all. He was referring to her birth in China, the daughter of missionaries. "Well, I spoke only Mandarin Chinese until I was five," she told Merv.

Merv's favorite show on TV at the time was *The Honeymooners*, where Audrey played Alice Cramden at that two-burner stove in her Chauncey Street kitchen. As Merv had coffee with her, he noticed that she was a chain smoker. The actress would later die of lung cancer in Beverly Hills in 1996.

"I almost didn't get the role of Alice," Audrey said. "Jackie Gleason thought I was too chic and too pretty to be Ralph Kramden's wife. I made myself up for the part and wore frumpy clothes and sent him photographs of me. He went for it. You know Gleason. He's short and has a Napoleonic complex. That's why he hires short actors. I'm five feet nine so he made me wear flats."

Audrey had just married Robert Six, the CEO of Continental Airlines. When Merv shook his hand, Merv indiscreetly blurted out, "You were married to Ethel Merman. Why would anyone in his right mind marry Ethel Merman?"

Merv was also introduced to Edie Adams, the actress, singer, and comic, who was also starring in *The Wonderful World of Toys*. He'd just seen *The Apartment* in which she'd co-starred with Shirley MacLaine, Fred MacMurray, and Jack Lemmon. It had been Edie's first major film.

In the movie Lemmon played a guy at the bottom of the ladder, who is trying to work his way up by lending the key to his apartment to his higher-ups—in this case MacMurray—for trysts.

Over lunch that day with Edie, Merv confessed that he too had lent his home in Los Angeles to illicit lovers. Although Merv around most people kept his own life closeted, he was often indiscreet in revealing the love affairs of his friends.

Reportedly, Merv told Edie a secret that day, revealing that Rosemary Clooney had been using his New York apartment to have an affair with Robert Kennedy that had to be kept a dead secret since his brother was the president of the United States. Other sources claim that Merv revealed that secret to Elsa Maxwell, not Edie.

"Unlike Lemmon in the movie, I'm not trying to advance my career this way," Merv allegedly said. "But I do believe in the secret life. Not all affairs were meant for public consumption."

Johnny Riley later claimed that Merv allowed his secret hideaway to be used by a number of stars conducting off-the-record weekends. "I think he got a vicarious thrill out of it," Johnny said. "I encountered Bob Kennedy and Rosemary on several occasions. Who am I to judge? I'm not exactly a candidate for sainthood myself."

Merv liked Edie and sent his condolences to her when her husband, Ernie Kovacs, died a few months later in a car accident in 1962 following a party at Milton Berle's home where Kovacs had had too much to drink. Upon his death, Kovacs owed half a million dollars in back taxes to the Internal Revenue Service. When Merv had met Kovacs, the comedian told him that the American tax system was "unfair, unjust, and illegal. That's why I'm not going to give those fuckers a penny of my money." Merv told him he was playing a dangerous game.

After the death of Kovacs, Edie refused to go along with her lawyers, who urged her to declare bankruptcy. She took every job she could until she'd paid every cent back to the IRS.

Years later, Merv, head of his own production company, saw a proposal for a film that seemed to have the endorsement of Edie. It was to be based on the life of Kovacs, and Merv understood that Edie wanted George Clooney to play her late husband. Merv passed on the script. He'd already seen a 1984 TV movie, *Ernie Kovacs: Between the Laughter*, starring Jeff Goldblum, and thought the movie was unsuccessful.

Elsa Maxwell, the short, stout American hostess and celebrity tattle-tale columnist, had also been cast in *The Wonderful World of Toys*. At the time Merv met her on set, he'd seen every episode of her controversial appearances on *The Jack Paar Tonight Show*. Merv was already telling friends like Peter Lawford and Rosemary Clooney that he was one day going to replace Paar as emcee of the show.

"When I do, Elsa is just the type of guest I'm seeking," Merv said. "She's never boring, and she knows everybody's secrets—perhaps my own. Elsa's parties for royalty and high society figures of her day earned her the nickname of "the hostess with the mostest.""

Elsa spread gossip, but was also its victim. He knew that she was a lesbian and had actively pursued Maria Callas, who was repulsed by her. Even so, Callas appreciated Elsa's introduction to Aristotle Onassis. Elsa was quickly discarded as the Greek shipping tycoon and the Greek-born opera singer launched their own torrid and tormented affair.

Merv met Elsa at the end of her celebrity-studded life. She was to die in New York on November 1, 1963, when she'd declared that "I didn't do bad at all—not bad for a short, fat, homely piano player from Keokuk, Iowa, with no money or background, who decided to become a legend and did just that."

During the filming, Elsa invited Merv to a party at the Plaza Hotel. She already knew about Rosemary's affair with Robert Kennedy—in fact, she knew everybody's darkest secrets. She even confessed to Merv that she'd introduced Patricia Kennedy Lawford to the notorious Porfirio Rubirosa, and that they'd had an affair.

"My darling Rubi has affairs with anything that moves. When he gets drunk, he doesn't give a damn what kind of legs are open to him. He's going to be at my party tonight. I'll introduce you to him."

The party was a star-studded event, but Merv had eyes only for Rubirosa. Stories about the size of his penis were legendary. Jerome Zerbe, the society photographer, claimed that the penis "looked like Yul Brynner in a black turtleneck sweater." The tobacco heiress, Doris Duke, Rubirosa's third wife, told anyone who was interested, that "it is the most magnificent penis I have ever seen."

From gossips, Merv already knew that Rubirosa's conquests had included Ava Gardner, Veronica Lake, Marilyn Monroe, Susan Hayward, and countless others, ranging from chambermaids to the upper crust of royalty and international society, even multi-millionaire male size queens with a preference for their own sex.

At the party, Merv noticed that Rubi was drinking heavily, and Merv knew that at some point the handsome, dashing stud would have to heed nature's call at a hotel urinal.

Merv waited for his chance, and followed the

Celebrity hostess **Elsa Maxwell:**
The dyke from Keokuk

346

former diplomat of the Dominican Republic into the men's room, where he stationed himself at the urinal immediately next to Rubi's.

The playboy of the Western world sensed at once that Merv wanted him to put on a show. Rubi unbuttoned his trousers and let it all hang out. He was used to having men, even merely curious straight ones, follow him into urinals around the world. In fact, the legend of his penis was such that men, including Merv, called for a "Rubirosa" when they wanted the waiter to bring a giant peppermill to table.

Merv was not disappointed at Rubi's show, later telling Johnny that it looked like "a fat baby's arm dangling from his pants."

Zipping up and shaking himself dry after his show, Rubi shook Merv's hand. "I would have shown it to you hard," Rubi said, "but it takes so much blood to get it up that I would have passed out. And you would have passed out at the size of it. When it gets hard, I can balance a phone book on it. For my virility, I drink Japanese mushroom tea."

Merv would learn a lot more about Rubi when he became a friend of Zsa Zsa Gabor, who had had a notorious affair with the playboy during his marriage to the Woolworth heiress, Barbara Hutton.

One morning in 1965 Merv picked up the newspaper to read that Rubi, at the age of fifty-six, had wrapped his sports car around a tree in Paris' Bois de Boulogne and was dead.

Paul Schone was sitting opposite Merv having his morning coffee.

"I don't think I could have handled it even if Rubi had given me the chance," Merv said. "Six inches in circumference is a bit large even for my big mouth."

Finally, the final star of *The Wonderful World of Toys*, Eva Gabor, came onto the set and immediately enchanted Merv. "She even invited me to a lunch of salami and champagne, which I later learned was her favorite snack," Merv said.

Playboy **Porfirio Rubirosa:**
The size queen's favorite

Before meeting Eva, Merv had seen her hilarious TV appearances with Jack Paar. When Merv was first introduced to Eva, she was deep into her fourth marriage, this time to Richard Brown.

Years later, as Merv recalled his first luncheon with Eva, she rather cautiously told him virtually nothing about herself but spent most of the time complaining about her sister, Zsa Zsa, and her "eternal fascination with that awful George Sanders. He was a complete scoundrel throughout his entire marriage to Zsa Zsa."

Eva went on to assert that her sister knew that George had been cheating on her throughout the course of their marriage. "Hedy Lamarr, Marilyn Monroe, Lucille Ball, you name her. The bastard even slept with Doris Duke. But Zsa Zsa got even with George by having an affair with Porfirio Rubirosa, Doris Duke's former husband. Zsa Zsa taunted George by telling him that Rubi was three times the man he was, at least in one department, and could go all night."

Releasing additional details about her sister Zsa Zsa, Eva maintained that "Throughout the course of the marriage, George humiliated Zsa Zsa by insisting that he should have married a rich woman. But by marrying George, Zsa Zsa had relinquished the alimony that was coming in from her earlier marriage to Conrad Hilton. And then, as a means of taunting her, George had the cruel bad taste to tell everybody that when it came to women, 'there is no greater aphrodisiac than money.'"

At the time of their first luncheon together, Merv was not sexually attracted to Eva, even though he found her fascinating and "incredibly beautiful."

As Merv later recalled, when they parted that day she gave him a light kiss on the lips. "Someday when we're older," she predicted, "we'll be great friends. We Hungarians are like gypsies. We know of such things. But, right now, both of us have too much living to do."

The glamorous **Eva Gabor:**
"Too much living to do."

Chapter Eight

As 1958 neared its end, Jack Paar was the king of late-night television.

Evoking Merv's own experiences in Hollywood, Paar's screen career had gone nowhere, despite having been cast in a role opposite Marilyn Monroe in *Love Nest* (1951). Paar's TV guests included, among others, a drunken Judy Garland making fun of Marlene Dietrich. Hungarian sexpot Zsa Zsa Gabor could also be trotted out for a laugh. But Paar could get serious too, as when, in 1960, he brought on both John F. Kennedy and Richard Nixon, appearing separately, when they were running for president. Robert F. Kennedy had also granted Paar his first televised interview after the assassination of JFK in Dallas.

Merv would watch nearly every line-up of Paar's guests, using his methods as a role model. Frequently, Paar would book, as part of the same show, both serious authorities in their respective fields and guests who could be counted on for light amusement. What Merv chose not to imitate was Paar's unpredictable emotional style.

Biographer Laurence Leamer called Paar an "emotional hemophiliac—scratch him and he bled all over the media." Leamer went on to say, "Paar took his private neuroses and turned them into a public spectacle. Eight million viewers waited every night for Paar's catharsis of the moment. He might walk off the show, break into tears, steamroller a guest, insult a politician or a commentator, or threaten to quit altogether."

"He's a total shithead, but I still watch him," Frank Sinatra told Merv in a phone call. "If you get a call to sub for him, don't do it. It'll mean your graveyard. His devotees love him too much, and they would hate you. And those who'd love you—that is, those who hate Jack Paar—wouldn't be watching anyway."

When Paar encountered Merv's agent, Marty Kummer, at a restaurant, he told him that Jack been impressed with their impromptu encounter on *Play Your Hunch*, and he wanted Merv to sub for him.

At long last Merv's dream had come to be. But he stayed up the night before wondering if this big chance would turn into a nightmare.

For Merv's Monday night debut on *The Tonight Show*, the regular production team took the evening off, not wanting to be linked to what they forecast as a potential disaster. "Putting Merv Griffin in Jack Paar's chair is like asking Jayne Mansfield to sit in for the President of the United States," said a jealous Robert Q. Lewis to anyone who wanted to listen.

As a producer for his debut, Merv was assigned Bob Shanks, a grassroots American who grew up in Indiana. This was viewed as a lucky break for Bob as well—his first chance to be the producer of a TV show. Up to that point, he had been a pre-show interviewer for Paar's guests. Before landing on the Paar show, Shanks had been a struggling actor and freelance writer.

Meeting Bob for the first time, Merv formed one of those instant friendships he'd become known for, although he could hardly imagine he was meeting the future producer of *The Merv Griffin Show*, both for NBC-TV and CBS-TV.

Right before showtime, Marty Kummer phoned all the network executives he knew, urging them to watch Merv's inaugural performance on *The Tonight Show*. With knees knocking and hands quivering, Merv walked out in front of millions of *Tonight Show* fans to sub for Paar. From the live audience, there arose a murmur of disappointment, which did little to quell Merv's anxieties.

"I knew I was bombing only three minutes into the show," Merv said. "After seven minutes when we broke for commercials, I bolted from my seat. I couldn't go on any more. I was overcome with panic. The worst stage fright of my life."

Behind the curtains he collided with Bob Shanks. "I'm out of here," Merv said. "Get someone to fill in for me. I'm going home. I can't do this."

Bob gripped Merv firmly by the arm. "You're going to turn your ass around and get back out there in front of the camera and deliver a show better than any that Paar has ever done."

Bolstered by Bob's encouragement, Merv walked back on stage to finish the show. Seated in Paar's chair once again, he felt a renewed confidence. "I was going to bring on Mickey Rooney tonight," he told the live audience, thinking he was on air. "But Jack kicked him off for having one too many." The audience laughed before a member of the crew signaled Merv that broadcasting would begin in five seconds.

Years later there was a lot that he didn't remember from that night except for

When Titans clash:
(left) **Jack Paar** (right) **Merv**

Aretha Franklin, who was making her first talk show appearance on live TV. "She was just great," Merv claimed, "a phenomenal entertainer. The audience loved her."

He had long supported black entertainers, but it was because of Aretha's stunning performance that he decided that if he ever got his own talk show, he would book frequent appearances of black entertainers, both the known and the unknown, both male and female.

After the show, backstage, Merv embraced Bob warmly. "You saved my TV career tonight, and I'll always be grateful. If I go on from here and get my own talk show, you're the producer, kid."

Paar sat up that night watching Merv's performance, and liked it. "He's not as warm and personal with the audience as I am," Paar later told Bob, "but he's a natural. Invite him back as the host this coming Monday night. I'm taking off to have dinner with Judy Garland."

On his second Monday night appearance on *The Tonight Show*, Merv did something provocative, so daring that it could have raised the ire of Paar and led to Merv getting kicked off the show forever: Merv summoned Woody Allen for an appearance on the show again.

Woody had gotten his start at the age of fifteen, writing one-liners to gossip columns. Behind those thick glasses he always wore, he would later become famous for his one-liners: "Join the army, see the world, meet interesting people—and kill 'em," or "Not only is there no God, but try getting a plumber on weekends."

Bob Shanks, who served as a kind of talent scout for Paar, had caught Woody's act at The Duplex in Greenwich Village and, with Paar's consent, had booked him on *The Tonight Show*.

Paar, who had not met Woody before the show, later claimed that he looked like "he'd been plugged into an electric socket and someone had flipped the switch." Merv later claimed that impression as his own opinion, publishing it word for word in his second autobiography.

Paar found Woody's act vulgar. He particularly objected to one line, "The difference between sex and death is, death you can do alone and nobody will laugh."

As Woody finished his act, the cameras cut back to Paar, who was obviously enraged. In front of his audience, he angrily said, "Whoever booked that man and knew what he was going to say, I want to see in my office immediately

"The difference between sex and death is, death you can do alone, and no one will laugh."
Woody Allen

following this show." Fortunately for Merv's future in TV, Bob Shanks wasn't fired that night.

Merv had been watching Paar's show on the night the Brooklyn-born comedian made his TV debut, and despite the gaffes, recognized Woody's talent and audience appeal. Paar had given Merv total control over booking any guest he wanted to while he filled in for him, but Bob was nonetheless shocked when Merv asked him to book Woody Allen for a comeback. Defying Paar, Bob booked Woody once again—and he was a big hit. "Even though Woody had a peculiar New York kind of humor, audiences seemed to eat it up, probably because Woody was so different," Merv later said.

Woody later went on to face spectacular success as a writer, a film director, an actor, a comedian, a playwright, and to a somewhat lesser extent, a jazz musician.

To Merv's dismay, Paar for decades dined out on the claim that he'd "discovered" Woody Allen and exposed him for the first time to nationwide attention. Woody, of course, would later be nominated for more awards than Charlie Chaplin, Buster Keaton, or Harold Lloyd.

For years, Merv and Paar competed about which of them had actually "discovered" Woody Allen. Merv, however, would also take credit for saving Woody from potential injury and disaster.

Years later, when Frank Sinatra, former husband of Mia Farrow, learned that Woody was having an affair with her adopted daughter, Soon-Yi Previn, he called Mia and threatened to have "my boys" work over the comedian.

When Merv learned of that, he phoned Frank and asked him to call off his boys and spare Woody. "After all, Frank, you owe me one." Frank called off his boys, but spent the rest of his life raging against what he called "that incestuous bastard."

On the nights Merv did not join his family—and there were many of those—he might be sitting next to Johnny Riley watching Paar on *The Tonight Show*.

"Merv had this incredible instinct that Paar was about to commit *hari-kiri* right in front of the *Tonight* audience," Johnny said. "And so he did."

Paar sealed his doom on the evening of February 10, 1960, although it would be months before he was off the air. One of his harmless jokes was cut from a broadcast by studio censors. It involved a woman writing to a vacation resort and asking about the availability of a W.C., meaning water closet or toilet. The person who received the letter thought W.C. meant "wayside chapel." The full joke was filled with *double entendres* that seemed innocent even back in 1960. Paar became so angered at the censorship that he walked off the show, but then allowed himself to be lured back. However, his days with the network were numbered. Claiming that he was "bone tired," he signed off for the last time at the end of his show of March 29, 1962.

"Merv practically jumped out of his seat," Johnny later reported. "I've never seen him so elated. He announced to me, 'I'm taking over *The Jack Paar Show.*'"

While the network debated a replacement, Merv, as he'd anticipated, was called by NBC to fill in for Paar on many a night. In all, Merv's gig totaled six weeks. He was not the only guest emcee, however. Temporarily occupying what was known as Paar's "tear-soaked seat," were other entertainers. They included Jerry Lewis, Soupy Sales, Steve Lawrence, Mort Sahl, Joey Bishop, Jan Murray, and Peter Lind Hayes.

In spite of this competition, Merv still clung to the belief that he was Paar's heir apparent. One night his agent, Marty, rained on Merv's parade. "I've got the scoop," Marty said. "NBC's first choice is Johnny Carson. But you're second choice if Johnny doesn't sign."

Merv was horribly disappointed. "At least they're not offering the deal to that fuck-face, Robert Q. Lewis," he said. His face brightened. "Frank Sinatra's always claiming he owes me one for saving his life. Maybe I should call Frank and ask him to have his boys work over Carson so much he won't emcee any show."

"I hope you're joking," Marty said.

"It's no joke!"

Paar watched all the appearances where Merv took over for him on *The Tonight Show* and had this comment: "Merv is a quick study. I would have to give him an 'A' in economics, because he knows more about the money end of television than anyone. He will never need food stamps. He will probably outlast Johnny Carson and all the rest because of his 'laid-back' approach. He is a decent and likable man."

That was Paar's public opinion. Privately he had a darker one. He told Johnny Carson and the NBC suits, "I still can't believe all those stories about Merv being a homosexual. I hear he likes well-built, well-endowed men and attends orgies staged by his best pal, Liberace. The evidence is overwhelming from countless sources: Merv Griffin is gay. Yet, amazingly, he doesn't come off as mincing or limp-wristed like most faggots. To give him his due, he conceals his homosexuality very well, although I predict that one day all that man chasing will get him into serious trouble."

It was Paar's discomfort with Merv's homosexuality that led him to endorse Johnny Carson for the late-night slot. Carson signed the deal.

"Merv later claimed that at the time, he fully expected Carson to take over the show," said Johnny Riley. "But that wasn't true at all. He thought he had the inside track. When he got the bad news, he went into an incredible depression, thinking his TV career—his big chance—was gone forever. I did everything I could to bolster his ego and make him believe in himself again. We were never closer than we were during this period. And then something happened. I fell in love with a guy. Nobody special. But I loved him. I was never in love with Merv. We were bedmates, but never lovers in the full sense of the word. The only problem was, I couldn't tell Merv the bad news—not when he was down."

***

As it turned out, NBC did not want to cut the umbilical cord with Merv. In July of 1962, he was offered a 55-minute daytime chat show to be launched in October. Hailing Merv as an entertainer of "star magnitude," NBC's Mort Werner, one of the network's vice presidents, promised that Merv's new show would be "amusing, adult, articulate, and alive."

Although elated to have his own talk show, Merv was terribly disappointed that it was scheduled for broadcasting every weekday at two o'clock in the afternoon. "That is the graveyard for daytime TV," he claimed. Merv's show was positioned within the orbit of his newly established Merv Griffin Productions, which gave him creative control of the guests he could book.

NBC made a mistake in announcing that Merv's show was going to be part of their autumn line-up. When he found this out, Merv had not yet signed a contract, so with his lawyer, Roy Blakeman, he pounced.

Meeting with Herb Schlosser from NBC, Merv listened politely as the executive offered $8,000 a week.

"Merv had us by the cojones," Schlosser said, "since we'd already announced him as part of our team. He refused to accept the $8,000 and wanted another $10,000 a week to sweeten the kitty. No one in those days made that kind of dough. When I faced the executives at NBC, I was shocked that they agreed to the $18,000. It was just unheard of."

In the wake of that decision, Merv reached out for "my savior," Bob Shanks, raising his salary as producer from $200 to $1,000 a week.

Call it beginner's luck, but Merv managed to hire a trio of the most talented young writers in television, each man headed for future acclaim. Dick Cavett was the first to sign on. He'd come from Nebraska, a state that had produced such other talents as Henry Fonda, Marlon Brando, and Montgomery Clift.

"Thank Zeus I finally made it here with a contract," Dick told Merv. "I once applied for a job as a page at NBC's office in Rockefeller Center but was turned down." Merv discovered that Dick was one of the most brilliant comics he'd ever encountered, but he suffered from a manic-depressive disorder that had begun during his freshman year at Yale. Both Dick and Merv's rival,

Johnny Carson, were also magicians, Merv learned.

He told Dick that, "The salary that I'm shelling out to you will more than pay for your $51 a month walk-up."

Although Merv liked the material Dick submitted, years later he would complain to associates that "Cavett writes better lines for Johnny Carson than he ever did for me." Merv especially liked it when Dick had Carson say, "Having your taste criticized by Dorothy Kilgallen is like having your clothes criticized by Emmett Kelly."

Years later, Merv expressed a kind of malicious glee when Cavett got his own talk show and competed against Carson in the same time slot. But after that, Merv came to view Dick "as more competition than Carson himself."

Paul Schone, Merv's friend, said, "If you want to make our boy angry, just compare him to Dick Cavett."

A critic for a New York newspaper had already done just that. "Cavett is an intelligent, penetrating interviewer who is not afraid to ask probing questions or even insult an obnoxious guest, the way Jack Paar did. After listening to Timothy Leary blabber on, Cavett right on the air told him, 'I really think you're full of crap.' Merv Griffin on the other hand is Mr. Nice Guy on the air. Being interviewed on his show is like having a steak-and-potato dinner with an insurance salesman from Kansas City."

Pat McCormick was the most outrageous writer Merv ever hired. Over the course of Pat's career, he would also write for Bill Cosby, Don Rickles, and Jonathan Winters. When doing so, he tested the barriers of what was acceptable as comedy on TV.

Merv was startled the first day Pat, all 270 pounds of him, lumbered into his office. Standing 6'6", he had blond curly hair and a big walrus mustache adorning his ruddy face. After Pat's first week on the job, Merv told Bob Shanks that "Pat's weird, but he can deliver one-liners as good as Woody Allen."

Pat's most notorious appearance was not on Merv's show but on Johnny Carson's show. On an episode of Carson's *Tonight Show* in 1974, while Carson was delivering his opening monologue, Pat suddenly emerged from behind the curtains. Totally nude, he streaked across the stage behind Carson.

Today Pat is best remembered for playing Big Enos Burdette alongside Burt Reynolds in *Smokey and the Bandit* (1977) and its two sequels.

The third writer Merv hired was David

Brilliant, witty,
and manic-depressive:
Dick Cavett

355

Lloyd. Mild-mannered and unobtrusive, he evolved into one of the top writers on serial television, creating 30 episodes of *The Mary Tyler Moore Show* in the 1970s. He also wrote many episodes of series which included *Taxi*, *Cheers*, *Wings*, and *Frasier*.

With creative freedom over who would appear on his show, Merv hired Woody Allen as a performer, getting him to sign a contract for an appearance every Friday. Welcoming the exposure, Woody gladly accepted the deal.

Merv wanted big names for his debut shows, and he asked his former roommate, Harry Belafonte, to come on. When Harry showed up at the studio, however, Merv realized that he'd lost his youthful beauty and even much of his charm. "But I embraced him and treated him like my best and long lost friend," Merv said. "People in show business do that all the time."

Merv recalled that Harry "seemed a bit full of himself," reminding Merv of some of his achievements. Frank Sinatra had recruited Harry to perform at the inaugural gala of President Kennedy, and Harry's latest album, *Jump Up Calypso*, had become another of the star's million sellers. Also, Harry reminded Merv that whereas he'd succeeded in the movies, Merv had not.

To the surprise of Bob Shanks and the rest of the staff, one of Merv's most interesting and most provocative guests was an acquaintance from the 1930s. Adela Rogers St. Johns had met Merv when she'd played tennis with his Uncle Elmer. Merv had been her "ball boy."

Adela was a famous and well-connected American journalist, novelist, and screenwriter. She'd reported on everything from the controversial Jack Dempsey-Gene Tunney "long-count" fight in 1927 to the 1935 trial of Richard Bruno Hauptmann for kidnapping and murdering the son of Charles Lindbergh. "She knew where all the bodies were buried in Hollywood," Merv said. "And I mean *all*. The stories she'd privately tell about Rudolph Valentino, Gloria Swanson, and Greta Garbo would shock the unshockable."

In anticipation of one of the several shows he did with Adela, Merv called on Joan Crawford, not knowing if she would even speak to him after their last disastrous encounter. The aging movie queen accepted the offer to appear on the show, treating Merv as if she'd never met him before.

Later, Merv said he regretted that he didn't let Adela interview Joan, as the columnist had done so many times in the past. On the air, Merv asked Joan if she'd ever felt any romantic attraction toward any of her leading men. Assuming a wide-eyed, innocent look, Joan claimed that she had not.

"Now, Joan, you *married* three of them," Adela butted in. "You *must* have had *some* feelings."

Backstage Merv walked into a screaming argument between Joan and Adela. "HOW DARE YOU EMBARRASS ME LIKE THAT?" Joan shouted. "WHY DIDN'T YOU JUST ASK WHAT IT'S LIKE TO FUCK CLARK

GABLE? But, of course, you could have answered that one yourself." Then Joan grandly stormed out of the studio.

After she'd left, Adela turned to Merv and said, "That Joan! From Henry Fonda to Glenn Ford, she's fucked more of her leading men than Lassie has taken shits. You should have asked her what it was like going to bed with President Kennedy."

Initially, Merv attracted bigger-name guests than the then relatively unknown Johnny Carson. Merv asked Danny Kaye's agent if the star would come on the show, and was rather surprised when Danny accepted. Merv wondered if Danny resented the fact that he'd done far better with his recording of "I've Got a Lovely Bunch of Coconuts" than the star had done with his. But when Danny came onto Merv's show, no mention was made of the Coconuts song.

Merv often bonded with his guests, but not with Danny. Privately Merv wanted to ask Danny all the big questions ("Tell me about your long-standing affair with Laurence Olivier." "What's it like fucking Princess Margaret?") but didn't dare.

After the show, Danny graciously invited Merv and a few members of the staff back to an apartment he was temporarily occupying. There he prepared what Merv called "the best Chinese dinner I've ever had in my life."

Over after-dinner drinks, Danny told amusing stories about his fabulous career in Hollywood. Suddenly, he abruptly said, "Nobody wants to fuck Danny Kaye."

"I do," Merv said, chivalrously, smiling to indicate he just might be joking.

"I don't mean it that way," Danny said. "Samuel Goldwyn himself uttered that statement about me, telling his associates that I don't have sex appeal. In *The Court Jester* I had to show off my legs in tights. Frankly, my gams aren't that great. I called in this expert costume designer, and he had me wear symmetricals. You might know them as leg falsies. That's why in that picture I had the shapeliest legs ever shown on the screen. But they weren't really mine."

"The other day I heard that Edward G. Robinson is proud of his shapely legs and likes to show them off every chance he gets," Merv said.

There was a sudden silence in the room. After Merv's flippant remark, the party died. Merv never became the intimate friend with Danny that he'd

Joan Crawford with **Merv**
Wide eyed innocence,
screaming denunciations

357

wanted to be.

Hoping for another big name, Merv called yet another former roommate, Monty Clift, who had forgiven him for not recognizing him that night he'd showed up at Merv's apartment following his plastic surgery in the wake of his terrible automobile accident.

Merv hadn't seen Monty in months, so he placed a call to his friend Lee Remick for an update. She'd filmed *Wild River* with Monty. "His body is bird-like," Lee said. "He's all skin and bones—practically half the man he was. If you put your arms around him, it's like hugging yourself."

Monty showed up at the studio drunk, and Merv tried to sober him up with black coffee. He'd never seen the once startlingly handsome star look this awful. At first Merv considered canceling Monty's appearance and bringing in a substitute guest.

"Monty did appear on the show," Merv said, "and I hated every minute of it. At times, he was so incoherent that he seemed retarded. The drugs in his body did all the talking—not Monty. I was on the edge of my seat all during the interview. I felt that Monty was going to have a nervous breakdown in front of millions of people."

Backstage, Merv asked Monty if he'd join him for dinner "for old time's sake."

Monty turned down the offer. "It's not that I don't want to hang out with you, but I don't want to talk about the past."

"Well, we'll talk about the future," Merv said.

"There is no future, at least not for me." Monty embraced Merv and walked away.

***

The Merv Griffin Show had been on the air for less than a month before Johnny Riley told Merv that he was moving out and moving on. His new boyfriend was much older and a TV executive. Johnny would be living on the Upper East Side in the future, not in Merv's secret hideaway, which was still used infrequently for trysts between Rosemary Clooney and Robert Kennedy.

"It was the strangest thing," Johnny later recalled. "Merv showed almost no reaction. He seemed neither elated to get rid of me nor terribly disappointed. He wished me well. If anything, it showed me that we should have always remained friends and should never have attempted a love affair. It wasn't a love affair, really. Call it an affair. If anything, Merv seemed to relish his new-found freedom. He already had the stability of a family. I think he wanted to play the field in his spare time, and not be tied down with any one person on the outside."

Johnny moved on, but Merv continued to maintain the hideaway with Paul Schone and Bill Robbins, neither of whom showed any indication that they wanted to settle down with anyone. It would be three years before Johnny saw Merv again, although Johnny continued to see his friends, Paul and Bill, apart from Merv, on the side.

Not only did Merv lose Johnny, but he temporarily lost his show as well. NBC pulled it off the air in favor of the Giants/Yankees World Series.

During the interim, Merv flew to London to tape a series of interviews. Through a publicist, one of the interviews was arranged with a young actor, Peter O'Toole, who had just completed filming *Lawrence of Arabia* (1962). Marlon Brando had foolishly rejected the leading role in this film, and at the time, the media was filled with talk and speculation about this movie.

When Merv with his TV crew showed up at Peter's home outside London, Peter wasn't there. Merv later learned he was drinking at the local pub. The interview was re-scheduled for the following day, at a locale in central London, although Merv was so furious at being stood up that he almost cancelled the gig altogether.

This time, Peter and his publicist showed up. As Merv would later tell Bill Robbins, "I found him devastatingly handsome with steely blue eyes and beautiful brown hair. He wore socks that were the brightest green I've ever seen."

"I always wear one item of green clothing," the actor explained, "because I take pride in my Irish ancestry."

A brilliant Shakespearian actor, the hard-drinking O'Toole was the son of an Irish metal worker, football player, and racetrack bookmaker. His father had taught Peter much about life, introducing him to hard drinking and teaching him how to escape from a racecourse with gambling proceeds even when the wrong horse ran past the post.

The interview with Peter went so well that the actor agreed to appear on Merv's show in three months, when he'd scheduled a trip to America for the preview of *Lawrence of Arabia* in December.

Merv had called Noel Coward the previous evening. Although the playwright was too busy to see him, during their phone dialogue Merv told Noel that he was about to interview Peter O'Toole.

Peter O'Toole (Lawrence of Arabia) and **Omar Sharif:** Rendezvous with a transsexual

"I saw the dear chap only the other night," Noel said. "I

359

told him if he were any prettier, the movie would have to be called *Florence of Arabia*."

During his interview with Peter, Merv found him the most candid star he'd ever met. Noel had already told Merv that only Richard Burton had seduced more women. Peter confessed to Merv that at the age of twelve, when he was a schoolboy in Leeds, he formed the Mutual Masturbation Society with his male friends. "We called ourselves the MMs," Peter said. "Even when the headmaster found out about our club, he wasn't appalled. He felt it was a healthy alternative to ordinary sex. But three years later, I had sex with a woman, a trollop. From then on, no more masturbation for me. There is nothing on earth as good as a man and woman coming together."

"I suppose that would depend on your taste," Merv said.

What Merv really wanted to ask Peter involved details of his involvement with a British transsexual, a young model named April Ashley. Born in Liverpool in 1935 as George Jamieson, she was destined to become the most famous transsexual in the UK. Peter and his costar, the Egyptian actor, Omar Sharif, had met April in Spain where some scenes from *Lawrence of Arabia* had been filmed.

Peter, Omar, and April had been seen out together almost every night. In Spain, they had appeared together at the opening of a new bodega in Jerez de la Frontera at a party staged for the press by the Marques de Domecq d'Usquain. Omar was on one of April's arms, Peter on the other.

Later, April joined Omar and Peter in their shared suite. Peter's biographer, Michael Freedland, claimed, "Peter found her deliciously feminine—soft, creamy skin, gently curving hips and breasts that would have delighted the readers of *Playboy*."

April later recalled, "When Peter strips off his clothes, he's like an El Greco." She had also, she related, visited Omar's bed as well. It was while Omar was making love to her that April allegedly told him that she'd once been a sailor in Her Majesty's Navy.

Merv was intrigued with Omar Sharif, and he asked Peter to help arrange an interview with him. As the years went by, Merv avidly followed Omar's career both on and off the screen as the Egyptian launched into serial seductions of his leading ladies. They included Ingrid Bergman (*The Yellow Rolls-Royce*, 1964); Julie Christie (*Doctor Zhivago*, 1965), Sophia Loren (*More Than a Miracle*, 1967), both Catherine Deneuve and Ava Gardner (*Mayerling*, 1968), and Barbra Streisand (*Funny Girl*, 1968). After Omar romanced Streisand on screen, a furor erupted in his native Egypt. The actress was not only Jewish, but she'd raised money for Israel.

The best story Merv ever heard about Omar was a tale the actor relayed about himself. The actor claimed that when he was in Dallas, a woman with a handgun broke into his hotel room. Aiming the gun at him, she demanded that he strip off all his clothes and make love to her. He looked down at his flaccid penis. "It's not possible at the moment," he told the disappointed woman.

***

That night in London, back in Merv's suite, a call came in from Noel Coward, claiming that he was so disappointed that they couldn't get together. "I'm sending Graham over to keep you company." Within the hour, Graham Payn arrived, having lost his Jamaican suntan.

The actor spent the night with Merv. "Somehow it wasn't as romantic as it had been in Jamaica," Merv later told Paul Schone. As if sensing that there was no longer a spark between them, the resourceful Graham suggested that he show Merv "some of the pleasures of London" the following night.

In a taxi en route to Belgravia, Graham told Merv that he was taking him to a pub, The Grenadier, which had been a former hangout for officers serving under the Duke of Wellington. Behind the scarlet door of the pub, Merv during the course of a long evening was introduced to five of the Queen's guardsmen, each of whom were known to Graham. Merv had agreed to give each of them twenty pounds if they'd return, with Graham, to his hotel suite. None of the guardsmen had ever been paid that much for their sexual services before.

Merv did not go into great detail when he flew back to New York, but he told Bill Robbins and Paul Schone that he and Graham had had an orgy with these guardsmen. "Merv claimed it was one of the most thrilling adventures of his life," Bill said. "That night in London set a pattern for Merv. He would set up many orgies in the future with young models and actors. But he always claimed that Liberace was better at staging orgies than he was."

***

As promised, Peter O'Toole and his publicist showed up at the pre-arranged time in New York for an interview on *The Merv Griffin Show*. Merv, however, did not meet the actor backstage before he was summoned to go on. Later Merv recalled, "It was the most disastrous interview of my life."

When Peter, now a platinum blond, walked out onto the set, Merv did not recognize him. At first he thought Bob Shanks was pulling some joke on him, having hired some British actor to impersonate Peter. Before his arrival in America, Peter had dyed his hair so that audiences would recognize the look he'd had in *Lawrence of Arabia*.

After a few minutes with the sullen guest and an interview going nowhere,

Merv asked Peter why he'd dyed his hair, although by this point in the interview, he'd figured it out for himself.

"I'd rather not discuss that, Mr. Griffin," was Peter's acidic response.

From that point on, Peter mumbled one-word answers to Merv's increasingly desperate questions. The interview would evoke a future appearance of Anne Bancroft on *The Johnny Carson Show* when she responded in much the same way.

In exasperation, Merv finally asked Peter if he'd like to return to England.

"I would, yes," Peter said.

"Thank you for coming," Merv said. "Goodbye."

Peter got up and walked off the show. The audience could hear Peter yelling backstage. "GRIFFIN'S A SON OF A BITCH." This appearance, which became notorious, was America's first introduction to the degree to which O'Toole had become a temperamental diva.

After the show, Merv talked to his staff, asking, "What pissed this guy off so?"

"By asking if he'd bleached his hair, maybe he thought you were suggesting that he was a faggot," said a staff member.

Another member of his staff had a different answer. "I hear he gets belligerent when he's drunk, and he's always at least a little bit drunk."

The disastrous interview with Peter O'Toole was the exception to an otherwise rather benign rule. Nearly all the guests Merv brought on related to him and gave relatively uncontroversial interviews. Merv rarely probed too deeply into a star's personal life, even though he had a gossipy nature and knew a great deal about the personal lives of his subjects. For example, he interviewed many gay actors who presented themselves as straight, and Merv dutifully went along with their charade, never wanting to embarrass or force a guest to reveal more than he or she wanted to air before the public.

With Bob Shanks, Merv made the decision to bring onto his program stars who had been blacklisted during the infamous Communist witch hunt launched by Senator Joseph McCarthy in the early 1950s.

One of his first guests, the Brooklyn-born comedian, Jack Gilford, was on the Red Channels list of both real or suspected Communist sympathizers. Gilford and his wife, the actress Madeline Lee Gilford, were specifically cited as Communist sympathizers by choreographer Jerome Robbins in his testimony before the House Un-American Activities Committee.

After interviewing Gilford, the witty but rather ugly comedian, on his show, Merv said, "He seemed harmless to me, not exactly a Russian bear or The Red Menace that his detractors claimed."

In the years ahead, Merv noted that in spite of a distinguished acting career, Gilford became best known to millions of Americans when he appeared in television commercials for Cracker Jack.

Much to the annoyance of the "suits" at NBC, Merv also booked the New York born-and-bred character actor, Phil Leeds. He won the audience over by announcing at the beginning of Merv's interview, "I'm not pretty, but I'm warm and feisty." Even though he'd entertained American troops in the Pacific during World War II, Leeds found himself caught up in McCarthy era, anti-Communist hysteria. He too joined a list of entertainers who had already been blacklisted and in most cases, were out of work.

As regards booking Leeds onto his show, Merv defiantly announced, "I've never paid any attention to the Red Channels list, and I don't intend to now."

One star wasn't officially blacklisted, but had her career derailed anyway when she was forced to appear before the House Un-American Activities Committee. That was Judy Holliday, who'd won the Oscar as Best Actress for her portrayal of Billie Dawn in the 1950 *Born Yesterday*. By winning that award, she beat out such formidable contenders as Gloria Swanson for *Sunset Blvd.* and Bette Davis for her role in *All About Eve*. Even though Judy had an IQ of 172, her lawyers advised her to "play dumb like Billie Dawn" during her appearance before the committee. Even though the committee's chairman repeatedly threatened to ruin Judy's career, she steadfastly did not reveal the names of other alleged Communist sympathizers. Having no real charges against Judy, the committee was forced to let her go. But despite the fact that she was cleared of all charges, the stigma of being called for interrogation before the committee caused her to lose major job offers, especially from TV.

"Book Judy," Merv told Bob Shanks, "and to hell with any blacklist. Bring her on."

Merv bonded with Judy so well on the air that he wanted to socialize with her. She readily accepted his invitation to dinner because she claimed to have some personal matter to talk over with him.

Two nights later Merv invited Judy to an Italian restaurant in Greenwich Village, after she'd assured him of her fondness for Mediterranean food.

In the early part of the evening, she amused him with stories of her career in Hollywood. Her funniest story occurred when she was called into the office of 20th Century Fox mogul Darryl F. Zanuck. He told her that all the women at the studio "belong to me."

"Then he whipped out his super-size dick and exposed himself to me," Judy said. "'Have you ever seen a whopper like this?' he asked me. At that point I removed my falsies and threw them in his face. 'Well,' I said, 'I guess these belong to you too!'"

"Don't ask, don't tell"
Judy Holliday

363

With the understanding that Merv was a bisexual like herself, Judy was very candid with him, even hinting that she'd had an affair with Katharine Hepburn during the making of the MGM film *Adam's Rib* in 1949.

Before the end of the evening, Merv and Judy openly discussed their sex lives. She claimed that she'd lost her virginity to a New York policewoman, Yetta Cohn. She also alleged that her first sexual encounter with a man involved the handsome English actor, John Buckmaster, who had raped her. John happened to have been the son of the famous actress, Gladys Cooper, and the brother-in-law of Robert Morley. In the 1930s, John had had an affair with Vivien Leigh, Merv found these revelations fascinating.

Judy seemed to be delaying discussing the personal matter she'd mentioned several days previously. Almost as a means of avoiding it, they chatted about crossword puzzles, both of them claiming to be experts in solving them. Throughout the meal, Merv noticed that she was such a chain-smoker that she'd developed a cough. This heavy smoking would lead to her death from breast cancer in 1965 at the age of forty-three.

Finally, she revealed what had been on her mind all evening. She said that she'd met and befriended Hadley Morrell when he was being supported by Robert Q. Lewis. Lewis had dropped Hadley, cutting off his support, and Merv's former friend was working at a grocery store on 8th Street to pay his bills. "I hope you don't mind," she said, "but I've invited him here tonight. I know you guys still love each other, and I want you to talk things over with him."

Merv later claimed that he felt trapped when Judy got up from her seat, and was almost immediately replaced by Hadley, who had been watching him from outside the restaurant.

Recalling that night years later, Hadley said the one hour he spent with Merv that night was filled with recriminations, Merv accusing him of "betrayal and sleeping with the enemy."

Hadley revealed that it took a month before Merv let him move back into the hideaway with Bill and Paul. "But it was never the same again between us," he said. "Merv agreed that we should remain friends, but he told me we'd never be lovers again."

Merv did allow Hadley to quit his job, promising that he'd give him a hundred dollars a week in cash. It seemed that Merv was getting too well known because of his TV show, and he needed a discreet intermediary to help him arrange sexual liaisons with young actors and models.

"He said I could be his 'Minister of Mischief,' and I know how corny that sounds," Hadley said. "Merv found the word pimp too hard to pronounce. I thought about it and finally decided it might even be fun for me. Little did I realize at the time that I'd just assigned myself to the role of Back Alley Friend for life, one that Merv was ashamed of. Year after year I swore I'd break away and find other, more dignified, employment. But I never did. The night I moved back in with the boys, I'd doomed my life but hardly knew that at the time. There would be many thrills in store for me, but also a heavy dose of pain."

***

Months before Merv's interviews from London, his friend Mark Goodson had asked him and Betty White to go through the trial run of a new TV game show called *Password*. Betty and Merv were so good they sold the idea to "the suits." Because of other commitments, it was understood that Merv would not be the show's emcee.

Ironically, *The Merv Griffin Show* eventually ended up in the same afternoon time slot as *Password*, and soon *Password* began out-rating Merv's show by a four-to-one margin. "It was killing me in the Nielsen ratings," Merv said.

At long last Johnny Carson had found his voice on *The Tonight Show*. He was not only getting four times more advertising revenue, but he was also luring many of the big-name guests who had originally launched the debut of Merv's show.

On April 1—April Fool's Day—1963, NBC notified Merv that his show was being taken off the air. "You have too much polish, too much sophistication for daytime TV," one of the NBC "suits" told him.

Adela Rogers St. Johns was one of Merv's last guests. "It was one of the most tender moments I've ever seen on daytime TV," she said. "The stage was dark, almost black. Suddenly, a spotlight shone down on Merv as he emerged with tears in his eyes. He was carrying a battered suitcase, a hat, and a raincoat. 'I'm so sorry,' he said to his audience. 'I just hate ending the show. Haven't we had a good time?' Then he sang 'Lost in the Stars.' I found myself shedding a tear or two, and in Hollywood they call me Hard-Hearted Hannah."

Merv had some hope that year of salvaging his pride when he was nominated for Outstanding Performance in a Variety, Musical, or Series. He was up against competition which included Danny Kaye, Andy Williams, and Edie Adams. The award went to Carol Burnett. "Just to prove that there is no justice in the world," Merv said, "the Best Supporting Actor award went to Don Knotts. He beat out Robert Redford. You figure."

Adela Rogers St. Johns
Merv brought her on just to insult other guests--and she did.

As thousands of letters poured in from NBC, protesting the cancellation of Merv's show, he said goodbye to his friends in New York and headed for Europe for a vacation. He later estimated that the studio received nearly 175,000 letters of protest from viewers, which at the time was an all-time high for any network. The "suits" at NBC belatedly realized that they had let a valuable property escape and that they had committed to Johnny Carson too early.

Paris and London were fine with Merv—"That is," he said, "if you like the charms of yesterday." But when his feet touched the soil of Ireland, he felt he'd come home again, as this was the green land from which his ancestors had sailed to the New World so long ago.

While NBC tried to find the proper showcase to woo Merv back on the air, he signed a two-play contract on the straw-hat circuit after having been inspired watching Judy Garland perform in her 1950 movie *Summer Stock*.

The comedy, *The Moon Is Blue*, was presented at the Bucks County Playhouse in New Hope, Pennsylvania. Many of Merv's friends, including Hadley, Bill, and Paul, drove down from New York to see him emote. The comedy by F. Hugh Herbert seems harmless today, and it is almost inconceivable that it could have caused nationwide protests in 1953 when Otto Preminger had brought it to the screen in a version that starred William Holden, David Niven, and Maggie McNamara.

At one point, Maggie herself came to Bucks County to see Merv in the play, which had been her one crowning moment on screen, thanks partly to the Oscar nomination she'd earned for her performance. The play involved two aging playboys who were attracted to the same young woman.

Backstage, Maggie told Merv that her movie had been the first to use the words "virgin,""seduce," and "mistress" on screen. In the more permissive 60s, Merv told her that he'd been aware of no protests at all.

The pert, perky actress had been charming on the night Merv met her. In 1978 he was saddened to read about the failure of her career. She'd ended up barely supporting herself as a typist, and had killed herself with an overdose of sleeping pills.

When not performing on stage in Bucks County, Merv rushed to and from New York to host *Talent Scouts* for CBS-TV, the summer replacement for *The Red Skelton Hour*.

The series was an attempt to revive Arthur Godfrey's popular 1950s show. With Merv as host, the show went on the air for CBS on July 3, 1962. Young newcomers were asked to perform, and they were introduced on stage by such stars as Jim Backus, George Maharis, Ann Sheridan, Lauren Bacall, Hugh O'Brien, Liza Minnelli, and "Mama" Cass Elliot.

Merv wanted to make a name for himself by discovering exceptional talent like Godfrey had done. Many young performers who got their first major exposure on Godfrey went on to great success. They included Pat Boone, Tony Bennett, Rosemary Clooney, Eddie Fisher, Connie Francis, Steve Lawrence, and Patsy Cline. Merv expressed a certain sense of glee when hearing how wrong Godfrey could be in appraising talent. He had turned down both Elvis Presley and Buddy Holly.

During his hosting of *Talent Scouts*, Merv did showcase some new talent, but made no great discoveries like Godfrey. George Carlin, Charles Nelson Reilly, and Vaughn Meader did go over big, however, and Meader did an impression of JFK which led to a hit album.

Merv's next acting gig was *Come Blow Your Horn*, the first play written by Neil Simon. It had premiered on Broadway in 1961. Even though Frank Sinatra and Dean Martin had starred in the movie version in 1963, "The play still had legs," according to Merv. "William Bendix and I sold out every seat."

As a footnote to this play, the offstage character of Felix Ungar later became one of the onstage protagonists of Simon's *The Odd Couple*. Reportedly, the producers of the show had considered Merv for the role of Felix, but he turned them down, claiming that the character he'd have played "is that of a menacing queen." Eventually, the part went to another closeted gay, Tony Randall.

Merv's costar in the play, William Bendix, hated him on sight. By the time he met Merv, Bendix's star had faded. He'd been popular in the 1940s, playing a dim-witted but lovable lug. In 1944 he'd starred in the radio series, *The Life of Riley*, which had made him a household name.

In Warren, Ohio, Merv overheard Bendix telling the director, "I've starred with Hepburn and Tracy, with Bob Hope and Bing Crosby, even Kirk Douglas and Groucho Marx. And now you give me Merv Griffin, a mediocre leftover from the Big Band era."

"Well, at least you don't have to wear a dress in this play," the director told Bendix, referring to his drag role in *Abroad With Two Yanks* in 1944.

Merv knew that Bendix had appeared during that same war year with Tallulah Bankhead in her greatest film, *Lifeboat*, directed by Alfred Hitchcock. Merv wanted to swap Tallulah stories with Bendix, but the actor cut him off. "I do not know Miss Bankhead," he said. "Nor do I care to."

Merv's stage nemesis:
William Bendix

367

After that encounter, Bendix never spoke to Merv again except on the stage. Actually, he didn't speak to him then, either, addressing comments meant for Merv to the audience instead. The former star did what he could to sabotage Merv's performance, "but I turned out to be a trouper," Merv recalled. "I would have been more understanding if I'd known that Bendix was in great pain during the run of the play." Suffering from a long bout with cancer, the actor died the following year, 1964, just before Christmas.

During his lonely nights in a hotel room in Bucks County, Merv worked on an idea for a television quiz show. He continued to perfect his idea in Warren, Ohio during other lonely nights, although a handsome young Ohio-born stagehand relieved the bleakness of many of those nights.

That show of Merv's was tentatively called *What's the Question?* Even if Merv dreamed of its future success, he could hardly have imagined that it would become the rock on which he'd build a billion dollar fortune.

***

Merv returned to television with his own show, *Word for Word*, for which he was both producer and star. The "suits" at NBC had wanted to cast him in a show which, in their opinion, might be more popular, but Merv held out for *Word for Word*, which was tied in with his passion for word games.

Contestants tried to extract the greatest number of three- or four-letter words out of a bigger word. Launched in October of 1963, the show was not a critical or popular success. The reviews were bad, the worst coming from some nameless critic in Newark, who wrote, "Watching Merv Griffin perform in *Word for Word* is about as exciting as scrubbing your kitchen floor with a very stinky mop." Most reviewers, however, found Merv a "likable but mediocre performer—the show just has no excitement."

One executive at MGM gave Merv some very bad advice. "I think you should look elsewhere," he said. "Game shows are not your *forte*." Even Merv grew bored with the show, later comparing it to "sleepwalking." The audience, of course, picked up on his boredom.

Merv's boredom was relieved when he got what he called "the most surprising invitation of my life." From the White House, he received an invitation to emcee the 1963 White House Correspondent's Dinner in Washington for President John F. Kennedy. "I started quivering like a bowl of jelly and didn't have a clue about what to say in my monologue. I immediately called Pat McCormick."

As a gag writer, Pat reigned supreme, and was an expert at offbeat, often warped humor. "No one did topical jokes better than Pat," Merv said. "He could even make politicians laugh at their own mistakes, and if you could pull that one off, you could get away with murder…at least. My favorite Pat story was when he celebrated the baptism of his baby boy. He invited some buddies over for dinner. After plowing them with booze, he went into the kitchen, emerging later with his naked baby child on a silver platter surrounded by cooked vegetables like carrots and onions. He gently took hold of his little boy's wee wee and asked his friends, 'Who wants the Pope's nose?'"

Merv's job was not only to entertain the President but the press corps, members of Congress, Supreme Court justices, the President's Cabinet, and the Diplomatic Corps.

Previously, he'd worked a few times with Edie Adams, so he contacted her and she agreed to appear. He also called the comedian Guy Marks, whom he would book on several of his future talk shows. Guy was a top-notch entertainer who was known as a master of impersonations. "He could do anybody or anything—birds, animals, even inanimate objects," Merv said. "He sounded more like Bogie than Bogie himself. I just knew he'd be a big hit."

During the early planning stages of the event in Washington, Merv received a surprise call from the White House. It seemed that on the night of May 12, 1963, the president was watching Dinah Shore's popular NBC talk show when he became mesmerized by the appearance of a young singer, Barbra Streisand. Merv was informed that Kennedy wanted Barbra to sing at this big event.

Merv would later admit that he'd been the last talk show host to appreciate Barbra's singing talent. Jack Paar had been one of her early supporters, but Merv had turned down her agent's request five times. "I just don't dig her voice," he told her agent. "Not my thing at all."

Of course, he would honor the President's request and book Barbra, but he warned the White House aide, "I still can't believe Streisand is the President's cuppa. Maybe she can get a nose job before the dinner. She's completely sexless. Not the President's type. Why don't you let me contact Marilyn Monroe? Isn't she more the president's type?"

Unholy trio, polluted protocol:

Merv (lower right) arranges for **Barbra Streisand** (above) to sing for **JFK** (upper right).

"The President doesn't have a type," the young White House aide stiffly informed Merv. "But if he does, she's Mrs. Kennedy herself."

Against Merv's better judgment, he booked Barbra for the show. Nervously standing in front of the august audience, including the President, Merv introduced "the little girl from Brooklyn with the powerful voice."

Barbra made a spectacular entrance wearing a satin gown that showed plenty of cleavage. She wowed the audience, including the President, with "Happy Days Are Here Again." At no point in her song did she take her eyes off the President.

"Knowing Kennedy's penchant for whore-mongering," Merv said, "Barbra readily signaled him that she was ready, willing, and able to do his bidding."

Merv was a smooth emcee and kept the President and the audience laughing. After the reception, Merv and Barbra, along with the others, were invited to join a receiving line to meet the President. A White House aide had warned them in advance that it was impolite to ask for the President's autograph.

Barbra stood in the receiving line before Merv. When she was introduced to the handsome, charismatic president, she curtsied as if meeting the Queen of England. He smiled at her and asked, "How long have you been singing?"

Without losing a beat, she shot back, "About as long as you've been President." He laughed and smiled at her. Defying the White House aide, she stuck the evening's program into Kennedy's face and handed him a pen. "Mr. President, if I don't get your autograph, my mother back in Brooklyn will never allow me into the house again."

Peter Daniels, Barbra's accompanist, was standing nearby, and he quickly offered the President his back to write on. Accepting the autographed program, Barbra said, "You're a doll, Mr. President, and thanks. I'd sing for you any night."

Merv was shocked at her blatant disregard of protocol and how she'd been so suggestive with the President.

When he had breakfast with Edie, Guy, and Barbra the following morning, he chastised Barbra. "For God's sake, why did you have to go and ask for his autograph?"

"Because I wanted to," she said rather grandly.

"At least you could tell us what he wrote," Merv said.

"He wrote, 'Fuck You, the President,'" she said.

Later Barbara confessed to friends that he'd actually written, "Best Wishes, John F. Kennedy." She also admitted that she'd lost the autographed program. "I slipped it inside my dress and it must have fallen out somewhere."

Later that morning when Merv read the newspapers, he realized how clever Barbra had been. He suspected she didn't really want the President's autograph. A nearby photographer had snapped a picture of Barbra standing next to the President as he autographed the program on Peter's back. That picture made the front page of newspapers across the nation, and became one of the biggest publicity breaks of Barbra's career.

Throughout the course of breakfast that morning, Merv kept a secret from Barbra, Guy, and Edie, but later confided it to his friends, Hadley, Bill, and Paul. In the receiving line the previous evening, as Kennedy was shaking Merv's hand and congratulating him on a job well done, he whispered an invitation in his ear. "Join me and some of my friends upstairs for some cigars and brandy." He motioned to an aide to escort Merv upstairs.

"Thanks, Mr. President," Merv said. "I'm honored."

"It was the most vulgar gathering of macho men I'd ever attended," Merv later said. "All these guys did was talk about cheating on their wives and the various specialties of prostitutes they'd encountered. Senator George Smathers of Florida was one of the guests. One very unattractive man—I don't have a clue as to who he really was—told the President about his encounter with this incredibly beautiful showgal who was called 'the Queen of Anal Sex in Las Vegas.' Apparently, Frank Sinatra and countless others had had her. The President announced that he'd arrange for Peter Lawford to hook him up with this backdoor whore."

After Kennedy retired for the evening, an aide in white gloves escorted Merv down the steps toward the door. At the foot of the steps, Merv encountered Jacqueline Kennedy. She kissed him on the cheek. "Truman tells me you're a delight." She was referring to her friend, Truman Capote. "Let's lunch. I'll call you."

"And then she just seemed to disappear," Merv said. "At first I thought I'd just dreamed her appearance. She was one of the most beautiful and enchanting creatures I'd ever met. She moved with the grace of a summer butterfly. Of course, I didn't really expect her to call me. I thought it was just a polite thing to say. I was wrong about that. Jackie Kennedy, or so I learned, always meant what she said."

***

After their joint appearance in Washington, Merv did a complete "about face" as regards his opinion of Barbra Streisand. He was so impressed at how she'd gone over at the White House that he called Liberace and suggested that he hire Barbra for his opening act at the Riviera in Las Vegas.

Taking Merv's suggestion, Liberace signed the young star as an extra-added attraction, granting her a salary of $7,500 a week.

Regrettably, on opening night and on the two following nights as well,

Barbra bombed in front of Liberace's older blue-haired ladies. His fans seemed startled by her innovative belting style and didn't get her act at all.

A critic for the *Hollywood Reporter* wrote, "Her makeup made her look like something that just climbed off a broom. When she sang, it was like the wailing of a banshee bouncing up and down on marionette strings. Her outrageous grooming almost nullifies her talent."

At this point Liberace intervened, showing the same over-the-top flair he'd used in salvaging Elvis's act after his first appearance in Las Vegas. In Barbra's dressing room, Liberace tossed out her dull gray wardrobe and replaced it with an almost electric gold lamé gown with dangling earrings. Remembering what Shirley Temple's mother had told her moppet star, Liberace said, "Sparkle, Barbra, sparkle! This is Vegas."

The gimmick worked. When Barbra made her fourth and most stunning appearance, her act ended with thunderous applause.

Liberace called Merv the next day and thanked him for hooking him up with Barbra. "The gal is gonna go far," Liberace predicted. "Maybe even become a bigger name than both of us."

"No one in show business will ever become as big as you, Sadie," Merv assured him.

"That's true, Fannie Mae," Liberace said. "Now let's get down to some serious gal talk. I want to know who's fucking you now—and don't leave out a single detail, regardless of how sordid. After you've spilled the beans, I'll tell you who I had last night. You won't believe it!"

"You don't mean. . . ." Merv said.

"Yes, I do mean *that one*," Liberace said. "The straightest man in show business. Mr. Skirt-Chaser himself. And we're not talking Sinatra either. I'll leave *that* conquest for you. After having that man of my dreams, I can only say those Vegas showgals didn't lie. It's a whopper."

"I bet he left you singing 'That's Amore.'"

"Not only that," Liberace said. "I won't be able to sit down at my piano for a month."

***

During her next trip to New York, Jackie Kennedy called Merv and arranged a luncheon meeting. She preferred the bar of the Carlyle Hotel because she was assured of more privacy there. Watched over by the Secret Service, she greeted Merv warmly. When he appeared reluctant to kiss her on the cheek, she said. "You can touch me. After all, I'm not the Queen of England."

Throughout their rendezvous that afternoon, he wanted to look into her

372

eyes, but she kept them hidden behind large dark glasses.

Unlike the serene princess she evoked in front of TV cameras, in person, she was warm and rather earthy. She obviously had a love of gossip, and she pumped Merv for scandalous revelations in the movie industry. She was particularly interested in who was sleeping with whom. Merv filled her in on some shocking details, carefully avoiding speaking of his friend Marilyn Monroe. Actually, he'd wanted to ask her about her own affairs with various movie stars, notably Marlon Brando and William Holden, but he didn't dare.

Jackie spoke candidly about their mutual friends, especially Truman Capote and Peter Lawford. "I know that Truman befriends me to my face," she said, "then spreads the vilest gossip about me behind my back. But I still adore him. He tells me more about what's really going on in the world of celebrities than any other person. As for Peter . . ." She hesitated, putting down her glass. "I don't know how to say this. He's confided to me about your own involvement with him, so we can speak frankly. Peter's in love with me, and I don't know how to handle it." She didn't say anything for a long moment, perhaps realizing she'd revealed too much.

To rescue her from her embarrassment, he immediately changed the subject. He urged her to come onto his show. "Talk about ratings. We'd blow everybody else off the air."

He could only imagine the mischief reflected in her eyes when she came up with an idea for one of his shows. "I could list all the men in the world I'd like to seduce—that is, if I haven't gotten around to some of them already."

"Name names," he said. "I'm all ears."

"Henry Kissinger."

"But he's so ugly," he said.

"Beautiful women down through the ages have not always sought out equally beautiful men," she said. "Perhaps just the opposite. A woman can be attracted to a man's brain. Or his power. Look at all those silly German housewives throwing themselves in the path of Hitler."

"I think beautiful women should bed ugly men, and only for their money," he said.

Later in her life when Jackie married Aristotle Onassis, Merv told Hadley, "I think I planted the idea in her head."

Back at the Carlyle, Jackie seemed to be enjoying their game. She continued to name names. "Prince Philip, of course. He's so handsome, so stately. John Glenn, most definitely. André Malraux. Dr. Christiaan Barnard. Robert

Jacqueline Kennedy
as First Lady

373

McNamara. General Maxwell Taylor. If they weren't gay, I'd add Cary Grant and Rudolph Nureyev to the list. Did you know that Jack often calls Cary Grant because he likes to hear the sound of his voice? I could go on and on. Alistair Cooke. Franklin Roosevelt Jr., Gianni Agnelli. And out of deference to your opinion, Eugene R. Black. If you want money, who better than the president of the World Bank?"

Months later, shocked and horrified at the assassination of John F. Kennedy in Dallas, Merv sent his condolences to Jackie. A few weeks later he received a warm reply, thanking him.

At the beginning of her marriage to Aristotle Onassis, Merv received another call from Jackie. She was seriously tempted to go on nationwide television to counterattack headlines around the world calling her a gold-digger. Such rumors had existed since she was first seen with Onassis. But these rumors exploded when a steward on the shipping tycoon's yacht wrote a tell-all book.

In it, he claimed that he'd personally witnessed Jackie sign a 170-clause marriage contract that stipulated, among other agreements, that man and wife would occupy separate bedrooms throughout the marriage. According to the steward, the contract also called for her getting an allowance of $585,000 a year. In case of a divorce, she was to be given $20 million in cash.

"Such lies!" Jackie said to Merv. "The day I married Ari, my annuity from the Kennedy Estate was cut off. I also lost my widow's pension from the government, which I'd been drawing since Jack died. There was no prenuptial agreement with Ari. Right now I have less than five thousand dollars in my bank account. To manage, I have to charge everything to Olympic Airlines."

Merv was elated at the prospect of such an appearance on his show by Jackie, knowing it would be one of the most watched interviews in the history of television. But two weeks later she phoned him again. "You must forgive me," she said. "I called you in a fit of madness. I can't go on your show and make a public spectacle of myself."

"But you are a spectacle, Jackie." he said. "Through no fault of your own, of course."

"Such an appearance would be too personal," she said. "Only make more unwelcome headlines." She seemed near tears as she put down the phone.

***

In the summer of 1964, Merv decided to go back onto the straw-hat circuit, contracting to appear in a revival of the George Abbott and Philip Dunning play, *Broadway*, which had originally opened in 1926.

Over the years since then, the play had been presented in many different productions across America and Europe. The chanteuse Greta Keller had starred in the Viennese production of the play, with a young Marlene Dietrich in the chorus line. Backstage and in various boudoirs, she entertained Greta and the other showgirls by playing her saw. Later Marlene entertained Greta in a more intimate way.

Merv met the playwright, who'd journeyed from New York to New Hope in Pennsylvania to see the latest production of his play. Born in 1887, George Abbott was still going strong. Merv mistakenly assumed that Abbott was on his last legs. As the years went by Merv was amazed that the playwright "was the man who refused to die." Merv heard that at the age of ninety-nine, Abbott was revising and directing a production of *Damn Yankees*. In 1995, when Abbott died three weeks short of his 108th birthday, Merv was astonished to read that a week and a half before his death, he was dictating revisions to the second act of *Pajama Game*. Merv told friends that he wanted to be like Abbott, plotting his new game show as he neared birthday number 110.

***

Working night after night at the dining table of his New York apartment, Merv slowly developed a new TV quiz show concept. Initially calling it *What's The Question?*, he later changed the title to the more dramatic *Jeopardy!*

TV quiz shows had enjoyed tremendous popularity in the 1950s until headline-making scandals broke in the latter part of the decade. Contestants came forth to testify that they were often supplied with the answers by producers desperate to make the shows more entertaining. "We got around that problem by openly supplying the answers to our contestants, and then letting them figure out what the question was," Merv said.

Contestants faced such dilemmas as:

ANSWER: JOHN BILLINGTON, WHO ARRIVED ON THIS BOAT, IS GENERALLY CONSIDERED AMERICA'S FIRST MURDERER.
QUESTION: WHAT WAS THE *MAYFLOWER*?

OR

ANSWER: HE COMMANDED AT THE SECOND BULL RUN AND IS SAID TO HAVE DEVISED A SPORT THAT LATER USED A BULLPEN.
QUESTION: WHO WAS ABNER DOUBLEDAY?

To make the show livelier, Merv inter-jected such concepts as the "Daily Double," which was inspired by his love of horse racing. This would lead to objections from the network. Executives felt the term was too suggestive of gambling. But Merv stood his ground and the feature was retained.

When he first presented the show to Mort Werner, head of NBC, he didn't like it, finding the "answers" to the questions too hard. His assistant, Grant Tinker, however, urged him to buy it. Tinker later became producer of such programs as *The Mary Tyler Moore Show* and later, president of NBC.

Although reluctant, Werner bought *Jeopardy!* for NBC early in 1964. Remembering a long-ago promise, Merv called Bob Murphy, his schoolmate in San Mateo, hiring him to interview potential contestants. In time, Bob would climb Merv's corporate ladder to producer status of *The Merv Griffin Show*.

Until *Jeopardy!* found its voice and its audience, its history was shaky. Basically, it was a quiz show based on trivia about such topics as literature, music, pop culture, history, and science, among other topics. The show first aired on NBC on March 30, 1964. Eventually it found an audience, running until January 3, 1975.

As the emcee of the show, Merv hired Art Fleming, an actor who'd made his Broadway debut at the age of four. Standing 6' 4", he was a former carnival barker and naval hero. When he signed on, Art thought it was a temporary gig that might pay his rent for a few months, hardly realizing that he'd be the host of 2,858 shows before his eventual termination.

Merv later claimed that *Jeopardy!* wasn't canceled because of bad ratings, but because eleven years after its debut, NBC wanted to "redecorate" its daytime lineup of programming. "That time period has never since duplicated the ratings strength of *Jeopardy!*" Merv said. "Chalk it up to a bad roll of the dice."

Three years after its cancellation, between October 2, 1978 and March 2, 1979, *Jeopardy!* was temporarily revived, with Art Fleming functioning as host. But the second time around, the show was not particularly successful, and once again it was canceled.

But like the beast that wouldn't die, *Jeopardy!* was brought back for an encore, going on TV again in September 10, 1984—and still running until this day. Various foreign-language versions of *Jeopardy!* were adapted for international audiences as well.

Lin Bolen, in charge of programming, conflicted with Merv on many an occasion. She activated her plan to fire Art Fleming, preferring to jettison old men and bring in "young studs" like Alex Trebek. Reportedly, Faye Dunaway based her character of the take-no-prisoners executive in the movie, *Network*, on Bolen.

Trebek was well known to Merv, having filled in as a substitute host on Merv's other show, *Wheel of Fortune*, when its regular emcee, Chuck Woolery, became sick. Under Trebek, *Jeopardy!* became the second-most watched game show in the history of syndicated television, the first spot being occupied by Merv's own *Wheel of Fortune*.

Art was bitterly disappointed when his contract wasn't renewed, claiming that his emcee gig on *Jeopardy!* "was the high point of my life." He ended up hosting a trivia show Sunday nights in St. Louis. With his glory days on *Jeopardy!* long behind him, he died in Florida in 1995.

Under the Canadian-born Trebek's hosting, *Jeopardy!* achieved its greatest success. He won two Emmy Awards for his role in the show, and the show itself has won eleven Emmys, a record for a quiz show. In January of 2001, *TV Guide* ranked *Jeopardy!* as Number 2 among the *50 Greatest Game Shows of All Time*.

***

During the early months of 1965, despite the success of *Jeopardy!*, Merv was restless. He still yearned to be a big-time talk show host, and a deal was slow in coming. He had, however, received a number of offers to sing on variety shows or to emcee other game shows.

The biggest offer involved his hosting of a TV series that would travel around the world, introducing international circus acts. He instructed his agent to turn it down, the job subsequently going to a fallen movie star, Don Ameche, instead.

Merv eagerly wanted to return *The Merv Griffin Show* to television. Each night as he watched Johnny Carson on late-night TV, he bit his nails. "I was always a nail biter," he told friends. "To me, nothing relieves anxiety as much as biting your nails. It also cuts down on manicure bills."

Early in 1965, Chester H. (Chet) Collier—at the time, VP of Group W, the Westinghouse Broadcasting company—made an appearance in Merv's life. Two years younger than Merv, Chet with his balding head, waist bulge, and double chin looked fifteen years older.

Merv had been impressed with how Chet had launched *The Mike Douglas Show* in Cleveland in 1961, later transferring its base to Philadelphia. Thanks to its syndication of original programs, that show had signaled the debut of a new era in television. No longer did a successful show have to be created by teams affiliated with CBS, ABC, or NBC.

Chet also had a formative hand in returning Steve Allen to television with his own show and jump-starting the career of Regis Philbin. Still active in the mid-1990s, Chet joined Rupert Murdoch and Roger Ailes in the launching the Fox News Channel.

Chet convinced Merv to sign with Westinghouse, an organization best known at the time for its manufacture of washing machines. "You could be the master of your own show," Chet promised Merv, "and you wouldn't be censored by NBC or CBS, as you were in the past." Merv interpreted that argument as a powerful lure.

Trusting Chet's vision, Merv signed with Westinghouse in February of 1965, calling Chet a "one-man think tank." There was only one significant drawback. At the time, the company's broadcast division was active in only five regional markets: Philadelphia, Boston, Baltimore, Pittsburgh, and Merv's native San Francisco. Chet promised Merv that he would soon be broadcasting coast to coast, including Canada.

As headquarters for his efforts, Merv was assigned the intimate Little Theater (later renamed the Helen Hayes Theater) on 44th Street in New York City, close to Sardi's. Originally the show was slated for a daytime slot, with Merv's faithful Bob Shanks functioning as producer and with Kirk Alexander directing.

Over strong objections from almost all of his associates, Merv kept his promise to hire Arthur Treacher as his sidekick. Chet referred to the selection of Arthur as "Merv Griffin's folly." The executive producer finally gave in, however, since he'd promised Merv creative control. Every objection involved the Englishman's age. "Wasn't Treacher born back when Queen Victoria sat on the throne?" Bob Shanks asked Merv.

Left photo: "Let 'em eat cake!" Merv's trenchant sidekick, **Arthur Treacher**, faces another birthday bash.
Right photo: Merv with his role model **Steve Allen**, creator of the TV talk show.

Arthur signed with Merv and thanked him. "I knew you'd come through for me one day, you dear little man," Arthur told Merv.

Long of face and tall in stature, Arthur stood before Merv's TV audience using crisp diction and what appeared to be a snobby disdain for almost everybody except Merv himself. "Look sharp!" he told the audience. "Here's the dear boy himself. Merrrrvyn!" At the ripe age of seventy-one, Arthur would deliver that same introduction countless times.

What Merv's producers didn't realize was that Arthur had previously developed a fan base of young people who'd seen him play the constable in the hit film *Mary Poppins*, which had been released a year before Merv's new show went on the air. These teenagers referred to Arthur as "granddaddy" and followed him down 44th Street every night after the show, clamoring for autographs and demanding that he sign his name as "Constable Jones," the character he played in the Poppins film, instead of Arthur Treacher.

Merv's fans never knew what Arthur was going to say, especially when a politician came on. He never liked politicians. Merv might be interviewing Hubert Humphrey and Arthur would make some wisecrack on the side. The audience would burst into laughter. Merv was constantly having to remind his guest, "Don't mind Arthur."

After some preliminary dialogue with Merv, Arthur would retreat to the far end of the sofa, which became known as "Treacher's Corner." He didn't try too hard to be entertaining, feeling perhaps that he'd done his job. After all, his philosophy of acting was simple: "Say the words. Get the money. Go home."

The most embarrassing incident occurred when Dan Dailey came onto the show. Arthur had known this singer/dancer/actor back in their vaudeville days. During one broadcast, Dan was telling Merv that shortly after he signed with MGM, Louis B. Mayer had cast him as a Nazi in *The Mortal Storm* in 1940. "Looking at the rushes, Mayer realized I was no Nazi. From then on, it was musicals for me."

Just as Dan was telling Merv about his onscreen appearance with a then relatively unknown Marilyn Monroe in *A Ticket to Tomahawk* (1950), Arthur woke up and noticed Dan. "Hello, Dan," Arthur said. "Are you still wearing dresses?" Merv's offscreen staff immediately cut to a commercial.

Unknown to the general public, Dan, a bisexual, often dressed in drag. He often "borrowed" (or stole, depending on how his actions were interpreted at the time) the gowns of his co-star, Betty Grable, then showed them off at crossdressing parties throughout Hollywood.

***

In 1965, Roddy McDowall was appearing in a movie, *Inside Daisy Clover*, starring Natalie Wood and Robert Redford. There was an uncredited part in it for a radio announcer, and Roddy called and asked if Merv would take it, pending the approval of the director. When approval was granted, Merv signed on.

Appearing in archive footage were some of the great stars of Hollywood. After the completion of his work, Merv said, "At least I can claim to have appeared in a movie with John Barrymore, Humphrey Bogart, Clark Gable, and Tyrone Power. Alas, I had no love scenes with them."

"Mickey Rooney was also in the film," Roddy said jokingly.

"Forget it!" Merv said.

The trenchant and gritty film provided an account of Daisy's rise as a Hollywood star in the 1930s, but upon its release, and despite its all-star cast, it misfired. One reviewer condemned it for portraying "caricatures instead of people."

***

"Guess what?" came a familiar early morning voice over the phone. "I just married Judy Garland."

A sleepy Merv recognized the voice at the other end. It was Mark Herron, with whom he'd enjoyed a brief affair. "I don't know whether to congratulate you or sympathize with you," Merv said. "Judy—and I know her well—is not your typical doting American housewife."

Somewhat shocked at the news, Merv was eager for details. The decision to get married had been made in May of 1964 when Mark and Judy spent a week vacationing together in Hawaii. The press had described Mark as "Garland's new escort."

Judy had married Mark in Las Vegas' Little Church of the West on November 14, 1965, at 1:30am. After the wedding, they'd attended Don Rickles' late, late night club act. As was his oft-repeated style, the comedian gave the newlyweds a terrific ribbing before the couple flew to San Francisco for their honeymoon. "Liza approves," Mark assured Merv. "She calls us the Scott and Zelda of the 1960s."

"If you've read anything about F. Scott Fitzgerald and Zelda, that's not exactly a compliment," Merv said.

"Judy's going to promote my career," Mark said. "We're going to star together in plays—dramas, not musicals. She wants us to do Tennessee Williams' *Sweet Bird of Youth*."

"I'm not sure that's a good idea," Merv cautioned. "People might get the wrong idea. After all, that play is about an aging actress who takes up with a

380

young gigolo."

There was a long silence on the other end of the phone. "You've got a point there."

As part of their honeymoon, Mark and Judy completed eight months together of hopping around the world. Their tour included stopovers in Hong Kong and an appearance in London, where Peter Allen became a hit with the critics as Judy's opening act.

Mark and his new bride finally landed back in the United States in 1965. Mark called Merv and wanted to get together for drinks and dinner. Merv gladly accepted and said he was bringing Hadley. "That's fine," Mark said. "I'll bring my boyfriend as well."

"Boyfriend?" Merv asked. "You mean, Judy won't be there?"

"She's flown to Los Angeles," Mark said.

"Well, bring him on," Merv said. "I'm eager to see who's captured your heart."

At a secluded restaurant and bar in Greenwich Village, Hadley and Merv were introduced to Peter Allen. Both of them were mesmerized by this charismatic young Australian with ginger hair, an infectious exuberance, and a lopsided but very engaging smile.

Gradually, Merv pieced together the story of these complex relationships. While Judy was in a hospital in Hong Kong, Mark had gone to the Starlight Room of the Hong Kong Hilton to catch an act by "The Allen Brothers" from Australia. After one of the best shows he'd seen in many a year, Mark went backstage and introduced himself to Peter.

"We made love that night," Mark said in front of Peter. "And we've been making love every night we can since then. London. And now New York."

"Does Judy know about the affair?" Merv asked.

"I don't think so," Peter said. "But there's one complication. Judy has introduced me to Liza, who's fallen in love with me."

"Judy's had one gay husband already," Merv said. "During their marriage, Vincente Minnelli spent more time getting fucked by Gene Kelly than he did fucking Judy. And now Mark. She could write a book on gay husbands."

Other than wanting to show off his new boyfriend, Mark had a motive for introducing Peter to Merv. He wanted Peter to appear as a guest on Merv's show.

Peter filled Merv in on his background. Born in a small town in Australia, he'd begun his career in show-biz by entertaining rowdy crowds at the local pub. Later he'd teamed with Chris Bell, a guitarist and singer, the duo billing themselves as "The Allen Brothers." In the spring of 1964, they'd toured Asia together and ended up in Hong Kong.

When Judy was released from the Chinese hospital, Mark took her to see

Peter's act. She was so impressed that she booked him as her opening act in London.

Mark revealed to Merv that it was Judy who had introduced Peter to her daughter, Liza Minnelli. "Judy is encouraging Liza to go after Peter, even though she knows Peter is gay," Mark said.

"I do make that rather obvious," Peter said.

"Liberace should be your role model," Merv advised Peter. "If he could be flamboyant and campy in the 50s, you can sure get away with that in the 70s."

Ironically, Peter would eventually become a household word in America, but not as Merv's guest, but because of his appearances on Johnny Carson's *Tonight Show*.

***

Like Johnny Carson before him, Mike Douglas became Merv's TV rival, based on ratings, advertising revenues, and on the "celebrity quotient" of their guests. Merv was jealous when Mike became the first syndicated TV talk show host to win an Emmy.

Right from the beginning, and based partly on the similarity of their names, the public confused Merv and Mike. Their backgrounds were similar. Merv had been a big band singer with Freddy Martin, and Mike had been a big band singer with Kay Kyser. Many fans came up to Merv and said, "Please, Mr. Douglas, may I have your autograph?" Merv hated that.

"I was often confused with Merv Griffin," Mike said. "We were both the same height, the same weight, and we were both Irish tenors." Unlike Merv, however, Mike had had a recent hit recording with his 1966 version of "The Men in My Little Girl's Life."

Merv found the song corny and was amused to hear that Elvis Presley had shot out the TV screen in his hotel suite at the Las Vegas Hilton while watching *The Mike Douglas Show*. Later, Merv learned that Elvis did not hate Mike, but couldn't stand his co-host, Robert Goulet.

As the battle for TV ratings between Merv and Mike intensified, the two men came to loathe each other. Sometimes they competed for the same guests, and Mike often won out, snaring everybody from Truman Capote to

That other Irish tenor from the big band era:
Mike Douglas

Richard Nixon. After Rosemary Clooney appeared on Mike's show, Merv called her. "How could you do that to me, you Benedict Arnold?"

Zsa Zsa Gabor appeared on both shows. After she made a vulgar insult to Morey Amsterdam on *The Mike Douglas Show*, Mike's shows were no longer taped live. Mike's highest ratings were achieved when John Lennon and Yoko Ono co-hosted the show with him. Reaching six million viewers every day, he saw his salary rise to $500,000 a year.

Much to Merv's regret, Mike extracted unusual performances on air from his guests, getting Barry Goldwater to play the trombone or golf prodigy Tiger Woods to putt before cameras. Both Barbra Streisand and Joan Crawford each agreed to co-host Mike's show for a whole week. Mike even persuaded Judy Garland to sing "Over the Rainbow" when she was reluctant to perform that song any more.

On looking back at TV programming in the mid-60s, Merv said, "It was a great time for a guy like me to have a talk show. The whole nation was having a debate over which direction to take. Hippies everywhere battling the Establishment. An unpopular war in Vietnam. Even religion itself had come under assault."

Privately, Merv told Hadley, "If you ever wondered how that studly jock on your football team was hung, you've got a chance now. Nudity's everywhere. Somewhere, some place he's taking off his clothes and letting his thing cool in the breeze."

When some right-wingers attacked Merv for having Communistic leanings, he proclaimed, "I've arrived! I loved it. It meant I was reaching them, that the show wasn't just a piece of fluff. Of course, I had controversial guests, but some of them—most of them—in fact, were booked just for the fun of it, including my very first guest, Miss Carol Channing."

***

Saucer-eyed and scratchy in voice, Carol Channing, in Merv's view, was "a space cadet but always good for a laugh." He'd first seen her playing Lorelei Lee in the original stage version of *Gentlemen Prefer Blondes* in 1949, eventually losing the movie role to Marilyn Monroe as she'd also lose the title role in *Hello, Dolly!* to Barbra Streisand.

As Merv's first guest, Carol came across as a larger-than-life personality, just as he expected her to. Privately, he knew that the most famous blonde on Broadway was part African-American on her father's side. She wasn't blonde at all but wore a wig, as she was allergic to bleach.

Carol claimed that she'd first met Merv when he sang at Lowell High School in San Francisco, although somehow the years don't seem to match up here. If Merv sang at her high school, he would have been thirteen years old. Carol was born in 1921, Merv in 1925. She also claimed that she became "fast friends" with Merv in New York, which was a bit of an exaggeration.

Merv did come to her rescue when she was starring in *Hello, Dolly!* at the St. James Theater on 44th Street and he was a few buildings away at the Little Theater broadcasting his show.

When there was a power breakdown at Con Edison, and the St. James went black, Merv ordered his crew to snake a series of extension cables over to Carol's stage. The Little Theater was on a different electrical system than the St. James.

"The air-conditioning went off, and it was in the middle of summer—terribly hot," Carol said. "Merv came over with a huge box of Kleenex and went up and down the aisles giving everyone a tissue so they could mop up the sweat. Merv stayed through the whole performance and told the crew exactly where to focus the lights because he'd seen the show so many times. Oh, I loved him. Everybody did!"

Merv didn't just stick to Broadway legends like Carol, or even to movie stars. He brought back his "regulars" like Woody Allen, but he also searched for new talents, including Dick Cavett, his future late-night rival. "If I knew that Cavett and I would one day compete for the same audience, I wouldn't have brought him on at all," Merv said. "But how can you predict who will be tomorrow's competition?"

When Merv, or others, tried to get Cavett to tell them, "What is Johnny Carson really like?" he deflected the queries with humor. "Just because everybody says he is a drug-addicted, sadistic, commie sex pervert, he never showed me that side of himself. He *is* cold. One day he was napping in the nude in his dressing room, and I shoved a thermometer up his ass and the mercury froze."

Word spread quickly across Broadway that Merv was showcasing new talent. "Dozens of performers tried every gimmick in the book to get on my show," Merv said. "One stripper wanted to come on with a python. Only a few got booked, and years later I was proud to have discovered so many of them. Great talents."

George Carlin and Richard Pryor were little-known stand-up comics performing in dives in Greenwich Village when Merv discovered them in 1965. Merv signed both of them to multi-show contracts.

Carlin made successful appearances on Merv's show, beginning in 1965. The astringent stand-up comedian was the natural heir to Lenny Bruce. Network "suits" were worried, claiming he "assaulted the barricades of censorship," but Merv loved his indignant counter-culture humor, and always laughed. In all, Carlin made 29 appearances on Merv's shows.

"Want to hear an oxymoron?" Carlin asked the audience. "Military intelligence."

Before every performance, Carlin faithfully promised Merv he would not use his infamous schtick about "Seven Words You Can Never Say on Television."

"By the way, George, what are those words again?" Merv often asked.

Carlin dutifully replied, "Shit, Piss, Fuck, Cunt, Cocksucker, Motherfucker, and Tits."

Richard Pryor, whom Merv had known for years, had become a friend by the time he appeared on the show. Merv knew a lot about this controversial African/American actor/comedian, the son of a prostitute who was reared in his grandmother's brothel. Richard had survived child molestation—once at the age of six by a teenage neighbor and later by his local priest.

"Our own little Richie Pryor," Merv would tell his audience as he brought on the gangly, wide-eyed kid from Peoria. Merv sometimes referred to him as "a comic genius."

Sadly, Merv realized early in their relationship that Richard was struggling with drug addiction. When Merv went to see him portray a drug-addicted piano player in *Lady Sings the Blues (1972),* Merv defined it as type casting.

As the years went by, Merv witnessed Richard sinking deeper into drug addiction. In the early 80s, Merv heard that Richard had attempted to commit suicide after free-basing cocaine. Richard's managers tried to make it seem like an accident, but according to several reports, Richard had very clearly tried to kill himself by setting himself on fire.

Merv always remembered Richard's enigmatic statement: "It's been a struggle for me because I had a chance to be white—and I refused." He once told Merv, "I'm a survivor with no pity, and that got me through eight mar-

Three of Merv's favorites: **Carol Channing (center)**, big-mouthed, saucer-eyed, and spacy.

Merv referred to **George Carlin** (left) and **Richard Pryor** (right) as
the most vulgar acts in show business.

385

riages—twice to the same woman." He told Merv's audience that he had served in the U.S. Army but spent "most of that gig in the brig." Along with some other blacks, he became annoyed when a white soldier seemed "a bit too amused" at the racially charged sections of *Imitation of Life*, the Lana Turner movie. Richard and three other black soldiers beat up the white soldier and stabbed him. Fortunately, the beating and stabbing weren't fatal.

Merv liked Richard before he developed his raw and racially provocative style. When he took his nephew to see Pryor perform in a theater in Baltimore, Merv later said, "I was shocked. The filthiest routine I've ever heard in my life."

Richard Zoglin, in an appraisal of Merv's career as a TV talk-show host, accurately summed it up. "Your ultimate goal was to land on Johnny Carson's *Tonight Show*. But for many up-and-comers who weren't yet on Carson's radar, the first TV stop was the friendlier, more accessible, less high-pressure showcase that Merv provided. His show didn't have the cachet or the clout of Carson's. But Merv and his producers were smart enough to realize that to compete they had to take more chances with guys like George Carlin or Richard Pryor."

The tunnel-mouthed comedienne, Jo Anne Worley, stood tall with piled-on jet-black hair and had Merv's audiences laughing long before she wowed them on Rowan & Martin's *Laugh-In* (1968). Merv found the brassy, indefatigable performer a delight both before and off the camera. He knew that she'd been Carol Channing's stand-in for *Hello, Dolly!* But as Jo Anne told Merv, "Channing is known for never missing a performance."

"I have this big mouth," she told Merv, "and I've always had it. When I sang in the church choir, I only mouthed the words so I wouldn't drown everybody else out."

Merv had discovered Jo Anne when she created her own nightclub act in Greenwich Village. He was so impressed with her talents that she became a regular on his show, eventually making two hundred appearances.

She later recalled, "I became part of Merv's family, you know, his on-air family of people."

Reni Santoni, an American actor of French and Spanish heritage, started his career as a comedy writer, and frequently entertained and amused guests on Merv's show. In 1967, he was on the dawn of his breakthrough role in Carl Reiner's *Enter Laughing*. Merv predicted "big things," for Reni, but he never became a top star, even though he played memorable roles in such films as Clint Eastwood's *Dirty Harry* in 1971 or Howard Stern's *Private Parts* in 1987.

Straight from the "Borscht Belt" in the Catskills, where he'd perfected his brand of Jewish humor, Sandy Baron had made his Broadway debut in *Tchin-*

Tchin in 1962. Sandy found inspiration for comedy in such unlikely subjects as hate, prejudice, and bigotry.

Years later, he achieved his greatest fame playing the role of Jack Klompus on the NBC sitcom, *Seinfeld*. His character became the comical nemesis of Jerry Seinfeld's retired father.

Sandy met with notoriety when he released his controversial album, *God Save the Queens*, in 1972. It was an earnest but now-dated attempt to break down the stereotypes and mystique about homosexuality. Sandy promoted his album on Merv's show, causing a lot of "snickers in the audience," he later recalled. "My promoters urged me not to go on the Griffin show and be so open about my album. They feared the audience would think I was a fag. As predicted, there was much talk that I was queer. If I refuted it, they'd say, 'Me thinks the lady doth protest too much.' What did I have to do to prove I was straight? Bring the audience into my bedroom and let them see me penetrating my woman?" Years before his death, Sandy said, "My false reputation as a gay came about from Griffin's show. There's still all this talk that I'm gay, which I'm not. The irony is that it was Griffin—not me—who is gay."

Sandy continued to make appearances on Merv's show in the 1970s. He was so influenced by comedian Lenny Bruce that many fans thought he was Bruce. He did impersonate him in the show *Lenny* in Hollywood in 1972.

Like Sandy, Stanley Myron Handelman was another Brooklyn-born comedian who went over with Merv's daytime TV audiences. He performed comedy egghead schticks, some of it inspired by his relationship with his mother.

Tall and gangly looking, he wore large, dark-rimmed glasses, like Merv's nemesis, Robert Q. Lewis, and stood with a nerdy demeanor under a porkpie cap. Years later, he sent Merv a copy of one of his latest films, *Linda Lovelace for President*. Lovelace, of course, was the star of the highest grossing porn film of all time, *Deep Throat*.

Merv claimed that John Denver, the son of an Air Force officer, was an instant hit the first time he appeared on Merv's show. He found John appealing with his longish blond hair cut in a Dutch boy style. He wore bell-bottom jeans and cowboy boots.

Merv liked John so much he invited him out for drinks. "I thought he had an offbeat sex appeal," Merv later confided to Hadley Morrell, "and I was hoping to get lucky. Boy, could that boy drink. I made a pass at him but I think he was too drunk to even know it."

John later had two drunk driving arrests, and he was to die in 1997 when a private plane he was piloting crashed into Monterey Bay in California. "Sigh," Merv told his friends. "Sean Connery got away from Noel Coward. John Denver got away from me."

Most of Merv's audience could relate to him, but he liked to shock his fans by bringing on an occasional "alien from Outer Space."

Taking his name from the crippled lad in Charles Dickens' *A Christmas Carol*, Tiny Tim stunned audiences when Merv introduced him. The ukulele-playing singer of 1920s ditties confused yet amused audiences, many of whom asked, "Is this guy for real?" His falsetto voice became an instant hit, and he was on his way to becoming an icon of the 60s. As one critic put it, "Tiny Tim became a cultural specimen that elucidated the *Zeitgeist* of that era."

When it was made known that Tiny Tim had fallen in love, Merv wanted him to marry "Miss Vicki," his 17-year-old girlfriend (Victoria Budinger), on the air, as part of the programmed content of *The Merv Griffin Show*. Merv was furious when the performer selected Johnny Carson's show instead as the wedding's TV venue. That ceremony drew the biggest audience ever record-ed for a nighttime talk show, garnering 85% of all TV viewers.

Muhammad Ali (a.k.a. Cassius Clay) appeared on Merv's show. "He was not the brightest bulb, but he was a colorful figure," Merv said. Suddenly real-izing the implication of that remark, he said, "I don't mean the color of his skin."

Merv said that he learned that the world heavyweight boxing champion, through a distant link with his maternal grandmother, had Anglo-Saxon ori-gins. He was linked by blood to Presidents William Henry Harrison, John Tyler, Zachary Taylor, and Benjamin Harrison, as well as to Confederate gen-eral Robert E. Lee.

Before Cassius arrived at the studio, an assistant had shown Merv a pic-ture of the boxer in trunks with his penis hanging out the leg of his shorts, which he'd pulled up to expose himself. The picture had been printed in underground gay magazines and was sometimes sold in porno stores. At first, Merv wanted to quiz the boxer about his reaction to this exposure, but staff members talked him out of it.

Instead Merv asked him what it was like meeting The Beatles. The boxer had posed with The Fab Four in the ring. "They're the greatest," he said, "but I'm still the prettiest." Later he modified that praise. "I don't admire nobody but Elvis Presley," he said. "He was the sweetest, most humble, and nicest man you'd ever meet."

Merv had intended to see Barbra Streisand on Broadway in *Funny Girl* but when he got to the theater, he was disappointed when the stage manager announced that her understudy, Lainie Kazan, was going on in her place. Barbra had a throat problem that night.

Lainie's dynamic performance, however, won Merv over, and he invited the Brooklyn-born actress and singer to appear on his show. She was so suc-cessful that she was asked back. He agreed with her own personal summation of her voice.

"I get a sensual feeling from my own singing voice," she said. "When I am right, whether I'm moaning it or winging it, I just fly. I soar. I get all caught up in myself. And, baby, when that happens, you just know the audience has to be with me, having a ball."

Merv was also having a ball doing the show, but "I was getting itchy," he said. I wanted to expand the show. The Little Theater was making me claustrophobic. I wanted to get out and see the world and bring on a whole new set of guests. 'Let's go to Europe,' I told Bob Shanks. 'Hang out with Princess Grace. Attend the Cannes Film Festival. Fly to London. Maybe have a cuppa with Queen Elizabeth.'"

Privately, he told Hadley in jest: "Maybe I can get Prince Philip to fuck me. I hear the Queen married him only when she found out he's got a big one. She had to bring some different genes into the House of Windsor. After all, her kin, including the Duke of Windsor, were known for having history's smallest dicks."

***

Before Merv arrived in Monaco to interview Grace Kelly, he'd heard all the stories about her wild, promiscuous days in New York and Hollywood and about her affairs with Bing Crosby, William Holden, Ray Milland, Marlon Brando, and her unrequited love for Clark Gable. Merv had also heard that she'd had affairs with Cary Grant, although he was mostly gay, James Stewart, Frank Sinatra, David Niven, Oleg Cassini, and Prince Aly Khan. Gary Cooper had told Merv that "She looked like a cold dish until you got her pants down. Then she'd explode."

Except for his control over some of the most expensive real estate in Europe, Merv didn't consider His Most Serene Highness, Rainier, the Sovereign Prince of Monaco, as "much of a catch." Grace had put on weight since her movie days, and Merv had heard gossip that she'd been drinking heavily. Yet she remained elegant, nurturing a prim white-gloves-wearing image which she presented to the public and his cameras. Back in Hollywood, director Henry Hathaway's wife had already proclaimed, loudly and in public, "Grace Kelly wore those white gloves, but she was no saint. In the old days they'd call her a whore."

Even off-camera, Grace was all charm and style to Merv, inviting him back to her kingdom on some future occasion. Nonetheless, he still found her just a bit of an "Ice Queen," and their friendship would always be superficial.

During the introductions at the palace, Merv had become aware of a strikingly handsome young man, perhaps French, who looked almost like the twin brother of Alain Delon. No matter where she moved, the young man followed Grace with his eyes. Merv had been introduced to him but couldn't remember his name. He later told Hadley, "I wanted to take him home as a party favor."

Grace had a commitment that night for dinner, but invited Merv to join her for after-dinner drinks at a small private party in a salon within the Monte Carlo Casino. He showed up at ten o'clock and found a very different Grace there. No longer the prim and proper princess, she was tipsy, light hearted, and full of fun. The young man Merv had seen earlier in the day sat beside her.

Ava Gardner had already told Merv, "Give her a couple of dry martinis, and Her Serene Highness becomes just another girl who likes to dish the dirt." Rock Hudson had told him, "Grace likes to get ripped to the tits and then begs you to fuck her, even though you want to fuck her boyfriend instead."

The Princess looked puffy, and had lost that stunning beauty that she'd displayed in such films as *To Catch A Thief*.

Before the evening ended, Grace seemed to be aware that Merv was evaluating her through the cruel eyes of a Hollywood camera. "I've been svelte all my life," she said. "What's the point of trying to maintain an image of long ago?" She looked Merv up and down. "You look like you could lose a few pounds yourself. Let's face it: I'm older now, but so are you."

"Your Majesty," Merv said, "you will always live in the public's mind as the most beautiful blonde who ever graced the screen. The one with the most class."

In 1956, Merv defined it as "The Wedding of the Century."
Ranier, the Sovereign Prince of Monaco and his bride, movie star **Grace Kelly**

Grace graciously kissed Merv on each cheek before heading out the door. She walked with an uncertain step. The mysterious Alain Delon look-alike followed her.

Merv turned to a trusted staff member. "If I'm judging the scene right, and I'm never wrong about these things, the Princess of Monaco is going to get the fucking of her life tonight. Gary Cooper may have been the best hung man in Hollywood, but he had no ass to push it with. That boy going to that door has not only the goods up front, but, as those tight pants reveal, the world's greatest ass as well. Lucky Grace. When will my Prince Charming ever come? Forget that pudgy Rainier. I bet he has a two-inch dick. Let's get the fuck out of here and head for Cannes. Monaco is too dull for me."

***

After Monte Carlo and his interview with Grace Kelly, Merv journeyed west to Cannes for the famous film festival. His bookers had already arranged for an interview with Sean Connery, who was scheduled to appear the following day.

In the meantime, Merv had met a young man of nineteen from the old papal city of Avignon. Hadley had not been invited along for the trip and Merv was lonely.

The young man, whose name is not known, seemed only too willing to help Merv through his nights . . . and some French francs, of course.

When Merv learned that the slender, strikingly handsome beach boy wanted the equivalent of only twenty U.S. dollars a day, Merv struck up a deal with him, even though language was a barrier.

The boy spoke only a few words of English. "We used the universal language known to aging men and young hustlers the world over," Merv boasted to Hadley upon his return from France.

On the beach in Cannes, Merv was on a *chaise longue* figuring out a crossword puzzle, waiting for the return of his young Frenchman, who had gone for a walk on the sands. He rushed up to Merv, brimming with excitement. At the time Beatlemania was sweeping England, the United States, and Europe. "Lennon, John Lennon," the young boy said. "Over there. Look! Beatles."

At first Merv thought the boy was mistaken. He pointed in the direction of a young man who was in swimming trunks and lying on a padded quilt, reading a book all by himself on the beach. Merv thought he

A beach encounter with
John Lennon

391

was seeing things. Surely Lennon would be surrounded by bodyguards, or else he'd be mobbed by adoring fans.

Merv walked over to discover that it was indeed John Lennon. Introducing himself, Merv learned that Lennon was to some degree vaguely familiar with his name already. To Merv's surprise, Lennon agreed to an interview. It would mark his first interview on an American talk show. With no preparation, Merv called his camera crew and spontaneously interviewed Lennon on the beach.

His studio in New York viewed this as a major coup, and Merv even rewarded his French boy with a hundred dollar bill before he flew back home from the Nice airport.

"When the film was developed," Merv recalled to his friends, "we realized that at one point, Lennon had raised his legs, exposing his uncut cock and balls. Apparently, his trunks didn't have a lining to hold himself in. Lennon didn't seem to notice or care. Of course, the editors had to cut that bit from the film. I guess it didn't matter if Lennon showed the full monty or not. Both he and Yoko Ono would reveal the full monty—or whatever you call that thing between her legs—to the whole world when they posed for that notorious album cover."

***

Merv's encounter with Sean Connery included not only an interview for *The Merv Griffin Show,* but also an insight into his self-image as a singer. Unknown to many of his fans, the Scottish actor in his pre-James Bond days had already sung in films. But few of his 007 fans had ever seen him. He had starred in Walt Disney's unsuccessful movie *Darby O'Gill and the Little People* in 1959. In the film, he sang "Pretty Irish Girl" to his onscreen love interest, and his version of that song was eventually released as a single.

Although Sean remained reticent throughout their time together, Merv at least got Sean to confirm one rumor. During his adolescence in Scotland, he had worked as a coffin polisher.

Merv wanted a juicier interview, but Sean closed the doors to his private life. In England, Sean had filmed *Another Time, Another Place* (1958) with the sultry Lana Turner. They'd engaged in a torrid affair. When word of that tryst reached Lana's gangster boyfriend, Johnny Stompanato, he showed up on the set, threatening to shoot both Lana and Sean. Sean managed to wrestle the gun from him and eject him from the set. Then he went about his business, making love to Lana on the screen, and for his pleasure, making love to Lana off the screen as well.

"He didn't even whip it out for me," Merv complained in a transatlantic phone call to Hadley. "But at least now I know why Noel Coward is so 'Mad About the Boy.'"

The following Christmas, Noel sent Merv a drawing of Sean in a G-string; a female student had drawn it in Edinburgh when Sean was posing nude for one of her art classes. As a joke, Noel also included a photograph of himself taken in a G-string on a beach in Jamaica.

***

Michael Chaplin agreed to appear on Merv's show. The third son of Charlie Chaplin, he was born in Beverly Hills in 1946, eventually moving to Switzerland with "The Little Tramp" and his mother, Oona O'Neill, the estranged daughter of playwright Eugene O'Neill. As a ten-year-old, Michael had been cast in his father's final film, *A King in New York* (1957).

Michael had written a book, *I Couldn't Smoke the Grass on My Father's Lawn*. Even though he grew up in luxury with his parents, surrounded by swimming pools and servants, Michael had rejected his father and was highly critical of him.

Fleeing from home at the age of fifteen, Michael descended into a twilight world of poverty, radical politics, and LSD. In London, reporters tracked him down to a seedy dive in Hampstead, where he was living on a National Assistance grant of ten pounds a week.

When he interviewed Michael, Merv suggested that nineteen was a bit young to be penning memoirs.

"Not when you've led the life I had," Michael said. "I've packed sixty years of living into my first twenty years."

Merv wanted to know what it was like to be born "to the most famous movie star of all time."

"To be the son of a great man can be a disadvantage," Michael said. "It is like living next to a huge monument. One spends one's life circling around it, either to remain in the shade, or to avoid its shadow."

***

In London, Merv wanted to bring on some "heavyweights" as he called them. "I was attacked throughout my career for interviewing drag queens, drug addicts, child molesters, or commie sex perverts, but we could have class too."

One of those heavyweights was Bertrand Russell, the British philosopher, historian, and logician. A world-famous advocate for social reform, he'd won the Nobel Prize for Literature in 1950.

393

Merv was mildly surprised when he met Lord Russell at his bone-bare flat in Chelsea. "I didn't expect him to be so old. He was ninety-three at the time, but he was sharp of mind and still articulate."

Russell's views on sexuality shocked Merv's audiences. He attacked Victorian notions of morality, advocating sex out of wedlock, even trial marriages, and he was one of the first to endorse sex education and widespread access to condoms. He also advocated a change in the law regarding homosexual practices in Britain, and lived to see homosexuality legalized there in 1967.

Privately, after the taping, Russell told Merv that his efforts to have homosexuality legalized "will make the world a finer place for men such as yourself to live a long and happy life."

Merv appeared shocked. "Oh, please, Mr. Russell," he said, "you've been misinformed. I'm a happily married man. I'm not a homosexual."

"Have it your way," Russell said. "But there is homosexuality in all men." He turned and walked away.

As a pacifist, Russell used Merv's show as a platform to attack the United States for its war in Vietnam.

After the airing of Merv's interview with Russell, massive protests poured into the studio, most of them objecting to Russell's views on the war. He'd called America's policies "near-genocidal."

Russell's denunciation of the Vietnam War and charges of genocide against the United States contributed to the most controversial show ever presented on the air by Merv. Even though he specifically stated that he was air-

"What did the fag have to say today?"
(Left to right) Pacifist and Nobel Prizewinner **Lord Bertrand Russell, Merv,** and **President Richard Nixon.**

394

ing Russell's viewpoint—and not his own—Merv was nonetheless denounced across the country. Newspaper editorials referred to him as a Communist and a traitor, despite his well-established status as a conservative Republican.

Months after the Russell interview, Merv himself came to oppose the Vietnam War, much to the annoyance of Richard Nixon. In one incident, Nixon reportedly asked an aide, "What did the fag have to say today?"

***

The British journalist, author, and satirist, an English gent named Malcolm Muggeridge, became a familiar face on American TV chat shows. Merv was eager to interview him, not knowing what the former communist sympathizer, former British spy, former alcoholic, former heavy smoker, and former womanizer was going to say. "That's what made him a fascinating media personality," Merv said.

In his role as editor of *Punch Magazine* from 1953 to 1957, Muggeridge had written an article, "Does England Really Need a Queen?" The reaction to the article was so violent that the BBC banned him for months, and his contract with Beaverbrook newspapers was canceled.

When he came onto Merv's show, he railed against the "Pills and Pot" of the late 1960s, attacking both birth control pills and marijuana. He even blasted The Beatles, calling them "four vacant youths . . . dummy figures with tousled heads and no talent." The audience booed him.

Years later, Merv was surprised to hear that during his final years, at the age of 79, Muggeridge had converted to Roman Catholicism. He became known as the "discoverer" of Mother Teresa and launched her legend in a TV documentary he filmed in Calcutta. It was called *Something Beautiful for God*, as was his best-selling book of the same name. "I liked him better when he was a down-and-dirty whore-mongering drunk, before he started protesting against the commercial exploitation of sex and violence," Merv said. "What's wrong with the media exploiting sex? Of course, we don't need the violence."

Merv continued to have what he called "thinkers" on his show. After Muggeridge, he booked Buckminster Fuller to come on, though some members of his research staff dismissed this architect, author, designer, futurist, and inventor as a "hopeless utopian."

Fuller coined the term "Spaceship Earth" and was one of the world's first advocates of renewable sources of energy such as solar or wind-derived electricity. He contributed a wide range of ideas, designs, and inventions to the planet, among the most visible of which was the geodesic dome. This visionary wasn't always right. For example, he predicted that the world would successfully conquer poverty by the year 2000.

"A lot of what he said went over my head," Merv later admitted. "I was finally reduced to asking him a question like, 'Why do you wear three watches, Mr. Fuller?'"

"I'm a frequent flier," he said. "I have one watch for the time zone I'm in, another from the zone I've just left, and a third watch for the time zone I'm flying into."

Feeling out of his depth, Merv in desperation asked Fuller, "Can you conclude with some advice for all of us."

"Yes," Fuller said. "Stop using the words 'up' and 'down.' They are awkward in that they refer to a planar concept of direction that's inconsistent with human experience. Use the words 'in' or 'out' instead. They better describe an object's relation to the gravitational center, the earth."

As he went off the air, Merv looked puzzled. "I don't know how yet, but somehow I'm going to work in Buckminster as an answer on *Jeopardy!* See if one of the guests can come up with the question."

***

Unlike Arthur Treacher, Merv rarely insulted a guest. "Sometimes the chemistry wasn't right between a guest and me," Merv said. "Peter O'Toole is a case in point. I also struck out with Al Pacino, whom I found very hostile right from the beginning." Merv brought the young actor onto his show long before he achieved fame in *The Godfather*.

Knowing he came from an urban neighborhood of the Bronx before breaking into show business, Merv asked, "How did you make it from the Bronx to Broadway?"

"By subway," Pacino said, garnering loud laughter from the audience.

Years later, Pacino told an interviewer that he'd abandoned talk shows forever "after being asked a completely stupid question by Merv Griffin."

Although Pacino is hailed as one of the greatest and most influential

Various degrees of provocation, *chez Merv,* on daytime TV
Left to right: Al Pacino, Buckminster Fuller, and Lily Tomlin

actors of all time, Merv was not impressed. He once claimed to a reporter that, "I've never seen one of his films and I've never had him on my show," even though millions of Merv's fans knew otherwise. He once told Roddy McDowall, "Pacino's asshole is too tightly clenched for my dick."

In contrast with Pacino, Merv bonded immediately with Lily Tomlin, the American actress and comedian who made her first television appearance on *The Merv Griffin Show* in 1965. She told him that her first "professional gig" was as a waitress at Howard Johnson's on Broadway near Times Square. "There was a mike in the restaurant, and I delivered zingers. I was a lousy waitress but I had the customers in stitches."

Merv laughed at her one liners. "There will be sex after death—we just won't be able to feel it," or "The trouble with the rat race is that even if you win, you're still a rat!"

Merv was delighted when five years later she shot to fame as a cast member of the slapstick sketch show, *Rowan & Martin's Laugh-in*. He always claimed that her impersonation of the wacko telephone operator Ernestine was one of the best comedic acts ever broadcast on TV.

At the time of her appearance on Merv's show, Lily was living in a shanty near the rail tracks in Yonkers. "She might have been skipping a meal or two," Merv said. "But I knew this gal was going places." He paused. "There was the lesbian thing, of course, but somehow I didn't think that was going to hold her back."

***

To Merv, Mark Herron's marriage to Judy Garland followed a predictable pattern. Merv could almost anticipate the urgent calls before receiving them.

After *Time* magazine wrote that "Judy Garland may have gone over the rainbow for the last time," she took a lethal overdose of Seconal. Mark saved her life when he found her in a coma and rushed her to the hospital.

Mark called Merv on August 16, 1966, announcing that he planned to sue Judy for a divorce.

"This does not come as a surprise," Merv said. "I've talked to Judy. She claims that the marriage was never consummated."

"That's a question for the courts," Mark said. "I let her give me two or three blow-jobs. Does that constitute consummation?"

"You got me on that one, kid" Merv said. "I've had entire relationships that consisted of one-way blow-jobs, with me blowing in the wind."

On December 3, 1966, Judy counterattacked, amending her plea in court from divorce to annulment, and indeed citing that the marriage to Mark had never been consummated.

Judy's divorce from Mark was finalized on April 11, 1967. She spoke to Merv two weeks later. "I've changed my name," she proclaimed.

"You did pretty well with Judy Garland," Merv said. He advised her to hang on to her name.

"Believe it or not, my legal name has been Frances Ethel Gumm Rose Minnelli Luft Herron. Today I'm officially Judy Garland."

"Well, *Miss* Judy Garland," Merv said, "I've got a great idea. I want you to come onto my show. You'll be spectacular. I'll get back to you with details. After all, you're only the biggest star in the world."

"Oh, yeah," she said. "If that's true, why am I perpetually broke?"

"Good question," he said before hanging up.

Merv announced his plans to bring Judy onto his show. He was also considering designating her as hostess while he went on vacation. But in April of 1966 he received a midnight call from Peter Lawford in Hollywood. "I think Judy's gone over the deep end."

"You mean, *again*?"

"You haven't seen her in quite a while," Peter said. "She's crazy most of the time. Totally out of control. Her most recent rage against Mark Herron was the most violent ever. During the course of that so-called marriage, she phoned me one night claiming that Mark had attacked her with a razor. I think she called me because she knew that at the time, I was having an affair with Mark. I rushed to her house, nearly getting ticketed along the way by a cop for speeding. When I got there, I ran upstairs to her bedroom. Judy's face was a mass of blood. It had been cut badly in several places. The maid was trying to stop the blood. I couldn't find any disinfectant, so I used the vodka by her bedside. I doused her with that while the maid called for an ambulance. She's become completely self-destructive. She'll be dead in a year or so. I just know it."

"Thanks for the grim news," Merv said, "but I still believe in Judy's ability to put on a show. In spite of all her suicide attempts, she's eternal."

"We'll see," Peter said with a sigh before hanging up.

Although he'd sounded optimistic on the phone with Peter, Merv had second thoughts about bringing Judy onto his show. He called her on the afternoon of the following day. At first he didn't believe it was Judy on the phone. She spoke in a voice angry and bitter.

Superstar **Judy Garland**
"Over the Rainbow
a few times too many"

During the course of their talk, she denounced Mark, calling him a "faggot," and he'd never heard her use that word before. She even called her loyal fans, especially the gay ones, "sons-of-bitches!" He assumed that she was either drunk or drugged—perhaps both.

On an impulse he called her again the next day. This time, the voice that came over the phone was more conciliatory. It was the Judy he'd known and loved. Vulnerable, yes, but not bitter, although she maintained her gallows humor.

Putting aside his doubts, he decided to arrange for her to come onto his show. "Fasten your seat belt," he told Bob Shanks. "It's gonna be a bumpy ride."

***

A week before she was scheduled to go on the show, Merv finally succeeded in speaking to Judy "after calling all over the country." She was a patient in a private hospital, where she was registered under a false name, trying to recover from an overdose of drugs which, mixed with her huge alcoholic intake, had almost killed her.

She was desperate, aggressively denouncing Sid Luft, her former husband before Mark Herron. "He's trying to sabotage my career. He took all my arrangements, even my wardrobe. I have nothing. Not a penny. In my state, no one in his right mind would want to give a booking to the broken down old hag from yesterday, Judy Garland. If MGM remakes *Meet Me in St. Louis*, I can take the Marjorie Main part."

She meant it when she claimed that she was broke. He wired the train fare she'd need to come to New York, and reserved a suite for her at the Americana Hotel. He also promised to hire a designer for her wardrobe. "As for musical arrangements, Mort Lindsey is my conductor," Merv said. "He's conducted music for you for years. Just leave it to old Mort."

After putting down the phone, Merv booked her into the hotel at his expense and called Christian Dior, ordering an expensive sequined gown for Judy. He also phoned Mort to prepare arrangements for her appearance.

It was agreed in advance that she would sing, "I'd Like to Hate Myself in the Morning," followed by "Have Yourself a Merry Little Christmas" and "The Trolley Song."

Judy's train arrived in New York the following evening. She took a taxi to the Americana. The night manager had not been informed about the details of her arrival, or that her expenses would be covered by Merv.

When she got there, the night manager ordered her out of the hotel lobby. Unknown to Merv, Judy had run up a big, and unpaid, bill at the Americana during a previous visit. Management had issued a standing order to eject her if she came back and didn't settle her way overdue account.

Humiliated and out on the street, Judy called a girlfriend in Brooklyn and spent the night with her. When Judy phoned the next morning and explained the situation, Merv swung into action. He called the New York Hilton and arranged a suite for her, and then he hired a messenger to rush some cash to Brooklyn so she could get a facial and book the town's best hairdresser. She'd warned him that she couldn't deposit a check into any bank because the Internal Revenue Service was systematically confiscating her funds to pay off a tax lien.

Basking in Merv's beaming approval, and with her beloved Mort Lindsey backing her up, Judy wowed Merv's audiences and her millions of fans. "You've still got the magic," Merv told her after the show, hugging her and kissing her.

He startled her by asking her to take over his show while he flew to Zurich for a Christmas holiday in Switzerland. Merv suggested that she bring on as guests some of her most loyal friends.

She began to tick them off immediately. "Burt Lancaster, of course, he adores me. James Mason, my most loyal fan. We'll get Gene Kelly. Naturally, you must let me have Liza on."

Merv was shocked the next day when his staff reported that each of the "friends" had turned Judy down. Liza had claimed she'd be out of town on an engagement. Merv belatedly learned that Liza hadn't spoken to her mother in months.

Burt Lancaster said, "I wouldn't trust that drunk on the air" before slamming down the phone. James Mason declined, claiming that their roles in *A Star Is Born* should have been reversed. "Judy should have played the broken down drunk who walks into the sea." Ethel Merman, who'd once adored Judy and had reportedly had an early lesbian relationship with her, called Merv personally. "I can't go on the show. I'll be *conveniently* busy. Got that?"

Merv managed to conceal from Judy that all her "dear friends," including her own daughter, had turned her down.

When the show was taped on December 23, 1968, Merv's staff had arranged for Judy's line-up to consist of Margaret Hamilton and Moms Mabley. Judy's loyal friend from her MGM days, Van Johnson, also agreed to come onto the show. She'd once had a crush on him in the 40s.

On the air, Margaret Hamilton confided that ever since the release of *The Wizard of Oz* in 1939, in which she'd played "The Wicked Witch of the West," children had scorned her, asking her why she was so mean to Dorothy. For nostalgia's sake, Judy asked her to deliver her most famous line from *Wizard*. Switching into the green-faced and (at least to children) terrifying character from long ago, Margaret screeched, "I'll get you, my pretty, and your little dog, too!" She then burst into her witch's cackle.

Billed as "The Funniest Woman in the World," Moms Mabley was an African American who had a "bag lady" persona and a sharp wit. She had Judy in stitches. "There ain't nothing an old man can do for me except bring me a message from a young one." Moms had no apparent feminine characteristics. Her cackling, scratchy voice led to various rumors that she was actually a female impersonator.

Judy and Arthur Treacher wooed the audience with "The Only Girl in the World" and "Just in Time."

The show marked Judy's last American television appearances. Regrettably, the studio lost its archival tape, although it exists in a grainy pirated version that some young Judy fan recorded by actually filming what appeared on the TV screen.

The day after Judy's appearance, fans flooded the studio with letters. A typical comment: "Judy did not look good, thin as a rail. Sang awful and was out of it. Where the hell was Liza? Or Sid? Or any number of her supposed friends? Any one of them should have taken her and saved her. Watching her I realized it was all over except for the funeral."

Other fans responded more positively. "On Judy's worst day, she's better than most on their best day."

***

As a footnote to Merv's career, he created the game show, *Reach for the Stars*, which aired on NBC on weekday mornings. Launched in January of 1967, it ran for a total of 65 episodes. Longtime broadcaster Bill Mazer hosted the show, which was similar to the more enduring *The Match Game*. A correct answer allowed a contestant to "reach for a star" on a game board, but a wrong answer meant the loss of a star. Later Merv called the show "one of my minor efforts."

***

Robert Kennedy was assassinated in the early hours of June 5, 1968, at the Ambassador Hotel in Los Angeles. Merv's close friend, Rosemary

Clooney, had spent months campaigning across the country for the man she wanted to be president and the lover she could never have just to herself. She'd been forced to share him not only with this wife, Ethel, but with Marilyn Monroe, Lee Remick, and surprise surprise, Rudolph Nureyev, who had also enjoyed the charms of Jacqueline Kennedy.

The days had long passed when Robert and Rosemary conducted their sexual trysts in Merv's hideaway. Even though Robert had long ago moved on to other lovers, Rosemary was still madly in love with him.

"Bobby was the passion of Rosie's life," Merv confided to Hadley. "He never really loved her—he was still in love with Ethel—but he wanted her friendship and support. He abandoned her bed, but he never abandoned the friendship."

With two of her five children in tow, Rosemary arrived at the second floor Embassy Room of the Ambassador. The crowds were overflowing that night, and at one point Rosemary went to the floor below and entertained the burgeoning crowd with "When Irish Eyes Are Smiling" and "This Land Is Your Land."

"I was in the VIP section," Rosemary later said, "and I never got to say a final goodbye to Bobby. After his victory speech, he was supposed to come into the roped-off VIP area to greet us and thank us. Instead some aide led him toward the adjoining banquet room, where he was directed to take a short-cut through the kitchen." Tears welled in her eyes. "Even now, I can't stand to think of what happened next."

Other than Ethel Kennedy, perhaps no woman in America suffered the death of Robert Kennedy more than Rosemary. "She literally went into exile," Merv said. "Reports reached me that she had begun dangerously mixing excessive booze with drugs. The pain in her heart was just too great. She had to dull it. She literally became a basket case. I knew she'd always loved Bobby and had for years, but until I went to see Rosie at the hospital, where she'd collapsed into a nervous breakdown, I never realized the full extent of that obsessive love. After Bobby's death, he was all she could think about. I'd never seen anything like it. She was behaving like the grieved widow, as if she were the mother of all of Bobby's children."

"Other than Ethel Kennedy, no woman in America suffered the death of RFK more than **Rosemary Clooney**"

After his visit that day to the hospital, Rosemary cut Merv out of her life and wouldn't answer his urgent phone calls. Years went by before he finally reached her by showing up, unannounced, on her doorstep. "A nanny or somebody let me in," Merv said, "and I marched immediately to her bedroom and confronted her. 'For God's sake,' I told her, 'get the hell out of that God damn bed and get on with your life. Bobby's dead. He's not coming back.'"

At least this is the story that Merv told his friends in Los Angeles. In his second autobiography, he claimed he reached her on the telephone.

After that painful reunion and confrontation, Merv admitted that he nagged the singer day after day. Even so, it took weeks before she agreed to come onto his show.

Merv had predicted to Rosemary that she'd be a big hit if she appeared in public again—and she was. The fans in the studio responded with massive applause after her beautiful rendition of "What Are You Doing the Rest of Your Life?" Merv admitted that he teared up at the end of that song.

He brought her back on the show time and time again until Rosemary pleaded with him, "Your audience will get tired of hearing me sing 'Come On-a My House.'"

For the rest of her life, Merv stayed in touch with her, even though most of their friendship was conducted over the phone. He called frequently and offered his moral support during Rosemary's eventual bout with lung cancer. Then a call he'd dreaded came in on June 29, 2002. Rosemary had died in Beverly Hills.

As Merv later told the press, "Those lungs that gave us some of the most beautiful music of the 20th century will breathe no more. I was hoping until the very end that she'd pull through. I called her as often as I could. She was one of my closest friends. The spot she occupied in my heart will never be filled by anyone else."

***

In 1968, Merv made an ill-fated move, bringing a liberal producer, David Susskind, onto the same show on which he'd booked Richard Nixon, who at the time was making what would turn out to be a successful run for the presidency.

Nixon had never been at ease on camera and seemed to be especially upset at the presence of David Susskind. When the producer suggested that many anti-Catholic Democrats had voted for him, and not for John F. Kennedy, in the 1960 election, Nixon was furious but masked it until Merv broke for a commercial.

At the beginning of the commercial break, Nixon got up and shook Merv's hand, telling him that he was walking off the show. After the commercial ended, when Merv came back on the air, he explained that Nixon had been called away on urgent business.

The next day Merv got a call from Herb Klein, Nixon's communications director, who urged him not to run the interview. Defying him, Merv ran the tape of Nixon's appearance anyway.

***

For a vacation, Merv flew to Hawaii, where he retained memories of Monty Clift and Frank Sinatra during the filming of *From Here to Eternity*. While walking through the lobby of his hotel, wearing his tennis whites on the way to his game, he encountered Queen Elizabeth and Prince Philip. "She couldn't take her eyes off my bare legs," he later said. "I think she wanted to fuck me."

More and more, Merv was having fun and paying for sex, as he'd long ago learned to do. Much of the actual day to day management of his various enterprises had been handed over to Murray Schwartz, who was now the president of Merv Griffin Productions. During the period when Merv had been represented by the William Morris Agency, Schwartz had been his agent.

***

Merv's beloved Tallulah Bankhead died in 1968, a nurse telling Merv that her final words were a desperate outreach for "bourbon" or "codeine."

In the years leading up to her death, the indomitable "Tallu" had been one of the most popular, most memorable, and amusing guests on Merv's daytime talk show.

After filming an episode for the *Batman* TV series, Tallulah had appeared twice on Merv's shows. Her last appearance was on January 23, 1968, eight days before her sixty-fifth birthday. She was so ill that Merv had to order his chauffeur to physically carry Tallulah from her bedroom to the waiting limousine. From the limousine, she was then carried through the studio to her dressing room.

Before they went on the air, Merv ordered his cameraman to steer clear of her face. Suffering from emphysema, she was having a hard time breathing. On the air Merv handed her a tumbler of water, or so it appeared. Actually it was filled with gin.

For her farewell appearance, she spoke of her favorite politicians, including Harry S. Truman, her fondness for bridge games, her various illnesses, and even her loneliness. So many of her favorite people in the world had died.

As the credits were rolling, he popped one final question, wanting to know why she'd gone to so much trouble to appear on his show. "I wanted to prove to all my fans that I'm not dead, *dah-ling.*"

Back at her home, her condition over the following months continued to worsen until she had to be taken to a hospital. She ranted and raged with the hospital staff, and had an intravenous tube injected into her body. One night as she was tossing and turning, she ripped the tube from her arm and immediately lapsed into a coma, from which she never recovered. She died on the night of December 12, 1968. Merv wept openly upon hearing the news. Privately, he journeyed to Frank Campbell's Funeral Home in Manhattan to see her body before her casket was closed. The coffin was lined in baby blue. "Pink is for *little* girls," Tallulah always said.

He couldn't help but notice that cigarette burns were etched into the silk wrapper that draped her body.

"Good night, sweet lady," Merv whispered to her before bending over to kiss her cheek. Rising up, he turned to one of his staff. "There will never be a hell-raisin' gal like Tallulah Bankhead ever again. God threw away the formula."

***

Merv met Mickey Deans when he was managing a club called Sybil Burton's Arthur Discothèque in New York. With the divorced wife of Richard Burton showing up frequently, it was the most popular disco in town. Merv had gone there one evening with Hadley and had been enchanted with the charismatic manager. "Mickey Deans knows how to treat a star like a star," Merv said. "That boy's going places. He's made this damn disco the most popular and entertaining place to be at night in all of America."

The following day, the first place Mickey went was into Merv's bed. Their sexual bonding was so successful that the two men became a "couple" the very next day, at least according to Hadley. Throughout the course of their brief relationship, Hadley acted as go-between between Merv and Mickey, carrying messages back and forth and arranging their private times together.

Merv was adamant that no member of his staff or family and especially the press got wind of this new relationship.

Through Mickey, Merv arranged to rent Arthur's one evening as the venue for his staff's Christmas party. As a courtesy, Merv invited Judy Garland to attend.

Ignoring Merv and the business of hosting a party, Mickey spent all evening at a table in a remote corner of the disco talking to Judy.

Every now and then Merv looked over at Judy and Mickey, both of whom had been drinking heavily all evening. Shortly after midnight, a waiter tapped

Merv on the shoulder, saying that Judy wanted him to come over to her table. Once there, she handed the phone to Merv. "[The columnist] Earl Wilson wants to talk to you," she said.

"Hi, Earl," Merv said, not knowing what to expect.

"Is Judy Garland drunk or is she marrying Mickey Deans for real?"

"Just a minute." Merv looked into the eyes of both Judy and Mickey. "You two getting married—or not?"

Judy claimed that she'd accepted Mickey's proposal of marriage only an hour before.

"They're getting married," Merv said to Earl. "Print it!" He put down the phone and walked away.

Judy called after him. "Aren't you going to congratulate us?"

Merv was furious. Before leaving the club that night, he had an angry confrontation with Mickey in his private office. "I can't believe you're doing this to me?" he said. "You're my boy friend, or at least you were until tonight."

"All of us have to move on," Mickey said. "Life is about change."

"Don't give me that God damn cliché," Merv shouted at him.

"C'mon, you've got to understand," Mickey said. "What gay man on the planet would turn down a chance to marry Judy Garland?"

Rumor had it that Mickey had originally met Judy when, at the suggestion of a friend, he'd rushed to her hotel suite with a bagful of amphetamines.

Mickey was good looking, with piercing blue eyes, and a voice so deep it seemed to emanate from a cave. He was ruggedly masculine, and his lovers reported that he was "well endowed."

"There was a kind of John Garfield toughness to Mickey Deans," said author Gerold Frank. "Mickey was a sturdy, muscular man, who could wheel and deal as well as sing, play the piano, entertain, manage a discothèque—all of which must have attracted Judy. It was his I-can-handle-it assurance that was reminiscent of Sid Luft."

London gossips kept Merv up to date with what was going on within the marriage. Judy was said to have caught Mickey in bed with the singer Johnnie Ray, with whom she was living for a time. Johnnie, like Judy, was also falling in popularity.

The marriage managed to survive that embarrassment. By now Judy must have been familiar with catching one or another of her husbands in bed with other men.

Singer **Johnny Ray** *(left)* slept with **Judy Garland**'s final husband, **Mickey Deans** *(right)* on the night before her wedding to yet another gay husband.

406

On June 22, 1969, Merv was informed that Mickey was on the phone calling from London about Judy. Merv was still furious at the way Mickey had dumped him for Judy, and at first, he decided not to take the call. But his secretary returned, telling Merv how urgent the call was. He picked up the receiver to hear Mickey's distressed voice. "Judy's dead," he announced bluntly.

Merv later told Hadley, "I'm ashamed of myself. My response was too bitchy."

Over the transatlantic line, Merv said, "I'm not surprised. I guess you'll start trying to get a book offer today." Then he hung up the phone.

At Judy's funeral in New York, Merv noted that many of the people who had refused to come onto *The Merv Griffin Show* with Judy showed up at the funeral, along with 22,000 hysterical fans outside.

"James Mason gave the eulogy," Merv said. "But he wouldn't come onto my show when I invited him when Judy was still alive and needed his support."

Merv sent a stunning array of flowers to the funeral. He wrote on the card, "*Bonne Nuit*, Judy. With eternal love, Merv."

When he walked out of the funeral home, he heard Judy's voice on the portable radio of a fan.

"Forget your troubles and just get happy. Get ready for the judgment day."

***

When Roddy McDowall phoned and asked Merv if he'd appear as himself in a film called *Hello Down There* (1969), he accepted because of his long-standing relationship with the actor. It was only when filming began that Merv learned from one of the co-directors, Jack Arnold, that the role had originally been intended for Jackie Gleason.

Merv enjoyed seeing Roddy again, his passion for the handsome actor a distant memory. Their relationship had evolved into a deep friendship. Merv also enjoyed a reunion on the set with Janet Leigh.

The film was a silly 60s comedy about a family living in an underwater house off the coast of Florida. Appearing as himself, Merv interviewed the "aqua family" for his TV show.

Merv's life-long contempt for the star of the film, Tony Randall, stemmed from their dealings together on the set of *Hello Down There*. Through Rock Hudson, Merv had learned that Randall was a closeted homosexual. Yet when he was around someone he suspected of being gay, Randall often launched into bitter putdowns.

In front of Merv, and without provocation, Randall attacked homosexuals. "I've had to give up the ballet," he said. "I'm surrounded there by a bunch of fags. Definitely not my bag. Friends of mine even showed me a gay male porno film. It was disgusting but it confirmed a long-held suspicion of mine. Homosexuals don't really like sucking each other's cocks. Throughout the film the guys didn't even get aroused, unlike the kids who do straight porn. Straight couples really go at it."

"If gays don't enjoy it, then why do they do it?" Merv asked.

Anger flashed across Randall's face. Usually quick with a comeback, he at first seemed stuck for an answer. "They just do it to defy society. It's a way of saying 'fuck you' to the Establishment. In fact, there's no such thing as homosexuality. It's all a joke. They just pretend to dig each other. Actually homosexuality is just a manifestation of self-hatred."

"Tony, sweet babycakes," Merv said mockingly. "Don't get so worked up about it. You're fooling no one. Rock Hudson told me you're one of the best cocksuckers in Hollywood." Merv turned and walked away.

***

Not just Ronald Reagan and Richard Nixon, but other U.S. presidents came onto Merv's show, including Gerald Ford and Jimmy Carter. But an anticipated interview with Dwight Eisenhower slipped through his fingers.

Merv almost got to interview Eisenhower in retirement with Mamie at his Gettysburg farm. He journeyed to Pennsylvania to personally ask Ike if he'd agree to be interviewed. What Merv discovered was a frail, greatly weakened man who no longer looked as strong and powerful as he did when he was commanding Allied forces during World War II. The presidency and a harsh life in the military had taken a great toll. Merv was reassured when Ike firmly shook his hand and told him that he and Mamie were "faithful watchers" of his talk show.

After agreeing to allow Merv's camera crew to film at his farmstead, Ike immediately discussed money, suggesting that his fee for appearing would be donated to charity. Merv's show at Westinghouse always paid guests under one-thousand dollars for their appearances. Ike wanted $30,000.

Merv was taken aback by the figure. He later wrote, "I knew that that was a lot more toasters than Westinghouse would ever pay."

Back in New York, Merv was pondering where he'd get the money when a bulletin came over television. Ike had died of a heart attack in Washington, D.C. The date was March 28, 1969.

Merv watched stunned as television stations across the country broadcast film clips of Ike, going back to the State of Texas where he was born in 1890, though he'd been raised in Abilene, Kansas.

"Maybe it's just as well that I didn't get to interview Ike," Merv later said.

"I was saving two provocative questions for the end of the show. I wanted to ask him why he had tried to hide his upbringing as a Jehovah's Witness. Then I was going to deliver the zinger. I wanted to know if Kay Summersby, his aide, was really his wartime mistress. After asking the bombshell, I guess his Secret Service guys would have kicked me off that farm in Gettysburg."

***

As the 1960s came to their tumultuous end, Merv was in his 40s and deep into middle age. But at long last, and after many failures, he'd found success. His game shows, *Let's Play Post Office, One in a Million, Talk It Up*, and *Reach for the Stars* had been purchased and aired, although, unlike *Jeopardy!*, each had had a short life.

One TV critic noted that Merv's game shows appealed to viewers "with a lot of time to waste." He specifically singled out *Let's Play Post Office*. On that show, three contestants were read letters from celebrities one line at a time. They tried to guess the identity of the letter's author. As each subsequent line from the mystery letter was read on air, the money value of the prize decreased.

Despite his many successes, Merv was bored and desperately wanted a challenge. Later, as events unfolded, "The tooth fairy must have heard me and granted my wish," Merv said. "And how!"

Retired President **Dwight D. Eisenhower** agreed to an exclusive interview with Merv, but priced himself too high.

He's pictured here, on the left, with his then-Vice-President **Richard Nixon**

Merv

Chapter Nine

In 1967, despite the popularity of *The Merv Griffin Show*, Westinghouse, its sponsor, seemed to be "dragging its feet" (Merv's words) about renewing his contract.

Then an unexpected call came in from CBS, asking Merv if he'd signed his contract. When Merv responded that he had not, "the suits" began secret negotiations with Merv about hosting a late-night talk show on CBS.

As negotiations continued, Merv demanded that CBS pay him "twice the money" that Carson was hauling in. "There were a lot of bank vaults in New York that needed filling," Merv said, only half kidding.

At the time, Carson was pulling in $40,000 a week, which meant that Merv was demanding $80,000. The negotiators at CBS were outraged, one executive calling the salary demand "highway robbery." Nevertheless, CBS was desperate, as they'd been running old movies in an unsuccessful attempt to lure late-night audiences away from Carson. "Not that many people wanted to see Kay Francis in *Transgression*," said an executive at CBS, referring to a movie the star had made in 1931.

When Merv's salary demands moved upstairs at CBS, the brass there agreed to it almost without protest. Merv was told that lawyers would begin drawing up the contract immediately. "It was the shock of my life," he said. "I couldn't believe they'd pay me a salary that was to the moon—unprecedented in the history of television."

For a combined total of two million dollars in renovation costs, CBS converted the 1912 Cort Theater, on West 48th Street in Manhattan, into Merv's television studio.

As soon as his contract with Westinghouse expired, thanks to CBS, Merv returned to network TV, taking on the other talking heads, notably Johnny Carson. From August 18, 1969 to February 11, 1972 at 11:30pm on weeknights, he challenged the more popular Carson to a duel for viewers and market share.

Carson's show was carried by two hundred and twelve stations, with Merv in second place with one hundred and fifty outlets. Merv scored best in his native San Francisco and also opened strong in Los Angeles, pulling thousands upon thousands of viewers away from Carson, whose appeal was the greatest in metropolitan New York.

It was an uphill battle for Merv. After a few months, when Merv's style didn't catch on with their late-night audiences, many stations dropped him, some of them opting instead for a roster of old movies from the 1930s and 40s. "I found myself competing with everybody from Betty Grable to John Wayne," Merv said.

In his scrabbling for audiences, Merv faced other hurdles—and not just from Carson. "I was in a rat race with a lot of other rats, all of us vying for the same piece of cheese," Merv said.

CBS wanted Merv to slay Carson as well as a lineup of other "dragons," especially an ABC-affiliated Rat Packer appearing nightly as host of "The Joey Bishop Show." Some nights, Merv's audiences were slightly larger than Carson's, but "Johnny always bounced back like gangbusters. But at least I managed to stay ahead of Joey, holding in second place," Merv said.

Perpetually glum, the Bronx-born stand-up comedian, Joey Bishop, was best known at the time for being a member of Frank Sinatra's Rat Pack. Carson felt particularly betrayed when Bishop competed with him on air, since the comedian had guest-hosted *The Tonight Show* more times than anyone else before breaking away for his own ninety-minute late-night talk show.

The Joey Bishop Show ran from 1967 to 1969, with then-newcomer Regis Philbin percolating cheerfully as the show's co-host. Merv was always a bit contemptuous of Bishop, claiming that his face had the look of "an untipped waiter." (The put-down may not have been original to Merv.) When Bishop told an interviewer that he'd never seen Dean Martin or Frank Sinatra drunk, and Merv heard about it, Merv mocked the claim openly among his friends and colleagues.

In the battle for ratings, Bishop proved no match for Merv and Carson, and ABC eventually dropped the show from its listings. Dick Cavett was hired to fill the late-night talk show void at ABC.

When asked privately about Merv, Bishop said, "He's an asshole, and I don't fuck assholes. I'm a pussy man myself—and married to Sylvia Ruzga since 1941." But despite what Merv and Bishop might have said privately, the

Talk Show King and Wannabe:
Johnny Carson (left), **Joey Bishop** (right)

412

two competitors seemed like the dearest of friends when Bishop, years later, in 1978, appeared on Merv's show.

Even after the demise of Joey Bishop as a competitor, Merv still had to compete for guests with Mike Douglas, who was luring stars to Philadelphia for his afternoon show. "All these talk shows, fighting for guests, were eating up interesting people the way a dinosaur might devour an animal for lunch," Merv claimed. "There were just so many times that I could bring on Eva Gabor."

As regards the décor of his late-night interviewing style, Merv preferred the old desk-and-sofa setup that Steve Allen, Dave Garroway, and Jack Paar had popularized years before. As Merv recited later, "Johnny Carson, Joey Bishop, and I sat there every night, playing a game with viewers called 'Pick Your Host.' Or more likely 'Pick Your Guest.'"

More than Bishop and Carson, Merv seemed to genuinely like surprising his viewers with the unexpected. Examples included Max Yasgur, the upstate New York dairy farmer who had rented his land to the Woodstock Music and Art Fair, or writer Billie Young, who, using the pseudonym Penelope Ashe, had contributed to the text of *Naked Came the Stranger*.

Naked Came the Stranger, published in 1969, was a literary hoax perpetrated by a group of prominent journalists. The project was conceived by Mike McGrady of *Newsday*, who assembled a committee of two dozen journalists to write a deliberately terrible book with a lot of sex to illustrate their point that American literary culture had become brainlessly vulgar. The text was deliberately mediocre, a dysfunctional pseudo-literary hodge-podge, with heavy editing of any segment which was too well written. Fulfilling the committee's cynical expectations, the book was wildly successful, even appearing briefly on *The New York Times* Bestseller List, perhaps a result of the intensive sales and marketing campaign associated with its release. As sales increased, some of the co-authors felt guilty about the money they were earning, and went public. At least some of the fallout from the hoax was explored on *The Merv Griffin Show.*

Naked
Came
The
Stranger
by Penelope Ashe

***

David Frost, an articulate, breezy import from London, was perceived as another talk-show dragon for Merv to slay—and doing so became a formidable challenge.

During its heyday, *The David Frost Show* presented serious competition for every other talk show host in the world. Frost's weekly routine involved taping his show in America during the week, and then flying to England every weekend for an appearance on *London Weekend Television*. Eventually, thanks to his ability to articulate complicated social, political, artistic, and intellectual trends, David Frost became known as "the Charlie Rose of his day."

Merv was usually furious when the press compared him unfavorably to Frost, whose shows were critiqued as "having more depth, with more intelligent conversation." In time Frost would interview every living U.S. president, as well as every living British Prime Minister, with Margaret Thatcher scoring the highest ratings.

As a counter-punch to Frost's string of VIPs, Merv brought on a controversial and deeply eccentric African American who had run for president, but not been elected. Dick Gregory had run for the nation's highest office in 1968 as a write-in candidate for the Freedom of Peace Party.

One amusing tale that Gregory related on Merv's show involved a publicity stunt his campaign had run, printing, as a satire on American presuppositions about power and wealth, U.S. $1 bills with Gregory's image on them. Some of these counterfeit bills were circulated within the money supply and used as currency in cash transactions. The Federal government moved in for punitive action, but Gregory wasn't charged. On the air, he joked with Merv that the bills "won't ever be accepted as legitimate cash because everyone knows a black man's image will never make it onto a U.S. dollar."

In later years, Gregory, like Harry Belafonte, became too provocative and too Left Wing for Merv, or at least for appearances on his show. The final straw, at least for Merv, came when Gregory angrily and publicly denounced the United States, referring to it as "the most dishonest, ungodly, unspiritual nation that ever existed in the history of the planet. As we talk now, America represents five percent of the world's population and consumes ninety-six percent of the world's hard drugs."

In reaction to the provocative nature of some of his guests, Merv received frequent memos, many of them addressed to "Mervin Griffith," from corporate executives within CBS.

The suits would, for example, object to Zsa Zsa Gabor's plunging *décolletage* and, predictably, her off-color chatter and gossip. Both on and off the air, she spared no one, especially former husbands such as George Sanders and Conrad Hilton. One memo from a CBS executive to Merv read, "The bitch is out of control. Expect a lawsuit filed for libel."

"Merv's polar opposite"
David Frost

Merv received constant objections to guests who attacked the Vietnam War. Jane Fonda ("Hanoi Jane," as her enemies called her), proved especially annoying to the suits.

CBS had almost had it with Merv in March of 1970 when he booked the prominent antiwar activist Abbie Hoffman, co-founder of the Youth International Party ("Yippies"), onto his show. Abbie had been arrested and tried for conspiracy and inciting a riot as a result of his role in the violent confrontations with the police during the 1968 Democratic National Convention in Chicago. Along with Jerry Rubin and Tom Hayden, Hoffman, during his prosecution, was widely referred to by the press as a dangerous subversive--a member of "The Chicago Seven."

Hoffman appeared on Merv's show wearing a red, white, and blue shirt whose pattern evoked the American flag. The censors at CBS interpreted this as objectionable, and blurred Hoffman's image electronically so that his voice emanated from "a jumble of lines." When Merv saw this, he was furious and complained loudly to CBS, to no avail.

"The way it appeared on screen, it looked like I was talking to an empty chair," Merv said.

CBS's legal department declared that broadcasting the image of Hoffman wearing an American flag might be illegal in some states. Ironically, that very night, TV commercials touting the Ford Motor Company starred "The King of the Cowboys," arch-conservative Roy Rogers, and his wife, "The Queen of the Cowgirls," Dale Evans. Both of them were nattily dressed in more or less the same shirt Hoffman wore onto Merv's show.

CBS shot off harshly worded protests to Merv, denouncing his habit of bringing on guests who attacked the Vietnam War. "In the past six weeks, thirty-four anti-war statements have been made on your show and only one pro-war statement by John Wayne," one memo read.

Merv fired back. "Find me someone as famous as Mr. Wayne to speak out in favor of the war, and we'll book him."

***

Censored Red, White, and Blue:
Abbie Hoffman

Although Merv's selection of guests in the late 60s and early 70s sometimes infuriated CBS, it appealed to many critics. Merv's "aw-shucks" style was effective at both catalyzing and controlling controversy in a sometimes frantic effect to woo viewers away from Carson. In the words of one critic, "Griffin brought on more would-be makers of controversy than all the David Susskinds combined. Merv's parade of politically oriented comedians such as Dick Gregory was the most controversial in show business."

Merv also invited classic, relatively uncontroversial, comedians as well, including Bob Hope and Jack Benny. Benny was a great success when he first appeared on Merv's show, telling hilarious anecdotes about his early days making movies. After the show, Merv visited his dressing room to congratulate him. "Mr. Benny, forgive me, but I've always wanted to pop the big question to you."

"A marriage proposal," Benny said. "I'm already taken."

"No, something else," Merv hesitated. "Are you gay?"

"Takes one to know one," Benny said without missing a beat. "And shut the door on your way out, sweetie."

Peter Barsocchini functioned as the producer of *The Merv Griffin Show* between 1980 and 1986, during which he won two Emmys. He was also the co-author of Merv's first autobiography, *Merv*, published by Simon and Schuster in 1980. In 2006, he once again attracted attention for his role as screenwriter of *High School Musical,* an Emmy Award-winning television film that inspired at least four franchised spinoffs. Originally released in January of 2006, it became one of the most successful movies that the Disney Channel Original Movie organization ever produced.

When Merv interviewed such guests as Sophia Loren, Henry Fonda, Bette Davis, or James Stewart, "the energized curiosity we all saw on the screen was real," claimed Barsocchini. "He usually did not socialize in advance with guests who appeared on his show, because he felt it would dampen the freshness of his interviews. I think there was always part of Merv who saw himself as the kid on the other side of the fence, watching the rich and famous, wondering about them."

Like Merv's autobiography itself, Barsocchini's statement is only half true. Merv was extremely intimate with many of his guests prior to their arrival on his show. A good example is Rosemary Clooney. In some instances, as in the case of both Marlon Brando and Montgomery Clift, he'd even had sex with them.

A few of his TV guests appeared on competing talk shows on the same night, as in the case of Senator Hubert Humphrey, who landed on *The David Frost Show* and then had to be hustled into a limousine to face Merv's cameraman. Jerry Lewis set the all-time record, appearing on the Carson show, the Cavett show, and Merv's line-up—all on the same night. "The double crosser didn't tell me what he was up to," Merv said. "So if you tuned in that night you got Jerry Lewis, Jerry Lewis, and Jerry Lewis. How unappetizing! A little of Jerry goes a long way."

All this stress led to Merv undergoing a physical change right in front of the TV cameras. "I grew fat and then fatter and then more fat," he said. As

1969 segued into 1970, he actually gained thirty-five pounds, a development that became obvious to many of his viewers and fans. Simultaneously, he was smoking three packages of cigarettes a day. "A great way to give yourself cancer," he later said.

He smoked so much on the air that some viewers complained that he was obscuring the faces of his guests. "I'd rather look at Hedy Lamarr—at least what's left of her—than see Griffin go up in a cloud of smoke," claimed one viewer from New Jersey.

***

Although TV talk shows exploring a specific, pre-defined theme are relatively commonplace today, thanks partly to their later evolution by Oprah Winfrey, Merv pioneered a style of theme show wherein several guests discuss and debate the same (usually controversial) issue on a single show. He introduced programs devoted to once-unmentionable issues such as incest and child molestation. And at one point he brought on Christine Jorgensen, the most famous transsexual in America, who'd migrated to Copenhagen as George, a former G.I., and had returned as an elegant, articulate, and well-spoken lady.

Merv later seemed jealous of the success of Oprah Winfrey. "The bitch has never acknowledged her debt to me."

Johnny Carson sometimes made fun of Merv's provocative shows. "Catch Merv on the tube tomorrow," Carson said mockingly. "He's bringing on five women who left the nunnery and are now running a brothel in Las Vegas." Despite that, during the closing years of the 1960s, Merv captured the ferment of the revolutionary era that changed American life for all time.

He was never awed by celebrities, regardless of their fame and stature. He recalled that in the course of his career, he was intimidated by only one guest—"and that was Miss Rose Kennedy."

One observer noted Merv's "lean-in close-talker style of interviewing. You were sure that at any moment he was going to end up in the lap of Jane Fonda or Roger Vadim." Before bringing that notorious couple onto the show, Merv had spent time at their farmhouse outside Paris, presumably familiarizing himself with issues he'd raise (or not raise) on camera later.

Merv's folksy style was remarkably different from that of the more aloof and sometimes chillier Johnny Carson. With his guests, Carson was a sardonic outside observer with a rapier wit. In distinct contrast, Merv appeared like a well-established friend at a gabfest, a style which translated into genuinely intimate interviews with such old acquaintances as Grace Kelly or Ronald and Nancy Reagan.

Merv's talk show career will be forever compared to that of Carson, "the King of Late Night Talk" between 1962 and the late 1980s. Ironically, Merv began his first daytime talk show on NBC the same day as Carson began his reign on NBC's *The Tonight Show*.

The two men were very different. Nebraska-born Carson had emerged from the Hollywood of the mid-1950s. For his inspiration, Merv looked elsewhere, especially to such liberal and edgy TV journals as David Susskind's *Open End* and Mike Wallace's *Night Beat*.

For his celebrity line-up, Merv didn't just stick to movie stars, singers, and comedians. Among many others, he brought on such "high brow" guests as cellist Pablo Casals and Will and Ariel Durant, the brilliant and provocative Pulitzer Prize-winning historians.

Critic John Colapinto in *Rolling Stone* best summed up Merv's appeal as a schmoozy talk-show host. "His talk show, with its unabashed celebrity worship and cozy *intime* atmosphere, offered the illusion of entering a living-room salon where a slightly risqué cocktail party was in progress. As a host, Merv used a cunning combination of obsequious fawning and probing interrogation to elicit disclosures more revealing than the stars would offer anywhere else."

When Merv heard that Carson had had a falling out with his younger brother, Dick Carson, and that Dick had quit after six years of directing *The Tonight Show*, Merv hired him. "That will show Johnny," Merv claimed.

Dick remained with the Griffin organization for nearly three decades, becoming director of *The Merv Griffin Show,* before eventually retiring in 1999. "My brother's kind of famous for standing off," Dick later said. "But Merv made working fun. Johnny was not like Merv, who appears very comfortable in any situation."

***

In a call from his old friend, Harry Belafonte, Merv was told that Martin Luther King Jr. might agree to an interview. "But I thought his Excellency didn't do talk shows," Merv said.

"I think I can persuade him, especially if you'll let me introduce him," Harry said.

Merv agreed, pushing hard to finalize the arrangements. At this point in his career, Merv had drifted more and more toward the Republican Party, mainly because of the growing influence of his friend, Ronald Reagan. Merv had actually taken objection to some of Dr. King's previous remarks, although he personally opposed the war in Vietnam.

The interview was widely publicized in advance, and millions tuned in.

But despite the advance ballyhoo, Merv's "Dr. King" show bombed.

On camera, Dr. King repeated his already-familiar opposition to the Vietnam War, claiming that the U.S. was in Southeast Asia with the intention of "occupying it as an American colony. The Vietnam War wastes money that should be spent on the War on Poverty...A nation that continues year after year to spend more money on military defense than on programs of social uplift is approaching spiritual death."

Merv later revealed that in advance of Dr. King's arrival, his staff had prepared some explosive questions to ask Dr. King on-camera. J. Edgar Hoover, director of the FBI, had submitted incriminating and embarrassing evidence about Dr. King's womanizing. "On the one hand," Merv told his confidants, "King holds himself up as a great moral leader, but in hotel rooms around the country he's acting like a Tom Cat in an alley after dark."

The day before Dr. King's appearance, an array of provocative information about Dr. King had already been splashed across magazine and other nationwide media. *Life's* editors had denounced Dr. King's anti-U.S. tirades as "demagogic slander that sounded like a script for Radio Hanoi." *The Washington Post* had also condemned King, charging that the leader had "diminished his usefulness to his cause, his country, his people." The newspaper was responding to King's outrageous claim that the United States had "killed a million Vietnamese, mostly children."

But fearing viewer backlash, and in advance of the interview, Merv had already decided not to bring up anything that was potentially embarrassing to Dr. King. During his interview, Merv listened politely to Dr. King as he condemned America's war policy.

Aggressively, and in a style that polarized the audience and transformed the interview into a complete disaster, Harry Belafonte, who had configured himself as part of the "package" associated with having Dr. King on-air in the first place, virtually took over the show, lavishing praise on Dr. King—and then a long list of additional tributes. Merv's audience began to drift off, many switching to other channels.

Dr. M. L. King, Jr.
Merv's critics were screaming

Backstage, when it was over, Merv chatted in a very friendly manner with Dr. King, who congratulated him for his effective use of *The Merv Griffin Show* as a platform for up-and-coming black entertainers. He'd been particularly amused by the appearances of Dick Gregory and Richard Pryor—"and the singers too," he

419

interjected.

"Speaking of singing," Merv said impishly, "my staff came up with the nugget that you'd sung as part of a church choir at the 1939 Atlanta premiere of *Gone With the Wind*. As you know, many African-Americans don't like the way your people were depicted in that movie. Did you, in fact, sing at the premiere?"

"There are things in any man's life that are best forgotten." Dr. King said before turning and heading out of the studio.

Then Harry embraced Merv as part of his goodbye. "I know Dr. King is a bit to the left of some of your own political views, but remember—dissent is central to any democracy."

After their departure, Merv turned to some of his key staff members. "The show got so boring that at one point I was tempted to ask Belafonte to sing 'Yellow Bird.'"

***

From the days of his early childhood, Merv had been raised on John Wayne movies. As such, he was delighted when "The Duke" agreed to be interviewed. Aired in January of 1971, the show was called "Duke and I— Merv Visits John Wayne."

As part of the experience, Merv and his crew spent a Thanksgiving weekend at the cowboy star's 22,000-acre ranch near Phoenix.

Wayne and Merv got drunk together the first night, and Merv later revealed how shocked he was at The Duke's candor. He admitted that "women scare the hell out of me," yet during the course of his long career, he'd already seduced such screen goddesses as Clara Bow, Joan Crawford, Carmen Miranda, and Claire Trevor.

"Marlene Dietrich was the best lay I ever had," Wayne claimed. He'd co-starred with her and Randolph Scott in *Pittsburgh* in 1942. "Things didn't work out too well with Joan Crawford, though."

"Things didn't work out between Crawford and me either," Merv confessed.

Wayne had made *Reunion in France* with Joan in 1942, the same year he'd appeared with Dietrich. Crawford later told her gay pal, William Haines, "Get Duke out of the saddle and you've got nothing."

Wayne kept Merv amused until the rooster crowed, relating stories of his career. He spoke of the time he'd starred with the British bisexual actor, Laurence Harvey, in the 1960 *The Alamo*.

"Please, Duke," Wayne quoted Harvey as saying to him. "Tonight. Just one time. I'll be the queen, if you'll be the king." Wayne claimed he turned down "my chance to be a king with a queen."

Because of his strong, perhaps obsessive, political views, Wayne was asked if he'd ever consider running for political office. "I've already been asked, and I turned it down. George Wallace wanted me to run as his Veep on his American Independent Party. 'No way,' I told Wallace, although I do agree with a lot of his positions."

Before dawn, Wayne shocked Merv by confessing, "Ever since I arrived in Hollywood, women have been attracted to me like flies on a steak dinner left in the sun. Men, too. You know, don't you, that John Ford is gay? But there's a downside to all this. When I take them to bed, they expect me to be hung like King Kong. I'm afraid I've disappointed quite a few of them. Paulette Goddard actually complained about my pecker. I guess that thanks to her getting regularly fucked by Charlie Chaplin, I couldn't satisfy her. Nowadays, when I can still get it up, I warn the gals, "If you want the Montana Mule, call Gary Cooper. In bed, I'm more pony than horse."

***

In the 1970s, as pornography became more prevalent and more or less legal, Merv developed an interest in the medium, especially after Hadley brought him a copy of *Boys in the Sand*, released in 1971. A landmark in gay pornography, and viewed today as a "classic," the film was directed and written by a former Broadway choreographer, Wakefield Poole. It starred "Casey Donovan," a well-built, well-educated actor and model. Born in 1943 in East Bloomfield, New York, he'd had an employment history which included a stint as a teacher in a private school on Central Park West in New York City, experience as a romantic lead in several summer stock productions, and moonlight jobs as a male hustler. His birth name was John Calvin ("Cal") Culver.

Merv was so enchanted with the film that he insisted that Hadley run it three times. According to Hadley, Merv thought Cal Culver was "Guy Madison, Tab Hunter, and Troy Donahue—all rolled into one bankable commodity."

Hadley claimed that Merv "let out a gasp of joy" when the image of a naked Cal first appeared. The clip of Cal emerging from the ocean like Venus, or rather Apollo, rising from the sea, is today interpreted as an iconic moment in gay porn.

The scene on shore that immediately followed became very graphic, with a dark, bearded Peter Fisk, who was Poole's real-life lover, performing oral sex on Cal. Later Cal penetrates Fisk on screen.

The most controversial segment of the film, called "Inside," involved

421

interracial sex, which was very daring at the time. An African-American telephone repairman was played by Tommy Moore. Most of this segment involved Cal's fantasies about sexual encounters with the studly "pole man," including scenes where Cal sniffs poppers and penetrates himself with a mammoth black dildo.

The three segments that make up the film were each shot at Cherry Grove on Fire Island, a gay beach resort off the southern coast of New York's Long Island, in just three successive weekends. Amazingly, its budget was only eight thousand dollars.

Boys in the Sand became the first gay porn movie to be both reviewed and advertised in *The New York Times*. *Variety* carried a full-page ad on it. Reviews, both appreciative and scathing, appeared in newspapers and magazines across the nation. *Variety* claimed, "there are no more closets," and *The Advocate* made the boast that, "Everyone will fall in love with this philandering fellator."

Merv, along with virtually everybody else, was astonished at the success of this film. *Boys in the Sand*—the title inspired by the Matt Crowley play (and later film) *The Boys in the Band*—was the first gay movie to achieve mainstream crossover success. It preceded Linda Lovelace's *Deep Throat* by almost a year.

Almost overnight, "Casey Donovan" became an underground celebrity. Wherever he went in Los Angeles, San Francisco, or New York, he was immediately recognized, and in many cases, propositioned. Although he'd pursued a legitimate career as a screen God, his hopes for that were dashed with the release of this controversial film. Instead of offers for legitimate stage and film roles, he was hired for ever-increasing roles in porn flicks. Also, an intense and lucrative demand had emerged for his services as a paid male escort.

Merv wanted to host a show that focused on the emergence of gay porn as a legitimate art expression whose freedom had recently been approved by the courts. His vision involved interviews with both Cal and his director, Wakefield Poole. He wasn't sure about what other guests to invite, but considered the avant-garde gay filmmakers, Kenneth Anger and Andy Warhol.

Merv asked his staff to provide

Merv's plaything, and
the world's most famous gay porn star
Cal Culver, aka Casey Donovan

background material on Wakefield Poole. As for Cal, Merv asked Hadley to privately arrange "an audition."

Poole's name was already known to Merv. The director had been a well-known Broadway choreographer. Both Poole and Merv had shared the sexual favors of Rock Hudson, and the choreographer had previously collaborated onstage with such big names as Hal Prince, Stephen Sondheim, Jane Powell, and Debbie Reynolds. Poole even knew the campy aspects of both the good and bad witches from *The Wizard of Oz* thanks to his friendships with Billie Burke and Margaret Hamilton.

Poole's banishment from the Great White Way came when he sued Richard Rodgers in court—and won—for the show, *Do I Hear a Waltz?* The waltz in the show had been staged and choreographed by Poole, who had received no credit and no royalties. Even though he won the case, he found himself suddenly barred from future involvements on Broadway because he'd dared to sue a theatrical icon like Rodgers.

Merv's staff retrieved evidence that Poole had wanted to make a serious statement with *Boys in the Sand*, a somewhat highbrow but highly commercial onscreen fusion of art and hardcore sex. As he later recorded in his autobiography, *Dirty Poole*, "I wanted to present high profile homosexuality without the guilt." Merv learned that prior to filming, Poole had issued a command to his actors and collaborators on Fire Island—"No top, no bottom, just two men discovering each other."

Hadley contacted Cal and arranged a private meeting with Merv. "Merv was eagerly anticipating Cal's arrival," Hadley said. He expected some dumb blond with a big dick and a small brain.

"When Cal came into the apartment," Hadley said, "he had the big dick—we'd already seen that on the screen—but he was well educated, a cultured young gentleman."

"He's an elegant, buttoned-down male courtesan," Merv later told Hadley.

This blond California Golden Boy, with a healthy appetite for the pleasures of the flesh, sometimes described himself as "Robert Redford's younger brother."

During Cal's conversations with Merv about the theater, he seemed to

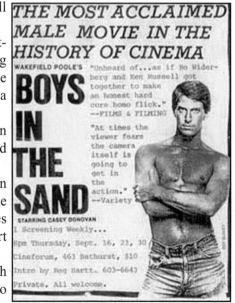

THE MOST ACCLAIMED MALE MOVIE IN THE HISTORY OF CINEMA

WAKEFIELD POOLE'S

"Unheard of...as if No Widerberg and Ken Russell got together to make an honest hard core homo flick."
—FILMS & FILMING

"At times the viewer fears the camera itself is going to get in the action."
—Variety

BOYS IN THE SAND

STARRING CASEY DONOVAN...

1 Screening Weekly...

8pm Thursday, Sept. 16, 21, 30

Cinaforum, 463 Bathurst, $10

Intro by Reg Hartt. 603-6643

Private. All welcome.

423

have inside knowledge about show business personalities. "Merv was fascinated, imagining that Cal was somebody you could invite to the Queen's Garden Party," Hadley said. "He was very preppy, wearing a dark blue suit, white shirt, and red tie. He was the old Arrow Shirt man of yesteryear come back to life. He was gracious and charming, not some hardened hustler. And he was a real blond—no bleach. Actually his hair was golden like wheat, and he had blue eyes that would put Paul Newman to shame. His sex appeal was natural, not some girly man on the screen pretending to be macho. The press had described him as the boy next door. Any gay man should have been so lucky to live next door to Cal Culver, especially if that man had a strong pair of binoculars."

Hadley said that when he saw that the chemistry between Merv and Cal was bubbling, he excused himself and went around the corner to the local gay bar. Later Cal claimed, "I liberated Merv sexually that night. He was one uptight dude until I had raunchy sex with him. When it came to sex, Merv was rather vanilla. I taught him to put some gooey chocolate fudge over that white vanilla sundae."

When Johnny Carson learned that Merv intended to host a TV show devoted to gay porn, he said, "Why not? Griffin's already interviewed transsexual witches from Transylvania and boy-lovers wanting to revive the ancient Greek tradition of sodomy." Carson obviously was speaking tongue in cheek.

Perhaps because of Carson's mockery, or perhaps for personal reasons, Merv decided not to forge ahead with the show. His rival, David Susskind, turned out to be more receptive to the idea of doing a TV talk show devoted to gay porn.

Merv had to tell a disappointed Cal that he had abandoned the idea of such a show. "That does not, however, have to mean the end of our friendship."

Cal later claimed that Merv clearly suggested that it would be "extremely lucrative" if Cal continued their relationship, especially the sexual aspects of it.

"Sign me up," Cal told him.

***

When Merv tired of Cal after eighteen months, he shipped him off to the beds of both Liberace and Rock Hudson. Through various connections established by these stars and others, Cal , whenever he wasn't shooting porn, eventually obtained full employment as a gay male escort. In a claim he made in Key West, where he functioned briefly as the unsuccessful manager of an unsuccessful gay guesthouse, The Casa Donovan, he said, "For several years

424

I was America's number one star fucker, and I owe it all to Merv Griffin for getting me launched."

Ever the sexual opportunist, Cal detected an interest on Merv's part in young emerging porn stars. He saw a chance to make money by arranging discreet introductions to male stars who intrigued Merv after Cal showed him porno films, which often starred Cal interacting with a prospective lover for Merv.

As the months went by, Cal more or less evolved into Merv's pimp, linking him up to "big names" in the porn business. Collectively, Cal and his associates managed to replace the array of otherwise unknown models, out-of-work actors, and surfers that Hadley might have otherwise proposed as sexual diversions for Merv.

***

"Our old gang was breaking up," Paul Schone lamented. "Once in San Mateo Bill Robbins, Johnny Riley, and Hadley Morrell had each promised Merv that they'd be his friends for life."

But it didn't work out that way. Johnny was the first of the quintet to move on, establishing himself as a kept boy in a new relationship.

Merv, too, had moved on to other friendships, other relationships, and other business affairs, finding that he had less and less time for his old friends of yesteryear.

Sometime during the 70s, Merv parted company with both Paul and Bill. "There was no final goodbye, and no little bonus for the way we'd served him so well over the years," Paul lamented.

Both Paul and Bill called Merv repeatedly, leaving messages, but the calls were never returned. "I don't think he was actually angry with us," said Bill. "I think he just outgrew us. We were going nowhere in life, and Merv was shooting to the top."

More than Johnny, Paul, and Bill, Hadley had been the most intimately involved with Merv. "But as time went by, I too was replaced in Merv's life," Hadley said. "He'd developed other friendships by then, and Cal Culver seemed to be supplying him with tricks, and eventually, I simply wasn't needed."

Consequently, when Hadley's ailing mother, who had moved to Texas, became seriously ill, Hadley and Merv more or less separated, and remained apart for years. Then, after his mother died, Hadley came briefly back into Merv's life in the late 1980s or early 90s. But Hadley grew tired of being a friend that Merv kept hidden in the closet. Perhaps he also grew tired of the servant role as well. Since he'd been bequeathed some money from his mother's estate, Hadley knew he could retire in reasonable comfort if he watched

425

his spending. According to some reports, Merv gave him $50,000 in cash. Presumably, Hadley returned to West Texas to live out his days in his mother's house and was never heard from again.

***

As a means of making money, and perhaps in a spirit motivated partly by jealousy and revenge, Paul and Bill began drafting page after page of sometimes negative memoirs about their experiences with Merv. It's because these notes and memoirs were circulated in the 1970s to publishers and literary agents (including the Jay Garon-Brooke & Associates Agency), whose president and namesake, Jay Garon, referred to them as "explosive") that we know some of the details of Merv's early life.

Jay Garon had a reputation as a ruthless and to some degree sleazy marketer of the often embarrassing memoirs of the rich and terribly famous, as proven with his successful launch of Hedy Lamarr's *Ecstasy and Me,* as well as an intensely embarrassing expose of Bette Davis by her estranged daugher.

Garon's enthusiasm for the Bill Robbins/Paul Schone memoirs dampened however, after months of shopping it around privately and unofficially to editors he knew personally at, among others, Doubleday, Random House, Simon & Schuster, and a paperback publishing house, Manor Books.

In every case, the Robbins/Schone book proposal was rejected, editors fearing with ample justification that Merv would sue for libel if such a book were ever published.

Presumably, Paul and Bill eventually left New York, their fate unknown. And having previously fallen out with Johnny, they lost track of him too. Then, after many a year, Johnny too disappeared from the radar screen.

Predictably, at one point, both Johnny and Hadley also floated and somewhat half-heartedly marketed their own rough drafts of memoirs, neither of which was as negative or as scandalous as that penned earlier by Paul and Bill. But whereas Paul and Bill felt deeply betrayed by Merv, Johnny and Hadley harbored feelings that were more benign. And when it had become obvious that the vitality of the relationship with Merv had faded, Johnny and Hadley departed without protest to pursue other lives.

The book proposal submitted by these former boyhood friends of Merv's after he'd dropped them amounted to an Outing of Merv as a homosexual. News of Merv's gender preference quickly spread along the cocktail circuit in New York City.

The mass media, large-scale press Outing of Merv would be delayed until 1991, when two other men, with different agendas, exposed Merv to the public as a homosexual by initiating legal action against him.

426

***

Merv appreciated any chance he could get to interview a celebrity on location, outside a studio, and he was delighted when Richard Burton agreed to let him tape an interview in Oroville, California. It was there that the Welsh actor with the great Shakespearean voice was filming *The Klansman* (1972).

Richard had arrived in town two weeks before Elizabeth Taylor, who had promised to join him on location after she'd satisfied some prior commitment. In the meantime, Richard, as Merv soon learned, was sleeping with a beautiful local girl. Merv was introduced to her at the time, but later couldn't recall her name.

The actor bragged to Merv, "If there's a dame in this town I can't screw, my name's not Richard Burton."

To Merv's surprise, Richard was completely candid in boasting about his sexual conquests. That tendency had been noted earlier by the cast of *Cleopatra* (1963) when Richard strode onto the set and announced to Rex Harrison and others: "I finally fucked E. Taylor in the back seat of my Cadillac last night."

Richard tried to explain his womanizing to Merv. "I fucked them all—Zsa Zsa Gabor, Ava Gardner, Sophia Loren, Jean Simmons, Lana Turner, even a toothless old maid in Jamaica. But Elizabeth is my only love. She's more a mistress than a wife. She's pornography, but only the dreamy version through a veil. She's Sunday's child and can even tolerate my drunkenness. Come to think of it, she's a drunk herself. When I'm away from her, there's a tight grip in my stomach, worse than any belly ache, so I lose myself in other women."

Merv joined Richard for a night on the town in Oroville. They hit one bar which remained open for them until six o'clock in the morning. Merv absorbed Richard's tall tales like a sponge. Perhaps out of deference to Merv's own homosexuality, which must have been known to him, Richard admitted that, "I was once a homosexual but it didn't take. Nevertheless, during that period I got to fuck Laurence Olivier, Noel Coward, your buddy Roddy McDowall, Michael Wilding, Emyln Williams. I even let John Gielgud give me a blow-job. Victor Mature and I did a sixty-nine when we filmed *The Robe*. He wanted to fuck me, but I demurely said no. The guy doesn't have a prick. It's more like a club. But except for a few dalliances here and there, I think of myself as straight. I guess that's true. No, it isn't. All actors are homosexuals. Some of them mask that with drink. I'll tell you a secret I've told no one. Rex Harrison and I, as you know, played two gay lovers in *Staircase* (1969). To make our roles more believable, we actually went to bed together. What I've done for the sake of my art."

427

"That surprises me," Merv said. "Sexy Rexy. Such a ladies' man."

"Those are the most suspicious types," Richard said. "Tyrone Power. Errol Flynn. Robert Taylor. Howard Hughes. Marlon Brando. The beat goes on. I'll tell you one final story, but with the understanding that I want to leave open the possibility that I might be joking. One night in Rome, when I was trying to break up Elizabeth's marriage to Eddie Fisher, I raped him just to humiliate him. Noel Coward was right. He has a great ass."

"Surely not!" Merv said.

"You'll never know," Richard said. With that parting line, he lifted himself up from his bar stool, reached for his young woman, and headed out to greet the California dawn.

***

Merv especially enjoyed interviewing his octogenarian friend, journalist and Hollywood columnist Adela Rogers St. Johns, as a vehicle for the deflation of the sometimes bloated egos of his other guests.

When Truman Capote had come on, basking in the glory of his non-fiction novel, *In Cold Blood* (1966), Adela hadn't read it and didn't mind telling Truman why not. "Why should I read a book about a page eighteen murder?" she asked the astonished author.

Years later, Merv brought Adela on once again to deflate another author's ego. He booked her on a show with Erica Jong, who'd written the feminist lifestyle guide *Fear of Flying* (1973). The book became the literary sensation of the nation. Adela wasn't impressed, claiming on the air that it was "too dull to read."

***

Like everything else in America at the time, viewer reaction to *The Merv Griffin Show* was mixed. One member of the audience wrote, "Merv is a bit of a bore. Arthur Treacher on the other hand is amusing." Yet another disappointed fan said that the only good thing about the program was Jack Sheldon on the trumpet and Mort Lindsey's Orchestra. "I often watched the show because with clueless Merv in

Confessions of a satyrist:
Richard Burton discusses rape.

428

charge, a train wreck was inevitable, especially when Merv got serious. And what was it about Merv and the Stephen Bishop song, 'On and On'? He sang that thing about three times a week. The sets were cheap. Merv couldn't carry a tune and got fatter by the year."

One viewer claimed that Merv's "interviewing skills were non-existent. The guest line-up was terrible. You know it's bad when the most entertaining thing about the program is Miss Miller. How on earth did Merv get so rich and successful? He's incompetent!"

Most of the fans, however, approved of Merv, citing his "wonderful smooth style—one cool dude." And most of these viewers genuinely liked his lineup of regular guests, who included Zsa Zsa Gabor and Moms Mabley. Actor Pat O'Brien could be counted on to appear every St. Patty's Day, spinning wonderful yarns. Demond Wilson from *Sanford and Son* came on, singing Kiki Dee's "I Got the Music in Me." Fans wrote in, claiming, "he was absolutely horrible . . . couldn't sing a note!"

***

In 1973, Spiro Agnew was forced to resign as Vice President of the United States. Merv invited him on his show and was surprised that the disgraced politician accepted. He admitted that he and Nixon hadn't spoken to each other since he'd left office. "He called several times, but I've refused to take his phone calls," Agnew claimed.

Polls early in 1973 had shown Agnew as the front leader for the 1976 presidential nomination, with California governor Ronald Reagan a distant second.

Out of office, Agnew became more controversial than ever. He dared to suggest, as TV cameras were rolling, that Nixon and Alexander Haig would have assassinated him if he had refused to resign the Vice Presidency. He claimed that Haig told him "to go quietly . . . or else."

The former Veep also became embroiled in controversy because of his anti-Zionist statements, calling for the United States to withdraw its support for Israel because of its bad treatment of Christians.

Merv complimented Agnew on his alliterative epithets such as "pusillanimous pussyfoots," "hopeless hysterical hypochondriacs of history," and "nattering nabobs of negativism." Agnew dismissed such praise, claiming these epithets were the creation of White House speech writers William Safire and Pat Buchanan.

On the show, Agnew discussed his new friendship with Frank Sinatra, who had been a lifelong Democrat until he felt rejected by Robert Kennedy. Agnew said that Sinatra had helped him pay back the $160,000 in back taxes he owed the government.

Merv later revealed that, backstage and after the show, Agnew tried to lure him into some dubious business associations. "A political cartoonist once lampooned Nixon with a caricature under which was written, 'Would you buy a used car from this man?' The same question could be asked of Agnew. I just didn't trust him. Even though he promised me I could make millions in some scheme in the Middle East, I turned him down."

***

One of Merv's most controversial guests was writer Gore Vidal, who could always be counted upon to shock and polarize an audience. Merv focused a lot of attention on Gore's kinship with Jacqueline Kennedy. His mother Nina had married Jackie's stepfather, Hugh Auchincloss. Even though acquainted with, and to some degree, related to, the Kennedys, Gore sometimes demonstrated a scathing contempt for the President. "Jack wanted the presidency, and his father bought it for him," Gore charged.

Merv later told friends that he'd never read a book by Gore Vidal except for the mysteries he'd written under the pseudonym of Edgar Box.

Gore was always consistently negative about how his plays had been adapted by Hollywood into movies, objecting strenuously to the casting of Jerry Lewis as the lead in the movie version of Gore's *Visitor to a Small Planet* (1960).

When Merv asked Gore why he was running for governor of California against the incumbent governor, Jerry Brown, Gore said that "the chance to compete against a Zen Space Cadet is too good to pass up."

The author could always deliver a shocker, as when he told stories about working on the screenplay of *Ben-Hur* in 1959, the picture directed by William Wyler. "To explain the animosity between Ben-Hur and Messala, I inserted a gay subtext, suggesting that the two had been lovers," Gore said. "Stephen Boyd played it gay but Charlton Heston didn't have a clue that he was playing a homosexual love scene."

A murmur would go up in the audience whenever Gore expounded on his sexual theories. "The human race is divided into male and female. Many human beings enjoy sexual relations with their own sex; many don't; many respond to both. That plurality is a fact of our nature and not worth fretting about. Therefore, there are no homosexual people, only homosexual acts."

Bagman and disgraced VP
Spiro Agnew

***

Although Gypsy Rose Lee had evolved into the most famous stripper in America, she never completely undressed, never fully exposing her breasts and always retaining a wisp of a G-string as a means of allowing viewers' imaginations a bit of free rein. Her roster of emotional involvements was impressive: When the burlesque mystery novel she'd written, *The G-String Murders*, was made into the film *Lady of Burlesque* (1943), she'd had an affair with Barbara Stanwyck. And between two of her three marriages, she'd enjoyed an affair with the director, Otto Preminger. A son was born to them, Eric Lee Preminger.

Years after the huge success of the film, *Gypsy* (1962) which had starred Natalie Wood in the title role, Merv was intrigued by the stripper and eager to interview her on his show.

When the aging burlesque queen appeared on Merv's stage, Mort Lindsey, the orchestra leader, broke into a strip number. As she'd done countless times in the past, Gypsy immediately—and to some degree, automatically—launched into her familiar bump-and-grind routine, dropping her drawers during the finale, cupping her breasts and revealing herself clad only in a G-string.

Almost instantly, the network cut her off, hastily filling in with clips from a show that Merv had filmed with his childhood friend and possible molester, Bishop Fulton J. Sheen.

Later, despite the censorship disaster associated with her appearance on his show, Merv said, "Gypsy was a real-life Auntie Mame. Her humor rivaled that of Judy Garland and her spirit was indomitable. My God, when her son, Erik, grew up, she hired him as her dresser. Imagine that!"

***

During the early 70s, it seemed inevitable that Merv would cross paths with pop artist Andy Warhol. By that time, Merv had succeeded in getting hundreds of people to open up and talk to him as they were being televised. But even in private, he found that Andy was no great talker, and he was forced to agree with the artist's self-assessment: "I am a deeply superficial person," Andy rightly claimed.

The homosexual and endlessly campy arbiter of pop went on to tell Merv, "I'm also the most celebrated of the celebrated, and I know them all: Jackie, Mick Jagger, Truman Capote, Calvin Klein, John and Yoko, Elizabeth Taylor, Bob Dylan. My life is nothing but parties, galas, art openings, chic clubs. I

431

once jerked off Marlon Brando in an elevator going down. He wanted me to blow him but settled for masturbation."

In anticipation of the upcoming show, Merv bluntly asked Andy, "Can I drop vague hints about your lifestyle?"

Andy looked at Merv as if he were an alien just descended to Earth. "I'd prefer to remain a mystery," he said. "I never like to give my background. At any rate, I make it all up differently every time I'm asked. It's not just that it's part of my image not to tell everything—it's just that I forget what I said the day before—and then I have to make it up all over again."

After his interview, Andy invited Merv to Studio 54—at the time, the most celebrated disco in the world—where he was introduced to Troy Donahue, the pretty-boy heartthrob of the late 50s and early 60s. Troy had always been Merv's dream fantasy. Merv, like many others of Troy's fans, overlooked his lack of acting talent and reveled instead in his image as a male pin-up and pop icon.

Merv had heard enticing stories about Troy from Henry Willson, who already took credit for discovering a then-new actor on the circuit, Merle Johnson Jr. It had been Henry who had changed Merle's name to Troy Donahue. Originally, he'd thought of naming him Paris, after the lover of Helen of Troy, but then he concluded, "No celebrity can be named Paris. That's a city in France. Let's go with Troy and throw in the Donahue."

"Don't mix me up with Tab Hunter," Troy said to Merv that night at Studio 54. "He's the other blond, blue-eyed actor. I'm the straight one."

At that point Liza Minnelli danced by, stopping to evaluate Troy with her eagle eye, and then whispered in Merv's ear. "The boy's a real looker—go for it!"

When Merv met Troy, his career was fading. He wanted work and Andy had a film project in mind. Before auditioning Troy, Andy had tossed the idea to three other stars, including Mick Jagger, and each of them had rejected it.

Merv was astonished when he learned more about Andy's film proposal. For the entire length of the movie, Andy wanted the camera to focus only on Troy's facial expression as he received a blow-job from a sixteen-year-old Vietnamese boy, hailed at the time as the most talented fellatio artist in Greenwich Village.

At first Troy thought Andy was joking. "That's the picture you want me to star in?" an incredulous Troy asked. As the evening progressed, however, and Andy

Addictively exhibitionistic:
Gypsy Rose Lee

432

kept pitching the proposal, Troy came to realize that the filmmaker was serious. "You're out of your mind," Troy said. "There's no way in hell I would do that!" He rose from the sofa and headed for the door.

"Oh, fuck," Andy said. "I really wanted Troy but I'm sure Joe Dallesandro will do it. I've always been fascinated by my superstar. I did my first painting of him. That was before Elizabeth Taylor and Marilyn Monroe."

"You've already shot *Blow Job*," Merv said. "You don't need to do it again." He was referring to a film which had starred DeVeren Bookwalter, who at the time was supposedly receiving oral sex from filmmaker Willard Maas, although the camera never tilts down to see the action.

That night at Studio 54 was not the last time Merv would see Troy. Within a few months, Merv received a call from Henry Willson. "Your dream has come true. Troy Donahue is coming to New York. He's completely broke and needs a place to stay for about a month until he can land a job. He also needs someone to pay his expenses."

"Troy Donahue," Merv said in astonishment. "Old and gray, pot-bellied and bald, that hunk can put his shoes under my bed any night he wants."

"Oh, and could you part with a thousand dollars a week in spending money?" Henry asked. "I mean, this star of yesterday is really broke."

"Tell Boy Troy he's got a deal," Merv said. "Send him on."

Merv's dream did not come true with Troy. It was more like a nightmare. When the actor arrived at Merv's apartment, he was deep into drug addiction and alcoholism. When they had sex together, Merv closed his eyes and tried to imagine what Troy used to look like in *A Summer Place* (1959).

Merv later told Hadley, "Troy has a hard time getting it up. And when he does manage to get it up, there ain't much there."

Troy's worst days were yet to come. In the 1980s, he was discovered sleeping in a cardboard box in Central Park.

***

National pinup and
ruined teen idol
Troy Donohue

The Merv Griffin Show on CBS was simply not working out. Merv had to do something to save the show and his own career. "I knew I had to come up with something, but I didn't know what. Then one afternoon an idea occurred to me. It was an impulse, but I acted on it at once. I decided to return to my roots."

Without bothering to go home to pack, Merv called his wife from the airport to tell her he was flying to California, address uncertain. He promised he'd

433

stay in touch.

Landing in Los Angeles, he rented a red convertible and drove to Malibu, where he talked to a real estate agent who rented him a house on the beach that was often leased to movie stars for off-the-record weekends, especially if those weekends were for gay old times.

On the fourth night, Liberace sent him what he called a "party favor."

The "prize" Liberace shipped over to Merv was John C. Holmes, a well-hung actor popularly known as both "Johnny Wadd" and "The King of Porn." Merv had already seen three of his movies.

Pop journalist John McAbee once wrote, "In the world of dicks, John Holmes was the D-Day, the 1969 NASA moon landing, the JFK assassination, and the invention of television all rolled up into one big, giant cock. His penis truly defined a dick generation that came, but hasn't gone yet."

Hadley later reported that Merv claimed that his weekend with the star was "the wildest of my life." As a favor to his usually faithful Hadley, Merv promised that, "You can have Johnny, too, but only after I've finished with him."

"Always sloppy seconds for me," Hadley protested.

After that weekend, Merv called Liberace, who was vacationing in Palm Springs. "Thanks, but no thanks," he said to his longtime friend.

"You didn't enjoy it?" Liberace asked. "I sure did. But then I can take a man's arm up my overworked ass. Where are you calling from?"

"I'm in the hospital about to get stitches!"

***

When his California binge was over, Merv flew back to New York to announce to CBS that he was moving his show's base of operations to Television City in Los Angeles, even though it meant abandoning the network's two-million dollar investment in restoring the Cort Theater. He was convinced he'd attract better and more interesting guests on the West Coast, where he wouldn't have to compete with so many other talking heads like Johnny Carson. "Nearly all guests wanted to go on Carson," Merv claimed. "But if they couldn't get a spot on Carson, Frost, or Cavett, they'd come to me."

"King of Porn"
John C. Holmes
(Johnny Wadd)

Merv's decision to move his show from New York to Los Angeles forced him to re-evaluate the role of

Arthur Treacher within the show's revised lineup. For months, CBS had been pressuring Merv to replace Arthur with a younger, better-looking sidekick. When Merv approached Arthur with the news, he was relieved to hear that he did not want to "move to a place where the earth shakes. Virginia and I want to remain in the East." He was referring to his wife, Virginia Taylor, whom he had married back in 1940.

Briefly, Merv supported the idea of naming Desi Arnaz Jr., the then-eighteen-year-old son of Lucille Ball and her estranged husband, Desi Arnaz, as a replacement. But eventually, the suits at CBS decided that Desi wasn't the right choice. Despite CBS's objections to Desi Jr., he did collaborate temporarily, co-hosting a few of Merv's shows.

From his home back on the East Coast, Arthur watched Desi Jr. in dismay, horrified at the show's new direction. Fortunately, he didn't need the income from Merv any more, as he'd signed to be the spokesman and figurehead for a fast-food chain (Arthur Treacher's Fish and Chips) which by then encompassed at least five hundred locations throughout the United States.

As Arthur aged, his loyalty and enthusiasm for Merv waned, and a barely controlled bitterness set in. In a final interview, he referred to Merv as "that wretched little man."

Merv's second choice as a replacement for Arthur Treacher had been Sonny and Cher. The proposal, like many that had preceded it, elicited strenuous objections from CBS, but this time Merv persisted, and eventually won.

Ironically, CBS was so impressed that eventually, they hired Sonny and Cher as hosts of their own variety show. "They became the hottest act on TV," Merv said. "My judgment prevailed once again over CBS."

Merv was disappointed when his longtime producer, Bob Shanks, announced that he preferred to remain in the East. As a result, Merv hired a new producing team, Ernest Chambers and Saul Ilson. Other than that, however, he managed to retain most of his key staff members, paying the expenses of their moves to Los Angeles and helping them find homes there.

One viewer summed up the aftereffects of Merv's westward migration to California. "When Merv was in New York he brought on people like Norman Mailer and Jimmy Breslin. I also remember a special show that was broadcast from the streets of Harlem when John Lindsay was mayor. 'Give a Damn' was the big slogan in the city. Burt Lancaster was there as a guest. But when Merv went Hollywood, boy did he go off the deep end. From Mailer and Breslin to Charo. Wow!"

In December of 1975, Bob Shanks called Merv from New York to tell him that Arthur had died of a heart attack. Merv later recalled, "It was the saddest day of my life. I cried and cried some more and then made a decision. No one could replace Arthur. I'll just go out there at the beginning of every show and introduce myself to the audience."

And so he did for the run of the show.

***

Merv's stint with CBS lasted for thirty tortuous months, and Merv's move to the West Coast, in clear opposition to the objections of the network suits, marked what Merv called "the beginning of the end."

Public reaction to Merv's move to Los Angeles evolved rapidly. Merv rented a house temporarily on North Bedford Drive in Beverly Hills. On his first morning there, some tourist buses stopped in front of the house. "My God," he said, "they've already found out where I live."

That afternoon, however, he discovered that he wasn't the main attraction. He'd rented the house where the boyfriend of Lana Turner, gangster Johnny Stompanato, had been stabbed to death. Cheryl Crane, Lana's daughter—a teenager at the time— was blamed for the stabbing, but Hollywood insiders such as Howard Hughes and Frank Sinatra knew that it was Lana herself who killed Stompanato, with Cheryl being blamed because she'd get off with a lighter sentence.

From his new base in "the murder house," Merv had more time to go swimming, boating, and to play tennis, as he'd done in his youth. He was still battling "the suits" at CBS whose roster of complaints had expanded to include the way Eva Gabor exposed so much of her bosom, and Merv's bringing the outspoken cast of *All in the Family* onto one of his shows. Right before that sitcom shot to number one, the executives at CBS informed Merv that it was about to be removed from the airwaves.

Merv's ratings continued to fall, and as a result, he lost stations. Behind the scenes, CBS plotted to replace his show with other contenders, one proposal which focused coverage, instead, on current arts-industry news. In a format evocative of *Broadway Open House*, it would have featured a theatrical program of breezy chitchat and musical numbers.

As his relationship with CBS deteriorated, Merv began secret negotiations with Metromedia for syndicated, nationwide broadcasting of *The Merv Griffin Show,* with less censorship and with less program-related interference from "the suits" upstairs. The president of the company told Merv, "You're welcome aboard at any time."

Meanhile, after months of private debates among management, CBS lowered the boom on Merv, firing him. By ending his contract in February of 1972, prior to its expiration, CBS was forced to pay him $250,000 in severance pay. That was in the dollars of the early 70s, which would be equivalent to about a million dollars today

436

CBS's management team was shocked to learn that Merv had already negotiated a deal with Metromedia, where *The Merv Griffin Show* would remain as a staple fixture for the next thirteen years. "I'd no sooner left CBS than I was popping up on TV screens everywhere, based on the syndication successes of Metromedia. I won that round with CBS."

His newly reconfigured show made its debut for Metromedia on March 13, 1972 at the old Hollywood Palace Theater. Because of its ongoing direction by Dick Carson, Johnny Carson's brother, it seemed to carry an automatic, inbuilt form of one-upmanship for Merv against Johnny. Merv's producer was Bob Murphy, with Mort Lindsey once again conducting an eighteen-piece orchestra. A thinner, more visibly happy Merv greeted his guests, who on that important day included Milton Berle, Dinah Shore, Dom DeLuise, Angie Dickinson, and Dionne Warwick.

As one of the many regrettable administrative policies in the history of television, nearly all of Merv's film archives from the thirty months of shows and interviews he did in association with CBS were erased.

The "suits" decided to erase the tapes and use them again to record other shows. "Some of the great moments in television were lost forever," Merv lamented when he heard about CBS's "tragic mistake, an action that showed CBS's utter contempt for what I'd done."

"CBS could have made a fortune on those old tapes," Merv claimed. "I'll give you just one example—there are so many more. One of my greatest shows was when I re-assembled, on air, the stars of all those *Road* movies. Bob Hope, Dorothy Lamour, and Bing Crosby were wonderful. It was a moment lost to TV history unless somewhere, some place out there in America, somebody recorded our show."

In 1973, following Merv's example, Johnny Carson also moved his show westward, in his case to "beautiful downtown Burbank." Merv didn't feel the competition with Carson as intensely as he had before. Carson still went on weeknights at 11:30pm, with Merv taking the afternoon slot.

Once, perhaps as a means of stirring up a bit of drama, Dick Carson arranged for his brother, Johnny Carson, to appear on Merv's show as an unannounced surprise guest. After Merv recovered from his shock, he sat down and did a friendly hour-long interview with Carson.

***

In spite of its failure under the CBS umbrella, Merv Griffin Productions continued to grow, with nearly four-hundred employees plus an annual gross that, in 1970, came close to ten million dollars. The company's assets included not only TV game shows, but radio stations, real estate (some of it platinum and within Rockefeller Center), and a high-tech outfit known as Racing Patrol, Inc., developers of a closed-circuit TV system used at racetracks throughout the country.

Merv's drinking sometimes led to bizarre behavior on the air. On one show with Vincent Price that focused on the actor's talents as a gourmet cook, Eva Gabor and Merv drank wine until Merv got bombed. "Quite accidentally, I spilled wine on Eva's décolletage," he said. "On another night I was singing with the microphone over my head."

Seeking treatment, it was revealed that he had hypoglycemia. "I had to give up booze," he said. "And whereas I could live with that, my having to give up Rocky Road ice cream was more than I could bear."

In Los Angeles, Merv began to relish life as a bachelor, enjoying the privacy the sprawling city afforded. George Cukor, who lived near Merv, became a close friend. Merv got invited to the director's all-male parties. George was something of a procurer, introducing Merv to a steady supply of some of the most handsome young men in Hollywood.

Merv often took his choice for the night, perhaps an actor or model, back to the small cottage in the hills above the Sunset Strip. The house had once been occupied by Susan Hayward, who had died of cancer in 1975, no doubt from making the John Wayne film, *The Conqueror*, on locations that were very close to a highly radioactive site, a former atomic test site in Nevada.

In October of 1974, Merv knew that he'd "arrived" when his name became a permanent part of the Hollywood Walk of Fame. He was number 1601, and his star still shines there today.

***

Merv made it a point, after his return to Los Angeles, to visit Rock Hudson. Accompanied by his pal Roddy McDowall, he found Rock "in a panic" about having turned fifty. "Can you believe that?" Rock asked Merv. "Me, fifty? Rock Hudson stands for youthful virility."

Rock and Roddy shared memories of a birthday bash that had recently been staged for Rock at his house. The band hired for the night struck up "You Must Have Been a Beautiful Baby" as Rock made his entrance at the top of the stairs. He strutted down the grand staircase in a diaper as friends who included Carol Burnett and Buddy Hackett howled with laughter.

After an evening of memories and drinking, Rock invited Roddy and Merv to join him upstairs in bed. "Let's find out if we middle-aged old farts can still cut the mustard."

***

438

It was a sad day when Merv was reunited with his old friend, Henry Willson, who had been moved into the Motion Picture Country Home for Indigent Show People at Woodland Hills. "I'm reduced to charity," he told Merv. "It's all gone now."

They talked nostalgically of the beautiful hunks they'd shared in common. But there was bitterness associated with Henry's memories of Rock Hudson. He'd never forgiven Rock for deserting him.

As Henry confided to Merv, he'd continued to live for a few years as richly as he had during his heyday by selling off his silverware, antiques, and other valuables.

Before driving away, Merv left Henry five hundred dollars as a no-strings-attached gift. On November 2, 1978, he was saddened to learn about Henry's death at the age of 67 from cirrhosis of the liver.

Rock sent flowers to Henry's funeral. Merv did too, but did not identify where they had come from, as it was still considered dangerous for one's career to be associated too closely with Henry Willson.

***

Merv was particularly enchanted by athlete Jim Palmer, whom he invited onto his show. Palmer had built a worldwide fan base thanks partly to his ads for Jockey underwear, especially the tight-fitting bikini kind. Merv said that the sight of Palmer in his bikini underwear "gives new meaning to the term 'pitcher's mound.'"

Before the camera, within the context of his show, Merv urged Palmer to take off his pants and reveal to the studio audience what underwear he was wearing that day. Palmer refused but did admit that he filled out his jockey pouch with no padding from wardrobe. Merv looked disappointed when the star pitcher for the Baltimore Orioles wouldn't perform a striptease.

Merv continued his fascination with underwear models, sometimes bringing young men onto the show who looked like they didn't really know why they were there. Jeff Aquilon, a Bruce Weber model and one of the most famous male images of the 70s and early 80s, was Merv's all-time fantasy male. "His rear end is classic," Merv told Hadley. "There's nothing wrong with his front part either."

In the late 1970s, Merv had first seen a fashion spread of the handsome beefy model in *GQ*. He was modeling a pair of Speedo briefs. "Daddy, buy me some of that," he said to Hadley. Merv was also shown a flagrantly erotic photo of Jeff reclining on a bed, wearing seductively unbuttoned long johns.

Merv tried, perhaps a bit too strenuously, to attach social significance to Jeff's appearance on his show. Merv had been told about how fashion photographer Bruce Weber, in *GQ*'s own words, had discovered a college water polo player from California and in the pages of *GQ* redefined the American man. "We changed forever the look of magazines, photography, and advertising," Weber said. He claimed that Jeff became "the most famous face—and body—of the modern *GQ*. Ah yes, I seem to recall his physical splendor—in intimate detail!"

***

Merv had stayed in constant touch with the porn star, Cal Culver, and when he landed in California, he often spent nights with Merv. Cal had continued to arrange introductions, hooking Merv up with handsome young actors and models. "A lot of studs back then wanted to meet THE Merv Griffin," Cal said. "And Merv continued to be generous with me for the work I did for him."

After Rock Hudson and Liberace tired of Cal, he went through the predictable conquests in Hollywood, including Peter Lawford, George Cukor, and "the usual suspects." He'd even received a call from Sammy Davis Jr. who informed Cal that "I'm partial to blonds of any sex."

Cal related to Merv some of the details associated with his seduction by George Cukor. "I managed to get through a night with old liver lips. He was repulsive but I kept my hard-on."

"It's unbelievable some of the calls I get from stars," Cal told Merv. "I didn't know some of these guys were secretly gay. Orson Welles, Richard Harris. Even Christopher Reeve. Who'd have thought it? Someday I'll tell you what Steve McQueen wanted me to do."

Cal's greatest dream was to play the runner, Billy Siuve, in *The Front Runner*, a best-selling novel by Patricia Nell Warren. Paul Newman had acquired the screen rights and had announced that he was going to play the gay coach. "Paul and I have been going at it like gangbusters," Cal said. "You know, of course, that he's bi. All those rumors are true."

The movie, regrettably, was never made. And although he'd seriously considered the project, Newman, in Cal's words, "chickened out."

According to Merv,
"**Jim Palmer** in bikini briefs gives new meaning to the term 'pitcher's mound.'"

There were high hopes at the time that Cal would get the leading part in the movie adaptation of Mary Renault's novel, *The King Must Die*. "This Greek gentleman, who's really interested in me, has purchased the rights. He's agreed to star me in spite of my background in porn." Regrettably, this became just another impossible dream that never came true for Cal.

In 1976, Cal told Merv that it was almost certain that he'd be awarded the protagonist's role of Numie, the male hustler, in the Key West-based film, *The Last Resort*, starring, among others, Eartha Kitt. The film was based on a steamy, widely publicized novel by Darwin Porter, *Butterflies in Heat*, which Manor Reviews had described as:

"THE MOST SCORCHING NOVEL OF THE BIZARRE, THE FLAMBOYANT, AND THE COR- RUPT SINCE <u>MIDNIGHT COWBOY</u>. THE STRIKINGLY BEAUTIFUL BLOND HUSTLER, NUMIE CHASE, HAS COME TO THE END OF THE LINE. HERE, IN THE SEARING HEAT OF TROPICAL TORTUGA KEY, HE AROUSES PASSIONS IN SIX FLAMBOYANT BUT VULNERABLE PEOPLE THAT EXPLODE UNDER THE BLOOD-RED SUN."

After several "casting couch" auditions with Cal, the film's producer, Jerry Wheeler, decided to cast another blond male, supermodel Matt ("The Marlboro Man") Collins, into the role instead. His reasoning? "Having a real-life porno star playing the romantic lead in *Butterflies* would send the wrong signal—after all, we're not making *that* kind of movie."

Resentful that another chance for legitimate film success had eluded him, Cal briefly toyed with the idea of writing an autobiographical memoir. He had noted the fame and success of such roughly equivalent tell-all books as Michael Kearns' *The Happy Hustler* and Marc Stevens' aptly named confessional, *10½*. Cal wanted to produce a memoir, too, but in a style radically different from the others.

Cal Culver After Dark

"I want to depict two different *personas* in the book," he told Darwin Porter. "I want to write from the viewpoint of both Casey Donovan and Cal Culver. Casey will be the hustler, who will do anything, either on screen or at private parties, as long as he gets paid. Cal, however, will represent the serious side of me, a legitimate actor who became corrupted. A man who wanted to lead a quiet, respectable life with his lover, Tom Tryon."

Cal was referring to his older companion, the handsome Yale-educated actor and best-selling novelist, Tom Tryon. He had played important roles in Darryl F. Zanuck's *The Longest Day* (1962) and in Otto Preminger's *The Cardinal* (1963).

Tryon had later publicly referred to Preminger as "a Nazi." After filming *The Cardinal*, Tryon had suffered a nervous breakdown and had spent time in a psychiatric ward.

In Key West, during his attempt to nab a leading role in *Butterflies in Heat/The Last Resort*, Cal relayed in great detail his wild adventures as a star fucker, with a special focus on his affairs with Merv Griffin and Rock Hudson.

He also revealed that he'd had a brief affair with the older, Sweden-born megastar Ingrid Bergman, "even though pussy isn't my thing," he said. "She taught me everything I know about being a star," Cal said, citing his brief onstage appearance with her in a revival in the early 1970s of George Bernard Shaw's 1901 drama, *Captain Brassbound's Conversion.*

Although Cal struggled for several months to find a voice and a market for the memoir he had threatened, its content and style were weak, unfocused, and uninteresting. "I guess I'm not that great at self-analysis," he finally admitted. Much to the relief of Merv and other clients across the country, Cal's tell-all book project was eventually abandoned

***

As the 70s seguéd into the 80s, Merv and Cal stayed in touch by phone. Merv was mainly interested in hearing what movie stars Cal had seduced, although Cal also took the opportunity to relate many of the manic and usually fruitless details of his fast-fading career. It became obvious to Merv and everyone else that Cal, to an increasing degree, was walking on the shadowy side of the boulevard of broken dreams.

During the final months of Cal's life, he called upon Merv for a favor. Sexual relations between the two men had long ago ceased, but Cal wanted his old friend to devote the theme of one of his upcoming shows to AIDS. Cal agreed to appear on the show and confess to the world that he too had AIDS. "Your friend,

Ronald Reagan, never mentions the subject," Cal told Merv. "Someone has to. It's the Black Death, and it's queer—and it's here to stay."

On Sunday, August 10, 1987, some unknown associate of Merv's called to tell him that Cal had died of a lung infection associated with AIDS, in Inverness, Florida, after a stint as a spokesman for the Gay Men's Health Crisis, advocating techniques to avoid the spread of the disease.

In the wake of his death, Cal was eulogized by Jay McKenna in *The Advocate*, who described him as a "gay Adam, the first widely embraced gay symbol to appear during the post-Stonewall years."

For obvious reasons, Merv did not attend Cal's funeral at a church in Greenwich Village.

***

Merv's most lucrative idea for a TV quiz show originated with a game he used to play with his sister in the back seat of the family car during long rides with his parents in California. The game was called "Hangman." Decades later, during a staff meeting, he proposed the adaptation of this contest into a televised game show. The final touch came when Merv remembered an annual church bazaar in San Mateo when a giant wheel used to spin around like a roulette wheel in a casino with various prizes written on the wheel's various spokes.

From this rather casual staff meeting, the concept for *Wheel of Fortune* was born. Millions of dollars of profits lay in the future.

Wheel of Fortune eventually became so profitable that, for large amounts of money, Merv was able to license international variations of the game in countries as diverse as Norway, Peru, Taiwan, and France.

Inaugurated in 1975 on NBC Daytime TV, *Wheel* didn't explode in popularity until a nighttime syndicated edition was conceived in 1983. The show became solidly profitable in 1984, and it's been going strong ever since. The show's 26th nighttime season, by then within the orbit of Sony Pictures Studio, premiered on September 8, 2008. Its theme song, "Changing Keys," was written by Merv himself for the show's 1983-89 run. Since then, that same song has been officially adapted into at least three different musical configurations.

On *Wheel*, three contestants—or in some cases, three separate pairs of contestants—compete against each other in finding a solution to a word puzzle. The name of the show derives from a large wheel whose lettering determines the prizes and dollar amounts won or lost by the contestants.

The original host of *Wheel of Fortune* was Chuck Woolery. A handsome, devout, born again Christian from Kentucky, he was not always Merv's cuppa, as Merv himself put it. Woolery's religious background didn't prevent him from entering into four marriages.

Woolery remained as host of the show until his contract expired in the early 80s. Originally Merv paid him $65,000 a year. As incentive to sign on again, Woolery demanded $500,000. Merv came back with a counter-offer of $400,000 a year, which Woolery turned down, later confessing, "I made a big mistake."

Throughout his gig on *Wheel of Fortune,* Woolery had remained an enthusiastic bass fisherman with a talent for selling his own line of fishing products, and he had an obsession with jewelry. He eventually amassed more than four hundred diamond rings and a bass guitar encrusted with diamonds. When Merv learned that Woolery had rejected his offer, he said, "Let him go fishing. We'll find someone even better."

Anyone who's ever seen *Wheel of Fortune* is likely to remember the show's svelte and enigmatic assistant, Vanna White, whose every sinuous movement seemed to celebrate the spinning wheel's drama and propel the game forward.

The day he met her, Merv selected Vanna from a line-up of other contestants, and later said, "Even I could not have predicted the cult of Vannamania." Although treated as a campy joke in some circles, the beautifully coiffed and elegantly dressed Vanna soon became indelibly associated around the globe as a key element in the ongoing allure of *Wheel of Fortune.*

Hailing from South Carolina, where she was known in high school as "Vanna Banana," she made her first national television appearance on June 20, 1980 on an episode of the game show *The Price Is Right.* Vanna's first episode, where she functioned as Pat Sajak's assistant presenter, and a replacement for the show's original hostess, Susan Stafford, was aired on December 12, 1982, and she remained as a highly visible component of the show until its cancellation in 1991.

When the show moved to a prime time evening slot in September of 1983, Vanna was credited in part with making *Wheel* the highest rated syndicated program in broadcast television. Yet in fact, she rarely spoke, and her role in the show was almost purely decorative.

She was candid about her role on *Wheel*, claiming that "I don't have the most intellectual job in the world, but I do have to know the letters." She also said, "And I enjoy getting dressed up as a Barbie doll."

In the early 1980s, during her initial involvement in the show, Merv had been impressed with Vanna's handsome boyfriend, John Gibson, a former Chippendale dancer. A copy of *Playgirl* had featured him as a nude centerfold. "I could go for the hunk myself," Merv told Hadley. Vanna became engaged to Gibson, but tragically, he died in a plane crash in 1986.

In 1987, Vanna released her autobiography, *Vanna Speaks!*, and it became an immediate bestseller. That same year she was featured in a *Playboy* pictorial. The photos of her wearing see-through lingerie were shot prior to the debut of her career on *Wheel of Fortune*. Since she'd signed a release at the time the pictures were taken, there was no way legally that she could prevent the magazine from publishing these revealing photos.

In 1992, Vanna entered the *Guinness Book of World Records*, as the globe's most frequent "clapper." Vanna puts her hands together for contestants some 28,080 times a season—an average of 720 times per show.

Always proud of the fact he had personally selected Vanna as his original choice for *Wheel*, Merv, with Pat Sajak and Alex Trebek, showed up when Vanna was awarded the 2,309[th] Star on the Hollywood Walk of Fame.

A former TV weatherman, Pat Sajak, the son of a Polish American trucking foreman, took over for Woolery in 1981. Merv, who appreciated his jocular TV style, had personally selected him for the job. Sajak functioned as host of the daytime version of *Wheel of Fortune* between December 28, 1981 and January 9, 1989, and as the host of the syndicated evening version of *Wheel of Fortune* beginning on September 19, 1983.

Previously, Sajak's bid for his own late-night talk show had failed. Pitted unsuccessfully against Johnny Carson, Sajak's show had aired between January 9, 1989 and April 13, 1990, when CBS dropped it. "You were more successful than I was in battling Carson," Sajak told Merv. "My gut feeling is that the only way to beat Carson is for him to retire."

Like Merv, Sajak was a conservative Republican, and as such, they rarely conflicted over politics.

After Merv sold his rights to *Wheel of Fortune* and no longer functioned as Sajak's boss, they remained life-long friends. Sajak visited Merv in the hos-

Spinmeisters:
(left to right) **Vanna White, Pat Sajak, Chuck Woolery**

pital shortly before he died. Merv's final words to his long-time collaborator were, "Goodbye, Pat. Give my love to Lesly and the kids."

"When you were with Merv, you rubbed shoulders with the most exciting and famous people on the planet," Sajak claimed after Merv's death. "He was a bigger-than-life person. The solar system of which he was the center was filled with bright stars who seemed to gravitate toward him. Whether on a TV talk show or in a living room, no one could make you feel more alive than Merv Griffin. His entire life was a celebration."

Between 1999 and the publication of this book, Harry Friedman was producer of both *Wheel of Fortune* and *Jeopardy!*, earning credit for many of the innovative ideas that kept both shows fresh and vital. During his childhood in Omaha, Friedman to a large extent witnessed the birth of television from the vantage point of his father's appliance store in Omaha. His father was the first retailer in the area to sell TV sets.

Thanks to his involvement in Merv Griffin Productions, Friedman is a seven-time Emmy Award winner. In September of 2006, and under his direction, both *Wheel* and *Jeopardy!* became the first syndicated TV shows to broadcast in High Definition.

In 2003, Friedman lifted the five-day limit for contestants on *Jeopardy!*, allowing returning champions to continue playing as long as they remained winners. This change of the rules led to the famous winning streak of Ken Jennings, a software engineer from Utah. In a history-making, seventy-four-day consecutive run, he won $2.5 million. During his appearance, viewership increased by thirty percent, leading to *Jeopardy!* becoming the single most talked about TV show in America.

In its 2007-2008 season, *Wheel of Fortune* became the longest running syndicated TV program in history, celebrating twenty-five seasons, during which $180 million worth of cash and prizes had been distributed to its contestants.

***

As the decades moved closer to the millennium, Merv's so-called "movie career" sputtered on. In most of the films he agreed to appear in, he was either cast as himself or appeared in brief walk-ons. Sometimes only his voice was used, evoking the screen credits he'd compiled during his 1950s career at Warner Brothers.

In 1976, Merv returned to the screen in *Two-Minute Warning*, a thriller that starred Charlton Heston, whom Merv had not seen since that day he came on to him in Hollywood back when they were struggling actors. No mention was made of that incident.

The film was about a psychotic man who's being hunted by both the police and a SWAT team. Armed with a rifle, he goes on a sniping spree. A great star of the 1940s, Walter Pidgeon, had been cast in a minor role as a pickpocket. Ruefully, Walter told Merv, "Show business sure does have its ups and downs, doesn't it?"

So what did Merv do in this cliffhanger? He appeared as himself, singing the National Anthem.

In *One Trick Pony* (1980), Paul Simon was cast as an aging rock star trying to write and record a new album in the face of an indifferent record label, a failing marriage, and a talentless producer. Some critics suggested that the film made many references to Paul's own life. For reasons known only to himself, Merv appeared, uncredited, as an *à capella* singer. He jokingly told Hadley, "I turned down the role of a blonde girl groupie. I didn't like the wig."

On the set, Merv encountered Tiny Tim playing himself. "Tiny, what are you doing in this thing?" Merv asked him.

"Mr. Griffin," Tiny Tim said, "I need the money. But I might ask, what are *you* doing in this thing?"

A Jerry Lewis movie, *Slapstick (Of Another Kind)*, whose plot had been adapted from a story by Kurt Vonnegut, premiered in 1982. The voice (but not the image) of Orson Welles intoned the words of the "Father of the Aliens." It was Welles who persuaded Merv to accept the role of "Anchorman." The plot, Merv found out on the day he showed up for work, focused on a rich, beautiful couple who give birth to deformed (and alien) twins. When their heads are together, and when they concentrate on a shared goal, they turn out to be the smartest kids on the planet.

"Oh, my God," Merv told his friends. "I've bottomed out. I'm appearing in a Jerry Lewis movie. If my family finds out, they'll think I've gone on relief."

In 1983, Ron Clark wrote and directed a film called *The Funny Farm* with a talented cast that included Peter Aykroyd, Miles Chapin, Jack Carter, and Eileen Brennan. The film was about a group of young entertainers performing at a comedy club called The Funny Farm. Clark asked Merv if he'd perform in the film as "The Voice of Merv Griffin."

"Why not?" Merv told Clark. "No one does Merv's voice better than me."

In 1985, *Alice in Wonderland,* based on a work by the Victorian writer Lewis Carroll, brought Merv to the silver screen once again. It wasn't the film but the cast that Merv enjoyed. It included Shelley Winters playing "The Dodo Bird" and Sammy Davis Jr. as "The Caterpillar." Merv got to meet and talk to Martha Raye, who played, in what turned out to be her final screen appearance, "The Duchess."

In November of 1998, Merv appeared in an episode of the TV series

Hercules. He told his friends, "If you don't watch it, there will be no hard feelings."

At the millennium's end, Merv decided that he wanted to be cast by director Harvey Frost in a comedy/drama called *Murder at the Cannes Film Festival*. Because Merv was one of the film's executive producers, Frost could hardly say no. Released in 2000, the film starred French Stewart, with much of the attention going to Bo Derek in a supporting role.

After the release of the film, Merv told Eva Gabor, "I think I'll abandon my film career. Or has it abandoned me? Okay, so I never became as big as Debbie Reynolds. But look what happened to her. She ended up having to sleep in her car."

***

Every year for an eight-week period, Merv left his luxurious Trans-American Video Studios (TAV) in Hollywood, and moved his staff and base of operations to Caesars Palace in Las Vegas.

One of the guests Merv persuaded to appear at Caesars was Bing Crosby. "Bing wanted to visit this dental expert in Vegas. I called the penny-pinching singer and agreed to pay his airfare if he'd appear at Caesars—and he agreed to it. He got his teeth fixed, he sang at Caesars, and flew home on my dime."

Merv's most dangerous on-air moment was associated with the appearance of Siegfried and Roy as guests on his Las Vegas-based show. At one point in the segment, one of their Bengal tigers escaped, leaving Merv alone, on the set, with the potentially lethal cat. "The cameraman ran and the orchestra fled into the dressing room," Merv said. "The damn tiger sat on my foot. Siegfried and Roy, who are just fabulous, started talking in German. Finally, they got the beast to walk away. That's why I'm still alive today."

***

One day, Merv told his then-producer, Bob Shanks, that he wanted Salvador Dalí, the mad Catalán surrealist painter, to be interviewed on his show. "He's an odd bird. No one had a clue as to what he'd say or do," Merv said. Dalí, however, agreed that he'd appear on the show after filming a TV commercial for Lanvin chocolates.

The artist arrived with a chair-sized leather replica of a rhinoceros, and refused to sit on anything else. On the show, he uttered a series of statements that some viewers found baffling: "The only difference between me and the surrealists is that I am a surrealist. Dalí is immortal and will not die."

448

Backstage, he was even more entertaining than before the TV cameras. Talking with Merv, Dalí seemed fascinated by masturbation, letting it be known that back in 1929, he'd named one of his most celebrated paintings *The Great Masturbator*.

Dalí invited Merv to visit him at his studio on Spain's Costa Brava, north of Barcelona. "I have this sculpture which depicts a large armpit of the Christ figure. If you visit, I'll want you to strip off all your clothes and lie in a fetal position in this armpit. I'll take photographs of you as you masturbate. I ask many of my male friends to do this for me."

"I'll get back to you on that," Merv said.

Before leaving, Dalí kissed Merv on the lips, using tongue. He also gave him a miniature painting of an erect penis. "It looks very small in the painting, but actually in perspective, the penis is fourteen inches when fully erect," Dalí claimed.

Merv took the penis home, but it was later stolen, perhaps by an overnight trick.

Merv was furious. "Who knows?" he asked. "That God damn penis might have brought me three million dollars one day."

***

Merv once told some friends that Zsa Zsa Gabor was more fascinating than Eva. Previously, columnist Earl Wilson had told Merv, "Zsa Zsa is unbelievable—you can't believe a damn thing the *dollink* says. You can't even trust her on when she lost her virginity. Once, she told me she lost it to her first husband, a Turkish diplomat, Burhan Belge. On another occasion, she told me that as a teenager she surrendered the cherry to the liberal Turkish dictator, Kemal Atatürk."

"What I found the most fascinating," Merv said, "was her marriage to Jack Ryan. Do you know he's the guy who invented the Barbie doll?"

Merv once tried to compile a list of Zsa Zsa's lovers. They included the most notorious and fascinating playboys in the world—Rafael Trujillo Jr. (son of the dictator of the Dominican Republic); Prince Aly Khan (the playboy and spiritual leader of the world's Ismailian Muslims who had married Rita Hayworth); and Porfirio Rubirosa, (the Dominican diplomat and playboy who had married both of the world's richest women, Woolworth heiress Barbara Hutton and tobacco heiress Doris Duke).

Merv's list also included an armada of actors and singers, ranging from British imports Richard Burton and Sean Connery to singers Frank Sinatra and Mario Lanza, with whom she'd co-starred in *For the First Time* in 1959. The most intriguing man on Zsa Zsa's list was President John F. Kennedy.

"When Jackie found out," Zsa Zsa told Merv, "she refused to speak to me after that." Reportedly, Zsa Zsa also sampled the wares of Jackie's second husband, Aristotle Onassis.

After Zsa Zsa's final marriage to the German so-called nobleman, Frederick von Anhalt, Merv with his tongue in his cheek introduced her as Princess von Anhalt, the Duchess of Saxony.

He could spend hours listening to Zsa Zsa's stories of her conquests, and he was equally enthralled with the men who didn't hit it lucky. "I turned down Howard Hughes because Lana Turner told me he gave her syphilis. When I was dancing close to Errol Flynn, he put my hand inside his zipper. 'As you can clearly feel,' he told me, 'I have something in common with the stallions on my property.'"

Zsa Zsa laughed when she told Merv that Wayne Hays, a Democratic senator from Ohio, on the Senate floor had referred to her as "the most expensive courtesan since Madame de Pompadour."

She also confided in Merv that her older sister, Magda, had married her discarded ex-husband, George Sanders. During the heat of passion on their wedding night, George had telephoned Zsa Zsa for comfort and advice. "The marriage went downhill after that," Zsa Zsa said.

In another gossipy tidbit, Zsa Zsa revealed that she had known Princess Grace—whom she referred to as "a bricklayer's daughter from Philadelphia"—for years. Both of them had been stars—or starlets in Zsa Zsa's case—at MGM. "She had more boyfriends in a month than I had in a lifetime," Zsa Zsa rather inaccurately claimed.

She also asserted, utterly without satire, that Prince Rainier had wanted to marry her instead of Grace. "Actually, he really wanted to marry Marilyn Monroe."

Merv's Mad Europeans:
Left: Catalán surrealist **Salvador Dalí.** Center: **Merv** with **Zsa Zsa Gabor**

Right: Zsa Zsa predicted that her sister Eva, if Merv would marry her, would become a 21st-century version of **Madame de Pompadour** (mistress to French king Louis XV)

450

At any dinner party, Zsa Zsa tended to be more outrageous than she ever was on Merv's television show. "Both Mike Todd and Richard Burton told me that I was far better in bed than Elizabeth Taylor. Of course, Nicky Hilton, my son-in-law and Liz's first husband, preferred my lovemaking to hers. But she was young and inexperienced when my darling Nicky took this poor girl to bed."

Merv wanted to know which man was the better lover—Sean Connery or Richard Burton. "I've never been to bed with either of them," Merv confided to Zsa Zsa, "and I'm curious."

"Oh, Richard, most definitely," Zsa Zsa said, "although Sean certainly had the more impressive equipment."

Merv was once asked which was the most outrageous story that Zsa Zsa ever told him. "She claimed that she introduced The Beatles at a charity event in London called *Night of a Thousand Stars*. Later she invited them all back to her hotel suite. Naturally, it was the London Hilton."

According to Merv, Zsa Zsa told him, "I loved the humor of those boys, their irreverence about institutions which most of the Western world viewed as sacred. They seduced me one at a time. Ringo Starr went first, then Paul McCartney, then John Lennon. George Harrison was last, and he was the best of the lot."

In her memoirs, *One Lifetime Is Not Enough*, Zsa Zsa claimed that "I wasn't involved with any of them romantically," which in a sense was the truth.

Her other most outrageous claim, according to Merv, involved the way Elvis Presley had seduced her during one of his gigs at The Flamingo in Las Vegas. She'd received a message that Elvis wanted to meet her in his dressing room.

"In her book, Zsa Zsa said she and Elvis didn't make it that night," Merv said. "But face-to-face, she told me a different story...namely, that she actually learned firsthand what 'Love Me Tender' meant. In her memoirs, however, all she said was that she found Elvis 'gorgeous and sexy, a cross between a gentleman and a big black sexy snake. He radiated sexuality'"

As time when by, she grew increasingly confidential with Merv, yet he often suspected that she was holding back, not revealing the most shocking indiscretions of her private life. He knew that Zsa Zsa confided everything to Eva, so one night Merv asked Eva for details about the most shocking affair her older sister had ever had.

"It was with Prince Philip," Eva said casually, using a voice that she might have used to read from a grocery list. "She met him at Windsor outside London when he was playing polo. The Queen and the Queen Mother were also watching that day. When Philip met Zsa Zsa, he was smitten. They had an affair that lasted on and off for several years."

"Anything more shocking than that?" Merv asked.

"Zsa Zsa knew Lord Mountbatten of Burma," Eva said. "A great war hero as you know. He was also the favorite uncle of Prince Charles. Zsa Zsa told me that when Charles was a teenage boy, he was regularly sodomized by his uncle."

"Okay, okay, I'm saturated," Merv said. "My head is spinning. To cap our lovely dinner, do you have a whopper that will keep me up all night?"

"Yes, I do," Eva said coyly, and "it happened right after Zsa Zsa appeared on your show, the one you taped with her at Caesars Palace in Las Vegas. If I remember correctly, and I do, she told the audience that 'Richard Nixon is one of the greatest presidents of modern times. He was the man who opened Russia and China for us. Why don't you give the guy a break?'"

The audience booed her.

The next day Nixon called Zsa Zsa and thanked her for his public display of support. One call led to another, and Zsa Zsa, at least according to Eva, found herself flying to Key Biscayne where she evolved into a guest of Nixon's best friend, Bebe Rebozo.

"Nixon?" Merv said in astonishment. "I didn't believe he had it in him."

"Actually, *dalink,* I read in the paper that arch-conservatives and Republicans have better sex than liberal Democrats. You should do a show on that subject one day."

Once, when Zsa Zsa and Merv were dining alone, she asked him a provocative question. "Why don't you marry Eva and make an honest woman out of her? If not that, you could at least take her for your mistress. She could be Madame de Pompadour to your Louis XV."

Heeeeeere's Merv!

Chapter Ten

Eva Gabor, the youngest of the three Gabor Sisters—was known as the last great courtesan of the 20th century. At the age of sixteen, Eva was the first member of her colorful family to emigrate from her native Hungary to America. In time, her sisters, Zsa Zsa and Magda, and their mother, Jolie, followed. As they matured, and grew more glib in the ways of America's entertainment industry, Eva and her outspoken sister, Zsa Zsa, were hailed as the world's most beautiful, desirable, and glamorous women.

Before Merv became more intimately linked with Eva, he often referred to Zsa Zsa and Eva as "my favorite and most amusing guests on TV," the "Gorgeous Gabors" and "The World's Greatest Sister Act."

He later claimed that what especially attracted him to both Zsa Zsa and Eva was their keen ability to deliver one-line zingers. "Take marriage for instance," Merv said. "Zsa Zsa told me, 'I believe in large families—every woman should have at least three husbands.'" On another occasion, Eva instructed Merv that "marriage is too interesting an experiment to be tried only once or twice."

Before her association with Merv, Eva had followed her own advice, entering into five equally ill-fated marriages: Dr. Eric Drimmer, a psychologist who had served at one time as the in-house shrink at MGM studios; realtor Charles Isaac; surgeon Dr. John E. Williams; stockbroker Richard Brown, and, finally, Frank Jamieson, vice president of the manufacturing and electronics giant, North American Rockwell. (North American Rockwell, after a complicated series of mergers, acquisitions, and spinoffs, later changed its name to Rockwell International.)

Ultimately, her intention involved making Merv her sixth husband. In that, of course, she never succeeded.

Eva may have had only one-third the lovers—her estimate—that her sister Zsa Zsa did, but Eva's beaux were strictly A-list: Glenn Ford, Tyrone Power, Frank Sinatra.

Of the fabled Gabor sisters, Eva was labeled "the good Gabor." She was also an acute businesswoman, founding a wig company. "A girl likes to look her best, even if she cheats a bit, or especially if she cheats a bit. All women have to deceive the world, especially about their age."

Sometimes Zsa Zsa reacted badly to Eva's comments about her on Merv's show. One comment, in particular, infuriated Zsa Zsa. As the cameras rolled, Eva said, "I was the first actress in the family, and am still the *only* actress in the family. I shouldn't be saying it. It just slipped out."

Although Eva appeared in many less-than-memorable movies and made a debut on Broadway in Rodger and Hammerstein's *The Happy Times*, it was a fluffy TV sitcom that's usually cited as her most memorable Hollywood achievement. She appeared as the glamorous female lead in *Green Acres,* a relentlessly cheerful sitcom which is still regularly broadcast worldwide. She played a "kind of dumb and kind of smart," well-intentioned Park Avenue socialite who had humored her husband, as played by Eddie Albert, by moving to a rustic farm staffed by bewildered but amusing hicks. Loaded with innuendos about sophisticated urbanites coping with the realities of life in the middle of nowhere, the sitcom, with its canned laughs and pratfalls, ran for six consecutive years.

Merv was often asked if Eva were like the character she played on *Green Acres*.

"She was a smart business woman, but sometimes she could be just like her character," Merv said. "I remember once when I invited Eddie Albert and her to stay at my ranch. That morning Eva came down the stairs in a feather boa. Eddie is a big animal rights guy, and he was outraged. 'Eva, don't you know where those feathers come from?' he yelled at her. She screwed up her face, very quizzical, and said, 'Pillows?'"

One of Merv's fondest memories of Eva as a guest on his talk show involved the episode when she appeared with Eddie Albert, her *Green Acres* co-star, alongside the then-most-powerful TV critic in the industry, Cleveland Amory. "He'd panned their show," Merv said, "And on-camera, both Eddie and Eva attacked him. He might have been the nation's number one television critic, but he left that show really scathed. I learned from that broadcast that you never wanted to get on the bad side of Eva."

Merv once claimed that "Eva was born to appear on TV talk shows." In 1951 she'd been a guest of Steve Allen on his first talk show for CBS. Allen, in fact, did even more than Merv to introduce the Gabor Sisters to American television. "The glamour and humor of the

Life on the farm
Eva Gabor with **Eddie Albert**

454

Gabors came into family living rooms across the nation," Merv said, "And Zsa Zsa was even better at the *double entendre* than Eva."

Sometimes, especially when Merv had been drinking, he privately asked Eva outrageous questions. "Is it true that when you worked on *Artists and Models* with Jerry Lewis and Dean Martin, you slept with both men? And is it true that Jerry has three inches, Martin ten?"

"No woman should ever reveal a man's most closely guarded secret, even to his enemies," Eva diplomatically responded.

Ultimately Zsa Zsa came up with funnier and more sophisticated answers to Merv's questions than Eva. Zsa Zsa was quick on the response. "How many husbands have I had?" she asked. "You mean apart from my own?"

Eva would say things whimsical, gracious, and charming, such as "All any girl needs at any time in history is simple velvet and diamonds." On the other hand, Zsa Zsa would utter something funnier. "I wasn't born, *dahlink*, I was ordered from room service."

Eva had humor, but she tended to be kinder than Zsa Zsa, who could at times be biting. As an example, Merv referred to Zsa Zsa's remark about her husband, actor George Sanders. "Ven I was married to George Sanders, we were both in love with him. I fell out of love with him, but he didn't."

After watching so many appearances by both Eva and Zsa Zsa "on the couch" on TV talk shows, author Anthony Turtu said, "Eva's turns were always glamorous, witty, and serene—unlike appearances by her unpredictable sister, who could always be counted on for her brand of fireworks."

Merv called Zsa Zsa, Magda, and Eva "*Vonderful Vimmen*. They conquered kings, princes, playboys, movie stars, and millionaires, broke hearts while amassing fortunes, and became adored by the world at the same time. Of course, all women held tightly on to their husbands when one of them walked into the room. They were the Budapest bombshells."

***

On an impulse in 1979, Eva called Merv and asked him to join her vacation party on their upcoming tour of Asia. In dire need of a long holiday, Merv told Eva, "What the hell? You only live once." So Merv arranged for several shows to be pre-taped in advance of his time away, and agreed to join Eva and her then-husband, Frank Jamieson, on the tour, with the understanding that it would include stops in South Korea, Hong Kong, Taiwan, and the Philippines.

They were guests of William Rockwell Jr., the CEO of Rockwell International (a manufacturer of advanced weapons systems), and his wife, Constance. For Rockwell, this was a major showcasing of the company's

455

products. For others in the party, including Eva and Merv, it was just a bit of vacation fun. Rockwell and his entourage were flown aboard a converted 727.

Preoccupied with the serious business of PR, corporate politics, and weapons sales, Frank "tolerated" Merv. Eva, however, adored him. It was the first time she'd ever spent a great deal of time with him.

"You really know how to enliven a boring party," Eva told Merv, looking directly at her husband as she said that.

Rockwell's converted 727 had scheduled a stop on Midway Island, famed for a role during World War II as a battleground between the naval forces of the U.S. and the Empire of Japan.

When Merv landed there, he discovered that several hundred Navy personnel and their wives followed a daily routine which involved watching *The Merv Griffin Show* on a communal wide screen TV. During the broadcast, business in the Midways virtually came to a halt. "It was an important ritual for them in those remote islands," Merv wrote in his second autobiography. "It was one of the ways they maintained a connection to home."

When Merv, Eva, and members of the Rockwell contingent walked in, with fanfare, at the end of one of the broadcasts, it caused pandemonium.

After Eva's divorce from Frank in 1983, she turned to Merv for comfort. "Despite the many husbands she'd had, Eva was crushed by the final divorce," Merv claimed. "In her way, she really loved Frank and hated losing him."

He invited her to visit his ranch in the cool mountain air over the Carmel Valley. "She came to heal herself, and we grew close," he said. He generously offered her long-term use of one of the half dozen guest cottages on site. "Stay here forever," he told her. "You're most welcome."

Like the protagonist in the play, *The Man Who Came to Dinner*, Eva moved in, interpreting as a literal fact Merv's invitation to stay forever. It cemented the long-enduring friendship that would last almost until her death.

Merv recalled that at the ranch she'd get up early every day. "I'd get up an hour later and walk down to the stable. By then, every horse in the pasture would have red lipstick on it."

In the next few months, Eva became Merv's "arm candy," going on trips with him and appearing with him at premieres and public events.

"Eva had a love for Merv, but at his age and at his weight it was not sexual," Jolie Gabor confided to friends. "Every day of my life I tried to get Merv to marry my daughter. I knew if she married Merv, she would be secure for life and never worry about having to sell wigs or appear in some dumb TV sitcom."

As Merv revealed in his second autobiography, he and Eva often passed the day together lying on sofas in his living room. "I'd get on one couch, Eva on the other," Merv said. "We'd lie there for days at a time—laughing, sleeping, laughing, watching television, laughing, eating, and laughing some more. We almost never argued except when we watched *Wheel of Fortune*. She'd get furious because I knew all the answers in advance."

Zsa Zsa knew the full details of the "arrangement" between Merv and Eva, but in her second autobiography, *One Lifetime Is Not Enough*, she chose to be discreet. "She is happily involved with Merv Griffin and has a marvelous life with him," Zsa Zsa claimed. "I like Merv a great deal, did hundreds of shows with him, and am glad that Eva is now so happy."

Behind the scenes, Zsa Zsa, like her mother, was constantly urging Merv to marry Eva and "make an honest woman out of her. There are many marriages without sex. It's an old Hungarian custom. Men marry, have children with their wives, and then stash them away so they can spend the rest of their lives with various mistresses."

Merv got a taste of Zsa Zsa's famous temper after she'd been thrown in jail for slapping the policeman who stopped her for a traffic violation. "All my friends came to support me in court," Zsa Zsa told Merv. "But not you—and not Eva." She took particular exception to a quote by Eva that appeared in the press. The item quoted Eva as saying, "Mrs. Kirk Douglas and I just had lunch, and we agreed that if Zsa Zsa hadn't talked so much, this stupid thing would never have happened."

Before slamming down the phone, Zsa Zsa told Merv, "I'll never speak to the bitch ever again."

But in a few days, Merv succeeded as peacemaker, bringing the two warring sisters together for dinner. Over wine, with tears, both Eva and Zsa Zsa poured out their "undying love" for each other.

***

As the 80s dawned, famous guests from Burt Reynolds to Orson Welles were showcased on *The Merv Griffin Show*.

Even during the early 70s, when Burt was still relatively unknown, Merv liked having the sexy, handsome actor on his show, almost preferring him to one of his underwear models.

Merv had booked Burt's first appearance after a strong pitch from the actor's agent. When Burt came on, Merv was enthralled by the good looks, wit, and charm of this half-Cherokee from Georgia, who would in the years to come (1978-82) become the number one box office attraction in America. Burt's appearances got even higher ratings after April of 1972, when he appeared "virtually nude" (but with genitals discretely concealed) for a centerfold in *Cosmopolitan* magazine.

Burt's first appearance went over so big with daytime audiences that Merv subsequently booked him for a series of twenty shows.

He'd been launched as a megastar after his appearance in *Deliverance* in 1972 with Jon Voigt, and Merv followed his career avidly. Hadley always claimed that Burt represented Merv's all-time macho male fantasy. In Merv's case, he could only dream, as he had no chance of ever seducing Burt Reynolds, as he had other stars such as Rock Hudson when he was younger.

Burt got a big laugh when he said, "When I die, what they're going to write on my tombstone is 'Here lies Burt Reynolds. The first guy to pose nude in a magazine.'"

Actually, Burt had been Cosmo's fourth choice as beefcake for their nude centerfold. The offer went first to football great Joe Namath, who declined the honor, as did, subsequently, both Steve McQueen and Clint Eastwood.

First wife Judy Carne admitted that Burt beat her up on occasion but then went on to assert, "He has the most divine little ass." Dolly Parton wasn't so kind. "Burt and I are too much alike to be involved. We both wear wigs and high heels, and we both have a roll around the middle." Actress Sarah Miles said, "A *toupée* and lifts—the man's an imposter."

Merv's ardor for Burt cooled when he learned about the lifts and the toupée. A killing blow came when Mamie Van Doren, a platinum-haired bombshell who struggled with unfavorable comparisons to Marilyn Monroe, and a one-time lover of Johnny Carson, revealed that Burt is "high on jive but low on substance." On their first night together, Burt said that he considered himself "the male Mamie Van Doren," an idea which she found off-putting in a man.

Years later in her autobiography, *Playing the Field*, Mamie revealed what she thought of Burt's nude, almost-full-monty layout in *Cosmopolitan*. "I could only laugh," she wrote. "An exaggeration. A cigar would have covered it nicely."

Once Burt admitted, "I'm not a superstud, though I'm labeled as one. The reason I get myself into these kinds of situations is because I talk too much."

Merv revealed to Hadley that the reason he kept booking Burt onto the show, long after he'd lost his fantasy passion for him, is "because he's such a great guest. Fabulous sense of humor and you never know what he's gonna say next."

In 1981, Burt met his future wife, Loni Anderson, during a taping of *The Merv Griffin Show*. Merv later said,

A charming, hairy beast
Burt Reynolds

"They seemed so happy, so right for each other. But that was before Burt—and-Loni-gate broke with all the cheesy accusations. What a messy breakup. Thank God I avoided that in my own life, even though I paid, and paid dearly, for my own divorce."

***

In 1980, Merv went to the movies with Hadley to see *The Blue Lagoon* starring Brooke Shields. At the age of nineteen, Christopher Atkins played opposite Brooke. Merv was thrilled by his male beauty, especially when he appeared fully nude on screen at a time when male frontal nudity in movies was rare.

Wherever he went after the release of the film, female fans—and some gay males—literally tore off his clothes. Atkins appeared on the cover of the September 1983 edition of *Playgirl*, posing nude for a pictorial inside. In the wake of that, Merv booked him for an appearance on his show. As the cameras rolled, Atkins talked about "the weenie cloth" he wore in *The Blue Lagoon*. Throughout the interview, "Merv was practically drooling over the kid," one viewer claimed.

***

The renowned filmmaker and intellectual, Orson Welles, and Merv became friends, and subsequently became known as television's odd couple.

Most of Orson's friends thought he'd have dismissed Merv as a creative lightweight, but they bonded the first day they met.

The French author, filmmaker, and *enfant terrible,* Jean Cocteau, defined Orson Welles as "a giant with a child's face, a tree inhabited by birds, a dog who has broken his chains to sleep on a bed of flowers."

As their friendship evolved, Orson became Merv's most popular guest, appearing fifty times on his show.

Merv didn't actually meet Orson at the time of his first televised appearance. In 1967, Merv's assistants arranged for a camera crew to record Orson's responses to pre-articulated questions. Orson responded, on tape, with his predictably cadenced style. It wasn't until 1976 that Orson made a live

Christopher Atkins
The Blue Lagoon

459

appearance on Merv's show, face-to-face, with cameras rolling.

Merv's staff had spent weeks researching the director's life. But once the interview began, Merv virtually had to throw out all his notes. Appearing for ninety minutes on a show devoted entirely to him, Orson was a self-generating machine, directing and channeling the flow of conversation in his witty way.

Merv usually preferred to interact with his guests only as the cameras rolled, but in advance of many of Orson's shows he went backstage for some chitchat.

At first Orson was intimidating. "Okay, okay, let's get it out of the way. You think *Citizen Kane* was the greatest film of all time."

"As a matter of fact, I do," Merv said.

"That just shows that you have good taste," Orson said, checking his makeup.

Orson startled Merv when he warned him, "I do not want to dwell on my past career. Nor do I want to talk about the past in general. Also, I might as well come clean right now. Seventy-five percent of what I say in interviews is false."

The show that day was followed by a luncheon with Merv. As it turned out, Orson was to some degree captivated by Merv. "I thought you'd be bland. After all, I'm used to hanging out with Marlene Dietrich. But you're not. You're actually a good listener. For some reason, I think I can confide in you."

And over the years Orson did just that.

"I've toured the world, learned everything, done everything and everybody," the great man said. "I've tasted the wares of every star, including Judy Garland and Marilyn Monroe, as well as all the women in the brothels between Singapore and Shanghai. I practically auditioned every beautiful married woman during the time I lived in Brazil. I even tried out a concubine of the Moroccan Pasha of Marrakesh. In all my world travels, would you like to hear the most important trick I learned?"

Thinking he was about to learn some new sexual technique, Merv said, "I'm all ears."

"A gypsy in Rome taught me how to walk with a live chicken between my legs."

It was three years before Orson got really confidential with Merv, getting down to what Merv called "the good stuff."

"I lost my virginity when I was nine years old to some of my female cousins," Orson confessed. "On my mother's side. The place, and I remember it well, was Woodstock, Illinois. These girls had their way with me."

"Nine years old," Merv said in astonishment. "I don't think I could even get it up back then."

"Oh, please, childhood sexuality is a big thing. I started masturbating when I was five years old. Italian men, especially, believe that any young boy is meat for a quick seduction, and that seduction will have no effect on him or on his masculinity when he grows up."

One chilly night in a Greenwich Village restaurant, when Orson was having dinner with Merv and Hadley, Hadley dared ask the question that he and Merv had speculated about for weeks. "Did you ever walk on the wild side like Merv and me?"

"You mean, gay?" Orson said. "Of course, my dear boy. I'm especially fond of seducing black women—take Eartha Kitt or Lena Horne, for example—and beautiful boy ass. In fact, I always seduce my actors and make them fall in love with me. From my earliest years in Hollywood, I was the Lillie Langtry of the older homosexual set. All of them lusted for me. Lucille Ball started all those rumors about me being queer in Hollywood because I couldn't get it up for the bitch one night. Let's face it: Hollywood has never been comfortable with the queer thing. One night at the Brown Derby, Guinn 'Big Boy' Williams came up to me and accused me of being queer in the loudest voice possible. There was sudden silence throughout that busy restaurant. A lot of people thought 'Big Boy' was going to punch me out. He pulled out this pocket knife. I thought he was going to stab me, but he merely cut off my red tie and then stormed out of the restaurant."

Merv liked it when Orson told stories about his early life and his encounters with Hollywood greats. "As a young kid, I worshipped John Barrymore and got to know him well. When he was appearing in *Hamlet* on Broadway, he wanted me to give him a blow-job in his dressing room before he went on stage. When he was performing *Hamlet*, I stood in the wings of the theater with a bucket of champagne. Between scenes he'd come to me and lustily drink from that bubbly."

In April of 1982, during one of his many interviews, Orson said to Merv, "I try to be a Christian, but I don't pray really because I don't want to bore God."

Merv appeared with Orson for a final taping on October 8, 1985. Before the show, Orson summoned Merv backstage and told him "we can gossip a bit on your

With minutes to live
Orson Welles

461

show tonight."

"You mean all those gossipy questions I've wanted to ask for years about Marlene and Rita?"

"Yes," Orson said. "Ask *anything* you want. Even questions about *Citizen Kane*, and you know I don't like to speak about that."

Merv had never seen Orson look so bad. He was haggard, his eyes sunken deep into his head, and despite being supported with a cane, he could barely stand up. "Maybe there's one question I won't answer."

"What's that?" Merv asked.

"If I hadn't gone into films, I would have been a dress designer like Coco Chanel. I love women's clothes. I love the women who wear them. When I was young, I used to dress up like a woman. Not any more. No one designs tents to fit all this whale blubber I carry around."

Merv did not really take advantage of this taped opportunity for final insights into Orson, and as the cameras rolled, both his questions and Orson's responses were innocuous and rather bland.

After the show, Merv walked Orson to the limousine he'd arranged for him. Before getting into the car, Orson said, "I think what gives dignity and tragedy, as well as meaning and beauty to life, is the fact that we will die. It is one of the great gifts of God, if you happen to believe in Him, that we *are* going to die. It would be terrible if we weren't."

Merv watched as Orson hobbled to the waiting limousine, where the chauffeur helped him into the back seat. As the car drove off, Orson waved *adieu*. "I had this gut feeling I'd never see him again. Fifty shows. Imagine that. Fifty fucking shows."

A call from Hadley came in for Merv two hours later. "It just came on television. A bulletin. Orson is dead."

As a commemoration of Orson's life, and as a sad footnote to his departure, Merv booked Rita Hayworth onto his show to talk about Orson. During their time together before the cameras, Merv was stunned when she said she didn't remember ever having met him before, despite the fact that she'd used his home in Los Angeles for her romantic tryst with Aldo Ray. At this point in her life, she'd begun showing signs of Alzheimer's disease, which as the years went by, would eventually destroy her life. As the cameras rolled, she said nothing of interest about Orson, her remarkable career, or

Rita Hayworth
"Merv, I hardly knew you."

462

the tabloid-ready aspects of her somewhat lurid personal life, which had included a widely publicized marriage to the Prince Aly Khan and a deep personal friendship with Marlene Dietrich.

"Rita is a fascinating person," Merv said. "I know that. But none of it came across that night. Except for her bizarre dress, I could have been interviewing a housewife from Duluth."

Merv told the press that Orson "was my favorite guest. An awesome character who was conversant on any topic I could think of. He'll be dearly missed."

"Days after Orson died, Merv received a hand-scribbled card mailed by an unknown person, probably whomever had cleaned up Orson's apartment in the wake of his death. On it, Orson had scribbled a final message to Merv:

"We're born alone, we live alone, and we die alone. Only through our love and friendship can we create the illusion for the moment that we're not alone."

***

Both Merv and Nancy Reagan shared the same birth date (July 6). Both of these old friends also shared a fascination with the zodiac, living under the astrological sign of Cancer, the crab.

Nancy remembered watching an episode of *The Merv Griffin Show* in which he interviewed a panel of the country's leading astrologers. Merv later remembered introducing Nancy to Joan Quigley, a Vassar graduate and Nob Hill (San Francisco) socialite who wrote books on astrology.

Every morning, Merv read his horoscope before working the crossword puzzles. He and Nancy often talked about astrology, and both of them were firm believers in consulting the stars before making any big decision.

Ronald Reagan and Nancy had been heavily influenced by astrology even before he became governor of California. In those days, they relied on Jeanne Dixon for prophecy. When she accurately predicted specific details about the assassination of President John F. Kennedy, she became the best known astrologer and psychic in America.

Nancy had arranged several meetings between her husband, who wanted to be president in 1976, and Dixon, most of them within the Mayflower Hotel in Washington, D.C

When Dixon announced that Reagan's wish to become president did not coincide with the position of the stars, both he and Nancy broke off relations with her.

Merv first introduced Joan Quigley to Nancy when they appeared together on an episode of *The Merv Griffin Show* in the early 70s. After that meeting, Quigley called Nancy several times to discuss Reagan's future. But the astrologer and the First Lady did not really intensify their relationship until a deranged John Hinckley attempted to assassinate Reagan on March 30, 1981.

In the highly emotional aftermath of that attempted assassination, Merv was instrumental in bringing Quigley and Nancy together. He called Quigley to get her reaction, and was astonished to learn that she could have predicted it. Then he called Nancy at the White House and told her what Quigley had said.

In her book, *My Turn*, Nancy revealed that she said to Merv, "Oh, my God. *I could have stopped it?*"

"I'm such a worry-wart," she revealed to Merv. "My weight has dropped from 112 pounds to just 100 pounds. I just can't hold down food." She also told Merv that she would suddenly burst into tears with no provocation. After her dialogue with Merv, she hung up the phone and called Quigley.

After that, Nancy became "hooked" on Quigley and turned to her almost daily for advice. They became fast friends and confidants during the remaining years of the Reagan administration. To enable her to talk privately with Quigley, who advised her on matters both political and personal, Nancy had special, high-security phone lines installed in both the White House and at Camp David.

Nancy revealed to Merv that thanks to her status as First Lady, she received many services for free, including those of her hairdresser. But she claimed that Quigley charged her $3,000 a month. Merv graciously agreed to discretely factor those bills into his own payroll, but Nancy turned him down.

After the assassination attempt, Nancy became obsessed with tinkering with her husband's schedule, sometimes keeping him a virtual prisoner in the White House because Quigley considered it too dangerous for him to meet the public. At one point in his administration, the president did not appear in public for 120 consecutive days. Quigley justified this at the time with the assertion that there were "malevolent movements of Uranus and Saturn," and she feared not only the danger of another assassination attempt, but also the possibility of impeachment.

Nancy's concerns led to conflicts with Donald Regan, her husband's chief of staff

Nancy and **Merv:**
Her link to a notorious obsession

and a former bigwig at Merrill Lynch, as regards the details of Ronald's schedule. It was obvious almost from the beginning of his appointment that Nancy aggressively disliked Regan—and vice versa.

Quigley's input became so influential in White House affairs that it was she who picked the opening time and date for the summit meeting in Reykjavik, Iceland; the optimum time for the signing of an arms control treaty, and the best time for a presidential flight to Moscow.

Throughout these consultations, Nancy confided to Merv that "Ronnie is not just indulging me. He believes in astrology too. Regardless of the headlines, he reads first his horoscope and then the funnies before he peruses world headlines."

It was Nancy who played a crucial role in getting the chief of staff fired. He resigned in 1987 after the Iran-Contra affair and the distribution of mixed reviews about his job performance. He got even, however, writing a book entitled *For the Record: From Wall Street to Washington*. In that book, which generated headlines throughout the world, Regan described "Mrs. Reagan's dependence on the occult." As the First Lady was mocked and ridiculed throughout the land, especially on late-night TV, Merv called to offer his support. "Hold in there," he advised her.

Public reaction throughout the late 1980s was the most unrelentingly negative of Nancy's career. Carl Sagan, writing an article entitled "The Demon-Haunted World," was particularly harsh. "Some portion of the decision-making that influences the future of civilization is plainly in the hands of charlatans."

As a result of this publicity, Quigley was dismissed as the White House astrologer. Nancy called her and demanded that she "lie and never tell anyone anything." Quigley's response? In 1990, she wrote and published a book, revealing everything.

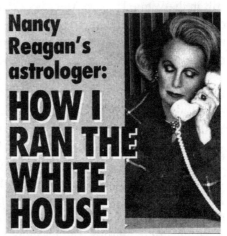

In her tell-all, *What Does Joan Say? My Seven Years as a White House Astrologer to Nancy and Ronald Reagan*, Quigley described herself as the power behind the throne. Her book even announced that she had advised the times and dates when Air Force One could safely take off. As she claimed within her book:

Joan Quigley

465

"Not since the days of the Roman emperors—and never in the history of the United States presidency—has an astrologer played such a significant role in a nation's affairs of State."

Prior to the publication of Quigley's book, when Nancy had returned to her home in California, she increasingly relied on Merv, calling him "My Rock." On some days, he found she had been crying for hours. He tried to revive her spirits by urging her to get dressed and accompany him either for lunch or for dinner at little hidden places known to him along the California coastline. Gradually, she began to accept these invitations, relying on Merv more and more as her best friend and closest confidant.

In the late 1980s, shortly after her departure from the White House, Nancy had often checked with Merv about statements she planned for insertion in *My Turn: The Memoirs of Nancy Reagan* as co-authored with William Novak. It was Merv who urged her to include a section on astrology and to explain, in simple terms, her interest in psychic phenomena. Immediately below is an excerpt which resulted from Merv's intervention:

"What it boils down to is that each person has his or her own ways of coping with trauma and grief, with the pain of life, and astrology was one of mine. Don't criticize me, I wanted to say, until you have stood in my place. This helped me. Nobody was hurt by it—except, possibly, me."

Merv had been privy to one of the darkest secrets of the Reagan White House, learning that the president had contracted Alzheimer's disease while still in the White House. Merv was kept abreast of the devastating effects the disease had on the former president, as each day he escaped from reality into a world of his own, resurfacing only briefly before retreating again into his own private space.

"The coming years—maybe it will be only months—will be the most difficult of my life," Nancy confided to Merv. "*Please*, be there for me."

"It will be the greatest honor of my life to stand by you," Merv said gallantly.

***

In the 1980s, Merv formed an unlikely friendship with the notorious wheeler-dealer, Armand Hammer, the flamboyant U.S. business tycoon who, like the decade itself, was in his 80s. Noted for his fabulous art collections, his occasional philanthropy, and his close ties to the Soviet Union, the mogul was associated with Occidental Petroleum. Merv became friendly with Armand's third wife, Frances Barrett, a wealthy and stylish widow whom Armand had married in 1956.

Armand's claim to fame: "I am the only man in history to have been friendly with both Ronald Reagan and Vladimir Lenin."

Hammer dabbled in politics and made large illegal contributions to the Richard Nixon campaign. He was convicted for this, but was later pardoned by another Republican "buddy" of his, President George Herbert Walker Bush. Merv always suspected, perhaps accurately, that Armand laundered money for the Soviets.

Hammer hated *Jeopardy!* but loved *Wheel of Fortune*. Whenever he traveled, he ordered his staff to tape *Wheel* so he wouldn't miss a show. Later, in Moscow, he sold these tapes to the Russians, who used them as inspiration for the launch of their own Soviet version of *Wheel*. Merv never got one cent of royalties.

Armand kindled a passion in Merv for Arabian stallions, an interest that he retained for the rest of his life. Merv and Armand often journeyed together to Scottsdale, Arizona for auctions of these stunning horses. Armand would rhapsodize about the beauty of an animal, the shape of its head, its high tail carriage, its intelligence and stamina, its spirit. "They have speed, refinement, endurance, and good bones," Armand told Merv. "Their bloodlines are the finest of any horse in the world. The Bedouin people used to bring the horses into their tents at night to protect them."

"I don't want to sleep with one," Merv said jokingly. "Their dicks are too big. But I'd like to purchase one."

Thus began Merv's collection of these Arabian stallions. He paid one-hundred and fifty thousand dollars for a particularly fabulous specimen. Soonafter, the market for the animals collapsed. The monetary worth of the horses fell to an average of less than $3,000 each. But Merv wasn't interested in making money from his ownership of the horses. He wanted to own the most prized stallions in America.

Armand proposed a deal to Merv that seriously tempted him. For forty-five million, Armand said he would purchase half of Merv Griffin Enterprises, whose most valuable nuggets included *Wheel of Fortune* and *Jeopardy!* To negotiate the fine points of the deal, Armand brought in the famed attorney Louis Nizer.

To counterpunch, Merv flew in Bobby Schulman, considered in legal circles to be the best tax attorney in the world. When Schulman discovered that Armand planned to put up "zero capital," he urged Merv to veto the deal and flew back to London.

Years later Merv said, "Thank God Armand fucked up that deal. Around the corner was waiting the sweetheart deal of my life, only I didn't know it at the time."

Appearing on TV with Bill Cosby, Armand proclaimed that a cure for cancer was imminent, but he died of bone marrow cancer in December of 1990 before living to see that happen.

***

Whereas the death of Rock Hudson in 1985 brought out the loyalty and courage of such friends as Elizabeth Taylor, a certified and secure heterosexual, it did not inspire anything particularly admirable in Merv.

The world had changed many times since the halcyon 1950s when both men, each born in 1925, were part of a small, secretive colony of gay men in the Greater Los Angeles area. Since then, both Merv and Rock had become big stars. But whereas Rock's career had virtually collapsed, Merv's fame and earning capacity were bigger than ever.

AIDS had driven Rock kicking and screaming out of his closet, but Merv preferred to keep the doors of his own closet tightly locked. He feared that with reporters and paparazzi hanging out at Rock's estate, "The Castle," he would be tainted with the suspicion of homosexuality for having come to call on his dying comrade.

To visit or not to visit was the question he fretted over before an unexpected call came in from Ronald Reagan at the White House. Like Merv, both Ronnie and Nancy had been longtime friends of Rock's. The President was flying to the West Coast with Nancy, and he felt that it might be appropriate for them to call on Rock for a final goodbye.

Knowing about Merv's private relationship with the stricken star, the President suggested that he accompany them to The Castle as part of their visit. Merv could not turn down a request from the President, and he agreed to go. He told aides "It'll be safe if I arrive there with Nancy and Ronnie on each of my arms."

That very afternoon, after accepting the President's invitation, Merv received a shocker phone call from one of his attorneys (name not known). To his dismay, Merv learned that from his sickbed, Rock had been dictating an authorized tell-all autobiography. Because he desperately didn't want to be Outed in Rock's book, Merv became even more eager to accompany the Reagans during their visit. Merv's plan involved remaining behind with

Nancy and Ronnie:
The Republican Lip-Lock

468

Rock after the Reagans' departure so that Merv could then discuss what Rock planned to include in the book.

Two days later, Merv received another call from the White House. With his trademark humor and charm, Reagan informed Merv that his advisers thought that it would be "politically unwise to call on Rock. It's a hot political potato, and Nancy and I can't pick it up without getting burned. We've always been fond of Rock, but we can't stand by him in his hour of need. He'll be in both of our prayers, however."

Merv said he understood and, before hanging up, sent his love to Nancy. The Reagan withdrawal left Merv alone with his dilemma. With the future book looming, Merv finally opted to call on Rock with his final request, with or without the Reagans.

Somehow Merv managed to slip in and out of The Castle without detection. It is suspected that Rock's closest friend, the gay actor, George Nader, arranged the secret rendezvous, without alerting Rock's staff or even his own lover, Mark Miller. Merv wanted his visit to be totally secretive, and he knew that George was trustworthy and capable of keeping a secret.

Lying on his deathbed, Rock was gaunt, frail, and enfeebled. Hollow-cheeked and sunken-eyed, he was a shell of his former robust self, and his weight had dropped to an alarming ninety-eight pounds. AIDS, like some devouring cancer, seemed to be feeding on his body. He told Merv that the only food he could hold down was tapioca pudding.

Suffering from acute metastatic liver disease, he had lost control of his bodily functions, and his pajamas had to be changed frequently by a nurse.

Merv later told Eva Gabor that he was shocked by Rock's appearance. "My memory of him was of this big, strapping truck driver kind of guy in tight blue jeans. He was the sex symbol of the 50s. All of us wanted him, and I was among the lucky few whose dreams came true. When I saw him in his bed, he looked like he'd died already, except that the corpse hadn't been buried."

Seeing Merv, Rock expressed his bitterness that the President and First Lady had refused a final visit based on their fear of offending the Moral Majority. Rock had arranged for his former lover, Tom Clark, to deliver a brief statement to reporters and the paparazzi clustered around the gates to The Castle. It read:

> *"Reagan is yet to actually say the word AIDS in public. He and his people are so afraid of the Far Right. Fuck them all!"*

Exactly what transpired between Merv and Rock that day will never be known. What little *is* known came from Eva Gabor, who talked indiscreetly to her network of friends. Merv did tell Eva that Rock claimed "the vultures are circling over me."

Merv departed from The Castle that night with Rock's firm commitment that he would not be Outed in his autobiography. He told Eva that Rock had claimed that his book would not be "the authentic story of my life. It's a vanilla version." Apparently, Rock feared that if he wrote an authentic tell-all, he would reveal details about the private lives of many famous men in Hollywood, who might then possibly sue his estate for libel.

Merv also told Eva that Rock had confessed to love affairs with three of the biggest stars in Hollywood, "names never before tarred with the lavender brush," Merv said.

"Never trust a man, *dahlink*," Eva responded. "When they're horny, any available hole will do."

It appeared that the main support for Rock's will to live were the cards, letters, telegrams, and gifts pouring in from around the world. And although the Reagans weren't standing by him, he was being contacted by dozens of luminaries who admired his courage and wished him god speed. They included Marlene Dietrich, Madonna, and Ava Gardner.

When Elizabeth Taylor organized a benefit dinner for Rock in Los Angeles, other stars also publicly stood up. They included Burt Reynolds, Ricardo Montalban, Burt Lancaster, Shirley MacLaine, and Linda Evans. Later, however, Elizabeth reported that dozens of other stars, including Frank Sinatra, had turned her down, not wanting to identify themselves with either AIDS or its victims.

When Roddy McDowall learned of Merv's encounter with Rock, he told friends, "Merv is not a crusader. I don't remember that he ever advocated anything politically—or artistically for that matter. Even though he has access to the Reagans, who could help our kind, his closet keeps him shockingly silent. His voice would make a huge difference if he'd speak out about all the suffering and horrific deaths occurring in America. But that's probably too much to expect from him. Let's face it: He created TV programs that entertained millions of people around the world. He has his fans to think of. Merv will do anything to preserve his image. You just have to admire his greatness and forget those moments when he's small."

It was George Nader who called Merv on October 2, 1985. "Rock left us at 8:45 this morning."

Perhaps because he was dismayed and shocked, or perhaps because he didn't know how to respond, Merv uttered one of the blandest statements he'd ever made, so innocuous that at the time, it appeared insensitive. "Well, all of us have to go sometime."

Another, more sensitive, acknowledgment of Rock's death came from Michael Nader, the nephew of George Nader. Michael had appeared with

Rock in nine separate episodes of the hit TV series *Dynasty* in 1984 and 1985. "Rock's gone," Michael told the press. "But the most important thing is that he was *here*—that he was a wonderful guy while he was here."

The website, *QueerTwoCents.com*, did not admire Rock's courage, claiming, "The sad truth of the matter is that had he not contracted HIV and developed AIDS, Rock Hudson, like Merv Griffin, most likely would have continued to live his life in a 'glass closet,' no doubt abetted by the mainstream media."

***

In 1986, at the ripe age of sixty, while Merv vacationed in Rio de Janeiro, Columbia Entertainment, a branch of the Coca-Cola Company, was concluding its negotiations to buy him out. Merv Griffin Enterprises had originated in 1964 as Merv Griffin Productions, a name that had endured for two decades.

Even before his return to the U.S., the deal was cemented for a cool $250 million. He'd retain creative control of both *Jeopardy!* and *Wheel of Fortune*, and he'd also occupy a seat on the board of directors of Columbia Entertainment. At the time, that company was led by Frank Biondi, who would later take over Viacom, reporting directly to its aging chairman, Sumner Redstone.

"The syndicated Merv Griffin programs have fully penetrated American culture," said Robert J. Thompson, founding director of the Bleier Center for Television and Popular Culture at Syracuse University. "He was a producer who understood how those kinds of programs worked with viewers. We tend to be watching those types of shows when diapering a child or preparing a meal, waiting for the chaos of everyone coming home in the afternoon."

After the sale was signed and sealed, Merv was bewildered, not only by getting such a bundle of cash, but in wondering what he was going to do with the rest of his life. "I'm too young to retire," he told a staff member. "I'm too active, too much alive. I can't see myself sitting out in the California sun waiting around for lunch."

He considered various options, including the purchase of Hebrew National Foods, which produced kosher products such as all-beef hot dogs.

Merv learned that his friend, Malcolm Forbes, had placed him on the list of the four-hundred richest men and women in America. He was less impressed when he learned that Forbes' editorial board had also included a dead woman on the list. Griffin knocked Bob Hope off the list as the richest performer in entertainment history.

***

Having sold his major media assets to Columbia, Merv made another career-changing decision, opting to retire from his involvement with *The Merv Griffin Show.* He announced that the final episode of the show would be aired on September 5, 1986.

As he made clear to his staff, "There's nobody left to talk to unless you want to book Zsa Zsa Gabor one more time. At least she's interesting, unlike those soap opera stars we've been booking. Do I really care about what some blonde bimbo starlet thinks about the way Ronnie is running the U.S. government or hear that she thinks Nancy depends too much on the color red?"

Merv sat with Peter Barsocchini the night before he recorded his last talk show. It would include a compilation of clips from the dozens of shows presented since he first went on the air with *The Merv Griffin Show* back in 1962.

According to Barsocchini, both men talked in his dressing room as Merv summoned the energy for a final appearance.

"Do you know what this feels like?" Merv said to Barsocchini. "It's like I've been at the best dinner party ever given—and that it's about to end."

Thousands of fans felt the same way, and Merv was bombarded with letters from all over America, lamenting the demise of the show. One housewife from Yonkers said she'd never missed a single Merv show since its inauguration in 1962, and that she'd followed him faithfully year after year as he moved from channel to channel.

Merv estimated that during his career as a talk show host, he'd had on-the-air dialogues with twenty-five thousand people. "I've interviewed almost everybody important in the world, from all walks of life," he told Eva Gabor. "And now, I've had it. I've decided to devote time to my game shows and a lot of time to just having fun."

To Hadley, he said, "Life's too short not to have fun. I've been holding back. And anyway, what beautiful guy would agree to have sex with me without the exchange of a few hundred dollar bills?" Hadley was instructed to continue arranging "fun and games" for Merv. And he wasn't talking about TV game shows.

After abandoning his show forever, and as the years went by, a reporter asked Merv if he missed talking to millions of Americans every day. "Sure, I do," he said, "but what I miss most is introducing new talent to the world. Imagine giving a jump start to the careers of Whitney Houston and Jerry

Carmel's most stately resident

472

Seinfeld. Of course, they would have eventually done very well on their own."

After taping his last episode of *The Merv Griffin Show*, he disappeared "into nowhere" with his young aide, Ronnie Ward. Although it was widely understood that Ward is straight, their sudden disappearance led to unfounded speculation.

With Ward behind the wheel, Merv ordered him to, "Just drive—wherever the car will take us. We'll stop at any place that amuses us." As Merv later recalled, the couple ended up in the gambling town of Laughlin, Nevada, close to the California border.

"I talked Ronnie's ear off," Merv later recalled to his friends. "I guess I was really talking to myself, trying to figure out where to go from here. More than friends or family, I was married to my career—always, ever since I sang with Freddy Martin's band."

At the end of that long ride into the desert, Merv made a decision to promote Ward, at the time only in his twenties, as his personal assistant. Prior to that Merv had defined Ward as his secretary, even though his typing skills hadn't advanced beyond the hunt-and-peck system.

"I've never felt as compatible with anyone as I have with Ronnie," Merv told his associates. "If I ask him to do something for me, I know he'll carry it out beautifully. I trust him completely."

By December of 1995, most of Merv's business interests fell within the orbit of an entity known as Merv Griffin Entertainment. He took great pride in naming Ward as Vice Chairman of his newly organized company. He was put in charge of "establishing the strategy and focus" of Merv's many investments and business interests.

Merv told the press, "Ronnie has been with me for twenty-five years. Not only is he a brilliant facilitator of our established projects, but he also has a remarkable aptitude for spotting new areas of profitability. In addition to overseeing Merv Griffin Entertainment, he heads my thoroughbred operation, Merv Griffin Ranch Company, and he was responsible for the formation of our newest company, Worldwide L.P., which specializes in high-end residential real estate."

Ronnie Ward would not be the only young man Merv would pluck from relative obscurity and hurl into fame, the spotlight, and fortune.

***

At this point in his life and career, Merv could buy any home he wanted. He purchased a spectacular home in Pebble Beach on Carmel Bay, near where he'd once worked as a struggling singer. Here he could "find peace and tranquility," and entertain whatever private guests he wanted, away from the prying eyes of the press. Liberace continued to send him "only the most prized of specimens."

Whereas some of his neighbors, including Kim Novak and Jean Arthur, tended to be somewhat reclusive, others, such as Clint Eastwood were genuinely friendly and accessible to him. Another neighbor, Jane Wyman, remembered Merv "from the old old days."

Whenever he needed "arm candy," Merv enrolled Eva Gabor, or perhaps Barbara MacFarland, who dealt in valuable antiques in a shop in Carmel. The paparazzi snapped dozens of pictures of Merv and Eva attending Eastwood's premier of *The Man Who Loved Cat Dancing*. They were accompanied by the film's star, Burt Reynolds, who at the time was deep into his affair with an older woman, Dinah Shore.

Clint Eastwood had introduced Merv to Transcendental Meditation, which fascinated him. Merv later cited TM for removing stress from his life, and he started meditating twenty minutes in the morning, followed by another twenty minutes at sunset. Years before, as the cameras rolled, he had interviewed the leader of the TM movement, Maharishi Mahesh Yogi. That episode of *The Merv Griffin Show* was credited with attracting almost fifty thousand converts to TM.

Merv's friendship with Clint had begun back in the 1960s, when Merv joined Clint as a resident of Carmel. An icon of macho, Clint was an unlikely candidate for the role of one of Merv's best friends. As owner of two homes within the region (one in Pebble Beach and one in the Carmel Valley), Merv supported Clint when he successfully ran for mayor of Carmel-by-the-Sea. "We share the same political views," Merv told reporters.

Merv loved hearing Clint's stories of his early days in Hollywood, going back to when he was a contract player at Universal International. Just before firing him, a director said, accusingly, "your Adam's Apple is too big." That same director, that same day, also fired another contract player, Burt Reynolds.

It is presumed that Clint knew Merv was gay. If he did, that was hardly a problem for him. He once said, "The most gentle people in the world are macho males, people who are confident in their masculinity and have a feeling of well-being in themselves. They don't have to kick in doors, mistreat women, or make fun of gays." Clint served as mayor of Carmel from 1986 to 1988.

Growing up in Northern California, Clint had been a fan of Merv's long before he actually met him. He recalled listening to him on radio KFRC, broad-

Dirty Harry
Clint Eastwood

474

casting from San Francisco. The two men launched a tennis tournament at Pebble Beach that for years brought in a lot of celebrities. When Merv died, Clint noted that he had been a loyal friend to a lot of people, and recalled a dinner at his house in Carmel Valley that included Cary Grant, Lucille Ball, and James Stewart. Clint also revealed that Merv in later life became a close friend of Johnny Carson, their sometimes bitter rivalry for late-night ratings a thing of the past.

Even though they developed some semblance of a friendship later in life, Merv said he never really approved of Carson. "He was sad, depressed, probably in need of a shrink. He cheated on his wives. He stayed at this penthouse at Caesars Palace with a private pool. He'd invite all the beautiful showgirls up for skinny dipping, some two dozen on a good night. He had many of them. A real Sultan in his harem. He never visited his son when he was confined to a mental hospital. He was just as cold as his mother, who, or so I heard, was colder than any icicle in Nebraska in February."

***

In his converted black military helicopter, Merv traveled the traffic-saturated 130 miles between Los Angeles and his elegant, 240-acre spread, La Quinta Ranch, which he'd purchased with his newly acquired millions. The sprawling ranch stood in the Coachella Valley near Palm Springs.

The compound's airy, Moroccan-themed main house was modeled on Yves St. Laurent's mansion in Marrakesh, Morocco. The estate boasted horse barns housing some fifty thoroughbreds; a manmade lake, Lac Merveilleux; a private racetrack, and some 3,000 cultivated roses.

Like Merv himself, Cary Grant was also a closeted homosexual, and during his late middle-aged years, he occasionally visited La Quinta. "Why would you ever want to leave this place? It's Shangri-la." Cary stood at twelve-foot high French windows, opening onto a panorama of a fifty-foot-high geyser spouting from the waters of Lac Merveilleux.

The next morning Cary joined Merv for breakfast, traversing one of the world's biggest Persian carpets, set atop floors crafted from purple and white marble, within a living room decorated with Moroccan rifles inlaid with ivory and silver.

Working on a crossword puzzle, Merv sat on his terrace under a mammoth umbrella painted with sunflower yellow butterflies and pink flamingos. He was eating oatmeal and smoking a lot of cigarettes.

Over breakfast, the two superstars spoke of retirement and their upcoming deaths. "To me, death is retirement," Merv told him. "I'll never retire. On the way to my grave, I'll be devising some new TV game show. I'm still working. After breakfast, I'll be on the phone reaching out to my empire. It keeps me alive. Why don't you go back to work?"

"There are no good scripts anymore," Cary said, "and at my age I don't do nude scenes."

Out of earshot of Cary, Zsa Zsa had called Merv. "They keep telling me what a great lover he is, but you can't prove that by me."

Cary and Merv discussed opportunistic hustlers who might try to expose them. "Of course, when we're dead, all the books will write about our homosexuality. But at least we can suppress it while we're still alive." He warned Merv never to go to court on a sexual harassment or alimony charge. "Anything can happen before a jury," Cary said. "Some son of a bitch could get millions."

Privately he told Merv, who in turn told Eva, that he'd once been arrested going down on a young sales clerk in the men's room of a department store in Los Angeles. "Howard Hughes intervened for me and paid off the cops. I was released and the matter was hushed up."

"Another, somewhat similar case was instigated by a woman," Cary said. "She claimed I picked up her teenage son along the highway and made advances toward him. Once again, Howard came through for me. He'd faced similar incidents himself."

Before parting, Cary gave Merv one final piece of advice: "Always wear women's nylon panties when traveling. They're easier to wash and hang up to dry."

***

Jolie Gabor, mother of the three most famous living courtesans in the world, took delight in Merv, even though, despite her urging, he constantly refused to marry her daughter, Eva.

"My God, Jolie," Merv said in protest. "Between the three of them, your daughters have already had twenty-one husbands. You really don't need to add me to the list."

Sometimes, Jolie cooked dinner for Merv, using lots of paprika and sour cream. But one night he found hot dogs in her stew. "Her stuffed goose neck, though, was the world's best," Merv said. Jolie always asserted that Merv loved her goulash. "As anybody can see from the looks of him, he could never get enough of it."

Merv would annoy her by constantly pestering her

Confessions from
a men's room:
Cary Grant

to reveal her age. "I am a timeless wonder," she told him. "Ageless. An enchantress."

Merv could sit and listen to Jolie for hours as she told tall tales about her remarkable life. He didn't know if they were true or not. Did President Dwight Eisenhower really make a pass at her?

"I don't think it would have done any good if I had accepted," she told Merv. "I heard he was impotent. Poor Mamie. I failed with her too. I constantly tried to get her to cut her bangs and adopt a new hair style, but she refused."

One night over wine Jolie confided to Merv that Zsa Zsa and Eva wanted as their escorts men with money. "And, God knows, you have money, Merv. Everything you touch turns to gold. Midas would be jealous. I, however, always followed my heart, and that's why I fell for Edmund de Szigethy of Transylvania. He had no money but he wanted to marry me even though I was an older woman. God, I detest that expression. He had only twenty-seven dollars when we went out on our first date. Twenty-two of those dollars he spent on roses for me. After that gesture, I had to marry him."

"Oh, that Conrad Hilton," Jolie told Merv one night. "He was such a louse. Zsa Zsa had a poor divorce settlement with him. She should have taken him for millions, and she should have gotten free accommodations at Hiltons for the rest of her life, even a permanent suite for her at the Plaza. Whenever Zsa Zsa stays at a Hilton, she has to pay. Stupid! Ridiculous!"

"But Zsa Zsa got even with Conrad," she claimed. "She slept with his son Nicky and told me that he was a much better lover than her husband, his father. Of course, you'll have to check with Elizabeth Taylor for the lowdown on Nicky."

"I don't need to check with anybody about Nicky Hilton," Merv claimed.

"Oh, I see," Jolie said, raising an eyebrow. "I have a theory about notorious womanizers. To them, all cats are gray at night."

"Zsa Zsa's great love was Porfirio Rubirosa, and I desperately wanted him to be my son-in-law," she said. "He was suave and sophisticated and knew how to treat a lady. But he dumped Zsa Zsa for Barbara Hutton instead. After all, she was one of the richest women in the world. Once, I spirited Rubi away from news reporters by dressing him in drag."

"Rubi in drag is a bit much for my meager mind to conjure up," Merv said.

"I've never told anybody this before, but once, at a formal dinner, I sat next to Rubi," she said. "At one point he discreetly took my hand and placed it over his genitals. I had never felt anything like that in my life. Surely he rivaled any bull. Rubi told me, 'That's what keeps Zsa Zsa as contented as a cow.'"

"Unlike my daughters, I have never pursued men with large penises," she claimed. "Four or five inches are adequate for me, though three is too small. What about your tastes? What do you consider as the ideal penis size for a man?"

"Eight and a half inches," he said. "Anything above that and you're a show-off."

"Magda and Zsa Zsa had to double up on that rogue, George Sanders," Jolie said. "I called George 'The Deep Freeze,' although I was tempted to go to bed with him myself just to see what sex appeal he had that enthralled my two daughters so much that they married him. Eva told me George once tried to seduce her as well, but thank God Eva had enough sense to avoid him."

"Clark Gable also asked me to marry him, but I said no," she confessed. "Too many women told me how inadequate he was in bed. He also had a homosexual side, believe it or not."

She used to brag to Merv that in 1939 she had arrived in New York from Hungary with "only one hundred dollars and a diamond ring. I later ended up owning a jewelry shop on Madison Avenue. Even Elizabeth Taylor came to me in those days to buy her diamonds."

When Merv visited Jolie at her modest home on Oscalete Road in Los Angeles, he was amazed at how she'd glamorized the place. "I like to make from nothing a something," she told him.

Over the years, Merv concocted many schemes to bring Jolie onto his show, including once when he wanted to have all four Gabors on at the same time. "Jack Paar called me years ago and proposed the same thing," she told Merv. On another occasion, Merv wanted to bring out five mothers of famous daughters for a gabfest. "Sounds more like a bitchfest to me," Jolie countered.

Months before Jolie's death in 1997, Merv paid her a visit. "I found her disconnected from reality," he later said. "She didn't remember that Eva, her youngest daughter, had died on July 4, 1995. I certainly didn't tell her. And at that point, I'm not sure if she even knew who Eva was."

When Jolie died at Rancho Mirage in California on April 1, 1997, Merv was saddened and sent a huge bouquet. He noticed that many newspaper accounts listed her age as ninety-six, but Eva had told Merv that Jolie was actually an astonishing 104.

"My beloved mother lived in an era when women lied about their age," Zsa Zsa said. "She always told me that a woman should lie by decades, not just five or six years. It's easier to remember dates that way if you lie by decades."

The world's oldest living courtesan:
Jolie Gabor

478

Jolie's final advice to Merv, back when she was still coherent, was "pawn a diamond if you have to keep the champagne flowing. Life's a gamble. You must know how to play it—and you sure did play it more than anybody else I've ever known. Kings and royalty I have known were often penniless. They still have the title and no money. You have no title and lots of money. Zsa Zsa still loves titles, and even I married a penniless count myself. But I have decided in the end that it's money that is more important than worthless European titles of long ago."

Asked to comment on Jolie's death, Merv told his aides, "If she hadn't trod on this Earth, Dominick Dunne would have had to invent her. Jolie was Euro before the word Eurotrash was invented. Her emeralds may have been flawed or faux but Jolie Gabor was the real thing."

***

At least five months before he died in 1987 at the age of sixty-seven, Liberace knew he had AIDS. He summoned Merv to his side. Slipping into Palm Springs, Merv drove himself to Liberace's elegant estate, The Cloister.

Merv later revealed to Hadley that he almost wanted to scream when he saw Liberace's wasted body and gaunt face. "He was a shadow version of himself, almost ghoulish. In his eyes I noticed this terrible fear. It was heartbreaking. He didn't want to talk about the present, only the past, only the good times around his pool, which had once been peopled with the most beautiful boys ever assembled. Oh, those pool parties of his. Rock Hudson with all his beautiful boys could never give pool parties like Lee. I never knew where he found all those guys. No one has ever seen the likes of Lee before—and perhaps never will again."

A correspondent for *Newsweek*, Bill Barol, summed it up best when he reviewed a Liberace event at Manhattan's Radio City Music Hall. "Liberace flew in from the wings suspended on a wire; introduced his valet/chauffeur; put on a purple sequined and feathered robe; took it off; played Chopin on a Lucite piano with lacework trim; did a soft shoe; bestowed a selection of gifts on a audience member; shamelessly plugged his new book and Las Vegas restaurant; drove onstage in a red, white, and blue Rolls-Royce; peeled away a red, white and blue sequined-and-feathered robe to reveal red, white and blue satin hot pants, and grabbed a red, white, and blue sequined baton to lead the Rockettes in 'The Stars and Stripes Forever.' This was all before intermission."

Sitting up in bed, Liberace told Merv that, "A lot of those gay libbers are writing pestering me, demanding that I finally come out of the closet and admit I'm gay. I'm not going to do it, and I don't think you should do so either.

Admitting I'm gay in my final hours would destroy what I've worked for for more than four decades. More than being an entertainer, I was this ethereal concept. I pleased everybody, offended no one. You should do the same. Besides, I'm not a crusader. Let Paul Newman or Marlon Brando do that. You and I should forever remain in the closet, although I have no doubt that biographers will Out us after we're dead. It's inevitable."

When Merv complimented Liberace on the black lace negligée he was wearing, the entertainer asserted, "I've always liked drag. As a teenager, I was a student at West Milwaukee High. Every year we dressed up in costumes of famous people. I came as Greta Garbo. Slinky gown. Blonde wig. Heavy makeup. I won first prize."

Liberace was so tired and ailing that he managed a dialogue with Merv for less than an hour before he told him he'd have to leave. "I want you to go now, dear old friend. But I don't want you to remember me as a pathetic old queer dying in bed of AIDS."

He asked Merv to go out into the garden and then return to the living room in fifteen minutes. A male aide came in to help Liberace out of bed and slowly walk him to the living room, where he seated himself at his piano.

After his interval in the garden, Liberace told him, "I'm going to play my theme song, 'I Don't Care,' and I want you to leave and not look back. Just walk out the door to the sound of my music."

Merv kissed Liberace's forehead and departed as he'd been instructed. Outside, the tears rolled down his cheeks. He later told friends, "I felt that I was leaving part of my life in that house with my dying friend. It was one of my most painful moments."

Within the hour, Merv had fled, incognito, from Palm Springs.

After his death, Liberace's aides lied to the press, issuing a statement about how the flamboyant entertainer had died of congestive heart failure. Shortly thereafter, a coroner's inquest asserted that he'd died of complications resulting from AIDS. Ironically, even after his death, Wladziu Valentino Liberace remained locked in the closet, denying his homosexuality even from beyond the grave.

Merv, probably motivated by a fear of "Outing" himself, never publicly discussed his enduring friendship with Liberace. His only comment, delivered with a giveaway wink, was, "He certainly was one of the great peacocks of our century." He went on to assert that Liberace had "paved the way" for such androgynous superstars as Michael Jackson, Elton John, and Boy George.

Face-lifted **Liberace:**
The final cover-up.

480

After his funeral, a reporter summarized one of show business's longest-running acts. "Liberace's was a life of exquisite paradox involving flamboyance and repression, kitsch and concealment."

***

In 1955, the year of its opening, the Beverly Hilton Hotel was hailed as "the most sumptuous hotel in the world" as part of an opening celebration presided over by Conrad Hilton himself. Richard Nixon showed up as part of the ceremony, recalling a time when the land adjacent to Wilshire Boulevard was mostly farmland. In the audience, listening to Nixon, was a photogenic "Hollywood couple" affectionately known as Ronnie and Nancy.

It was at this same hotel that Merv appeared years later to celebrate President Reagan's 80th birthday dinner gala.

At the 1955 inauguration, Esther Williams, MGM's mermaid, had swum through thousands of floating gardenias as part of the launch of the Hilton's Aqua Star Pool, the largest in Beverly Hills. All but a few of the U.S. presidents, from John F. Kennedy to Bill Clinton, had been involved in sexual trysts within the hotel's presidential suite. Kennedy came to view the Beverly Hilton as the Western White House. Through the lobby paraded every movie star from Judy Garland to Elizabeth Taylor.

Dale Olsen, longtime Hollywood publicist and journalist, summed it up nicely: "There hasn't been a celebrity in Hollywood for the past fifty years that hasn't been to the Beverly Hilton at least several times. It is the gathering place of the stars."

From the very beginning, the hotel was known for secret liaisons among the stars. Unfounded rumors spread quickly. Was Tony Curtis really seen late at night leaving the room of Laurence Olivier? Did Barbra Streisand and Steve McQueen share a suite for a night?

With the passing of decades, as celebrities flocked to newer and more cutting-edge properties, the 1950s landmark had become a bit battered and had lost much of its prestige,

For years, Merv had been "itching" to get into the hotel business, dreaming of restoring the Beverly Hilton to its former glory. When it came onto the market, he went for it. On November 16, 1987, Merv bought the hotel from Hilton Hotels Corporation and the Prudential Insurance Company. After the deal was signed, he spent $60 million restoring it.

The Beverly Hilton had been an old stamping ground for Merv, and it was associated with what he called "one of the great nights of my life." In the hotel's International Ballroom, he'd been presented with the Will Rogers Memorial Award by the Beverly Hills Chamber of Commerce.

Orson Welles waddled in that night to pay a public tribute to Merv, and even the latest incarnation of Freddy Martin's Orchestra turned out to provide the music. "As in olden days," Merv said, "I sang with Freddy's boys once again, warbling 'Tonight We Love.'"

After Merv's takeover of the hotel, he asked Eva Gabor to decorate the women's bathroom in the International Ballroom. She chose a soft pink marble, claiming, "I want to make it a room where a lady likes to linger while powdering her nose." Caught in the can in 2000 at the Golden Globe Awards, Renée Zellwegger was blasting off as her name was called to accept the award.

The Beverly Hilton had been hosting the Golden Globe Awards since March 16, 1961, when Stanley Kubrick's *Spartacus* took the award for Best Picture.

Merv was delighted when his hotel could host a Royal Tribute to Cary Grant on October 17, 1988, an evening that netted more than a million dollars for the Princess Grace Foundation. Everyone from Monaco royalty to A-list entertainers came.

Merv later told Hadley that during the break, "I found myself standing at the urinals side by side with Frank Sinatra, Burt Lancaster, and Cary Grant. Cary and Burt came up a little short, but Frank let it dangle with no hand needed. He lit a cigarette as all three of us took in the view."

Within the hotel, in 1998, Merv launched The Coconut Club, the latest incarnation of the Cocoanut Grove where he'd once sung with Freddy Martin's Orchestra. Merv loved the word coconut, probably because it evoked his Big Band hit, "I've Got a Lovely Bunch of Coconuts."

For decorations, he commissioned a faux-tropical setting with gold and silver palm trees and wild-eyed monkeys. After the club's launch, Merv defined it as "The Supreme Dance Floor on the West Coast." Somewhat bitchily, his critics said he'd created the club just as a means of having a showroom in which he could perform.

Faced with declining revenues, the Coconut Club closed its doors forever in 2002. But during Merv's regime, a remarkable array of celebrities was spotted on its dance floor.

They included Billy Crystal, Hugh Hefner, Mickey Rooney, Victoria Principal, Tom Cruise, Antonio Banderas, Michael Jackson, Jerry Lewis, Mark Wahlberg, Vanna White,

The Beverly Hilton Hotel:
Merv's kingdom on Earth

Mel Brooks, Anne Bancroft, Jackie Collins, Ted Danson, and Robert Vaughn.

***

At this point in his life, and as new business opportunities were proposed and promoted, Merv recalled that, "I felt I had other dragons to slay. New challenges to meet. I was antsy to get on with the final phase of my life. I dared dream dreams of conquest in the business world that would have terrified me years before. I was ready to take chances."

From the eighth floor of the Beverly Hilton, where Merv maintained a luxurious apartment, he looked out every night at a hilltop where he dreamed of building his own San Simeon to rival the castle of William Randolph Hearst. The site was the highest point in Beverly Hills.

He owned one hundred and fifty seven acres of this choice real estate, which he'd purchased from Princess Shams, the sister of the Shah of Iran. These Persian royals had wanted to turn the site into a sanctuary for the Peacock Throne in exile. Merv's plans for the site had included an elaborate Palladian villa on the hilltop's summit, along with stables and a trio of lakes. But Merv unexpectedly changed his mind, selling the real estate to Mark Hughes of Herbalife, the nutritional supplement company, for nine million dollars.

Around the same time, Merv bought a vineyard, the Mount Mervillian Winery, and sunk money into Merv Griffin Events, an outfit specializing in the organization of large-scale fashion events for enterprises like Tommy Hilfiger and Gucci.

In the 1990s and beyond, Merv would buy and sell some seventeen hotels. Many of these became hangouts for celebrities, and occasionally one of his hotels would make headlines. Such was the case on July 22, 2002 when Robert Downey Jr. was arrested on charges of drug possession at Merv Griffin's Resort Hotel in Palm Springs. After that, Merv claimed his resort was deluged by clients wanting to book the room where Downey was arrested.

On September 15, 1993 Merv purchased Florida's Deerfield Beach/Boca Raton Hilton from the Prudential Realty Group, based in Newark, New Jersey. Some real estate agents in Florida wondered why Merv wanted a business travelers' hotel positioned at the intersection of Interstate 95 and Hillsboro Boulevard. "It's not his usual style," said Danny Toldman, a real estate broker. "I doubt if Merv Griffin would even stay there. It's not grand enough. But who can figure out why Merv Griffin buys anything?"

In March of 1998, Merv acquired the Givenchy Hotel and Spa in Palm Springs from its owner, Rose Narva. The fourteen-acre luxury property had been developed by the legendary fashion icon Hubert de Givenchy and had opened in 1995. As justification for its purchase, Merv told the press that he had enjoyed the hotel and spa since the day it opened.

By 2003, Merv's love affair with the Beverly Hilton was nearing an end. "It no longer has magic for me," he confided to friends. Even so, *tout* Hollywood was shocked when he announced that he was selling his once beloved property to an investment group.

"After seventeen years," Merv told the press, "I am pleased to turn over the reins, and I'm confident the new owners will continue the proud traditions of this extraordinary property." On the last night of his ownership, Merv was seen "walking every inch" of the nine acres surrounding the hotel.

***

When the Reagans returned home to California in 1988, after occupying the White House for eight momentous years, Merv threw a $25,000-a-table homecoming gala.

Inspired partly by his friendship with the Reagans, Merv had become a heavy donor to Republican causes and in 2003 publicly blasted CBS for the unfavorable slant of their two-part TV biopic, *The Reagans*. (Yanked by CBS because of massive right-wing protests, it was later picked up by Showtime and subsequently earned seven Emmy Award nominations.)

Merv seemed on top of the world. Everything in his life was "coming up roses," as he put it. But at his first private luncheon with Nancy, she issued a dire warning: Her latest astrologer had told her that the upcoming 1990s were going to be the darkest years of both of their lives.

"I don't believe it," he said boastfully. "I'm about to take on Donald Trump, and he ain't seen nothing 'til he's dealt with this feisty Irishman."

Chapter Eleven

Known for his extravagant lifestyle and his devotion to beautiful women, all of whom have given him high marks as a lover, New Yorker Donald Trump is America's most famous real estate developer. His celebrity is spread by the success of his NBC TV reality show, *The Apprentice* ("You're fired!"), of which he is the host and executive producer. "The Jewish Don" is also the founder of Trump Entertainment Resorts, which brought him into contact with Merv Griffin in 1988.

The idea of transforming a resort like Atlantic City or the one on Paradise Island in The Bahamas into a touristy destination linking entertainment with gambling appealed to Merv. "Big stars—or at least big stars from yesterday—with high rollers, what a combination!" Merv told Dale Scutti, a car dealer from upstate New York, who at the time was a shareholder in Resorts International.

With his newly materialized millions, and with perhaps a need for attention, Merv began to covetously eye Donald Trump's Resorts International. "The Donald" owned eighty percent of the voting stock and controlled a huge hunk of Paradise Island. He also owned two Atlantic City hotels and casinos, one of them an antiquated relic (The Resorts Atlantic City Hotel), as well as the as yet-to-be-completed Taj Mahal, which, when it opened, was the largest and costliest hotel-casino ever built along the New Jersey shoreline.

As a means of rounding out his ownership of Resorts International, Donald had originally offered to buy the outstanding shares of that organization for $15 a share. Later, under threat of lawsuits, he raised his offer to $22 a share. Behind the scenes, as part of a complicated bidding war, Merv outbid him, offering an astonishing $35 per share.

"You mean, Merv Griffin?" Donald asked in astonishment. "That boy singer with Freddy Martin's boys?"

The counter offer brought Merv into gladiatorial combat with the powerful New York mogul.

Merv sued Donald as a means of sabotaging his attempt to purchase the remaining shares of Resorts for $22 a share. Merv then announced that he was willing to offer just under $300 million for ownership of the entire corporation, including the 85% controlled by Trump.

Donald's reaction was immediate. "Is Merv Griffin fucking crazy? In fact, his offer is so crazy that I don't think I should ask for more. Normally, I might say, 'Merv, make it $40 a share and it's yours, sweetheart.' Not in this case. Talk about *Jeopardy!* He will learn what *Jeopardy!* is when he gets deep into the shit of the gaming business."

Flying into New York on a private jet, Merv had arranged a showdown meeting with his adversary at Trump's penthouse office on Fifth Avenue.

No one will ever really know what transpired that day high above the streets of Manhattan between Merv and Donald. The accounts both men have rendered are self-serving and contradictory.

Donald later claimed that he put some hard questions to Merv. "As a guy who's never built anything bigger than a *Wheel of Fortune* set, do you feel prepared to deal with the contractors, unions, bureaucrats, and politicians who stand between you and success?"

At the end of that afternoon in the glass penthouse, Donald agreed to sell out his ownership interest in most of Resorts International, but held onto the Taj Mahal and the Steel Pier in Atlantic City. Merv ended up with Bahamas-based Paradise Island (which had been known years before as "Hog Island,") and the less desirable of the two hotels in Atlantic City, Resorts Atlantic City. Originally known as Haddon Hall, it was the first Atlantic City hotel-casino launched after gaming was legalized there in 1976. An Atlantic City insider told author Gwenda Blair that Haddon Hall "used to be our shithouse along the boardwalk. After Trump converted the old building, we called it a shithouse with carpeting."

After endless legal and financial hassles and "closing adjustments," the sale was concluded on May 27, 1988.

Merv's own lawyer, Tom Gallegher, called it "the deal from hell," But Merv seemed unflappable. In looking back upon dealing with Trump, Gallegher said, "there was the good twin and the bad twin. In many ways Trump is a Jekyll-and-Hyde guy. He can be enormously charming and you get the feeling he's nice, decent, and warm. That's

The Nemesis:
Donald Trump

486

when the bad twin emerges."

Merv had been able to pull off the deal by transferring ownership of $325 million of Michael Milken's junk bonds as the currency that was used to purchase Resorts International.

After the deal was signed, Trump encountered Merv and shook his hand. "Enjoy your Resorts, which is falling apart. Enjoy Paradise, which is the worst dump you've ever seen. Have a lot of fun."

"I kicked his ass!" Trump told his friends. "It was a great deal for me. I got the Taj Mahal—he got shit!"

Most Wall Street financiers agreed that Merv got a bad deal from Trump. As Michael Craig put it, "Griffin was right to be so reluctant to complete the transaction. The deal was a horrible loser right from the start. For more than $700 million—the cost of buying out Trump and other shareholders and assuming all the debt, minus Trump's payment for the Taj Mahal—all Griffin got was decrepit Resorts, not especially well run, and in dire need of restoration."

Merv went so far as to call Trump's account of their negotiation, as printed within the pages of his memoir, *Surviving at the Top*, "a novel."

He later charged that Trump had completely misled him, claiming that he could "fix up" the Atlantic City resort for 15 million dollars," when Merv knew it would take that much money just to renovate the lobby.

After taking over from Trump, Merv found himself saddled "with interest payments that equaled the treasury of many small countries." His company president, David Hanlon, told the press that "museum-piece elevators and a leaky roof have kept Merv from trading on his cachet to book celebrities."

Just paying the interest on the loans was more than Merv's money advisors could cope with. The money just wasn't there, unless the debt could be restructured.

As clever as Merv had been in his negotiations, often outwitting "The Donald" and his lawyers, he did not foresee the oncoming recession, with the hardships that lay ahead. Waking up one morning in 1989 he found himself $925 million in debt. Most of that debt, $600 million, had been assumed when he'd purchased Resorts International. To retain his twenty percent equity, Merv had to plow another $30 million of his own money into the company. Working behind the scenes, he was able to reorganize Resorts under Chapter 11 of the Federal bankruptcy laws.

To publicize his resorts, Merv began to invite stars for high-visibility visits, often friends from yesterday, including Burt Lancaster and Dinah Shore. He even brought in one of the nation's best-selling novelists, Sidney Sheldon, for a book signing.

For entertainment he booked such stars as the operatic great, Roberta

Peters, or "my old buddy," Tony Bennett, who on one drunken night in California, had been mistakenly introduced to the audience by Merv as Tony Martin.

Merv admitted that "I tried every trick in the book to gain business and publicity, at one point giving away $150,000 in thousand dollar bags to fifteen people every hour."

Even so, he was forced to restructure the organization's debt again in 1994, Trump mockingly referring to it as "Griffin's Chapter 22."

In 1996, Merv's promotional ploys for his New Jersey hotel, Resorts Atlantic City, brought in revenue of $64 million, up from the $16 million it was earning when he took it over in 1988. By 1996 Merv was able to terminate his tumultuous venture into gaming, selling out at $20 a share to Sol Kerzner, the South African real estate developer.

All in all, it is estimated that Merv personally lost $50 million in his flirtation with the gaming industry.

Merv took the money from Kerzner and invested it in Player's International, an outfit that launched and maintained riverboat casinos in Louisiana, Missouri, and Illinois. He sold his investment to Harrah's at a profit in 2000.

As part of a final kiss-off to "The Donald," Merv called him in the 90s, when he was first considering a run for president in the Republican primaries. "Donald, I'm going to contribute one hundred dollars to your campaign. I've thought it over and that's all I can afford."

"As always, generous to a fault," Trump said. "I can't accept the money because I plan to drop out of the race. There are too many hands to shake. Germs, you know. In Atlantic City, I was in the men's room and this guy comes out of a booth after taking this big crap and wants to shake my hand."

During the recession of the early 90s, Merv had been secretly delighted when Trump's most prized investments, including the Taj Mahal in Atlantic City and the Plaza Hotel in Manhattan, racked up a total of more than $1 billion in debt. In an interview with host Jim Palmer on WBAL Radio, Merv was promoting his second autobiography. "You wrote about Donald Trump in your book, Chapter 7 isn't it?" Palmer asked.

"Actually," Merv said with a grin and a wink, "he's in Chapter 11 now."

***

In 1982, when Liberace's live-in boyfriend of five years, Scott Thorson, sued his longtime companion for $113 million in palimony charges after an acrimonious split-up, it sent chills through Merv. He was terrified that someone might file either a palimony suit or a sexual harassment suit against him, although there wasn't enough fear there to get Merv to change his old habits. He still actively and aggressively pursued young men.

Double jeopardy came for Merv in 1991 when, at the age of sixty-five, he was slapped with both a palimony suit and a sexual harassment suit. Filing the complaint was a handsome thirty-seven-year-old former employee, Brent Plott. He had previously been Merv's "secretary/driver/horse trainer/and bodyguard." In his complaint, Brent stated that in addition to the duties cited, he'd been Merv's lover.

He also charged that he'd been Merv's business consultant and was entitled to a share of the Griffin fortune. As an example, Brent maintained that he'd played a big role in the creation of *Wheel of Fortune*, and he also took credit for personally selecting Vanna White as hostess of the show.

The lawsuit sought in excess of $200 million, according to Miami attorney Ellis Rubin, who filed the claim with Los Angeles attorney Stephen Kolodny.

Brent had left Merv's employment in 1985, moving to Florida. It is not known why he waited until 1991 to file the lawsuit.

"We lived together, shared the same bed, the same house," Brent told NBC news. "Merv told me he loved me, and he promised to take care of me for the rest of my life, to provide solace and emotional support."

Through his attorneys, Merv issued a statement, denying Brent's claims, maintaining that the relationship was strictly professional, not sexual.

"This is a shameless attempt to extort money from me," the statement said. "This former bodyguard and horse trainer was paid $250 a week, lived in one of two apartments underneath my former house as part of his security function, and left my payroll six or seven years ago. His charges are ridiculous and untrue."

Merv filed a counter-suit against Brent. "I said, 'Well, I'm not going to pay him off.' That's an admission of guilt. We go to court. I'm not going to pay hush money. I forget what it was—five million that he wanted? Five million, my ass!" Merv was later reminded that it wasn't just five million, but $200 million.

Brent claimed that he'd suffered emotional distress and illness at the end of a nine-year relationship because "of the wrongful and malicious acts of the defendant, Merv Griffin."

In his affidavit, Brent stated that he had met Merv in Monte Carlo in 1976, the year of Merv's divorce, and that Merv had been instantly attracted

The $200 million man:
Brent Plott

489

to him. The handsome young man had been stationed in Germany as part of a three-year stint in the U.S. Army. During one of his leaves, he'd taken a train to Monte Carlo.

Brent claimed that from the beginning, Merv had urged him to come back to America and live with him. Brent said that even before the end of his tour of duty, he'd received constant calls from Merv, urging him to come to California and "to enter into a cohabitation agreement on a full-time basis."

In 1981 Merv finally convinced Brent to give up his job and to "move in with me in return for financial support." In December of that year Brent flew from Paris to Los Angeles to become Merv's lover.

Then-President George Herbert Walker Bush offered Merv his sympathy at a party at the home of Jerry Weintraub. Merv told the President that the lawsuit was "a lot of garbage."

"Garbage or not," the president said, "it can get you in a lot of do-do." He wisely advised Merv to settle out of court.

The lawsuit launched a media feeding frenzy. The story was carried by the Associated Press and appeared in major newspapers and magazines across the country, including *The New York Times* and *People*. "It was the official outing of Merv Griffin," claimed editor Dennis Holder. "All of us in media knew that Merv was gay, but this became a legal reason for us to expose this closeted old queen. I was a Mike Douglas man myself."

Many of Merv's neighbors in Carmel told the press that they always knew Merv was gay. "It's no big deal," claimed Adam Kramer, a local art dealer.

Suddenly, eyewitnesses to Merv's gayness began to emerge. One waiter at the swank Lodge at Pebble Beach said that he often served Merv an early breakfast. "He was always in his bathrobe, and he was always in the company of very handsome and virile looking young men. Each one I saw was different from the rest. I just assumed they were high-paid hustlers. Why else would these good-looking guys want to go to bed with fat Merv?"

One typical case was cited in the book, *Queer in America*, by Michelangelo Signorile. It involved "Hal," who was described as a very pretty young boy, who had worked himself up from the mailroom to Merv's inner office staff. Hal claimed that one day at work, he was dressed in tight-fitting jeans and also a tight-fitting T-shirt. "Griffin placed his hand on my chest and said, 'Oh, you're getting pecs.'" Hal claimed he brushed Merv's hand away. "After that, I was demoted back to the mailroom. I was told that Griffin thought I acted too gay. That wasn't the case at all. I got demoted because I didn't respond to his advances. Other guys in the company were much more willing to sleep with Griffin to advance their careers."

Signorile noted that "if you worked for Merv, and he found out you were 'Out,' you were out the door."

After Merv's death, other outrageous examples of his aggressive sexual behavior were cited. David Ehrenstein posted a column called "Mervgate!" in *The Huffington Post*. He recalled a dinner in the early 1980s for the Los Angeles Film Critics Association, attended by, among others, Peter O'Toole and Dustin Hoffman.

The surprise of the evening, according to Ehrenstein, was "a gaggle of gorgeous muscle boys in multi-colored Izod shirts running about hither thither and yon. They did all sorts of things: Showing us to our tables, delivering messages from the stars to an offstage Merv and such. There's no doubt Merv hired each and every one of them personally," said Ehrenstein. "It was a male harem to rival Hef's Playboy bunnies in every way. And the message was clear from Merv. 'Look at what I've got!'"

In spite of the evening's blatant exhibitionism, Merv was still known for firing gays for being too open. Ehrenstein claimed that a "secretary-executioner would tell a hapless homo—'We don't want your kind here.'"

Rolling Stone, in a piece written about Merv in 2006, analyzed the issues associated with Brent's palimony suit and the subsequent sexual harassment suit.

"Merv does not refute the underlying implication in both cases: that he is gay," the magazine claimed. "Nor does he admit to it. Instead, he mentions the high-profile relationship that he began with actress Eva Gabor at the time of his legal troubles. They were photographed everywhere: Atlantic City, La Quinta, Hollywood premieres. Merv says that they discussed marriage, and he parries any direct questions about his sexual orientation. 'You're asking an eighty-year-old man about his sexuality right now!' he cries. 'Get a life!'"

Brent had alleged that Merv's relationship with Eva Gabor was a cover-up. "Every picture she's in, I am there too," he claimed. "She went where Merv and I went. The editors crop me out."

***

The most insiderish look into Eva's relationship with both Merv and Brent was published by Camille (also known as Camyl) Sosa Belanger in her memoir, *Eva Gabor: An Amazing Woman*, in 2005. Camille had worked as a personal assistant to Eva for some twenty years.

In February of 1991, Camille recalled

Eva on the town with **Merv:**
Happy together?

that she had been at Eva's home when Merv and Eva returned together from a trip to Palm Springs.

"*Dahlink*, can I tell Camille?" Eva asked.

"Sure, why not?" Merv said.

"Merv and I are getting married," Eva told her friend.

Camille had been urging the marriage for years—"a better catch, forget it." Her book makes it obvious that Camille knew that it would be a marriage based on financial security, not romance. The next day Eva told her that Merv was insisting on a prenuptial agreement.

After Brent filed his palimony suit in April of that year, Camille said that "all hell broke loose." Merv called Eva, because he wanted her to know what had happened before it appeared in the news media.

After the call from Merv, Eva turned to Camille. "Remember Brent?"

Camille said that, of course, she remembered Brent. "Is he back?"

At one point Eva admitted to Camille that "the kid deserves all the money he's asking for. It is no peanuts. He wants millions. No wonder Merv asked me to marry him. He knew all along that Brent was planning to sue him."

Camille later asserted that news of the lawsuit did not come as a shock to Eva because she knew about "the close relationship" between Brent and Merv right from the beginning.

Eva called her friends, including Zsa Zsa, and Eva's voice was filled with remorse. "We've known for decades that Merv was a homosexual. Now the public will know. The whole world will know. The secret is finally out in the open."

Camille wrote about Eva's tolerance, about her acceptance of Merv's homosexuality, and specifically about his love affair with Brent. "Eva was at the time really annoyed and humiliated because, after all, Eva loved and respected her friend, and seeing him like a wounded soul was no joy to Eva. Eva knew it all along, and she lived with them, and they went out to places together and to long trips on the road and to Europe, so Eva was used to that kind of life and she did not care."

Camille wrote that Eva enjoyed "traveling like a queen and with expenses paid."

Many of Eva's friends later admitted that "she's one of the most gay-friendly women in Hollywood, where the competition for that title is keen."

Camille herself was saddened by the lawsuit, because she too had seen the relationship between Merv and Brent first hand. "How can anyone destroy many years of happiness and drag each other in the 'Mud' when there was so much love during the young fresh years when one had eyes 'only' for each other? From what I had seen during the fresh years, it was love and equality and eating from the same table."

In the days and weeks ahead, Eva was hounded by the national media for an articulation of her reaction to the lawsuit. The *Star*, the *Globe*, and the *Enquirer* were virtually harassing her day and night. Camille claimed that both men, Brent and Merv, had treated Eva with "love and kindness like a little sister, especially after her last divorce." Camille claimed that Eva respected both Merv and Brent, and it was obvious to Eva's friends that her loyalties were tested. In the end, of course, she sided with Merv.

Putting up a brave public front, Eva told the press, "I've been with Merv for nine years, and I can tell you, this is ridiculous." Privately to her friends, Eva had maintained all along that Merv was gay and that her relationship with him was platonic.

In an outrageous statement on *The Joan Rivers Show*, Zsa Zsa suggested that it was Eva who should be suing for palimony. "After all, she lived with Merv for nine years."

In November of 1991, Brent's case against Merv came before Judge Diane Wayne of the Los Angeles Superior Court. She dismissed it "with prejudice," meaning that the case could not be refiled. The court also fined Brent two thousand dollars for bringing the case against Merv. A spokesman for Merv claimed, "This was a totally baseless suit from a guy trying to make a quick buck."

Many observers disagreed with that opinion, thinking the case "had a lot of legs." Others were surprised at the quick dismissal.

When news reached Camille and Eva that the lawsuit against Merv had been dropped, Camille asked Eva about the status of Merv's marriage proposal.

Eva's answer was somewhat enigmatic. "Come on, *dahlink,* don't play dumb. It is out in the air and that is all—and there is nothing to worry now."

***

Not intimidated by the failure of Brent's case, Deney Terrio filed a sexual harassment suit against Merv in December of 1991, a month after Brent's case was dismissed.

Deney was seeking $11.3 million from his former boss, who he claimed had constantly propositioned him in 1978 when he was hosting Merv's *Dance Fever*.

Deney was a choreographer and former film actor. He achieved fame when he coached John Travolta in his dance numbers for *Saturday Night Fever*. As an actor, he appeared in such films as *The Idolmaker* and *Star Trek II*.

In his affidavit, Deney claimed, "beginning in 1978, and continuing through the parties' business relationship, the Defendant, Merv Griffin, made on-going explicit homosexual advances toward me."

The young actor also claimed that "Griffin persisted in said advances." Deney alleged that Merv spoke of substantial financial gains if Deney would become his bed partner. Attorneys for Merv claimed that the allegations were "totally false."

Like the case that preceded it, this second lawsuit was widely publicized by the media.

Deney charged on *A Current Affair* that Merv attacked him in 1978. "Griffin fell on top of me and started grabbing me and tearing my shirt off," he said. "It shocked me. I was terrified. I kept pushing him back, saying, 'Merv, I'm not ready.'"

Shock jock, trash-talking Howard Stern also booked Deney for two episodes of his show in 1991 and 1992 to air his sexual harassment charges against Merv.

As in the case of Brent, Merv claimed that Deney's suit was motivated by greed. "It was after they started printing the money stuff," he said. "After the sale of *Wheel of Fortune* and *Jeopardy!*, I was a target."

Prompted by the case's media exposure, gay men in the discos of Los Angeles could be seen dancing in pink T-shirts with the slogan, I TOO SLEPT WITH MERV GRIFFIN.

In June of 1992, a judge dismissed the second lawsuit against Merv.

In retaliation against Deney's lawsuit, Merv threatened to destroy the young actor's career. He never carried through with this threat.

Deney went on to appear as a guest star on such popular TV series as *The Love Boat*. In the 90s he toured nightclubs and judged dance contests. In July of 2005 he was hosting his own disco radio show for Sirius satellite radio network.

In 1993, after the two lawsuits were dismissed, activist and journalist Michelangelo Signorile, who specializes in "outing," cited Merv as one of the "closeted power brokers still keeping the homophobic machine going. It's highly unlikely that Merv Griffin, for instance, will ever publicly discuss his sexuality, even though it would probably do him a world of good and would have an effect on

Deney Terrio

494

the way his own gay employees, as well as gay people throughout the industry, are treated."

"I've been in the public eye for more than fifty years as Merv Griffin—not as somebody else's creation," Merv said. "I've never pretended to be someone I wasn't. If there was anything really important that people didn't know about me by now, then I would have to be the world's greatest actor. Forget Brando. Forget Hoffman. Forget De Niro. I would have to be the best."

"Since his entire life was based on concealing his true self from the public, Merv deserved an Oscar for deception," said Marlon Brando, who was far more open than Merv (and virtually anybody else as well) about the various outlets of his own sexual expression.

Merv tried to deflect the issue whenever he was asked if he was gay. "I tell everybody that I'm a *quartre*-sexual. I will do anything for a quarter."

***

Marshall Blonsky, author of *American Mythologies* (Oxford University Press, 1992*)*, crafted one of the most controversial interviews of Merv ever written. Their meeting took place over lunch at the Beverly Hilton.

As Merv rose to "greet an ex-movie queen," Blonsky contemplated "his Beverly Hills image, far removed from the professorial tweeds or Wall Street subdued sharpness. He is the greedy, contemporary Sidney Greenstreet, dressed in an oversize, richly textured sweater braided with black leather. His pants are black, and I realize: This is Hollywood, Merv is entertainment royalty, and Merv is dressed in robes, then about to build his Versailles on a plateau in West L.A., a project that will collapse when, reaching for the Maltese Falcon in the form of Resorts International, he finds a nasty surprise inside it. Happily unclairvoyant, I had left the finance capital to enter the fantasy capital, two poles, flesh and fantasy, base and superstructure, content and form."

In his unflattering portrait of Merv, Blonsky described him as financially successful but artistically limited. He noted that the key to Merv was "a desperate drive to be accepted by the rich and powerful," and he credited Murray Schwartz with much of Merv's financial success. The two partners separated in the 1980s. Blonsky did admit, however, that Merv had a genius for creating game shows on TV.

When the interview was published, Merv claimed, about Blonsky, "He tricked me, seduced me."

In his article, Blonsky aptly summed up Merv's unique character as a phenomenon still anchored in the 1950s. "It's everything I love," Merv said, speaking of the Beverly Hilton. "Ballrooms, bands, singing, entertaining." At one point Merv leaned forward and began to sing, *Dancing in the Daaark . .*"

"I had the craziest image of Merv Griffin whirling me around the ball-room," Blonsky said. "For Merv, show-business heaven is still a ballroom, and in his ballroom fantasy he moves from one dream to another, and, as with our own dreams, they're always incomplete, inchoate. He ends up disillusioned and immediately begins a new fabrication. Failure is the end of the dream and the driving force to change again."

Eva, whether by fault of her accent or because she was making an ironic joke, always referred to Merv as a "typhoon," not a tycoon.

Merv's success caused amazement in others, including Mike Dann, the chief programming executive at CBS. "For a guy like Griffin to have made it to the top is like Joe the Plumber becoming a best-selling novelist." This Joe the Plumber reference was said years before John McCain immortalized another Joe the Plumber during one of his presidential debates in 2008.

Merv too was sometimes awed by how far he'd gone in show business. "I could have become even bigger," he often said. Years after his $250 million sellout was concluded, many Wall Street financiers told him that had he waited another four or five years, he might have gotten one billion.

"Bankers like that are trying to give me a heart attack—and to think I seriously considered bailing out for $45 million," Merv said.

***

On numerous occasions and over many years, Merv had encountered Ronald and Nancy Davis Reagan, including that embarrassing run-in at Robert Walker's house when she was "not dressed for the occasion." As for "Ronnie" (as Merv then called him), Doris Day had introduced him to Merv back on the Warner's lot in the early 50s.

The Reagans' relationship with Merv remained casual until Nancy and Reagan, back when he was Governor of California, made a joint appearance on Merv's talk show. The on-camera banter among the three of them had been personal and intimate, but hardly revelatory. The Reagans weren't former movie stars who revealed their darkest secrets to millions in front of TV sets.

"Beginning with that talk show, the Reagans and Merv bonded," Hadley claimed. "He talked about them all the time. Although they didn't see that much of each other, they talked a lot on the phone. Merv was much closer to Nancy than Ronald, as was to be expected. Merv and Nancy have much in common, including their joint interest in astrology. A true friendship between Merv and the Reagans didn't really blossom until he was invited to the White House. That was sometime around March—or maybe April, I don't remember—in 1983."

As Merv relates in his second autobiography, he arrived at the White House around eleven in the morning and was ushered into the private apartments of the First Family. He'd worn what he called "my best dark suit," but found them dressed in clothes they might have worn at their ranch in California. "Oh, that's just great!" he said to them. "Here I am dressed like Herbert Hoover and you two look like Roy Rogers and Dale Evans."

That broke the ice between them, and the couple chatted like old friends over lunch that day. "Even though temporarily misplaced on the East Coast, Nancy, Ronnie, and I were Californians at heart, I being a native and they being transplants," Merv said. "Their pleasant afternoon was broken by a grim visit to Andrews Air Force Base to salute a plane carrying sixteen Americans who had been killed at the bombing of the U.S. Embassy in Beirut."

When the Reagans returned to the White House, Nancy—and later the President himself—showed Merv around the family quarters. The President also took him into the Oval Office where Merv noticed big jars of multicolored jelly beans.

"You sure do love those jelly beans," Merv said. "Not me. Pure sugar. They'd make me fatter than I already am."

"Actually, I'm not crazy for jelly beans at all," Reagan revealed. "Someone just wrote that in the press. After that I get daily deliveries of jelly beans, which we accept politely and Nancy sees that thank you notes are sent out."

"If not jelly beans, what is your passion?" Merv asked.

"Aside from Nancy," he said, "peanut brittle."

From that day on, until the Reagans left the White House, Merv always sent the most expensive and best-tasting peanut brittle that money could buy.

As President, Reagan respected what he viewed as Merv's media savvy. He called Merv on several occasions, seeking his advice on how to handle the press.

Toward the end of his administration, Reagan even called Merv to ask for advice about how to treat Jane Wyman in his memoir, *An American Life*. "Nancy doesn't want me to mention her at all," Reagan said.

"You can't do that," Merv cautioned. "Of course, you're the President and can do what you like. But you have to mention her. My God, you were married to her for eight years. She was a famous movie star. An

The Lion in Winter

497

Oscar winner. If you don't mention her, it'd be a sin of omission. The press would mock you for it."

"But Jane and I agreed at the time of our divorce not to write about each other or give interviews about our marriage."

"You've still got to mention her, Mr. President."

Finally, after mulling it over, and after overcoming Nancy's protests, the President called Merv with what he'd personally written. He read from a printed page.

The same year I made the Knute Rockne movie, I married Jane Wyman, another contract player at Warners. Our marriage produced two wonderful children, Maureen and Michael, but it didn't work out, and in 1948 we were divorced."

The President paused for a long moment. "What do you think, Merv?"

"Short but sweet, Mr. President."

Presumably, the subject of homosexuality reared its head only rarely in the relationship between Merv and Reagan. It can be assumed that Nancy had told her husband that Merv was a homosexual. In private Reagan wasn't as anti-gay as he was often depicted.

Very rarely did he want to bring up the subject, however. "Reagan lived in an era when homosexuals were locked up in the closet so they wouldn't frighten guests in the parlor," said Truman Capote, no great admirer of the Reagans. "During his administration, with the outbreak of the world's AIDS disaster, the President didn't want to mention that either, thinking it a gay disease. But God likes to play tricks on men like Reagan. That's why God herself gave him Ron Reagan Jr. for a son."

In a private phone call to Merv, Reagan said, "I have to bring up a delicate matter. It's about my son, Skipper. Because he's into ballet, the press is making a lot of insinuations...." He paused. There was an awkward silence.

"They're saying he's gay, you mean?" Merv said.

"Exactly," Reagan said. "We've checked him out. He likes girls. The rumors are untrue. What can I do?"

"You can ignore it, Mr. President," Merv advised. "It's suggested all the time in the press or somewhere—mostly idle gossip—that I'm a homosexual, too. As we both know, that's not true. If some jerk in the press asks you if Skipper is gay, just deny it—and move on. That's the only way. The less said the better."

"Yes," the President said, "the less said the better. That's the way I've always treated the subject of homosexuality, and I'd like to live my life the way I was brought up. Did you know that I didn't know what a homosexual was until I got to Hollywood?"

"Hollywood," Merv said. "Well, that's the place to find out all about it."

"After being introduced to Errol Flynn, I learned far more about homosexuality than I'd ever wanted to know," Reagan said. Abruptly changing the subject, the President invited Merv to dinner with Nancy and himself.

Merv eagerly accepted.

The Reagans were so impressed with Merv that they allowed him to return to the White House about five months later to interview them in their private space, the President filling in the first forty-five minutes, with Nancy making an appearance for the final 15-minute segment of the hour-long show.

***

The private encounters between Merv and the President and his Lady would never be known if Merv hadn't insisted on providing most of the details to his friends. Although he shared stories about the Reagans with his intimates, he never did so at their expense. "I think Merv had a genuine affection for the President, but he developed a deep, loving friendship with Nancy," said Rosemary Clooney. "Like any good friend, he knew her faults and shortcomings, and she was willing to overlook some of the more sordid aspects of Merv's life. I'm sure all those gossips in California she surrounded herself with kept her well supplied with anecdotes about Merv's nocturnal life."

In the years to come, Merv would become Nancy's closest male confidant. Since he was homosexual, the President would not get jealous of Merv the way he was with his wife's attention and devotion to Frank Sinatra, on whom she maintained a lifelong crush.

After her tenure as First Lady, Merv often took Nancy to Holmby Hills, an affluent neighborhood adjacent to Beverly Hills. There, they visited the mansion of real estate mogul Marge Everett, where the former First Lady and Merv often sang duets together at the piano. Johnny Mathis sometimes joined them. Nancy's favorite number was "Our Love Is Here to Stay."

Once, during his business involvement in The Bahamas, and after their tenure in the White House, Merv asked Ronald and Nancy Reagan to join him on Paradise Island. One afternoon when she was having her hair done, Merv invited Ronald to a bar for drinks.

Living well is the best revenge.

499

"Nancy was furious at me when she found out," Merv recalled. "I told her, 'Come on, lots of people drink at bars. John Wayne drinks at bars.'"

Nancy shot back, "John Wayne is not the former President of the United States."

In 1994, when the ex-President wrote his famous letter to "My Fellow Americans," informing them that he was afflicted with Alzheimer's disease, he accurately predicted that he had begun "the journey that will lead me into the sunset of my life."

Merv shared in that journey, being with Reagan whenever he was invited by Nancy to see the President. He saw a lot more of Nancy and was almost in daily contact with her, if not in person, then by phone.

When Merv first saw Reagan after he'd written that famous letter, the former President seemed cheerful and optimistic. "My mother always said that if life hands you lemons, make lemonade."

Merv had a front-row seat to watch the slow but steady post-presidential decline of his friend Ronald Reagan. He shared the gruesome details with Eva Gabor, who, without any malicious intent, shared those same details with her close friends—and that is why we know today about Merv's role in the life of the Reagans.

On several occasions, Merv attended private luncheons, arranged by Nancy, at Reagan's post-presidential office at Century City in Los Angeles. The former President arrived there late every morning and left early. He was incapable of doing any actual work except—perhaps—pose for a picture with some Girl Scouts.

It had been recommended to Nancy that Alzheimer's patients needed some sense of routine—hence, Reagan's ritual visits to his office five days a week. Nancy would write out a schedule for him for the day, just as his White House staff used to do, but it was filled only with busy work to keep his mind occupied. Merv was one of the few people she trusted to be alone with the former President.

In his first luncheon meeting, Merv was surprised when the former President tossed salt over his left shoulder. "I'm superstitious," he said.

Merv told Eva a secret he'd never told anyone. Over lunch, according to Merv, Reagan talked about two things—Doris Day and flying saucers. He said that when he was dating Doris, during the aftermath of his divorce from Jane Wyman, he was seriously considering proposing marriage to her. "He spent most of the lunch talking about what marriage to Doris would have been like," Merv told Eva, "but he hastened to add that he'd made the perfect choice in Nancy."

The remainder of the luncheon involved talk about flying saucers. The President informed Merv that he was an ardent believer in UFOs, claiming that in California, back in 1947, he'd seen flying saucers on three separate occasions. He also told Merv that he believed that aliens had been spying on the Earth for decades, and he feared that an invasion of the United States was imminent. "I just know it," Reagan said. "They've selected some desert somewhere in the West here to make their initial landing."

As the months went by, Merv couldn't help but notice that the President's condition, and especially his memory, had faded. "As long as he was able to go to his beloved Rancho del Cielo with Nancy, he seemed okay," Merv said. "The fresh air there, the chance to cut brush, those still romantic moments when he could walk hand-in-hand with Nancy to observe the beautiful sunsets—all of that seemed to keep his spirit alive."

One day Nancy called Merv to tell him that, "Ronnie has cleared his last brush." Her voice sounded melancholic. Ronnie had lost all interest in the ranch and didn't want to go there anymore. She was going to put it up for sale.

In 1997, Merv paid his last call on the President. He later told Eva, "Ronnie didn't know who I was. I respectfully addressed him as 'Mr. President.' He looked up at me confused. Very slowly, he asked me, 'President of what? I was never the President. That job belonged to Jack Warner.'"

After leaving the Reagans' home that day, Merv believed that Reagan had obliterated all memories of his years in the White House, as well as his memories of Sacramento when he was governor of California. "But he still retained some memory of being in films. His mind had gone back to a happier time, perhaps the 1940s when he was a movie star."

"When Nancy limited my access to the President," Merv said, "I understood completely. After all, she was the chief custodian of him— the gatekeeper, so to speak. In the end she wanted to protect the President from prying eyes. He had gone too far into that sunset he wrote about in the letter. Ronnie had already gone over the top of the world, and darkness—not even twilight—had set in. Ronnie had to be shielded. Old friends could no longer come to call and talk about the good times in Sacramento or Washington. At some point, and I'm guessing here, Ronnie no longer remembered even being a movie star, much less President."

In one candid moment, Merv claimed that

Nancy Reagan:
Deep in December

Nancy had been virtually under "house arrest for ten years when Ronnie was sick."

Even in the darkest of times, Merv brought humor into the former First Lady's life, including a Saturday lunch he had with her at Chez Mimi, a chic Santa Monica eatery favored by celebrities. "Merv's a real, real upper," Nancy said. "He will not let himself be depressed or low. He cheers you right up!"

When Merv visited Nancy after Ronald had surgery on a broken hip, he knew the end was coming. "But she was so brave. She also knew it was the end yet she appeared optimistic. The actress in her put up a front for me."

"He's going to get well, you'll see," she told Merv.

Nancy also revealed that she was "stretched to my limits," when she'd visited Reagan's first daughter, Maureen, and her husband on the same day at the same hospital.

"Of course, Nancy, without saying so, knew she was conducting a death watch for both Maureen and Ronnie at the same time," Merv told Eva.

Born in 1941, Maureen was the only biological child of Reagan and his first wife, Jane Wyman. She was active in Republican party politics, and the first daughter of a U.S. President to run for public office. She was defeated in both of the two elections she spearheaded. They included the race for US Senator from California in 1982, and a decade later, an unsuccessful race for California's 36th congressional district.

Maureen was never particularly close to Nancy (her stepmother) and sometimes endorsed political positions—including a pro-choice platform on abortion—that opposed the widely publicized tenets of her famous father. Death for Maureen from melanoma cancer came prematurely, in 2001, at the age of sixty.

Nancy had slept every night of her life that she could with her husband, even during the months before their marriage in 1952, when she'd become pregnant. "The saddest thing for Nancy was when she was told she could no longer sleep at Ronnie's side," Merv said. "She had to order a hospital bed with bars on either side so Ronnie would not fall out of bed again and injure his hip."

"That bed I wake up in every morning these days feels very lonely indeed," she told Merv.

Merv sent flowers when the Reagans celebrated their fiftieth wedding anniversary on March 4, 2003. "It wasn't much of a celebration," Nancy confided in him. "The cake was small and we sat in silence. Ronnie didn't know what we were celebrating."

Nancy called Merv on June 5, 2005, to tell her that "Ronnie has gone on his way." He promised to come over at once.

After the President died, Merv was among the first to visit Nancy with condolences. In tears she looked up at him. "The most painful thing for me to endure over the past few years was when the moment came that we could no longer share memories together."

To mask his grief, Merv turned a bright face to the press waiting outside the Reagans' Bel Air home. "In all the stories you're filing," Merv told the press, "don't forget to add that Ronald Reagan was the most successful actor in history. As for me, I'm going home to watch Ronnie and Nancy in *Hellcats of the Navy*."

***

In 1990 Merv created a television game show based on the parlor game *Monopoly*. Hosted by Mike Reilly, the show premiered on June 16, with three contestants competing to answer crossword puzzle-style clues and gain property on the Monopoly board. After only thirteen episodes, the show went bust. Many viewers claimed that Merv made the rules too complicated for the average viewer.

Recordings of each episode of the show survive, but so far no network has opted for reruns. In a touch of irony, it was announced in 2006 that Donald Trump, Merv's nemesis, was "going from boardroom to Boardwalk." *The Apprentice* star said he was going to become the executive producer of a reality show based on the classic board game.

***

In the spring of 1998, Merv granted an interview with Matt Tyrnauer of *Vanity Fair*. During their time together, Merv discussed Eva, who had died three years before. "Those years had great ups and downs," Merv said. "We really loved each other a lot, but sometimes we would leave each other and go to different people. She would go to someone else, and I would go to—say, Princess Elizabeth of Yugoslavia. We had broken up just before her death, but when we were together we traveled everywhere: Morocco, all the islands."

Herb Caen of the late *San Francisco Chronicle*, once said, "If Merv and Eva ever stopped laughing, they'd get married."

"Now everyone says, 'God, we really miss the two of you,'" Merv said. "We were like another version of Lucy and Desi."

Merv refused to tell Tyrnauer the reason he split from Eva, although he did confess that they'd planned to be married, with Nancy Reagan serving as the matron of honor. "There was a pre-marital agreement," Merv said. "But we could never agree which house we'd live in, and I couldn't agree which of her staff she would bring with her and that really drove us apart. It's awful, because there is so much more I can't tell. It was a monstrous problem and it wasn't mine—but I will never drag Eva's name through the mud."

The "monstrous" problem that Merv referred to was Eva's demand that he settle fifty million dollars on her for all the years she'd been his companion. If he didn't come across with the money, Eva was threatening to file a palimony suit against him, like his former companion Brent Plott had done.

After learning of her intentions, Merv could not forgive her, and ordered her from La Quinta and all of his other properties. When she'd returned to her own home and recovered from her immediate anger, Eva told her friends, "I don't know what got into me. My Hungarian temper, I suppose. I would never have sued Merv, but he should have made some financial settlement on me."

The unresolved marriage—or money—issues between them bubbled over when Merv fell madly in love with a young hustler and wanted to spend all his evenings with the handsome little stud—and no more evenings with Eva.

In June of 1995, after her split from Merv, Eva journeyed to Baja, Mexico, where she had a home. Bitterly disappointed over the failure of her relationship, she claimed she was in desperate need of a vacation.

On June 2, she "ate a bad piece of fruit" in her words and contracted viral pneumonia. As her condition weakened, she refused to seek help from Mexican doctors, having no faith in them. In her disoriented state, she collapsed on a staircase in her house, falling about ten steps to her foyer. Her hip was broken.

Eva's housekeeper placed a call to Merv, who claimed he was "devastated" to hear of Eva's injury. He immediately called for a private jet to transport Eva from Baja to the Cedars Sinai Medical Center in Los Angeles.

When Eva was admitted there on June 21, doctors discovered fluid in her lungs and a blood clot. She was also running a dangerous fever. Put on a respirator, she was given the drug heparin for the clotting and antibiotics for the pneumonia.

Experts have speculated that Eva may not have died of viral pneumonia, but of pneumococcal pneumonia, a horrible bug that can kill within twenty-four hours.

Under heavy medication and with her condition worsening by the hour, she slipped into a coma. Death came at 10:05 on Tuesday, July 4, 1995. Presumably, Eva was seventy-six years old, although some have disputed that.

The increasingly senile Jolie wasn't immediately informed of her daughter's death, but Zsa Zsa and Magda, her older sisters, attended a 7pm memorial service at the Good Shepherd Catholic Church in Beverly Hills. Eva had been cremated.

Paying his last respects was her faithful co-star of *Green Acres*, Eddie Albert. He embraced Merv, who also greeted fellow mourners Rosie

O'Donnell, Johnny Mathis, and Mitzi Gaynor. The matriarch of the Gabor clan, Jolie, and Eva's older sister, Magda, would each survive another two years, dying, respectively, on April 1, and June 11 of 1997.

From aboard his yacht, the *Griff*, Merv heard about Eva's death and went into shock. "Only because we'd had an argument, and we hadn't settled the argument yet, and I was mad, and I was off on my boat, and she died while I was gone. That was rough."

Reportedly, Merv's final words to Eva before they departed forever were, "I've loved a thousand times, but never been in love."

***

Merv knew the Prince and Princess of Wales somewhat distantly. "We circled each other," he later said, "although at a distance, but a respectful distance."

In the 80s, Merv threw a party for Charles and Diana in Palm Beach. The Prince of Wales had given his first American TV interview to Merv. After that, Merv developed an ongoing relationship with the royal couple that never became close.

"I adored Di, who for some reason I kept calling Lady Di," Merv said. "That stuck in my mind even when she became a royal princess. I simply adored her. But I also thought Prince Charles was wonderful—a really marvelous guy, funny and charming. Harry and William simply adored him, and he's wonderful with them."

When Princess Di was killed in Paris in 1997, Merv sent Prince Charles a condolence note. "I hate that Britain's royal family has become the heavies in the tragic death of Di. It's foolish. People are even saying that Charles had Di killed—or that Prince Philip did it. Such charges are baseless. Ridiculous. Beyond libel."

Although Merv's strongest attachment was to Princess Diana, he also got to meet Prince Charles' second bride, Camilla.

Merv admitted in 2000 that he "adored" George W. Bush, who invited him to the White House to attend a party for Prince Charles and Camilla.

"The President yelled at me across the room," Merv said. "'M-e-e-e-rv is here!'" Merv quoted the president as saying. "'Ooooh, I love him! He's funny. He's bright. He's intelligent. And he loves to have a good time. I wish everybody could get to know him personally.'"

***

Built in 1784, and surrounded by fifty-five acres of rolling green hills, "the most beautiful house in Ireland," St. Clerans Manor, a Georgian estate in Craughwell, County Galway, had been acquired after World War II by John Huston. When he was in residence, the famed director entertained Hollywood luminaries who included Elizabeth Taylor, Cary Grant, Montgomery Clift, Marlon Brando, Peter O'Toole, and Paul Newman.

After Merv bought the property in 1997, he restored the estate to its original splendor, lavishly upgrading and redecorating it before its launch as a luxury hotel made available to paying guests whenever Merv was not in residence.

John Huston's bedroom is now called the Griffin Suite. Its bathroom still has gilded taps shaped like swan's heads. The Angelica Suite is actually a small separate octagonal guest cottage, once the bedroom of Angelica Huston, John's daughter.

The opulently furnished dining room that had hosted kings, princes, consorts, and movie stars, now feeds rich tourists.

***

Merv responded to the challenge by the Federal Communications Commission to develop TV programs for young people that were more challenging than *Scooby Doo* and *Beavis and Butt-head*. Responding to the need for educational kids' programming, he created *Click*, a children's quiz show. "I want to do a fast-moving question-and-answer show," Merv said. "I want to do one with high speed, because kids react to questions faster than adults do."

He hired Ryan Seacrest as host of *Click*. Seacrest called Merv a perfectionist who personally oversaw the production of the show's first twenty-two segments. "Merv is very 'on,' very quick-witted," said Seacrest. "He's very hands-on. He has a vision. He knows exactly what he wants."

When Seacrest began his association with *Click*, in September of 1997, he was relatively unknown. The game show was based around computers and the then relatively novel medium of the Internet. *Click* aired in syndication from September of 1997 to August of 1999.

Ryan Seacrest / Merv

506

Other than Vanna White, Merv cited as one of his greatest achievements the discovery of Ryan Seacrest. Merv had developed a late-in-life crush on the handsome twenty-two-year old. "I saw energy in the boy. There's *the look* of him. Easy smile. He could do it!"

Seacrest, by now a familiar face on *American Idol*, was maliciously rumored to have slept with Merv to advance his career in media, and bloggers went to work posting these charges on the web. However, they were just that—rumors—and have never been proven.

Some of the blog postings were more humorous than real. "*Holy shee-it*, really?" wrote Fanatic. "I'd never heard the Merv rumor before. I thought when they said 'screwed over your idol to get the gig,' they meant 'screwed OVER your idol,' not literally banged. That's just too funny. Because Merv Griffin was actually my first 'celebrity crush' when I was only about three years old. I used to try to feed him potato chips through the television screen. So like, wow. My first celebrity crush and my last celebrity crush have apparently done the deed. Ain't that some shit? I've come full circle with my too foolish man-slut obsessions."

Other bloggers such as "Ladyjaney," took a more reasonable point of view. 'As far as Seacrest and Merv go, I refuse to believe it. Or I sure as heck don't want to anyway."

"GJJ," another blogger, summed up "this new-found lust for Seacrest. It couldn't be because he appears to be 'enhanced' by packing a pair of tube socks in his pants, could it?"

***

Merv's last *protégé* was Andrew Yani. At the age of thirty-one, he was appointed as head of Merv's television company. An extraordinarily handsome young man, Yani looks like a model for *GQ*. Merv's publicist, Marcia Newberger, claimed, "Merv loves having young guys around—it makes him feel young."

***

At the age of seventy, Roddy McDowall died in October of 1998. He and Merv hadn't sought one another out with any particular frequency during the final years of his life. By that time, their friendship was essentially a distant memory of their youth. However, they occasionally remained in touch, usually by telephone.

Merv was saddened by Roddy's death, feeling his own life slipping away as old friends of the 40s and 50s died. He said, "Roddy was living proof that not all former child stars were doomed to be either forgotten or else a drug user or alcoholic. He was the world's greatest movie fan, and a star in his own right. All of his friends, including Elizabeth Taylor, who appeared with him in *Lassie Come Home*, were saddened today. A friend told me that he died very peacefully at his home in Studio City, just the way he planned it."

Later, Merv revealed to close friends that he'd visited Roddy privately during the weeks before his death. "He took my hand and looked deeply into my eyes. 'This is not a time to be sad,' Roddy said. 'We've both had incredible lives. It was like a visit to Walt's Magical Kingdom. With all our pain and disappointments, it was a life that most people only dream about. Too bad it must end, like all good things.'"

***

Merv lived to accept many honors due him, including a lifetime achievement award at the Daytime Emmys. He was also honored by the Museum of Television and Radio, now known as the Paley Center for Media. Stuart N. Brotman, then president of the museum, said, "There really has been no one who has managed to have his type of success both in front of and behind the camera. He is a one-man conglomerate, and I can't think of anyone else who has had that reach."

In his final years, the awards came frequently. In 1994 he was honored with the Broadcasting and Cable Hall of Fame Award, sharing it with Dan Rather and Diane Sawyer. Throughout his life, Merv won fifteen Emmy Awards, including the 1993-94 Outstanding Game/Audience Participation Show Emmy for his role as executive producer of *Jeopardy!*. The John Wayne Cancer Institute presented Merv with "The Duke Award," and he was also honored by the American Ireland Fund and the SHARE organization. As the awards piled up, Merv soon lost count.

His last big honor came in 2005, when he was presented with Daytime Emmy's Lifetime Achievement Award at the organization's 32nd annual award ceremony.

***

In March of 2001, Merv released *It's Like a Dream,* a CD of mostly vintage songs he'd recently recorded. They included "A Nightingale Sang in Berkeley Square," as well as the album's title song, which he had himself composed.

Soon after, Merv endorsed a retrospective of the best of the thousands of televised interviews he'd conducted during his long and gregarious lifetime.

Containing three separate discs, it was entitled *The Merv Griffin Show: 40 of the Most Interesting People of Our Time.* Some of the younger viewers who played these discs were seeing *The Merv Griffin Show* for the first time.

In reviewing it, Ken Tucker, a TV critic writing in *Entertainment Weekly*, said that as a talk show host, Merv was about "as confrontational as Elmer Fudd. Not all of this stuff ages well. I'd been looking forward to seeing Totie Fields, a 60s comedian who's attained cult status as a pioneeringly ruthless female comic since her death in 1978, but the guest spot here finds her braying tired jokes about how expensive vacations are."

Merv's last "gig" would have involved singing at the Hollywood Bowl beginning on September 14, 2007, as an introduction to Pink Martini, a "little orchestra" devoted to a vintage blend of Latin, lounge, classical, and jazz music. Sadly, because Merv died the day before the scheduled date, his appearance at that event never came to be.

***

Often, Merv was asked by reporters to comment on his rapidly expanding waistline. "I've been very fortunate with my health," he said. "I smoke, I drink—not heavily, but I like my wine. I don't exercise. I take a cab to a cab. It's all in your DNA. My philosophy of life? Turn the page. If something falls through, turn the page. It's over with, get used to it, get on with it. Very simple. It's always worked for me."

When he turned eighty, Merv admitted that he'd tried all the diets—Atkins, Scarscale, Jenny Craig—"and just plain water. Now I've given up worrying about my weight." Critics claimed that he'd become "mountainous—he's taking to wearing polo shirts that drape his girth like a tent," wrote John Colapinto in 2006. "Life is too short for fat-free brownies," Merv said.

"I've outlived all of my diet doctors," Merv said. "My first diet doctor was Dr. Atkins. And then I went through Dr. Stillman, the water diet. I think he drowned on his own diet. And I had Dr. Tarnower, and his girlfriend shot him. So I gave up dieting."

He was referring to Herman Tarnower, the cardiologist who wrote *The Complete Scarsdale Medical Diet*. His lover, Jean Harris, the usually prim headmistress of a private girl's school, fatally shot him on March 10, 1980 when she discovered that the confirmed bachelor had been seducing other women. Merv also tried the doctor's *Quick Weight Loss Diet* (The Stillman Diet). A creation of Irwin Maxwell Stillman, it was an early incarnation of the high protein, low carbohydrate diet.

Merv had referred to Robert Atkins, a nutritionist and cardiologist who created the Atkins Diet, a controversial way of dieting that entails close control of carbohydrate consumption, relying on protein and fat intake instead. On April 28, 2003, at the age of seventy two, Dr. Atkins slipped on a patch of ice while walking to work, hitting his head and causing bleeding around his brain. The fall killed him.

Even as late as 2003, friends were urging Merv to cut back on the package of Marlboro Lights he smoked daily. "Any day now," he told them. "I'm likely to cold-turkey it. I've stopped countless times in my past. But, *ooooh,* that first cigarette after you go back. It's like your first time at Disneyland."

***

Facing death by 2005, Merv told *The New York Times,* "I know death is inevitable, but I'm happy for the time being. I've got great energy, and I've got all my hair. For my tombstone epitaph, I'm suggesting—*"I will not be right back after these messages."*

When Merv was told by Dr. Skip Holden that he needed immediate surgery for prostate cancer, he said, "I don't want anything sliced out of me. I've never had an operation in my life. No, I don't want that. And, then they told me about radiation. I said that I'd do that. And then I went off on my boat out in the Mediterranean for two months. The doctor called and said, 'Merv, you have to undergo treatment. What are you doing out there?' And, I said, 'Well I will. I will. I will.' By this time I had forgotten and he ruined my whole day. He said, 'You've got cancer, remember?' So, I came back."

Back in California, Merv, at the age of eighty-two, entered Cedars Sinai Medical Center on July 8, 2007 for a recurrence of prostate cancer. He'd been treated for the disease more than a decade before. Once there, he undertook radiation treatments five days a week.

Before checking in, Merv said, "I'd rather play *Jeopardy!* than live it. I feel ready for another vacation. Cedars Sinai Medical Center was not the destination I had in mind."

Even on his deathbed, as he lay in the hospital, Merv was working on a game show—in this case a proposed syndicated series called *Merv Griffin's Crosswords.*

Merv wouldn't live to see the show's debut on September 1, 2007. He had hoped that it would attain the success of *Jeopardy!,* but that appears to be a deathbed wish. The show's credits posthumously listed Merv as executive producer.

A frail Nancy Reagan, accompanied by Secret Service agents, made a bedside call on the Friday afternoon before Merv's death. She knew he didn't have long to live, but no mention was made of his grave condition.

She wisely listened to him talk about his success as a horse owner. His

510

colt, "Stevie Wonderboy"—named for entertainer Stevie Wonder—had won the $1.5 million Breeders' Cup Juvenile in 2005, and his mind was drifting back to happier times.

When the nurse signaled Nancy that her time was up, she kissed her friend of fifty years a final good-bye on his forehead.

Merv drifted in and out of consciousness, with feeding tubes and morphine drips. The cancer had spread to his bones, lungs, and liver.

His last words were to his son, Tony. "You were my life."

Merv died at one o'clock on Sunday morning, August 12, 2007.

Before he entered the hospital for the final time, Merv—perhaps knowing he was about to die—summed up his days on earth. "I like my life. When I look back on it, I don't have many regrets. It was all great fun."

"Regrets. I've had a few..."

Epilogue:
MERVGATE

On August 17, 2007, the invitation-only funeral of Merv Griffin was held in The Church of the Good Shepherd in Beverly Hills. The interior of the church had sometimes been used by film companies for fake funerals, including a scene from Judy Garland's 1954 *A Star Is Born*. Elizabeth Taylor had also married her first husband, Nicky Hilton, in this same church.

Merv's coffin was buried under a mass of white flowers, with one single rose.

A grief-stricken Nancy Reagan was an honorary pallbearer. Merv had been an honorary pallbearer at President Reagan's funeral in 2004.

When the news reached her in Bel Air, Nancy's reaction to Merv's death had been immediate. "This is heartbreaking, not just for those of us who had loved Merv personally, but for everyone around the world who has known Merv through his music, his television shows, and his business."

At the funeral, Nancy could be seen brushing away a tear as the choir sang "Amazing Grace."

The other most distinguished guest was Governor Arnold Schwarzenegger, who had made his U.S. talk show debut on Merv's show in 1974. He told the assembled guests that, "I can say today I wouldn't have gone as far in my career if it wouldn't have been for Merv Griffin. He had me on many times. I was on his show to teach him about fitness, and he would teach me about acting. Well, neither worked."

The governor spoke to five hundred mourners who included Alex Trebek, Vanna White, Larry King, Suzanne Somers, and Dick Van Dyke.

Pat Sajak, host of *Wheel of Fortune*, said, "I'm dealing with sadness and the realization that I will never hear that wonderful laugh of his again. He meant so much to my life, and it's hard to imagine it without him."

As a sign of changing times, Ellen DeGeneres and Portia De Rossi were caught walking hand in hand toward the chapel for Merv's funeral. Ellen later told

Funeral rites:
Nancy Reagan,
Arnold and Maria Schwarzenegger

the press, "Merv was, as you know, a genius. He was brilliant. He created all kinds of amazing shows. He sang, he danced, and he talked. I'm going to start singing in honor of Merv."

The entertainment mogul, David Geffen, who is also "out," was in attendance that day, too.

Yet another member of the audience was also "out." Rosie O'Donnell, who claimed that her popular show was "totally Merv-inspired. I didn't create anything. I just copied Merv Griffin."

Forgetting past disagreements, Zsa Zsa told the press, "I'm very upset at the news. He was a very close friend of ours, a good friend of mine, and a good friend of Eva's. He was a *vonderful, vonderful* man."

George W. Bush said, "For over half a century, Merv Griffin entertained America. He was a man of innovation and energy who greeted challenges with laughter and determination."

Speaking to *People* magazine, Ryan Seacrest said, "Merv was a dear friend and my idol. He gave me my first break into show business, and for that I will forever be grateful. Merv is a true legend and will continue to be an inspiration."

Seacrest also announced that as an empire builder, he wanted to become his generation's version of Merv. He also reminded *Entertainment Weekly* that, "I'm not gay."

In his usual tasteless way, gay-bashing Jerry Lewis announced to the press that "Griffin deserved to die," because he avoided treating his prostate cancer. The comedian claimed that he was furious at his friend, "because he had the same disease I did, and I was cured after seeing doctors. You can't have cancer and say, 'I'll be all right'. You're not going to be all right."

The remains of Merv were interred in the Westwood Village Memorial Park Cemetery, where he joined such ill-fated ghosts of yesterday as Marilyn Monroe and Natalie Wood.

***

All hell broke loose three days later, on August 20, when Merv was posthumously "outed." *Hollywood Reporter* scribe Ray Richmond wrote in his weekly column that Merv, the mega-mogul, was a "Big Ol' Gay Homosexual," which was hardly a secret within the film industry. As another mogul put it, "We knew that Merv was gay like we know our own names."

The story had been headlined, GRIFFIN NEVER REVEALED MAN BEHIND THE CURTAIN. The news agency, Reuters, picked up the story in its news feed and syndicated it internationally.

Merv's "people" called the *Reporter* and made several threats, including the yanking of advertising. Some of Merv's associates cancelled a tribute ad that they had planned to run in the *Reporter*.

The column was yanked by Editor Elizabeth Guider, who caved in to pressure from Merv's angry cohorts.

Her action led to a reverse reaction. Readers deluged the *Hollywood Reporter* with demands that the column be restored—and after a few hours it was. Reuters, however, refused to restore the syndication of the column, unbelievably claiming that "it did not meet our standard for news."

In outing Merv, Ray Richmond claimed, "I wanted to make sure that the truth was out there and not a version of it that allowed everyone to make Merv the subject of gossip or the butt of jokes. I wanted to put the truth out there in a loving and concerned way. One could make the point that it was his business alone, but I don't think this was true, because he was a public figure—and this was who the man was."

Pam Spaulding, writing for *Pandagon*, gave her reaction to Mervgate. "The real problem is the news media, which has no problem recounting the endless romances of stars (real or alleged). The 'legitimate' press can be ridiculously squeamish about reporting basic facts about gay public figures (such as the partner left behind)."

The gay and lesbian press also weighed in. *The Gay & Lesbian Review*, published this statement: "One doesn't speak ill of the dead, but does saying that someone was gay qualify, and isn't that being homophobic rather than polite? Of course, Merv could have saved a lot of agonizing if he had just come out of the closet and taken a lover to be 'survived by' (and to inherit his billions)."

In a surprise move, even *The New York Times* virtually "outed" Merv when they mentioned in his obit that he'd been the victim of a palimony lawsuit and a male-on-male sexual harassment lawsuit.

Michelangelo Signorile, the noted gay author, wrote after Merv's death, "Though he'd quietly led a gay life—and had his pool parties filled with young men in the years past, as well as a parade of boyfriends—that was viewed as 'private information' that was not discussed in mixed company. I had interviewed many gay men who'd known Griffin as gay, as well as men who told stories about how his closet had him doing horrendous things—and how he was threatened by openly gay people."

When the furor died down over his *Hollywood Reporter* column, Ray Richmond reflected on the uproar. "I have to wonder if the response in defense of keeping Griffin's secret life a secret post-mortem would have been as acute had he died penniless and forgotten. It would seem there is a direct relationship between the size of one's estate and the level of security guarding his or her heretofore undisclosed sexual orientation. And it appears that $1.6 billion will buy an awful lot of closet space."

***

In the wake of Merv's death, hundreds of persons came forward with either fond remembrances or critical attacks. Most of Merv's fans wished him God's speed, but many bloggers went to work, criticizing Merv for having led a closeted life. His sexual peccadillos were also aired, including several postings from men who had serviced Merv over the years. "In later life he ordered four or five male prostitutes at one time," the head of a male escort agency in Los Angeles charged.

In one notorious incident, which took place at New York's Palace Hotel, a callboy claimed he was paid $2,100—$700 an hour for three hours—to attend a private little bash with four other handsome young men, mostly models.

Merv had booked the Presidential Suite, one of whose features was a marble bathroom. "Merv had us strip and get in the huge bathtub, where he delighted in pouring the most expensive champagne over our tight, muscular bodies, and then licking the bubbly off our chests. He had his fun."

Merv's two tell-nothing autobiographies were called "a series of *shticky* sound bites," reducing a complicated, closeted life to a simple and very vanilla version fit for daytime network TV.

"Talk about an unexamined life," said book critic John Stafford. "A lot of sounding brass, signifying nothing."

One blogger predicted that "the books will come out, telling all his secrets, all about his life of LIES."

Reporter Jon Ponder noted that "Griffin's internalized homophobia was tragic, but it pales in comparison with the hypocrisy of the Reagans, who spent their professional lives in the company of gay people, but then exploited the homophobic Christian Right to gain power. Their silence persisted when Rock Hudson, their friend and a much bigger star than Ronnie ever was, contracted HIV and withered away. Unfortunately, for the Reagans, their hypocrisy on gay issues will be a permanent stain on their legacies. Ironically, for Griffin, despite his many accomplishments, including decades as a talk show host and creating game shows, needlessly living a lie the last thirty years of his life will likely be the only thing he is remembered for."

The strongest reaction to Merv's death came from Margie Phelps, of the famous Phelps family, the most homophobic in America. They live in Topeka, Kansas, which is the center of their hate ministry.

"Mindless millions sit around watching programs engineered by Merv Griffin," she charged. "His goal was to dumb down everyone so he could slip around in the back halls doing his filth. America is doomed. We've turned this nation over to feces-eating fags, and now you're *(sic)* children are coming home in body bags. It's too late for this nation. The siege is coming. You're going to eat your children."

A more reflective, more tolerant, and less psychotic view was posted on *The Data Lounge*. "A tiger does not change its stripes. Merv was from another time, another era. The times may have changed but he didn't. No stars/celebs from his day ever came out. It was career-killing. Not Liberace, not Rock Hudson (until AIDS kicked his closet door down), not Robert Reed, nor Van Johnson, who took his glass closet to the grave. A very few have, Richard Chamberlain, Tab Hunter, Johnny Mathis, and a few more. Good for them, but Griffin, like Tom Cruise, has set his cap to portray himself as straight and he could never change his sails. It would have disputed a lifetime's worth of public/self-image, and he could never have handled it emotionally, despite the fact that most people already knew. Who knows the innermost reasons WHY he never did? It is just not surprising nor particularly repugnant that he did not. I mean, did anyone ever even THINK that he would come out? Gay rights came along in the 60s and 70s, and a lot of things changed, but men who were young in the 40s and 50s simply did not discuss their homosexuality. Ever. Period. The few who found a way out of the closet, good for them. But Merv Griffin was not any different from millions of old guys out there today. They simply lived in a different time and will see the world in a different way until they die. I don't think they deserve our hate."

"I will not be back"

517

Acknowledgments

The first time I ever saw Merv Griffin was when my Aunt Bleeka took me to the premiere of *So This Is Love,* his first starring movie, in which he appeared opposite songbird Kathryn Grayson. We didn't really know who Merv Griffin was, but before the show there had been a parade along the main street of Knoxville, Tennessee. Our primary motivation involved a fascination with Miss Grayson, but as an aggressively promoted part of the venue, we saw Merv ride by, waving from the passenger seat of an open convertible. Teenage girls were screaming at him. Was a new matinee idol, like Rock Hudson or Tab Hunter, in the making?

I next encountered Merv in the late 50s when our University of Miami senior prom committee hired him to entertain us at our big bash. We paid him five hundred dollars for his singing engagement. This represented one of the university's last proms starring an old-fashioned crooner. In the rapidly approaching 1960s, rock 'n' roll would inevitably prevail.

Over the years, I encountered him many other times, mainly in California and New York at various parties. We often moved in the same circles, and knew many of the same people, including Montgomery Clift, Roddy McDowall, Guy Madison, Rock Hudson, and the agent and talent scout, Henry Willson.

As the decades passed, I accumulated enough "Merv stories" to fill three volumes. I have talked, literally, to hundreds of people associated with the entertainment industry, not just about Merv, but about dozens of other show business personalities as well. During countless conversations, Merv's name frequently cropped up. Everybody who'd met him had some story to relay, perhaps only a snippet of which I could use. But each of the pieces contributed to the interconnected puzzle of the star's private life.

Mentioned below are only some of the most significant contributors to this biography. Because I've had to leave out many people, I apologize, yet I am nonetheless grateful for their help. Of course, many people who discussed Merv did so strictly off the record.

When I lived in San Francisco, I made several visits to San Mateo, Merv's hometown. There, many of his friends who attended school with him and knew his family were still alive. Each was very helpful, including the musician, Cal Tjader.

The pals of Merv who contributed the most information about his early life were Johnny Riley, Paul Schone, and Bill Robbins. A great deal of the information in this book was provided by Hadley Morrell, Merv's longtime on-and-off again companion. After their departure from Merv, each of these men attempted some form of memoir. The Jay Garon-Brooke Agency of New York tried to combine these reminiscences into a comprehensive text evocative of *Elvis:What Happened?,* the memoir of three of that singer's closest but by-then-alienated companions. Every publisher we showed it to at the time deemed Garon's book proposal too hot and too potentially libelous to publish, and the project collapsed.

Other bits and pieces came from such witnesses as Janet Folsom, a source of the information about Merv and his days as an entertainer at the Pebble Beach Lodge. When Stanley Haggart and I worked with Joan Crawford on Pepsi-Cola commercials, she provided a tantalizing insight into her superficial relationship with Merv, whom she did not particularly admire.

Ralph Laven, a close friend of singer Guy Mitchell, attempted to explain the strange friendship that developed between Guy and Merv. When Rita Hayworth was considering appearing as the star of the film *The Last Resort,* which was based on my novel, *Butterflies in Heat,* she spoke frankly about her relationship with Merv.

Band leader Freddy Martin was a font of information about the Big Band era and about Merv in particular. In his later years, he was always receptive to granting interviews to reporters who wanted to document the heyday of the Bands during the early 40s and 50s.

Special thanks go to Carlo Fiore, longtime friend of Marlon Brando, who enlightened me about Merv's relationship with Brando. I am especially grateful to my departed friend, Henry Willson, who provided many juicy details about Merv—especially about his relationships with the likes of Guy

Madison, Rock Hudson, Troy Donahue, and others.

After many hours of dialogue, an aging Guy Madison in Thousand Oaks, California, turned down my offer to ghost-write his memoirs. But he was very revealing in uncensored, private talks about his glory years in Hollywood. It was he who provided the information about John Wayne and his affair with Guy's wife, Gail Russell, as well as insights into Merv's minor involvement in this secret liaison.

Peter Lawford and Roddy McDowall were each longtime friends, and neither spoke on record, but each of them were privy to much that was going on in the lives of Hollywood stars who included Merv. Roddy, for example, supplied details about the relationship between Merv and Richard Long, plus details about numerous other encounters as well. I met with Tom Drake on three separate occasions, when he was selling used cars, years after he could no longer pass as Judy Garland's "boy next door."

Much of the information about Howard Hughes appearing within this book came from Johnny Meyer, a former personal assistant—read that as "pimp"— of the great aviator.

Both Robert Clary and Robert Loggia have either written or spoken of their friendship with Merv. The link between Merv and his fan club "prexy," Carol Burnett, is well documented in many sources.

Dear, tumultuous Tallulah Bankhead told hilarious stories about her involvements with Merv. She related these incidents when she was a guest of Mrs. Albert Peirce in Key West, Florida, following her late 1950s road tour of *Crazy October.*

I am also grateful to the author Shaun Bradford for letting me read his unpublished manuscript on the tragic life of Robert Walker. Likewise, the unpublished memoirs of my friend, Brooks Clift (brother of Montgomery), shed great light on the troubled life of his brother and his link with Merv.

Marty Melcher, former husband of Doris Day, has gone on record in many different published sources about his wife and her relationship with Merv at Warner Brothers.

Rosemary Clooney, during the many evenings she spent at Ted Hook's Backstage Bar in New York City, was no great diva, but an honest straightforward woman who spoke nostalgically about the disappointments in her life. She had only the highest of praise for Merv and what he did for her own comeback.

Even after many years, Jose Ferrer, Rosemary's husband, was still resentful of Marlene Dietrich's intrusion into his marriage. He also remained deeply resentful of Robert Kennedy's involvement with Rosemary, and Merv's small role in that illicit romance.

Acting coach Mira Rostova, who would be the fascinating subject of any book devoted entirely to her, shared memories of both Merv and Monty Clift. She was introduced to me by Brooks Clift and Kim Stanley, his lover.

Ralph Richards, a close friend and personal assistant to Bill Orr, provided insights into what was going on behind the scenes at Warner Brothers during the 1950s. After leaving the studio, he was very candid about Jack Warner and Warner's son-in-law, Bill Orr.

Years after her involvement in show-biz, Phyllis Kirk was bright, perky, and filled with regrets about her days in Hollywood. She spoke honestly of her brief involvement with Merv and about why she felt that she was betrayed.

Sammy Cahn was also full of stories about the entertainment industry, including anecdotes about Merv, and to an even greater degree, tales about Frank Sinatra.

Fred Zinnemann provided remembrances of his horrendous experiences directing the actors and egos associated with *From Here to Eternity.*

Nick Adams, a friend of mine, shared memories of James Dean and his own encounters with Merv.

When I was a member of the student press in Miami, I got to meet Robert Francis, in town on a publicity tour. He graciously accepted my invitation to show him the glories of South Florida. During that time with him, I learned many stories about his attempt to become a big star in Hollywood, as well as his rather unattractive brief encounter with Merv. His loss in a plane crash was a great tragedy.

Meeting Lady May Lawford at a party in Santa Monica, I encountered the most tactlessly outspoken woman I'd ever met. The mother of Peter Lawford had vitriolic opinions about everybody, including her son. She had nothing but barbs for the Kennedys, Frank Sinatra, and others.

Through mutual friends,and on several occasions, I met Claudette Colbert. Her remembrances were always "laundered," highly censored, and very discreet.

Director Gordon Douglas never censored himself when he relayed tall tales about Hollywood, including stories about his involvements with Liberace and Merv. He directed Liberace in *Sincerely Yours*.

I am deeply indebted to Paul Richardson, Liberace's assistant, for his stories linking Merv and Liberace into a deep friendship. He was especially entertaining in relating the details of an evening which Merv and Liberace shared with Mae West.

Once married to Judy Garland, Mark Herron articulated stories too hot to print, many of them about his troubled days with Judy. After Judy died, he seriously considered writing a tell-all memoir, but the project was never completed. He spoke frankly about his brief flings with Merv and Tallulah, as well as equivalent involvements with Charles Laughton and the actor Henry Brandon. Herron also delivered a zinger about a notorious episode involving Merv's one-night involvement with Ol' Blue Eyes and sultry Lana Turner.

Truman Capote, in Key West, was characteristically candid about his relationships with both Merv and Montgomery Clift.

Agent Marty Kummer was a source for material about Merv's struggle in show business during the 1950s and early 1960s.

Actor George Grizzard, one evening at Ted Hook's Backstage Bar in New York, spoke with candor about his involvements with both Paul Newman and Merv during his appearance in *The Desperate Hours* on Broadway.

John Henry Faulk had only the fondest of memories of Merv when they co-hosted *The Morning Show* for CBS. In contrast, Robert Q. Lewis had only venom for Merv, his rival. And perhaps in a kind of karmic symmetry, Irving Mansfield, the husband and promoter of author Jacqueline Susann, had only venom for Lewis.

Although discreet in print, Graham Payn spent the rest of his life after the death of his lover, Noel Coward, sharing raucous and sometimes hilarious stories.

My attempt to ghost write a memoir with Cal Culver didn't work out, but my head is still reeling from learning the details of his personal involvement as "stud" to the stars, including Merv.

My dear friend, the Austrian *chanteuse,* Greta Keller, who lived for a year in my home in New York City, introduced me to her best friend, Jolie Gabor. Ms. Gabor arrived on many a summer night at my home and, perhaps without knowing it, provided material not only about herself, but about her daughter, Zsa Zsa, and especially about Merv and his relationship with Eva.

I am also deeply grateful to Monica Dunn for her tireless assistance during the preparation of this biography.

As a means of assisting readers of this book, within it I sometimes presented the stories related to me as "conversations remembered." If the wording isn't exactly right in some of these recitations, the points I've made in my use of this device are dead-on.

Darwin Porter
New York City
February, 2009

Selected Bibliography

Adams, Cindy. *Jolie Gabor.* New York: Mason Charter, 1975.

Amburn, Ellis. *The Most Beautiful Woman in the World— Elizabeth Taylor.* New York: HarperCollins, 2000.

Andersen, Christopher. *Barbra— The Way She Is.* New York: HarperCollins, 2006.

_____, *Citizen Jane—The Turbulent Life of Jane Fonda.* New York: Bantam, 1990.

Bacon, James. *How Sweet It Is—The Jackie Gleason Story.* New York: St. Martin's Press, 1985.

Bankhead, Tallulah. *Tallulah.* New York: Harper and Brothers, 1952.

Behrens, Jack. *Big Bands & Great Ballrooms.* Indiana: Author House, 2006.

Belanger, Camyl Sosa. *Eva Gabor an Amazing Woman.* Nebraska: iUniverse, 2005.

Benson, Ross. *Charles—The Untold Story—Is He Fit To Be King?* New York: St Martin's Paperback, 1993.

Björkman, Stig. *Woody Allen on Woody Allen.* New York: Grove Press, 1993.

Blair, Gwenda. *The Trumps.* New York: Simon & Schuster, 2000.

Blonsky, Marshall. *American Mythologies.* New York: Oxford University Press, 1992.

Bockris, Victor. *Warhol The Biography.* London: Da Capo Press, 1989.

Bosworth, Patricia. *Montgomery Clift—A Biography.* New York: Harcourt, Brace, Jovanovich, 1978.

Bragg, Melvyn. *Richard Burton A Life.* Boston: Little, Brown and Company, 1988.

Bret, David. *Rock Hudson.* London: Robson Books, 2004

Brown, Peter Harry and Broeske, Pat H. *Down the End of Lonely Street— The Life & Death of Elvis Presley.* New York: Penguin, 1997.

Brown, Tina. *The Diana Chronicles.* New York: Doubleday. 2007.

Callan, Michael Feeney. *Sean Connery.* London: Virgin Books, 2003.

Carr, William H.A. *What Is Jack Paar Really Like?* New York: Lancer Books,1962.

Cavett, Dick, and Porterfield, Christopher. *Cavett.* New York: Harcourt, Brace, Jovanovich, 1974.

Chaplin, Michael. *I Couldn't Smoke the Grass on My Father's Lawn.* New York: G.P. Putnam Sons, 1966.

Clooney, Rosemary, and Barthel, Joan.*Girl Singer.*New York:Broadway Books,1999.

Deaver, Michael K. *Nancy— A Portrait of My Years with Nancy Reagan.* New York: William Morrow Co., Inc. 2004.

Diederich, Bernard. *Trujillo, The Death of the Goat.*Boston:Little Brown and Co 978.

Druxman, Michael B. *Merv.* New York: Universal Publishing, 1976.

Edmonson, Roger. *Boy in the Sand— Casey Donovan—All American Sex Star.* California: Alyson Books, 1998.

Edwards, Anne. *The Reagans— Portrait of a Marriage.* New York: St. Martin's Press, 2003.

Eells, George, and Musgrove, Stanley. *Mae West.* New York: William Morrow Co. Inc., 1982.

_____, *Hedda and Louella.* New York: G.P. Putnam's Sons, 1972.

Eliot, Marc. *Burt! Burt Reynolds the Unauthorized Biography.* New York: Dell Publishing, 1982.

Frank, Gerold. *Judy.* New York: Harper & Row, 1975.

_____, *Zsa Zsa Gabor— My Story Written for Me.* Ohio: World Publishing Co. 1975.

Freedland, Michael. *Peter O'Toole.* New York: St. Martin's Press, 1982.

_____, *Sean Connery— A Biography.* London: Orion Press, 1994.

_____, *The Secret Life of Danny Kaye.* New York: St. Martin's Press, 1986.

Gabor, Eva. *Orchids & Salami.* New York: Doubleday & Co, 1954.

Gabor, Zsa Zsa. *How To Catch a Man, How To Keep a Man, How To Get Rid of a Man.* New York, Doubleday, 1970.

Griffin, Merv and Barsocchini, Peter. *Merv—An Autobigraphy.* New York: Simon & Schuster, 1980.

Griffin, Merv and Bender, David. *Merv— Making the Good Life Last.* New York: Simon & Schuster, 2003.

_____, *From Where I Sit Merv Griffin's Book of People.* New York: Pinnacle Books, 1983.

Guiles, Fred Lawrence. *The Intimate Biography of Marion Davies.* New York:Bantam, 1972.

Guralnick, Peter. *Careless Love— The Unmaking of Elvis Presley.* New York: Little Brown & Co.,1998.

_____, *Last Train to Memphis—The Rise of Elvis Presley.* New York: Back Bay Books, 1994.

Hammer, Armand and Lydon, Neil. *Hammer.* New York: Perigee, 1988.

Harris, Harry. *Mike Douglas. The Private Life of the Public Legend.* New York: Award Books, 1976.

Haygood, Wil. *In Black and White—The Life of Sammy Davis Jr.* New York: Alfred A. Knopf, 2003.

Henry, William A., III, *The Great One—The Life and Legend of Jackie Gleason.* New York: Doubleday, 1992.

Heymann, C. David. *Liz—An Intimate Biography of Elizabeth Taylor.* New York: Carol Publishing 1995.

_____, *A Woman Named Jackie.* New York: Carol Communications, 1989.

_____, *R*F*K.* New York: Penguin Group, 1998

Higham, Charles. *Charles Laughton — An Intimate Biography.* New York: Doubleday & Co., 1976.

_____, *Orson Welles—The Rise & Fall of an American Genius.* New York: St. Martin's Press, 1985.

Hofler, Robert. *The Man Who Invented Rock Hudson— The Pretty Boys and Dirty Deals of Henry Willson.* New York: Carroll & Graf, 2005.

Hopper, Hedda. *The Whole Truth and Nothing But.*New York:Doubleday&Co. 1963.

Hudson, Rock & Davidson, Sara. *Rock Hudson— His Story.* New York: William Morrow Co., Inc. 1986.

Johnson, George. *The Real Jack Paar.* Connecticut: Fawcett Publications, 1962.

Kelley, Kitty. *Jackie Oh!* New York: Ballantine Books, 1978.

_____, *His Way—The Unauthorized Biography of Frank Sinatra.* New York: Bantam Books, 1986.

_____, *Nancy Reagan —The Unauthorized Biography.* New York: Simon & Schuster, 1991.

LaGuardia, Robert. *Monty. A Biography of Montgomery Clift.* New York: Arbor House, 1977.

Leamer, Laurence. *King of the Night — The Life of Johnny Carson.* USA: Leda Productions, 1989.

Leaming, Barbara. *Orson Welles- A Biography.* New York: Viking, 1985.

Lee, Gypsy Rose. *Gypsy a Memoir.* California: Frog, Ltd., 1986.

Leigh, Wendy. *One Lifetime Is Not Enough Zsa Zsa Gabor.* New York: Delacorte Press, 1991

_____, *True Grace —The Life and Times of an American Princess.* New York: St. Martins Press, 2007.

Lesley, Cole. *Remembered Laughter. The Life of Noel Coward.* New York: Alfred A.Knopf. 1977.

Liberace. *Liberace An Autobiography.* New York: G.P.Putnam's Sons, 1973.

_____, *The Wonderful Private World of Liberace.* New York: Harper and Row, 1986.

Lobenthal, Joel. *Tallulah! The Life and Times of a Leading Lady.* New York: HarperCollins, 2004.

Louvish, Simon. *Mae West It Ain't No Sin.* London: Faber and Faber Limited, 2005.

Madsen, Axel. *John Huston.* New York: Doubleday & Co, 1978.

Mark, Geoffrey. *Ethel Merman — The Biggest Star on Broadway.* New Jersey: Barricade Books, 2006

Marx, Arthur. *The Nine Lives of Mickey Rooney.* New York: Stein and Day, 1986.

Maxwell, Elsa. *R.S.V.P. Elsa Maxwell's Own Story.* Boston: Little Brown and Co., 1954.

McCluskey, Audrey Thomas. *Richard Pryor.* USA: Indiana University Press, 2008

McGilligan, Patrick. *Clint The Life and Legend.* New York: St. Martin's Press, 1999.

McMahon, Ed. *Here's Johnny! My Memories of Johnny Carson.* New York: Penguin, 2005.

Merman, Ethel, and Eells, George. *Merman, an Autobiography.* New York: Simon & Schuster, 1978.

Mongomery, Ruth. *The Phenomenal Jeane Dixon.* New York: Bantam, 1965.

Morella, Joe and Epstein, Edward Z. *Lana: The Public & Private Lives of Miss Turner.* New York: Dell Publishing, 1971.

Morris, Edmund. *Dutch A Memoir of Ronald Reagan.* New York: Random House, 1999.

Mungo, Ray. *Palm Springs Babylon.* New York: St. Martin's Press, 1993.

O'Brien, Timothy L. *Trump Nation — The Art of Being the Donald.* New York: Warner Business Books, 2005.

Paar, Jack. *An Entertainment.* New York: Doubleday, 1983.

Porter, Darwin & Prince, Danforth. *Hollywood Babylon — It's Back!* New York: Blood Moon Productions, Ltd., 2008.

Porter, Darwin. *Brando Unzipped.* New York: Blood Moon Productions, Ltd., 2005

_____, *Howard Hughes: Hell's Angel.* New York: Blood Moon Productions, Ltd., 2005

Preminger, Erik Lee. *Gypsy & Me.* New York: Little, Brown and Company, 1984.

Pyron, Darden Asbury. *Liberace, An American Boy.* Chicago: University of Chicago Press, 2000.

Ramer, Jean. *Duke: The Real Story of John Wayne.* New York: Universal Award House, 1973.

Randall, Tony. *Which Reminds Me.* New York: Delacorte Press, 1989.

Reagan, Nancy & Novak, William. *My Turn — The Memoirs of Nancy Reagan.* New York: Random House, 1989.

Reeves, Thomas C. *America's Bishop — The Life and Times of Fulton J. Sheen.* California: Encounter Books, 2001.

Reagan, Ronald. *An American Life.* New York: Simon & Schuster, 1990.

Reynolds, Burt. *My Life.* New York: Hyperion, 1994.

Richmond, Peter. *Fever — The Life and Music of Miss Peggy Lee.* New York: Picador, 2006.

Roberts, Randy and Olson, James S. *John Wayne — American.* New York: First Bison Books, 1995.

Rogers St. Johns, Adela. *The Honeycomb — An Autobiography.* New York: Doubleday, 1969.

Shanks, Bob. *The Cool Fire— How to Make It in Television.* New York: Vintage Books, 1976.

Sharif, Omar, and Guinchard, Marie-Thérése. *The Eternal Male.* New York: Doubleday & Co., 1977.

Shipman, David. *Judy Garland— The Secret Life of an American Legend.* New York: Hyperion, 1993.

Signorile, Michelangelo. *Queer in America —Sex, the Media, and the Closets of Power.* New York: Random House, 1993.

Slater, Robert. *No Such Thing as Over-Exposure. Inside the Life and Celebrity of Donald Trump.* New Jersey: Pearson, 2005.

Spada, James. *Peter Lawford – The Man Who Kept the Secrets.* New York: Bantam, 1991.

Summers, Anthony & Swan, Robbyn. *Sinatra — The Life.* New York: Alfred A Knopf, 2005.

Swanberg, W.A. *Citizen Hearst—* A Biography of William Randolph Hearst. New York: Scribner, 1961.

Thomas, Bob. *Liberace The True Story.* New York: St. Martin's Press, 1987.

Thomas, Evan. *Robert Kennedy.* New York: Simon & Schuster, 2000.

Thompson, Douglas. *Clint Eastwood — Billion Dollar Man.* London: John Blake Publishing, 2005.

Trebek, Alex & Griffin, Merv. *The Jeopardy! Challenge.* New York: HarperCollins, 1992.

Trump, Donald J. & Leerhsen, Charles. *Trump — Surviving at the Top.* New York: Random House, 1990.

Turner, Lana. *Lana, The Lady, The Legend, The Truth.* Boston: G.K.Hall & Co. 1983.

Turtu, Anthony, and Reuter, Donald F. *Gaborabilia.* New York: Three Rivers Press, 2001.

Vidal, Gore. *Palimpsest — A Memoir.* New York: Random House, 1995.

Wayne, Jane Ellen. *The Life of Robert Taylor.* New York: Warner, 1973.

Weatherby, W.J. *An Intimate Portrait of the Great One — Jackie Gleason.* New York: Pharos Books, 1992.

Welles, Orson & Bogdanovich, Peter. *This is Orson Welles.* New York: HarperCollins, 1992.

West, Mae. *Mae West On Sex, Health, and ESP.* London: W. H. Allen, 1975.

White, Vanna. *Vanna Speaks.* New York: Warner Books, 1987.

Wilding, Michael & Wilcox, Pamela. *The Wilding Way— The Story of My Life.* New York: St. Martin's Press, 1982.

Williams, Tennessee. *Tennessee Williams' Memoirs.* New York: Bantam, 1975.

Index

530

532

534

536

539

540

541

BLOOD MOON PRODUCTIONS

Entertainment about how America interprets its celebrities.

Blood Moon Productions originated in 1997 as *The Georgia Literary Association*, a vehicle for the promotion of obscure writers from America's Deep South. Today, Blood Moon is based in New York City, and staffed with writers who otherwise devote their energies to *THE FROMMER GUIDES*, a trusted name in travel publishing.

Four of Blood Moon's recent biographies have been extensively serialized (excerpted) by the largest-readership publications of the U.K., *The Mail on Sunday* and *The Sunday Times*. Other serializations of Blood Moon's titles have appeared in Australia's *Women's Weekly* and *The Australian*.

Our corporate mission involves researching and salvaging the oral histories of America's entertainment industry--those "off the record" events which at the time might have been defined as either indecent or libelous, but which are now pertinent to America's understanding of its origins and cultural roots. For more about us, click on **www.BloodMoonProductions.com,** or refer to the pages which immediately follow.

Thanks for your interest, best wishes, and happy reading.

Danforth Prince, President, Blood Moon Productions

Salvaging the unrecorded
oral histories of America's "off the record" past

& its affiliate, the Georgia Literary Association

Entertainment you wouldn't necessarily expect from
America's Deep South

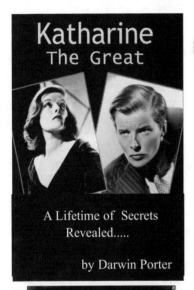

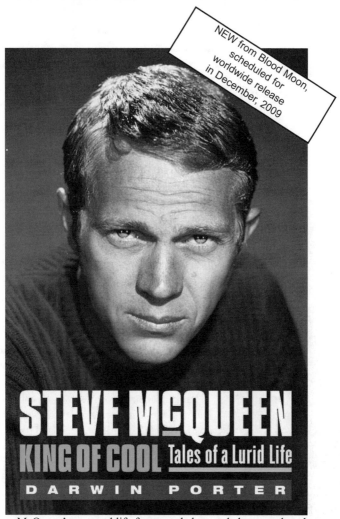

STEVE McQUEEN
KING OF COOL Tales of a Lurid Life
DARWIN PORTER

The drama of Steve McQueen's personal life far exceeded any role he ever played on screen. Born to a prostitute, he was brutally molested by some of his mother's "johns," and endured gang rape in reform school. His drift into prostitution began when he was hired as a towel boy in the most notorious bordello in the Dominican Republic, where he starred in a string of cheap porno films. Returning to New York before migrating to Hollywood, he hustled men on Times Square and, as a "gentleman escort" in a borrowed tux, rich older women.

And then, sudden stardom as he became the world's top box office attraction. The abused became the abuser. "I live for myself, and I answer to nobody," he proclaimed. "The last thing I want to do is fall in love with a broad."

Thus began a string of seductions that included hundreds of overnight pickups--both male and female. Topping his A-list conquests were James Dean, Paul Newman, Marilyn Monroe, and Barbra Streisand. Finally, this pioneering biography explores the death of Steve McQueen. Were those salacious rumors really true?

Steve McQueen   King of Cool   Tales of a Lurid Life
by Darwin Porter

ISBN 978-1-936003-05-1   Available December 2009   Hardcover   **$26.95**

From the Georgia Literary Association,
in cooperation with the Florida Literary Association
and Blood Moon Productions

THE RENAISSANCE OF A CULT CLASSIC

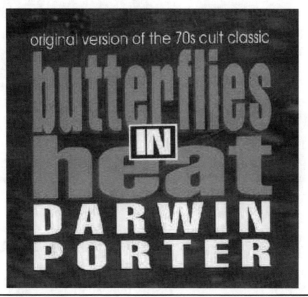

*You first heard about it in the 70s,
when it was the most notorious and gossipped-
about book in Key West. Now it's back.*

"Darwin Porter writes with an incredible understanding of the milieu--
hot enough to singe the wings off any butterfly"
James Kirkwood, co-author, **A Chorus Line**

"I'd walk the waterfront for Numie Chase [*Butterflies'* doomed hero] anytime"
Tennessee Williams

"How does Darwin Porter's garden grow? Only in the moonlight, and only at midnight,
when man-eating vegetation in any color but green bursts forth
to devour the latest offerings"
James Leo Herlihy, author of **Midnight Cowboy**

MIDNIGHT IN SAVANNAH

BY DARWIN PORTER   ISBN 09668030-1-9   Paperback   **$14.95**

A saga of corruption, greed, sexual tension, and murder that gets down and dirty in the Deep Old South, this is the more explicit and more entertaining alternative to John Berendt's *Midnight in the Garden of Good and Evil.* .

If you've ever felt either traumatized or eroticized south of the Mason-Dixon Line, you should probably read this book.

"In Darwin Porter's <u>Midnight</u>, *both Lavender Morgan ("At 72, the world's oldest courtesan") and Tipper Zelda ("an obese, fading chanteuse taunted as "the black widow,") purchase lust from sexually conflicted young men with drop-dead faces, chiseled bodies, and genetically gifted crotches. These women once relied on their physicality to steal the hearts and fortunes of the world's richest and most powerful men. Now, as they slide closer every day to joining the corpses of their former husbands, these once-beautiful women must depend, in a perverse twist of fate, on sexual outlaws for* <u>le petit mort.</u> *And to survive, the hustlers must idle their personal dreams while struggling to cajole what they need from a sexual liaison they detest. Mendacity reigns, Perversity in extremis. Physical beauty as living hell. CAT ON A HOT TIN ROOF'S Big Daddy must be spinning in his grave right now."*   **EUGENE RAYMOND**

The author, Darwin Porter, a native Southerner, is co-author of ***The Frommer Guides*** to the City of Savannah and the State of Georgia. During his research, he formed some startling conclusions about the <u>real</u> Savannah, The Deep South, and the city's most famous murder

552

553

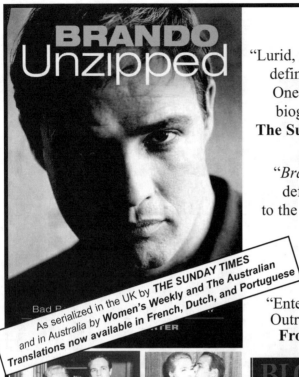

"Authoritative, exhaustive, and essential, it's the queer girl's and queer boy's one-stop resource for what to add to their feature-film queues. The film synopses and the snippets of critic's reviews are reason enough to keep this annual compendium of cinematic information close to the DVD player. But the extras--including the special features and the Blood Moon Awards--are butter on the popcorn."

Richard LaBonte, Books to Watch Out For

"Blood Moon's Guide to Gay and Lesbian Film is like having access to a feverishly compiled queer film fan's private scrapbook. Each edition is a snapshot of where we are in Hollywood now. It's also a lot of fun..."

Gay Times (London)

"Startling. It documents everything from the mainstream to the obscure, detailing dozens of queer films from the last few years."

HX (New York)

"Includes everything fabu in the previous years' movies. An essential guide for both the casual viewer and the hard-core movie watching homo."

Bay Windows (Boston)

"From feisty Blood Moon Productions, this big, lively guidebook of (mostly) recent gay and gayish films is not meant to be a dust-collecting reference book covering the history of GLBT films. Instead, it's an annual running commentary on what's new and what's going on in gay filmmaking. *Mandate*

Volume One (published 2006)
ISBN 978-0-9748118-4-0 $19.95

Volume Two (published 2007)
ISBN 978-0-9748118-7-1 $21.95

The Secret Life of
HUMPHREY BOGART
THE EARLY YEARS (1899-1931)　　　BY DARWIN PORTER

The Secret Life of
Humphrey Bogart
The Early Years
(1899 - 1931)
Darwin Porter

This myth-shattering biography gives a controversial CLOSEUP of a young, hot and horny Bogart pre-Casablanca, pre-Bacall, pre-African Queen Revealing for the first time what was under the trench coat of history's most famous movie star

Loaded with information once suppressed by the Hollywood studios, this is the most revealing book ever written about the undercover lives of movie stars during the 1930s. Learn what America's most visible male star was doing during his mysterious early years on Broadway and in Hollywood at the dawn of the Talkies--details that Bogie worked hard to suppress during his later years with Bacall.

The subject of more than 80 radio interviews by its author, and widely covered by both the tabloids and the mainstream press, it's based on never-before-published memoirs, letters, diaries, and interviews from men and women who either loved Bogie or who wanted him to burn in hell. No wonder Bogie, in later life, usually avoided talking about his early years.

Serialized in three parts by Britain's *Mail on Sunday*, it demonstrates that Hollywood's Golden Age stars were human, highly sexed, and at least when they were with other Hollywood insiders, remarkably indiscreet.

"This biography has had us pondering as to how to handle its revelations within a town so protective of its own...This biography of Bogart's early years is exceptionally well written." **JOHN AUSTIN, *HOLLYWOOD INSIDE***

"In this new biography, we learn about how Bogart struggled for stardom in the anything goes era of the Roaring 20s." ***THE GLOBE***

"Porter's book uncovers scandals within the entertainment industry of the 1920s and 1930s, when publicists from the movie studios deliberately twisted and suppressed inconvenient details about the lives of their emerging stars."
TURNER CLASSIC MOVIE NEWS

"This biography brilliantly portrays a slice of time: In this case, the scandal-soaked days of Prohibition, when a frequently hung-over Bogie operated somwhat like a blank sheet of paper on which other actors, many of them infamous, were able to design their lives. The book is beautifully written."
LAURENCE HAZELL, PhD. University of Durham (UK)

Softcover. 527 pages, with photos.　ISBN　**0-9668030-5-1**　**$16.95**

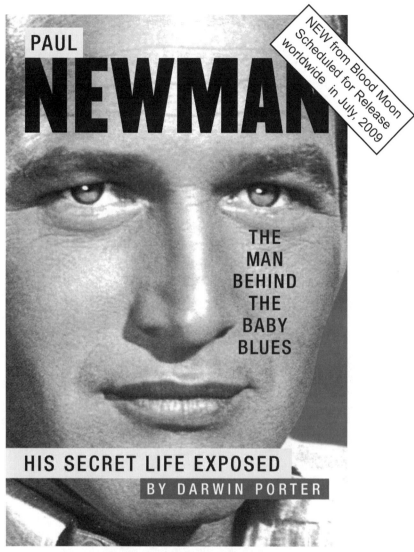

PAUL NEWMAN

THE MAN BEHIND THE BABY BLUES

HIS SECRET LIFE EXPOSED

BY DARWIN PORTER

NEW from Blood Moon
Scheduled for Release
worldwide in July, 2009

The private Newman was remarkably different from the public face he revealed to the world. He became one of the most potent, desirable, and ambiguous sex symbols in America. A former sailor from Shaker Heights, Ohio, he parlayed his ambisexual charm into one of the most successful careers in Hollywood.

From celebrity chronicler Darwin Porter, this is a compelling postmortem description of the dirt, the glory, the bad, the beautiful, the giddy heights, and the agonizing lows of a great American star.

Compiled over a period of nearly 50 years from firsthand interviews with insiders who knew Paul Newman intimately, this is the world's most revelatory biography of Hollywood's pre-eminent male sex symbol, with dozens of potentially shocking revelations.

Hardcover, available in July, 2009.
ISBN 978-0-9786465-1-6   **$26.95**

ABOUT THE AUTHOR

Darwin Porter's contacts with Merv Griffin began in college. As chief editor of the Student Press at the University of Miami, Darwin hired Merv as the featured entertainer for the graduating class's senior prom. From there, a friendship continued, as well as the systematic compilation of information over the decades which made its way into this book.

Merv Griffin is but one of the subjects in Darwin's list of biographies of show-biz personalities. Other celebrities he's profiled include award-winning overviews of Humphrey Bogart, Katharine Hepburn, Marlon Brando, Howard Hughes, and Michael Jackson. Several of these have been serialized in Britain, in either the MAIL ON SUNDAY or THE SUNDAY TIMES, which defined *Brando Unzipped* as "Lurid, raunchy, perceptive, certainly worth reading...one of the best show-biz biographies of the year."

In 2008, Darwin's *Hollywood Babylon-It's Back!* was cited as the decade's best overview of exhibitionism, sexuality, and sin as filtered through 85 years of Hollywood scandal.

One of America's foremost travel authorities, Darwin is the widely read author of more than 50 ongoing titles--most of them associated with coverage of Europe and the Caribbean--within *The Frommer Guides,* the world's best-selling travel series.

Most of the time, Darwin lives in New York City, with frequent trips to Los Angeles, London, and various other Frommer-related points around the world.